THE PRACTICAL SKEPTIC

READINGS IN SOCIOLOGY

Sixth Edition

Lisa J. McIntyre

Washington State University

Mc
Graw
Hill
Education

THE PRACTICAL SKEPTIC: READINGS IN SOCIOLOGY, SIXTH EDITION

Published by McGraw-Hill Education, 2 Penn Plaza, New York, NY 10121. Copyright © 2014 by McGraw-Hill Education. All rights reserved. Printed in the United States of America. Previous editions © 2011, 2009, and 2006. No part of this publication may be reproduced or distributed in any form or by any means, or stored in a database or retrieval system, without the prior written consent of McGraw-Hill Education, including, but not limited to, in any network or other electronic storage or transmission, or broadcast for distance learning.

Some ancillaries, including electronic and print components, may not be available to customers outside the United States.

This book is printed on acid-free paper.

1 2 3 4 5 6 7 8 9 0 DOC/DOC 1 0 9 8 7 6 5 4 3

ISBN 978-0-07-802688-1
MHID 0-07-802688-1

Senior Vice President, Products & Markets: *Kurt L. Strand*
Vice President, General Manager, Products & Markets: *Michael Ryan*
Vice President, Content Production & Technology Services: *Kimberly Meriwether David*
Managing Director: *Gina Boedeker*
Brand Manager: *Courtney Austermehle*
Marketing Manager: *Philip Weaver*
Marketing Coordinator: *Ryan Viviani*
Director of Development: *Rhona Robbin*
Freelance Development Editor: *Nomi Sofer*
Director, Content Production: *Terri Schiesl*
Content Project Manager: *Mary Jane Lampe*
Buyer: *Nichole Birkenholz*
Cover Designer: *Studio Montage, St. Louis, MO*
Cover Image: *Digital Vision/Getty Images*
Typeface: *10/12 Palatino LT std*
Compositor: *Laserwords Private Limited*
Printer: *R. R. Donnelley*

All credits appearing on page or at the end of the book are considered to be an extension of the copyright page.

Library of Congress Cataloging-in-Publication Data

McIntyre, Lisa J.
The practical skeptic : readings in sociology / Lisa J. McIntyre. — Six Edition.
    pages cm
  ISBN 978-0-07-802688-1 (alk. paper)
1. Sociology. I. Title.
  HM586.M55 2014
  301—dc23
                                                                            2013008645

The Internet addresses listed in the text were accurate at the time of publication. The inclusion of a website does not indicate an endorsement by the authors or McGraw-Hill Education, and McGraw-Hill Education does not guarantee the accuracy of the information presented at these sites.

www.mhhe.com

PREFACE

There are dozens of anthologies available for introductory-level sociology classes, but I think that this one is different. It's different because as I compiled and edited these articles, I kept the needs of introductory students in mind. That's important. When sociologists write for their professional colleagues, they take for granted (as they should) that their readers are equipped with a great deal of knowledge. Student readers, by contrast, generally lack this sort of preparation; consequently, many students find that reading the works of sociologists is not so much a challenge as an onerous chore. I suspect that beginning students assigned to read sociology feel much like the theatergoer who stumbles into a foreign film that lacks subtitles. No matter how dramatic or comedic the action, unless one can follow the dialogue, the movie is boring.

In this volume, I have tried to bridge the gap between the sociologists who wrote these articles and the students who will read them. Each article begins with a brief introduction to help orient students to the author's aims and point of view, includes footnotes containing explanations of concepts that are likely to be unfamiliar to novice sociologists, and concludes with some questions that will help students sort through and make sense of what they have read. My goal is to replace boredom with intellectual challenge, to make sociology not "easy," but accessible.

Both classic and contemporary articles were selected because they help to illustrate the importance of understanding the social contexts through which people move and to highlight some of the core concepts that sociologists and other social observers use to make sense of the social world. The classic articles especially were selected to illustrate the foundational concepts that most contemporary writers take for granted. But while these fundamentals might seem old hat to professional sociologists, they still contain important revelations for beginners.

New to This Edition

In the final selection in this edition, Randall Collins suggests that the core of sociology is not a "set of texts or ideas." It is, he tells us, "an activity." This sixth edition of the reader continues to emphasize articles that provide students the opportunity to do the activity that sociologists do: to reexamine the familiar and to rethink conventional understandings of these understandings. Moreover, I want to invite students to contemplate in new ways their own participation in the social world.

Supplements for Text and Reader

Visit our Online Learning Center website at http://www.mhhe.com/mcintyre6e for robust student and instructor resources. This is a combined website for both *The Practical Skeptic: Core Concepts in Sociology* and its companion reader, *The Practical Skeptic: Readings in Sociology.*

FOR STUDENTS

Student resources for the *Core Concepts* text include self-quizzes, defined key concepts, practical applications, and other chapter study aids.

FOR INSTRUCTORS

The password-protected instructor portion of the website includes the *Core Concepts* text instructor's manual (written by the author), containing discussion questions and activities, examples of lectures, tips specifically targeting new instructors, a comprehensive test bank and computerized test bank, and all the tools available to students. Also included are a separate test bank and computerized test bank for the reader with multiple choice, true/false, and essay questions for each reading.

The Practical Skeptic: Core Concepts in Sociology

Created to serve as a companion to the reader, *The Practical Skeptic: Readings in Sociology,* this text focuses on core concepts as the central building blocks for understanding sociology. Written in a lively, conversational style, this text includes numerous pedagogical features to help students grasp key sociological concepts.

ACKNOWLEDGMENTS

We thank the following reviewers whose suggestions and shaped the sixth edition:

Susan Eichenberger, Seton Hill University; Stacy Evans, Berkshire Community College; Kelly Fulton, The University of Texas at Austin; Catherine

Leone, University of Wisconsin-Manitowoc; Pamela McMullin-Messier, Central Washington University; Janice L. Milner, Century College; Megan Peterson, William Rainey Harper College; Lissa J. Yogan, Valparaiso University.

Thank you to the following reviewers whose helpful comments and suggestions helped us in our preparation of the fifth edition: Elizabeth Larsen, California University of Pennsylvania; Lynda Dickson, University of Colorado at Colorado Springs; Kiren Ghei, Delta College; Thomas B. Gold, University of California at Berkeley; Patti Guiffre, Texas State University; Michael Collins, UW Fox Valley in Menasha; Linda C. Evans, Drake University; Carolyn Kapinus, Ball State University; Carla Norris-Raynbird, Bemidji State University, C. Stephen Glennon, Iowa Western Community College; Doug Degher, North Arizona University; Kim Hennessee, Ball State University.

The fourth edition was reviewed by the following people, who responded with suggestions and pointed out necessary revisions, for which I am deeply grateful: Chris Adamski-Mietus, Western Illinois University; James Cassell, Henderson State University; Lindsay Custer, Bellevue Community College; Martha Doyle, Mercy College of Health Sciences; Yasmiyn Irizarry, Indiana University; Christine K. Oakley, Washington State University; Kennon Rice, Albright College; and Elizabeth Underwood, Eastern Kentucky University.

I would like to thank the reviewers of the third edition for their insightful feedback: Deborah A. Abowitz, Bucknell University; Jarl Ahlkvist, University of Colorado-Colorado Springs; Cheryl Albers, Buffalo State College; Sue Cox, Bellevue Community College; Derek Greenfield, Highline Community College; Tiffany Hayes, Green River Community College; Louise Hull, Green River Community College; Barbara Karcher, Kennesaw State University; John Poindexter, West Shore Community College; Susan Ross, Lycoming College; Ericka Stange, Central Washington University; Ann S. Stein, College of Charleston; Deborah Thorne, Ohio University; and Jamee K. Wolfe, Roanoke College.

For the second edition, the following individuals provided thoughtful reviews and recommendations: Deborah J. Baiano Berman, Framingham State College; Jerry Barrish, Bellevue Community College; Valerie S. Brown, Cuyahoga Community College; Margo Rita Capparelli, Framingham State College; Debra Cornelius, Shippensburg University; Jamie Dangler, SUNY Cortland; Laurel R. Davis, Springfield College; Gloria Y. Gadsden, Fairleigh Dickinson University; Alan G. Hill, Delta College; Susan E. HumphersGinther, Moorhead State University; Katherine Johnson, Niagara County Community College; Barbara Karcher, Kennesaw State University; Debra C. Lemke, Western Maryland College; Patricia A. Masters, George Mason University; Susan McWilliams, University of Southern Maine; Kristy McNamara, Furman University; Dan Pence, Southern Utah University; Marcella Thompson, University of Arkansas; and Brenda S. Zicha, Charles Stewart Mott Community College.

The following colleagues reviewed the manuscript and choice of articles for the first edition and made many helpful suggestions: Sheila Cordray, Oregon State University; Rebecca Erickson, University of Akron; Allen Scarboro, Augusta State University; and Martha L. Shockey, St. Ambrose University.

Lisa J. McIntyre

CONTENTS

1

THE PROMISE

C. Wright Mills

"The Promise," published in 1959 by C. Wright Mills, is probably the most famous essay ever written by a modern sociologist. In this article, Mills captures the essential lesson of sociology: To truly understand people's behavior, we must look beyond those individuals to the larger social contexts in which they live. Individuals make choices, to be sure, but their choices are constrained by social, historical, cultural, political, and economic factors. Most important, people frequently do not even realize the extent to which their lives are affected by things that are external to them and outside of their control. Mills's point is that if we are to understand people's behavior, we must take into account these nonindividual factors. (This is not an especially easy article to read, but it is fundamental. You might find it helpful to read the section on Mills in *The Practical Skeptic: Core Concepts in Sociology*, chapter 2, before you tackle this reading.)

Nowadays men often feel that their private lives are a series of traps. They sense that within their everyday worlds, they cannot overcome their troubles, and in this feeling, they are often quite correct: What ordinary men are directly aware of and what they try to do are bounded by the private orbits in which they live; their visions and their powers are limited to the close-up scenes of job, family, neighborhood; in other milieux[1] they move vicariously and remain spectators. And the more aware they become, however vaguely, of ambitions and of threats which transcend their immediate locales, the more trapped they seem to feel.

Underlying this sense of being trapped are seemingly impersonal changes in the very structure of continentwide societies. The facts of contemporary history are also facts about the success and the failure of individual men and women. When a society is industrialized, a peasant becomes a worker; a feudal lord is liquidated or becomes a businessman. When classes rise or fall, a man is employed or unemployed; when the rate of investment goes up or down, a man takes new heart or goes broke. When wars happen, an insurance salesman becomes a rocket launcher; a store clerk, a radar man; a wife lives alone; a child grows up without a father. Neither the life of an individual nor the history of a society can be understood without understanding both.

---

[1]*Milieux* is French; it means "social environments." (*Milieux* is plural; *milieu* is singular.)—Ed.

Yet men do not usually define the troubles they endure in terms of historical change and institutional contradiction.[2] The well-being they enjoy, they do not usually impute to the big ups and downs of the societies in which they live. Seldom aware of the intricate connection between the patterns of their own lives and the course of world history, ordinary men do not usually know what this connection means for the kinds of men they are becoming and for the kinds of history-making in which they might take part. They do not possess the quality of mind essential to grasp the interplay of man and society, of biography and history, of self and world. They cannot cope with their personal troubles in such ways as to control the structural transformations that usually lie behind them.

Surely it is no wonder. In what period have so many men been so totally exposed at so fast a pace to such earthquakes of change? That Americans have not known such catastrophic changes as have the men and women of other societies is due to historical facts that are now quickly becoming "merely history." The history that now affects every man is world history. Within this scene and this period, in the course of a single generation, one sixth of mankind is transformed from all that is feudal and backward into all that is modern, advanced, and fearful. Political colonies are freed; new and less visible forms of imperialism installed. Revolutions occur; men feel the intimate grip of new kinds of authority. Totalitarian societies rise, and are smashed to bits—or succeed fabulously. After two centuries of ascendancy, capitalism is shown up as only one way to make society into an industrial apparatus. After two centuries of hope, even formal democracy is restricted to a quite small portion of mankind. Everywhere in the underdeveloped world, ancient ways of life are broken up and vague expectations become urgent demands. Everywhere in the overdeveloped world, the means of authority and of violence become total in scope and bureaucratic in form. Humanity itself now lies before us, the super-nation at either pole concentrating its most coordinated and massive efforts upon the preparation of World War Three.

The very shaping of history now outpaces the ability of men to orient themselves in accordance with cherished values. And which values? Even when they do not panic, men often sense that older ways of feeling and thinking have collapsed and that newer beginnings are ambiguous to the point of moral stasis. Is it any wonder that ordinary men feel they cannot cope with the larger worlds with which they are so suddenly confronted? That they cannot understand the meaning of their epoch for their own lives? That—in defense of selfhood—they become morally insensible, trying to remain altogether private men? Is it any wonder that they come to be possessed by a sense of the trap?

It is not only information that they need—in this Age of Fact, information often dominates their attention and overwhelms their capacities to assimilate it. It is not only the skills of reason that they need—although their struggles to acquire these often exhaust their limited moral energy.

---

[2]Mills is using the term *institution* in its sociological sense—which is a bit different from the way this term is used in everyday or conventional speech. To the sociologist, institution refers to *a set of social arrangements, an accepted way of resolving important social problems.* Thus, the institution of the family is our society's way of resolving the important social problem of raising children. The institution of the economy is how we resolve the problem of distributing goods and services (for example, in the case of the United States, capitalism). The concept of institutional contradiction refers to situations in which the demands of one institution are not compatible with the demands of another institution. For example, there is institutional contradiction when the institution of the family is based on the norm that dad goes to work and mom stays home with the kids but the institution of the economy is such that it takes two employed adults to support a family. You will find more examples of institutional contradictions in reading 2 by Stephanie Coontz. You can read more about the nature of institutions in *The Practical Skeptic: Core Concepts in Sociology,* chapter 9, "Society and Social Institutions."—Ed.

What they need, and what they feel they need, is a quality of mind that will help them to use information and to develop reason in order to achieve lucid summations of what is going on in the world and of what may be happening within themselves. It is this quality, I am going to contend, that journalists and scholars, artists and publics, scientists and editors are coming to expect of what may be called the sociological imagination.

I

The sociological imagination enables its possessor to understand the larger historical scene in terms of its meaning for the inner life and the external career of a variety of individuals. It enables him to take into account how individuals, in the welter of their daily experience, often become falsely conscious of their social positions. Within that welter, the framework of modern society is sought, and within that framework the psychologies of a variety of men and women are formulated. By such means the personal uneasiness of individuals is focused upon explicit troubles and the indifference of publics is transformed into involvement with public issues.

The first fruit of this imagination—and the first lesson of the social science that embodies it—is the idea that the individual can understand his own experience and gauge his own fate only by locating himself within his period, that he can know his own chances in life only by becoming aware of those of all individuals in his circumstances. In many ways it is a terrible lesson; in many ways a magnificent one. We do not know the limits of man's capacities for supreme effort or willing degradation, for agony or glee, for pleasurable brutality or the sweetness of reason. But in our time we have come to know that the limits of "human nature" are frighteningly broad. We have come to know that every individual lives, from one generation to the next, in some society; that he lives out a biography, and that he lives it out within some historical sequence. By the fact of his living he contributes, however minutely, to the shaping of this society and to the course of its history, even as he is made by society and by its historical push and shove.

The sociological imagination enables us to grasp history and biography and the relations between the two within society. That is its task and its promise. . . . And it is the signal of what is best in contemporary studies of man and society.

No social study that does not come back to the problems of biography, of history and of their intersections within a society has completed its intellectual journey. Whatever the specific problems of the classic social analysts, however limited or however broad the features of social reality they have examined, those who have been imaginatively aware of the promise of their work have consistently asked three sorts of questions:

1. What is the structure of this particular society as a whole? What are its essential components, and how are they related to one another? How does it differ from other varieties of social order? Within it, what is the meaning of any particular feature for its continuance and for its change?

2. Where does this society stand in human history? What are the mechanics by which it is changing? What is its place within and its meaning for the development of humanity as a whole? How does any particular feature we are examining affect, and how is it affected by, the historical period in which it moves? And this period—what are its essential features? How does it differ from other periods? What are its characteristic ways of history-making?

3. What varieties of men and women now prevail in this society and in this period?

And what varieties are coming to prevail? In what ways are they selected and formed, liberated and repressed, made sensitive and blunted? What kinds of "human nature" are revealed in the conduct and character we observe in this society in this period? And what is the meaning for "human nature" of each and every feature of the society we are examining?

Whether the point of interest is a great power state or a minor literary mood, a family, a prison, a creed—these are the kinds of questions the best social analysts have asked. They are the intellectual pivots of classic studies of man in society—and they are the questions inevitably raised by any mind possessing the sociological imagination. For that imagination is the capacity to shift from one perspective to another—from the political to the psychological; from examination of a single family to comparative assessment of the national budgets of the world; from the theological school to the military establishment; from considerations of an oil industry to studies of contemporary poetry. It is the capacity to range from the most impersonal and remote transformations to the most intimate features of the human self—and to see the relations between the two. Back of its use there is always the urge to know the social and historical meaning of the individual in the society and in the period in which he has his quality and his being.

That, in brief, is why it is by means of the sociological imagination that men now hope to grasp what is going on in the world, and to understand what is happening in themselves as minute points of the intersections of biography and history within society. In large part, contemporary man's self-conscious view of himself as at least an outsider, if not a permanent stranger, rests upon an absorbed realization of social relativity and of the transformative power of history. The sociological imagination is the most fruitful form of this self-consciousness. By its use men whose mentalities have swept only a series of limited orbits often come to feel as if suddenly awakened in a house with which they had only supposed themselves to be familiar. Correctly, or incorrectly, they often come to feel that they can now provide themselves with adequate summations, cohesive assessments, comprehensive orientations. Older decisions that once appeared sound now seem to them products of a mind unaccountably dense. Their capacity for astonishment is made lively again. They acquire a new way of thinking, they experience a transvaluation of values; in a word, by their reflection and by their sensibility, they realize the cultural meaning of the social sciences.

2

Perhaps the most fruitful distinction with which the sociological imagination works is between "the personal troubles of milieu" and "the public issues of social structure." This distinction is an essential tool of the sociological imagination and a feature of all classic work in social science.

Troubles occur within the character of the individual and within the range of his immediate relations with others; they have to do with his self and with those limited areas of social life of which he is directly and personally aware. Accordingly, the statement and the resolution of troubles properly lie within the individual as a biological entity and within the scope of his immediate milieu—the social setting that is directly open to his personal experience and to some extent his willful activity. A trouble is a private matter: values cherished by an individual are felt by him to be threatened.

Issues have to do with matters that transcend these local environments of the individual and the range of his inner life. They have to do with the organization of many such milieux into the institutions of an historical society as a whole, with the ways in which various milieux overlap and interpenetrate to form the larger structure of social and historical life. An issue is a public matter: some value cherished by publics is felt to be threatened. Often there is a debate about what that value really is and about what it is that really threatens it. This debate is often without focus if only because it is the very nature of an issue, unlike even widespread trouble, that it cannot very well be defined in terms of the immediate and everyday environments of ordinary men. An issue, in fact, often involves a crisis in institutional arrangements, and often too it involves what Marxists call "contradictions" or "antagonisms."

In these terms, consider unemployment. When, in a city of 100,000, only one man is unemployed, that is his personal trouble, and for its relief we properly look to the character of the man, his skills, and his immediate opportunities. But when in a nation of 50 million employees, 15 million men are unemployed, that is an issue, and we may not hope to find its solution within the range of opportunities open to any one individual. The very structure of opportunities has collapsed. Both the correct statement of the problem and the range of possible solutions require us to consider the economic and political institutions of the society, and not merely the personal situation and character of a scatter of individuals.

Consider war. The personal problem of war, when it occurs, may be how to survive it or how to die in it with honor; how to make money out of it; how to climb into the higher safety of the military apparatus; or how to contribute to the war's termination. In short, according to one's values, to find a set of milieux and within it to survive the war or make one's death in it meaningful. But the structural issues of war have to do with its causes; with what types of men it throws up into command; with its effects upon economic and political, family and religious institutions,

with the unorganized irresponsibility of a world of nation-states.

Consider marriage. Inside a marriage a man and a woman may experience personal troubles, but when the divorce rate during the first four years of marriage is 250 out of every 1,000 attempts, this is an indication of a structural issue having to do with the institutions of marriage and the family and other institutions that bear upon them.

Or consider the metropolis—the horrible, beautiful, ugly, magnificent sprawl of the great city. For many upper-class people, the personal solution to "the problem of the city" is to have an apartment with private garage under it in the heart of the city, and forty miles out, a house by Henry Hill, garden by Garrett Eckbo, on a hundred acres of private land. In these two controlled environments—with a small staff at each end and a private helicopter connection—most people could solve many of the problems of personal milieux caused by the facts of the city. But all this, however splendid, does not solve the public issues that the structural fact of the city poses. What should be done with this wonderful monstrosity? Break it all up into scattered units, combining residence and work? Refurbish it as it stands? Or, after evacuation, dynamite it and build new cities according to new plans in new places? What should those plans be? And who is to decide and to accomplish whatever choice is made? These are structural issues; to confront them and to solve them requires us to consider political and economic issues that affect innumerable milieux.

In so far as an economy is so arranged that slumps occur, the problem of unemployment becomes incapable of personal solution. In so far as war is inherent in the nation-state system and in the uneven industrialization of the world, the ordinary individual in his restricted milieu will be powerless—with or without psychiatric aid—to solve the troubles this system or lack of system imposes upon him. In so far as the family as an institution turns women into darling little slaves and men into their chief providers and unweaned dependents, the problem of a satisfactory marriage remains incapable of purely private solution. In so far as the overdeveloped megalopolis and the overdeveloped automobile are built-in features of the overdeveloped society, the issues of urban living will not be solved by personal ingenuity and private wealth.

What we experience in various and specific milieux, I have noted, is often caused by structural changes. Accordingly, to understand the changes of many personal milieux we are required to look beyond them. And the number and variety of such structural changes increase as the institutions within which we live become more embracing and more intricately connected with one another. To be aware of the idea of social structure and to use it with sensibility is to be capable of tracing such linkages among a great variety of milieux. To be able to do that is to possess the sociological imagination. . . .

Questions

1. What is the sociological imagination? (You might begin with quoting Mills's definition, but try to describe this phenomenon in your own words as well.)

2. In brief, what kinds of questions are asked by those who possess a sociological imagination?

3. What are "personal troubles of milieu"? What are "public issues of social structure"? Why does Mills say that the distinction between troubles and issues is "an essential tool of the sociological imagination"?

2

HOW HISTORY AND SOCIOLOGY CAN HELP TODAY'S FAMILIES

Stephanie Coontz

In this 1997 article (the introductory chapter to her book *The Way We Really Are*), Stephanie Coontz demonstrates the sociological imagination as she discusses the nature of relations between men and women and between parents and kids. Again, these issues *seem* personal; but Coontz demonstrates how taking the larger—sociological and historical—view is very important if we want to find practical answers to such crucial questions as "What's wrong with male–female relationships in modern society?" and "What's happening to today's youth?"

When lecture audiences first urged me to talk about how family history and sociology were relevant to contemporary life, I wasn't sure I wanted to abandon the safety of my historical observation post. But my experiences in recent years have convinced me that people are eager to learn whether historians and social scientists can help them improve their grasp of family issues. And I've come to believe that it's our responsibility to try.

I don't want to make false promises about what history and sociology offer. I can't give you five tips to make your relationship last. I don't have a list of ten things you can say to get your kids to do what *you* want and make them think it's what *they* want. Nor can I give kids many useful pointers on how to raise their parents.

But a historical perspective can help us place our personal relationships into a larger social context, so we can distinguish individual idiosyncrasies or problems from broader

Stephanie Coontz, "How History and Sociology Can Help Today's Families" (editor's title) from *The Way We Really Are*. Copyright © 1997 by Basic Books, a division of HarperCollins, Inc. Reprinted by permission of Basic Books, a member of Perseus Books Group.

dilemmas posed by the times in which we live. Understanding the historical background and the current socioeconomic setting of family changes helps turn down the heat on discussion of many family issues. It can alleviate some of the anxieties of modern parents and temper the recriminations that go back and forth between men and women. Seeing the larger picture won't make family dilemmas go away, but it can reduce the insecurity, personal bitterness, or sense of betrayal that all of us, at one time or another, bring to these issues. Sometimes it helps to know that the tension originates in the situation, not the psyche.

Putting Teen–Parent Conflicts in Perspective

Consider the question of what's happening to American youth. It's extremely difficult for parents today to look at a specific problem they may have with their teenager, whether that is sneaking out at night or experimenting with alcohol and drugs, without seeing it as a sign of the crisis we are told grips modern youth. Parents tell me they are terrified by headlines about the "epidemic" of teen suicide and by chilling television stories about kids too young to drive a car but old enough to carry an AK-47.

Concerns over adolescent behavior are not entirely new. "Let's Face It," a *Newsweek* cover story of September 6, 1954, declared: "Our Teenagers Are Out of Control." The 1955 film, *Blackboard Jungle,* claimed that teens were "savage" animals because "gang leaders have taken the place of parents." Still, there *are* new structural and historical changes in American life that have recently complicated the transition from early adolescence to young adulthood, making youth–adult relations seem more adversarial.

It doesn't help us understand these changes, however, when people exaggerate the problems of today's teens or turn their normal ups and downs into pathologies. Most teens do not get involved in violence, either as criminals or victims. While teen suicide rates have indeed been increasing, any growth from a low starting point can sound dramatic if presented as a percentage. For example, a 1995 report from the Centers for Disease Control stated that suicides among 10- to 14-year-old youths had "soared" between 1980 and 1992. What this meant in real figures, points out researcher Mike Males, was that 1 in 60,000 youths in this age group killed themselves in 1992, compared to 1 in 125,000 in 1980. The actual death rate among teens from firearms and poisoning has scarcely changed since the 1950s, but the proportion attributed to suicide has risen dramatically, while the proportion attributed to accident has declined (Holinger 1994; Males 1996).

Furthermore, many "teen" suicide figures are overstated because they come from a database that includes people aged 15 to 24. Suicide rates for actual teenagers, aged 13 to 19, are among the lowest of any age group. In fact, notes Kirk Astroth, "teens as a whole are *less likely* to commit suicide than any other age group *except* preteens. . . . Occupational surveys

consistently show that parents and teachers are *twice* as likely, counselors and psychologists are *four* times as likely, and school administrators are *six* times as likely to commit suicide as are high school students" (Astroth 1993, 413). (When I read this statistic to a teenage acquaintance of mine, he told me dourly, "Yeah, but they'll just say we drove them to it.")

It's not that we have more bad parents or more bad kids today than we used to. It's not that families have lost interest in their kids. And there is no evidence that the majority of today's teenagers are more destructive or irresponsible than in the past. However, relations between adults and teens are especially strained today, not because youths have lost their childhood, as is usually suggested, but because they are not being adequately prepared for the new requirements of adulthood. In some ways, childhood has actually been prolonged, if it is measured by dependence on parents and segregation from adult activities. What many young people have lost are clear paths for gaining experience doing responsible, socially necessary work, either in or out of the home, and for moving away from parental supervision without losing contact with adults.

The most common dilemma facing adolescents, and the one that probably causes the most conflicts with adults, is their "rolelessness" in modern society. A rare piece of hard data in all the speculation about what makes adolescents tick is that young people do better on almost every level when they have meaningful involvement in useful and necessary tasks. This effect exists independently of their relationships with parents and friends. Teens also benefit from taking responsibility for younger or less-fortunate children. As one author observes, teens "need some experience of being older, bigger, stronger, or wiser" (Hamburg 1992, 201; Maton 1990, 297).

But today's adolescents have very few opportunities to do socially necessary work. The issue of rolelessness has been building for eighty years, ever since the abolition of child labor, the extension of schooling, and the decline in farm work that used to occupy many youths in the summer. The problem has accelerated recently, as many of the paths that once led teenagers toward mastery of productive and social roles have turned into dead ends. Instead of having a variety of routes to adulthood, as was true for most of American history, most youngsters are now expected to stay in high school until age 17 or 18.

High schools were originally designed for the most privileged sector of the population. Even now they tend to serve well only that half of the high school population that goes on to college. Non-college-bound students often tell me they feel like second-class citizens, not really of interest to the school. And in recent decades a high school degree has lost considerable value as a ticket to a stable job. Even partial college work confers fewer advantages than in the past. Because of these and other trends, researcher Laurence Steinberg claims, adolescence "has become a social and economic holding period" (1992, 30).

Parents are expected to do the holding. In 1968, two researchers commented that most teen–parent conflicts stemmed from the fact that "readiness for adulthood comes about two years *later* than the adolescent claims and about two years *before* the parent will admit" (Stone and Church 1968, 447; emphasis added). There is some evidence that the level of miscalculation has widened for *both* parents and kids.

From the point of view of parents, it is more necessary than ever for kids to stay in school rather than seek full-time work, and to delay marriage or pregnancy. After all, the age at which youths can support themselves, let alone a *family*, has reached a new high in the past two decades. From the kids' point of view, though, this waiting period seems almost unbearable. They not only know a lot more than their folks about modern technology but they feel that they also know more

about the facts of life than yesterday's teens. Understandably, they strain at the leash.

The strain is accentuated by the fact that while the age of economic maturation has been rising, the age of physical maturation has been falling. The average age of puberty for girls, for instance, was 16 in 1820, 14 in 1900, and 13 in 1940. Today it is 12, and may still be dropping. For boys, the pace and timing of pubertal development is the most important factor in determining the age at which they first have sex; the influence of parents, friends, income, and race is secondary. Although parents and friends continue to exert considerable influence on the age at which girls begin to have sex, there are obvious limits to how long parents can hold their teenagers back (Nightingale and Wolverton 1988, 1994).

And even as the job market offers fewer and fewer ways for teens to assert their independence and show that they are more grown up than younger kids, consumer markets and the media offer more and more. Steinberg points out that while teens "have less autonomy to pursue societally-valued *adult* activities" than in the past, they "have more autonomy than did their counterparts previously in matters of leisure, discretionary consumption, and grooming." As a result, adolescents "find it easier to purchase illicit drugs than to obtain legitimate employment" (Steinberg 1992, 30).

Another problem for parent–child relations is society's expectation that teens abide by rules and habits that grown-ups have abandoned, and that parents ought to be able to *make* them do so. In preindustrial societies most kids were integrated into almost all adult activities, and right up until the twentieth century there were few separate standards or different laws for teens and adults. For centuries, youth and adults played the same games by the same rules, both literally and figuratively. From "blind man's bluff" to "follow the leader," games we now leave to children were once played by adults as well. There were few special rules or restrictions that applied solely to teens. *All* premarital sex was supposedly out of line in the nineteenth century; teen sex was not singled out as a special problem. In fact, as late as 1886, the "age of consent" for girls was only 10 in more than half the states in the union (Luker 1996). However, girls or women who *did* consent to premarital sex were ostracized, regardless of their age.

Today's adults have moved on to new amusements and freedoms, but we want teens to play the old games by the old rules. There may be some good reasons for this, but any segregated group soon develops its own institutions, rules, and value systems, and young people are no exception.

Sports is virtually the only adult-approved and peer-admired realm where teens can demonstrate successive gains in competency, test their limits, and show themselves bigger, stronger, and better than younger children. But for teens who aren't good at sports, or those who reject it as busywork designed to keep them out of trouble, what's left? Music, clothes, drugs, alcohol—the choices differ. Many kids experiment and move on. Others get caught in the quagmire of seeking their identity through consumption. What we often call the youth culture is actually adult marketers seeking to commercially exploit youthful energy and rebellion. But sometimes consumerism seems the only way teens can show that they are growing up and experimenting with new social identities while adults try to keep them suspended in the children's world of school or summer camp.

Of course, many teens get a lot out of school and summer camp. But the dilemmas of rolelessness often put adolescents and their parents on a collision course. Young people feel that adults are plying them with make-work or asking them to put their lives on hold as they mature. They're pretty sure we didn't put *our* lives on hold at comparable levels of maturity, so they suspect us of hypocrisy. Often, they have a point.

On the other hand, while many parents recognize that risk taking among teenagers hasn't changed much since their own youth, they feel that there are more serious consequences for those behaviors than there used to be, given the presence of AIDS (acquired immune deficiency syndrome), high-tech weapons, and new potent drugs. So adults are not necessarily being hypocritical when they hold kids to higher standards than they met themselves. Many of us fear that the second chances and lucky breaks we got may not be available to the next generation.

Balancing the legitimate fears of adults against the legitimate aspirations of teens is not easy. But it helps for both teens and adults to realize that many of their conflicts are triggered by changes in social and economic arrangements, not just family ones. The best way I've found to personally confirm the sociological studies of rolelessness is to ask older men to talk about their life histories. Some of the most interesting discussions I've had over the past few years have been with men over age 60, whose memories extend beyond the transitional period of the 1960s and 1970s to what teen life was like in the 1930s, 1940s, or early 1950s.

The conversations usually start with comments on irresponsible behavior by today's teenage males. "I'd have had my hide tanned if I'd been caught doing that," someone always says, which generally leads to examples of how they got "whomped" or "taught a lesson." Soon, though, the subject switches to the things these upstanding men *didn't* get caught doing in their youth. And most of the time, it turns out the first lesson they learned by getting whomped was how not to get caught.

When they talk about what *really* set them on the right path, almost every older man I've talked with recalls his first job. "I was supporting myself when I was 17" (16, 18, 19, even 15), or "I was in the army with a job to do," the stories go: "What's the matter with today's kids?"

And soon they provide their own answers. The typical job a teenager can get today provides neither the self-pride of economic independence nor the socializing benefits of working alongside adult mentors. Teens work in segregated jobs where the only adult who ever comes around is the boss, almost always in an adversarial role. Few jobs for youth allow them to start at the bottom and move up; the middle rungs of the job ladder have been sawed off. Marking time in dead-end jobs that teach no useful skills for the future, teens remain dependent on their parents for the basic necessities of life, simultaneously resenting that dependence and trying to manipulate it.

The stories older men tell about their first jobs are quite different from those told by today's teens. Even men who later became businessmen or highly educated professionals say that their first jobs were in construction, factory work, or some menial setting where they worked beside older men who were more skilled or highly paid. The senior men teased the youngsters, sending them out for a left-handed hammer or making them the butt of sometimes painful practical jokes, but they also showed kids the ropes and helped protect them from the foreman or boss. And they explained why "putting up with the crap" was worth it. After older men talk for a while about what these work experiences meant to them, they are almost always surprised to find themselves agreeing that the loss of nonparental male mentoring may be a bigger problem for boys today than the rise of single-mother homes.

Even allowing for nostalgia, such work relations seem to have been critical experiences for the socialization of many young men in the past. Such jobs integrated youths into adult society, teaching skills they would continue to use as they aged, instead of segregating them in a separate peer culture. As late as 1940, about 60 percent of employed adolescents aged 16–17 worked in traditional workplaces, such as farms, factories, or construction sites. The jobs

they did there, or at least the skills they used, might last well into their adult lives. By 1980, only 14 percent worked in such settings (Greenberger and Steinberg 1986).

Girls, who were excluded from many such jobs, have lost less in this arena of life. Up through the 1960s an adolescent girl typically had more responsibilities at home, from washing dishes to taking care of siblings, than she does today. While such tasks may have prepared girls for adult roles as wives and mothers, they also held girls back from further education or preparation for future work outside the home. The change in work patterns for girls has thus made it *easier* for them to see that they have paths toward adult independence. On the other hand, it raises a different set of tensions between girls and their parents. The decline of the sexual double standard, without an equal decline in economic and social discrimination against women, leads parents to worry that their daughters may have too much opportunity, too early, to engage in sexual risk taking for which girls still pay a far higher price than boys.

Another issue facing teens of both sexes is their increasing exclusion from public space. People talk about how kids today are unsupervised, and they often are; but in one sense teens are under *more* surveillance than in the past. Almost anyone about the age of 40 can remember places where young people could establish real physical, as opposed to psychic, distance from adults. In the suburbs it was undeveloped or abandoned lots and overgrown woods, hidden from adult view, often with old buildings that you could deface without anyone caring. In the cities it was downtown areas where kids could hang out. Many of these places are now gone, and only some kids feel comfortable in the malls that have replaced them.

Much has been written about the gentrification of public space in America, the displacement of the poor or socially marginal from their older niches, followed by fear and indignation from respectable people suddenly forced to actually see the homeless doing what they always used to do. Over the years we have also seen what I think of as an "adultification" of public space. Kids are usually allowed there, as long as they're young enough to be in their parents' charge. But where in your town are teenagers welcome on their own?

Teens today have fewer opportunities than in the past for gradual initiation into productive activities, both at home and in public, and fewer places to demonstrate their autonomy in socially approved ways. At the same time, though, they have more access to certain so-called adult forms of consumption than ever before. This makes it hard for adults to avoid the extremes of overly controlling, lock-'em-up positions on the one hand and frequent breakdowns of supervision on the other. Some parents clearly underprotect their kids. We've all seen parents who are too stressed to monitor their kids effectively or who have had their limits overrun so many times that they have given up. Other parents, however, overprotect their kids, trying to personally compensate for the loss of wider adult contacts and of safe retreats. Both extremes drive kids away. But, in most cases, both are reactions to structural dilemmas facing parents and teens rather than abdications of parental responsibility.

What Social Science Tells Us About Male–Female Conflicts

The same kind of perspective can be useful in sorting through conflicts between modern couples. I vividly remember the first people who forced me to bring my historical and social analysis down to individual cases. Following one of my talks, a couple stood up and described a conflict they were having in their marriage. She complained about how unappreciative he was of the effort she took in making

gourmet dinners and keeping the house clean. He said: "Hang on a minute. I never asked her to do any of those things. I can't help it if she has higher standards than I do. I don't *care* what we have for dinner. I don't *care* if the floor gets mopped twice a week." They wanted me to comment on their situation.

This is not fair, I thought, as I tried to wriggle out of doing so. I've just summed up the history of family diversity and changing gender roles since colonial times and they want me to settle a marital argument—over housework, of all things? I'm not a counselor; I don't know anything about mediating these issues. I tried to change the subject, but they wouldn't let up, and the audience was clearly on their side. You think family history is relevant, they seemed to be saying. Prove it.

Trapped, but unwilling to pretend I had therapeutic expertise, I cast about for something in my own research or training that might by any stretch of the imagination be helpful. The only thing that came to mind was a concept I had read about in an academic journal. "So," I said, feeling a bit silly, "perhaps the problem we have here lies in what social scientists would call your 'situated social power'" (Wartenberg 1988).

It sounded very academic, even downright pompous, but the more we talked about it, the more I realized this *was* a useful concept for them. In plain English it means that various groups in society have unequal access to economic resources, political power, and social status, and these social differences limit how fair or equal a personal relationship between two individuals from different groups can really be. Such social imbalances affect personal behavior regardless of sincere intentions of both parties to "not let it make a difference."

Teachers, for example, have social power over students. I tell my students that I want them to speak their minds and express their disagreements with me. And I mean it. But often I don't even notice that they continue to defer until someone finally gets angry at me for "dominating the discussion." Even after all these years, my initial reaction is usually indignation. "I told you to speak up," I want to say; "it's not my fault if you hold back." Then I remind myself that in any situation of unequal power, it's the party with the most power who always assumes that other people can act totally free of outside constraints.

When a person with power pretends not to have it, people with less power feel doubly vulnerable. Although they continue to be unequal, they are now asked to put aside the psychological defenses they have constructed against that inequality, including a certain amount of self-protective guardedness. So they clam up or get sore, which leaves the more powerful person feeling that his or her big-hearted gestures are being rebuffed. This tension arises between people of different races and classes, between employees and supervisors, and between men and women, as well as between my students and me.

With this awareness, I try to remember that my students are never going to feel as free criticizing my work as I'm going to feel criticizing theirs. I have to adjust the structure of my class to facilitate discussion. I need to institute protected spaces for criticism, such as providing anonymous evaluation forms for assessing my performance. But I also have to recognize that our power imbalance will always create tensions between us. I should neither blame my students for that nor feel that I've failed to communicate my "authentic self" to them. None of us exists independently of the social relations in which we operate.

Remembering how helpful this concept is to me in depersonalizing conflicts with students, I reminded the couple that men and women have different options in our society, outside and independent of their personal relationships. Research shows that men are happiest in a relationship when they don't have to do much housework and yet meals get made, clothes get ironed, and the house looks good. This doesn't mean they are chauvinist pigs. Who *wouldn't* be happier under those conditions?

But the wives of such men tend to be depressed. A wife may feel, especially if she jeopardized her earning power by taking time off to raise children, that she can't give up the domestic services she performs, because if her husband *does* get dissatisfied, she has fewer options than he does in the work world, and will be far worse off after a divorce.

Consciously or not, the wife in this particular marriage seemed to be assessing the risk of not keeping a nice house or putting delicious meals on the table, and finding it too high to just relax and let the housework go. But she was also resenting her husband's unwillingness to help out. This very common pattern of seemingly voluntary sacrifice by the woman, followed by resentment for the man's failure to reciprocate, originates outside the individual relationship. The man was probably completely sincere about not caring if the work got done, but he was missing the point. His wife had looked around, seen what happened to wives who failed to please their husbands, and tried extra hard to make her husband happy. He could not understand her compulsion, and resented being asked to participate in what he saw as unnecessary work. Counseling and better communication might help, but would probably not totally remove the little kernel of fear in the wife's heart that stems from her perfectly reasonable assessment of the unequal social and economic options for men and women.

Similarly, two people trying to raise a child while they both work full-time are going to get stressed or angry. Part of the problem may be that the man isn't doing enough at home (on average, research shows, having a man in the house *adds* hours to a woman's workday) (Brace, Lloyd, and Leonard 1995; Hartmann 1981). Part of the problem may be that the woman is sabotaging her own stated desire to have the man do more—treating him as an unskilled assistant, refusing to relinquish her control over child-raising decisions, and keeping her domestic standards too high for him to meet. But another part of the problem will remain even if they are the most enlightened individuals in the world.

There's no nonstressful way to divide three full-time jobs between two individuals. Better communication can make the sacrifices more fair, or help clear away the side issues that get entangled with the stress, but the strains are a social problem existing outside the relationship. The solution does not lie in Martians learning to talk Venusian or Venusians being tolerant of the cultural oddities of Martians, as one pop psychologist describes the differences between men and women, but in changing the job structures and social support networks for family life. Until businesses and schools adjust their hours and policies to the realities of two-earner families, even the best-intentioned couples are going to have difficult times.

Improving communication or using the shortcuts offered by self-help books can alleviate some of the conflicts between men and women in this period of rapidly changing roles and expectations. But addressing communication problems alone ignores the differing social options and the patterned experiences of inequality that continually *re-create* such problems between men and women. So people move from one self-help book to another; they try out new encounter groups and memorize new techniques; they slip back and must start all over again. They are medicating the symptoms without solving the problem.

For example, the Venusian–Martian reference comes from best-selling author John Gray, who has found a strikingly effective analogy for getting men and women to realize that they bring different assumptions and experiences to relationships: Men and women, he says, come from different planets. They need to learn each other's culture and language. Gray tells women why men's periodic

withdrawals from communication do not mean lack of interest in a relationship. Martians, he says, like to retreat to caves in times of stress, while Venusians tend to crowd around, offering each other support and empathy. He explains to men that women are often just asking for reassurance, not trying to control men's lives, when they pursue subjects past the male comfort zone (Gray 1992).

But Gray doesn't urge either sex to make any big changes, merely to take "tiny steps toward understanding the other." He offers women hints on how to ask their partners for help without antagonizing them or making them feel manipulated, but he doesn't demand that men share housework or that women accept the responsibilities that go with egalitarian relationships. For Gray, a healthy relationship exists "when both partners have permission to ask for what they want and need, and they both have permission to say no if they choose." This is certainly better than no one feeling free to ask, but it leaves a rather large set of issues unresolved (Gray 1992, 265; Peterson 1994).

The problem is that many advice books refuse to ask hard questions about the division of household work and decision-making power. In a section called "scoring points with the opposite sex," for example, Gray's advice to women revolves around issues such as not criticizing men for their driving or choice of restaurants. Men, by contrast, are advised: "offer to make dinner," "occasionally offer to wash the dishes," "compliment her on how she looks," "give her four hugs a day," and "don't flick the remote control to different channels when she is watching TV with you" (Gray 1992; Sen 1983).

Now, most women will say that the book would be worth its weight in gold if their husbands would just follow that last tip, but the fact remains that the unequal bargaining power and social support systems for men and women are not addressed, *or even acknowledged,* in this kind of advice. In the long run, failure to address the roots of gender differences perpetuates the problem of communication, or merely replaces one set of misunderstandings with another. As therapist Betty Carter writes, communicating about feelings rather than addressing issues of power and daily behavior can lead to manipulation that eventually degenerates into mutual blame and psychological name-calling (Carter 1996).[1] If we're going to think of men and women as being from different planets, they need more than guidebooks and language translations; we must make sure that the social, economic, and political treaties they operate under are fair to both parties.

It's not only women's dissatisfactions that are addressed by a historical and sociological perspective. Men often complain that feminists ignore male insecurities and burdens, and they have a point. Men *do* feel injured and alienated, despite their economic and political advantages over women of the same social group. But history and sociology can identify the sources of men's pain a lot more accurately than myths about the loss of some heroic age of male bonding when Australian aborigines, Chinese sun kings, and Greek warriors marched to their own drumbeat. Going "back to the woods" makes a nice weekend retreat, but it doesn't help men restructure their long-term relationships or identify the social, economic, and political changes they need to improve their family lives (Bly 1990).[2]

Male pain is the other side of male power. Not all men, contrary to the rhetoric of masculinity, can be at the top of the pyramid. The contrast between rhetoric and reality is very painful for men whose race, class, health, or even height does not allow them to wield power, exercise authority, or just cut a figure imposing enough to qualify as a "real man." Even successful men pay a high price for their control and authority. The competitive, hierarchical environments men are encouraged to operate in cut them off from intimacy and penalize them for letting down their guard. The myth that male power is all individually achieved, not socially structured, means masculinity can be lost if it is not constantly proven in daily behavior (Brines 1994; Lehne 1989).

Structural analysis helps us get beyond the question of "who hurts more" to explore the different rewards and penalties that traditional gender roles impose on today's men and women. For girls, societal pressures descend heavily at about age 11 or 12, penalizing them for excelling and creating a sharp drop in their self-esteem. There is overwhelming evidence, for example, that girls are treated in ways that hinder their academic and intellectual development. But sometimes this discrimination takes the form of too easy praise and too little pressure to complete a task, leading boys to feel that "girls get off easy." And almost any parent can testify that boys are subject to a much earlier, more abrupt campaign to extinguish the compassion, empathy, and expression of feelings that young boys initially display as openly as girls. The list of derogatory words for boys who don't act masculine is miles longer than the list of disparaging words for girls who don't act feminine. Boys who don't get the message quickly enough are treated brutally. Those who do get the message find that the very success of their effort to "be a man" earns mistrust and fear as well as admiration. In an article that my male students invariably love, Eugene August points out that people always talk about "innocent women and children" in describing victims of war or terrorism. Is there no such thing as an innocent man? (August 1992; Gilligan and Brown 1992;

[1]As Andrew Greeley points out (1989), women's morale has declined far more significantly than men's. Unless their frustrations with the marriage bargain are addressed more directly, not just placated, men and women *could* end up on different planets.

[2]For a critique of Bly's point of view, see Connell 1992.

Gilligan, Lyons, and Hammer 1990; Kann 1986; Orenstein 1994; Sadker and Sadker 1994).

It's good to get past caricatures of female victims and male villains, but it is too simplistic to say that we just have to accept our differences. A man's fear of failure and discomfort with intimacy, for example, come from his socially structured need to constantly have others affirm his competence, self-reliance, or superiority. This is the downside of what he must do to exercise power and privilege. For women, lack of power often leads to fear of *success*. The downside of women's comfort with intimacy is discomfort with asserting authority.

As three researchers in the psychology of gender summarize the tradeoffs, boys "get encouraged to be independent and powerful, possibly at the cost of distancing themselves from intimacy." The result is that boys "tend to be overrepresented in the psychopathologies involving aggression." Girls, by contrast, "get rewarded for being compliant and for establishing intimate relations, possibly at the cost of achieving autonomy and control over their choices." This may be why girls are "overrepresented in the psychopathologies involving depression" (Cowan, Cowan, and Kerig 1993, 190).

The solution suggested by historical and social analysis is not for men and women to feel each other's pain but to equalize their power and access to resources. That is the only way they can relate with fairness and integrity, so that unequal and therefore inherently dishonest relations do not deform their identities. Men must be willing to give up their advantages over women if they hope to build healthy relationships with either sex. Women must be willing to accept tough criticism and give up superficial "privileges" such as being able to cry their way out of a speeding ticket if they hope to develop the inner resources to be high achievers. . . .

References

Astroth, Kirk. 1993. "Beyond Ephebiphobia: Problem Adults or Problem Youths?" *Phi Delta Kappan,* January.

August, Eugene. 1992. "Real Men Don't: Anti-Male Bias in English." Pp. 131–141 in Melita Schaum and Connie Flanagan (eds.), *Gender Images: Reading for Composition.* Boston: Houghton Mifflin.

Bly, Robert. 1990. *Iron John: A Book About Men.* Reading, MA: Addison-Wesley.

Brace, Judith, Cynthia Lloyd, and Ann Leonard, with Patrice Engle and Niev Duffy. 1995. *Families in Focus: New Perspectives on Mothers, Fathers, and Children.* New York: The Population Council.

Brines, Julie. 1994. "Economic Dependency, Gender, and the Division of Labor at Home." *American Journal of Sociology* 100.

Carter, Betty. 1996. *Love, Honor, and Negotiate: Making Your Marriage Work.* New York: Pocket Books.

Connell, R. W. 1992. "Drumming Up the Wrong Tree." *Tikkun* 7.

Cowan, Philip A., Carolyn Pape Cowan, and Patricia K. Kerig. 1993. "Mothers, Fathers, Sons and Daughters: Gender Differences in Family Formation and Parenting Styles" in Philip Cowan et al., (eds.), *Family, Self, and Society: Toward a New Agenda for Family Research.* Hillsdale, NJ: Erlbaum.

Gilligan, Carol, and Lynn Mickel Brown. 1992. *Meeting at the Crossroads: Women's Psychology and Girls' Development.* Cambridge, MA: Harvard University Press.

Gilligan, Carol, Nona Lyons, and Trudy Hammer. 1990. *Making Connections: The Relational World of Adolescent Girls at Emma Willard School.* Cambridge, MA: Harvard University Press.

Gray, John. 1992. *Men Are from Mars, Women Are from Venus.* New York: HarperCollins.

Greeley, Andrew. 1989. "The Declining Morale of Women." *Sociology and Social Research* 73.

Greenberger, Ellen, and Laurence Steinberg. 1986. *When Teenagers Work: The Psychological and Social Costs of Adolescent Employment.* New York: Basic Books.

Hamburg, David. 1992. *Today's Children: Creating a Future for a Generation in Crisis.* New York: Times Books.

Hartmann, Heidi. 1981. "The Family as the Locus of Gender, Class and Political Struggle: The Example of Housework." *Signs* 6.

Holinger, Paul. 1994. *Suicide and Homicide Among Adolescents.* New York: Guilford.

Kann, Mark. 1986. "The Costs of Being on Top." *Journal of the National Association for Women Deans* 49.

Lehne, Gregory. 1989. "Homophobia Among Men: Supporting and Defining the Male Role." Pp. 416–429 in Michael Kimmel and Michael Messner (eds.), *Men's Lives.* New York: Macmillan.

Luker, Kristin. 1996. *Dubious Conceptions: The Politics of Teenage Pregnancy.* Cambridge, MA: Harvard University Press.

Maddrick, Jeffrey. 1995. *The End of Affluence: The Causes and Consequences of America's Economic Dilemma.* New York: Random House.

Males, Mike. 1996. *The Scapegoat Generation: America's War on Adolescents.* Monroe, ME: Common Courage Press.

Maton, Kenneth. 1990. "Meaningful Involvement in Instrumental Activity and Well-Being: Studies of Older Adolescents and At Risk Urban Teenagers." *American Journal of Community Psychology* 18.

Nightingale, Elena, and Lisa Wolverton. 1988. "Adolescent Rolelessness in Modern Society." Working paper, Carnegie Council on Adolescent Development, September.

———. 1994. "Sex and America's Teenagers." New York: Alan Guttmacher Institute.

Orenstein, Peggy. 1994. *School Girls: Young Women, Self-Esteem, and the Confidence Gap.* New York: Doubleday.

Peterson, Karen. 1994. "A Global Ambassador Between the Sexes." *USA Today*, March 28.

Sadker, Myra, and David Sadker. 1994. *Failing at Fairness: How American Schools Cheat Girls.* New York: Scribner.

Sen, Amartya. 1983. "Economics and the Family." *Asian Development Review* 1.

Steinberg, Laurence. 1992. "The Logic of Adolescence." In Peter Edelman and Joyce Ladner (eds.), *Adolescence and Poverty: Challenge for the 1990s.* Washington, DC: Center for National Policy Press.

Stone, L. J., and J. Church. 1968. *Childhood and Adolescence: A Psychology of the Growing Person.* New York: Random House.

Wartenberg, Thomas. 1988. "The Situated Concept of Social Power." *Social Theory and Practice* 14.

Questions

1. Would Mills conclude that Coontz has a sociological imagination? Why or why not?

2. What is "rolelessness"? As a teenager, did you experience (or are you now experiencing) this phenomenon? Explain.

3. What is "situated social power"? Describe an example of situated social power that you have experienced or witnessed personally.

4. Consider the concept of "adultification." To what extent did it exist in the place(s) where you grew up? Explain. How might this problem be resolved?

3

HERNANDO WASHINGTON

Lisa J. McIntyre

One of the things that sets sociologists apart from ordinary people is their concern for the social. In their professional lives, sociologists tend to ignore individual cases and focus on aggregates or groups. For example, Émile Durkheim studied suicide in order to discover what factors contributed to fluctuations in the overall rates of suicide; he had no interest in what might lead particular individuals to take their lives.

Professional sociologists study *social* facts simply because these are interesting (at least to us). But to the layperson trying to live life in society, social facts may seem irrelevant. Why a society's crime rate goes up and down seems much less intriguing than why *my* house was robbed, or why *I* was mugged on the street. Likewise, the social forces that propel the unemployment rate are not nearly as interesting as the matter of why I am having a difficult time finding a job.

As C. Wright Mills pointed out, however, having a sociological imagination allows us to make connections between individuals and the societies in which they live. And, for the student of sociology, the acquisition of this imagination brings with it an enhanced ability to make sense of the behavior of individuals. Recall what Mills stressed as the "first fruit" of the sociological imagination: "the idea that the individual can understand his own experience and gauge his own fate only by locating himself within his period." It was in this sense that Stephanie Coontz (in the previous reading) brought to bear the sociological concept of "situated social power" to help her understand her own relationships with her teaching assistants, as well as the personal troubles of the woman whose husband did not appreciate her heroic housework.

From the viewpoint of the professional sociologist, the following reading may seem out of place in a sociology reader, because its focus is on an individual and how he responded to his immediate social milieu. But I have included it for the benefit of nonsociologists; written in 1999, it provides an example of how having an understanding of the impact of the social milieu can help us to understand the all-too-frequently unintelligible behaviors of individuals in our environment.

To get a Ph.D., one has to write something called a dissertation. It's essentially a research paper, and sometimes a very long research paper. Mine, for example, ended up being two hundred plus pages. I wrote my dissertation on public defenders—those attorneys who are paid by the state to defend people who are accused of crimes but can't afford to hire their own lawyer. The basic question was this: How can these attorneys defend individuals they know are guilty of crimes, especially if they are terrible crimes? Ultimately, I arrived at my answer by looking not just at the private consciences of the public defenders but also at what Mills would have called their social milieux or surroundings.

I met a number of murderers in the course of my research, but Hernando was my first one; and in part because he was my first, he left a large impression on me. But this crime also made a big impression on me because it seemed so bizarre. It never should have happened the way it did. But you can judge for yourself. I will tell you the story as I learned it.

Warning: The first time I heard this story, I remember being shocked. I remember, in fact, feeling nauseous. It's not because anyone showed me terrible pictures of the crime scene; it's just because the whole thing seemed so awful. And it *seemed* so awful because it *was* awful. That led me to wonder, Should I share this story with college students? Possibly, no one is (or should be) worldly enough to hear about this sort of thing.

The Case

This story takes place in Chicago. The major player in the story is a man named Hernando Washington. At various times, his nicknames included the Reverend and the Deacon, because he was president of the youth choir. His other nickname was Prince, because he was so charming and good-looking.

Before I get to the story, let me tell you a bit about the neighborhood in which Hernando lived, or as Mills would put it, his *social milieu*. It was on the South Side of Chicago. In his 1973 song "Bad, Bad Leroy Brown" songwriter Jim Croce describes Chicago's South Side as the "baddest" section of the city. That was an astute observation. It is the baddest part of town; chances are, if you lived on the South Side, you'd never be able to get a cab driver to take you home at night; some cabs won't even venture there in the daytime.

The police refer to a murder that involves a man and woman on the South Side as a "South Side divorce." A great deal of its reputation involves the fact that the South Side of Chicago is heavily populated by people who are poor—mostly African Americans. Perhaps that's why the police tend to disrespect the people who live there. The police often call murders that involve African American killers and victims as "63rd Street misdemeanors." Police also take much longer to respond to calls on the South Side. The clear message to the people who live there is that they really aren't a part of the community that the Chicago police are pledged to "serve and to protect." This, I think, is an important fact.

[handwritten margin note: the police does not care about them]

On April 1, 1978, Hernando "Prince" Washington was arrested and charged with robbery, aggravated kidnapping, rape, and murder. His victim, 29-year-old Sarah Gould, was the wife of a physician and the mother of a small child. Sarah Gould had the great misfortune to be one of the 787 people in Chicago and one of the 20,432 people in the United States who were murdered that year.

When I say that Sarah had the "great misfortune" to be murdered, I mean that. Statistically, she should not have been a murder victim. Nationally, the murder rate for white women in 1978 was 2.8 per 100,000 population. For white men, it was 9.0; for black women, 12.8; and for black men, 58.1. Not only was Sarah white, but she was killed by a stranger. And in 1978, most murder victims were killed by people they knew—friends, lovers, family members, acquaintances, or neighbors. Of all the recorded acts of criminal violence—batteries, assaults, murders—in 1978, less than a third were committed by strangers. This was especially true for women: When the violent act was committed by a stranger, the victim was typically male.

Finally, Sarah Gould was white while Hernando was black. This was one of the more unusual aspects of the case. Most violence, and certainly most murders, involve persons of the same race.

So, the odds were really against Sarah Gould being murdered—however you want to look at it.

That year, April 1, April Fool's Day, fell on a Saturday. The story actually begins two days earlier. That Thursday afternoon, Hernando went out to do his sister Leah a favor. She had just bought a car, a used two-year-old Oldsmobile Cutlass, and the dealer had called the day before to tell her it was ready to be picked up. Hernando offered to do this for her, partly because he wanted to drive the car. His sister, who is ten years older than Hernando, said that would be fine as long as Hernando came to pick her up when she was done with work. Leah worked at the post office and got off work ten minutes before midnight.

Hernando picked up the car, but of course he didn't drive it straight home. Instead, he cruised around his South Side neighborhood for a while. However, he didn't see any of his friends, so he decided to cruise up to the north part of the city.

For Sarah Gould, that was a fatal decision.

Hernando later said he didn't have any particular plan, but eventually he admitted that just maybe, in the back of his mind, he thought he might rob someone. But it was nothing definite. He would simply drive around and see what happened.

Once up north, he drove to Northwestern University's hospital parking lot. He got out of his car and sat on the steps of a nearby building.

ROBBERY AND ABDUCTION

Around 7:30 P.M., Hernando saw a woman getting out of a reddish-orange VW Rabbit. He approached her, gun in hand, and demanded her money. Sarah gave him $25, explaining that it was all the money she had, but he grabbed her by the arm, dragged her back to his car, and shoved her inside.

Later, when asked why he did that, he told his lawyers that he'd noticed a bunch of people walking toward them and he didn't want them to know that he had just robbed this woman. He said he was afraid that she'd scream or run or something.

Once Hernando got Sarah into the car, he was still afraid that she'd somehow make trouble, so he ordered her to take off her slacks and underpants. He threw her clothing underneath her car and then drove off.

In his confession to the police, Hernando had this to say:

> She was real excited, you know, asking me not to hurt her and I was constantly telling her I wouldn't hurt her, that all I want is money. She was sitting in the front seat alongside of me. We drove off, and she asked me, "What are you going to do to me?" and I told her that I would take her away from the area, so I would have a chance, you know, to get away without being caught.

He kept assuring her that he would not hurt her.

THE PHONE CALL

After Hernando drove around for several hours, Sarah said that he should let her go because her husband and son would be getting worried about her. He considered this for a while and then asked her if she'd like to call home. He stopped at a gas station that was closed for the evening but it had a phone booth.

Sarah's husband, who was indeed worried about her, later told police that she had said something to the effect that she was okay. He asked her, "When are you coming home?" There was a pause, and then he could hear Sarah asking someone when she'd be home. In the background, he heard a male voice saying "an hour." He then asked, "Where are you?" She asked, "Where are we?" Her husband heard the answer: "You'll be home in an hour, bitch, come on."

After the phone call, Hernando told police,

I turned from the phone, going around the car and at this time, when I, you know, walked around to my car, she broke and ran. I was running after her. I asked her, I said, "Why are you acting like that? I have not hurt you, I told you I will let you go, I just want to make it as safe for me as you want it safe for yourself."

Then, as it was approaching midnight, Hernando pulled the car into a dark alley. He explained to Sarah that he had to go pick someone up and that she couldn't stay in the front seat of the car while he did this. Perhaps for a moment Sarah thought he was going to let her go, but instead, he forced her into the trunk telling her that if she was quiet, everything would be okay.

At exactly 11:50 P.M., Hernando was where he was supposed to be—in the car in front of the main post office. His sister Leah came out and got into the front seat with him. As he drove her home, they talked about the sorts of things that you would expect a brother and sister to talk about—mostly about the new car.

When they got home, Hernando waited in the car until Leah was inside the house. He had always been very concerned about her safety.

A few years earlier, Leah had been raped on her way home from work. Two men grabbed her, dragged her into an alley, stripped off her clothes, and raped her repeatedly. Afterwards, she crawled out of the alley and was relieved to see a police car there. The two officers looked at her, a black woman with her face bleeding and her clothes torn up, and said "Get home by yourself, bitch." Maybe they didn't want her to mess up the back of their patrol car.

Usually, Hernando met his sister after work— but that night he'd had a bike accident and was running late.

Indeed, Hernando's family had not had a great deal of luck when it came to dealing with the police. A few years earlier, Hernando's brother James had been at a party when he was shot by one of the neighborhood guys. Some of James's friends took

him to the emergency room, but they were afraid to stay with him because gunshot wounds tend to attract attention. They left him in the emergency room, where he bled to death before the medical staff got to him. "Everyone knew" who had shot Hernando's brother, but for some reason the police didn't take him into custody. It was at that point that Hernando bought his first gun.

Then Hernando drove a few blocks away, stopped, and let Sarah out of the trunk. She reminded him of his promise to let her go, but he said they'd have to go back and get her clothes, because he didn't want to let her go until she was fully dressed again. He drove back to the hospital parking lot, but her clothes were gone; by now, the police had them.

When Sarah had driven into that parking lot earlier in the evening, she was on her way to a Lamaze class she was supposed to teach that night. Eventually, her students became worried about her, called her husband, and found out that she wasn't home. And, of course, he thought she was in class. Next, the class notified hospital security, which investigated and found Sarah's car in the parking lot. When they saw her keys in the ignition and her pants and underpants under the car, the security officers were naturally concerned. They called her husband, who immediately called the police to file a missing person's report.

Finding the clothes missing from under the car scared Hernando. Sarah told him that it didn't matter, that she could go home without them—she was covered enough, she said, by her long raincoat. But he was adamant that he wasn't going to let her go until he'd found her something to wear or, as he put it, until she was "decent" again. He said, "I've got to think of somewhere to get you some clothes."

THE RAPE

By now, it was well past midnight. Hernando thought it was much too late to go to a friend's house and borrow some clothes, so instead, he drove them back down to the South Side. On the way, he stopped and bought a pint of rum, leaving Sarah alone in the car for a moment. Then, he drove to a motel, got out of the car (again leaving Sarah in the front seat alone), registered for a room—in his name. He later told police, "I let her wash up. First she was kind of skeptical. I guess she was frightened. I kept reassuring her that I would not do anything to her. After a while, she went into the bathroom and washed up." Then, he told police, they both went to sleep.

But that was a lie. What really happened next, as Hernando admitted to his attorneys, was that he raped Sarah.

The next morning, Hernando left Sarah alone in the room while he checked out. After they left the motel, he stopped the car and put her back into the trunk. Then he drove to his parents' house to get a change of clothing for himself.

A few blocks later, Hernando let Sarah out of the trunk. Then he drove to a northwestern suburb where he had an appointment. On the way, he again stopped in an alley and forced her into the trunk while he "took care of some business."

What was this urgent appointment? Hernando's "appointment" was in one of the felony trial courtrooms in Cook County, Illinois. At the time all this was going on, Hernando was out on bail. A year earlier, Hernando had been arrested on charges of rape and aggravated kidnapping. His parents had taken out a loan, paid his bail, and hired him a private lawyer, who told Hernando that he would probably beat the rap and not to worry.

In any case, that Friday, March 31, was the scheduled trial date for the year-old rape case. When the case was called, however, the prosecutor requested a continuance, which the judge granted. Feeling good, Hernando walked out of the courtroom a relatively free

man; he even offered his lawyer's assistant a ride back downtown.

When Hernando got back to his car, he saw a couple of people standing near it, seemingly talking to his trunk. Hernando told them to get lost and sped away. But one of the people got Hernando's license plate number and called it in to the police. The dispatcher who took the call about a "woman in the trunk" relayed the message to the detective division; someone placed it on a detective's desk.

Unfortunately, that particular detective had taken off—unannounced—for the weekend, and so no one found the message until the next morning. By then, it was too late. Sarah was dead.

Hernando let Sarah out of the trunk and told her he was disappointed that she'd tried to get help. After all, hadn't he told her that he wasn't going to hurt her and that he would let her go as soon as she got some clothes?

Hernando drove around for a while, and then, as he later told his lawyers, he noticed how dirty her raincoat was. Once again, he told Sarah that he just had to find some decent clothes for her. And once again, she protested that it really wasn't necessary, that she could get home without being fully dressed. Instead, Hernando went to the home of an old girlfriend to borrow some clothes. But he ended up not getting any clothes, claiming that he just didn't quite know how to ask and that her boyfriend was home and he didn't want the boyfriend to hear.

So he released Sarah from the trunk and drove around some more.

As evening approached, Hernando put Sarah back into the trunk of the car and went to meet some friends at a bar. Actually, they ended up going to several bars. He was, he said, getting pretty tired, but he liked being with his friends. And he was "reluctant" to go back to his car because he knew he'd have to deal with this problem. Finally, well after midnight, he returned to the car.

At this point, as they were listening to Hernando tell his story, one of his attorneys asked him, "If you were beginning to be uncomfortable about your situation, why didn't you just let her go, then and there?" Hernando said, "Because the neighborhood I was in wasn't a safe neighborhood for a white woman to be alone in."

Instead of letting her go, he took Sarah to another motel and again raped her. Details about the rape are sketchy because Hernando was a "little shy," as he put it, when it came to talking about "sex." And that's how he referred to the rapes—as sex.

THE MURDER

Early the next morning, Hernando checked out of the motel, drove around for about an hour, and then came to a decision: Clothing or no clothing, it was time to let Sarah go. He parked the car on a residential street, gave her some change, and told her to get on the bus. He said he told her, "All you got to do is walk straight down the street there and get on the bus. Go straight home."

And Sarah, as Hernando always emphasized when he got to this part of the story, Sarah Gould *promised* him that she would get on the bus and go straight home. And, of course, she *promised* not to tell the police.

Hernando let Sarah out of the car, and as he drove away, she was walking toward the bus stop. But, as soon as he was out of sight, she changed her course, walked up to a house, and rang the doorbell.

The house belonged to a Chicago firefighter, who was getting ready for work. He opened the door and saw Sarah—messy, dirty, bruised, and distraught. She told him that she needed help; he told her that he would call the police and that she should stay right there on the porch. Then he closed the door and went to phone the police.

Meanwhile, Hernando had begun to wonder whether Sarah had kept her promise and gotten on the bus. So he doubled back to where he had left her. He saw Sarah standing on the porch of that house; he saw the firefighter talking to her; he saw the firefighter close the door.

As Hernando recounted it, he felt betrayed—she had broken her promise to him. He parked and got out of the car. He said that he called out to her. In Hernando's words, here's what happened next:

> I called to her and she came down. I took her by the arm and around the corner to the alley.
>
> I said, "What are you doing? All you had to do was get on the bus. You promised that you would get on the bus."
>
> She protested that I was hurting her, that I was going to kill her.
>
> I said, "No. All you had to do was get on the bus!"
>
> She screamed, "You are going to kill me!"
>
> I said, "No, you said you was going to get on the bus. All you had to do was to get on the bus. Stop screaming. I'm not going to hurt you."
>
> She said, "You are going to kill me."
>
> I said, "I am not going to kill you, shut up, stop screaming."
>
> She said, "You are going to kill me. You are going to kill me."
>
> I said, "I am not going to kill you."
>
> She said, "You are going to kill me. I know you are going to kill me."
>
> So I shot her. Then I shot her again. She fell. I looked at her, then I broke and ran to my car.

The Chicago firefighter kept his promise and called the police, but they were too late to save Sarah. Around one of her wrists was a cloth stamped with Hernando's father's name. When the police asked the firefighter why he didn't let Sarah into his home, he said that when he saw how beat up she was and saw a black man out on the street calling to her, he assumed it was a domestic dispute and didn't want to get in the middle of it.

Shortly thereafter, the police found Hernando at his parents' home, washing the trunk of his car. At first, he denied everything. Then, when police confronted him with the fact that witnesses had said he had a woman in the trunk of his car, he said it was a prostitute. He varied his story every time the police introduced more information. The police were gentle with him; they read him his Miranda rights, they offered him food and drink. But they confused him with their questions, and it didn't take too long for Hernando to confess to having robbed, kidnapped, and murdered Sarah.

But when police asked Hernando to sign the confession, he refused, saying that it might make his attorney mad. It didn't matter. That attorney didn't really want to have anything to do with Hernando the murderer, and besides, his parents had no money left to pay him.

Before his trial, his new attorneys—public defenders—persuaded him that his only chance to beat the death penalty was to plead guilty. This was one of those cases that defense attorneys in Chicago, not without a certain amount of irony, call a "dead bang loser case"—one in which "the state has everything but a videotape of the crime." At first, Hernando didn't want to plead guilty; he didn't want his parents to know that he was guilty. But ultimately, in hopes of saving his own life, he did plead guilty.

It didn't work. In January 1980, Hernando was sentenced to death. Finally, on March 25, 1995, after his appeals were exhausted, Hernando was executed by lethal injection.

Hernando's lawyers spend a lot of time trying to find some explanation for what happened. Maybe if they could understand what had been going on in his mind, it would help to save his life. But Hernando couldn't really say. What he kept saying, in essence, was, "What is the big deal? Why is everyone so upset with me?" It was not that, in his mind, Hernando did not understand that robbery, kidnapping, rape, and murder are against the law. The fact that he at first denied doing them helped to prove that. So, Hernando was not legally insane—in the sense that he didn't know right from wrong. It was simply that he could not understand why everyone was so worked up about what he had done.

This is difficult for most of us to understand. Why would someone be surprised at getting into really serious trouble for robbing, kidnapping, raping, and murdering another human being? At first, I could not make any sense of Hernando's confusion on this point. But eventually, as my horror receded, I was able to bring a more sociological perspective to bear on the whole subject. In other words, I had to call upon my sociological imagination—I had to look for the general in the particular.

Let me begin my explanation with an analogy. Last semester, in my introductory class, two students decided to turn in the same paper. They weren't in the same section, so I guess they thought they could get away with it. Unfortunately for them, in my department the professors discuss the papers because we want to be sure that we are all grading consistently. We noticed that the two students had submitted the same paper, so we called them in and said, "Hey, you cheated. And, as it says in the syllabus, if you cheat, you flunk."

At first, in each case, the students denied the accusation. However, when confronted with positive proof (copies of the papers with their names on them), they admitted what they had done. But, they said, our reaction was way out of line. Yes, they had read in the syllabus that getting caught cheating meant flunking the course. But flunking was simply *too much* punishment. In one case, flunking meant more than getting an F; it meant losing scholarship and loan money.

Hernando's reaction was much the same: "Okay, I did this, but you shouldn't punish me; certainly you shouldn't punish me this much."

You may be thinking that my analogy isn't really appropriate, that there is no way to compare students who cheat with people who murder. And, of course, I would not compare the behaviors. What I am comparing is how the individuals thought about their acts, and especially their reactions to the punishment.

Both the murder and the cheating were done in hopes of not getting caught; and in neither case did the perpetrators plan on getting caught. Furthermore, when they were caught, each thought the punishment was way out of proportion to the crime. In the case of the students, they argued that the consequences were much too severe, that cheating on a paper wasn't that bad and that losing a scholarship is unfair. In part, too, I think the students were shocked to find that we actually were going to flunk them. I suspect that to the degree they thought about it in advance, they expected to be given another chance, or to receive some lesser punishment. It's possible that they knew of other students who had been caught but not punished for cheating. In any case, their view was that punishment was unfair.

Hernando's reaction was much the same. He acted as if he thought that people were simply too worked up over his deeds. Being sentenced to death was just not acceptable to him. Like our students, he showed no real remorse for what he had done. He was only sorry that he had been caught and had to deal with the consequences.

Again, I suspect that some of you won't like my analogy. Perhaps you can understand why the students might feel that the punishment for cheating was too harsh. But you might wonder how Hernando could think that he should not be given the more serious punishment for what he'd done wrong.

This is where having a sociological imagination becomes helpful. The students felt abused because they did not see cheating as such a horrendous crime. After all, cheating happened all the time, and in any case, it was only a class paper.

The same kind of logic can be used to explain Hernando's reaction. Recall that Hernando had grown up on Chicago's South Side, where, when a husband killed his wife, it was jokingly referred to by police as a "South Side divorce." That sort of attitude from officials teaches people that life is not very valuable. And, as I mentioned previously, Hernando had learned some more personal, and painful, lessons about the low value placed on life. When his sister was raped, the police would not help her; they would not even give her a ride home. Also, when his brother was murdered, no one moved to identify the killer, much less to arrest him.

What I did not stress was the degree to which Hernando himself had committed violent acts against others. I did mention that he was out on bail on a rape and kidnapping charge, but in addition to that, he had raped at least three other women. No charges were brought in any of those cases—perhaps because they were not reported, for his victims knew there would be little point. *Those* victims also lived on the South Side.

What about the one charge he did have against him? Hernando's parents had mortgaged their home to get him a private lawyer, who told him he would beat the rape charge. Again, Hernando got the same message: His acts had no consequences. As a result of his life experiences, Hernando had learned that human life doesn't count for too much and that it's okay to take what you want. That's why he was so surprised that he was in so much trouble.

Let's look at what two psychiatrists had to say about Hernando.

> He appeared to mask any signs of strong emotions and states that "this is typical for me." He gave an example of—if he were upset about something and it pertained mostly to himself, he wouldn't reveal it to anyone. He would give the impression that he didn't have any feelings, and that he does not reveal his real emotions. . . . He shows a recall of dates and times not in synchrony with reality—this,

together with his difficulty with complex problem solving and concept formation—shows impairment, possibly indicative of minimal brain dysfunction. . . .

The evaluation of this man indicates that he is suffering from a borderline personality disorder with episodic deterioration in reality testing and thought processes with episodic psychotic thinking. There is the impression of someone who may be seen as withdrawn or aloof, with a superficial intellectual achievement in the use of language which masks a lowered intellectual achievement. There is also the indication of a minimal brain damage, which combined with his psychological profile, would indicate that at times of stress (as existed prior to the commission of the alleged offense) he lacks the ability to plan and to comprehend the consequences of action.

He has at best a fragile purchase on reality. He feels overwhelmed by external stimulation and must constantly narrow his perceptual field in order to manage it. These overwhelmed feelings include those of inferiority and paranoia. While he generally stays close to the normal bounds of reality, he does occasionally lapse into abnormal perception and thinking. His capacity to recover from such lapses is the major reason for forgoing a diagnosis of schizophrenia. In general, his thinking and perception are idiosyncratic. He often does not see what others see. The mode of this distortion is to experience and understand the world in ways that are egocentric and sociopathic. . . . [The results of projective tests] present a picture of a highly impoverished internal world where fantasy and imagination are often enacted according to the most basic laws of "kill or be killed," or "eat or be eaten."

Note that this second psychiatrist stressed his expert opinion that *Hernando did not have much of a grasp of reality.* The psychiatrist made that judgment because Hernando persisted in seeing the world as a jungle in which the rule is to kill or be killed.

If this psychiatrist had possessed a sociological imagination, he might have realized that Hernando actually had an uncannily accurate grasp of reality. The understanding of his world as one in which the most basic law was kill or be killed was no delusion or misunderstanding; that was the way things worked on the South Side of Chicago. The very structure of social life in that part of the city meant that people were vulnerable—without help from the police, they had only themselves to fall back on.

But Hernando, too, lacked a sociological imagination—the ability to see beyond his own immediate social milieu, to understand that there are different rules for different people in places like Chicago. On the South Side, where the population is mostly poor and mostly African American, people don't have much power to call on "the establishment" to help them, so life is like a jungle. But on the North Side, things are different. When Hernando drove his sister's car to the North Side of Chicago, he made a fatal error because he drove into a part of the world where life does have value.

On the face of it, we seemingly can never understand what Hernando did. However, it is easier to understand if we use our sociological imagination (as Mills told us to do) and look past Hernando to his social milieu or environment. Then, things begin to make sense.

Don't get me wrong! I'm not saying that we should excuse Hernando for what he did because of the harsh environment in which he grew up. That's not the point. And certainly, that's not the *sociological* point. The goal of sociology is to understand and make predictable people's behavior, to explain what can lead people to act as they do.

What's the benefit of this sort of sociological thinking? What if it were your job to help prevent such crimes? Wouldn't you want to understand how the social environment affects people so that you could, if possible, make changes in that environment? Wouldn't you want to have a sociological imagination?

Mini-Glossary

borderline personality disorder a personality disorder characterized by a long-standing pattern of instability in mood, interpersonal relationships, and self-image. Frequently severe enough to cause extreme distress or interfere with social and occupational functioning.

egocentric centered around and focused on the self.

idiosyncratic a personal reaction (not shared by other people).

minimal brain dysfunction a relatively mild impairment of brain function which has subtle effects on perception, behavior, and academic ability.

psychotic a form of thinking in which the individual has inaccurate perceptions. Specific symptoms of psychosis include delusions, hallucinations, markedly incoherent speech, disorientation, and confusion. Psychotic individuals generally do not know that they are confusing reality and fantasy.

sociopathic like "psychopathic," a term for what is now usually called "antisocial personality disorder." This disorder is characterized by chronic and continuous antisocial behavior (and is not due to severe mental retardation, schizophrenia, or manic episodes). This behavior pattern, which is more common in males than in females, generally begins before the age of 15 with such infractions as lying, stealing, fighting, truancy, vandalism, theft, drunkenness, and substance abuse. It then continues after age 18 with at least four of the following manifestations: inability to work consistently, inability to function as a responsible parent, repeated violations of the law, inability to maintain an enduring sexual relationship, frequent fights and beatings inside and outside the home, failure to repay debts and provide child support, travel from place to place without planning, repeated lying and conning, and extreme recklessness in driving and other activities.

Questions

1. After I tell them about Hernando, students frequently ask me: "Why didn't Sarah Gould escape? She seemed to have so many chances, why didn't she take advantage of them?" Because I never had an opportunity to speak with Sarah, I will never know the answers for sure, but like my students, I can't help but wonder about it.

   The sociologist Max Weber introduced sociologists to the concept of *verstehen*—that's a German term meaning "empathic understanding." According to Weber, one way to better our understanding of people's behavior is to use empathy to put ourselves in their places to determine what they were thinking and feeling about their situations. With this concept in mind, why do you think Sarah didn't try to escape from Hernando?

2. Assume that you are a sociologist who is presented with the opportunity to act as an investigator for Hernando's defense team. In that role, you have the opportunity to ask questions of everyone involved in the case—Hernando himself; his attorneys, family, friends, and psychiatrists; and Sarah Gould's family and friends. Who would you want to interview? What questions would you ask?

3. Suppose you are the mayor of Chicago and you've just read all the facts of Hernando's murder of Sarah Gould. In a memo to your chief of police, what suggestions might you make to improve the structure of the city's law enforcement to help prevent this sort of crime from happening again?

4

ADOLESCENT HUMOR DURING PEER INTERACTION

Stephanie Sanford and Donna Eder

In the following article, authors Stephanie Sanford and Donna Eder study the role played by humor among adolescent friends. They find that depending on size and the closeness of the group, different types of humor are used: memorized jokes, funny stories, practical jokes and humorous behavior. As you read the article, pay special attention to *how* the researchers obtained their data and how they justified their methods.

Introduction

Recently there has been a growing awareness of the importance of peer interaction for child development and socialization. While humor has been identified as a fundamental aspect of children's interaction (Fine, 1977; McGhee and Chapman, 1980), we know very little about the nature of humor in naturally occurring interaction. We know even less about humor among adolescent peers.

Research on adults indicates that humor serves a variety of social functions. For example, adults use humor both to challenge and strengthen relationships with others (Kane et al., 1977; Giles et al., 1976). Humor may also be

We would like to thank Bill Corsaro, Diane Felmlee, Gary Fine and Cathy Evans for their helpful suggestions. This research was supported by Spencer Grant No. 44-329-02 and NIMH Grant No. MH 36680-01. A version of this paper was presented at the American Sociological Association Meetings, San Francisco, September, 1982. Requests for reprints should be sent to Donna Eder, Department of Sociology, Indiana University, Bloomington, IN 47405.

Stephanie Sanford and Donna Eder, "Adolescent Humor During Peer Interaction," *Social Psychology Quarterly*, Vol. 47, no. 3 (Sept. 1984): 235–243. © 1984. Reprinted by permission of SAGE Publications via Copyright Clearance Center, Inc.

used to strengthen within-group ties while, at the same time, maintaining hostilities between groups (Chapman et al., 1980). Previous research on preadolescent boys and adolescent girls suggests that humor is often used to express curiosity about taboo topics such as sexuality (Fine, 1977, 1981; Ransohoff, 1975; Sacks, 1978).

This paper examines the role of humor in peer interaction among adolescents. It is part of a larger study of early adolescent peer relations and socialization. During the course of this study we were surprised by the frequency with which adolescents utilize humor in their daily informal interactions. While we had not anticipated this, we found that humor was an important means for communicating attitudes towards others. As we examined humor more closely, we found that its ambiguous nature allows adolescents to convey feelings without being held accountable for them.

We also found that humor plays a central role in adolescent socialization. Its ambiguous nature allows adolescents to explore sensitive issues like sexuality without having to reveal explicitly the extent of their actual knowledge in this area. Also, it is an indirect means for communicating peer and adult expectations for behavior. Finally, it is clear that an important aspect of peer group socialization is learning how to use different types of humor and how to interpret the potentially ambiguous messages being conveyed.

In this paper we look at four distinct types of humor: (1) memorized jokes; (2) funny stories; (3) practical jokes; and (4) humorous behavior. The four different types are distinguishable based upon the form each takes and according to how each is used in adolescent interaction. At the same time all four types have a common characteristic, i.e., they are indirect, and thus ambiguous modes of communication. The value of this aspect of humor for adolescent interaction as well as the potential problems it can lead to are also considered.

Methods

The data for this report were collected as part of an extensive study of adolescent peer interaction in a middle-school setting.[1] The school which was selected for this study was chosen because it enrolls students from a range of socioeconomic backgrounds, from upper middle class to lower class.[2] It is located in a medium-size midwestern community and is also attended by students from surrounding rural areas. While most of the students are white, a small number of black students are also enrolled. The school itself is relatively large, with approximately 250 students per grade.

The unit of analysis for this study was lunch periods. Both researchers observed lunch periods twice weekly, one for a five-month period and one for a nine-month period, for a total of 242 lunch periods. The study was designed to collect data on interaction among adolescents of different ages and social backgrounds. Thus, both researchers attended lunch periods for each of the three grades (sixth, seventh, and eighth). In addition, one observer usually sat on the side of the cafeteria where students from predominantly middle- to lower-middle-class backgrounds typically sat and the other sat on the side occupied largely by working- and lower-class students.[3] Most of the groups we observed were all-female groups, although we did observe a few mixed-sex groups. Altogether we observed 9 groups and have data on approximately 120 students. This includes nearly one-third of the girls who were in the school at the time of the study.

Besides observing lunchroom interaction, both researchers also observed other school events in which peers interact, including before and after school activities, athletic games and practices, and school parties, picnics and other social events. In this study we focus mainly on lunchroom interaction since it provides the only opportunity at school for sustained interaction with friends on a regular basis. Also, data from lunch periods are the most representative of the female students at the school since all students ate lunch at school, whereas only some students participated in athletic and other social events.

Another advantage of the lunch period was that we could participate in the same activity with students, namely, eating lunch with them, and thus were able to establish good rapport fairly quickly. This, along with the fact that we were in the setting on a regular basis for an extended period of time, makes us quite confident that our data represent typical examples of adolescent humor during lunchtime.[4]

---

[1]For a discussion of norms governing adolescent, peer interaction see Eder and Sanford (1982).

[2]Occupational information was obtained by asking all sixth-grade students in the school to list their parents' occupation and place of work. The census occupational classification system was used to code occupations. Based on this coding 23% of the students have fathers in professional and managerial occupations, while 77% have fathers in clerical and blue-collar occupations.

---

[3]This division of the cafeteria according to social class was done at the initiative of the students themselves and was most apparent in the older grades, particularly in eighth grade.

[4]One indication that we were accepted by students was their willingness to swear openly even though swearing is against school rules and, thus, not normally done in the presence of adults. Some students also informed others that we were "one of them" and could be trusted.

Although we informed students that we were doing a study of adolescent interaction and friendship, we did not take notes openly. Between lunch periods we took brief notes and immediately after leaving the setting we recorded detailed notes by tape recorder. During the last two months we also tape recorded many lunch periods and took full notes both before and after listening to these recordings.[5]

Our field notes were coded for type of event, including all humorous events. Humorous events were identified mainly through laughter,[6] although on some occasions students would specifically identify certain acts as being jokes, funny stories, or practical jokes or would talk about a comment or behavior being "funny." Altogether there were 154 humorous events recorded in our field notes. Field notes from 44 percent of the lunch periods we observed had at least one humorous event, with some having as many as five. It should be noted that this does not reflect the total amount of humor during lunch periods since we may not have remembered all the humorous events that occurred on a given day. It does indicate that humor was a frequent activity among adolescent girls.

Memorized Jokes

Sharing "memorized" jokes is an activity in which students at all three grade levels engaged.[7] These jokes are gathered from a variety of sources—parents, siblings, television programs, etc.—and are repeated to friends at school. The following example is representative of the joke-telling episodes we observed:

From there, the interaction between Lynne[8] and Jean continued. Gayle was involved in this as well as Sarah. Then other people got involved as the joke telling started. Lynn told the same jokes that she had told me two days earlier. There was one, "Why is a chicken so ugly?" "Because it's got a pecker right between its eyes." Then there was one about a Russian and an American and the communication between them was misinterpreted by the Russian and the Russian ran back to the camp and said, "This man's going to swim across the lake and fuck me so hard my eyeballs come out!" (That's how he interpreted what was a more straightforward kind of a message.) And then another joke about a chicken, "What's the difference between a man and a chicken?" "A chicken can pick up corn with its pecker." (S.S., 4/23)[9]

The context in which this episode occurs is important for understanding how joke telling is utilized by adolescents. On this particular day, Lynne was a newcomer to this group of friends. She and Jean had talked to each other on several occasions due to the fact that they were both interested in the same boy. This was the first time Lynne actually joined the group Jean sat with. We observed several other incidents in which memorized joke telling was used as an initial way of interacting with a new group of people.

The jokes in the episode above also point to another common feature of adolescent joking—joking often has to do with sexual topics such as intercourse, menstruation, and genitalia. Sexual jokes are told in mixed groups as well as in all-girl groups. In fact, in mixed groups girls will sometimes choose sexual topics about which they have more information, such as menstruation:

Andrea then told a joke . . . There was a bar and three vampires came in for a drink. The

---

[5]These recordings are currently being transcribed and will be used for future analyses.

[6]Occasionally laughter occurred when students were embarrassed and not amused. However, the nature of laughter, as either a response to being amused or to just being embarrassed, was usually readily apparent from the immediate context or from our background information.

[7]Joke telling was commonly found in mixed-sex groups; all other types of humor occurred primarily in groups of girls.

---

[8]All names used are pseudonyms.

[9]Field notes by S.S. concern students from primarily lower-class backgrounds, while field notes by D.E. concern students from primarily middle-class backgrounds.

first one came up to the bar and said, "I'd like a glass of fresh blood," took the blood and drank it. The second one came up to the bar and said, "I'd like a glass of fresh blood" and got a glass of blood and drank it. The third one came up and said, "I'd like a glass of hot water please" and the bartender said, "What are you going to do with hot water? You're a vampire." And the vampire pulled out a used "tampax" and said, "Teatime" . . . Not many people laughed outright to that, and, in fact, Andrea looked at John and said, "Do you understand it?" . . . He nodded but he hadn't laughed very naturally either. So I wonder if he understood it. But the consequence was that John then launched into a series of what he considered to be more sexual or "dirtier" jokes. (S.S., 3/30)

The telling of sexual jokes is one way for adolescents to exchange information about sexuality. Sexual jokes provide adolescents with an opportunity to deal with this potentially embarrassing, and yet highly salient, topic in an indirect way. Through these jokes they can talk about words and information they are unsure of without being held accountable for precise meanings or details. This indirect nature of humor is one of its key assets, making it an extremely important form of communication for adolescents.

A third feature of joke telling is apparent in the example above. That is, group members become engaged in a contest to "do one better" as far as joke telling is concerned. Engaging in such a contest has other advantages as well—one can hide the fact that s/he didn't understand the joke just told. In the next example it seems very likely that John was not only feeling competitive but that he wished to mask his embarrassment:

Gwen told a joke—first she told it to me and then to John, and . . . it was "How many knees do you have?" And you always say "two." And then she said, "No." Speaking to me, she said "You have three, a right knee, a left knee and a hinie." And to John she said, "You have a left knee, a right knee, a hinie, and a weenie."

And everybody thought that was pretty funny, and John looked a little bit embarrassed, but he came back right away with a joke, "Okay, Gwen . . . Three monkeys, Do, Re, Mi, were sitting in a tree . . . Do and Re fell down, and who was left?" And you're supposed to say "Me" but everyone there knew the answer to that one. So, instead of saying "Me" Gwen said "You." (S.S., 2/24)

The theme that much of adolescent behavior is directed toward acting "grown-up" is a common one. For the students in the lower grades at Woodruff "grown-up" means acting like seventh or eighth graders. For eighth graders it means acting like a high schooler. This characteristic is easy to identify—many conversations have to do with people's acquaintances in the higher grade levels.

Having the knowledge and ability to tell risque jokes is treated as a sign of maturity. There is the assumption (as is the case among adults, most likely) that the joke teller understands the sexual behavior being described in the joke (e.g., listeners seldom accuse the teller of failing to understand his or her own joke).

In general, adolescents appear to have high regard for those peers who discuss topics which are essentially prohibited in the school. For example, school rules dictate that students may not use "swear words"; there is also a rule that boys and girls may not hold hands. Swearing and telling sexual jokes are both done frequently and people who engage in these behaviors are admired in many groups.

In one episode, for example, Ilene concluded her story of having a fight with another girl with the self-characterization that she has a "German temper" and thus she'll say just what she means. Ilene's friends all agreed with her and pointed out that she was always getting into trouble for saying bad things. At this point Ilene recited a limerick which referred to a man with "96 pounds of meat" who had intercourse with a woman who "farted softly on the ground." After the intercourse, the man's "meat" was "shredded." Ilene and her friends found this "joke" very amusing and, importantly, in telling it Ilene provided proof of her prior claim that she had a "bad mouth." Likewise, one group of 7th graders frequently told jokes in a manner meant to attract attention from others in the room. They often shouted out the "bad" words contained in jokes loudly enough to cause others in the lunch room to turn their heads and look. By behaving in this manner the girls established that they were sophisticated by virtue of using prohibited expressions and fearless to do so in such an open manner.

Other general types of humor are tied much more directly to the immediate adolescent "culture." That is, the fact that "dirty" jokes are told with frequency, and the fact that they are utilized to "make conversation" in situations where it may be unclear as to what to talk about otherwise, certainly says something about what topics interest adolescents. Nevertheless, memorized jokes are frequently borrowed from older acquaintances and adults.

Adolescents create their own humor as well primarily through telling funny stories, playing practical jokes, and engaging in humorous behavior. In fact this is a large proportion of the occurrences of female adolescent humor (80%). Funny stories and practical jokes are as easily identifiable as memorized jokes—all three normally occur as specific incidents or episodes. The fourth type, humorous behavior is normally integrated into ongoing interaction.

Funny Stories

In contrast to memorized jokes, which are told to new acquaintances, funny stories are shared primarily among friends.[10] Both types

of humor are presented in a similar manner: interactants take turns building a series of jokes or tales. Also, like memorized jokes, funny stories are relatively context independent. Often they are set apart from the ongoing conversation with an introductory remark such as "I have a funny story to tell."

The content of funny stories differs dramatically from that of memorized jokes in that most stories concern events in the daily lives of adolescents. The most common subject of humorous stories was some type of rule violation involving either adolescents themselves or their acquaintances. Through these stories, adolescents shared knowledge about peer and adult norms and also conveyed information about situations in which norm violations were permissible or at least possible.

By describing rule violations involving other students, adolescents often clarified their own views concerning acceptable social behavior. For example, one day two seventh graders were describing the behavior of a boy on their bus. They said that if food was being passed around on the bus he would eat it all when it got to him. While they found his behavior humorous, their discussion of his behavior made salient the importance of sharing food among friends.

On a different occasion, Betty and Mary shared stories which described situations in which the norm that boys and girls remain physically separated is upset:

> Mainly they were talking about their boyfriends, telling stories about them. Betty told a story about how Sue was changing her clothes in the girls' bathroom and Fred was chasing someone who had his coat and almost went into the bathroom when Sue was changing her clothes. Mary's story was about how she and some other girls had carried somebody—a boy—by his leg and arms. (D.E., 10/24)

In the first story, a boy almost enters the girls' restroom, where someone is at least partially nude. In the other, girls make physical contact

---

[10]"Funny story" is a term used by the students themselves. Many story-telling episodes were initiated with statements like "I've got a funny story to tell you!"

with a boy and actually "overpower" him. When one friend relates such a narrative to another, she is inviting that friend to explore the issue with her: how did the people in the story behave and what is the proper response to such behavior?

In other cases, humorous stories provide information about situations in which violations of adult norms are permissible. For example, one day Karen told the following story about her father:

> Karen said, "You know what my daddy was doing last night," and then told a short story about how he had gone to wash the truck and when he came home, he came in the house and said, "Goddamn birds. Got the whole damn truck to shit on and they shit on the windshields." And she was saying how she was sitting there saying, "Calm down, dad. Calm down." Julie's response to the story was, "Your dad said that?" (D.E., 517)

Part of what makes this story humorous is Karen's adultlike, calm behavior in comparison to her father's frustrated, angry behavior. At the same time, this story provides information about situations in which adults feel free to swear, i.e., when they are extremely angry or frustrated.

Through other stories peer norms were defined by contrasting them with adult norms. For example, Sharon entertained her friends by telling them how "hung up" her mother was about cleanliness and by imitating her mother's comments and habits in this regard. By doing so, she was implying that her own standards are different from those of her mother.

Getting in trouble during choir was a topic of several funny stories told by a group of eighth-grade girls. One day several girls collaboratively told a story about the altos getting in trouble for not singing at a school concert.

> Penny said she (the music teacher) was saying how three altos were fighting about it and how they weren't going to sing that song. Mardi then imitated the teacher, who said, "Well, I'm not going to play it. I'm not going to baby you." Then Karen said they only sang it for Joy, Tami and Sherry but not for Peggy. Then Penny said something about how she had heard the choir teacher saying that "You guys begged her." They made fun of that, "Oh yes, we were down on our knees, pulling her dress, begging her to let us sing." (D.E., 5/21)

This story clarifies a peer norm regarding appropriate reasons for singing for others by contrasting it with the adult norm, i.e., students should sing when instructed to sing. They clearly reject this norm, but do end up singing. They explain that they only sing for their friends, indicating at the same time whom they consider their friends and whom they consider their enemies.

Funny stories thus reveal another important function of humor for adolescents, i.e., to share and convey information regarding peer and adult norms. Through funny stories, students provide information about what they consider to be appropriate behavior. At times this is accomplished by contrasting peer expectations with those of adults. Funny stories also convey information about the appropriate use of peer and adult norms by indicating situations in which norm violations are permissible. In general, funny stories provide an important vehicle for indirectly conveying important information about appropriate behavior.

Practical Jokes

While practical jokes are also clearly definable events, they are more context dependent than either memorized jokes or funny stories. The themes of practical jokes are closely tied to the immediate situation and often have to do with taking and/or destroying someone's food or property (papers and books, for example). Practical jokes are played for two contradictory reasons: (1) to reinforce friendships; or (2) to show dislike for certain people. Because

practical joking serves these two very different functions, ambiguity often arises during
the course of a joke.

Since practical joking brings attention to the
joke's recipient, it can be used between friends
as a means of flattery. That is, for some people,
at least, being the "center attraction" among a
group of friends is a desirable position to be in:

> Ilene tried to distract Julie by telling her to look
> at a certain table and then when she did that she
> took her bag of chips from her. Julie appeared
> not to notice for quite awhile, and during this
> time they passed the bag of chips all the way
> down along one side and over to Bonnie. Then
> all of a sudden Julie said, "Oops! She (her
> mother) left something out." And then she said,
> "My chips are gone." But she said it in a way as
> if she realized they had taken them and she was
> playing along with them. (D.E., 5/5)

Here, although she is the "target" of the joke,
Julie helps her friends to "pull it off." When
she finally claims to notice that something is
going on, her reaction is not one of anger or
despair, for the joke playing has made her the
center of attention among her friends.

At the opposite extreme, practical joking is
used among friendship groups to relay negative messages to the "less desirable" members.
Many of the groups we observed had at least
one member who was seen by the others as
being less desirable. While occasionally dislike
or disapproval was conveyed directly to these
girls, it usually was conveyed indirectly—
often by making them the target of practical
jokes. For example, Nancy was viewed by her
group as being less desirable, in part, because
other group members thought that she did not
dress as well as they did, e.g., did not wear
name-brand jeans and sports shoes. One day
Bonnie brought an Easter egg for everyone in
the group. Nancy's was the only one which
was not hard boiled, and when she cracked it
open she got raw egg all over her hand.

In another group, Betty was becoming
increasingly less popular because she refused

to share her lunch and openly made fun of
other group members, both of which were
considered to be violations of group norms.
One day she was the target of a practical joke:

> As soon as Betty left, Linda said to Mary and
> Carol, "Let's take her shake." They took it and
> put it at the other end of the table. When Betty
> came back she said, "Okay, where's my shake?"
> She got mad immediately and said, "Well I don't
> care then." Linda went and got the shake and
> continued joking, asking Sally, "Do you want
> some of this shake? It's really a good shake."
> Betty didn't joke at all. She was really mad at
> Linda for taking her shake and didn't say much
> until they gave it back to her. It was interesting
> that everyone wanted to play a joke on her and
> that Betty didn't respond at all in a joking way
> but instead got really angry. (D.E., 3/3)

The fact that this form of humor is utilized
for two very different purposes helps explain
why many instances of practical joking are
met with ambiguity by the recipients. In other
words, many times it is apparently not clear
to the recipient whether the joke is meant as
a show of friendship or whether it should be
taken as a sign of dislike:

> Lisa then played a trick on Wendy. She tiptoed
> all the wayaround the table and then she stood
> behind Wendy and put her index finger to her
> mouth, telling everyone to be quiet and not let
> Wendy know that she was behind her. And
> she didn't [know] . . . because another girl was
> standing next to her talking to her. And then
> Lisa dropped a piece of wrapper into Wendy's
> milk, which made Wendy turn real red and
> made her more angry than anything else.
> Wendy first turned to Renee and said, "Do you
> have 20¢ I could borrow to buy a new milk?"
> And finally Wendy turned to Lisa and said,
> "Lisa, give me 20¢ to buy a new milk." And
> then Lisa said, "Here, you can have my milk."
> And at that point Wendy laughed a little bit
> about it. (S.S., 3/12)

In the above episode, it wasn't until Lisa
had established the friendly nature of her
act by agreeing to give Wendy her own milk

that Wendy treated the joke as an exchange between friends. On the same day, only a short time later, Lisa pulled a similar joke on Helen. Lisa "got away" before Helen could see her and it was not until someone else explained that Lisa had done it that Helen calmed down and stopped fuming. Although her initial reaction had been one of anger, it took only the knowledge that Lisa had been the perpetrator to get Helen to view the episode as a friendly joke in the end.

The potentially ambiguous nature of practical jokes has some useful as well as some negative consequences. Because these jokes are often ambiguous, they allow students to express feelings indirectly. This is especially useful in regard to negative feelings which can be conveyed through jokes without expressing open dislike. At the same time, this ambiguity can be confusing, especially to new group members or members who are unsure about their standing in the group. They may not know how to interpret a joke and may assume a negative message is being conveyed when the exact opposite message was really intended.

Humorous Behavior

Humorous behavior is very different in form from memorized jokes, practical jokes, and funny stories. It seldom composes an entire episode or segment of interaction. Instead, it is usually interjected into the normal flow of interaction. Humorous behavior may be verbal, nonverbal, or both; it is closely tied to the ongoing interaction and conversation. Thus, this type of humor is both spontaneous and context dependent.

Humorous behavior varies in degree of complexity. In the most simple form, it is used among female friends within small groups as a means of acting out and expressing what are normally "taboo" topics. Specifically, within this context, girls are much more likely to

bring up aspects of sexuality which affect females most directly, such as pregnancy, menstruation, and breast development. Three examples follow:

> they were joking about pregnancies today. This has come up before. A girl was blowing up her ice cream wrapper . . . and they were saying it was pregnant, and she thought that was really funny. And later on Tami was putting a basketball underneath her sweater so she looked pregnant. It's interesting how this idea is very funny to them. (D.E., 11/10)
>
> Jean got some catsup on her sweatshirt . . . and she tried to wipe it up and Lynne made the comment, "What are you leaking today?" And that "grossed out" everybody at the table. I said, "use some cold water and it will probably come out." Lynne said, "Yeah *blood* does that." And everybody went, "Oh, that's really gross." (S.S., 1/29)
>
> They were joking around about breasts again. One girl said she wanted a milk shake and shook her breasts as she said this. Afterwards they commented on how dumb this was. (D.E., 12/15)

All of these examples typify the kind of humorous behavior that occurs frequently in interaction among small groups of girlfriends. In most of the groups we observed, female sexual development was "discussed" only through some form of humor, and certain topics, such as menstruation, were never discussed in a serious manner. Nevertheless, the frequency with which groups of female friends raised topics regarding sexual development through humorous behavior underlies the importance to girls of sharing such information.

In its more complex form, humorous behavior conveys information about social norms and a message concerning the ongoing interaction or the existing relationships. Often a humorous remark is funny because it represents a violation of a social norm, as in this example among a group of close friends:

> There was some talk about the eighth-grade dance which was initiated by Lisa when she

asked Bob if he was going to go. He said yes and then [she asked] who he was going to take. And he said he didn't know. Then . . . Penny said, "Well, who are you going to take, Lisa?" And Lisa laughed and said *she* wasn't going to take anybody . . . (S.S., 4/21)

What makes Penny's question to Lisa a clever and humorous one is the fact she ignored the rules typically followed in dating at this school, among students of this age—i.e., boys ask girls out and not vice versa. At the same time, Penny succeeds in "smoothing over" a potentially embarrassing situation in which Lisa might be viewed as prying into things that Bob is not willing to share with this particular group of friends.

Other times humorous behavior clarifies a particular group's norms by contrasting them with those of adults and other groups. For example, one day a group of sixth-grade girls who did not wear make-up or have elaborate hair styles made fun of a teacher who did:

[They] talked a lot about gym class and about . . . a gym teacher. First one person said she hates her. Another person said, "I hate her too," then someone else said, "I hate her three," which was followed by "I hate her four" and "I hate her five." They were also talking about how thick her make-up is and how her face is really small but it gets really thick when she puts all this make-up on. Then Heidi was saying . . . "Oh, I have to go now . . . my fiance is coming in 3 hours and I have to fix my hair." And they joked and joked about how funny it was that she would have to spend 3 hours fixing her hair and about how this one hair is out of place. (D.E., 2119)

These girls are using humorous behavior both to clarify group norms about appropriate behavior and to convey a negative attitude toward the gym teacher—showing the complexity of this form of humor.

In the previous episode an adult's behavior served as the basis of comparison when defining a group norm. A similar episode took place in an 8th-grade group in which a student's behavior served as the basis of comparison:

Then they started talking about some other girl, maybe the girl that was running for queen, and about how much make-up she wore. Cindy said, "Her face is probably this thin and the rest of it is make-up." (D.E., 4/12)

This episode shows how norms regarding appropriate behavior can vary across peer groups. While this particular group of girls did not wear make-up, girls in other groups did. Through humorous behavior, girls can reinforce their own group norms as well as reinforce certain friendship boundaries, in this case by conveying a negative attitude toward a non-group member. This also illustrates an important difference between communicating negative attitudes through practical jokes versus humorous behavior. While practical jokes are always aimed at someone who is present, humorous behavior often focuses on someone who is outside the immediate situation. When this person is another student, it allows members to reinforce friendship distinctions as well as normative distinctions.

Because humorous behavior is often very complex, it can be an ambiguous form of communication. The following example of humorous behavior points to the ambiguity which frequently goes hand in hand with this type of humor. This is the case even in situations like the following which take place among relatively close friends for the purpose of essentially reinforcing that friendship:

Bill came by . . . and Tami said to sit across from her and so he did. He had both of his arms across the table toward her and he indicated that her boyfriend Kevin was walking by. He was . . . teasing Kevin by being friendly to Tami, and then told Tami why he was doing that. (D.E., 10/10)

In this example, Bill challenges the norm for exclusive boy–girl interaction, while conveying positive feelings toward his friend Kevin by teasing him. Bill, however, feels a need to clarify the nonserious nature of this act. By doing so he avoids the potential conflict which could arise from violating an important interactional norm.

This episode illustrates the importance of shared interpretations when a peer group's own norm is the subject of humorous behavior. When this occurs, the behavior can reinforce the norm by drawing attention to it and, at the same time, reinforce the friendship by drawing positive attention to the other person. However, if the behavior is misinterpreted, it may be seen and treated as a violation of the group's own standards and may also weaken, rather than strengthen, interpersonal ties.

Discussion

In general, we found that adolescents use different types of humor in different situations. When they were in large groups or among students they did not know well, adolescents relied primarily on memorized jokes for entertainment. On the other hand, when they were with students they knew well, they told funny stories, played practical jokes, and engaged in humorous behavior.

We also found that different types of humor were used for very different purposes. Memorized jokes were often used to establish one's identity, especially a sophisticated identity. This sometimes took on a competitive nature, with students attempting to be the most "sophisticated." In contrast, humor among good friends was seldom competitive and was used to communicate normative information often by challenging adult norms. In addition, some forms of humor such as practical jokes and humorous behavior were often used either to reinforce friendships or convey dislike. While contextual information could be used to interpret the positive or negative direction of these messages, we found some cases where

the nature of the message was so ambiguous that explicit clarification was needed.

The fact that such different forms of humor were found in different groups has important implications for the development of social skills. Specifically, it is important to consider the different skills learned by students who have a group of close friends versus those who do not. Students without close friends would be less likely to participate in funny stories, practical jokes, and humorous behavior. Since these types of humor are often used to convey both positive and negative messages, lack of experience with such humor could have important implications. For example, these students could either miss or misinterpret a message intended to convey affiliation. Likewise, they might miss or misinterpret a message intended to convey dislike and remain in a group where they are not wanted. At the same time these students would be less aware of appropriate norms for peer group behavior and may not be able to distinguish adult norms from those of their peers.

One common theme throughout is the use of humor to deal indirectly with sensitive topics and issues. Humor was a useful way to bring up sensitive topics like sexuality and to discuss embarrassing experiences. It was also a useful way to convey positive and negative feelings indirectly, allowing students to make their feelings toward other group members known without being held accountable for them. In this regard, humor has many of the same advantages as nonverbal communication, which is also less direct and more ambiguous.

The indirectness which is an essential aspect of humor makes it a very useful tool in peer socialization, allowing adolescents to discuss topics which might be too embarrassing to discuss directly. At the same time, because humor is an indirect and complex form of communication, adolescents first need to learn how to use and interpret it. In many of the examples, the use of humor was clarified, or explained, showing how adolescents teach each other to use this valuable form of communication.

Most of the groups of good friends in our study were female. We do know that groups of boys often use humor in a competitive way much like the mixed-groups in our study (Labov, 1972; Fine, 1977). It would be important to see if groups of male friends use other types of humor, such as those used by girls in this study, and to determine whether boys develop similar or different skills than girls through their participation in humorous events.

In summary, humor was found to play an important role in peer interaction. Its indirect nature allowed adolescents to discuss sensitive topics and convey feelings towards others without being held accountable. Many of the types of humor used by adolescents were found to be complex, often ambiguous, forms of communication. Extensive interaction with peers would thus be needed before many of these types of humor could be comprehended and effectively utilized. Likewise, further in-depth research is needed before the role of humor in peer interaction will be adequately understood.

References

Chapman, A. J., J. R. Smith, and H. C. Foot 1980 "Humor, laughter, and social interaction." P. E. McGhee and A. J. Chapman (eds.), Children's Humour. New York: John Wiley and Sons, Ltd.

Eder, D., and S. Sanford 1982 "The development and maintenance of interactional norms among early adolescents." Paper presented at the International Sociological Association Meetings, Mexico City.

Fine, G. A. 1977 "Humor in situ: The role of humour in small group culture." Pp. 315–18 in A. J. Chapman and H. C. Foot (eds.), It's a Funny Thing, Humour. Oxford: Pergamon Press. 1981 "Rude words, insults, and narration in preadolescent obscene talk." Maledicta 5:51–68.

Giles, H., R. Y. Bourhis, N. J. Gadfield, G. J. Davies, and A. P. Davies 1976 "Cognitive aspects of humour in social interaction: a model and some linguistic data." Pp. 139–54 in A. J. Chapman and H. C. Foot (eds.), Humour and Laughter: Theory, Research and Applications. Chichester: Wiley.

Kane, T. R., J. M. Suls, and J. Tedeschi 1977 "Humour as a tool of social interaction." P. 16 in A. J. Chapman and H. C. Foot (eds.), It's a Funny Thing, Humour. Oxford: Pergamon Press.

Labov, William 1972 Language in the Inner City: Studies of Black English Vernacular. Philadelphia: University of Pennsylvania Press.

McGhee, P. E., and A. J. Chapman 1980 Children's Humour. New York: Wiley.

Ransohoff, R. 1975 "Some observations on humor and laughter in young adolescent girls." Journal of Youth and Adolescence 4:155–70.

Sacks, H. 1978 "Some technical considerations of a dirty joke." Pp. 249–69 in J. Schenkein (ed.), Studies in the Organization of Conversational Interaction. New York: Academic Press.

Questions

1. In this research, the authors used observational methods to obtain their data. Can you think of any other technique that could have been used?

2. According to the authors, what lessons do students learn from the humor?

3. The authors claim that humor can help clarify norms. Explain how this happens.

4. According to the article, telling "memorized jokes" help establish one's identity. Explain how this is so.

5. This article focused on *adolescent* humor. In your experience, do adults use humor differently?

5

MISCOUNTING RACE: EXPLAINING WHITES' MISPERCEPTIONS OF RACIAL GROUP SIZE

Charles A. Gallagher

What proportion of the United States is white? African American? Asian? Latino? White people tend to get the answers wrong. In this article, Gallagher investigates the phenomenon of "racial innumeracy" in an attempt to discover why white people tend to get the numbers wrong? Does it matter?

The extent to which whites overestimate the nonwhite population and underestimate the white population is well documented. A 2001 Gallup poll found that the "average American" thinks the United States is 33 percent black, almost three times the actual percentage (Gallup 2001). A recent poll conducted by the Kaiser Foundation found that whites estimated the black population at 29 percent, more than twice the actual number (Kaiser Family Foundation 2001). Another study found that 54 percent of the U.S. population thinks that blacks account for at least 30 percent of the population, with almost one in seven believing they comprise more than 50 percent of the total population (Nadeau, Niemi, and Levine 1993). A Kaiser Family Foundation survey in 1995 found that white Americans believe the United States is 50 percent white (Patterson 1997). It appears that a sizable number of white Americans go about their day thinking that whites are a thin majority nationally and that nonwhites, lumped together, are as large or larger than the white population. The actual census figures tell a different story. In 2000 the U.S. population was 75.1 percent white, 12.7 percent black, 0.9 percent American Indian, and 3.6 percent Asian. Latinos, who can be of any race, comprised 12.5 percent of the total population (U.S. Bureau of the Census 2002).

Survey research on perceptions of racial group size describes which populations are more likely to overestimate the nonwhite population; these are individuals with low incomes, those with a high school degree or less, and those under thirty years of age (Carrol 2001; Gallup 2001; Gallup and Newport 1990; Gilens 1999; Giles and Evans 1985; Loeb 1994; Nadeau, Niemi, and Levine 1993; Quillian 1996). Why the dominant group exaggerates the nonwhite population has not been explored. I attempt to fill the gap in the existing literature on perceptions of racial group size by exploring the accounts whites offer in individual interviews and focus groups.

How the dominant group perceives racial group size and the narratives they draw on to explain their own racial innumeracy has important implications for race relations. Because racial attitudes develop as part of a relational, group-level process (Blumer 1958; Bobo, Kluegel, and Smith 1997; Lewis 2002), uncovering the sources of racial innumeracy will help us to gain knowledge of the images or circumstances that shape perception of

Charles A. Gallagher, "Miscounting Race: Explaining Whites' Misperceptions of Racial Group Size" from *Sociological Perspectives* 46, no. 3: 381–396. Copyright © 2003 by Pacific Sociological Association. Reprinted with the permission of University of California Press Journals.

group size and will provide a window into how whites see their own group standing in relation to other racial groups. This knowledge can also provide important information about how perceptions of group size may influence racial attitudes. The major focus of this exploratory study is to give white respondents from various social backgrounds and levels of exposure to racial minorities the opportunity to detail why they misconstrue the nonwhite population. This study will allow us to examine if whites explain their estimates of the population by drawing on narratives of threat, status anxiety, or the effects of residential segregation, or offer new explanations that have not been identified previously.

Research on Racial Innumeracy

In their survey on how the size of the black population influences whites' attitudes on race, Fossett and Kiecolt (1989) found that whites feel threatened by blacks as their group size and proximity to the black population increases. Other research has demonstrated that when the concentration of the nonwhite population increases, whites feel threatened by a loss of social status that is associated with living in majority white neighborhoods (Blumer 1958; Feagin and Vera 1995; Giles and Evans 1985; Hacker 1995; Massey and Denton 1993; Schuman et al. 1997; Sigelman and Welch 1993). Threats to white economic, political, and social standing are thought to be most acute when whites find themselves competing with nonwhites over resources and the various social structures that control their allocation (Bonilla-Silva 2001; Feagin and Vera 1995; Gallagher 1997; Giles and Evans 1985; Wellman 1997).

Challenges to the social arrangements that benefit whites have been offered as one possible reason why whites' estimates of the nonwhite population, particularly the black population,

are greatly exaggerated (Gilens 1999; Loeb 1994; Nadeau, Niemi, and Levine 1993). This threat to white status resulting from high concentrations of racial minorities has also been linked to lack of support among whites for race-based social policies aimed at alleviating racial inequality, such as affirmative action and integration (Bobo and Zubrinsky 1996; Fossett and Kiecolt 1989; Giles and Evans 1985; Hacker 1995; Nadeau, Niemi, and Levine 1993).

In his classic statement about the relationship between segregation, racial group size and perceived threat, Allport ([1954] 1979) hypothesized that the lack of black-white contact results in the numerical inflation of racial minorities by whites. Allport posited that residential segregation "markedly enhances the visibility of a group, it makes them seem larger and more menacing" (p. 269). The lack of contact between racial groups and the perceived hypervisibility of blacks by whites is thought to be one factor that breeds ignorance, hostility, and discrimination toward racial minorities. Residential segregation may contribute to the exaggeration of the nonwhite population by whites, but sharing social space does not mean that whites will come to view nonwhites as less "menacing" or smaller in relative group size. Reviewing the literature on racial interaction and racial attitudes, Sigelman and Welch (1993, 784) found that "only under highly auspicious circumstances should a favorable attitude change be anticipated." These circumstances must include a noncompetitive, nonthreatening environment, where interaction is legally and socially sanctioned and contact between parties is both sustained and of equal status (Jackman and Crane 1986). One is hard pressed to find many social environments or institutionalized arrangements that satisfy all of these conditions. In fact, Farley (1988, 35) notes that without conditions that promote positive racial interaction, "any contact that evokes fear and defensiveness runs the risk of making intergroup relations worse, not better."

why whites #aerestimaty

The literature, then, suggests that whites overestimate the nonwhite population, particularly blacks, because (1) they believe that their social status is diminished when they share space with racial groups they perceive as being socially stigmatized and (2) the lack of physical or social contact creates the impression that these groups are larger and constitute a potential threat to white privilege. In his review of the literature on whites' racial attitudes toward blacks, Feagin (2000) reconciles this apparent contradiction. He argues that "the focus on black men and women as physically dominant, deviant, or dangerous in the media and in various legislative and other public discussions appears to create in the white mind the impression that there are more blacks in society than there actually are" (p. 117). Research on race relations suggests it is almost exclusively blacks who are the central focus of discussion for whites when the topic of race relations is broached (Feagin 2000; Feagin and Vera 1995). These observations are consistent with the dynamic that took place in my interviews. Racial minorities may be concentrated in different parts of the United States, but the overwhelming majority of my white respondents launched into explanations of their own innumeracy in terms of a white/black dichotomy.

Arguing that group position reflects placement in a racial hierarchy that is both a relational and a competitive process, Blumer (1958) states that it is often opinion makers, political leaders, and the popular culture industry that are able to manufacture a "collective image" of racial groups that serves to maintain group dominance or group stereotypes, even if members from different races have *little or no contact* with one another. These "story lines" or "interpretive repertoires," Bonilla-Silva (2001, 66) explains, promotes a color-blind version of race relations that maintains white privilege by rendering those privileges as a historical artifact.

My data on racial innumeracy cannot test directly previous research related to overestimates of the nonwhite population, but it can provide valuable information on the sources whites identify as shaping their views of racial group size and how internalizing a racial "minority" status may result in ignoring or rejecting claims of white privilege.

Data and Methods

I use data from eight focus groups and eighteen semistructured individual interviews with white adults.[1] A total of seventy-six respondents were interviewed. Three of the eight focus groups took place in two rural counties in Georgia. The participants in the remaining five focus groups were chosen randomly from a list generated by the office of the registrar at Peak College, an elite liberal arts institution in the Rocky Mountains. The individual interviews were selected through snowball sampling with the explicit intent of recruiting respondents from urban, rural, and suburban settings.

Mountain County, Georgia, was selected for two of these focus groups because it is almost entirely white (99.54 percent). According to the U.S. Census (1996), there are no blacks, eighteen Latinos, and eleven Asians out of a population of 6,754, making it the "whitest" county in the state. Conducting interviews there allowed me to examine how whites who have little or no interaction with racial minorities described the size of racial groups and how they reconcile answers that

---

[1] A "focus group" is a research technique in which a group of people are asked to discuss a particular topic. Unlike a group interview, the point is to get people to talk with one another about a topic.

In a structured interview, the respondent is asked closed-ended questions and chooses from specific answer categories. Interviewers are required to not deviate from the interview script. In a semi-structured interview, respondents are asked open-ended questions and, depending upon their answers, may be asked follow up questions that occur to the interviewer.—Ed.

differ from the actual census figures. Using the principal of the Mountain County High School as my initial contact, I employed snowballing techniques to interview an additional six adult white respondents in Mountain County. The remaining site in Georgia, Farmer County, was selected because it contained the smallest statewide proportion of whites (20 percent) and the largest proportion of blacks (80 percent). No Asians or Latinos reside in Farmer County. Whites interacted with blacks in this county on a daily basis. Interviewing whites in this county provided me with the opportunity to examine if the narratives whites provide about racial group size vary from those provided by whites with little or no interaction with racial minorities.

Twenty-three of the Peak College respondents in the five focus groups came from large cities or the suburbs of large metropolitan areas, the majority of which had sizable nonwhite populations. All these respondents were traditional college age, ranging from seventeen to twenty-one. The focus groups were composed of fourteen men and eleven women. Respondents described their class background as ranging from middle to upper middle class and had varying degrees of interaction with racial minorities. As a demographic group, they resembled a sizable segment of the white population in the United States who live in white suburbs that surround racially mixed urban centers (Massey and Denton 1993).

The remaining twelve respondents were selected to include urban, suburban, and rural environments. Six of the respondents were raised in rural and/or agrarian settings. The remaining six respondents were born and lived in large metropolitan areas with a sizable population of racial minorities. While this sample is not representative of the total white population, the diverse range of those who have had different levels of exposure to racial minorities allows for comparisons between whites from different social backgrounds

and to examine if any recurring or divergent themes emerged in my interviews.

"They're All Over the Place": Media Influences on Racial Perceptions

My respondents estimated that whites, on average, made up 49.9 percent of the U.S. population. Blacks and Asians were estimated, on average, at 32 percent and 15 percent, respectively. The perception that blacks were overrepresented in the media, particularly on the local television news, was the most frequently cited reason whites offered as an explanation for their overestimates of the nonwhite population. Describing how local television news shaped his impression of racial group size, Jeb, an eighteen-year-old from a Mountain County focus group who thought the United States was 44 percent black, noted, "Well, like on TV, when you hear of a murder or something, the first thing you think of and hear, is a black person." Three middle-aged Mountain County women who worked at a state social service agency and collectively agreed that the United States was 40 percent black, offered a similar explanation: "From watching the news, you see, it consists of blacks. . . . The things you hear, the bad things, it's black people, and I guess it seems like there are so many of them they are overriding . . . most of the robberies and the domestic violence, the majority of what you see is colored people."

These women confided that they rarely left Mountain County, and when they did it was to visit relatives in adjacent counties that were also overwhelmingly white. In 1995 the largest city (population 637) in Mountain County was chosen by CNN as the safest place to retire among 183 retirement communities in the nation (Mountain County, Chamber of Commerce 1999). It is important to note that the closest sizable black population is located more than one hundred miles from this community.

For members of this community, the media is the medium through which race relations are lived and experienced.

Zach, a nineteen-year-old from Mountain County estimated that the United States was 60 percent black. When told that blacks account for about 13 percent of the population, he explained, "[I]t's just . . . you hear more about black people, or I do. And you see them on TV, there's lots of them on TV, you go to the city, there's a lot down there." Jake, who was in the same focus group as Zach, explained that over-representation of blacks on television warped his perception of blacks in America: "I believe it's television, because every time you turn it on, they're all over the place."

Carol, a fifty-three-year-old, college-educated executive secretary who had lived in Atlanta all her life, estimated that the United States was "40 to 50 percent Caucasian, 35 to 40 percent black, and the rest evenly divided." When asked what might be the reason for her inaccurate estimate of the black population, Carol discounted television as an influence, explaining that she watched very little and was in fact quite contemptuous of television programming in general: "I would rather read than watch TV. I watch the news and love the weather channel because I love geography. So, but, I just don't care for TV. I think there is trash on TV."

When I asked Mary, a middle-aged, well-educated woman who had lived in several large cities, why so many people distort the racial composition of the United States, she responded:

> There is so much in the media about black people and there's so much about numbers of black people, you know, 90 percent of the black male population, well I don't know if that's the right number, but you can hardly read anything about the prison population, without reading that 90 percent of them being black. . . . [T]here has been so much attention paid to the black population and particularly in big cities where they are not a minority. I think that is one of the things.

Kelly, a twenty-nine-year-old mother of two who runs a Christian curio shop in Mountain County, also linked local news explicitly to black criminality. Kelly said she estimated that blacks made up 55 percent and whites 45 percent of the U.S. population in part because of what she sees on the local news:

> I do watch it [the local news] and I don't know why, probably for the weather. It just seems, now this may seem like I'm a racist but I'm not, but if I'm watching the news and there are like crimes committed. They are usually by blacks and Hispanics, and, not to say that white people can't do it, because they do it every day.

Professional sports as portrayed on television and in other mass media was offered by male respondents as the reason they overestimated the nonwhite population. For example, Luke, a young Philadelphian who had said that blacks constitute 50 percent of the U.S. population, told me, without a hint of irony or sarcasm, that he "liked the NBA [National Basketball Association]." He and the other young men in a Mountain County focus group also pointed to playing basketball and football as the reason they overestimated the black population. The following exchange is illustrative:

BLAKE: Yeah, I had 42 percent [black].
C.G.: Forty-two percent, now how do you reconcile the 12.7 percent with your number? That is an enormous difference, so you're thinking the United States is a black country.
BLAKE: I mean, I play basketball and we go places to play and like 90 percent of the teams that we play are all black.
JOE: Football too . . .

In the 1996–97 season blacks made up 79 percent of the NBA and 66 percent of the National Football League (Lapchick and Matthews 1999). As these young men's comments suggest, selective attention to sports may contribute to their double and triple counting of the black population.

Effects of the Media

A Gallup Poll found that 79 percent of white Americans watch the local news at least four days a week (McAneny 1994). In his study of the way in which blacks are represented in television news, Entman (1992, 329) found that "exposure over time to local TV news presents viewers with an accumulation of images that make blacks appear consistently threatening, demanding and undeserving of accommodation by government." Many of my white respondents' comments confirm Entman's findings; local news both constructs a negative image of the black population as a whole and seems to create the kind of "menace" Allport claims is responsible for people distorting the size of minority populations.

The extent to which racial minorities are overrepresented in the local news also reflects where news centers are located and how news is "created." Gans (1979) found that because news centers are located in urban areas with sizable minority populations, reporters can conveniently and cheaply "find" news stories that focus disproportionately on the social problems of a narrow segment of the non-white population. Many white respondents seem to associate the focus of local news on black crime with the size of the black population (Giroux 1996; Gray 1995). Among a sizable portion of my respondents from majority white rural counties or suburbs, black America was reduced to a negative newscast, broadcast from a city that was often more than one hundred miles away.

It is also likely that watching the local news and sporting events, rather than viewing television shows with a majority black cast, influence perceptions of racial group size. A 1996 study on television viewing habits by race found that white and black television viewing preferences overlap very little. In the year of this study, only ER, Monday Night Football, and NBC's Monday Night Movie appeared on both the black family

and total household ratings records (Gillespie 1996). In 1998 the number one show in black households (the Steve Harvey Show) ranked 112 among whites, while the number one show in white households (Friends) ranked 91 in black households (Sterngold 1998). It becomes difficult to reconcile statements like "Blacks are all over the place" in the media when outside of local news and professional sports, television viewing patterns are quite segregated. It is more likely that whites pay particular attention to blacks while ignoring the extent to which whites dominate the media. For many whites in this study, selective attention to blacks in the media appears to shape perception of racial group size.

"They Get All the Attention": Identity Politics and Racial Hypervisibility

The perception among some whites that blacks make inappropriate or excessive "demands" for racial equality also appears to contribute to why some whites overestimate the size of the black population. Pam, a fifty-one-year-old paralegal from Farmer County, explained why she overestimated the black population:

PAM: You know, I think it's because, it seems to us [whites], that they [blacks] are at the forefront all the time. They get all the attention.
C.G.: The forefront of what?
PAM: I don't know how to say it, it's politically correct to make sure black people are not in any way mistreated or whatever, it seems like we're going overboard maybe. . . . I think that blacks are more vocal about what they want, wanting their rights. . . . [I]t's just like in this county when blacks wanted the right to vote, . . . they didn't hesitate to get out, march up and down the street calling attention to themselves. And we, the white people, will sit around

and gripe about it, but we won't get up and take to the streets and march. . . . [W]e are not as obvious out there. . . . [W]e tend to, I think, sit back and maybe gripe about things, and the blacks will get up, march around and be vocal and, you know, and demand what they want.

Seth, a young man in a focus group at Peak College who grew up in a white suburb of Washington, D.C., explained that he overestimated the nonwhite population because blacks bring attention to themselves by focusing on their racial identity. Asked how he accounts for the fact that he thought whites were 30 percent, Asians 40 percent, and blacks 25 percent of the U.S. population, he replied:

Easily, because I've never been asked to go to a white meeting or white awareness or anything like that. I was looking at the [bulletin] boards on campus and it's all like, Black Awareness Month, Black Week, you know, come to this, talk about this, it seems basically they make more of a statement about, we don't have an NAACP [for whites], and stuff like that, and I guess it seems they have a stronger voice right now.

Seth's comments are especially interesting because he estimated that Asians were the single largest racial population in the United States but identifies blacks as the group who engage in racial politics.

The perception by many whites that it is blacks, but not Asians, who make "demands" for social change is consistent with the depiction of Asian Americans as a "model minority." This perspective holds that as a group Asian Americans have embraced a work ethic based on individual upward mobility and socioeconomic assimilation instead of making group claims to address racial inequality. The notion of blacks embracing racial identity as a way to highlight racial inequality was also evident in an exchange I had with a group of senior citizens in Mountain County. Asked why they thought the United States was 50 to 60 percent black, Jane and Martha explained:

JANE: Because we don't know any different, we're up here where it is all white. We are not around colored people.
C.G.: But you didn't say 4 percent, you didn't say a small number, you said a big number.
JANE: I know it, but still we're not, we just don't have them, we don't have many up here.
C.G.: So if you don't have many up here, then why didn't you say 5 percent?
MARTHA: Well, they're out there every time. They are out front of everything, everything that's going. That's the reason we see more of them, on TV. . . . I hate to say this, you hear so much complaining about segregation and all that, I just thought there was more of them here.

Rather than view blacks' demands for civil rights or the mobilization to end discrimination as a fundamental right or legitimate grievance, these actions were viewed as incessant, group-level "complaining about segregation."

Aaron, a lawyer from Farmer County, provides insight into how whites might be subtly influenced by representations of black political figures on television. He explains that racial overestimates of the U.S. population might be "partially a function of places like Atlanta, Washington, D.C., Miami, and Birmingham. Whenever you see the mayor on television, it's a black person. Whenever you see the chairman of the city commission, it's a black person. Whenever you see the police chief, it's a black person, on *television*" (my emphasis).

Like others in this study, Carmen, a middle-aged butcher from Philadelphia, estimated that the United States was not a white country: "Thirty-five percent white, 35 percent black, and I think the other 30 percent would be Asians, but the Asians are moving up fast." Sal, a thirty-one-year-old owner of an Italian specialty food shop in Philadelphia, calculated that "Asians may be 20 percent, white is probably about 45 to 50, and the black would be what's left, . . . about 20 percent, you know 30 percent." When asked to explain his answers after he was told the actual percentages, he replied, "[There are] so many of them in the neighborhood that's why I said that. I mean this neighborhood just exploded with an Asian population. That's why I said that. Or what could it be, 10 percent [the Asian percentage nationally]."

Sal's observations reflect demographic changes that have taken place in this part of Philadelphia. For much of the twentieth century the neighborhood was dominated by Italian American merchants. Vietnamese and Korean merchants now stand side by side with Italian American shopkeepers. Although Sal now lives in an all-white suburb of Philadelphia, his estimate of the white and non-white population for the nation was based on where he works rather than on where he lives.

Tommy, a young man from a rural suburb of Atlanta, used the homogeneity of his community to explain why he thought that whites made up only 47 percent of the U.S. population:

> I'm certainly from a sheltered area. I've grew up twenty minutes south of Atlanta in a 95 percent white county. I haven't traveled much beyond the southeastern U.S. From this experience, I don't see much other ethnic groups. Therefore I don't have much of an idea of the breakdown of the ethnic groups.

Similarly, Lauren, a Peak College student who grew up in a New York City suburb, did not overestimate the white population even though her social networks were almost entirely white. She explained that blacks constituted 35 percent of the population in this way: "White is the majority in the country as far as percentage-wise, but, like I guess the area that I grew up in was—I don't think

I have a really clear picture as to what the rest of the country is other than New York City and northern New Jersey."

Lauren, like many of my respondents raised in the suburbs, and the young men in rural Mountain County parallel each other in two ways: each group lives in a racially homogeneous area, and each views the United States as being more racially diverse than it was. What is significant sociologically is that Lauren and Tommy were raised in a white environment and had little contact with racial minorities but seriously underestimated the size of the white population. Their lack of contact or exposure did not lead them to guess the United States was 90 percent or even 75 percent white. Nor did Sal's daily exposure to whites in his suburban enclave lead him to overestimate the size of the white population in the United States. Overestimating the nonwhite population occurred when respondents had very little as well as considerable contact with racial minorities.

The Effects of Identity Politics and Black Hypervisibility

My respondents' perception that racial minorities, especially African Americans, embrace racial identity politics as a way to address racial inequality or to challenge white privilege appeared to play a role in how large whites imagine other racial groups to be. National polling data reveal a chasm between whites' and blacks' perceptions of race relations in the United States. Not only do a majority of whites believe that blacks have "as good a chance as whites" to procure housing and employment or achieve middle-class status (Gallup 1997), but a 1995 survey of white adults found that a majority (58 percent) believed that African Americans were "better off" finding a job than were whites (Shipler 1998). Whites and blacks also differ significantly in their support for affirmative action (Moore 1995), the perceived fairness of the criminal justice system (Moore and Saad 1995), the ability to achieve the "American Dream," and the extent to which whites have benefited from past discrimination (Kaiser Foundation 1995). Attitudes on symbolic issues are no less divergent. A recent poll found that 67 percent of whites opposed but 65 percent of blacks favored legislation that would have the government officially apologize to American blacks for the slavery practiced before the Civil War (Newport 1997). Much of white America sees a level playing field, whereas a majority of black Americans see a field that is still uneven.

Blumer (1958, 100) notes that the tendency for the dominant group to focus on racial differences, the use of stereotypes to characterize racial minorities, and the belief that racial minorities "harbor designs on the prerogatives of the dominant group" may have the effect of raising group consciousness. He argues that a threat to the dominant groups' placement in the racialized hierarchy is created when the dominant group perceives its privileges as being eroded or challenged. As racial groups see themselves in competition over political, economic, and cultural resources, in-group identity is reinforced. Among my respondents, distorting the size of the black population appears to accelerate or at least exacerbate this process as whites come to view themselves as a racial minority.

Reports from the Census: Whites as a Minority

Magazines and newspaper articles have described the changing complexion of the United States and projected that whites would soon be the "new" racial minority. Many of my respondents reported hearing from a friend or "something" in the media that whites are, or were soon to be, a racial

minority in the United States. Sarah, a Peak College focus group respondent who grew up in San Francisco and defined whites as a minority, explained, "Somebody told me that we [whites] are not actually a majority in the U.S." Dylan, a nineteen-year-old Peak College respondent who was raised in a suburb of Seattle, confessed: "I thought that the blacks were growing because I heard people say that in a few years the blacks will be the majority, but I guess they have a long way to go. I also thought that there were more Asians because of the large companies and the smarts that Asians are supposed to have."

Sophia, a Peak College respondent from Boston, explained the hypervisibility of the black population in this way: "I heard on the radio that the whites are going to be a minority in the year 2010 or something like that." Miles, also a Peak College respondent, thought that it was Latinos who would be the largest minority group in the United States: "I had heard figures that say that by 2015 that Hispanics will be the majority population in the United States so I assumed that the percentage was greater now than what it actually is."

Misinformation about changing demographic patterns in the United States seems to play a role in the perception of racial group size. What has been lost on the general public is that this great racial sea change wherein whites are no longer a majority will not occur until 2050. It also assumes that the variables demographers use to predict this transition, like immigration rates or the way in which the U.S. Census defines race, will not once again change (Warren and Twine 1997).

Changing Demography

reason estimation wrong

The belief expressed by whites in this study that they are now or will soon be a minority may be tapping into growing fears that white privilege is eroding (Bonilla-Silva 2001; Gallagher

1997; Omi and Winant 1994; Wellman 1997). These concerns, coupled with the fact that many whites internalize television images of racial minorities that are negative and stereotypical, may explain how "subjective meanings become objective" facts (Berger and Luckmann 1966, 18). The social construction of racial group size has consequences for race relations because individuals act on this distorted information as if it were real. These subjective renderings of racial groups become loosely structured "interpretive communities" (Chiricos, Eschholz, and Gertz 1997), providing each racial group with an understanding of their social status relative to other racial groups. Perceptions of group size may function crudely as a proxy of how powerful or vulnerable a group is perceived to be and what portion of society's resources each group is thought to deserve (Blumer 1958; Frankenberg 2001; Omi 2001).

It seems reasonable that urban whites would exaggerate the nonwhite population because they have more contact with racial minorities than do those who live in the suburbs. But city dwellers like Carol, Sal, and Carmen are linked to those like Zach and Jake from rural settings in Mountain County in their inaccurate depiction of the size of the nonwhite population. The rural county respondents with no African American or Asian neighbors and the urban and suburban respondents who live in areas with sizable racial minorities both exaggerate the nonwhite population. For whites in this study, the hypervisibility of nonwhites transcends the urban-rural divide. This finding is consistent with what researchers have found nationally concerning perceptions of racial group size. Whites who live in states where blacks constitute less than 1 percent of the population are as likely as whites who live in states where blacks constitute more than 20 percent of the population to give estimates that almost double the size of the national black population (Gilens 1999).

Conclusion

My finding that white respondents from suburban, urban, and rural areas uniformly exaggerate the size of the nonwhite population is consistent with previous research on racial innumeracy. In my data three narratives emerged to account for this: (1) exposure to racial minorities in the media, particularly the way in which blacks are represented on local television newscasts; (2) the perception that blacks make collective demands for racial justice; and (3) the belief that demographic changes had made whites a minority. These accounts support, at least indirectly, previous research findings that the fear of threat, status anxiety, and the effects of segregation each play a role in the tendency of a majority of whites to overestimate the nonwhite population.

Several respondents were bothered by what they saw as group demands as the means to ameliorate racial inequalities. Various studies confirm the anxious coexistence between the almost universal belief that equal opportunity should be afforded to all Americans regardless of skin color and the resistance to using group membership as a means to address inequalities rooted in past and present discrimination. For many whites, the American creed of equal opportunity is understood culturally as an individual, not a group, right (Hochschild 1995; Lipset 1996). If group size becomes a proxy for power, then viewing the size of the white population as being similar to other racial groups may serve to reinforce the idea that we are now a color-blind nation. Not only does this perspective mask and maintain white privilege; it hides the extent to which racism still shapes the life chances of racial minorities.

My findings also raise an important question concerning race and social justice. What are the implications for race relations when the dominant group mistakenly believes they no longer constitute a majority? The most obvious concern is that whites can ignore, discount, or negate claims that being white affords its members social, political, or economic privileges because there is the perception that with parity in size comes equal access to social resources. Maintaining and simultaneously masking racial dominance is consistent with the idea that U.S. race relations are embedded in ongoing racial projects that continually reinterpret and redefine group dynamics in order to maintain white control and dominance (Lipset 1996; Omi and Winant 1994). If group size is defined as being synonymous with political and economic power, then any suggestion that the state needs to (or should) take an active role in ameliorating racial inequality can be rejected on the grounds that such measures are no longer needed because numerical parity implies social and economic parity. "Race-based" government programs such as affirmative action and social welfare initiatives can be viewed, at least in part, as both unnecessary and unfair to whites since the playing field is perceived to have been leveled. As one respondent in this study noted, there are no white versions of the NAACP to promote white interests. White respondents' underestimation of the white population appears to have the effect of framing whites as a group who are now socially disadvantaged, or at least not socioeconomically different from any other racial group.

In addition, this study has implications for how we conduct research on race relations. Researchers must be cautious about using the size of the racial population when examining racial attitudes. To what extent, if any, would group threat, antiblack prejudice, or the perception that racial minorities are "taking over" decrease if whites were informed of the size of the black population before questions that measure racial attitudes are administered? To what extent has race relations research advanced claims

about intergroup relations that did not take into account and differentiate between how individuals perceive the size of racial groups and how race relations informs their day-to-day racial interactions? Research on racial attitudes suggests that when individuals are provided with counterarguments that frame racial inequality in structural terms, most respondents change their minds about race-specific policy issues (Gallagher 1999; Sniderman and Piazza 1993). Given that previous research has demonstrated that racial group size is inflated, the majority of research on group size and racial attitudes has provided us with only one account of how individuals view race relations. Future research on group size and attitudes needs to rectify this omission.

References

Allport, Gordon. [1954] 1979. *The Nature of Prejudice*. New York: Addison Wesley.

Berger, Peter L., and Thomas Luckmann. 1966. *The Social Construction of Reality*. Garden City, NY: Anchor Books.

Blumer, Herbert. 1999. "Race Prejudice as a Sense of Group Position." Pp. 99–105 in C. A. Gallagher (ed.), *Rethinking the Color Line: Readings in Race and Ethnicity*. Mountain View, CA: Mayfield Publishing Company.

Bobo, Lawrence. 1983. "Whites' Opposition to Bussing: Symbolic Racism or Realistic Group Conflict?" *Journal of Personality and Social Psychology* 45(6): 1196–1210.

———. 1997. "Race, Public Opinion, and the Social Sphere." *Public Opinion Quarterly* 61: 1–15.

Bobo, Lawrence, J. Kluegel, and R. Smith. 1997. "Laissez-faire Racism: The Crystallization of a Kinder, Gentler, Anti-Black Ideology." Pp. 15–42 in S. A. Tuch and J. K. Martin (eds.), *Racial Attitudes in the 1990s: Continuity and Change*. Westport, CT: Praeger.

Bobo, Lawrence, and Camille L. Zubrinsky. 1996. "Attitudes Toward Residential Integration: Perceived Status Differences, Mere In-Group Preference, or Racial Prejudice?" *Social Forces* 74: 883–909.

Bonilla-Silva, Eduardo. 2001. *White Supremacy and Racism in the Post-Civil Rights Era*. Boulder, CO: Lynne Rienner.

Carrol, Joseph. 2001. "Public Overestimates U.S. Black and Hispanic Populations." *Gallup Poll Analyses*, June 4.

Chiricos, Ted, Sarah Eschholz, and Marc Gertz. 1997. "Crime, News and Fear of Crime: Toward an Identification of Audience Effects." *Social Problems* 44: 342–57.

Doane, Ashley W., Jr. 1997. "Dominant Group Ethnic Identity in the United States: The Role of 'Hidden' Ethnicity in Intergroup Relations." *Sociological Quarterly* 38(3): 375–97.

Ehrlich, Howard. 1999. "Reporting Ethnoviolence: Newspaper Treatment of Race and Ethnic Conflict." Pp. 319–30 in F. Pinkus and H. Ehrlich (eds.), *Race and Ethnic Conflict: Prejudice, Discrimination and Ethnoviolence*. Boulder, CO: Westview Press.

Entman, Robert. 1992. "Blacks in the News: Television, Modern Racism and Cultural." *Journalism Quarterly* 69(2): 341–61.

———. 1994. "Representation and Reality in the Portrayal of Blacks on Television News." *Journalism Quarterly* 7(4): 509–20.

Espiritu, Yen Le. 1992. *Asian American Panethnicity: Bridging Institutions and Identities*. Philadelphia: Temple University Press.

Feagin, Joe. 2000. *Racist America: Roots, Current Realities and Future Reparations*. London: Routledge.

Feagin, Joe, and Heran Vera. 1995. *White Racism: The Basics*. New York: Routledge.

Fossett, Mark A., and K. Jill Kiecolt. 1989. "The Relative Size of Minority Populations and White Racial Attitudes." *Social Science Quarterly* 70(4): 820–35.

Frankenberg, Ruth. 2001. "The Mirage of an Unmarked Whiteness." Pp. 72–96 in B. B. Rasmussen, E. Klinenberg, I. Nexica, and M. Wray (eds.), *The Making and Unmaking of Whiteness*. Durham: Duke University Press.

Gallagher, Charles A. 1995. "White Reconstruction in the University." *Socialist Review* 24: 165–87.

———. 1997. "White Racial Formation: Into the Twenty-first Century." Pp. 6–11 in R. Delgado and J. Stefancic (eds.), *Critical White Studies: Looking Beyond the Mirror*. Philadelphia: Temple University Press.

———. 1999. "Research Race, Reproducing Racism." *Review of Education/Pedagogy/Cultural Studies* 21(2): 165–91.

Gallup, George, Jr., and Frank Newport. 1990. "Americans Ignorant of Basic Census Facts." *Gallup Poll Monthly*, no. 294: 1–5.

Gallup Poll Social Audit. 2001. "Black-White Relations in the United States 2001 Update." Washington, DC: Gallup Organization.

Gans, Herbert. 1979. *Deciding What's News*. New York: Pantheon.

Gilens, Martin. 1996. "Race and Poverty in America: Public Misperceptions and the American News Media." *Public Opinion Quarterly* 60: 515–41.

———. 1999. *Why Americans Hate Welfare: Race, Media, and the Politics of Antipoverty Policy*. Chicago: University of Chicago Press.

Giles, Michael W. 1977. "Percent Black and Racial Hostility: An Old Assumption Reexamined." *Social Science Quarterly* 58: 412–17.

Giles, Michael W., and Melanie A. Buckner. 1993. "David Duke and the Black Threat: An Old Hypothesis Revisited." *Journal of Politics* 55(3): 702–13.

Giles, Michael W., and Arthur S. Evans. 1985. "External Threat, Perceived Threat and Group Identity." *Social Science Quarterly* 66: 55–66.

Gillespie, Nick. 1996. "Ratings Race." *Reason* (October): 48–49.

Giroux, Henry A. 1996. *Fugitive Cultures: Race, Violence and Youth*. New York: Routledge.

Gray, Herman. 1995. *Watching Race: Television and the Struggle for "Blackness."* Minneapolis: University of Minnesota Press.

Hacker, Andrew. 1995. *Two Nations: Black and White, Separate, Hostile and Unequal*. New York: Charles Scribner's Sons.

Hochschild, Jennifer. 1995. *Facing Up to the American Dream*. Princeton: Princeton University Press.

Jackman, Mary R., and Maria Crane. 1986. "'Some of my Best Friends are Black . . .': Interracial Friendship and Whites' Racial Attitudes." *Public Opinion Quarterly* 50(4): 459–86.

Kaiser Foundation. 1995. *The Four Americas: Government and Social Policy through the Eyes of America's Multi-Racial and Multi-Ethnic Society.* Menlo Park, CA: Kaiser Family Foundation.

Lapchick, Richard E., and Kevin J. Matthews. 1999. "The 1997 Racial Report." Pp. 390–408 in C. A. Gallagher (ed.), *Rethinking the Color Line: Readings in Race and Ethnicity.* Mountain View, CA: Mayfield.

Lewis, Amanda. 2002. "Whiteness Studies: Past Research and Future Directions." African American Research Perspectives 8(1).

Lipset, Seymour Martin. 1996. *American Exceptionalism: A Double Edged Sword.* New York: Norton.

Lipsitz, George. 1995. "The Possessive Investment in Whiteness: Racialized Social Democracy and the 'White' Problem in American Studies." *American Quarterly* 47(3): 369–87.

Loeb, Paul. 1994. *Generations at the Crossroads: Apathy and Action on the American Campus.* New Brunswick, NJ: Rutgers University Press.

Massey, Douglas, and Nancy Denton. 1993. *American Apartheid: Segregation and the Making of the Underclass.* Cambridge, MA: Harvard University Press.

Moore, David. 1995. "Americans' Most Important Source of Information: Local News." *Gallup Poll Monthly* (September): 2–5.

Moore, David, and Lydia Saad. 1995. "No Immediate Signs that Simpson Trial Intensified Racial Animosity." *Gallup Poll Monthly* (October): 2–5.

Nadeau, Richard, Richard G. Niemi, and Jeffrey Levine. 1993. "Innumeracy about Minority Populations." *Public Opinion Quarterly* 57: 332–47.

Newport, Frank. 1997. "Whites Oppose Formal Apology for Slavery." *Gallup Poll Monthly* (July): 21–22.

Omi, Michael. 2001. "(E)racism: Emerging Practices of Antiracist Organizations." Pp. 266–93 in B. Rasmussen, E. Klinenberg, I. Nexica, and M. Wray (eds.), *The Making and Unmaking of Whiteness.* Durham: Duke University Press.

Omi, Michael, and Howard Winant. 1994. *Racial Formation in the United States: From the 1960s to the 1990s.* New York: Routledge.

Patterson, Orlando. 1997. *The Ordeal of Integration: Progress and Resentments in America's Racial Crisis.* Washington, DC: National Academy Press.

———. 1999. "What to Do When Bussing Became Irrelevant." *New York Times,* July 18, p. A17.

Quillian, Lincoln. 1996. "Group Threat and Regional Change in Attitudes Toward African-Americans." *American Journal of Sociology* 3: 816–60.

Shipler, David K. 1998. *A Country of Strangers: Blacks and Whites in America.* New York: Vintage Books.

Sigelman, Lee, and Susan Welch. 1993. "The Contact Hypothesis Revisited: Black-White Interaction and Positive Racial Attitudes." *Social Forces* 71(3): 781–95.

Sniderman, Paul, and Thomas Piazza. 1993. *The Scar of Race.* Cambridge, MA: Harvard University Press.

Sterngold, James. 1998. "A Racial Divide Widens on Network TV." *New York Times,* December 19, pp. Al, A12.

Taylor, Marylee C. 1998. "How Whites Attitudes Vary with the Racial Composition of Local Populations: Numbers Count." *American Sociological Review* 63(4): 512–35.

U.S. Bureau of the Census. 1996. *State Profiles: Georgia, Towns County.* www.census.gov.

———. 1999. *Population Profile of the United States.* www.census.gov.

Warren, Jonathan W., and France Winddance Twine. 1997. "White Americans, the New Minority? Non-Blacks and the Ever-Expanding Boundaries of Whiteness." *Journal of Black Studies* 28(2): 200–18.

Waters, Mary. 1990. *Ethnic Options: Choosing Identities in America.* Berkeley: University of California Press.

Wellman, David. 1997. "Minstrel Shows, Affirmative Action Talk, and Angry White Men: Marking Racial Otherness in the 1990's." Pp. 311–31 in R. Frankenberg (ed.), *Displacing Whiteness: Essays in Social and Cultural Criticism.* Durham: Duke University Press.

Questions

1. Why did Professor Gallagher decide to use focus groups and semi-structured interviews in his research (rather than, for example, a survey)?

2. To what factors does Gallagher attribute whites' tendency to *under*estimate the proportion of U.S. society that is white?

3. Presumably, Latinos, blacks, and Asians are subjected to the same media influences as whites, yet it is usually whites who are more likely to misperceive the size of minority groups. What accounts for this?

6

DOING THE RIGHT THING

Ethics in Research

Lisa J. McIntyre

There is more to doing sociological research than choosing variables, picking respondents, gathering data, and doing an analysis. More than ever before, every choice the social researcher makes must be informed by considerations of ethics. At base, doing the right thing means not subjecting the people we study and (those around them) to unnecessary risk of harm. What's behind the increasing stress on ethics in research? What are the responsibilities of the ethical researcher? Above all, what is "harm"? This 1999 paper explores these questions.

Ethical guides are not simply prohibitions; they also support our positive responsibilities. For example, scientists have an obligation to advance knowledge through research. They also have a responsibility to conduct research as competently as they can and to communicate their findings accurately to other scientists.

—Diener and Crandall 1978

To begin, it is important to note that the term *ethics* has both a conventional (or everyday) meaning and a technical meaning. The fact that there are two ways to use this term causes a great deal of confusion. In the conventional or everyday sense, ethics is synonymous with morality, and doing the ethical thing simply means doing the moral thing. Conversely, unethical behavior is immoral behavior.

Ethics: Technical Meaning and Origins

In the technical sense, ethics and morals are different. Although in many cases there may be an overlap between ethical and moral

behavior, there are no guarantees that this will occur. The following two scenarios give examples of how morals and ethics may diverge.

Scenario 1
Chris confesses to a friend to having killed someone and hidden the body under a pile of garbage near an old shack at the lake. The police can't find the missing victim, nor do they know that Chris is the killer. The friend calls the police and tells them where to find Chris and the victim's body.

Has the friend done something moral or immoral? In spite of the fact that there is a widely accepted rule in society against snitching on one's friends, most people probably would say that the friend did the moral thing. It is not right to allow murderers to go free, and the victim certainly has a right to a proper burial.

Scenario 2
Chris hires an attorney and then confesses the murder and burial to that attorney. The police can't find the missing victim, nor do they know that Chris is the killer. The lawyer isn't all that sure about Chris's story and drives up to the lake to check it out. A search through the

garbage reveals the body. After taking a Polaroid of the body, the lawyer reburies it in the garbage. Returning to town, the lawyer urges Chris to go to the police but does not call the police.[1]

Because the lawyer does not turn in the murderer, he or she does not seem to be acting morally. But there is an important consideration: Whereas in scenario 1 the friend may have a moral obligation to turn Chris in to the police, the lawyer has an ethical obligation to keep the client's confidence—even when the client is a murderer! This is not a gray area, either; this ethical requirement is spelled out clearly in the legal profession's *Code of Professional Responsibility:* "The lawyer must hold in strictest confidence the disclosures made by the client in the professional relationship. The first duty of an ethical attorney is 'to keep the secrets of his clients'" (Ethical Consideration 4-1). Preserving a client's secrets is such an important ethical obligation that had the lawyer turned Chris in, that attorney could have been disbarred and never again allowed to practice law.

In the technical sense, *behavior is ethical insofar as it follows the rules that have been specifically oriented to the welfare of the larger society and not to the self-interests of the professional.* So, ethics are designed to promote the welfare of others. You might be wondering how this lawyer could be promoting the welfare of others. The short answer is this: The legal profession is committed to the idea that people are innocent until proved guilty, that everyone accused of a crime has a right to the best defense, and that this is possible only if those accused of crimes can trust their attorneys. No client would trust an attorney who did not keep his or her secrets.

To be ethical, professionals have the burden of having to do things that others might consider to be immoral. For lawyers, in addition to keeping possibly nasty secrets, being ethical involves the duty to defend what may be unpopular cases and vicious criminals.

To become a professional, one must promise to abide by the relevant professional ethical codes. This is not a matter of personal choice—if you want to be a physician, you must follow the medical rules of ethics. To act unethically is to act unprofessionally.

It is important to be precise here: What do I mean by "professional"? In conventional language, we use the term at least three different ways. Sometimes, we apply the word to a job that is well done: "You did a very professional job of building that doghouse." Other times, we label someone a professional because he or she is paid to do something, regardless of the quality of the outcome: "John was a professional baseball player—but he never could hit a curve ball."

When sociologists use the term *professional,* however, they generally mean something else. Sociologically speaking, a professional is a member of a special kind of occupational group. Originally, only three occupational groups qualified as professions: lawyers, physicians, and clergy. These three groups have several things in common that set them apart from other occupations:

1. Their practitioners study for years to acquire technical knowledge and skills.

2. The knowledge they possess involves traditions and secrets that are not shared by outsiders.

3. Their knowledge is useful to outsiders and frequently means the difference between life and death.

From the first three characteristics of the professional derives a fourth—and this is really what sets the professional apart from other workers:

4. The work of a professional cannot be judged or supervised by anyone who is not a member of the same profession.

---

[1]A very similar case happened several years ago in Lake Pleasant, New York.

As sociologists see it, these qualities are characteristics of doctors, lawyers, and clergy, but not of plumbers or hairstylists. Although people in any occupational group may refer to themselves as professionals ("I am a professional hairstylist" or "I am a professional plumber"), relatively few occupations really are professions.[2]

The nature of the professional's job is such that *how* it is done is as important as (if not more important than) what the outcome is. The problem is that as laypeople, we cannot judge how well the job was done. For example, if patient Q's family suspects that the surgeon wasn't competent and that this incompetence led to Q's death, they might want to sue the surgeon for malpractice. Q's family might feel righteous in claiming that if the surgeon had done the job right, Q would still be alive. But that is not necessarily true (recall the old saying, "The operation was a success, but the patient died"). The views of Q's family are legally irrelevant and will hold no water in court. According to the law, only another physician can judge whether the surgeon was truly negligent. So, Q's family will have to find another surgeon who is willing to testify that it was the poor quality of the surgeon's work that led to the patient's death.[3]

Even though they could not tell if their doctor, lawyer, priest, or rabbi was doing all that ought to be done, for a long time people trusted these professionals to do the right thing. But by the mid-nineteenth century, many people were growing increasingly suspicious of professionals and were beginning to suggest that perhaps professionals ought not to be given so much freedom and autonomy.

Professionals responded by emphasizing the fact that their actions were prompted not by self-interest, but by their concern for their clients, patients, or parishioners. According to members of the medical profession, then, doctors do not perform surgery simply to make money, but to relieve people's suffering. And according to members of the legal profession, then, lawyers do not represent clients simply for the money, but because everyone has a right to representation.

One of the ways that professionals emphasized their commitment to the public welfare over self-interest was to promulgate or announce codes of ethics. They promised that they would follow these codes of ethics and punish any member of their profession who failed to do so. As we moved into the twentieth century, however, it became increasingly clear that at least one aspect of professional work was not being regulated properly by the professionals themselves: research.

Research Atrocities

Gross abuses of professional power in research became public knowledge after World War II. When Nazi physicians were brought to trial at Nuremberg in the late 1940s, the tales of their "research" horrified the world:

> Physicians forced people [in concentration camps] to drink seawater to find out how long a man might survive without fresh water. At Dachau, Russian prisoners of war were immersed in icy waters to see how long a pilot might survive when shot down over the English Channel and to find out what kinds of protective gear or rewarming techniques were most effective. Prisoners were placed in vacuum chambers to find out how the human body responds when pilots are forced to bail out at

---

[2]I do not mean to disrespect members of any occupational group by claiming that they are not professionals. I simply mean to illustrate how sociologists use the term *professional* to highlight the qualities of certain occupational groups.

[3]There are exceptions. Some errors are so obvious that the law does not require an expert witness to testify—as when a surgeon cuts off the wrong leg or sews a surgical instrument into the wound. (The legal phrase for such exceptions is *res ipsa loquitur,* a Latin term meaning "the thing speaks for itself.")

high altitudes. . . . At Auschwitz, physicians experimented with new ways to sterilize or castrate people as part of the plan to repopulate Eastern Europe with Germans. Physicians performed limb and bone transplants (on persons with no medical need) and, in at least one instance, injected prisoners' eyes with dyes to see if eye color could be permanently changed. At Buchenwald, Gerhard Rose infected prisoners with spotted fever to test experimental vaccines against the disease; at Dachau, Ernst Grawitz infected prisoners with a broad range of pathogens to test [different cures]. . . . Hundreds of people died in these experiments; many of those who survived were forced to live with painful physical or psychological scars. (Annas and Grodin 1992, 26)

At their trials, many Nazi physicians protested that they "had only been following orders." But much evidence suggested otherwise: "Contrary to postwar apologies, doctors were never forced to perform such experiments. Physicians volunteered—and in several cases, *Nazi officials actually had to restrain overzealous physicians from pursuing even more ambitious experiments*" (Annas and Grodin 1992, 26; emphasis added).

What could have motivated these physicians, these professional healers, to misapply their professional skills so horribly? At the time, many Americans believed that there was something fundamentally wrong with the German "personality type." For one thing (or so it was thought), Germans were all too quick to follow orders without exercising independent judgment. Certainly, such things could never happen in the United States!

What many people did not know or appreciate was the long tradition among U.S. physicians of conducting questionable research. For example, in the nineteenth century, orphans, the "feeble-minded," and hospital patients frequently were made the unwilling victims of medical experiments.

In his autobiography, physician J. Marion Sims described how, between 1845 and 1849, he kept several black female slaves at his hospital to test his discovery of a repair for vesicovaginal fistula. The fistulas, allowing urine or feces to leak through the vaginal opening, caused great discomfort and distress. . . . Sims performed dozens of operations on the women—this in the days before anesthetics—and praised their "heroism and bravery." (Lederer 1995, 115–116)

There have even been cases in which U.S. military personnel were required to participate in surgical experiments—under threat of court-martial!

In any case, outraged at the evidence they heard, the judges at Nuremberg promulgated the Nuremberg Code. The ten principles of the code were written to protect the rights of research subjects. Never again, the judges said, would humans be placed at risk of serious harm by being used as unwilling guinea pigs. But less than 30 years later, there was another research scandal. This time, the physicians were not only Americans but were employed by the United States Public Health Service! This study, known as the Tuskegee Syphilis Experiment, began in 1932 when public health workers came to Macon County, Georgia, in search of African American men who suffered from syphilis. The physicians preyed on the poverty of the men and recruited research subjects by offering to "pay" for their participation—free medical exams, transportation to and from the medical facilities where the exams would be held, and free meals on examination days. The biggest incentive was that the families of each subject would be paid $50 to help with burial expenses.

Not one of the subjects was told that he had syphilis—though each was told that he had "bad blood." And, although a cure for syphilis was widely available throughout most of the 30-year period during which the study was conducted, not one of the men was given this medication despite the fact that it would have

---

The Nuremberg Code

1. The voluntary consent of the human subject is absolutely essential. . . .

2. The research should be such as to yield fruitful results for the good of society, unprocurable by other methods or means. . . .

3. The research should be so designed . . . so that the anticipated results will justify the performance of the experiment.

4. The research should be so conducted as to avoid all unnecessary physical and mental suffering and injury.

5. No research should be conducted where there is . . . reason to believe that death or disabling injury will occur.

6. The degree of risk to be taken should never exceed that determined by the humanitarian importance of the problem to be solved by the research.

7. Proper preparations should be made . . . to protect the research subject against even remote possibilities of injury, disability, or death.

8. The research should be conducted only by scientifically qualified persons. . . .

9. During the course of the research the human subject should be at liberty to bring the research to an end if he has reached the physical or mental state where continuation of the research seems to him to be impossible.

10. During the course of the research the scientist in charge must be prepared to terminate the research at any stage, if he has probable cause to believe . . . the continuation of the research is likely to result in injury, disability, or death to the research subject.

Note: The writers of the original code emphasized the need to protect subjects in experimental research. Because social scientists use a variety of techniques, I have substituted the word "research" for "experiment."

---

saved his life.[4] You see, the researchers were intent on studying the effects of *untreated* syphilis. The study continued until 1972 when its existence became public. At that point, the research was terminated because of public outrage (Jones 1981).

_____

[4]Alexander Fleming discovered the cure (penicillin) in 1928, but it would be another decade before the drug was used by medical practitioners. In the late 1930s, just in time for World War II, two British researchers, Ernst Chain and Howard Florey, discovered a process that purified penicillin and made it safe. The drug was widely used by the military in the war and in the civilian sector after the war.

The Case for Sociological Research

You might well think that members of the general public have little to fear from sociologists. After all, what harm can a bunch of geeks with clipboards do by asking questions?

There is potential for harm in any sort of research that involves human subjects. The potential harm in sociological research frequently involves not what we do or do not do to our research subjects, but what we find out about them. Sociologists and other social scientists find out information that people often would prefer to keep private.

One of the most famous examples of social science research that many believed crossed the ethical lines was Laud Humphreys' study, which he titled *Tearoom Trade* (1970).

Technically speaking, *Tearoom Trade* was a study of impersonal sexual activity between male homosexuals. Less technically speaking, Humphreys began his research (or so he later said) by trying to find an answer to a question posed by his graduate advisor: "Where does the average guy go just to get a blow job?"

As Humphreys discovered, the answer to that particular question was "a tearoom" (that is, a restroom in a public park). In these tearooms, Humphreys did observational research. More specifically, to hide the fact that he was a researcher, he took on the role of "watch queen" (a third man who serves as a lookout for those engaged in homosexual acts and obtains voyeuristic pleasure from his observations).

From his observations, Humphreys obtained a great deal of information about how men approach each other and negotiate sex. But, given the circumstances, he could not very well find out much else. Humphreys wanted to know, Who are these men? How do they spend the rest of their time?

So, in addition to making his secret observations, Humphreys recorded each participant's license plate number. He then took this list of numbers to the police, told them he was doing "market research," and obtained the names and addresses of each man.

But, then what? He could hardly show up at the men's doorsteps and announce, "Hi, I saw you engaging in homosexual sex in the park last month, and now I would like to ask you a few questions about the rest of your life." (Sometimes, the most straightforward approach simply does not work.)

Around that time, another researcher at the same university was conducting a study on issues related to health care. Humphreys persuaded this researcher to include the names of his tearoom players on the list of subjects for the health study and schedule them for interviews. Humphreys himself would interview these men. To reduce the chances that the men would recognize him, Humphreys waited a year and changed his hairstyle. Then, no doubt armed with that ubiquitous clipboard, Humphreys visited and interviewed each of the men. This way, posing as a health-care researcher, he was able to find out all about the men's socioeconomic status (mostly middle class), their educational level (pretty high), and their family life (mostly married with children). Humphreys discovered that the only nonconventional thing about these men was that they visited tearooms for anonymous sex.

What might be ethically questionable about Humphreys' research? Although some might object that the very topic of Humphreys' research was immoral, the nature of the topic is not an *ethical* concern. What is of concern ethically is the fact that Humphreys deceived his subjects—they never knew that they were participating in research, and they didn't have the opportunity to choose to participate. Moreover, Humphreys conducted his research during a time when homosexual behavior was illegal where the research was conducted. By recording their names and addresses, Humphreys was placing his research subjects in great jeopardy. After his book was published, what if the police had demanded that Humphreys turn over his list of subjects' names and addresses? There was a great risk not only of legal prosecution but of psychological and social harm as well. And, had their names been discovered, some of the men might even have been subjected to extortion.

Humphreys defended his research by pointing out that it is important for sociologists to know about such men and their activities in order to understand them. In point of fact, Humphreys' research did contradict many social myths about men who have sex in public bathrooms. Most were established members of the community with wives and children, and in practicing consensual sex, they were not hurting anyone and certainly not bothering children. Humphreys' research was published and widely cited and may well have played a role in decriminalizing some sexual acts between consenting adults.

Humphreys' research was perhaps extreme in this respect, but it is not unusual for sociologists to uncover embarrassing details. Sometimes, what we learn not only is embarrassing but may place the research subject in legal jeopardy. In such cases, we have to figure out what our duty is—do we keep the secrets only of those whom we respect as "good people"? The problem may be compounded by the fact that the people we study are often those who have little power in society: it almost seems as if sociologists are obsessed with marginalized people (the poor, the homeless, street criminals, and so on).[5]

There are few hard-and-fast rules about what is and is not ethical behavior in sociological research. As far as I am concerned, the only thing that is consistently unethical is to not think through the possible consequences of our research.

As we think through the possible consequences of our research, we need to remember that we have an obligation not only to our research subjects but to other sociologists, to the university, and to members of the community at large. Making ethical decisions involves weighing the costs and benefits of the research to all of these groups.

This takes a great deal of thought; frequently, our research may have consequences that extend beyond the obvious. For example,

in the early 1960s, a woman named Kitty Genovese was raped and murdered in New York City. What set the Genovese murder apart from the many other murders that happened that year was the fact that a number of people had heard her screams for help, which lasted for many minutes, but not a single one called the police.

The Genovese murder caught the imagination of social researchers in a big way. Under what conditions would people help strangers in trouble? What followed was a multitude of so-called bystander intervention studies. Some of these were pretty benign, such as a boy on crutches dropping all of his school books to see whether anyone would stop to help. Other versions included scenes of staged violence, such as a woman yelling from the bushes, "Help, rape." Soon, people grew leery and distrustful as they walked around college campuses and nearby neighborhoods—there were so many researchers out and about that one never knew when one might become an involuntary research subject.

Then, the inevitable but still unthinkable happened:

> At the University of Washington in Seattle in 1973, a male student accosted another student on campus and shot him. Students on their way to class did not stop to aid the victim, nor did anyone follow the assailant (who was caught anyway). When the campus reporters asked some students about their lack of concern over the murder, they said they thought it was just a psychology experiment. (Diener and Crandall 1978, 87)

In this case, the harm caused by the overdoing of bystander and other sorts of research in the field did not affect only the research subjects. It contaminated the researcher's world by making people distrust researchers. And, far worse, it may have contributed to the death of a college student.

---

[5]Part of the reason for this apparent obsession is that it is much easier to gain access to people with little power. It's easier to get permission to examine, say, prison inmates than executives of Ford Motor Company.

The Nature of Informed Consent

"Informed consent is the procedure in which individuals choose whether to participate in an investigation after being informed of facts that would be likely to influence their decision. Informed consent includes several key elements: (a) subjects learn that the research is voluntary; (b) they are informed about aspects of the research that might influence their decision to participate; and (c) they exercise a continuous free choice to participate that lasts throughout the study. The greater the possibility of danger in the study and the greater the potential harm involved, or the greater the rights relinquished, the more thorough must be the procedure of obtaining informed consent" (Diener and Crandall 1978).

Institutional Review Boards: The Dawn of a New Era

These days, before any member of the university community (student, faculty, or staff) can conduct research that involves humans, they must submit a research proposal to a university officer or committee charged with ensuring that research is done ethically. If there is any question of risk to the human subjects, a committee consisting of both faculty (from a variety of disciplines) and community members will scrutinize the proposal. These committees are commonly called Institutional Review Boards (IRBs). If the members of the IRB judge that the researcher has not created sufficient safeguards to protect the rights of the research subjects and the general public, and even the researcher him- or herself, the researcher is prohibited from going on.

Like the Nuremberg Code, contemporary ethical guidelines place a great deal of emphasis on treating research subjects with respect. In many cases, researchers must obtain not merely *consent* from potential subjects but *informed consent*. As a general rule, deception must be kept to the absolute minimum. Members of IRBs are particularly skeptical of any research that places research subjects at risk of injury (physical, psychological, emotional, or

legal) greater than the risk that surrounds the routine activities of everyday life.

How Heroic Must an Ethical Researcher Be?

To what extremes must the sociological researcher go to fulfill his or her ethical duty? As I noted previously, one of the reasons Laud Humphreys was criticized when he published *Tearoom Trade* was that homosexual acts were prohibited by law where he did his research. In theory, the district attorney could have subpoenaed the list of names and addresses of Humphreys' subjects and prosecuted these men.[6] Would being ethical have required Humphreys to choose jail over releasing his information? In fact, this course of action apparently was contemplated, though it never materialized.

A little over a decade later, another sociologist came even closer to being forced to decide between breaching confidentiality and

---

[6]A subpoena (sa-PEE-na) is nothing to fool around with. It is a command from a legal authority to appear and give testimony. If you refuse to comply with a subpoena, you can be charged with contempt of court and sent to jail until you change your mind (or until the judge accepts the fact that nothing is going to change your mind).

going to jail. Mario Brajuhas, a graduate student at the State University of New York at Stony Brook, was doing participant observation research as a waiter in a restaurant. When the restaurant burned down, the police suspected arson. Investigators knew of Brajuhas's research and of the fact that he had taken copious field notes; they suspected that those field notes might help identify the arsonist. The local prosecutor subpoenaed the notes, but Brajuhas refused to hand them over, even when threatened with jail. Finally (after 2 years), the major suspects in the fire died, and the prosecutor dropped the case.

In the early 1990s, Rik Scarce, a graduate student at Washington State University, took a vacation. He left an acquaintance of his, Rodney Coronado, behind as a housesitter. Scarce and Coronado had become acquainted when Scarce, prior to going to graduate school, had been researching a book on radical environmentalists entitled *Eco-Warriors: Understanding the Radical Environmental Movement* (1990). Coronado was involved with the Animal Liberation Front (ALF), which was adamantly opposed to the use of animals for research.

While Scarce was on vacation, the ALF raided a research laboratory at Washington State University. Several animals were set free, and the researchers' computers were destroyed. The university estimated the damage at about $100,000. Several months later, Scarce was subpoenaed and commanded to appear before a grand jury that had been convened to investigate the crime. Scarce did appear and answer several questions, but he declined to answer questions that, he said, required him to breach the confidentiality of his research subjects. Scarce quoted from the American Sociological Association's Code of Ethics, which states that "confidential information provided by research participants must be treated as such, even when this information enjoys no legal protection or privilege and legal force is applied." As Scarce later explained, "I told the judge that I

feared for my ability to earn a living as a sociologist if I were compelled to testify. Research subjects might not be willing to speak with me, and institutions might not be willing to hire an unethical researcher" (Scarce 1994).

The judge was not moved by Scarce's explanation. Ultimately, after he continued to refuse to testify, Scarce was sent to jail as a "recalcitrant [unwilling] witness." He spent more than 5 months in jail before the judge, finally convinced that Scarce could not be compelled to testify, freed him.

The Scarce case sounded a warning bell to sociologists everywhere. According to their ethical code, they have an obligation to keep confidential information to themselves even when they have no legal right to do so. This puts sociologists in a different position than lawyers and doctors. Communication between lawyers and clients and between doctors and patients is *legally privileged.* Lawyers and physicians have not only an *ethical duty* to keep information confidential but the *legal right* to do so. Sociologists, on the other hand, have no such clear legal right, although they do have an ethical duty.

References

Annas, George J., and Michael A. Grodin. 1992. *The Nazi Doctors and the Nuremberg Code.* New York: Oxford University Press.

Diener, Edward, and Rick Crandall. 1978. *Ethics in Social and Behavioral Research.* Chicago: University of Chicago Press.

Humphreys, Laud. 1970. *Tearoom Trade: Impersonal Sex in Public Places.* Chicago: Aldine.

Jones, James H. 1981. *Bad Blood: The Tuskegee Syphilis Experiment.* New York: Free Press.

Lederer, Susan E. 1995. *Subjected to Science: Human Experimentation in America Before the Second World War.* Baltimore: Johns Hopkins University.

Scarce, Rik. 1994. "(No) Trial (But) Tribulations: When Courts and Ethnography Conflict." *Journal of Contemporary Ethnography* 23: 123–149.

Scarce, Rik, 1990. *Eco-Warriors: Understanding the Radical Environmental Movement.* Chicago: Noble Press.

Questions

1. One problem that often crops up in survey research is that many people do not fill out and return questionnaires. Researchers have learned that it helps increase the "response rate" if survey respondents are sent a reminder a week or so after they are sent the questionnaire. This doesn't sound controversial, does it? Well, consider the following situation:

   > For her senior research project, Mary is doing an anonymous survey. In other words, she has stated on the cover of each questionnaire that responses will be totally anonymous—no names will be asked for or in any way recorded.
   >
   > From reading the literature on response rates, Mary expects that only about a third of those to whom she mails the questionnaire will send it back. She knows that she can perhaps double her response rate if she sends everyone a reminder. However, she barely had enough money to send out the questionnaire in the first place, and she can't afford to send a postcard reminder to everyone. She comes up with what she thinks is a great plan. She will embed a secret symbol somewhere in each questionnaire—a different symbol for each respondent. As each survey is returned, she will locate the symbol, consult the master list, and determine the name of each respondent. That way, she will be able to check off the name of each respondent who has returned his or her questionnaire. After a week or so, Mary will send reminder cards to respondents who have not yet returned their questionnaires.

   You are Mary's thesis advisor. What ethical issues would you raise with her?

2. A sociology professor offers her students extra credit for participating in an experiment. As far as the students are concerned, the down side is the fact that participating in this particular experiment will expose them to embarrassing situations; the up side is that obtaining the extra credit will have a big impact on their grades.

   Is a student's participation really voluntary when to not participate means he or she will miss out on some valuable rewards and possibly fail the class? What might this professor do to make her plan more ethical?

3. Bob is writing his senior thesis on "The Functions of Symbols in the Secret Rituals of College Fraternities." He plans to ask his fraternity brothers to give him their views on the ceremonies of their fraternity. In addition, he plans to secretly record an upcoming fraternity initiation ritual.

   As his thesis advisor, what ethical issues would you feel compelled to raise with Bob about his research?

7

IF HITLER ASKED YOU TO ELECTROCUTE A STRANGER, WOULD YOU? PROBABLY

Philip Meyer

When he reflected back on the tales of Nazi horror that surfaced after World War II, Stanley Milgram wanted to know how ordinary people could be led to participate in such brutality. Like many others, Milgram had persuaded himself that it was something about the German character or culture that allowed the Holocaust to happen; such a horrible thing could never take place, for example, in the United States. Milgram's original plan was to go to Germany to test his hypothesis. Before he could do that, however, he needed a point of comparison. So, he tried out his experiment in New Haven and Bridgeport, Connecticut. As Philip Meyer explains in this 1970 article, Milgram never got to Germany.

In the beginning, Stanley Milgram was worried about the Nazi problem. He doesn't worry much about the Nazis anymore. He worries about you and me, and perhaps, himself a little bit too.

Stanley Milgram is a social psychologist, and when he began his career at Yale University in 1960 he had a plan to prove, scientifically, that Germans are different. The Germans-are-different hypothesis has been used by historians, such as William L. Shirer,[1] to explain the systematic destruction of the Jews by the Third Reich. One madman could decide to destroy the Jews and even create a master plan for

getting it done. But to implement it on the scale that Hitler did meant that thousands of other people had to go along with the scheme and help to do the work. The Shirer thesis, which Milgram set out to test, is that Germans have a basic character flaw which explains the whole thing, and this flaw is a readiness to obey authority without question, no matter what outrageous acts the authority commands.

The appealing thing about this theory is that it makes those of us who are not Germans feel better about the whole business. Obviously, you and I are not Hitler, and it seems equally obvious that we would never do Hitler's dirty work for him. But now, because of Stanley Milgram, we are compelled to wonder. Milgram developed a laboratory experiment which provided a systematic way to measure obedience. His plan was to try it out in New Haven on Americans and then go to Germany and try it out on Germans. He was strongly motivated by scientific curiosity, but there was also some moral content in his decision to pursue this line of research, which

[1] William Lawrence Shirer began his career as a journalist. Shirer went to work for CBS in 1937, broadcasting the events of the war from both Europe and the United States. In 1940, Shirer took a job with the New York *Herald Tribune,* for which he wrote a column for a couple of years. In 1960, his book *The Rise and Fall of the Third Reich* won the National Book Award.—Ed.

Philip Meyer, "If Hitler Asked You to Electrocute a Stranger, Would You? Probably" from *Esquire* (February 1970). Reprinted with the permission of the author.

was, in turn, colored by his own Jewish background. If he could show that Germans are more obedient than Americans, he could then vary the conditions of the experiment and try to find out just what it is that makes some people more obedient than others. With this understanding, the world might, conceivably, be just a little bit better.

But he never took his experiment to Germany. He never took it any farther than Bridgeport. The first finding, also the most unexpected and disturbing finding, was that we Americans are an obedient people: not blindly obedient, and not blissfully obedient, just obedient. "I found so much obedience," says Milgram softly, a little sadly, "I hardly saw the need for taking the experiment to Germany."

There is something of the theatre director in Milgram, and his technique, which he learned from one of the old masters in experimental psychology, Solomon Asch, is to stage a play with every line rehearsed, every prop carefully selected, and everybody an actor except one person. That one person is the subject of the experiment. The subject, of course, does not know he is in a play. He thinks he is in real life. The value of this technique is that the experimenter, as though he were God, can change a prop here, vary a line there, and see how the subject responds. Milgram eventually had to change a lot of the script just to get people to stop obeying. They were obeying so much, the experiment wasn't working—it was like trying to measure oven temperature with a freezer thermometer.

The experiment worked like this: If you were an innocent subject in Milgram's melodrama, you read an ad in the newspaper or received one in the mail asking for volunteers for an educational experiment. The job would take about an hour and pay $4.50. So you make an appointment and go to an old Romanesque stone structure on High Street with the imposing name of The Yale Interaction Laboratory. It looks something like a broadcasting

studio. Inside, you meet a young, crew cut man in a laboratory coat, who says he is Jack Williams, the experimenter. There is another citizen, fiftyish, Irish face, an accountant, a little overweight, and very mild and harmless-looking. This other citizen seems nervous and plays with his hat while the two of you sit in chairs side by side and are told that the $4.50 checks are yours no matter what happens. Then you listen to Jack Williams explain the experiment.

It is about learning, says Jack Williams in a quiet, knowledgeable way. Science does not know much about the conditions under which people learn and this experiment is to find out about negative reinforcement. Negative reinforcement is getting punished when you do something wrong, as opposed to positive reinforcement which is getting rewarded when you do something right. The negative reinforcement in this case is electric shock. You notice a book on the table, titled *The Teaching-Learning Process,* and you assume that this has something to do with the experiment.

Then Jack Williams takes two pieces of paper, puts them in a hat, and shakes them up. One piece of paper is supposed to say, "Teacher" and the other, "Learner." Draw one and you will see which you will be. The mild-looking accountant draws one, holds it close to his vest like a poker player, looks at it, and says, "Learner." You look at yours. It says, "Teacher." You do not know that the drawing is rigged, and both slips say "Teacher." The experimenter beckons to the mild-mannered "learner."

"Want to step right in here and have a seat, please?" he says. "You can leave your coat on the back of that chair . . . roll up your right sleeve, please. Now what I want to do is strap down your arms to avoid excessive movement on your part during the experiment. This electrode is connected to the shock generator in the next room.

"And this electrode paste," he says, squeezing some stuff out of a plastic bottle and putting it on the man's arm, "is to provide a good contact and to avoid a blister or burn. Are there any questions now before we go into the next room?"

You don't have any, but the strapped-in "learner" does.

"I do think I should say this," says the learner. "About two years ago I was at the veterans' hospital . . . they detected a heart condition. Nothing serious, but as long as I'm having these shocks, how strong are they— how dangerous are they?"

Williams, the experimenter, shakes his head casually. "Oh, no," he says. "Although they may be painful, they're not dangerous. Anything else?"

Nothing else. And so you play the game. The game is for you to read a series of word pairs: for example, blue-girl, nice-day, fat-neck. When you finish the list, you read just the first word in each pair and then a multiple-choice list of four other words, including the second word of the pair. The learner, from his remote, strapped-in position, pushes one of four switches to indicate which of the four answers he thinks is the right one. If he gets it right, nothing happens and you go on to the next one. If he gets it wrong, you push a switch that buzzes and gives him an electric shock. And then you go to the next word. You start with 15 volts and increase the number of volts by 15 for each wrong answer. The control board goes from 15 volts on one end to 450 volts on the other. So that you know what you are doing, you get a test shock yourself, at 45 volts. It hurts. To further keep you aware of what you are doing to that man in there, the board has verbal descriptions of the shock levels, ranging from "Slight Shock" at the left-hand side, through "Intense Shock" in the middle, to "Danger: Severe Shock" toward the far right. Finally, at the very end, under 435- and 450-volt switches, there are three ambiguous X's. If, at any point, you hesitate, Mr. Williams calmly tells you to go on. If you still hesitate, he tells you again.

Except for some terrifying details, which will be explained in a moment, this is the experiment. The object is to find the shock level at which you disobey the experimenter and refuse to pull the switch.

When Stanley Milgram first wrote this script, he took it to fourteen Yale psychology majors and asked them what they thought would happen. He put it this way: Out of one hundred persons in the teacher's predicament, how would their break-off points be distributed along the 15-to-450-volt scale? They thought a few would break off very early, most would quit someplace in the middle and a few would go all the way to the end. The highest estimate of the number out of one hundred who would go all the way to the end was three. Milgram then informally polled some of his fellow scholars in the psychology department. They agreed that very few would go to the end. Milgram thought so too.

"I'll tell you quite frankly," he says, "before I began this experiment, before any shock generator was built, I thought that most people would break off at 'Strong Shock' or 'Very Strong Shock.' You would get only a very, very small proportion of people getting out to the end of the shock generator, and they would constitute a pathological fringe."

In his pilot experiments, Milgram used Yale students as subjects. Each of them pushed the shock switches, one by one, all the way to the end of the board.

So he rewrote the script to include some protests from the learner. At first, they were mild, gentlemanly, Yalie protests, but, "it didn't seem to have as much effect as I thought it would or should," Milgram recalls. "So we had more violent protestation on the part of the person getting the shock. All of the time, of course, what we were trying to do was not to create a macabre situation, but simply to generate disobedience. And that was one of the first findings. This was not only a technical deficiency of the experiment, that we didn't get disobedience. It really was the first finding: that obedience would be much greater than we had assumed it would be and disobedience would be much more difficult than we had assumed."

As it turned out, the situation did become rather macabre. The only meaningful way to generate disobedience was to have the victim protest with great anguish, noise, and vehemence. The protests were tape-recorded so that all the teachers ordinarily would hear the same sounds and nuances, and they started with a grunt at 75 volts, proceeded through a "Hey, that really hurts," at 125 volts, got desperate with, "I can't stand the pain, don't do that," at 180 volts, reached complaints of heart trouble at 195, an agonized scream at 285, a refusal to answer at 315, and only heart-rending, ominous silence after that.

Still, sixty-five percent of the subjects,twenty- to fifty-year-old American males, everyday, ordinary people like you and me, obediently kept pushing those levers in the belief that they were shocking the mild-mannered learner, whose name was Mr. Wallace, and who was chosen for the role because of his innocent appearance, all the way up to 450 volts.

Milgram was now getting enough disobedience so that he had something he could measure. The next step was to vary the circumstances to see what would encourage or discourage obedience. There seemed very little left in the way of discouragement. The victim was already screaming at the top of his lungs and feigning a heart attack. So whatever new impediment to obedience reached the brain of the subject had to travel by some route other than the ear. Milgram thought of one.

He put the learner in the same room with the teacher. He stopped strapping the learner's hand down. He rewrote the script so that at 150 volts the learner took his hand off the shock plate and declared that he wanted out of the experiment. He rewrote the script some more so that the experimenter then told the teacher to grasp the learner's hand and physically force it down on the plate to give Mr. Wallace his unwanted electric shock.

"I had the feeling that very few people would go on at that point, if any," Milgram says. "I thought that would be the limit of obedience that you would find in the laboratory."

It wasn't.

Although seven years have now gone by, Milgram still remembers the first person to walk into the laboratory in the newly rewritten script. He was a construction worker, a very short man. "He was so small," says Milgram, "that when he sat on the chair in front of the shock generator, his feet didn't reach the floor. When the experimenter told him to push the victim's hand down and give the shock, he turned to the experimenter, and he turned to the victim, his elbow went up, he fell down on the hand of the victim, his feet kind of tugged to one side, and he said, 'Like this, boss?' ZZUMPH!"

The experiment was played out to its bitter end. Milgram tried it with forty different subjects. And thirty percent of them obeyed the experimenter and kept on obeying.

"The protests of the victim were strong and vehement, he was screaming his guts out, he refused to participate, and you had to physically struggle with him in order to get his hand down on the shock generator," Milgram remembers. But twelve out of forty did it.

Milgram took his experiment out of New Haven. Not to Germany, just twenty miles down the road to Bridgeport. Maybe, he reasoned, the people obeyed because of the prestigious setting of Yale University. If they couldn't trust a center of learning that had been there for two centuries, whom could they trust? So he moved the experiment to an untrustworthy setting.

The new setting was a suite of three rooms in a run-down office building in Bridgeport. The only identification was a sign with a fictitious name: "Research Associates of Bridgeport."

Questions about professional connections got only vague answers about "research for industry."

Obedience was less in Bridgeport. Forty-eight percent of the subjects stayed for the maximum shock, compared to sixty-five percent at Yale. But this was enough to prove that far more than Yale's prestige was behind the obedient behavior.

For more than seven years now, Stanley Milgram has been trying to figure out what makes ordinary American citizens so obedient. The most obvious answer—that people are mean, nasty, brutish and sadistic—won't do. The subjects who gave the shocks to Mr. Wallace to the end of the board did not enjoy it. They groaned, protested, fidgeted, argued, and in some cases, were seized by fits of nervous, agitated giggling.

"They even try to get out of it," says Milgram, "but they are somehow engaged in something from which they cannot liberate themselves. They are locked into a structure, and they do not have the skills or inner resources to disengage themselves."

Milgram, because he mistakenly had assumed that he would have trouble getting people to obey the orders to shock Mr. Wallace, went to a lot of trouble to create a realistic situation.

There was crew cut Jack Williams and his grey laboratory coat. Not white, which might denote a medical technician, but ambiguously authoritative grey. Then there was the book on the table, and the other appurtenances of the laboratory which emitted the silent message that things were being performed here in the name of science, and were therefore great and good.

But the nicest touch of all was the shock generator. When Milgram started out, he had only a $300 grant from the Higgins Fund of Yale University. Later he got more ample support from the National Science Foundation, but in the beginning he had to create this authentic-looking

machine with very scarce resources except for his own imagination. So he went to New York and roamed around the electronic shops until he found some little black switches at Lafayette Radio for a dollar apiece. He bought thirty of them. The generator was a metal box, about the size of a small footlocker, and he drilled the thirty holes for the thirty switches himself in a Yale machine shop. But the fine detail was left to professional industrial engravers. So he ended up with a splendid-looking control panel dominated by the row of switches, each labeled with its voltage, and each having its own red light that flashed on when the switch was pulled. Other things happened when a switch was pushed. Besides the ZZUMPHing noise, a blue light labeled "voltage energizer" went on, and a needle on a dial labeled "voltage" flicked from left to right. Relays inside the box clicked. Finally, in the upper left-hand corner of the control panel was this inscription, engraved in precise block letters:

SHOCK GENERATOR TYPE ZLB
DYSON INSTRUMENT COMPANY
WALTHAM, MASS.
OUTPUT: 15 VOLTS–450 VOLTS

One day a man from the Lehigh Valley Electronics Company of Pennsylvania was passing through the laboratory, and he stopped to admire the shock generator.

"This is a very fine shock generator," he said. "But who is this Dyson Instrument Company?" Milgram felt proud at that, since Dyson Instrument Company existed only in the recesses of his imagination.

When you consider the seeming authenticity of the situation, you can appreciate the agony some of the subjects went through. It was pure conflict. As Milgram explains to his students, "When a parent says, 'Don't strike old ladies,' you are learning two things: the content and, also, to obey authority. This experiment creates conflicts between the two elements."

Here is a partial transcription from one of the experiments. The naïve "teacher" is a heavyset, worried-looking man with prematurely grey hair. He is wearing a polo shirt. He is very polite. He has just pushed the 180-volt lever. A hidden camera is recording the performance.

LEARNER (*who, from the teacher's point of view is heard but not seen, an offstage voice*): Ow, I can't stand the pain. Don't do that. . . .

TEACHER (*pivoting around in his chair and shaking his head*): I can't stand it. I'm not going to kill that man in there. You hear him hollering?

EXPERIMENTER: As I told you before, the shocks may be painful, but—

TEACHER: But he's hollering. He can't stand it. What's going to happen to him?

EXPERIMENTER (*His voice is patient, matter-of-fact.*): The experiment requires that you continue, Teacher.

TEACHER: Aaah, but, unh, I'm not going to get that man sick in there . . . know what I mean?

EXPERIMENTER: Whether the Learner likes it or not, we must go on, through all the word pairs.

TEACHER: I refuse to take the responsibility. He's in there hollering!

EXPERIMENTER: It's absolutely essential that you continue, Teacher.

TEACHER (*indicating the unused questions*): There's too many left here, I mean, Geez, if he gets them wrong, there's too many of them left. I mean who's going to take the responsibility if anything happens to that gentleman?

EXPERIMENTER: I'm responsible for anything that happens to him. Continue please.

TEACHER: All right. (*Consults list of words.*) The next one's "Slow—walk, truck, dance, music." Answer, please. (*A buzzing sound indicates the learner has signaled his answer.*) Wrong. A hundred and ninety-five volts. "Dance." (*Zzumph!*)

LEARNER: Let me out of here. My heart's bothering me! (*Teacher looks at experimenter.*)

EXPERIMENTER: Continue, please.

LEARNER (*screaming*): Let me out of here, you have no right to keep me here. Let me out of here, let me out, my heart's bothering me, let me out! (*Teacher shakes head, pats the table nervously.*)

TEACHER: You see, he's hollering. Hear that? Gee, I don't know.

EXPERIMENTER: The experiment requires. . . .

TEACHER (*interrupting*): I know it does, sir, but I mean—hunh! He don't know what he's getting in for. He's up to 195 volts! (*Experiment continues, through 210 volts, 225 volts, 240 volts, 255 volts, 270 volts, delivered to the man in the electric chair, at which point the teacher, with evident relief, runs out of word-pair questions.*)

EXPERIMENTER: You'll have to go back to the beginning of that page and go through them again until he's learned them all correctly.

TEACHER: Aw, no. I'm not going to kill that man. You mean I've got to keep going up with the scale. No sir. He's hollering in there. I'm not going to give him 450 volts.

EXPERIMENTER: The experiment requires that you go on.

TEACHER: I know it does, but that man is hollering in there, sir.

EXPERIMENTER (*same matter-of-fact tone*): As I said before, although the shocks may be painful . . .

TEACHER (*interrupting*): Awwww. He—he—he's yelling in there.

EXPERIMENTER: Start with "Blue," please, at the top of the page. Continue, please, Teacher. Just go ahead.

TEACHER (*concentrating intently on list of words in front of him, as if to shut everything else out*): "Blue—boy, girl, grass, hat." (*Buzz indicates answer.*) Correct. "Night—day, sky, job, chair." (*Buzz*) Wrong. The answer is "day." Two hundred and eighty-five volts. (*Zzumph!*)

LEARNER: *Ohhhuhhoohhh!*

EXPERIMENTER: Continue, please.

TEACHER: "Fat—man, lady, tub, neck." Answer, please. (*Buzz*) Wrong. The answer is "neck." Three hundred volts. (*Zzumph!*)

LEARNER: Ohhh. I absolutely refuse to answer any more. (*Shouting urgently, now*) Let me out of here. You can't hold me here. Get me out. Get—me—out—of—here.

EXPERIMENTER: Continue. The next word is "Green," please.

TEACHER: "Green—grass, hat, ink, apple." (*Nothing happens. No answering buzz. Just gloomy silence.*)

TEACHER: I don't think he is going to answer.

EXPERIMENTER: If the learner doesn't answer in a reasonable time, about four or five seconds, consider the answer wrong. And follow the same procedures you have been doing for wrong answers. Say "Wrong," tell him the number of volts, give him the punishment, read him the correct answer. Continue, please.

TEACHER: "Green—grass, hat, ink, apple." Answer, please. (*More silence. Teacher just sits there.*)

EXPERIMENTER: Go on with the procedure, please, Teacher.

TEACHER: Three hundred and fifteen volts. The answer is "ink." (*Zzumph!*)

LEARNER: Ohh, Ooohh.

TEACHER (*relieved to hear response*): Next one . . .

LEARNER: I absolutely refuse to answer.

TEACHER: You got to. You get a shock if you don't answer. (*Experiment continues with learner refusing to answer, and finally failing even to grunt or groan. At 375 volts, the teacher stands up. Has he had enough? Will he break off the experiment? Will he disobey?*)

TEACHER: I think something's happened to that fellow in there. I don't get no answer. He was hollering at less voltage. Can't you check in and see if he's all right, please?

EXPERIMENTER (*same detached calm*): Not once we've started. Please continue, Teacher.

TEACHER (*sits down, sighs deeply*): "Cool—day, shade, water, paint." Answer, please. Are you all right in there? Are you all right?

EXPERIMENTER: Please continue, Teacher. Continue, please. (*Teacher pushes lever. Zzumph!*)

TEACHER (*swiveling around in his chair*): Something's happened to that man in there. (*Swiveling back*) Next one. "Low—dollar, necklace, moon, paint." (*Turning around again*) Something's happened to that man in there. You better check in on him, sir. He won't answer or nothing.

EXPERIMENTER: Continue. Go on, please.

TEACHER: You accept all responsibility.

EXPERIMENTER: The responsibility is mine. Correct. Please go on. (*Teacher returns to his list, starts running through words as rapidly as he can read them, works through to 450 volts.*)

TEACHER: That's that.

EXPERIMENTER: Continue using the last switch on the board, please. The four-fifty switch for each wrong answer. Continue, please.

TEACHER: But I don't get no anything!

EXPERIMENTER: Please continue. The next word is "White."

TEACHER: Don't you think you should look in on him, please.

EXPERIMENTER: Not once we've started the experiment.

TEACHER: But what if something has happened to the man?

EXPERIMENTER: The experiment requires that you continue. Go on, please.

TEACHER: Don't the man's health mean anything?

EXPERIMENTER: Whether the LEARNER likes it or not . . .

TEACHER: What if he's dead in there? (*Gestures toward the room with the electric chair*) I mean, he told me he can't stand the shock, sir. I don't mean to be rude, but I think you should look in on him. All you have to do is look in the door. I don't get no answer, no noise. Something might have happened to the gentleman in there, sir.

EXPERIMENTER: We must continue. Go on, please.

TEACHER: You mean keep giving him what? Four hundred fifty volts, what he's got now?

EXPERIMENTER: That's correct. Continue. The next word is "White."

TEACHER (*now at a furious pace*): "White— cloud, horse, rock, house." Answer, please. The answer is "horse." Four hundred and fifty volts. (*Zzumph!*) Next word. "Bag— paint, music, clown, girl." The answer is "paint." Four hundred and fifty volts. (*Zzumph!*) Next word is "Short—sentence, movie . . . "

EXPERIMENTER: Excuse me, Teacher. We'll have to discontinue the experiment.
(*Enter Milgram from camera's left. He has been watching from behind one-way glass.*)

MILGRAM: I'd like to ask you a few questions. (*Slowly, patiently, he dehoaxes the teacher, telling him that the shocks and screams were not real.*)

TEACHER: You mean he wasn't getting nothing? Well, I'm glad to hear that. I was getting upset there. I was getting ready to walk out. (*Finally, to make sure there are no hard feelings, friendly, harmless Mr. Wallace comes out in coat and tie. Gives jovial greeting. Friendly reconciliation takes place. Experiment ends.*)

Subjects in the experiment were not asked to give the 450-volt shock more than three times. By that time, it seemed evident that they would go on indefinitely. "No one," says Milgram, "who got within five shocks of the end ever broke off. By that point, he had resolved the conflict."

Why do so many people resolve the conflict in favor of obedience?

Milgram's theory assumes that people behave in two different operating modes as different as ice and water. He does not rely on Freud or sex or toilet-training hang-ups for this theory. All he says is that ordinarily we operate in a state of autonomy, which means we pretty much have and assert control over what we do. But in certain circumstances, we operate under what Milgram calls a state of agency (after agent, n . . . one who acts for or in the place of another by authority from him; a substitute; a deputy. —*Webster's Collegiate Dictionary*). A state of agency, to Milgram, is nothing more than a frame of mind.

"There's nothing bad about it, there's nothing good about it," he says. "It's a natural circumstance of living with other people. . . . I think of a state of agency as a real transformation of a person: if a person has different properties when he's in that state, just as water can turn to ice under certain conditions of temperature, a person can move to the state of mind that I call agency . . . the critical thing is that you see yourself as the instrument of the execution of another person's wishes. You do not see yourself as acting on your own. And there's a real transformation, a real change of properties of the person."

To achieve this change, you have to be in a situation where there seems to be a ruling authority whose commands are relevant to some legitimate purpose; the authority's power is not unlimited.

But situations can be and have been structured to make people do unusual things, and not just in Milgram's laboratory. The reason, says Milgram, is that no action, in and of itself, contains meaning.

"The meaning always depends on your definition of the situation. Take an action like killing another person. It sounds bad.

"But then we say the other person was about to destroy a hundred children, and the only way to stop him was to kill him. Well, that sounds good.

"Or, you take destroying your own life. It sounds very bad. Yet, in the Second World War, thousands of persons thought it was a good thing to destroy your own life. It was set in the proper context. You sipped some saki from a whistling cup, recited a few haiku. You said 'May my death be as clean and as quick as the shattering of crystal.' And it almost seemed like a good, noble thing to do, to crash your kamikaze plane into an aircraft carrier. But the main thing was, the definition of what a kamikaze pilot was doing had been determined by the relevant authority. Now, once you are in a state of agency, you allow the authority to determine, to define what the situation is. The meaning of your action is altered."

So, for most subjects in Milgram's laboratory experiments, the act of giving Mr. Wallace his painful shock was necessary, even though unpleasant, and besides they were doing it on behalf of somebody else and it was for science. There was still strain and conflict, of course. Most people resolved it by grimly sticking to their task and obeying. But some broke out. Milgram tried varying the conditions of the experiment to see what would help break people out of their state of agency.

"The results, as seen and felt in the laboratory," he has written, "are disturbing. They raise the possibility that human nature, or more specifically the kind of character produced in American democratic society, cannot be counted on to insulate its citizens from brutality and inhumane treatment at the direction of malevolent authority. A substantial proportion of people do what they are told to do, irrespective of the content of the act and without limitations of conscience, so long as they perceive that the command comes from a legitimate authority. If, in this study, an anonymous experimenter can successfully command adults to subdue a fifty-year-old man and force on him painful electric shocks against his protest, one can only wonder what government, with its vastly greater authority and prestige, can command of its subjects."

This is a nice statement, but it falls short of summing up the full meaning of Milgram's work. It leaves some questions still unanswered.

The first question is this: Should we really be surprised and alarmed that people obey? Wouldn't it be even more alarming if they all refused to obey? Without obedience to a relevant ruling authority there could not be a civil society. And without a civil society, as Thomas Hobbes pointed out in the seventeenth century, we would live in a condition of war, "of every man against every other man," and life would be "solitary, poor, nasty, brutish and short."

In the middle of one of Stanley Milgram's lectures at C.U.N.Y. recently, some mini-skirted undergraduates started whispering and giggling in the back of the room. He told them to cut it out. Since he was the relevant authority in that time and that place, they obeyed, and most people in the room were glad that they obeyed.

This was not, of course, a conflict situation. Nothing in the coeds' social upbringing made it a matter of conscience for them to whisper and giggle. But a case can be made that in a conflict situation it is all the more important to obey. Take the case of war, for example. Would we really want a situation in which every participant in a war, direct or indirect—from front-line soldiers to the people who sell coffee and cigarettes to employees at the Concertina barbed-wire factory in Kansas—stops and consults his conscience before each action? It is asking for an awful lot of mental strain and anguish from an awful lot of people. The value of having civil order is that one can do his duty, or whatever interests him, or whatever seems to benefit him at the moment, and leave the agonizing to others. When Francis Gary Powers was being tried by a Soviet military tribunal after his U-2 spy plane was shot down, the presiding judge asked if he had thought about the possibility that his flight might have provoked a war. Powers replied with Hobbesian clarity: "The people who sent me should think of these things. My job was to carry out orders. I do not think it was my responsibility to make such decisions."

It was not his responsibility. And it is quite possible that if everyone felt responsible for each of the ultimate consequences of his own tiny contributions to complex chains of events, then society simply would not work. Milgram, fully conscious of the moral and social implications of his research, believes that people should feel responsible for their actions. If someone else had invented the experiment, and if he had been the naïve subject, he feels certain that he would have been among the disobedient minority.

"There is no very good solution to this," he admits, thoughtfully. "To simply and categorically say that you won't obey authority may resolve your personal conflict, but it creates more problems for society which may be more serious in the long run. But I have no doubt that to disobey is the proper thing to do in this [the laboratory] situation. It is the only reasonable value judgment to make."

The conflict between the need to obey the relevant ruling authority and the need to follow your conscience becomes sharpest if you insist on living by an ethical system based on a rigid code—a code that seeks to answer all questions in advance of their being raised. Code ethics cannot solve the obedience problem. Stanley Milgram seems to be a situation ethicist, and situation ethics does offer a way out: When you feel conflict, you examine the situation and then make a choice among the competing evils. You may act with a presumption in favor of obedience, but reserve the possibility that you will disobey whenever obedience demands a flagrant and outrageous affront to conscience. This, by the way, is the philosophical position of many who resist the draft. In World War II, they would have fought. Vietnam is a different, an outrageously different, situation.

Life can be difficult for the situation ethicist, because he does not see the world in straight lines, while the social system too often assumes such a God-given, squared-off

structure. If your moral code includes an injunction against all war, you may be deferred as a conscientious objector. If you merely oppose this particular war, you may not be deferred.

Stanley Milgram has his problems, too. He believes that in the laboratory situation, he would not have shocked Mr. Wallace. His professional critics reply that in his real-life situation he has done the equivalent. He has placed innocent and naïve subjects under great emotional strain and pressure in selfish obedience to his quest for knowledge. When you raise this issue with Milgram, he has an answer ready. There is, he explains patiently, a critical difference between his naïve subjects and the man in the electric chair. The man in the electric chair (in the mind of the naïve subject) is helpless, strapped in. But the naïve subject is free to go at any time.

Immediately after he offers this distinction, Milgram anticipates the objection.

"It's quite true," he says, "that this is almost a philosophic position, because we have learned that some people are psychologically incapable of disengaging themselves. But that doesn't relieve them of the moral responsibility."

The parallel is exquisite. "The tension problem was unexpected," says Milgram in his defense. But he went on anyway. The naïve subjects didn't expect the screaming protests from the strapped-in learner. But they went on.

"I had to make a judgment," says Milgram. "I had to ask myself, was this harming the person or not? My judgment is that it was not. Even in the extreme cases, I wouldn't say that permanent damage results."

Sound familiar? "The shocks may be painful," the experimenter kept saying, "but they're not dangerous."

After the series of experiments was completed, Milgram sent a report of the results to his subjects and a questionnaire, asking whether they were glad or sorry to have been in the experiment. Eighty-three and seven-tenths percent said they were glad and only 1.3 percent were sorry; 15 percent were neither sorry nor glad. However, Milgram could not be sure at the time of the experiment that only 1.3 percent would be sorry.

Kurt Vonnegut Jr. put one paragraph in the preface to *Mother Night,* in 1966, which pretty much says it for the people with their fingers on the shock-generator switches, for you and me, and maybe even for Milgram. "If I'd been born in Germany," Vonnegut said, "I suppose I would have *been* a Nazi, bopping Jews and gypsies and Poles around, leaving boots sticking out of snowbanks, warming myself with my sweetly virtuous insides. So it goes."

Just so. One thing that happened to Milgram back in New Haven during the days of the experiment was that he kept running into people he'd watched from behind the one-way glass. It gave him a funny feeling, seeing those people going about their everyday business in New Haven and knowing what they would do to Mr. Wallace if ordered to. Now that his research results are in and you've thought about it, you can get this funny feeling too. You don't need one-way glass. A glance in your own mirror may serve just as well.

Afterword

It has been nearly a half century since Stanley Milgram conducted his experiments and some wonder, would people still be so compliant with the orders of a scientist? One would hope not but recent evidence suggests that the power of the situation to evoke obedience remains. Although our new understanding of the ethical responsibilities of researchers prevents us from exactly replicating Milgram's research, in 2009 Jerry M. Burger published the results of his partial replication of the experiment.[2] In his version, Burger allowed some subjects to first witness another "teacher" who refused to continue. Surprisingly, seeing another person [refuse to continue shocking] had no apparent effect on obedience level. Burger concluded that the same situational factors that affected obedience in Milgram's participants still operate today. The similarity between my results and Milgram's is also noteworthy because of a few procedural changes I implemented that should have made it easier for the participants to resist authority. The participants were told explicitly and repeatedly that they could leave the study at any time and still keep their $50.

[2]Jerry M. Burger. 2009. "Replicating Milgram, Would People Still Obey Today?" *American Psychologist,* 64: 1–11.

Questions

1. Ultimately, Milgram conducted this experiment with thousands of individuals from all walks of life. One series of experiments involved the use of women in the teacher role. Milgram notes that their performance was "virtually identical to the performance of men," although women experienced a higher level of conflict than men did. One variation that Milgram did not attempt was using women as "learners." What effect might this have had on, say, male teachers' performance?

2. In your judgment, if the technician ("Jack Williams") had been female, would this have changed the outcome of the experiment? Why or why not?

3. Milgram has been criticized for being unethical in conducting this research. Why? How did he respond to these criticisms? Are you more persuaded by Milgram or by his critics? Why?

4. Meyer implies that Milgram's motives were something other than purely scientific—that his decision was in part a "moral one," "colored by his own Jewish background." Did Milgram's moral convictions lead him to invalid findings? Why or why not?

5. Elsewhere, Milgram wrote this:

> The problem of obedience, therefore, is not wholly psychological. The form and shape of society and the way it is developed have much to do with it. There was a time, perhaps, when men were able to give a fully human response to any situation because they were fully absorbed in it as human beings. But as soon as there was a division of labor among men, things changed. Beyond a certain point, the breaking up of society into people carrying out narrow and very special jobs takes away from the human quality of work and life. A person does not get to see the whole situation but only a small part of it, and is thus unable to act without some kind of over-all direction. He yields to authority but in so doing is alienated [separated] from his own actions. (Milgram, *Obedience to Authority* [New York: Harper & Row, 1975], p. 11)

Do you agree or disagree with Milgram? Why?

8

QUEER CUSTOMS

Clyde Kluckhohn

Clyde K. M. Kluckhohn (1905–1960) was born in Iowa and studied anthropology at Princeton, Wisconsin, Vienna, and Oxford universities. In 1935, Kluckhohn accepted a position at Harvard University, where he stayed for the remainder of his career. Kluckhohn's particular area of expertise was the Navajo. The following essay is excerpted from his 1949 book *Mirror for Man*, which Kluckhohn wrote in order to explain cultural theory to the lay public.

Why do the Chinese dislike milk and milk products? Why would the Japanese die willingly in a Banzai[1] charge that seemed senseless to Americans? Why do some nations trace descent through the father, others through the mother, still others through both parents? Not because different peoples have different instincts, not because they were destined by God or Fate to different habits, not because the weather is different in China and Japan and the United States. Sometimes shrewd common sense has an answer that is close to that of the anthropologist: "because they were brought up that way." By "culture" anthropology means the total life way of a people, the social legacy the individual acquires from his group. Or culture can be regarded as that part of the environment that is the creation of man.

This technical term has a wider meaning than the "culture" of history and literature.

A humble cooking pot is as much a cultural product as is a Beethoven sonata. In ordinary speech a man of culture is a man who can speak languages other than his own, who is familiar with history, literature, philosophy, or the fine arts. In some cliques that definition is still narrower. The cultured person is one who can talk about James Joyce, Scarlatti, and Picasso.[2] To the anthropologist, however, to be human is to be cultured. There is culture in general, and then there are the specific cultures such as Russian, American, British, Hottentot,[3] Inca. The general abstract notion

[1]Banzai is a Japanese war cry.—Ed.

Clyde Kluckhohn, "Queer Customs" from *Mirror for Man: The Relation of Anthropology to Modern Life.* Copyright 1949 by George E. Taylor. Reprinted with the permission of George E. Taylor.

[2]So, are you a cultured person by this definition? James Joyce (1882–1941) was an Irish author. His best-known book, *Ulysses,* was a novel about a day in Dublin (June 4, 1904). It was published in Paris in 1922 but was banned in the United States until 1937. Alessandro Scarlatti (1660–1725) was a Sicilian composer noted mostly for his operas. Pablo Picasso (1881–1973) was a prolific artist. Born in Spain (in Málaga), he spent much of his life in France. During his lifetime, he created more than 50,000 works—drawings, paintings, sculptures, and even ceramics and lithographs.—Ed.

[3]More properly called the *Khoikhoi*—a people mostly of Namibia, Africa. Nomadic and pastoral, their numbers were decimated by Dutch colonists in the seventeenth and eighteenth centuries.—Ed.

serves to remind us that we cannot explain acts solely in terms of the biological properties of the people concerned, their individual past experience, and the immediate situation. The past experience of other men in the form of culture enters into almost every event. Each specific culture constitutes a kind of blueprint for all of life's activities.

One of the interesting things about human beings is that they try to understand themselves and their own behavior. While this has been particularly true of Europeans in recent times, there is no group which has not developed a scheme or schemes to explain man's actions. To the insistent human query "why?" the most exciting illumination anthropology has to offer is that of the concept of culture. Its explanatory importance is comparable to categories such as evolution in biology, gravity in physics, disease in medicine. A good deal of human behavior can be understood, and indeed predicted, if we know a people's design for living. Many acts are neither accidental nor due to personal peculiarities nor caused by supernatural forces nor simply mysterious. Even those of us who pride ourselves on our individualism follow most of the time a pattern not of our own making. We brush our teeth on arising. We put on pants—not a loincloth or a grass skirt. We eat three meals a day—not four or five or two. We sleep in a bed—not in a hammock or on a sheep pelt. I do not have to know the individual and his life history to be able to predict these and countless other regularities, including many in the thinking process, of all Americans who are not incarcerated in jails or hospitals for the insane.

To the American woman a system of plural wives seems "instinctively" abhorrent. She cannot understand how any woman can fail to be jealous and uncomfortable if she must share her husband with other women. She feels it "unnatural" to accept such a situation. On the other hand, a Koryak woman of Siberia, for example, would find it hard to understand how a woman could be so selfish and so undesirous of feminine companionship in the home as to wish to restrict her husband to one mate.

Some years ago I met in New York City a young man who did not speak a word of English and was obviously bewildered by American ways. By "blood" he was as American as you or I, for his parents had gone from Indiana to China as missionaries. Orphaned in infancy, he was reared by a Chinese family in a remote village. All who met him found him more Chinese than American. The facts of his blue eyes and light hair were less impressive than a Chinese style of gait, Chinese arm and hand movements, Chinese facial expression, and Chinese modes of thought. The biological heritage was American, but the cultural training had been Chinese. He returned to China.

Another example of another kind: I once knew a trader's wife in Arizona who took a somewhat devilish interest in producing a cultural reaction. Guests who came her way were often served delicious sandwiches filled with a meat that seemed to be neither chicken nor tuna fish yet was reminiscent of both. To queries she gave no reply until each had eaten his fill. She then explained that what they had eaten was not chicken, not tuna fish, but the rich, white flesh of freshly killed rattlesnakes. The response was instantaneous—vomiting, often violent vomiting. A biological process is caught in a cultural web.

A highly intelligent teacher with long and successful experience in the public schools of Chicago was finishing her first year in an Indian school. When asked how her Navaho pupils compared in intelligence with Chicago youngsters, she replied, "Well, I just don't know. Sometimes the Indians seem just as bright. At other times they just act like dumb animals. The other night we had a dance in the high school. I saw a boy who is one of the best students in my English class standing off by himself. So I took him over to a pretty girl and told them to dance. But they just stood there with their heads down. They wouldn't even say anything." I inquired if she knew whether or not they were members of the same clan. "What difference would that make?"

"How would you feel about getting into bed with your brother?" The teacher walked off in a huff, but, actually, the two cases were quite comparable in principle. To the Indian the type of bodily contact involved in our social dancing has a directly sexual connotation. The incest taboos between members of the same clan are as severe as between true brothers and sisters. The shame of the Indians at the suggestion that a clan brother and sister should dance and the indignation of the white teacher at the idea that she should share a bed with an adult brother represent equally nonrational responses, culturally standardized unreason. . . .

Culture and Society

Since culture is an abstraction, it is important not to confuse culture with society. A "society" refers to a group of people who interact more with each other than they do with other individuals—who cooperate with each other for the attainment of certain ends. You can see and indeed count the individuals who make up a society. A "culture" refers to the distinctive ways of life of such a group of people. Not all social events are culturally patterned. New types of circumstances arise for which no cultural solutions have as yet been devised.

A culture constitutes a storehouse of the pooled learning of the group. A rabbit starts life with some innate responses. He can learn from his own experience and perhaps from observing other rabbits. A human infant is born with fewer instincts and greater plasticity. His main task is to learn the answers that persons he will never see, persons long dead, have worked out. Once he has learned the formulas supplied by the culture of his group,

most of his behavior becomes almost as automatic and unthinking as if it were instinctive. There is a tremendous amount of intelligence behind the making of a radio, but not much is required to learn to turn it on.

The members of all human societies face some of the same unavoidable dilemmas, posed by biology and other facts of the human situation. This is why the basic categories of all cultures are so similar. Human culture without language is unthinkable. No culture fails to provide for aesthetic expression and aesthetic delight. Every culture supplies standardized orientations toward the deeper problems, such as death. Every culture is designed to perpetuate the group and its solidarity, to meet the demands of individuals for an orderly way of life and for satisfaction of biological needs.

However, the variations on these basic themes are numberless. Some languages are built up out of twenty basic sounds, others out of forty. Nose plugs were considered beautiful by the predynastic Egyptians but are not by the modern French. Puberty is a biological fact. But one culture ignores it, another prescribes informal instructions about sex but no ceremony, a third has impressive rites for girls only, a fourth for boys and girls. In this culture, the first menstruation is welcomed as a happy, natural event; in that culture the atmosphere is full of dread and supernatural threat. Each culture dissects nature according to its own system of categories. The Navaho Indians apply the same word to the color of a robin's egg and to that of grass. A psychologist once assumed that this meant a difference in the sense organs, that Navahos didn't have the physiological equipment to distinguish "green" from "blue." However, when he showed them objects of the two colors and asked them if they were exactly the same colors, they looked at him with astonishment. His dream of discovering a new type of color blindness was shattered.

culture/sex

Every culture must deal with the sexual instinct. Some, however, seek to deny all sexual expression before marriage, whereas a Polynesian adolescent who was not promiscuous would be distinctly abnormal. Some cultures enforce lifelong monogamy; others, like our own, tolerate serial monogamy; in still other cultures, two or more women may be joined to one man or several men to a single woman. Homosexuality has been a permitted pattern in the Greco-Roman world, in parts of Islam, and in various primitive tribes. Large portions of the population of Tibet, and of Christendom at some places and periods, have practiced complete celibacy. To us marriage is first and foremost an arrangement between two individuals. In many more societies marriage is merely one facet of a complicated set of reciprocities, economic and otherwise, between two families or two clans.

The essence of the cultural process is selectivity. The selection is only exceptionally conscious and rational. Cultures are like Topsy. They just grew.[4] Once, however, a way of handling a situation becomes institutionalized, there is ordinarily great resistance to change or deviation. When we speak of "our sacred beliefs," we mean of course that they are beyond criticism and that the person who suggests modification or abandonment must be punished. No person is emotionally

indifferent to his culture. Certain cultural premises may become totally out of accord with a new factual situation. Leaders may recognize this and reject the old ways in theory. Yet their emotional loyalty continues in the face of reason because of the intimate conditionings of early childhood.

A culture is learned by individuals as the result of belonging to some particular group, and it constitutes that part of learned behavior which is shared with others. It is our social legacy, as contrasted with our organic heredity. It is one of the important factors which permits us to live together in an organized society, giving us ready-made solutions to our problems, helping us to predict the behavior of others, and permitting others to know what to expect of us.

Culture regulates our lives at every turn. From the moment we are born until we die there is, whether we are conscious of it or not, constant pressure upon us to follow certain types of behavior that other men have created for us. Some paths we follow willingly, others we follow because we know no other way, still others we deviate from or go back to most unwillingly. Mothers of small children know how unnaturally most of this comes to us—how little regard we have, until we are "culturalized," for the "proper" place, time, and manner for certain acts such as eating, excreting, sleeping, getting dirty, and making loud noises. But by more or less adhering to a system of related designs for carrying out all the acts of living, a group of men and women feel themselves linked together by a powerful chain of sentiments. Ruth Benedict gave an almost complete definition of the concept when she said, "Culture is that which binds men together." . . .

No participant in any culture knows all the details of the cultural map. The statement frequently heard that St. Thomas Aquinas was the last man to master all the knowledge of his society is intrinsically absurd. St. Thomas

---

[4]To grow like Topsy means to flourish without being purposefully tended. The roots of this odd-sounding expression are to be found in *Uncle Tom's Cabin*, by Harriet Beecher Stowe. In 1850, the Congress enacted a Fugitive Slave Act which required the return of runaway slaves who fled to states where slavery had been abolished. Beecher Stowe's novel was written in a protest against this law and slavery in general. The character Topsy was a young slave girl of about eight or nine years old. Purchased from an abusive family, Topsy is brought to New England to be raised by the pious Ophelia St. Clare. Asked by Miss Ophelia how old she is, Topsy says she has no idea: Another slave explains to Miss Ophelia that it is common practice in the South for speculators to purchase black infants and raise them for the slave market. When queried about her parents, Topsy says, "I spect I growed. Don't think nobody never made me."—Ed.

would have been hard put to make a pane of cathedral glass or to act as a midwife. In every culture there are what Ralph Linton has called "universals, alternatives, and specialties." Every Christian in the thirteenth century knew that it was necessary to attend mass, to go to confession, to ask the Mother of God to intercede with her Son. There were many other universals in the Christian culture of Western Europe. However, there were also alternative cultural patterns even in the realm of religion. Each individual had his own patron saint, and different towns developed the cults of different saints. The thirteenth-century anthropologist could have discovered the rudiments of Christian practice by questioning and observing whomever he happened to meet in Germany, France, Italy, or England. But to find out the details of the ceremonials honoring St. Hubert or St. Bridget he would have had to seek out certain individuals or special localities where these alternative patterns were practiced. Similarly, he could not learn about weaving from a professional soldier or about canon law from a farmer. Such cultural knowledge belongs in the realm of the specialties, voluntarily chosen by the individual or ascribed to him by birth. Thus, part of a culture must be learned by everyone, part may be selected from alternative patterns, part applies only to those who perform the roles in the society for which these patterns are designed.

Many aspects of a culture are explicit. The explicit culture consists in those regularities in word and deed that may be generalized straight from the evidence of the ear and the eye. The recognition of these is like the recognition of style in the art of a particular place and epoch. If we have examined twenty specimens of the wooden saints' images made in the Taos valley of New Mexico in the late eighteenth century, we can predict that any new images from the same locality and period will in most respects exhibit the same techniques of carving, about the same use of colors and choice of woods, a

similar quality of artistic conception. Similarly, if, in a society of 2,000 members, we record 100 marriages at random and find that in 30 cases a man has married the sister of his brother's wife, we can anticipate that an additional sample of 100 marriages will show roughly the same number of cases of this pattern.

The above is an instance of what anthropologists call a behavioral pattern, the practices as opposed to the rules of the culture. There are also, however, regularities in what people say they do or should do. They do tend in fact to prefer to marry into a family already connected with their own by marriage, but this is not necessarily part of the official code of conduct. No disapproval whatsoever is attached to those who make another sort of marriage. On the other hand, it is explicitly forbidden to marry a member of one's own clan even though no biological relationship is traceable. This is a regulatory pattern—a Thou Shalt or a Thou Shalt Not. Such patterns may be violated often, but their existence is nevertheless important. A people's standards for conduct and belief define the socially approved aims and the acceptable means of attaining them. When the discrepancy between the theory and the practice of a culture is exceptionally great, this indicates that the culture is undergoing rapid change. It does not prove that ideals are unimportant, for ideals are but one of a number of factors determining action.

Cultures do not manifest themselves solely in observable customs and artifacts. No amount of questioning of any save the most articulate in the most self-conscious cultures will bring out some of the basic attitudes common to the members of the group. This is because these basic assumptions are taken so for granted that they normally do not enter into consciousness. This part of the cultural map must be inferred by the observer on the basis of consistencies in thought and action. Missionaries in various societies are often disturbed or puzzled because the natives do not regard "morals" and "sex-code" as almost synonymous. The natives seem to feel that morals are concerned with sex just about as much as with eating—no less and no more. No society fails to have some restrictions on sexual behavior, but sex activity outside of marriage need not necessarily be furtive or attended with guilt. The Christian tradition has tended to assume that sex is inherently nasty as well as dangerous. Other cultures assume that sex in itself is not only natural but one of the good things of life, even though sex acts with certain persons under certain circumstances are forbidden. This is implicit culture, for the natives do not announce their premises. The missionaries would get further if they said, in effect, "Look, our morality starts from different assumptions. Let's talk about those assumptions," rather than ranting about "immorality.". . .

In our highly self-conscious Western civilization that has recently made a business of studying itself, the number of assumptions that are literally implicit, in the sense of never having been stated or discussed by anyone, may be negligible. Yet only a trifling number of Americans could state even those implicit premises of our culture that have been brought to light by anthropologists. If one could bring to the American scene a Bushman who had been socialized in his own culture and then trained in anthropology, he would perceive all sorts of patterned regularities of which our anthropologists are completely unaware. In the case of the less sophisticated and less self-conscious societies, the unconscious assumptions characteristically made by individuals brought up under approximately the same social controls bulk even larger. But in any society, as Edward Sapir said, "Forms and significances which seem obvious to an outsider will be denied outright by those who carry out the patterns; outlines and implications that are perfectly clear to these may be absent to the eye of the onlooker." . . .

Questions

1. According to Kluckhohn, what is the difference between culture and society? (Many people improperly use these terms interchangeably, but now that you know the difference you can avoid that error.)

2. What does Kluckhohn mean by the phrase "culturally standardized unreason"? Can you think of any examples of this sort of unreason from your own culture?

3. What does Kluckhohn mean by the concept of "behavioral pattern"? What is a "regulatory pattern"? Give a couple of examples from your own culture of instances in which behavioral and regulatory patterns are consistent. Then, give examples from your own culture in which behavioral and regulatory patterns are inconsistent. (Which was harder to do—to find examples of consistency or of inconsistency between behavioral patterns and regulatory patterns? Why do you think this is?)

9

BODY RITUAL AMONG THE NACIREMA

Horace Miner

? what's this?

The American anthropologist Horace Miner was one of the first to make public the results of anthropological research on the Nacirema. Although in the decades that followed the 1956 publication of Miner's work many more studies have been published, none more dramatically reveals the role of myth, magic, and ritual in the lives of this rather exotic group of people.

The anthropologist has become so familiar with the diversity of ways in which different peoples behave in similar situations that he is not apt to be surprised by even the most exotic customs. In fact, if all of the logically possible combinations of behavior have not been found somewhere in the world, he is apt to suspect that they must be present in some as yet undescribed tribe. This point has, in fact, been expressed with respect to clan organization by Murdock (1949, 71). In this light, the magical beliefs and practices of the Nacirema present such unusual aspects that it seems desirable to describe them as an example of the extremes to which human behavior can go.

Professor Linton first brought the ritual of the Nacirema to the attention of anthropologists [over seventy] years ago (1936, 326), but the culture of this people is still very poorly understood. They are a North American group living in the territory between the Canadian Cree, the Yaqui and Tarahumare of Mexico, and the Carib and Arawak of the Antilles. Little is known of their origin, although tradition states that they came from the east. According to Nacirema mythology, their nation was originated by a culture hero, Notgnihsaw, who is otherwise known for two great feats of strength—the throwing of a piece of wampum across the river Po-To-Mac and the chopping down of a cherry tree in which the Spirit of Truth resided.

Nacirema culture is characterized by a highly developed market economy which has evolved in a rich natural habitat. While much of the people's time is devoted to economic pursuits, a large part of the fruits of these labors and a considerable portion of the day are spent in ritual activity. The focus of this activity is the human body, the appearance and health of which loom as a dominant concern in the ethos of the people. While such a concern is certainly not unusual, its ceremonial aspects and associated philosophy are unique.

The fundamental belief underlying the whole system appears to be that the human body is ugly and that its natural tendency is to debility and disease. Incarcerated in such a body, man's only hope is to avert these characteristics through the use of the powerful influences of ritual and ceremony. Every household has one or more shrines devoted to this purpose. The more powerful individuals in the society have several shrines in their houses and, in fact, the opulence of

Horace Miner, "Body Ritual Among the Nacirema" from *American Anthropologist* 58: 3 (June 1956). Reprinted with the permission of the American Anthropological Association and the Estate of Horace Miner.

a house is often referred to in terms of the number of such ritual centers it possesses. Most houses are of wattle and daub construction, but the shrine rooms of the more wealthy are walled with stone. Poorer families imitate the rich by applying pottery plaques to their shrine walls.

While each family has at least one such shrine, the rituals associated with it are not family ceremonies but are private and secret. The rites are normally only discussed with children, and then only during the period when they are being initiated into these mysteries. I was able, however, to establish sufficient rapport with the natives to examine these shrines and to have the rituals described to me.

The focal point of the shrine is a box or chest which is built into the wall. In this chest are kept the many charms and magical potions without which no native believes he could live. These preparations are secured from a variety of specialized practitioners. The most powerful of these are the medicine men, whose assistance must be rewarded with substantial gifts. However, the medicine men do not provide the curative potions for their clients, but decide what the ingredients should be and they write them down in an ancient and secret language. This writing is understood only by the medicine men and by the herbalists who, for another gift, provide the required charm.

The charm is not disposed of after it has served its purpose, but is placed in the charm-box of the household shrine. As these magical materials are specific for certain ills, and the real or imagined maladies of the people are many, the charm-box is usually full to overflowing. The magical packets are so numerous that people forget what their purposes were and fear to use them again. While the natives are very vague on this point, we can only assume that the idea in retaining all the old magical materials is that their presence in the charm-box, before which the body rituals are conducted, will in some way protect the worshipper.

Beneath the charm-box is a small font. Each day every member of the family, in succession, enters the shrine room, bows his head before the charm-box, mingles different sorts of holy water in the font, and proceeds with a brief rite of ablution. The holy waters are secured from the Water Temple of the community, where the priests conduct elaborate ceremonies to make the liquid ritually pure.

In the hierarchy of magical practitioners, and below the medicine men in prestige, are specialists whose designation is best translated "holy-mouth-men." The Nacirema have an almost pathological horror of and fascination with the mouth, the condition of which is believed to have a supernatural influence on all social relationships. Were it not for the rituals of the mouth, they believe that their teeth would fall out, their gums bleed, their jaws shrink, their friends desert them, and their lovers reject them. They also believe that a strong relationship exists between oral and moral characteristics. For example, there is a ritual ablution of the mouth for children which is supposed to improve their moral fiber.

The daily body ritual performed by everyone includes a mouth-rite. Despite the fact that these people are so punctilious about care of the mouth, this rite involves a practice which strikes the uninitiated stranger as revolting. It was reported to me that the ritual consists of inserting a small bundle of hog hairs into the mouth, along with certain magical powders, and then moving the bundle in a highly formalized series of gestures.

In addition to the private mouth-rite, the people seek out a holy-mouth-man once or twice a year. These practitioners have an impressive set of paraphernalia, consisting of a variety of augers, awls, probes, and prods. The use of these objects in the exorcism of the evils of the mouth involves almost unbelievable

Weird month rituals

ritual torture of the client. The holy-mouth-man opens the client's mouth and, using the above mentioned tools, enlarges any holes which decay may have created in the teeth. Magical materials are put into these holes. If there are no naturally occurring holes in the teeth, large sections of one or more teeth are gouged out so that the supernatural substance can be applied. In the client's view, the purpose of these ministrations is to arrest decay and to draw friends. The extremely sacred and traditional character of the rite is evident in the fact that the natives return to the holy-mouth-men year after year, despite the fact that their teeth continue to decay.

It is to be hoped that, when a thorough study of the Nacirema is made, there will be careful inquiry into the personality structure of these people. One has but to watch the gleam in the eye of a holy-mouth-man, as he jabs an awl into an exposed nerve, to suspect that a certain amount of sadism is involved. If this can be established, a very interesting pattern emerges, for most of the population shows definite masochistic tendencies. It was to these that Professor Linton referred in discussing a distinctive part of the daily body ritual which is performed only by men. This part of the rite involves scraping and lacerating the surface of the face with a sharp instrument. Special women's rites are performed only four times during each lunar month, but what they lack in frequency is made up in barbarity. As part of this ceremony, women bake their heads in small ovens for about an hour. The theoretically interesting point is that what seems to be a preponderantly masochistic people have developed sadistic specialists.

The medicine men have an imposing temple, or *latipso*, in every community of any size. The more elaborate ceremonies required to treat very sick patients can only be performed at this temple. These ceremonies involve not only the thaumaturge but a permanent group of vestal maidens who move sedately about the temple chambers in distinctive costume and headdress.

The *latipso* ceremonies are so harsh that it is phenomenal that a fair proportion of the really sick natives who enter the temple ever recover. Small children whose indoctrination is still incomplete have been known to resist attempts to take them to the temple because "that is where you go to die." Despite this fact, sick adults are not only willing but eager to undergo the protracted ritual purification, if they can afford to do so. No matter how ill the supplicant or how grave the emergency, the guardians of many temples will not admit a client if he cannot give a rich gift to the custodian. Even after one has gained admission and survived the ceremonies, the guardians will not permit the neophyte to leave until he makes still another gift.

The supplicant entering the temple is first stripped of all his or her clothes. In everyday life the Nacirema avoids exposure of his body and its natural functions. Bathing and excretory acts are performed only in the secrecy of the household shrine, where they are ritualized as part of the body-rites. Psychological shock results from the fact that body secrecy is suddenly lost upon entry into the *latipso*. A man, whose own wife has never seen him in an excretory act, suddenly finds himself naked and assisted by a vestal maiden while he performs his natural functions into a sacred vessel. This sort of ceremonial treatment is necessitated by the fact that the excreta are used by a diviner to ascertain the course and nature of the client's sickness. Female clients, on the other hand, find their naked bodies are subjected to the scrutiny, manipulation and prodding of the medicine men.

Few supplicants in the temple are well enough to do anything but lie on their hard beds. The daily ceremonies, like the rites of the holy-mouth-men, involve discomfort and torture. With ritual precision, the vestals awaken their miserable charges each dawn and roll them about on their beds of pain while performing ablutions, in the formal movements of which the maidens are highly trained. At other times they insert magic wands in the supplicant's mouth or force him to eat substances which are supposed to be healing. From time to time the medicine men come to their clients and jab magically treated needles into their flesh. The fact that these temple ceremonies may not cure, and may even kill the neophyte, in no way decreases the people's faith in the medicine men.

There remains one other kind of practitioner, known as a "listener." This witch-doctor has the power to exorcise the devils that lodge in the heads of people who have been bewitched. The Nacirema believe that parents bewitch their own children. Mothers are particularly suspected of putting a curse on children while teaching them the secret body rituals. The counter-magic of the witch-doctor is unusual in its lack of ritual. The patient simply tells the "listener" all his troubles and fears, beginning with the earliest difficulties he can remember. The memory displayed by the Nacirema in these exorcism sessions is truly remarkable. It is not uncommon for the patient to bemoan the rejection he felt upon being weaned as a baby, and a few individuals even see their troubles going back to the traumatic effects of their own birth.

In conclusion, mention must be made of certain practices which have their base in native esthetics but which depend upon the pervasive aversion to the natural body and its functions. There are ritual fasts to make fat people thin and ceremonial feasts to make thin people fat. Still other rites are used to make women's breasts larger if they are small, and smaller if they are large. General dissatisfaction with breast shape is symbolized in the fact that the ideal form is virtually outside the range of human variation. A few women

afflicted with almost inhuman hypermammary development are so idolized that they make a handsome living by simply going from village to village and permitting the natives to stare at them for a fee.

Reference has already been made to the fact that excretory functions are ritualized, routinized, and relegated to secrecy. Natural reproductive functions are similarly distorted. Intercourse is taboo as a topic and scheduled as an act. Efforts are made to avoid pregnancy by the use of magical materials or by limiting intercourse to certain phases of the moon. Conception is actually very infrequent. When pregnant, women dress so as to hide their condition. Parturition takes place in secret, without friends or relatives to assist, and the majority of women do not nurse their infants.

Our review of the ritual life of the Nacirema has certainly shown them to be a magic-ridden people. It is hard to understand how they have managed to exist so long under the burdens which they have imposed upon themselves. But even such exotic customs as these take on real meaning when they are viewed with the insight provided by Malinowski when he wrote (1948, 70):

> Looking from far and above, from our high places of safety in the developed civilization, it is easy to see all the crudity and irrelevance of magic. But without its power and guidance early man could not have mastered his practical difficulties as he has done, nor could man have advanced to the higher stages of civilization.

References

Linton, Ralph. 1936. *The Study of Man*. New York: Appleton-Century.
Malinowski, Bronislaw. 1948. *Magic, Science, and Religion*. Glencoe, IL: Free Press.
Murdock, George P. 1949. *Social Structure*. New York: Macmillan.

Questions

1. What is a thaumaturge?

2. Why would it be ethnocentric to think of the Nacirema as weird—or even silly—for their beliefs?

3. Can you see any signs that Miner experienced "culture shock" as he investigated the Nacirema? Explain.

4. Do you think you would enjoy taking a vacation in the land of the Nacirema? Why or why not?

10

ACT YOUR AGE

Cheryl Laz

Sociologists tend to question many of the things that most people take for granted. In the process they have discovered surprising things about social life. In this article, Professor Laz manages to surprise even many sociologists when she focuses on something that even sociologists have taken for granted: age. Age, she argues, is not just something we have, it's something we perform. And how we perform it depends upon the expectations of those around us.

Introduction

To laypersons (and to many sociologists in their unguarded moments) it seems almost absurd to think about age as anything but a chronological fact and as something every individual simply *is*. Like race and gender, for most people most of the time, age is unproblematic. When asked "How old are you?" we offer the number of years since our birth. When someone directs us to act our age, we know what age is (the number of years since our birth), usually know what is being demanded of us, and often are prepared to account for our "misbehavior." We assume that as people get older, they will fulfill different roles in a predictable sequence. When the sequence or the timing is altered, we linguistically mark the discrepancy (teenage mothers, nontraditional students), and we want an explanation, an account, for being "off time."

As with race and gender, the apparently objective and factual nature of age make it ideal for sociological inquiry. Sociologists now understand race as a social construction rather than a biological "fact." Race is defined

by and constituted within social groups (How much "blood" makes one black or Native American?), and it is accomplished by individuals (What does it mean to "pass" as one race and not another?). Moreover, a sociological understanding of race has led us to appreciate more fully the relations of power and the pervasive normative ideas that create and sustain the supposedly biological "fact" of race.

Similarly, sociologists understand gender as a social construction and individual accomplishment. Gender is defined and constituted within social groups (What does masculinity entail for a heterosexual steelworker? a gay bank manager?), and it is accomplished by individuals in interaction (How does a woman in a male-dominated job "act" feminine?). Further, normative cultural ideas traditionally have equated gender with women. We view the dominant group, in this case men, as if its members had no gender.

There is much to suggest that age, like race and gender, is anything but natural and involves much more than the number of years since one's birth. "Act your age. You're a big kid now," we say to children to encourage independence (or obedience). "Act your age. Stop being so childish," we say to other adults when we think they are being irresponsible. "Act your age; you're not as young as you used

Cheryl Laz, "Act Your Age" from *Sociological Forum* 13, no. 1 (March 1998): 85–87, 98–110. Reprinted with the permission of Blackwell Publishing Ltd.

to be," we say to an old person pursuing "youthful" activities. The sanctioned actions vary, but the command "Act!" remains the same. When we say "act your age" we press for behavior that conforms to norms. However, the saying also expresses a commonsense understanding that age is not natural or fixed, and it implies that age requires work, i.e., physical or mental effort. As such, the saying encapsulates a fundamentally sociological view of age and provides us with the useful metaphor of *performance*. Age *is* an act, a performance in the sense of something requiring activity and labor, and age is normative. Whether we do it well or poorly, according to the dominant rules or not, our accomplishment of age—indeed age itself—is always collective and social. However, age is not simply *shaped* by social forces; it is *constituted* in interaction and gains its meaning in interaction and in the context of larger social forces. We all perform or enact age; we perform our own age constantly, but we also give meaning to other ages and to age in general in our actions and interactions, our beliefs and words and feelings, our social policies.

This essay develops a framework with which to understand age as *accomplished*. "Accomplish," and the closely related "perform," can refer to ongoing actions as well as to actions finished or carried through to completion. In this essay, I emphasize accomplishment not as the full or final completion of an action, but rather as ongoing action that is ultimately social and public. (Although it also may be private, the accomplishment of age is never only private.) Accomplishing age involves often routine, sometimes impressive, but always ongoing, recurring work. . . .

"Doing Gender"

In "Doing Gender," Candace West and Don Zimmerman argue that gender is an *accomplishment:* an emergent feature of social situations that is both an outcome of and a rationale

for the most fundamental division of society (1987; also West and Fenstermaker 1993, 151). Rather than viewing gender as a role, identity, or individual attribute, gender is a feature of social situations. It is embedded in and constituted by everyday interaction. We do gender in the actual or virtual presence of others, even when it seems irrelevant or unrelated to interaction. Casual conversation (Henley and Freeman 1989), making dinner (Devault 1991), working as an engineer (McIlwee and Robinson 1992) or a flight attendant (Hochschild 1983) are occasions for doing gender at the same time that they are conversations, meals, and work.

This distinctively sociological view is grounded in ethnomethodology, which "proposes that the properties of social life which seem objective, factual, and transsituational, are actually managed accomplishments or achievements of local processes" (Zimmerman 1978, cited in West and Fenstermaker 1993, 152). To see "the objective reality of social facts *as* an ongoing accomplishment," ethnomethodologists and other sociologists treat the commonplace and unproblematic as unfamiliar or "anthropologically strange" (Garfinkel 1967, vii).

West and Zimmerman show how even the most taken-for-granted aspects of social life (like the "fact" that there are two, and only two, sexes) are actually the result of socially guided conceptual, interactional, and micropolitical processes (1987, 126). That we describe, explain, rationalize, justify—account—for ourselves and our actions is central to these processes (Heritage 1984, 136). Further, we act with an eye toward accountability; that is, we anticipate how our actions may be characterized, understood or misunderstood, excused, condemned, etc., and act in ways that will minimize the need for accounting (since accounting holds the possibilities of being misunderstood, discounted, or contradicted). As a result, we often conform to dominant norms and conceptualizations, including those related to age and gender, even if we question or reject those norms.

predicting

In West and Zimmerman's view, when individuals do gender "right" (i.e., in accordance with dominant beliefs about women and men, masculinity and femininity), gender becomes invisible. As we collectively "do it right," dominant assumptions about gender become natural. Indeed, gender itself is naturalized. Moreover, "If we do gender appropriately, we simultaneously sustain, reproduce, and render legitimate the institutional arrangements that are based on sex category. . . . [Ultimately,] an understanding of how gender is produced in social situations will afford clarification of the interactional scaffolding of social structure and the social control processes that sustain it" (West and Zimmerman 1987, 146–147). West and Zimmerman are, in the end, less interested in the production of a *gendered self* than they are in the production of *gender itself*. They intend for this formulation to overcome the twin dangers of self-determination and overdetermination by pointing out the reciprocal relationship between interaction and social structure, between choice, negotiation, and constraint.

Doing Age

West and Zimmerman explain how gender is constituted in and through interaction and how its accomplishment sustains social organization and social order. Like gender, age is accomplished—not in the sense of something completed, but in the sense of something "brought to pass" or continually carried on. In accomplishing age, we create and maintain selves, roles, and identities. But we also participate in and constitute a larger shared universe in which we impart meaning to age in ways that influence but transcend us as individuals. In this section, I outline the idea of age-as-accomplished in relation to the assumptions about age described earlier.

Although age often feels like something we simply are, it feels this way because we enact

age in all interactions. Since we usually act our age in predictable ways—predictable given the particular context—we make age invisible. We make age *seem* natural.

Of course, age is not always invisible; occasionally it comes to the forefront of our consciousness and we must deliberately make sense of age, often in the context of particular events or milestones (birthdays, anniversaries, deaths of parents), changes in our physical appearance or physical condition, or social roles and norms (Eisenhandler 1991; Karp 1991). David Karp describes between ages 50 and 60 as "a decade of reminders . . . during which people, more sharply than before, are made to feel their age. . . . Contextual events giving rise to distinctive consciousness are correlated with age, but not determined by age" (1991, 67, 69). At these moments, age is momentarily denaturalized; its meaning cannot be taken for granted. Feminists in the 1970s referred to moments when gender or sex inequality was foregrounded in individual consciousness as a "click." "Clicks" are significant because they represent the point at which one can no longer take existing knowledge, relations, and practices as "givens."

While such reminders may be more frequent and intense at later ages, younger people are not exempt. During informal conversations over the past several years, colleagues not infrequently share their "age-click" anecdotes. One colleague (now in her mid-40s) confessed that the first time she refused to tell someone her "real" (i.e., chronological) age, something clicked; she was forced to examine what age meant to her personally and to women in general in the context of her social circles and in the larger society. Another relates the following anecdote. "Fifteen or 20 years ago (that makes me 30–35) I was sitting on the front step with D— and A—, and one of the children came up asking for a conflict resolution. I was all of a sudden struck by the fact that *we* were the 'grown ups.' I was shocked."

Perhaps the click comes from realizing that we are not acting our age or from noticing how effectively and unconsciously we have been acting our age. Or maybe we realize that we are "ahead of" or "behind time" (for example, more or less advanced in our careers or family lives in comparison to other people of the same chronological age or of the same cohort; observe the multiple ways to measure age). "Clicks" often require us to offer accounts to others or to ourselves, and accountability is social and interactional. Sociologists can study disruptions of "the normal," like the "clicks" described above, to explore how normalcy is accomplished, how "the natural" *becomes* natural.

Conceptualizing age-as-accomplished does not ignore the "fact" of chronology. Rather, it enables sociologists to examine the process by which chronology is *made* "factual" and to view the consequences of our acting *as if* chronology were natural. Moreover, viewing age-as-accomplished does not require rejecting the concepts of age norms or roles. Rather, it enables us to clarify how norms and roles work in social situations. Norms and roles are resources that individuals draw on in interaction. They are among the tools we use to act our age; they do not themselves constitute age. Conceptualizing age-as-accomplished also helps bridge the self-determined/overdetermined dichotomy by making explicit the "interactional scaffolding of social structure and the social control processes that sustain it" (West and Zimmerman 1987, 146–147). The reciprocal relationship between actors acting and structural factors constraining and enabling action is central. Finally, the idea of age-as-accomplished radically transforms the notion of age as a problem. If age is accomplished, then it is not a social problem in the sense of a troublesome condition requiring solution. It is, instead, a problem in the sense of a situation that presents uncertainty or difficulty that can be managed or negotiated, at best temporarily resolved, though never permanently eliminated.

Resources for Doing Age

If age is something everyone does, then how to act one's age is a "problem" each of us faces in innumerable encounters every day. How we act our age in any given situation is the product of the interpretations and choices (often unconscious) we make among available individual, cultural, and institutional resources. What are the resources from which we may choose? How do we choose among them? What shapes our accomplishment of age?

Ann Swidler has proposed "the image of culture as a 'tool kit' of symbols, stories, rituals, and world-views, which people may use in varying configurations to solve different kinds of problems" (1986, 273). When people solve problems they construct strategies of action—persistent (but not fixed or immutable) ways of ordering action through time. Culture is significant, "not in defining ends of action [i.e., providing values or goals], but in providing cultural components that are used to construct strategies of action. . . . To adopt a line of conduct, one needs an image of the kind of world in which one is trying to act, a sense that one can read reasonably accurately . . . how one is doing, and a capacity to choose among alternative lines of action" (Swidler 1986, 273, 275).

This conceptualization has the advantage of seeing individuals as active and skilled users of culture, rather than as passive "cultural dopes" (Swidler 1986, 277). It has the advantage of seeing how "action is necessarily integrated into larger assemblages [strategies of action]" (Swidler 1986, 276) rather than seeing actions as something people choose one at a time according to their values or interests. It admits the potential for using culture in new, challenging, or unpredictable ways at the same time that it explains continuities and order. And it bridges the self-determined/overdetermined dichotomy by positing active and skilled users of culture who nonetheless construct persistent ways of ordering action.

*cultural
dopes*

Norms/roles

THE TOOL KIT   *culture/age*

Our culture provides us with multiple images of and resources for doing age. These images and resources shape our consciousness of age, our expectations about the life course and life course changes, our behavior and feelings about our experiences, and our life chances. We draw on resources of different types from the most individual and personal—our bodies and interpersonal relations—to the organizational and institutional.

Resources are not simply "out there" waiting to be used in identical ways by all. Rather, in interaction we draw on and give meaning to available resources, then use that meaning as a guide to action. Arlie Hochschild's work on the sociology of emotions helps us understand how we make use of the available resources. Hochschild argues that emotions are culturally shaped and publicly displayed; the choice of display is constrained by macro social and cultural forces and by individual concerns for impression management and self-concept. Actors do "emotion work" in deciding how to feel and act in particular situations. In addition, Hochschild (1989) argues that emotions mediate between what people believe, say, and actually do; feelings mediate between ideals, goals, values, and actions and thus are crucial for understanding "strategies of action." In short, emotions function to transform available resources for acting one's age into the actual accomplishment of age.

I visualize available "age resources" as a set of concentric circles with the inner circle(s) consisting of personal and highly individualized resources—the body and interpersonal relationships. The outer circles consist of cultural, bureaucratic, institutional, and structural factors available to larger groups of people. Since individuals draw simultaneously on more personal (and possibly idiosyncratic) resources and impersonal bureaucratic and structural resources as they actively construct strategies of action, their strategies are ultimately patterned by age without being determined by age. Sociologists can thus generalize about age categories and age-related behaviors and statuses and at the same time appreciate variation and "deviance."

At the individual level, our bodies (appearance, physical capabilities, and changes) are a source of age consciousness and a resource for doing age. We interpret "internal" messages conveyed by bodies (stiffness in the morning, decreased agility) in the context of age. In addition, we get "external" messages about bodies (people comment on the presence or absence of grey hair or wrinkles). But the resources provided by our bodies require interpretation, and the experience and interpretation of bodies in relation to age is situational. For the "aging" table dancers—most in their late teens and early twenties—studied by Carol Ronai (1992), setting and situation, more than chronological age, give meaning to "old." Studies of nursing home residents (Gubrium 1977, 1993; Diamond 1992) also illustrate how the body and its functions are variously interpreted and acted upon.

Interpersonal interactions provide resources for and constraints on the accomplishment of age. For example, Gubrium *et al.* (1994, 139) show how juvenile delinquents "act their age" in encounters with the police. Officers exercise a great deal of discretion and, in interaction with juveniles, demeanor is a crucial factor shaping officer response. "Those who act their age—appearing neither overly immature nor worldly beyond their years—are generally not seen as problems" (Gubrium *et al.* 1994, 139). In this example, not acting one's age appropriately—appearing too immature or too worldly—might very well get one taken into custody. In the field of aging, research on housing and living arrangements (e.g., Margolis 1990), care giving (e.g., Abel 1991), and nursing homes (Gubrium 1977; Ross 1977; Hazan 1992) shows the ways that formal and informal attachments within and to social organizations and networks provide the setting for interpersonal relations and interaction, influence our feelings about age, and ultimately shape how we act our age.

Our culture, in the forms of language and cognitive and conceptual categories, provides yet another resource for accomplishing age. Hockey and James (1993, 10) show how metaphors of childhood (with their assumptions of dependency) provide frames of reference for everyday encounters with people in multiple age categories and lay the foundation for treating physically dependent adults as childlike. Gubrium *et al.* (1994) examine the ways that images of the life course are used by mental health and social service professionals with serious consequences (hospitalization or release, course of treatment, etc.) for individuals. Media

Institutions such as the media, advertising, education, medicine, and religion depend on and sustain our consciousness of age, and they provide us with additional resources. For example, from the mass media we get images of different age categories with which to compare ourselves. These messages are not always consistent, nor are they necessarily desirable or attractive, as studies of ageism and stereotyping (Butler 1996; Scrutton 1996) have shown. Yet, we situate ourselves vis-à-vis these images and as a consequence feel guilty or proud, ashamed or delighted, at our ability to "measure up."

Our legal system uses chronological age to regulate education, sexual intercourse, marriage, and labor force participation, to name just a few examples. Law, public policy, and bureaucratic requirements provide a resource for age consciousness and for actually accomplishing age since formal requirements enable and constrain strategies of action (Buchmann, 1989). For instance, much of how kids accomplish age is shaped by the requirements of teachers and administrators, the school day,

and the academic year (and this is historically specific; see Chudacoff, 1989). In addition, their accomplishment of age outside of school also is patterned by compulsory education. For example, for kids, getting older means getting to stay up later at night. But getting older also means an earlier start to the school day. During the school week, then, a 14-year-old's ability to act "grown up" and stay awake late is circumscribed.

Trends in the economy, employment, and labor markets influence life chances and the meaning and accomplishment of age. For example, the creation and extension of Social Security and employer pension plans make it possible (though not inevitable) to think of oneself as a retiree or future retiree. Conversely, assumptions about age, the typical life course, and life course transitions (especially education, marriage, childbearing, work, and retirement), in conjunction with assumptions about class, race/ethnicity, and gender, shape labor market practices and public policies such as Social Security.

In her studies of changes in labor force participation rates and early withdrawal (through disability, unemployment, and pension systems), Guillemard (1996) has found that "the age when persons stop working has been lowered significantly" in many Western industrialized countries. "The chronological thresholds used both to determine personal identities throughout the life course and to organize the transition to old age have been torn up during the last fifteen years" (Guillemard 1996, 180).

Guillemard argues that together welfare systems and work/retirement policies have had the effect of reorganizing the life course (1996, 181). Mayer and Müller (1986) argue that both the modern, bureaucratic welfare state and the contemporary life course are joint products of the same processes of societal development (rationalization, social differentiation, and social control).

SEX, AGE EDUCATION

AGE / beliefs of aging

CHOOSING FROM AMONG THE TOOLS

. . . Accomplishing age requires that individuals use and interpret available resources, have emotional reactions, and act accordingly. As a result, ideologies (beliefs about age and aging including roles and norms), "objective" factors (such as chronological age or physical condition), and macro societal policies or trends (for example, opportunities for early labor force withdrawal) provide clues but do not tell us how individuals actually will feel about and accomplish their age. Instead we can examine how, in particular contexts, individuals constitute and respond to the meaning of available resources.

It is worth observing that people do not necessarily act their age in an explicit or self-conscious manner. Rather, the accomplishment of age is mediated through characteristics we assume to be related to age categories (for example, dependence and independence, competence, maturity). These attributes, themselves social constructions, serve as proxies for age.[1] Thus, elementary school students and nursing home residents, each in their own way, act their age by demonstrating, in interaction and with the help of others, their "competence" (i.e., their ability to do the things that someone "of that age" should be able to do) (Gubrium *et al.* 1994, 118–154).

Two recent studies of old-age home residents illustrate both the complex process of "doing age" and a variety of possible outcomes. In his study of an Israeli old-age home designated for the "able bodied" aged, Haim Hazan describes residents as deliberately demonstrating "functioning" to other residents, staff, and administrators. In this case, "functioning" serves as a proxy for age. Because of the great number of applicants, the director is compelled to remove as large a number of "nonfunctioning" aged as often as possible. And because the cost of other institutions is much greater and because residents know transfer denotes physical deterioration, residents feel compelled to demonstrate their functioning. They know that administrators look favorably on officially sanctioned group activities. Hazan's description of the Talmudic study in the synagogue group is especially telling.

> The teacher [hired specifically for this purpose] reads and interprets in Yiddish, despite the fact that some 'students' do not understand the language. No questions are asked, and if remarks are made, these are usually digressions. Some participants do not even turn the pages . . . some whisper between themselves . . . [one] hums oriental melodies quietly to himself and glances at his watch every now and then, in order to see if the time has come for the lesson to end. He also does not turn over any pages—sometimes reading aloud a line or two, irrespective of what the teacher is saying. . . . It is absolutely clear that the participants do not comprehend the content of the lessons. . . . Nevertheless, many of the congregants wanted the treasurers to organize more lessons on weekdays . . . (Hazan 1992, 129)

In addition to their participation in sanctioned group activities, residents demonstrate their functioning in the public lobby, hallways, elevators, and dining room, in the possession and circulation of photographs, and in their clothing and appearance.

The dominant sociological approach (and a mainstream gerontological approach) might view these behaviors as indicative of some actual level of functioning or as signs of the necessity for certain kinds of programs or activities. Hazan, in contrast, sees them as ways that group members organize their own world of meaning in the context of power relations in an institutional setting. Each resident takes into account features of the organizational

---

[1]West and Zimmerman (1987) demonstrate that in "doing gender," women "do deference" and men "do dominance." In other words, we can tease out dimensions of gender (femininity, masculinity, domination, subordination) that are accomplished.

setting (the authority of the director; the director's obligation to transfer nonfunctioning adults), beliefs about age, health, and physical condition (functioning is defined by the director as "able-bodied"), and her/his own physical capabilities (Can I move about unassisted? Am I physically able to eat with others in the dining room?). Each resident has an emotional reaction (fear of being transferred, determination to participate in activities, pride in abilities) and acts accordingly (attending Talmudic study group).

In contrast to the residents Hazan studies are the residents of Les Floralies, an old-age home in a Parisian suburb where anthropologist Jennie-Keith Ross lived and did field work. Les Floralies residents make very different choices about how to act like old-age home residents. Health condition is a characteristic that residents often talk about, but unlike in the Israeli home, health and "functioning" are not the dominant principles for social organization and interaction. Instead, "sex and political identification are important principles of social organization in this community" (Ross 1977, 54–55).

The residents of Les Floralies are similar in some ways to the residents Hazan studies. Both groups are of similar ages (most residents are between 70 and 79 years old) and have similar (working) class and educational backgrounds. Their context for interaction, however, is significantly different. The Israeli home is much larger than Les Floralies (400 vs. 150 residents) and, most importantly, Les Floralies does not transfer "non able-bodied" residents. These features have significant effects on the meaning and nature of interaction among and between residents, staff, administrators, and "outsiders." The juxtaposition of these two studies (and the variations within each group of residents) illustrates how people can nonetheless accomplish age very differently given the combination of, and their reaction to, available resources.

Conclusion

. . . Like gender, age is "potentially omnirelevant." This means that age is not the property of "the elderly"; it is potentially relevant to people of all (chronological) ages. One effect, then, of the view of age-as-accomplished is to shift the focus away from "the elderly" to broader social processes that affect people in multiple age categories throughout their lives. The second implication of age as "potentially omnirelevant" is that, although we continually "act our age," age is not always or equally relevant—i.e., salient—in all situations. Qualitative research has revealed the ways that individuals notice, feel, and experience their age in varying ways in different settings and at different points in the life course (e.g., Luborsky and Rubinstein 1987). Moreover, statistical portraits, first-person and ethnographic accounts (Ross 1977; Hazan 1992), and age theory (e.g., Dannefer 1988) attest to diversity within age categories. The view of age-as-accomplished can deflect attention away from "success" in aging (so often the focus of gerontology) in order to devote more attention to diversity and the appreciation of variability.

In giving credit to actors and in granting them agency, I do not want to minimize the extent to which performances are constrained. Representations of age and the life course not only are resources but also are used as means of control (Gubrium *et al.* 1994). Beliefs about age and the life course permeate our mechanisms of formal control and are institutionalized in law, medicine, psychiatry, and education (Karp and Yoels 1982; Buchmann 1989). The familiarity of the phrase "act your age" and the frequency with which it is used to direct the actions of others (and ourselves) testifies to the pervasiveness of beliefs about age as a method of informal social control. In short, age is never accomplished outside of relations of power.

The emphases of the age-as-accomplished framework have implications for research

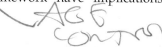
AGE
CONTROL

agendas. The effort to counter the dominant assumptions may be a guide for research into age-as-accomplished. The refusal to take chronological age as fixed or determinate and a focus on group process (in contrast to individual attributes) generate a variety of research possibilities including historical studies, ethnography, and cross-national comparisons as well as research into cognitive and conceptual categories. Relatively small-scale, ethnographic, and qualitative studies will enable sociologists to investigate the nuances of acting one's age. Secondary analysis involving comparisons between and among ethnographic studies will enable sociologists to understand patterns and sources of variation in the construction and accomplishment of age. Historical, statistical, and macro level studies, because they tend to stress structural factors as opposed to meaning, interpretation, and interaction, will not be supplanted by the age-as-accomplished framework. Rather, the framework of age-as-accomplished will benefit from and complement these studies.

In sum, the metaphor of acting and the idea of age-as-accomplished can make explicit what often goes unrecognized in the sociology of age: the performative, interactive work of accomplishing age, the emotion work involved in "becoming" and "being" an age, and the strategies people develop and use as they create and display themselves as aged (that is, as being of a particular age). To understand "age" as situated, contingent, and negotiated, and as continually constituted in interaction, provides the foundation for a sociology of age.

References

Abel, Emily K. 1991. *Who Cares for the Elderly?* Philadelphia, PA: Temple University Press.

Buchmann, Marlis. 1989. *The Script of Life in Modern Society: Entry into Adulthood in a Changing World.* Chicago: University of Chicago Press.

Butler, Robert. 1996. "Dispelling Ageism: The Cross-Cutting Intervention." Pp. 131–140 in Jill Quadagno and Debra Street (eds.), *Aging for the Twenty-first Century.* New York: St. Martin's.

Chudacoff, Howard P. 1989. *How Old Are You? Age Consciousness in American Culture.* Princeton, NJ: Princeton University Press.

Dannefer, Dale. 1988. "What's in a Name? An Account of the Neglect of Variability in the Study of Aging." Pp. 356–364 in James E. Birren and Vern L. Bengtson (eds.), *Emergent Theories of Aging.* New York: Springer Publishing.

Devault, Marjorie. 1991. *Feeding the Family.* Chicago: University of Chicago Press.

Diamond, Timothy. 1992. *Making Gray Gold: Narratives of Nursing Home Care.* Chicago: University of Chicago Press.

Eisenhandler, Susan A. 1991. "The Asphalt Identikit: Old Age and the Driver's License." Pp. 107–120 in Beth Hess and Elizabeth Markson (eds.), *Growing Old in America.* New Brunswick, NJ: Transaction Publishers.

Garfinkel, Harold. 1967. *Studies in Ethnomethodology.* Englewood Cliffs, NJ: Prentice-Hall.

Gubrium, Jaber. 1977. *Living and Dying at Murray Manor.* New York: St. Martin's.

———. 1993. *Speaking of Life: Horizons of Meaning for Nursing Home Residents.* New York: Aldine de Gruyter.

Gubrium, Jaber F., James A. Holstein, and David R. Buckholdt. 1994. *Constructing the Life Course.* Dix Hills, NY: General Hall.

Guillemard, Anne-Marie. 1996. "The Trend Toward Early Labor Force Withdrawal and the Reorganization of the Life Course: A Cross-National Analysis." Pp. 177–193 in Jill Quadagno and Debra Street (eds.), *Aging for the Twenty-first Century.* New York: St. Martin's.

Hazan, Haim. 1992. *Managing Change in Old Age: The Control of Meaning in an Institutional Setting.* Albany, NY: State University of New York Press.

Henley, Nancy, and Jo Freeman. 1989. "The Sexual Politics of Interpersonal Behavior." Pp. 457–469 in Jo Freeman (ed.), *Women: A Feminist Perspective.* Mountain View, CA: Mayfield.

Heritage, John. 1984. *Garfinkel and Ethnomethodology.* New York: Polity Press.

Hochschild, Arlie. 1983. *The Managed Heart.* Berkeley: University of California.

———. 1989. *The Second Shift.* New York: Avon.

Hockey, Jenny, and Allison James. 1993. *Growing Up and Growing Old.* London: Sage.

Karp, David A. 1991. "A Decade of Reminders: Changing Age Consciousness between Fifty and Sixty Years Old." Pp. 67–92 in Beth Hess and Elizabeth Markson (eds.), *Growing Old in America.* New Brunswick, NJ: Transaction Publishers.

Karp, David A., and William C. Yoels. 1982. *Experiencing the Life Cycle: A Social Psychology of Aging.* Springfield, IL: Charles C. Thomas.

Luborsky, Mark, and Robert L. Rubinstein. 1987. "Ethnicity and Lifetimes: Self Concepts and Situational Contexts of Ethnic Identity in Late Life." Pp. 35–50 in Donald E. Gelfand and Charles M. Barresi (eds.), *Ethnic Dimensions of Aging.* New York: Springer Publishing.

Margolis, Richard. 1990. *Risking Old Age in America.* Boulder, CO: Westview.

Mayer, Karl Ulrich, and Walter Müller. 1986. "The State and the Structure of the Life Course." Pp. 217–245 in Aage B. Sorensen, Franz E. Weinert, and Lonnie R. Sherrod (eds.), *Human Development and the Life Course: Multidisciplinary Perspectives.* Hillsdale, NJ: Lawrence Erlbaum.

McIlwee, Judith S., and J. Gregg Robinson. 1992. *Women in Engineering.* Albany: State University of New York Press.

Ronai, Carol Rambo. 1992. "Managing Aging in Young Adulthood: The 'Aging' Table Dancer." *Journal of Aging Studies* 6: 307–317.

Ross, Jennie-Keith. 1977. *Old People, New Lives: Community Creation in a Retirement Residence.* Chicago: University of Chicago Press.

Scrutton, Steve. 1996. "Ageism: The Foundation of Age Discrimination." Pp. 141–154 in Jill Quadagno and Debra Street (eds.), *Aging for the Twenty-first Century.* New York: St. Martin's.

Swidler, Ann. 1986. "Culture in Action: Symbols and Strategies." *American Sociological Review* 51: 273–286.

West, Candace, and Sarah Fenstermaker. 1993. "Power, Inequality and the Accomplishment of Gender: An Ethnomethodological View." Pp. 151–174 in Paula England (ed.), *Theory on Gender/Feminism on Theory.* New York: Aldine deGruyter.

West, Candace and Don H. Zimmerman. 1987. "Doing gender." *Gender & Society* 1: 125–151.

Questions

1. Obviously age is a chronological fact. Why, then, does Professor Laz insist age is a *social* construction?

2. Describe the kinds of circumstances under which someone is most likely to be told to act his or her age.

3. Is there one aspect of your life in which you don't "act your age"? If so, describe it. Is this something you hide or flaunt? If so, do you usually do it alone or in the company of others?

4. According to Laz, what are the possible consequences for not acting one's age?

11

THE CODE OF THE STREETS

Elijah Anderson

Except in the most general sense, it is wrong to speak of "American" culture as if it were a single entity. American society is not homogeneous, nor is its culture. In this 1994 article, Elijah Anderson focuses on a particular *subculture* that exists within the larger culture. In this subculture, the ubiquitous human search for respect creates what has been called a "perverse etiquette of violence," one from which it may well be impossible to escape.

Of all the problems besetting the poor inner-city black community, none is more pressing than that of interpersonal violence and aggression. It wreaks havoc daily in the lives of community residents and increasingly spills over into downtown and residential middle-class areas. Muggings, burglaries, carjackings, and drug-related shootings, all of which may leave their victims or innocent bystanders dead, are now common enough to concern all urban and many suburban residents. The inclination to violence springs from the circumstances of life among the ghetto poor—the lack of jobs that pay a living wage, the stigma of race, the fallout from rampant drug use and drug trafficking, and the resulting alienation and lack of hope for the future.

Simply living in such an environment places young people at special risk of falling victim to aggressive behavior. Although there are often forces in the community which can counteract the negative influences, by far the most powerful being a strong, loving, "decent" (as inner-city residents put it) family committed to middle-class values, the despair is pervasive enough to have spawned an oppositional culture, that of

"the streets," whose norms are often consciously opposed to those of mainstream society. These two orientations—decent and street—socially organize the community, and their coexistence has important consequences for residents, particularly children growing up in the inner city. Above all, this environment means that even youngsters whose home lives reflect mainstream values—and the majority of homes in the community do—must be able to handle themselves in a street-oriented environment.

This is because the street culture has evolved what may be called a code of the streets, which amounts to a set of informal rules governing interpersonal public behavior, including violence. The rules prescribe both a proper comportment and a proper way to respond if challenged. They regulate the use of violence and so allow those who are inclined to aggression to precipitate violent encounters in an approved way. The rules have been established and are enforced mainly by the street-oriented, but on the streets the distinction between street and decent is often irrelevant; everybody knows that if the rules are violated, there are penalties. Knowledge of the code is thus largely defensive; it is literally necessary for operating in public. Therefore, even though families with a decency orientation are usually opposed to the values of the

96

Code

code, they often reluctantly encourage their children's familiarity with it to enable them to negotiate the inner-city environment.

At the heart of the code is the issue of respect—loosely defined as being treated "right," or granted the deference one deserves. However, in the troublesome public environment of the inner city, as people increasingly feel buffeted by forces beyond their control, what one deserves in the way of respect becomes more and more problematic and uncertain. This in turn further opens the issue of respect to sometimes intense interpersonal negotiation. In the street culture, especially among young people, respect is viewed as almost an external entity that is hard-won but easily lost, and so must constantly be guarded. The rules of the code in fact provide a framework for negotiating respect. The person whose very appearance—including his clothing, demeanor, and way of moving— deters transgressions feels that he possesses, and may be considered by others to possess, a measure of respect. With the right amount of respect, for instance, he can avoid "being bothered" in public. If he is bothered, not only may he be in physical danger but he has been disgraced or "dissed" (disrespected). Many of the forms that dissing can take might seem petty to middle-class people (maintaining eye contact for too long, for example), but to those invested in the street code, these actions become serious indications of the other person's intentions. Consequently, such people become very sensitive to advances and slights, which could well serve as warnings of imminent physical confrontation.

This hard reality can be traced to the profound sense of alienation from mainstream society and its institutions felt by many poor inner-city black people, particularly the young. The code of the streets is actually a cultural adaptation to a profound lack of faith in the police and the judicial system. The police are most often seen as representing the dominant white society and not caring to protect inner-city residents. When called, they may not respond, which is one reason many residents feel they must be prepared to take extraordinary measures to defend themselves and their loved ones against those who are inclined to aggression. Lack of police accountability has in fact been incorporated into the status system: the person who is believed capable of "taking care of himself" is accorded a certain deference, which translates into a sense of physical and psychological control. Thus the street code emerges where the influence of the police ends and personal responsibility for one's safety is felt to begin. Exacerbated by the proliferation of drugs and easy access to guns, this volatile situation results in the ability of the street-oriented minority (or those who effectively "go for bad") to dominate the public spaces.

Decent and Street Families

Although almost everyone in poor inner-city neighborhoods is struggling financially and therefore feels a certain distance from the rest of America, the decent and the street family in a real sense represent two poles of value orientation, two contrasting conceptual categories. The labels "decent" and "street," which the residents themselves use, amount to evaluative judgments that confer status on local residents. The labeling is often the result of a social contest among individuals and families of the neighborhood. Individuals of the two orientations often coexist in the same extended family. Decent residents judge themselves to be so while judging others to be of the street, and street individuals often present themselves as decent, drawing distinctions between themselves and other people. In addition, there is quite a bit of circumstantial behavior—that is, one person may at different times exhibit both decent

Respect / Disrespect

and street orientations, depending on the circumstances. Although these designations result from so much social jockeying, there do exist concrete features that define each conceptual category.

Generally, so-called decent families tend to accept mainstream values more fully and attempt to instill them in their children. Whether married couples with children or single-parent (usually female) households, they are generally "working poor" and so tend to be better off financially than their street-oriented neighbors. They value hard work and self-reliance and are willing to sacrifice for their children. Because they have a certain amount of faith in mainstream society, they harbor hopes for a better future for their children, if not for themselves. Many of them go to church and take a strong interest in their children's schooling. Rather than dwelling on the real hardships and inequities facing them, many such decent people, particularly the increasing number of grandmothers raising grandchildren, see their difficult situation as a test from God and derive great support from their faith and from the church community.

Extremely aware of the problematic and often dangerous environment in which they reside, decent parents tend to be strict in their child-rearing practices, encouraging children to respect authority and walk a straight moral line. They have an almost obsessive concern about trouble of any kind and remind their children to be on the lookout for people and situations that might lead to it. At the same time, they are themselves polite and considerate of others, and teach their children to be the same way. At home, at work, and in church, they strive hard to maintain a positive mental attitude and a spirit of cooperation.

So-called street parents, in contrast, often show a lack of consideration for other people and have a rather superficial sense of family and community. Though they may love their children, many of them are unable to cope with the physical and emotional demands of parenthood, and find it difficult to reconcile their needs with those of their children. These families, who are more fully invested in the code of the streets than the decent people are, may aggressively socialize their children into it in a normative way. They believe in the code and judge themselves and others according to its values.

In fact the overwhelming majority of families in the inner-city community try to approximate the decent-family model, but there are many others who clearly represent the worst fears of the decent family. Not only are their financial resources extremely limited, but what little they have may easily be misused. The lives of the street-oriented are often marked by disorganization. In the most desperate circumstances people frequently have a limited understanding of priorities and consequences, and so frustrations mount over bills, food, and, at times, drink, cigarettes, and drugs. Some tend toward self-destructive behavior; many street-oriented women are crack-addicted ("on the pipe"), alcoholic, or involved in complicated relationships with men who abuse them. In addition, the seeming intractability of their situation, caused in large part by the lack of well-paying jobs and the persistence of racial discrimination, has engendered deep-seated bitterness and anger in many of the most desperate and poorest blacks, especially young people. The need both to exercise a measure of control and to lash out at somebody is often reflected in the adults' relations with their children. At the least, the frustrations of persistent poverty shorten the fuse in such people—contributing to a lack of patience with anyone, child or adult, who irritates them.

In these circumstances a woman—or a man, although men are less consistently present in children's lives—can be quite aggressive with children, yelling at and striking them for the least little infraction of the rules she has set down. Often little if any serious explanation follows the verbal and physical punishment. This response teaches children a particular lesson. They learn that to solve any kind of interpersonal problem one must quickly resort to hitting or other violent behavior. Actual peace and quiet, and also the appearance of calm, respectful children conveyed to her neighbors and friends, are often what the young mother most desires, but at times she will be very aggressive in trying to get them. Thus she may be quick to beat her children, especially if they defy her law, not because she hates them but because this is the way she knows to control them. In fact, many street-oriented women love their children dearly. Many mothers in the community subscribe to the notion that there is a "devil in the boy" that must be beaten out of him or that socially "fast girls need to be whupped." Thus much of what borders on child abuse in the view of social authorities is acceptable parental punishment in the view of these mothers.

Many street-oriented women are sporadic mothers whose children learn to fend for themselves when necessary, foraging for food and money any way they can get it. The children are sometimes employed by drug dealers or become addicted themselves. These children of the street, growing up with little supervision, are said to "come up hard." They often learn to fight at an early age, sometimes using short-tempered adults around them as role models. The street-oriented home may be fraught with anger, verbal disputes, physical aggression, and even mayhem. The children observe these goings-on, learning the lesson that might makes right. They quickly learn to hit those who cross them, and the dog-eat-dog mentality prevails. In order to survive, to protect oneself, it is necessary to marshal inner resources and be ready to deal with adversity in a hands-on way. In these circumstances physical prowess takes on great significance.

In some of the most desperate cases, a street-oriented mother may simply leave her young children alone and unattended while she goes out. The most irresponsible women can be found at local bars and crack houses, getting high and socializing with other adults. Sometimes a troubled woman will leave very young children alone for days at a time. Reports of crack addicts abandoning their children have become common in drug-infested inner-city communities. Neighbors or relatives discover the abandoned children, often hungry and distraught over the absence of their mother. After repeated absences, a friend or relative, particularly a grandmother, will often step in to care for the young children, sometimes petitioning the authorities to send her, as guardian of the children, the mother's welfare check, if the mother gets one. By this time, however, the children may well have learned the first lesson of the streets: survival itself, let alone respect, cannot be taken for granted; you have to fight for your place in the world.

Campaigning for Respect

These realities of inner-city life are largely absorbed on the streets. At an early age, often even before they start school, children from street-oriented homes gravitate to the streets, where they "hang"—socialize with their peers. Children from these generally permissive homes have a great deal of latitude and are allowed to "rip and run" up and down the street. They often come home from school, put their books down, and go right back out the door. On school nights eight- and nine-year-olds remain out until nine or ten o'clock (and teenagers typically come in whenever they want to). On the streets they play in groups that often become the source of their primary social bonds. Children from decent homes tend to be more carefully supervised and are thus likely to have curfews and to be taught how to stay out of trouble.

When decent and street kids come together, a kind of social shuffle occurs in which children have a chance to go either way. Tension builds as a child comes to realize that he must choose an orientation. The kind of home he comes from influences but does not determine the way he will ultimately turn out—although it is unlikely that a child from a thoroughly street-oriented family will easily absorb decent values on the streets. Youths who emerge from street-oriented families but develop a decency orientation almost always learn those values in another setting—in school, in a youth group, in church. Often it is the result of their involvement with a caring "old head" (adult role model).

In the street, through their play, children pour their individual life experiences into a common knowledge pool, affirming, confirming, and elaborating on what they have observed in the home and matching their skills against those of others. And they learn to fight. Even small children test one another, pushing and shoving, and are ready to hit other children over circumstances not to their liking. In turn, they are readily hit by other children, and the child who is toughest prevails. Thus the violent resolution of disputes, the hitting and cursing, gains social reinforcement. The child in effect is initiated into a system that is really a way of campaigning for respect.

In addition, younger children witness the disputes of older children, which are often resolved through cursing and abusive talk, if not aggression or outright violence. They see that one child succumbs to the greater physical and mental abilities of the other. They are also alert and attentive witnesses to the verbal and physical fights of adults, after which they compare notes and share their interpretations of the event. In almost every case the victor is the person who physically won the altercation, and this person often enjoys the esteem and respect of onlookers. These experiences reinforce the lessons the children have learned at home: might makes right, and toughness is a virtue, while humility is not. In effect they learn the social meaning of fighting. When it is left virtually unchallenged, this understanding becomes an ever more important part of the child's working conception of the world. Over time the code of the streets becomes refined.

Those street-oriented adults with whom children come in contact—including mothers, fathers, brothers, sisters, boyfriends, cousins, neighbors, and friends—help them along in forming this understanding by verbalizing the messages they are getting through experience: "Watch your back." "Protect yourself." "Don't punk out." "If somebody messes with you, you got to pay them back." "If someone disses you, you got to straighten them out." Many parents actually impose sanctions if a child is not sufficiently aggressive. For example, if a child loses a fight and comes home upset, the parent might respond, "Don't you come in here crying that somebody beat you up; you better get back out there and whup his ass. I didn't raise no punks! Get back out there and whup his ass. If you don't whup his ass, I'll whup your ass when you come home." Thus the child obtains reinforcement for being tough and showing nerve.

While fighting, some children cry as though they are doing something they are ambivalent about. The fight may be against their wishes, yet they may feel constrained to fight or face the consequences—not just from peers but also from caretakers or parents, who may administer another beating if they back down. Some adults recall receiving such lessons from their own parents and justify repeating them to their children as a way to toughen them up. Looking capable of taking care of oneself as a form of self-defense is a dominant theme among both street-oriented and decent adults who worry about the safety of their children. There is thus at times a convergence in their child-rearing practices, although the rationales behind them may differ.

Code = presentation of self

Self-Image Based on "Juice"

By the time they are teenagers, most youths have either internalized the code of the streets or at least learned the need to comport themselves in accordance with its rules, which chiefly have to do with interpersonal communication. The code revolves around the presentation of self. Its basic requirement is the display of a certain predisposition to violence. Accordingly, one's bearing must send the unmistakable if sometimes subtle message to "the next person" in public that one is capable of violence and mayhem when the situation requires it, that one can take care of oneself. The nature of this communication is largely determined by the demands of the circumstances but can include facial expressions, gait, and verbal expressions—all of which are geared mainly to deterring aggression. Physical appearance, including clothes, jewelry, and grooming, also plays an important part in how a person is viewed; to be respected, it is important to have the right look.

Even so, there are no guarantees against challenges, because there are always people around looking for a fight to increase their share of respect—or "juice," as it is sometimes called on the street. Moreover, if a person is assaulted, it is important, not only in the eyes of his opponent but also in the eyes of his "running buddies," for him to avenge himself. Otherwise he risks being "tried" (challenged) or "moved on" by any number of others. To maintain his honor he must show he is not someone to be "messed with" or "dissed." In general, the person must "keep himself straight" by managing his position of respect among others; this involves in part his self-image, which is shaped by what he thinks others are thinking of him in relation to his peers.

Objects play an important and complicated role in establishing self-image. Jackets, sneakers, gold jewelry, reflect not just a person's taste, which tends to be tightly regulated among adolescents of all social classes, but also a willingness to possess things that may require defending. A boy wearing a fashionable, expensive jacket, for example, is vulnerable to attack by another who covets the jacket and either cannot afford to buy one or wants the added satisfaction of depriving someone else of his. However, if the boy forgoes the desirable jacket and wears one that isn't "hip," he runs the risk of being teased and possibly even assaulted as an unworthy person. To be allowed to hang with certain prestigious crowds, a boy must wear a different set of expensive clothes—sneakers and athletic suit—every day. Not to be able to do so might make him appear socially deficient. The youth comes to covet such items—especially when he sees easy prey wearing them.

In acquiring valued things, therefore, a person shores up his identity—but since it is an identity based on having things, it is highly precarious. This very precariousness gives a heightened sense of urgency to staying even with peers, with whom the person is actually competing. Young men and women who are able to command respect through their presentation of self—by allowing their possessions and their body language to speak for them—may not have to campaign for regard but may, rather, gain it by the force of their manner. Those who are unable to command respect in this way must actively campaign for it—and are thus particularly alive to slights.

One way of campaigning for status is by taking the possessions of others. In this context, seemingly ordinary objects can become trophies imbued with symbolic value that far exceeds their monetary worth. Possession of the trophy can symbolize the ability to violate somebody—to "get in his face," to take something of value from him, to "dis" him, and thus to enhance one's own worth by stealing someone else's. The trophy does not have to be something material. It can be another person's sense of honor, snatched away with a

juice = wolves *stealing*

fighting

trophys = highrank

derogatory remark. It can be the outcome of a fight. It can be the imposition of a certain standard, such as a girl's getting herself recognized as the most beautiful. Material things, however, fit easily into the pattern. Sneakers, a pistol, even somebody else's girlfriend, can become a trophy. When a person can take something from another and then flaunt it, he gains a certain regard by being the owner, or the controller, of that thing. But this display of ownership can then provoke other people to challenge him. This game of who controls what is thus constantly being played out on inner-city streets, and the trophy—extrinsic or intrinsic, tangible or intangible—identifies the current winner.

An important aspect of this often violent give-and-take is its zero-sum quality. That is, the extent to which one person can raise himself up depends on his ability to put another person down. This underscores the alienation that permeates the inner-city ghetto community. There is a generalized sense that very little respect is to be had, and therefore everyone competes to get what affirmation he can of the little that is available. The craving for respect that results gives people thin skins. Shows of deference by others can be highly soothing, contributing to a sense of security, comfort, self-confidence, and self-respect. Transgressions by others which go unanswered diminish these feelings and are believed to encourage further transgressions. Hence one must be ever vigilant against the transgressions of others or even *appearing* as if transgressions will be tolerated. Among young people, whose sense of self-esteem is particularly vulnerable, there is an especially heightened concern with being disrespected. Many inner-city young men in particular crave respect to such a degree that they will risk their lives to attain and maintain it.

The issue of respect is thus closely tied to whether a person has an inclination to be violent, even as a victim. In the wider society

up down

people may not feel required to retaliate physically after an attack, even though they are aware that they have been degraded or taken advantage of. They may feel a great need to defend themselves *during* an attack, or to behave in such a way as to deter aggression (middle-class people certainly can and do become victims of street-oriented youths), but they are much more likely than street-oriented people to feel that they can walk away from a possible altercation with their self-esteem intact. Some people may even have the strength of character to flee, without any thought that their self-respect or esteem will be diminished.

In impoverished inner-city black communities, however, particularly among young males and perhaps increasingly among females, such flight would be extremely difficult. To run away would likely leave one's self-esteem in tatters. Hence people often feel constrained not only to stand up and at least attempt to resist during an assault but also to "pay back"—to seek revenge—after a successful assault on their person. This may include going to get a weapon or even getting relatives involved. Their very identity and self-respect, their honor, is often intricately tied up with the way they perform on the streets during and after such encounters. This outlook reflects the circumscribed opportunities of the inner-city poor. Generally people outside the ghetto have other ways of gaining status and regard, and thus do not feel so dependent on such physical displays. . . .

"Going for Bad"

In the most fearsome youths such a cavalier attitude toward death grows out of a very limited view of life. Many are uncertain about how long they are going to live and believe they could die violently at any time. They accept this fate; they live on the edge. Their manner conveys the message that nothing intimidates them; whatever turn the encounter takes, they maintain their attack—rather like a pit bull, whose spirit many such boys admire. The demonstration of such tenacity "shows heart" and earns their respect.

This fearlessness has implications for law enforcement. Many street-oriented boys are much more concerned about the threat of "justice" at the hands of a peer than at the hands of the police. Moreover, many feel not only that they have little to lose by going to prison but that they have something to gain. The toughening-up one experiences in prison can actually enhance one's reputation on the streets. Hence the system loses influence over the hard core who are without jobs, with little perceptible stake in the system. If mainstream society has done nothing *for* them, they counter by making sure it can do nothing *to* them.

At the same time, however, a competing view maintains that true nerve consists in backing down, walking away from a fight, and going on with one's business. One fights only in self-defense. This view emerges from the decent philosophy that life is precious, and it is an important part of the socialization process common in decent homes. It discourages violence as the primary means of resolving disputes and encourages youngsters to accept nonviolence and talk as confrontational strategies. But "if the deal goes down," self-defense is greatly encouraged. When there is enough positive support for this orientation, either in the home or among one's peers, then nonviolence has a chance to prevail. But it prevails at the cost of relinquishing a claim to being bad and tough, and therefore sets a young person up as at the very least alienated from street-oriented peers and quite possibly a target of derision or even violence.

Although the nonviolent orientation rarely overcomes the impulse to strike back in an encounter, it does introduce a certain confusion and so can prompt a measure of soul-searching, or even profound ambivalence.

Did the person back down with his respect intact or did he back down only to be judged a "punk"—a person lacking manhood? Should he or she have acted? Should he or she have hit the other person in the mouth? These questions beset many young men and women during public confrontations. What is the "right" thing to do? In the quest for honor, respect, and local status—which few young people are uninterested in—common sense most often prevails, which leads many to opt for the tough approach, enacting their own particular versions of the display of nerve. The presentation of oneself as rough and tough is very often quite acceptable until one is tested. And then that presentation may help the person pass the test, because it will cause fewer questions to be asked about what he did and why. It is hard for a person to explain why he lost the fight or why he backed down. Hence many will strive to appear to "go for bad," while hoping they will never be tested. But when they are tested, the outcome of the situation may quickly be out of their hands, as they become wrapped up in the circumstances of the moment.

An Oppositional Culture

The attitudes of the wider society are deeply implicated in the code of the streets. Most people in inner-city communities are not totally invested in the code. But the significant minority of hard-core street youths who have to maintain the code in order to establish reputations because they have—or feel they have—few other ways to assert themselves. For these young people the standards of the street code are the only game in town. The extent to which some children—particularly those who through upbringing have become most alienated and those lacking in strong and conventional social support—experience, feel, and internalize racist rejection and contempt from mainstream society may strongly encourage them to express contempt for the more conventional society in turn. In dealing with this contempt and rejection, some youngsters will consciously invest themselves and their considerable mental resources in what amounts to an oppositional culture to preserve themselves and their self-respect. Once they do, any respect they might be able to garner in the wider system pales in comparison with the respect available in the local system; thus they often lose interest in even attempting to negotiate the mainstream system.

At the same time, many less alienated young blacks have assumed a street-oriented demeanor as a way of expressing their blackness while really embracing a much more moderate way of life; they, too, want a nonviolent setting in which to live and raise a family. These decent people are trying hard to be part of the mainstream culture, but the racism, real and perceived, that they encounter helps to legitimate the oppositional culture. And so on occasion they adopt street behavior. In fact, depending on the demands of the situation, many people in the community slip back and forth between decent and street behavior.

A vicious cycle has thus been formed. The hopelessness and alienation many young inner-city black men and women feel, largely as a result of endemic joblessness and persistent racism, fuels the violence they engage in. This violence serves to confirm the negative feelings many whites and some middle-class blacks harbor toward the ghetto poor, further legitimating the oppositional culture and the code of the streets in the eyes of many poor young blacks. Unless the cycle is broken, attitudes on both sides will become increasingly entrenched, and the violence, which claims victims black and white, poor and affluent, will only escalate.

Questions

1. How would you define each of the following terms (used by Anderson in his article)?
   a. mayhem
   b. oppositional culture
   c. zero-sum

2. What factors of life on the street make it difficult for people to be "decent"?

3. In your judgment, are young men from more "middle-class" cultural settings at all preoccupied with earning respect? How do young men in middle-class culture earn the respect of others and prove themselves to be properly "manly"?

12

THE POWER AND MEANING
OF "GIRL WATCHING"

Beth A. Quinn

Sociologists understand that gender is not something people have, it's something people do. A man is not masculine unless he successfully performs in masculine ways; a woman is not feminine unless she acts in ways that persuade others that she indeed is feminine. The question is, when we do masculinity or femininity, who is our audience? In her article, Beth A. Quinn finds an answer that might surprise you.

Confronted with complaints about sexual harassment or accounts in the media, some men claim that women are too sensitive or that they too often misinterpret men's intentions (Bernstein 1994; Buckwald 1993). In contrast, some women note with frustration that men just "don't get it" and lament the seeming inadequacy of sexual harassment policies (Conley 1991; Guccione 1992). Indeed, this ambiguity in defining acts of sexual harassment might be, as Cleveland and Kerst (1993) suggested, the most robust finding in sexual harassment research.

Using in-depth interviews with 43 employed men and women, this article examines a particular social practice—"girl watching"—as a means to understanding one way that these gender differences are produced. This analysis does not address the size or prevalence of these differences, nor does it present a direct comparison of men and women; this information is essential but well covered in the literature.[1] Instead, I follow Cleveland and Kerst's

Beth A. Quinn, "Sexual Harassment and Masculinity: The Power and Meaning of 'Girl Watching'" from *Gender & Society* 16, no. 3 (June 2002): 386-402. Reprinted by permission of SAGE Publications.

(1993) and Wood's (1998) suggestion that the question may best be unraveled by exploring how the "subject(ivities) of perpetrators, victims, and resistors of sexual harassment" are "discursively produced, reproduced, and altered" (Wood 1998, 28).

This article focuses on the subjectivities of the perpetrators of a disputable form of sexual harassment, "girl watching." The term refers to the act of men's sexually evaluating women, often in the company of other men. It may take the form of a verbal or gestural message of "check it out," boasts of sexual prowess, or explicit comments about a woman's body or imagined sexual acts. The target may be an individual woman or group of women or simply a photograph or other representation. The woman may be a stranger, coworker, supervisor, employee, or client. For the present analysis, girl watching within the workplace is centered.

The analysis is grounded in the work of masculinity scholars such as Connell (1987, 1995) in that it attempts to explain the subject positions of the interviewed men—not the abstract and genderless subjects of patriarchy but the gendered and privileged subjects embedded in this system. Since I am attempting to delineate the gendered worldviews of the interviewed men, I employ the term "girl watching," a phrase that reflects their language ("they watch girls").

I have chosen to center the analysis on girl watching within the workplace for two reasons. First, it appears to be fairly prevalent. For example, a survey of federal civil employees (U.S. Merit Systems Protection Board 1988) found that in the previous 24 months, 28 percent of the women surveyed had experienced "unwanted sexual looks or gestures," and 35 percent had experienced "unwanted sexual teasing, jokes, remarks, or questions." Second, girl watching is still often normalized and trivialized as only play, or "boys will be boys." A man watching girls—even in his workplace—is frequently accepted as a natural and commonplace activity, especially if he is in the presence of other men.[2] Indeed, it may be required (Hearn 1985). Thus, girl watching sits on the blurry edge between fun and harm, joking and harassment. An understanding of the process of identifying behavior as sexual harassment, or of rejecting this label, may be built on this ambiguity.

Girl watching has various forms and functions, depending on the context and the men involved. For example, it may be used by men as a directed act of power against a particular woman or women. In this, girl watching—at least in the workplace—is most clearly identified as harassing by both men and women. I am most interested, however, in the form where it is characterized as only play. This type is more obliquely motivated and, as I will argue, functions as a game men play to build shared masculine identities and social relations.

Multiple and contradictory subject positions are also evidenced in girl watching, most notably that between the gazing man and the woman he watches. Drawing on Michael Schwalbe's (1992) analysis of empathy and the formation of masculine identities, I argue that girl watching is premised on the obfuscation

of this multiplicity through the objectification of the woman watched and a suppression of empathy for her. In conclusion, the ways these elements operate to produce gender differences in interpreting sexual harassment and the implications for developing effective policies are discussed.

Previous Research

The question of how behavior is or is not labeled as sexual harassment has been studied primarily through experimental vignettes and surveys.[3] In both methods, participants evaluate either hypothetical scenarios or lists of behaviors, considering whether, for example, the behavior constitutes sexual harassment, which party is most at fault, and what consequences the act might engender. Researchers manipulate factors such as the level of "welcomeness" the target exhibits and the relationship of the actors (supervisor-employee, coworker-coworker).

Both methods consistently show that women are willing to define more acts as sexual harassment (Gutek, Morasch, and Cohen 1983; Padgitt and Padgitt 1986; Powell 1986; York 1989; but see Stockdale and Vaux 1993) and are more likely to see situations as coercive (Garcia, Milano, and Quijano 1989). When asked who is more to blame in a particular scenario, men are more likely to blame, and less likely to empathize with, the victim (Jensen and Gutek 1982; Kenig and Ryan 1986). In terms of actual behaviors like girl watching, the U.S. Merit Systems Protection Board (1988) survey found that 81 percent of the women surveyed considered "uninvited sexually suggestive looks or gestures" from a supervisor to be sexual harassment. While the majority of men (68 percent) also defined it as such, significantly more men were willing to dismiss such behavior. Similarly, while 40 percent of the men would not consider the same behavior from a coworker to be harassing, more than three-quarters of the women would.

The most common explanation offered for these differences is gender role socialization. This conclusion is supported by the consistent finding that the more men and women adhere to traditional gender roles, the more likely they are to deny the harm in sexual harassment and to consider the behavior acceptable or at least normal (Gutek and Koss 1993; Malovich and Stake 1990; Murrell and Dietz-Uhler 1993; Popovich *et al.* 1992; Pryor 1987; Tagri and Hayes 1997). Men who hold predatory ideas about sexuality, who are more likely to believe rape myths, and who are more likely to self-report that they would rape under certain circumstances are less likely to see behaviors as harassing (Murrell and Dietz-Uhler 1993; Pryor 1987; Reilly et al. 1992).

These findings do not, however, adequately address the between-group differences. The more one is socialized into traditional notions of sex roles, the more likely it is for both men and women to view the behaviors as acceptable or at least unchangeable. The processes by which gender roles operate to produce these differences remain underexamined.

Some theorists argue that men are more likely to discount the harassing aspects of their behavior because of a culturally conditioned tendency to misperceive women's intentions. For example, Stockdale (1993, 96) argued that "patriarchal norms create a sexually aggressive belief system in some people more than others, and this belief system can lead to the propensity to misperceive." Gender differences in interpreting sexual harassment, then, may be the outcome of the acceptance of normative ideas about women's inscrutability and indirectness and men's role as sexual aggressors. Men see harmless flirtation or sexual interest rather than harassment because they misperceive women's intent and responses.

Stockdale's (1993) theory is promising but limited. First, while it may apply to actions such as repeatedly asking for dates and quid pro quo harassment,[4] it does not effectively explain motivations for more indirect actions, such as displaying pornography and girl watching. Second, it does not explain why some men are more likely to operate from these discourses of sexual aggression contributing to a propensity to misperceive.

Theoretical explanations that take into account the complexity and diversity of sexual harassing behaviors and their potentially multifaceted social etiologies are needed. An account of the processes by which these behaviors are produced and the active construction of their social meanings is necessary to unravel both between-and within-gender variations in behavior and interpretation. A fruitful framework from which to begin is an examination of masculine identities and the role of sexually harassing behaviors as a means to their production.

Method

I conducted 43 semistructured interviews with currently employed men and women between June 1994 and March 1995. The interviews ranged in length from one to three hours. With one exception, interviews were audiotaped and transcribed in full.

Participants were contacted in two primary ways. Twenty-five participants were recruited from "Acme Electronics," a Southern California electronic design and manufacturing company. An additional 18 individuals were recruited from an evening class at a community college and a university summer school class, both in Southern California. These participants referred 3 more individuals. In addition to the interviews, I conducted participant observation for approximately one month while on site at Acme. This involved observations of the public and common spaces of the company.

At Acme, a human resources administrator drew four independent samples (salaried and hourly women and men) from the company's approximately 300 employees. Letters of invitation were sent to 40 individuals, and from this group, 13 women and 12 men agreed to be interviewed.[5]

The strength of organizationally grounded sampling is that it allows us to provide context for individual accounts. However, in smaller organizations and where participants occupy unique positions, this method can compromise participant anonymity when published versions of the research are accessed by participants. Since this is the case with Acme, and since organizational context is not particularly salient for this analysis, the identity of the participant's organization is sometimes intentionally obscured.

The strength of the second method of recruitment is that it provides access to individuals employed in diverse organizations (from self-employment to multinational corporations) and in a range of occupations (e.g., nanny, house painter, accounting manager). Not surprisingly, drawing from college courses resulted in a group with similar educational backgrounds; all participants from this sample had some college, with 22 percent holding college degrees. Student samples and snowball sampling are not particularly robust in terms of generalizability. They are, nonetheless, regularly employed in qualitative studies (Chen 1999; Connell 1995) when the goal is theory development—as is the case here—rather than theory testing.

The interviews began with general questions about friendships and work relationships and progressed to specific questions about gender relations, sexual harassment, and the policies that seek to address it.[6] Since the main aim of the project was to explore how workplace events are framed as sexual harassment (and as legally bounded or not), the term "sexual harassment" was not introduced by the interviewer until late in the interview.

While the question of the relationship between masculinity and sexual harassment was central, I did not come to the research looking expressly for girl watching. Rather, it surfaced as a theme across several men's interviews in the context of a gender reversal question:

> It's the end of an average day. You get ready for bed and fall to sleep. In what seems only a moment, the alarm goes off. As you awake, you find your body to be oddly out of sorts. . . . To your surprise, you find that you have been transformed into the "opposite sex." Even stranger, no one in your life seems to remember that you were ever any different.

Participants were asked to consider what it would be like to conduct their everyday work life in this transformed state. I was particularly interested in their estimation of the impact it would have on their interactions with coworkers and supervisors. Imagining themselves as the opposite sex, participants were forced to make explicit the operation of gender in their workplace, something they did not do in their initial discussions of a typical workday.

Interestingly, no man discussed girl watching in initial accounts of his work-place. I suspect that they did not consider it to be relevant to a discussion of their average *work* day, even though it became apparent that it was an integral daily activity for some groups of men. It emerged only when men were forced to consider themselves as explicitly gendered workers through the hypothetical question, something they were able initially to elide.[7]

Taking guidance from Glaser and Strauss's (1967) grounded theory and the methodological insights of Dorothy Smith (1990), transcripts were analyzed iteratively and inductively, with the goal of identifying the ideological tropes the speaker used to understand his or her identities, behaviors, and relationships. Theoretical concepts drawn from previous work on the etiology of sexual harassment

(Bowman 1993; Cleveland and Kerst 1993), the construction of masculine identities (Connell 1995, 1987), and sociolegal theories of disputing and legal consciousness (Bumiller 1988; Conley and O'Barr 1998) guided the analysis.

Several related themes emerged and are discussed in the subsequent analysis. First, girl watching appears to function as a form of gendered play among men. This play is productive of masculine identities and premised on a studied lack of empathy with the feminine other. Second, men understand the targeted woman to be an object rather than a player in the game, and she is most often not the intended audience. This obfuscation of a woman's subjectivity, and men's refusal to consider the effects of their behavior, means men are likely to be confused when a woman complains. Thus, the production of masculinity through girl watching, and its compulsory disempathy, may be one factor in gender differences in the labeling of harassment.

Findings: Girl Watching as "Hommo-Sexuality"

[They] had a button on the computer that you pushed if there was a girl who came to the front counter. . . . It was a code and it said "BAFC"—Babe at Front Counter. . . . If the guy in the back looked up and saw a cute girl come in the station, he would hit this button for the other dispatcher to [come] see the cute girl.
—Paula, police officer

In its most serious form, girl watching operates as a targeted tactic of power. The men seem to want everyone—the targeted woman as well as coworkers, clients, and superiors—to know they are looking. The gaze demonstrates their right, as men, to sexually evaluate women. Through the gaze, the targeted woman is reduced to a sexual object, contradicting her other identities, such as that of competent worker or leader. This employment

of the discourse of asymmetrical heterosexuality (i.e., the double standard) may trump a woman's formal organizational power, claims to professionalism, and organizational discourses of rationality (Collinson and Collinson 1989; Gardner 1995; Yount 1991).[8] As research on rape has demonstrated (Estrich 1987), calling attention to a woman's gendered sexuality can function to exclude recognition of her competence, rationality, trustworthiness, and even humanity. In contrast, the overt recognition of a man's (hetero)sexuality is normally compatible with other aspects of his identity; indeed, it is often required (Connell 1995; Heam 1985). Thus, the power of sexuality is asymmetrical, in part, because being seen as sexual has different consequences for women and men.

But when they ogle, gawk, whistle and point, are men always so directly motivated to disempower their women colleagues? Is the target of the gaze also the intended audience? Consider, for example, this account told by Ed, a white, 29-year-old instrument technician.

> When a group of guys goes to a bar or a nightclub and they try to be manly. . . . A few of us always found [it] funny [when] a woman would walk by and a guy would be like, "I can have her." [pause] "Yeah, OK, we want to see it!" [laugh]

In his account—a fairly common one in men's discussions—the passing woman is simply a visual cue for their play. It seems clear that it is a game played by men for men; the woman's participation and awareness of her role seem fairly unimportant.

As Thorne (1993) reminded us, we should not be too quick to dismiss games as "only play." In her study of gender relations in elementary schools, Thorne found play to be a powerful form of gendered social action. One of its "clusters of meaning" most relevant here is that of "dramatic performance." In this, play functions as both a source of fun and a mechanism by which gendered identities, group boundaries, and power relations are (re)produced.

The metaphor of play was strong in Karl's comments. Karl, a white man in his early thirties who worked in a technical support role in the Acme engineering department, hoped to earn a degree in engineering. His frustration with his slow progress—which he attributed to the burdens of marriage and fatherhood—was evident throughout the interview. Karl saw himself as an undeserved outsider in his department and he seemed to delight in telling on the engineers.

Girl watching came up as Karl considered the gender reversal question. Like many of the men I interviewed, his first reaction was to muse about premenstrual syndrome and clothes. When I inquired about the potential social effects of the transformation (by asking him, Would it "be easier dealing with the engineers or would it be harder?") he haltingly introduced the engineers' "game."

KARL: Some of the engineers here are very [pause] they're not very, how shall we say? [pause] What's the way I want to put this? They're not very, uh [pause] what's the word? Um. It escapes me.
RESEARCHER: Give me a hint?
KARL: They watch women but they're not very careful about getting caught.
RESEARCHER: Oh! Like they ogle?
KARL: Ogle or gaze or [pause] stare even, or [pause] generate a commotion of an unusual nature.

His initial discomfort in discussing the issue (with me, I presume) is evident in his excruciatingly formal and hesitant language. The aspect of play, however, came through clearly when I pushed him to describe what generating a commotion looked like: " 'Oh! There goes so-and-so. Come and take a look! She's wearing this great outfit today!' Just like a schoolboy. They'll rush out of their offices and [cranes his neck] and check things

out." That this is a form of play was evident in Karl's boisterous tone and in his reference to schoolboys. This is not a case of an aggressive sexual appraising of a woman coworker but a commotion created for the benefit of other men.

At Acme, several spatial factors facilitated this form of girl watching. First, the engineering department is designed as an open-plan office with partitions at shoulder height, offering a maze-like geography that encourages group play. As Karl explained, the partitions offer both the opportunity for sight and cover from being seen. Although its significance escaped me at the time, I was directly introduced to the spatial aspects of the engineers' game of girl watching during my first day on site at Acme. That day, John, the current human resources director, gave me a tour of the facilities, walking me through the departments and offering informal introductions. As we entered the design engineering section, a rhythm of heads emerged from its landscape of partitions, and movement started in our direction. I was definitely aware of being on display as several men gave me obvious once-overs.

Second, Acme's building features a grand stairway that connects the second floor—where the engineering department is located—with the lobby. The stairway is enclosed by glass walls, offering a bird's eye view to the main lobby and the movements of visitors and the receptionists (all women). Robert, a senior design engineer, specifically noted the importance of the glass walls in his discussion of the engineers' girl watching.

> There's glass walls around the upstairs right here by the lobby. So when there's an attractive young female . . . someone will see the girl in the area and they will go back and inform all the men in the area. "Go check it out." [laugh] So we'll walk over to the glass window, you know, and we'll see who's down there.

One day near the end of my stay at Acme, I was reminded of his story as I ventured into the first-floor reception area. Looking up, I saw Robert and another man standing at the top of the stairs watching and commenting on the women gathered around the receptionist's desk. When he saw me, Robert gave me a sheepish grin and disappeared from sight.

PRODUCING MASCULINITY

I suggest that girl watching in this form functions simultaneously as a form of play and as a potentially powerful site of gendered social action. Its social significance lies in its power to form identities and relationships based on these common practices for, as Cockbur (1983, 123) has noted, "patriarchy is as much about relations between man and man as it is about relations between men and women." Girl watching works similarly to the sexual joking that Johnson (1988) suggested is a common way for heterosexual men to establish intimacy among themselves.

In particular, girl watching works as a dramatic performance played to other men, a means by which a certain type of masculinity is produced and heterosexual desire displayed. It is a means by which men assert a masculine identity to other men, in an ironic "hommo-sexual" practice of heterosexuality (Butler 1990).[9] As Connell (1995) and others (Butler 1990; West and Zimmerman 1987) have aptly noted, masculinity is not a static identity but rather one that must constantly be reclaimed. The content of any performance—and there are multiple forms—is influenced by a hegemonic notion of masculinity. When asked what "being a man" entailed, many of the men and women I interviewed triangulated toward notions of strength (if not in muscle, then in character and job performance), dominance, and a marked sexuality, overflowing and uncontrollable to some degree and natural to the male "species."

Heterosexuality is required, for just as the label "girl" questions a man's claim to masculine power, so does the label "fag" (Hopkins 1992; Pronger 1992). I asked Karl, for example, if he would consider his sons "good men" if they were gay. His response was laced with ambivalence; he noted only that the question was "a tough one."

The practice of girl watching is just that—a practice—one rehearsed and performed in everyday settings. This aspect of rehearsal was evident in my interview with Mike, a self-employed house painter who used to work construction. In locating himself as a born-again Christian, Mike recounted the girl watching of his fellow construction workers with contempt. Mike was particularly disturbed by a man who brought his young son to the job site one day. The boy was explicitly taught to catcall, a practice that included identifying the proper targets: women and effeminate men.

Girl watching, however, can be somewhat tenuous as a masculine practice. In their acknowledgment (to other men) of their supposed desire lies the possibility that in being too interested in women the players will be seen as mere schoolboys giggling in the playground. Taken too far, the practice undermines rather than supports a masculine performance. In Karl's discussion of girl watching, for example, he continually came back to the problem of men's not being careful about getting caught. He referred to a particular group of men who, though "their wives are [pause] very attractive—very much so," still "gawk like schoolboys." Likewise, Stephan explained that men who are obvious, who "undress [women] with their eyes" probably do so "because they don't get enough women in their lives. Supposedly." A man must be interested in women, but not too interested; they must show their (hetero)sexual interest, but not overly so, for this would be to admit that women have power over them.

THE ROLE OF OBJECTIFICATION
AND (DIS)EMPATHY

As a performance of heterosexuality among men, the targeted woman is primarily an object onto which men's homosocial sexuality is projected. The presence of a woman in any form—embodied, pictorial, or as an image conjured from words—is required, but her subjectivity and active participation is not. To be sure, given the ways the discourse of asymmetrical sexuality works, men's actions may result in similarly negative effects on the targeted woman as that of a more direct form of sexualization. The crucial difference is that the men's understanding of their actions differs. This difference is one key to understanding the ambiguity around interpreting harassing behavior.

When asked about the engineers' practice of neck craning, Robert grinned, saying nothing at first. After some initial discussion, I started to ask him if he thought women were aware of their game ("Do you think that the women who are walking by . . . ?"). He interrupted, misreading my question. What resulted was a telling description of the core of the game:

> It depends. No. I don't know if they enjoy it. When I do it, if I do it, I'm not saying that I do. [big laugh] . . . If they do enjoy it, they don't say it. If they don't enjoy it—wait a minute, that didn't come out right. I don't know if they enjoy it or not [pause]; that's not the purpose of us popping our heads out.

Robert did not want to admit that women might not enjoy it ("that didn't come out right") but acknowledged that their feelings were irrelevant. Only subjects, not objects, take pleasure or are annoyed. If a woman did complain, Robert thought "the guys wouldn't know what to say." In her analysis of street harassment, Gardner (1995, 187) found a similar absence, in that "men's interpretations seldom mentioned a woman's reaction, either guessed at or observed."

The centrality of objectification was also apparent in comments made by José, a Hispanic man in his late 40s who worked in manufacturing. For José, the issue came up when he considered the topic of compliments. He initially claimed that women enjoy compliments more than men do. In reconsidering, he remembered girl watching and the importance of intent.

> There is [pause] a point where [pause] a woman can be admired by [pause] a pair of eyes, but we're talking about "that look." Where, you know, you're admiring her because she's dressed nice, she's got a nice figure, she's got nice legs. But then you also have the other side. You have an animal who just seems to undress you with his eyes and he's just [pause], there's those kind of people out there too.

What is most interesting about this statement is that in making the distinction between merely admiring and an animal look that ravages, José switched subject position. He spoke in the second person when describing both forms of looking, but his consistency in grammar belies a switch in subjectivity: you (as a man) admire, and you (as a woman) are undressed with his eyes. When considering an appropriate, complimentary gaze, José described it from a man's point of view; the subject who experiences the inappropriate, violating look, however, is a woman. Thus, as in Robert's account, José acknowledged that there are potentially different meanings in the act for men and women. In particular, to be admired in a certain way is potentially demeaning for a woman through its objectification.

The switch in subject position was also evident in Karl's remarks. Karl mentioned girl watching while imagining himself as a woman in the gender reversal question. As he took the subject position of the woman watched rather than the man watching, his understanding of the act as a harmless game was destabilized. Rather than taking pleasure in being the object of such attention, Karl would take pains to avoid it.

So with these guys [if I were a woman], I would probably have to be very concerned about my attire in the lab. Because in a lot of cases, I'm working at a bench and I'm hunched over, in which case your shirt, for example, would open at the neckline, and I would just have to be concerned about that.

Thus, because the engineers girl watch, Karl feels that he would have to regulate his appearance if he were a woman, keeping the men from using him in their game of girl watching. When he considered the act from the point of view of a man, girl watching was simply a harmless antic and an act of appreciation. When he was forced to consider the subject position of a woman, however, girl watching was something to be avoided or at least carefully managed.

When asked to envision himself as a woman in his workplace, like many of the individuals I interviewed, Karl believed that he did not "know how to be a woman." Nonetheless, he produced an account that mirrored the stories of some of the women I interviewed. He knew the experience of girl watching could be quite different—in fact, threatening and potentially disempowering—for the woman who is its object. As such, the game was something to be avoided. In imagining themselves as women, the men remembered the practice of girl watching. None, however, were able to comfortably describe the game of girl watching from the perspective of a woman and maintain its (masculine) meaning as play.

In attempting to take up the subject position of a woman, these men are necessarily drawing on knowledge they already hold. If men simply "don't get it"—truly failing to see the harm in girl watching or other more serious acts of sexual harassment—then they should not be able to see this harm when envisioning themselves as women. What the interviews reveal is that many men—most of whom failed to see the harm of many acts that would constitute the hostile work environment form of sexual harassment—did in fact understand the harm of these acts when forced to consider the position of the targeted woman.

I suggest that the gender reversal scenario produced, in some men at least, a moment of empathy. Empathy, Schwalbe (1992) argued, requires two things. First, one must have some knowledge of the other's situation and feelings. Second, one must be motivated to take the position of the other. What the present research suggests is that gender differences in interpreting sexual harassment stem not so much from men's not getting it (a failure of the first element) but from a studied, often compulsory, lack of motivation to identify with women's experiences.

In his analysis of masculinity and empathy, Schwalbe (1992) argued that the requirements of masculinity necessitate a "narrowing of the moral self." Men learn that to effectively perform masculinity and to protect a masculine identity, they must, in many instances, ignore a woman's pain and obscure her viewpoint. Men fail to exhibit empathy with women because masculinity precludes them from taking the position of the feminine other, and men's moral stance vis-à-vis women is attenuated by this lack of empathy.

As a case study, Schwalbe (1992) considered the Thomas-Hill hearings, concluding that the examining senators maintained a masculinist stance that precluded them from giving serious consideration to Professor Hill's claims. A consequence of this masculine moral narrowing is that "charges of sexual harassment . . . are often seen as exaggerated or as fabricated out of misunderstanding or spite" (Schwalbe 1992, 46). Thus, gender differences in interpreting sexually harassing behaviors may stem more from acts of ignoring than states of ignorance.

THE PROBLEM WITH GETTING CAUGHT

But are women really the untroubled objects that girl watching—viewed through the eyes of men—suggests? Obviously not; the game may be premised on a denial of a woman's subjectivity, but an actual erasure is beyond men's power! It is in this multiplicity of subjectivities, as Butler (1990, ix) noted, where "trouble" lurks, provoked by "the unanticipated agency of a female 'object' who inexplicably returns the glance, reverses the gaze, and contests the place and authority of the masculine position." To face a returned gaze is to get caught, an act that has the power to undermine the logic of girl watching as simply a game among men. Karl, for example, noted that when caught, men are often flustered, a reaction suggesting that the boundaries of usual play have been disturbed.[10]

When a woman looks back, when she asks, "What are you looking at?" she speaks as a subject, and her status as mere object is disturbed. When the game is played as a form of hommosexuality, the confronted man may be baffled by her response. When she catches them looking, when she complains, the targeted woman speaks as a subject. The men, however, understand her primarily as an object, and objects do not object.

The radical potential of sexual harassment law is that it centers women's subjectivity, an aspect prompting Catharine MacKinnon's (1979) unusual hope for the law's potential as a remedy. For men engaged in girl watching, however, this subjectivity may be inconceivable. From their viewpoint, acts such as girl watching are simply games played with objects: women's bodies. Similar to Schwalbe's (1992) insight into the senators' reaction to Professor Hill, the harm of sexual harassment may seem more the result of a woman's complaint (and law's "illegitimate" encroachment into the everyday work world) than men's acts of objectification. For example, in reflecting on the impact of sexual harassment policies in the workplace, José lamented that "back in the '70s, [it was] all peace and love then. Now as things turn around, men can't get away with as much as what they

used to." Just whose peace and love are we talking about?

REACTIONS TO ANTI-SEXUAL HARASSMENT TRAINING PROGRAMS

The role that objectification and disempathy play in men's girl watching has important implications for sexual harassment training. Consider the following account of a sexual harassment training session given in Cindy's workplace. Cindy, an Italian American woman in her early 20s, worked as a recruiter for a small telemarketing company in Southern California.

> [The trainer] just really laid down the ground rules, um, she had some scenarios. Saying, "OK, would you consider this sexual harassment?" "Would you . . ." this, this, this? "What level?" Da-da-da. So, um, they just gave us some real numbers as to lawsuits and cases. Just that "you guys better be careful" type of a thing.

From Cindy's description, this training is fairly typical in that it focuses on teaching participants definitions of sexual harassment and the legal ramifications of accusations. The trainer used the common strategy of presenting videos of potentially harassing situations and asking the participants how they would judge them. Cindy's description of the men's responses to these videos reveals the limitation of this approach.

> We were watching [the TV] and it was [like] a studio audience. And [men] were getting up in the studio audience making comments like "Oh well, look at her! I wouldn't want to do that to her either!" "Well, you're darn straight, look at her!"

Interestingly, the men successfully used the training session videos as an opportunity for girl watching through their public sexual evaluations of the women depicted. In this, the intent of the training session was doubly subverted. The men interpreted scenarios that Cindy found plainly harassing into mere instances of girl watching and sexual (dis)interest. The antiharassment video was ironically transformed into a forum for girl watching, effecting male bonding and the assertion of masculine identities to the exclusion of women coworkers. Also, by judging the complaining women to be inferior as women, the men sent the message that women who complain are those who fail at femininity.

Cindy conceded that relations between men and women in her workplace were considerably strained after the training ("That day, you definitely saw the men bond, you definitely saw the women bond, and there was a definite separation"). The effect of the training session, rather than curtailing the rampant sexual harassment in Cindy's workplace, operated as a site of masculine performance, evoking manly camaraderie and reestablishing gender boundaries.

To be effective, sexual harassment training programs must be grounded in a complex understanding of the ways acts such as girl watching operate in the work-place and the seeming necessity of a culled empathy to some forms of masculinity. Sexually harassing behaviors are produced from more than a lack of knowledge, simple sexist attitudes, or misplaced sexual desire. Some forms of sexually harassing behaviors—such as girl watching—are mechanisms through which gendered boundaries are patrolled and evoked and by which deeply held identities are established. This complexity requires complex interventions and leads to difficult questions about the possible efficacy of any workplace training program mandated in part by legal requirements.

Conclusions

In this analysis, I have sought to unravel the social logic of girl watching and its relationship to the question of gender differences in the interpretation of sexual harassment. In the form analyzed here, girl watching functions simultaneously as only play and as a potent site where power is played. Through the objectification on which it is premised and in the nonempathetic masculinity it supports, this form of girl watching simultaneously produces both the harassment and the barriers to men's acknowledgment of its potential harm.

The implications these findings have for anti-sexual harassment training are profound. If we understand harassment to be the result of a simple lack of knowledge (of ignorance), then straightforward informational sexual harassment training may be effective. The present analysis suggests, however, that the etiology of some harassment lies elsewhere. While they might have quarreled with it, most of the men I interviewed had fairly good abstract understandings of the behaviors their companies' sexual harassment policies prohibited. At the same time, in relating stories of social relations in their workplaces, most failed to identify specific behaviors as sexual harassment when they matched the abstract definition. As I have argued, the source of this contradiction lies not so much in ignorance but in acts of ignoring. Traditional sexual harassment training programs address the former rather than the later. As such, their effectiveness against sexually harassing behaviors born out of social practices of masculinity like girl watching is questionable.

Ultimately, the project of challenging sexual harassment will be frustrated and our understanding distorted unless we interrogate hegemonic, patriarchal forms of masculinity and the practices by which they are (re)produced. We must continue to research the processes by which sexual harassment is produced and the gendered identities and subjectivities on which it poaches (Wood 1998). My study provides a first step toward a more process-oriented understanding of sexual harassment, the ways the social meanings of harassment are constructed, and ultimately, the potential success of antiharassment training programs.

Notes

1. See Welsh (1999) for a review of this literature.
2. For example, Maria, an administrative assistant I interviewed, simultaneously echoed and critiqued this understanding when she complained about her boss's girl watching in her presence: "If he wants to do that in front of other men . . . you know, that's what men do."
3. Recently, more researchers have turned to qualitative studies as a means to understand the process of labeling behavior as harassment. Of note are Collinson and Collinson (1996), Giuffre and Williams (1994), Quinn (2000), and Rogers and Henson (1997).
4. Quid pro quo ("this for that") sexual harassment occurs when a person with organizational power attempts to coerce an individual into sexual behavior by threatening adverse job actions.
5. This sample was not fully representative of the company's employees; male managers (mostly white) and minority manufacturing employees were underrepresented. Thus, the data presented here best represent the attitudes and workplace tactics of white men working in white-collar, technical positions and white and minority men in blue-collar jobs.
6. Acme employees were interviewed at work in an office off the main lobby. Students and referred participants were interviewed at sites convenient to them (e.g., an office, the library).
7. Not all the interviewed men discussed girl watching. When asked directly, they tended to grin knowingly, refusing to elaborate. This silence in the face of direct questioning—by a female researcher—is also perhaps an instance of getting caught.
8. I prefer the term "asymmetrical heterosexuality" over "double standard" because it directly references the dominance of heterosexuality and more accurately reflects the interconnected but different forms of acceptable sexuality for

men and women. As Estrich (1987) argued, it is not simply that we hold men and women to different standards of sexuality but that these standards are (re)productive of women's disempowerment.
9. "Hommo" is a play on the French word for man, *homme.*
10. Men are not always concerned with getting caught, as the behavior of catcalling construction workers amply illustrates; that a woman hears is part of the thrill (Gardner 1995). The difference between the workplace and the street is the level of anonymity the men have vis-à-vis the woman and the complexity of social rules and the diversity of power sources an individual has at his or her disposal.

References

Bernstein, R. 1994. "Guilty if Charged." *New York Review of Books,* January, 13.

Bowman, C. G. 1993. "Street Harassment and the Informal Ghettoization of Women." *Harvard Law Review* 106: 517–80.

Buckwald, A. 1993. "Compliment a Woman, Go to Court." *Los Angeles Times,* October, 28.

Bumiller, K. 1988. *The Civil Rights Society: The Social Construction of Victims.* Baltimore: Johns Hopkins University Press.

Butler, J. 1990. *Gender Trouble: Feminism and the Subversion of Identity.* New York: Routledge.

Chen, A. S. 1999. "Lives at the Center of the Periphery, Lives at the Periphery of the Center: Chinese American Masculinities and Bargaining with Hegemony." *Gender & Society* 13: 584–607.

Cleveland, J. N., and M. E. Kerst. 1993. "Sexual Harassment and Perceptions of Power: An Under-articulated Relationship." *Journal of Vocational Behavior* 42(1): 49–67.

Cockbur, C. 1983. *Brothers: Male Dominance and Technological Change.* London: Pluto Press.

Collinson, D. L., and M. Collinson. 1989. "Sexuality in the Workplace: The Domination of Men's Sexuality." In J. Heam and D. L. Sheppard (eds.), *The sexuality of organizations.* Newbury Park, CA: Sage.

———. 1996. "'It's Only Dick': The Sexual Harassment of Women Managers in Insurance Sales." *Work, Employment & Society* 10(1): 29–56.

Conley, F. K. 1991. "Why I'm Leaving Stanford: I Wanted My Dignity Back." *Los Angeles Times*, June, 9.

Conley, J., and W. O'Barr. 1998. *Just Words*. Chicago: University of Chicago Press.

Connell, R. W. 1987. *Gender and Power*. Stanford, CA: Stanford University Press.

———. 1995. *Masculinities*. Berkeley: University of California Press.

Estrich, S. 1987. *Real Rape*. Cambridge, MA: Harvard University Press.

Garcia, L., L. Milano, and A. Quijano. 1989. "Perceptions of Coercive Sexual Behavior by Males and Females." *Sex Roles* 21(9/10): 569–77.

Gardner, C. B. 1995. *Passing by: Gender and Public Harassment*. Berkeley: University of California Press.

Giuffre, P., and C. Williams. 1994. "Boundary Lines: Labeling Sexual Harassment in Restaurants." *Gender & Society* 8: 378–401.

Glaser, B., and A. L. Strauss. 1967. *The Discovery of Grounded Theory: Strategies for Qualitative Research*. Chicago: Aldine.

Guccione, J. 1992. "Women Judges Still Fighting Harassment." *Daily Journal*, 13 October, 1.

Gutek, B. A., and M. P. Koss. 1993. "Changed Women and Changed Organizations: Consequences of and Coping with Sexual Harassment." *Journal of Vocational Behavior* 42(1): 28–48.

Gutek, B. A., B. Morasch, and A. G. Cohen. 1983. "Interpreting Social-Sexual Behavior in a Work Setting." *Journal of Vocational Behavior* 22(1): 30–48.

Hearn, J. 1985. "Men's Sexuality at Work." In A. Metcalf and M. Humphries (eds.), *The Sexuality of Men*. London: Pluto Press.

Hopkins, P. 1992. "Gender Treachery: Homophobia, Masculinity, and Threatened Identities." In L. May and R. Strikwerda. (eds.), *Rethinking Masculinity: Philosophical Explorations in Light of Feminism*. MD: Littlefield, Adams.

Jensen, I. W., and B. A. Gutek. 1982. "Attributions and Assignment of Responsibility in Sexual Harassment." *Journal of Social Issues* 38(4): 121–36.

Johnson, M. 1988. *Strong Mothers, Weak Wives*. Berkeley: University of California Press.

Kenig, S., and J. Ryan. 1986. "Sex Differences in Levels of Tolerance and Attribution of Blame for Sexual Harassment on a University Campus." *Sex Roles* 15(9/10): 535–49.

MacKinnon, C. A. 1979. *The Sexual Harassment of Working Women*. New Haven, CT: Yale University Press.

Malovich, N. J., and J. E. Stake. 1990. "Sexual Harassment on Campus: Individual Differences in Attitudes and Beliefs." *Psychology of Women Quarterly* 14(1): 63–81.

Murrell, A. J., and B. L. Dietz-Uhler. 1993. "Gender Identity and Adversarial Sexual Beliefs as Predictors of Attitudes Toward Sexual Harassment." *Psychology of Women Quarterly* 17(2): 169–75.

Padgitt, S. C., and J. S. Padgitt. 1986. "Cognitive Structure of Sexual Harassment: Implications for University Policy." *Journal of College Student Personnel* 27: 34–39.

Popovich, P. M., D. N. Gehlauf, J. A. Jolton, J. M. Somers, and R. M. Godinho. 1992. "Perceptions of Sexual Harassment as a Function of Sex of Rater and Incident Form and Consequent." *Sex Roles* 27(11/12): 609–25.

Powell, G. N. 1986. "Effects of Sex-Role Identity and Sex on Definitions of Sexual Harassment." *Sex Roles* 14: 9–19.

Pronger, B. 1992. "Gay Jocks: A Phenomenology of Gay Men in Athletics." In L. May and R. Strikwerda (eds.), *Rethinking Masculinity: Philosophical Explorations in Light of Feminism*. Lanham, MD: Littlefield Adams.

Pryor, J. B. 1987. "Sexual Harassment Proclivities in Men." *Sex Roles* 17(5/6): 269–90.

Quinn, B. A. 2000. "The Paradox of Complaining: Law, Humor, and Harassment in the Everyday Work World." *Law and Social Inquiry* 25(4): 1151–83.

Reilly, M. E., B. Lott, D. Caldwell, and L. DeLuca. 1992. "Tolerance for Sexual Harassment Related to Self-Reported Sexual Victimization." *Gender & Society* 6: 122–38.

Rogers, J. K., and K. D. Henson. 1997. "'Hey, Why Don't You Wear a Shorter Skirt?' Structural Vulnerability and the Organization of Sexual Harassment in Temporary Clerical Employment." *Gender & Society* 11: 215–38.

Schwalbe, M. 1992. "Male Supremacy and the Narrowing of the Moral Self." *Berkeley Journal of Sociology* 37: 29–54.

Smith, D. 1990. *The Conceptual Practices of Power: A Feminist Sociology of Knowledge*. Boston: Northeastern University Press.

Stockdale, M. S. 1993. "The Role of Sexual Misperceptions of Women's Friendliness in an Emerging Theory of Sexual Harassment." *Journal of Vocational Behavior* 42(1): 84–101.

Stockdale, M. S., and A. Vaux. 1993. "What Sexual Harassment Experiences Lead Respondents to Acknowledge Being Sexually Harassed? A Secondary Analysis of a University Survey." *Journal of Vocational Behavior* 43(2): 221–34.

Tagri, S., and S. M. Hayes. 1997. "Theories of Sexual Harassment." In W. O'Donohue (ed.), *Sexual Harassment: Theory, Research and Treatment.* New York: Allyn & Bacon.

Thorne, B. 1993. *Gender Play: Girls and Boys in School.* Buckingham, UK: Open University Press.

U.S. Merit Systems Protection Board. 1988. *Sexual Harassment in the Federal Government: An Update.* Washington, DC: Government Printing Office.

Welsh, S. 1999. Gender and Sexual Harassment. *Annual Review of Sociology* 1999: 169–90.

West, C., and D. H. Zimmerman. 1987. "Doing gender." *Gender & Society* 1: 125–51.

Wood, J. T. 1998. "Saying Makes It So: The Discursive Construction of Sexual Harassment." In S. G. Bingham (ed.), *Conceptualizing Sexual Harassment as Discursive Practice.* Westport, CT: Praeger.

York, K. M. 1989. "Defining Sexual Harassment in Workplaces: A Policy-Capturing Approach." *Academy of Management Journal* 32: 830–50.

Yount, K. R. 1991. "Ladies, Flirts, Tomboys: Strategies for Managing Sexual Harassment in an Underground Coal Mine." *Journal of Contemporary Ethnography* 19: 396–422.

Questions

1. On the face of it, "girl watching" is about the "girls." Based on what you've read in this article, what role do women play in the process?

2. For men, what are the functions of "girl watching"? Does "girl watching" have any functions for the women who are watched?

3. Quinn suggests that "doing" masculinity sometimes requires the "narrowing of the moral compass." What did she mean? In what ways do men do masculinity without narrowing the moral compass?
   Can you think of any ways in which women must narrow their moral compass in order to do femininity?

13

THE GIRL HUNT: URBAN NIGHTLIFE AND THE PERFORMANCE OF MASCULINITY

David Grazian

This article continues the theme explored in the Quinn article on "Girl Watching." David Grazian explores the dynamics of male gender performance, by focusing on how young males interact with women and each other in order to prove themselves as men.

From Chicago's jazz cabarets to New York's gay discos to Las Vegas's strip clubs, sexualized environments have historically defined downtown zones of urban nightlife (Bernstein 2001; Chatterton and Hollands 2003; Chauncey 1994; Kenney 1993; Owen 2003). Hot nightclubs and cool lounges enforce sexualized norms of dress and body adornment and invite flirtation, innuendo, and physical contact among patrons engaged in rituals of courtship. Nightspots also rely on the attractiveness of service staff and the promise of eroticized interaction to recruit customers (Allison 1994; Lloyd 2005; Spradley and Mann 1975), while sexual relations among staff are frequently the norm (Giuffre and Williams 1994). Moreover, young urbanites identify downtown clusters of nightclubs as *direct sexual marketplaces,* or markets for singles seeking casual encounters with potential sex partners (Laumann et al. 2004).

Direct all correspondence to David Grazian, Department of Sociology, 290 McNeil Building, 3718 Locust Walk, University of Pennsylvania, Philadelphia, PA 19104-6299; *email:* dgrazian@soc.upenn.edu.

David Grazian, "The Girl Hunt: Urban Nightlife and the Performance of Masculinity as Collective Activity," *Symbolic Interaction*, Vol. 30, Issue 2 (Spring 2007): 221–243 © 2007 by the Society for the Study of Symbolic Interaction. All rights reserved. Reprinted by permission of John Wiley & Sons, Inc.

For these reasons, scenes of urban nightlife serve as particularly fitting sites for observing how men and women enact gender as a routine accomplishment in everyday life (West and Zimmerman 1987). In this article I examine girl hunting—a practice whereby adolescent heterosexual men aggressively seek out female sexual partners in nightclubs, bars, and other public arenas of commercialized entertainment. Recent sociological studies of sexual behavior analyze courtship patterns in relatively normative terms, concentrating on the logistics of sex partnering and mate selection in cities (Laumann et al. 2004). In contrast, in this article I wish to emphasize the more performative nature of contemporary flirtation rituals by examining how male-initiated games of heterosexual pursuit function as strategies of impression management in which young men sexually objectify women to heighten their own performance of masculinity. While we typically see public sexual behavior as an interaction between *individuals,* I illustrate how these rituals operate as collective and homosocial *group* activities conducted in the company of men.

The Performance of Masculinity as Collective Activity

According to the symbolic interactionist perspective, masculinity represents a range of dramaturgical performances individuals exhibit through face-to-face interaction (Goffman 1959, 1977; West and Zimmerman 1987). Like femininity, masculinity is not innate but an accomplishment of human behavior that appears natural because gendered individuals adhere to an institutionalized set of myths they learn through everyday interactions and encounters, and thus accept as social reality (Goffman 1977; West and Zimmerman 1987). Throughout their formative years and beyond, young men are encouraged by their parents, teachers, coaches, and peers to adopt a socially constructed vision of manhood, a set of cultural beliefs that prescribe what men ought to be like: physically strong, powerful, independent, self-confident, efficacious, dominant, active, persistent, responsible, dependable, aggressive, courageous, and sexually potent (Donaldson 1993; Messner 2002; Mishkind et al. 1986). In the fantasies of many boys and men alike, a relentless competitive spirit, distant emotional detachment, and an insatiable heterosexual desire, all commonly (but not exclusively) displayed by the sexual objectification of women (Bird 1996), characterize idealized masculinity.

Essentialist visions of masculinity obscure how both women and men resist, challenge, and renegotiate the meanings surrounding masculinity and femininity in their everyday lives (Chapkis 1986; Connell 1987, 1992, 1993, 1995; Connell and Messerschmidt 2005; Donaldson 1993; Hollander 2002). The inevitable disconnect between dominant expectations of normative masculinity, on the one hand, and actualized efforts at what West and Zimmerman (1987) refer to as "doing gender" as a dramaturgical performance, on the other, presents a challenging problem for

men, particularly because "the number of men rigorously practicing the hegemonic pattern in its entirety may be quite small" (Connell 1995:79). It is an especially acute dilemma for young men of college age (18–25) who, as "emerging adults" (Arnett 1994, 2000), display many of the physical traits of early adulthood along with the emotional immaturity, diminutive body image, and sexual insecurities of late adolescence (Mishkind et al. 1986).

The competitive ritual of *girl hunting* epitomizes this dilemma, as heterosexual adolescent males aggressively seek out female sexual partners in dance clubs, cocktail lounges, and other public arenas of commercialized entertainment in the city at night. While courtship rituals are by no means confined to nightlife settings—as evidenced by the relatively large numbers of romantic couples who meet through work and school (Michael et al. 1995:72)—in American culture, bars and nightclubs are widely considered more normative environments for actively pursuing anonymous sexual partners in a strategic manner (Laumann et al. 2004). In contrast to occupational and educational domains in which masculine power can be signaled by professional success and intellectual superiority, sexual prowess is a primary signifier of masculinity in the context of urban nightlife.[1] Indeed, the importance placed on competitive "scoring" (Messner 2002) among men in the highly gendered universe of cocktail lounges and singles bars should not be underestimated.

However, a wealth of data suggests that, contrary to representations of urban nightlife in popular culture, such as Candace Bushnell's novel *Sex and the City* ([1996] 2001) and its HBO television spin-off, rumors of the proverbial one-night stand have been greatly exaggerated (Williams 2005). According to the National Health and Social Life Survey, relatively few men (16.7 percent) and even fewer women (5.5 percent) report engaging in sexual activity with a member of the opposite sex within two days of meeting them (Laumann et al. 1994:239).[2] About 90 percent of women aged eighteen to forty-four report that they find having sex with a stranger unappealing (Laumann et al. 1994:163–65). Findings from the Chicago Health and Social Life Survey demonstrate that, across a variety of city neighborhood types, typically less than one-fifth of heterosexual adults aged eighteen to fifty-nine report having met their most recent sexual partner in a bar, nightclub, or dance club (Mahay and Laumann 2004:74).[3]

Moreover, the efficacy of girl hunting is constrained by women's ability to resist unwanted sexual advances in public, as well as to initiate their own searches for desirable sex partners. Whereas the ideological basis of girl hunting stresses vulnerability, weakness, and submissiveness as conventional markers of femininity, young women commonly challenge these stereotypes by articulating their own physical strength, emotional self-reliance, and quick wit during face-to-face encounters with men (Duneier and Molotch 1999; Hollander 2002; Paules 1991; Snow et al. 1991).

For all these reasons, girl hunting would not seem to serve as an especially efficacious strategy for locating sexual partners, particularly when compared with other methods (such as meeting through mutual friends, colleagues, classmates, or other trusted third parties; common participation in an educational or recreational activity; or shared membership in a civic or religious organization). In fact, the statistical rareness of the one-night stand may help explain why successful lotharios are granted such glorified status and prestige among their peers in the first place (Connell and Messerschmidt 2005:851). But if this is the case, then why do adolescent men persist in hassling women in public through aggressive sexual advances and pickup attempts (Duneier and Molotch 1999; Snow et al. 1991; Whyte 1988), particularly when their chances of meeting sex partners in this manner are so slim?

I argue that framing the question in this manner misrepresents the actual sociological behavior represented by the girl hunt, particularly since adolescent males do not necessarily engage in girl hunting to generate sexual relationships, even on a drunken short-term basis. Instead, three counterintuitive attributes characterize the girl hunt. First, the girl hunt is as much *ritualistic and performative* as it is utilitarian—it is a social drama through which young men perform their interpretations of manhood. Second, as demonstrated by prior studies (Martin and Hummer 1989; Polk 1994; Sanday 1990; Thorne and Luria 1986), girl hunting is not always a purely heterosexual pursuit but can also take the form of an inherently *homosocial* activity. Here, one's male peers are the intended audience for competitive games of sexual reputation and peer status, public displays of situational dominance and rule transgression, and in-group rituals of solidarity and loyalty. Finally, the emotional effort and logistical deftness required by rituals of sexual pursuit (and by extension the public performance of masculinity itself) encourage some young men to seek out safety in numbers by participating in the girl hunt as a kind of *collective* activity, in which they enjoy the social and psychological resources generated by group cohesion and dramaturgical teamwork (Goffman 1959). Although tales of sexual adventure traditionally feature a single male hero, such as Casanova, the performance of heterosexual conquest more often resembles the exploits of the dashing Christian de Neuvillette and his better-spoken co-conspirator Cyrano de Bergerac (Rostand 1897). By aligning themselves with similarly oriented accomplices, many young men convince themselves of the importance and efficacy of the girl hunt (despite its poor track record), summon the courage to pursue their female targets (however clumsily), and assist one another in "mobilizing masculinity" (Martin 2001) through a collective performance of gender and heterosexuality.

In this article, I focus on the ritual of girl hunting to analyze how heterosexual young men perform masculinity as a collective activity in the context of urban nightlife. Drawing on their self-reported narrative accounts, I document how these young men employ a set of collective "hunting" strategies designed to (1) reinforce what I call "the myth of the pickup" and other dominant expectations of masculine behavior; (2) boost confidence in one's performance of masculinity and heterosexual power; and (3) assist in the performance of masculinity in the presence of women. I am not suggesting that the presentation of a masculine self and its attendant peer status serves as the *only* desired or stated purpose or outcome of the girl hunt, as this activity is also clearly motivated by physical and romantic pleasure seeking (Collins 2004). It is also not my intention to suggest that all young men follow the protocols of girl hunting as collective activity in their sexual pursuits. Rather, in this article I wish to illustrate how groups of young heterosexual men employ the power of collective rituals of homosociality to perform heterosexual competence and masculine identity in the public context of urban nightlife, and to show how these rituals reproduce structures of inequality *within* as well as *across* the socially constructed gender divide between women and men.

Methods and Data

I draw on firsthand narrative accounts provided by 243 heterosexual male college students attending the University of Pennsylvania, an Ivy League research university situated in Philadelphia. These data represent part of a larger study involving approximately 600 college students (both men and women). The study was conducted at Penn among all students enrolled in one of two semester terms of a sociology course on media and popular culture taught by me during the 2003–4 academic year.[4] Respondents were directed to

explore Philadelphia's downtown nightlife by attending at least one nightlife entertainment venue (i.e., restaurant, café, dance club, sports bar, cocktail lounge) located in Philadelphia's Center City district for the duration of a few evening hours' time. They were encouraged to select familiar sites where they would feel both comfortable and safe and were permitted to choose whether to conduct their outing alone or with one or more friends, relatives, intimates, or acquaintances of either gender.

Upon the conclusion of their evening, students were instructed to document their experiences in detailed narrative accounts. Although some of the materials I assigned during the course address the elaborated performance of masculinity in public (i.e., Bissinger 1990; Geertz 1973; Grazian 2003; Grindstaff 2002), students were not necessarily expected to address these themes or issues in their accounts. After submitting their typed narrative accounts electronically to a team of research assistants (who in turn read them to ensure that each adhered to proper standards of protocol), the respondents' names were removed from their submissions to protect their anonymity. These accounts were then forwarded to me; I assigned them individual case numbers and systematically coded and analyzed them separately on the basis of gender.[5] An initial read-through of accounts submitted by my male respondents revealed recurring commonalities, including a pronounced goal of seeking out young women as potential sexual and romantic partners, and an ambitiously strategic orientation toward this end. Subsequent coding of these accounts highlighted the importance of collective behavior (including the ritualistic consumption of alcohol), a codependent reliance on one's peer group, and the deployment of team-oriented strategies deemed necessary for approaching women in public.[6]

The original sample of 243 heterosexual male students consists of 21.4 percent (n = 52) freshman, 36.6 percent (n = 89) sophomores, 21.8 percent (n = 53) juniors, and 20.2 percent (n = 49) seniors. Participants ranged from 18 to 24 years of age, with a mean age of 19.9 years. Reflecting the privileged social status of Ivy League university students, the racial and ethnic makeup of the sample is as follows: 78.2 percent (n = 190) white, 11.5 percent (n = 28) Asian, 4.5 percent (n = 11) non-Hispanic black, 2.9 percent (n = 7) Hispanic, and 2.9 percent (n = 7) mixed race/other.[7] Recent available statistics (*U.S. News and World Report* 2005) estimate the proportion of minority students at the University of Pennsylvania at 17 percent Asian, 6 percent black, and 5 percent Hispanic. In terms of residence prior to college, nearly three-quarters (70 percent) of the sample lived in suburban areas, while about one-quarter hailed from urban environments (26.3 percent) and the rest from rural areas (3.7 percent). Likewise, nearly three-quarters of the sample (70.4 percent) resided in the northeastern United States, with the rest closely divided among the Midwest (5.3 percent), South (9.1 percent), West (10.7 percent), and eight countries outside the United States (3.7 percent).[8]

STUDYING COLLEGE MEN

Because young people are likely to self-consciously experiment with styles of public behavior (Arnett 1994, 2000), observing undergraduates can help researchers understand how young heterosexual men socially construct masculinity through gendered interaction rituals in the context of everyday life. But just as there is not one single mode of masculinity but many *masculinities* available to young men, respondents exhibited a variety of socially recognizable masculine roles in their accounts, including the doting boyfriend, dutiful son, responsible escort, and perfect gentleman. In the interests of exploring the girl hunt as *one among many types* of social orientation toward the city at night, the findings discussed here represent only the accounts of those heterosexual young men whose accounts revealed commonalities relevant to the girl hunt, as outlined above.

These accounts represent about one-fifth of those submitted by my 243 hetero-sexual male respondents. While this subgroup comprises a substantial portion of the sample, the findings it suggests by no means represents the behaviors of *all* my students, and this should not be surprising. As Connell (1995), Messner (2002), and others argue, the dominance of hegemonic masculinity is often sustained by the aggressive actions of a minority within a context of normative complicity by a more or less "silent majority" of men who nevertheless benefit from the subordination and sexual objectification of women. Insofar as the ritual of the girl hunt symbolizes a celebrated form of hegemonic masculinity, it is therefore imperative that we examine how it is practiced in the context of everyday life, even if its proponents and their activities represent only one of many possibilities within the constellation of masculine performances and sexual identities available to men. As Connell and Messerschmidt (2005:850) observe, hegemonic masculinities are "to a significant degree constituted in men's interaction with women." Accordingly, examining how girl hunting is accomplished can help clarify how group interactions link gender ideologies to everyday social behavior.

To ensure informants' anonymity and confidentiality, I have assigned pseudonyms to all persons. However, I have identified all respondents by their reported age, school year, and racial and ethnic background.

The Girl Hunt and the Myth of the Pickup

As I argue above, it is statistically uncommon for men to successfully attract and "pick up" female sexual partners in bars and nightclubs. However, as suggested by a wide selection of mass media—from erotic films to hardcore pornography—heterosexual young men nevertheless sustain fantasies of successfully negotiating chance sexual encounters with anonymous strangers in urban public spaces (Bech 1998), especially dance clubs, music venues, singles bars, cocktail lounges, and other nightlife settings. According to Aaron, a twenty-one-year-old mixed-race junior:

> I am currently in a very awkward, sticky, complicated and bizarre relationship with a young lady here at Penn, where things are pretty open right now, hopefully to be sorted out during the summer when we both have more time. So my mentality right now is to go to the club with my best bud and seek out the ladies for a night of great music, adventure and female company off of the grounds of campus.

Young men reproduce these normative expectations of masculine sexual prowess—what I call *the myth of the pickup*—collectively through homosocial group interaction. According to Brian, a nineteen-year-old Cuban sophomore:

> Whether I would get any girl's phone number or not, the main purpose for going out was to try to get with hot girls. That was our goal every night we went out to frat parties on campus, and we all knew it, even though we seldom mention that aspect of going out. *It was implicitly known that tonight, and every night out, was a girl hunt.* Tonight, we were taking that goal to Philadelphia's nightlife. In the meanwhile, we would have fun drinking, dancing, and joking around. (emphasis added)

For Brian and his friends, the "girl hunt" articulates a shared orientation toward public interaction in which the group collectively negotiates the city at night. The heterosexual desire among men for a plurality of women (hot *girls*, as it were) operates at the individual and group level. As in game hunting, young men frequently evaluate their erotic prestige in terms of their raw number of sexual conquests, like so many notches on a belt. Whereas traditional norms of feminine desire privilege the search for a singular and specified romantic interest (Prince Charming, Mr. Right, or his less attractive cousin, Mr.

Right Now), heterosexual male fantasies idealize the pleasures of an endless abundance and variety of anonymous yet willing female sex partners (Kimmel and Plante 2005).

Despite convincing evidence to the contrary (Laumann et al. 2004), these sexual fantasies seem deceptively realizable in the context of urban nightlife. To many urban denizens, the city and its never-ending flow of anonymous visitors suggests a sexualized marketplace governed by transactional relations and expectations of personal noncommitment (Bech 1998), particularly in downtown entertainment zones where nightclubs, bars, and cocktail lounges are concentrated. The density of urban nightlife districts and their tightly packed venues only intensifies the pervasive yet improbable male fantasy of successfully attracting an imaginary surplus of amorous single women.

Adolescent men strengthen their belief in this fantasy of the sexual availability of women in the city—the myth of the pickup—through collective reinforcement in their conversations in the hours leading up to the girl hunt. While hyping their sexual prowess to the group, male peers collectively legitimize the myth of the pickup and increase its power as a model for normative masculine behavior. According to Dipak, an eighteen-year-old Indian freshman:

> I finished up laboratory work at 5:00 pm and walked to my dormitory, eagerly waiting to "hit up a club" that night. . . . I went to eat with my three closest friends at [a campus dining hall]. We acted like high school freshmen about to go to our first mixer. We kept hyping up the night and saying we were going to meet and dance with many girls. Two of my friends even bet with each other over who can procure the most phone numbers from girls that night. Essentially, the main topic of discussion during dinner was the night yet to come.

Competitive sex talk is common in male homosocial environments (Bird 1996) and often acts as a catalyst for sexual pursuit among groups of adolescent and young adult males. For example, in his ethnographic work on Philadelphia's black inner-city neighborhoods, Anderson (1999) documents how sex codes among youth evolve in a context of peer pressure in which young black males "run their game" by women as a means of pursuing in-group status. Moreover, this type of one-upmanship heightens existing heterosexual fantasies and the myth of the pickup while creating a largely unrealistic set of sexual and gender expectations for young men seeking in-group status among their peers. In doing so, competitive sexual boasting may have the effect of momentarily energizing group participants. However, in the long run it is eventually likely to deflate the confidence of those who inevitably continue to fall short of such exaggerated expectations and who consequently experience the shame of a spoiled masculine identity (Goffman 1963).

Preparing for the Girl Hunt Through Collective Ritual

Armed with their inflated expectations of the nightlife of the city and its opportunities for sexual conquest, young men at Penn prepare for the girl hunt by crafting a specifically gendered and class-conscious nocturnal self (Grazian 2003)—a presentation of masculinity that relies on prevailing fashion cues and upper-class taste emulation. According to Edward, a twenty-year-old white sophomore, these decisions are made strategically:

> I hadn't hooked up with a girl in a couple weeks and I needed to break my slump (the next girl you hook up with is commonly referred to as a "slump-bust" in my social circle). So I was willing to dress in whatever manner would facilitate in hooking up.

Among young college men, especially those living in communal residential settings (i.e., campus dormitories and fraternities),

these preparations for public interaction serve as *collective rituals of confidence building*—shared activities that generate group solidarity and cohesion while elevating the personal resolve and self-assuredness of individual participants mobilizing for the girl hunt. Frank, a nineteen-year-old white sophomore, describes the first of these rituals:

> As I began observing both myself and my friends tonight, I noticed that there is a distinct pre-going-out ritual that takes place. I began the night by blasting my collection of rap music as loud as possible, as I tried to overcome the similar sounds resonating from my roommate's room. Martin seemed to play his music in order to build his confidence. It appears that the entire ritual is simply there to build up one's confidence, to make one more adept at picking up the opposite sex.

Frank explains this preparatory ritual in terms of its collective nature, as friends recount tall tales that celebrate character traits commonly associated with traditional conceptions of masculinity, such as boldness and aggression. Against a soundtrack of rap music—a genre known for its misogynistic lyrics and male-specific themes, including heterosexual boasting, emotional detachment, and masculine superiority (McLeod 1999)—these shared ritual moments of homosociality are a means of generating group resolve and bolstering the self-confidence of each participant. Again, according to Frank:

> Everyone erupted into stories explaining their "high-roller status." Martin recounted how he spent nine hundred dollars in Miami one weekend, while Lance brought up his cousins who spent twenty-five hundred dollars with ease one night at a Las Vegas bachelor party. Again, all of these stories acted as a confidence booster for the night ahead.

Perhaps unsurprisingly, this constant competitive jockeying and one-upmanship so common in male-dominated settings (Martin 2001) often extends to the sexual objectification of women. While getting dressed among friends in preparation for a trip to a local strip club, Gregory, a twenty-year-old white sophomore, reports on the banter: "We should all dress rich and stuff, so we can get us some hookers!" Like aggressive locker-room boasting, young male peers bond over competitive sex talk by laughing about real and make-believe sexual exploits and misadventures (Bird 1996). This joking strengthens male group intimacy and collective heterosexual identity and normalizes gender differences by reinforcing dominant myths about the social roles of men and women (Lyman 1987).

After engaging in private talk among roommates and close friends, young men (as well as women) commonly participate in a more public collective ritual known among American college students as "pregaming." As Harry, an eighteen-year-old white freshman, explains,

> Pregaming consists of drinking with your "boys" so that you don't have to purchase as many drinks while you are out to feel the desired buzz. On top of being cost efficient, the actual event of pregaming can get any group ready and excited to go out.

The ritualistic use of alcohol is normative on college campuses, particularly for men (Martin and Hummer 1989), and students largely describe pregaming as an economical and efficient way to get drunk before going out into the city. This is especially the case for underage students who may be denied access to downtown nightspots. However, it also seems clear that pregaming is a bonding ritual that fosters social cohesion and builds confidence among young men in anticipation of the challenges that accompany the girl hunt. According to Joey, an eighteen-year-old white freshman:

> My thoughts turn to this girl, Jessica. . . . I was thinking about whether or not we might hook up tonight. . . . As I turn to face the door to 301, I feel the handle, and it is shaking from the music and dancing going on in the room.

I open the door and see all my best friends just dancing together. . . . I quickly rush into the center of the circle and start doing my "J-walk," which I have perfected over the years. My friends love it and begin to chant, "Go Joey— it's your birthday." I'm feeling connected with my friends and just know that we're about to have a great night. . . . Girls keep coming in and out of the door, but no one really pays close attention to them. Just as the "pregame" was getting to its ultimate height, each boy had his arms around each other jumping in unison, to a great hip-hop song by Biggie Smalls. One of the girls went over to the stereo and turned the power off. We yelled at her to turn it back on, but the mood was already lost and we decided it was time to head out.

In this example, Joey's confidence is boosted by the camaraderie he experiences in a male-bonding ritual in which women— supposedly the agreed-upon raison d'être for the evening—are ignored or, when they make their presence known, scolded. As these young men dance arm-in-arm with one another, they generate the collective effervescence and sense of social connectedness necessary to plunge into the nightlife of the city. As such, pregaming fulfills the same function as the last-minute huddle (with all hands in the middle) does for an athletic team (Messner 2002).[9] It is perhaps ironic that Joey's ritual of "having fun with my boys" prepares him for the girl hunt (or more specifically in his case, an opportunity to "hook up" with Jessica) even as it requires those boys to exclude their female classmates. At the same time, this men-only dance serves the same function as the girl hunt: it allows its participants to expressively perform hegemonic masculinity through an aggressive display of collective identification. In this sense the pregame resembles other campus rituals of male socialization and boundary maintenance, particularly those associated with fraternity life and violence against women (Boswell and Spade 1996; Martin and Hummer 1989; Sanday 1990).

During similar collective rituals leading up to the girl hunt, young men boost each other's confidence in their abilities of sexual persuasion by watching films about male heterosexual exploits in urban nightlife, such as Doug Liman's *Swingers* (1996), which chronicles the storied escapades of two best friends, Mike and Trent. According to Kevin, an eighteen-year-old white freshman:

> I knew that [my friend] Darryl needed to calm down if he wanted any chance of a second date. At about 8:15 pm, I sat him down and showed him (in my opinion, the movie that every man should see at least once—I've seen it six times)—*Swingers*. . . . Darryl immediately related to Mike's character, the self-conscious but funny gentleman who is still on the rebound from a long-term relationship. At the same time, he took Trent's words for scripture (as I planned): "There's nothing wrong with showing the beautiful babies that you're money and that you want to party." His mind was clearly eased at the thought of his being considered "money." Instead of being too concerned with not screwing up and seeming "weird or desperate," Darryl now felt like he was in control. The three of us each went to our own rooms to get ready.

This collective attention to popular cultural texts helps peer groups generate common cultural references, private jokes, and speech norms as well as build in-group cohesion (Eliasoph and Lichterman 2003; Fine 1977; Swidler 2001).[10] In this case, globally distributed mass-media texts (i.e., films, music recordings and videos, television programs, computer games, comic books) supply audiences with a familiar set of shared discursive strategies and symbolic resources that influence daily social behavior pertaining to gender and sexual expression at a more localized level (Connell and Messerschmidt 2005; Swidler 2001). Similar to the immersion in rap music, the incorporation of collective film viewing into the pregame ritual promotes male group solidarity. But in addition to generating a sense of collective energy, it provides a set of cultural frames useful for making sense of the girl hunt, just as Sanday (1990:129) documents how fraternity brothers habitually watch pornographic films together in their preparations for late-night parties. Of course, *Swingers* represents much tamer fare: yet like pornography, the film encourages the development of a hypermasculine identity while supplying young men with scripts for upcoming social interactions with women, reducing women to infantile objects of sexual desire ("beautiful babies"), generating collective excitement for the girl hunt, and giving young men the self-confidence necessary for competing in such a contest.[11]

Girl Hunting and the Collective Performance of Masculinity

Finally, once the locus of action moves to a more public venue such as a bar or nightclub, the much-anticipated "girl hunt" itself proceeds as a strategic display of masculinity best performed with a suitable game partner. According to Christopher, a twenty-two-year-old white senior, he and his cousin Darren "go out together a lot. We enjoy each other's company and we seem to work well together when trying to meet women." Reporting on his evening at a local dance club, Lawrence, a twenty-one-year-old white junior, illustrates how the girl hunt itself operates as collective activity:

> We walk around the bar area as we finish [our drinks]. After we are done, we walk down to the regular part of the club. We make the rounds around the dance floor checking out the girls. . . . We walk up to the glassed dance room and go in, but leave shortly because it is really hot and there weren't many prospects.

Lawrence and his friends display their elaborated performance of masculinity by making their rounds together as a pack in search of a suitable feminine target. Perhaps it is not sur-prising that the collective nature of their pur-suit should also continue *after* such a prize has been located:

> This is where the night gets really interesting. We walk back down to the main dance floor and stand on the outside looking at what's going on and I see a really good-looking girl behind us standing on the other side of the wall with three friends. After pointing her out to my friends, I decide that I'm going to make the big move and talk to her. So I turn around and ask her to dance. She accepts and walks over. My friends are loving this, so they go off to the side and watch. . . .
>
> After dancing for a little while she brings me over to her friends and introduces me. They tell me that they are all freshman at [a local college], and we go through the whole small talk thing again. I bring her over to my two boys who are still getting a kick out of the whole situation. . . . My boys tell me about some of the girls they have seen and talked to, and they inform me that they recognized some girls from Penn walking around the club.

Why do Lawrence and his dance partner both introduce each other to their friends? Law-rence seems to gain almost as much pleasure from his *friends'* excitement as from his own exploits, just as they are "loving" the vicari-ous thrill of watching their comrade succeed in commanding the young woman's atten-tion, as if their own masculinity is validated by his success.

In this instance, arousal is not merely individual but represents a collectively shared experience as well (Thorne and Luria 1986:181). For these young men the perfor-mance of masculinity does not necessarily require successfully meeting a potential sex partner as long as one enthusiastically par-ticipates in the ritual *motions* of the girl hunt in the company of men. When Lawrence brings over his new female friend, he does so to celebrate his victory with his buddies, and in return, they appear gratified by their

own small victory by association. (And while Lawrence celebrates with them, perhaps he alleviates some of the pressure of actually conversing with her.)

Along these lines, the collective quality of the girl hunt makes each male partici-pant accountable to the group as well as to himself. In this manner, young single men will goad each other on to persist in the hunt, deriding those who turn away poten-tial pickups. Michael, a nineteen-year-old white junior, reports on his evening out at McFadden's, an Irish-themed sports bar and nightclub:

> My friend Buddy beckoned to me from the dance floor. Not knowing what he wanted, I snaked my way through the crowd to join him. As I approached him, a girl several years my senior smiled at me. She looked like she wanted to start a conversation, but waited for me to initiate. Not particularly interested in her and with my friend waiting, I awkwardly moved past with what I am sure was a weird smile on my face. *Buddy had seen this entire exchange and said he was disappointed in me for not trying to hit on her.* (emphasis added)

Through their homosocial encounters, young men make one another accountable for their interactions with women, and their vigilance increases the chances that over time these men will eventually comply with the set of practices that sustain the ideals of hegemonic masculinity, *even in instances when such men disagree with those expectations* (Connell 1995; Demetriou 2001).

As Christopher remarked above on his rela-tionship with his cousin, the collective aspects of the girl hunt also highlight the efficacy of conspiring with peers to meet women: "We go out together a lot. We enjoy each other's company and we seem to work well together when trying to meet women." In the language of the confidence game, men eagerly serve as each other's shills (Goffman 1959; Grazian 2004; Maurer 1940) and sometimes get roped into the role unwittingly with varying degrees of success. Michael continues in his report by describing Buddy's exploits:

Buddy, a twenty-five-year-old University of Pennsylvania alumnus, is the kind of guy who is not afraid to flirt with as many girls as possible. Tonight he was putting his charm to good use, dancing with any girl who would give him the time of day. I realized he had called me over for the purpose of finding a girl for me. Turning to the girl nearest him on dance floor he said to her, "This is my friend Michael. He's a little shy." Waiting for him to introduce me to her, I realized after a moment that he didn't know these girls either. His introduction was actually one of the cheesiest pickup lines I had ever heard used that wasn't the punch line to a joke. I introduced myself to the girl whose name I found out was Rebecca, a twenty-four-year-old professional from South Philly. I talked to her for a few minutes and admitted my true age to her; surprisingly, she didn't blow me off too quickly, but her interest was definitely in Buddy rather than me at that point. Deciding to leave the two of them to get better acquainted, I excused myself to the bar to get a second beer.

In this instance, Michael politely disengages from the interaction without challenging the ideological basis of the girl hunt itself. Rather, his passive performance amounts to what Connell (1995) refers to as "complicit masculinity," insofar as Michael is able to support his friend's interaction and thus benefit from the "patriarchal dividend" (acceptance within a male homosocial group and the status associated with such membership) gained from the promotion of the ideals of hegemonic masculinity as represented by the girl hunt (also see Demetriou 2001).

Among young people, the role of the passive accomplice is commonly referred to in contemporary parlance as a *wingman*. Popularized by the 1986 film *Top Gun*, the term literally refers to the backup fighter pilots who protect the head of a military flying formation by positioning themselves outside and behind

(or on the wing of) the lead aircraft to engage enemy fire when necessary. In recent years, the term has been appropriated to refer to an accomplice who assists a designated leading man in meeting eligible single women, often at costs to his own ability to do the same. In male-oriented popular culture, the wingman has become institutionalized in men's magazines ("*Maxim*'s Wingman Training Manual" 2003), literature documenting young men's real-and-imagined sex lives (i.e., Max 2006; Strauss 2005), and how-to manuals with such dubiously promising titles as *The Guide to Picking Up Girls*. This last text provides a vulgar description of the colloquialism:

Everyone knows what a wingman must do. Your wingman must take the extra girl for you if there are two girls and you want to talk to one of them. The wingman must lay rap on your girl's friend as long as you rap with your girl. It does not matter that the girl's friend may be very ugly. The wingman must do his job at any cost. He must be able to pull his own weight and back you up. Otherwise, your girl may get pulled away by her friend whom your wingman has failed to entertain. (Fischbarg 2002:36)

In public rituals of courtship, the wingman serves multiple purposes: he provides validation of a leading man's trustworthiness, eases the interaction between a single male friend and a larger group of women, serves as a source of distraction for the friend or friends of a more desirable target of affection, can be called on to confirm the wild (and frequently misleading) claims of his partner, and, perhaps most important, helps motivate his friends by building up their confidence. Indeed, men describe the role of the wingman in terms of loyalty, personal responsibility, and dependability, traits commonly associated with masculinity (Martin and Hummer 1989; Mishkind et al. 1986). According to Nicholas, an eighteen-year-old white freshman:

As we were beginning to mobilize ourselves and move towards the dance floor, James noticed Rachel, a girl he knew from Penn who he often told me about as a potential girlfriend. Considering James was seemingly into this girl, Dan and I decided to be good wingmen and entertain Rachel's friend, Sarah.

Hegemonic masculinity is not only expressed by competitiveness but camaraderie as well, and many young men will take their role as a wingman quite seriously and at a personal cost to their relationships with female friends. According to Peter, a twenty-year-old white sophomore:

> "It sounds like a fun evening," I said to Kyle, "but I promised Elizabeth I would go to her date party." I don't like to break commitments. On the other hand, I didn't want to leave Kyle to fend for himself at this club. . . . Kyle is the type of person who likes to pick girls up at clubs. If I were to come see him, I would want to meet other people as well. Having Elizabeth around would not only prevent me from meeting (or even just talking to) other girls, but it would also force Kyle into a situation of having no "wing man."

In the end, Peter takes Elizabeth to a nightclub where, although he *himself* will not be able to meet available women, he will at least be able to assist Kyle in meeting them:

> Behind Kyle, a very attractive girl smiles at me. Yes! Oh, wait. Damnit, Elizabeth's here. . . . "Hey, Kyle," I whisper to him. "That girl behind you just smiled at you. Go talk to her." Perhaps Kyle will have some luck with her. He turns around, takes her by the hand, and begins dancing with her. She looks over at me and smiles again, and I smile back. I don't think Elizabeth noticed. I would have rather been in Kyle's position, but I was happy for him, and I was dancing with Elizabeth, so I was satisfied for the moment.

By the end of the night, as he and Kyle chat in a taxi on the way back to campus, Peter learns that he was instrumental in securing his friend's success in an additional way:

> "So what ever happened with you and that girl?" I ask. "I hooked up with her. Apparently

she's a senior." I ask if she knew he was a freshman. "Oh, yeah. She asked how old you were, though. I said you were a junior. I had to make one of us look older."

Peter's willingness to serve as a wingman demonstrates his complicity in sustaining the ideals of hegemonic masculinity, which therefore allows him to benefit from the resulting "patriarchal dividends"—acceptance as a member of his male homosocial friendship network and its attendant prestige—even when he himself does not personally seek out the sexual rewards of the girl hunt.

In addition, the peer group provides a readily available audience that can provide emotional comfort to all group members, as well as bear witness to any individual successes that might occur. As demonstrated by the preceding examples, young men deeply value the erotic prestige they receive from their conspiratorial peers upon succeeding in the girl hunt. According to Zach, a twenty-year-old white sophomore:

> About ten minutes later, probably around 2:15 am, we split up into cabs again, with the guys in one and the girls in another. . . . This time in the cab, all the guys want to talk about is me hooking up on the dance floor. It turns out that they saw the whole thing. I am not embarrassed; in fact I am proud of myself.

As an audience, the group can collectively validate the experience of any of its members and can also internalize an individual's success as a shared victory. Since, in a certain sense, a successful sexual interaction must be recognized by one's peers to gain status as an in-group "social fact," the group can transform a private moment into a celebrated public event—thereby making it "count" for the male participant and his cohorts.[12]

Of course, as argued above and elsewhere (Laumann et al. 1994) and demonstrated by the sample analyzed here, turning a heterosexual public encounter with a stranger into an immediately consummated sexual episode is a statistical rarity, especially when compared with the overwhelming degree of time, money, effort, and emotion that young men invest in such an enterprise. But if we focus on the *primary* goal of the girl hunt—the performance of normative masculinity—then it becomes clear that the collectivity of the endeavor allows peer group members to successfully enact traditional gender roles even when they ultimately fail at the sexual pursuit itself. Again, the performance of masculinity does not necessarily require *success* at picking up women, just so long as one participates in the endeavor enthusiastically in the company of men.

For instance, Sam, a twenty-two-year-old black senior, observes how one such peer group takes pleasure in one of their member's public rejection at the hands of an unimpressed woman:

> By this time it was around 1:30 am, and the party was almost over. . . . I saw a lot of the guys had their cell phones out while they were talking to the women. I figured the guys were trying to get phone numbers from the girls. So as I walked past one of the guys, I heard him ask a girl for her number. But she just laughed and walked away. That was real funny especially since his friends saw what happened and proceeded to laugh as well.

As young men discover, contrary to popular myths about femininity, it is increasingly uncommon for women to act passively during sexually charged confrontations, even those that may be physically precarious. In such situations, women often resist and challenge the advances of strange men in public through polite refusal or the expression of humor, moral outrage, outright rejection, or physical retaliation (Berk 1977; Hollander 2002; Snow et al. 1991).

Nevertheless, one participant's botched attempt at an ill-conceived pickup can solidify the male group's bonds as much as a successful one. According to Brian, the aforementioned nineteen-year-old Cuban sophomore:

> We had been in the club for a little more than half an hour, when the four of us were standing at the perimeter of the main crowd in the dancing room. It was then when Marvin finished his second Corona and by his body gestures, he let it be known that he was drunk enough and was pumped up to start dancing. He started dancing behind a girl who was dancing in a circle with a few other girls. Then the girl turned around and said "Excuse me!" Henry and I saw what happened. We laughed so hard and made so much fun of him for the rest of the night. I do not think any of us has ever been turned away so directly and harshly as that time.

In this instance, Marvin's abruptly concluded encounter with an unwilling female participant turns into a humorous episode for the rest of his peer group, leaving his performance of masculinity bruised yet intact. Indeed, in his gracelessness Marvin displays an enthusiastic male heterosexuality as emphasized by his drunken attempts to court an unsuspecting target before a complicit audience of his male peers. And as witnesses to his awkward sexual advance, Brian and Henry take pleasure in the incident, as it not only raises *their* relative standing within the group in comparison with Marvin but can also serve as a narrative focus for future "signifying" episodes (or ceremonial exchanges of insults) and other rituals of solidarity characteristic of joking relationships among male adolescents (Lyman 1987:155). Meanwhile, these young men can bask in their collective failure to attract a woman without ever actually challenging the basis of the girl hunt itself: the performance of adolescent masculinity.

In the end, young men may enjoy this performance of masculinity—the hunt itself—even more than the potential romantic or sexual rewards they hope to gain by its successful execution. In his reflections on a missed opportunity to procure the phone number of a law student, Christopher, the aforementioned twenty-two-year-old senior, admits as much: "There's something about the chase that I really like. Maybe I subconsciously neglected to get her number. I am tempted to think that I like the idea of being on the look out for her better than the idea of calling her to go out for coffee." While Christopher's excuse may certainly function as a compensatory face-saving strategy employed in the aftermath of another lonely night (Berk 1977), it might also indicate a possible acceptance of the limits of the girl hunt despite its potential opportunities for male bonding and the public display of adolescent masculinity.

Discussion

A consistent thread in symbolic interactionism concerns how structures of inequality are constituted and reproduced through recurrent patterns of ordinary social interaction. According to Collins (1981:987–88), the very foundations of the macrosocial world and its institutions can be reduced to the agglomeration of everyday face-to-face encounters conducted among humans over time. As he argues, "Strictly speaking, there is no such thing as a 'state,' an 'economy,' a 'culture,' a 'social class.' There are only collections of individual people acting in particular kinds of microsituations." Schwalbe et al. (2000) emphasize how the repetition of "generic processes" such as oppressive othering, identity work, boundary maintenance, and emotion management all contribute to the reproduction of inequality through their frequent deployment in varied social contexts.

Taken in this way, the "girl hunt" is shorthand for a composite of multiple types of collectively initiated interaction rituals capable of reproducing social inequality on the basis of gender. Group-based efforts at "mobilizing masculinity" (Martin 2001) during the pregame, and "girl watching" (Quinn 2002) in the context of nightclub interaction, operate as processes that fabricate gender difference and

male superiority while transforming women into targets of the collective male gaze and objects of sexual desire. By engaging in the "mutually supportive facework" provided by wingmen, would-be suitors reproduce myths of male dominance by cooperatively creating nocturnal selves that "foster impressions of competence and trustworthiness" through strategies of impression management, deception, and guile (Schwalbe et al. 2000:424). Of course, these generic processes occur not merely in a vacuum but within a social setting in which the regularity of sexist banter and asymmetric courtship rituals encourage the replication of such behaviors, along with the continually renewed ideologies of feminine subordination they promote.

But at the same time, it is equally noteworthy that the girl hunt promotes social inequality and subordinate behavior *among men*. Among participants in the girl hunt, the most dominant men enjoy a disproportionate degree of social prestige relative to their competitors, as is the case in other sexual contests (Wright 1995). Competitive sex talk among adolescent peers in the hours leading up to the girl hunt create an unrealistic set of sexual expectations for impressionable young men, particularly those who already suffer from anxiety over their body image and sexual development (Mishkind et al. 1986). Meanwhile, the repetition of collective rituals of masculine identification successfully conditions young men to suppress empathy for females targeted by the girl hunt, just as the training regimes of military and police units serve to diminish feelings of inhibition and fear among cadets (Schwalbe et al. 2000:437). As illustrated in the last section, male peers often rely on the cultural scripts associated with girl hunting to hassle one another to perform masculinity by behaving in ways that seem to counter their actual sexual desires. In the end, the interaction rituals associated with the girl hunt reproduce structures of inequality *within* as well as *across* the socially constructed gender divide between women and men.

Conclusion

In this article, I used the ritual of girl hunting to analyze how young men employ the power of collective rituals of homosociality to perform heterosexual competence and masculine identity in public. Drawing on self-reported narrative accounts, I documented collective strategies young men employ when girl hunting, suggesting that these strategies reinforce dominant myths about masculine behavior, boost confidence in one's performance of masculinity and heterosexual power, and assist in the performance of masculinity in the presence of women. While the presentation of a heteronormative masculine self and its attendant peer status does not necessarily serve as the only desired or stated purpose of the girl hunt, my goal in this article was to isolate and therefore emphasize the *ritualistic, performative,* and *homosocial* features of girl hunting as a *collective* strategy of impression management and mobilizing masculinity.

In emphasizing the collective aspects of girl hunting and the performance of masculinity in urban nightlife, this study follows a consistent thread within sociology that recognizes how rituals of dating and mating occur within specific interpersonal networks in which shared and collective meanings of sexuality are institutionally inscribed in social space (Anderson 1999; Laumann et al. 2004; Liebow 1967; Swidler 2001; Waller 1937). More specifically, this exploration of how men collectively perform gender and heterosexuality builds on more recent symbolic interactionist approaches to homosocial group dynamics, including the maintenance of hegemonic masculinity through homosocial behavior (Bird 1996), the mobilization of masculinities in public (Martin 2001), and the practice of "girl watching" as a collective form of sexual harassment (Quinn 2002). Likewise, this analysis of girl hunting illustrates the efficacy of homosocial rituals of solidarity not only as tools for mobilizing masculinities among men

in the moment but as engines of confidence building for subsequent public encounters.

While girl hunting employs collective group dynamics found in a variety of settings, the social context in which college students participate clearly shapes the collective character of their everyday behaviors, including the performance of adolescent masculinity and the pursuit of casual sex. While by no means "total institutions" (Becker 2003; Goffman 1961), modern American colleges and universities encourage collective behavior through the segregation of persons on the basis of age (as well as other social attributes such as race and class), officially recognized student groups (including fraternities, sororities, and athletic teams), shared residential housing, and the spatial concentration of campus life. As young adults undergoing the slow transition from adolescence to adulthood, college men may be more likely than their elder counterparts to desire the protection of their peers during risky encounters with strangers in public. Meanwhile, as men grow older and gain additional markers of status (i.e., occupational prestige), they may no longer require the pregaming rituals of confidence building once considered necessary preparation for the girl hunt. At the very least, they may replace collegiate forms of "pregaming" with more adult-oriented rituals, such as happy hour cocktails shared with colleagues after work.

The nightlife setting itself also appears to invite a more collective orientation to masculine performance and sexual pursuit than other contexts. Unlike professional settings where formal guidelines and official workplace norms (at least theoretically) censure sexually suggestive talk and behavior (Dellinger and Williams 2002; Quinn 2002), nightlife settings encourage aggressive sexual interaction among participants. As a result, such an environment may prove too intimidating for individuals unprotected by a surrounding peer group. Moreover, nightclubs and singles bars feature open floor plans where populous clusters of anonymous strangers can congregate and mingle, whereas coffeehouses, bookstores, sidewalks, and other public areas conducive to public interaction are less accommodating of large groups of people. In such settings, perhaps we would expect to see men participating in the girl hunt in smaller formations of two and three (the exception being the male "girl-watchers" who line downtown sidewalks during the lunch hour; see Whyte 1988). Future research on girl hunting in alternative public contexts (and among a wider variety of populations) will undoubtedly yield interesting findings about the collective nature of masculine performance and heterosexual pursuit.

Acknowledgments: This research was supported by grants from the University of Pennsylvania Research Foundation, Alice Paul Center for Research on Women and Gender, and the Penn Institute for Urban Research. I gratefully acknowledge Rachelle Brunn, Jan Jaeger, Colette Joyce, Taryn Kudler, Abigail Platten, Georges Reiners, Lindsay Rutherford, Elizabeth Vaquera, and Yuping Zhang for their invaluable research assistance. I also wish to thank Elizabeth Armstrong, Kathleen Bogle, Wayne Brekhus, Meredith Broussard, Keith Brown, Randall Collins, Maria Kefalas, Jennifer Lena, Peggy Reeves Sanday, and the editors and reviewers at *Symbolic Interaction* for their comments on an earlier draft of this article.

Notes

1. Other such signifiers include physical dominance and assertiveness relative to other men, skill at competitive bar games, and a high tolerance for alcohol.
2. The gender discrepancy here may reflect reporting biases, with men overreporting and women underreporting their sexual behavior (Laumann et al. 1994:239n12). For a critique of the National Health and Social Life Survey and the reliability of sex research more generally, see Lewontin 1995.
3. According to the Chicago Health and Social Life Survey, the exception to this statistic is the Mexican community area called "Westside," in which 23 percent of women (but only 19 percent of men) reported having met their most recent partner at a bar, dance club, or nightclub (Mahay and Laumann 2004:81).
4. For inclusion in the sample generated for this article, male students either voluntarily self-identified as heterosexual or else were coded as such from their written narrative accounts (i.e., referenced a female sex partner or generalized heterosexual desire). While it is certainly possible that those coded as heterosexual may *also* engage in homosexual or bisexual practices, this did not preclude them from inclusion in the sample, given the nature of the research question. (In my original pool of 267 eligible male subjects, 4 self-identified as gay and 34 opted not to disclose their sexual orientation; of the latter, 14 were eventually coded as heterosexual, while 20 remained nondescript enough to be removed from the sample.) The lack of data on the experiences of homosexual students is a clear limitation of this study; on the varied performances of gay men in the context of urban nightlife, see Brekhus 2003, Chauncey 1994, and Rupp and Taylor 2003.
5. All names were removed to ensure the anonymity and confidentiality of the participants. However, students were asked to supply basic demographic information (including gender, age, year of school, residence, racial and ethnic origin, and sexual orientation [optional]) to be used as a reference during coding and analysis, which was conducted with the help of NVivo, a qualitative data software package.
6. Of course, since these reports account for only one evening's worth of behavior and experience, I cannot validate whether they accurately characterize the lifestyles of my individual respondents, although peer-led focus groups later conducted among a smaller sample of thirty male respondents uncovered similar findings.
7. Nearly 40 percent of the Asian students in the sample are of Indian descent. While my data analysis did uncover very small differences in consumption patterns among my sample on the basis of race and ethnicity, I could not

detect notable differences relevant to the arguments presented in this article. Nevertheless, for the edification of the reader I identify the ethnoracial background of all participants cited in the rest of the article.

8. Students residing in Philadelphia prior to attending the University of Pennsylvania comprise 8.2 percent of the entire sample, while 22.2 percent hail from within the Commonwealth of Pennsylvania. Of those students from outside the Northeast, a disproportionate number resided in the populous states of California and Florida prior to college. The numbers are rounded off.

9. In this context, the male ritual of jumping in unison to loud music bears a close resemblance to the "circle dance" initiated by fraternity brothers immediately prior to an alleged incident of gang rape, as described in Sanday 1990.

10. Perhaps for this reason, Kevin's narrative account consistently draws on the slang employed by the film's lead characters: "Darryl, our newly decreed 'money' friend, shifts around, playing it cool, scanning the room for his tie." "Darryl was definitely in 'money' mode, because she sat close to him (after only a little to drink—so she must have seen something in him)."

11. In the last several years, my classroom surveys of undergraduate students and their favorite motion pictures reveal that male respondents consistently cite films that draw on similar themes to those in *Swingers*, including the party-hearty campus hijinks of college life (*National Lampoon's Animal House, Old School*); male vanity and the meaning of manhood (*American Psycho, Fight Club*); the camaraderie of violent men in secret societies and criminal gangs (The *Godfather, Goodfellas, Scarface, The Usual Suspects*); and the relentless pursuit of women (*There's Something About Mary*).

12. There are additional benefits to working as a collective as well. If the success of any single member can confer status on all other members, then traveling in a large group increases the odds that at least *someone* in the group will have a successful romantic encounter, provided the group does not *impede* the success of any single member by introducing competition to the setting or prove distracting to the proceedings.

References

Allison, Anne. 1994. *Nightwork: Sexuality, Pleasure, and Corporate Masculinity in a Tokyo Hostess Club.* Chicago: University of Chicago Press.

Anderson, Elijah. 1999. *Code of the Street: Decency, Violence, and the Moral Life of the Inner City.* New York: Norton.

Arnett, Jeffrey Jensen. 1994. "Are College Students Adults? Their Conceptions of the Transition to Adulthood." *Journal of Adult Development* 1(4):213–24.

————. 2000. "Emerging Adulthood: A Theory of Development from the Late Teens through the Twenties." *American Psychologist* 55(5):469–80.

Bech, Henning. 1998. "Citysex: Representing Lust in Public." *Theory, Culture & Society* 15(3–4):215–41.

Berk, Bernard. 1977. "Face-Saving at the Singles Dance." *Social Problems* 24(5):530–44.

Becker, Howard S. 2003. "The Politics of Presentation: Goffman and Total Institutions." *Symbolic Interaction* 26(4):659–69.

Bernstein, Elizabeth. 2001. "The Meaning of the Purchase: Desire, Demand, and the Commerce of Sex." *Ethnography* 2(3):389–420.

Bird, Sharon R. 1996. "Welcome to the Men's Club: Homosociality and the Maintenance of Hegemonic Masculinity." *Gender & Society* 10(2): 120–32.

Bissinger, H. G. 1990. *Friday Night Lights: A Town, a Team, and a Dream.* Reading, MA: Addison-Wesley.

Boswell, A. Ayres and Joan Z. Spade. 1996. "Fraternities and Collegiate Rape Culture: Why Are Some Fraternities More Dangerous Places for Women?" *Gender & Society* 10(2):133–47.

Brekhus, Wayne H. 2003. *Peacocks, Chameleons, Centaurs: Gay Suburbia and the Grammar of Social Identity.* Chicago: University of Chicago Press.

Bushnell, Candace. [1996] 2001. *Sex and the City.* New York: Warner.

Chapkis, Wendy. 1986. *Beauty Secrets: Women and the Politics of Appearance.* Boston: South End.

Chatterton, Paul and Robert Hollands. 2003. *Urban Nightscapes: Youth Cultures, Pleasure Spaces, and Corporate Power.* London: Routledge.

Chauncey, George. 1994. *Gay New York: Gender, Urban Culture, and the Making of the Gay Male World, 1980–1940.* New York: Basic Books.

Collins, Randall. 1981. "On the Microfoundations of Macrosociology." *American Journal of Sociology* 86(5):984–1014.

————. 2004. *Interaction Ritual Chains.* Princeton, NJ: Princeton University Press.

Connell, R. W. 1987. *Gender and Power: Society, the Person, and Sexual Politics.* Stanford, CA: Stanford University Press.

————. 1992. "A Very Straight Gay: Masculinity, Homosexual Experience, and the Dynamics of Gender." *American Sociological Review* 57(6):735–51.

————. 1993. "The Big Picture: Masculinities in Recent World History." *Theory and Society* 22(5):597–623.

————. 1995. *Masculinities.* Berkeley: University of California Press.

Connell, R. W. and James W. Messerschmidt. 2005. "Hegemonic Masculinity: Rethinking the Concept." *Gender & Society* 19(6):829–59.

Dellinger, Kirsten and Christine L. Williams. 2002. "The Locker Room and the Dorm Room: Workplace Norms and the Boundaries of Sexual Harassment in Magazine Editing." *Social Problems* 49(2):242–57.

Demetriou, Demetrakis Z. 2001. "Connell's Concept of Hegemonic Masculinity: A Critique." *Theory and Society* 30(3):337–61.

Donaldson, Mike. 1993. "What Is Hegemonic Masculinity?" *Theory and Society* 22(5):643–57.

Duneier, Mitchell and Harvey Molotch. 1999. "Talking City Trouble: Interactional Vandalism, Social Inequality, and the 'Urban Interaction Problem.'" *American Journal of Sociology* 104(5):1263–95.

Eliasoph, Nina and Paul Lichterman. 2003. "Culture in Interaction." *American Journal of Sociology* 108(4):735–94.

Fine, Gary Alan. 1977. "Popular Culture and Social Interaction: Production, Consumption, and Usage." *Journal of Popular Culture* 11(2):453–56.

Fischbarg, Gabe. 2002. *The Guide to Picking Up Girls.* New York: Plume.

Geertz, Clifford. 1973. "Deep Play: Notes on a Balinese Cockfight." In *The Interpretation of Cultures.* New York: Basic.

Giuffre, Patti A. and Christine L. Williams. 1994. "Boundary Lines: Labeling Sexual Harassment in Restaurants." *Gender & Society* 8(3):378–401.

Goffman, Erving. 1959. *The Presentation of Self in Everyday Life.* Garden City, NY: Anchor Books.

————. 1961. *Asylums: Essays on the Social Situation of Mental Patients and Other Inmates.* New York: Anchor.

————. 1963. *Stigma: Notes on the Management of Spoiled Identity.* New York: Simon & Schuster.

————. 1977. "The Arrangement between the Sexes." *Theory and Society* 4(3): 301–31.

Grazian, David. 2003. *Blue Chicago: The Search for Authenticity in Urban Blues Clubs.* Chicago: University of Chicago Press.

————. 2004. "The Production of Popular Music as a Confidence Game: The Case of the Chicago Blues." *Qualitative Sociology* 27(2):137–58.

Grindstaff, Laura. 2002. *The Money Shot: Trash, Class, and the Making of TV Talk Shows.* Chicago: University of Chicago Press.

Hollander, Jocelyn A. 2002. "Resisting Vulnerability: The Social Reconstruction of Gender in Interaction." *Social Problems* 49(4):474–96.

Kenney, William Howland. 1993. *Chicago Jazz: A Cultural History, 1904–1930.* New York: Oxford University Press.

Kimmel, Michael S. and Rebecca F. Plante. 2005. "The Gender of Desire: The Sexual Fantasies of Women and Men." In *The Gender of Desire: Essays on Male Sexuality,* edited by M. S. Kimmel. Albany: State University of New York Press.

Laumann, Edward O., John H. Gagnon, Robert T. Michael, and Stuart Michaels. 1994. *The Social Organization of Sexuality: Sexual Practices in the United States.* Chicago: University of Chicago Press.

Laumann, Edward O., Stephen Ellingson, Jenna Mahay, Anthony Paik, and Yoosik Youm, eds. 2004. *The Sexual Organization of the City.* Chicago: University of Chicago Press.

Lewontin, Richard C. 1995. "Sex, Lies, and Social Science." *New York Review of Books,* April 20.

Liebow, Elliot. 1967. *Tally's Corner: A Study of Negro Streetcorner Men.* Boston: Little, Brown.

Lloyd, Richard. 2005. *Neo-Bohemia: Culture and Capital in Postindustrial Chicago.* New York: Routledge.

Lyman, Peter. 1987. "The Fraternal Bond as a Joking Relationship: A Case Study of the Role of Sexist Jokes in Male Group Bonding." In *Changing Men: New Directions in Research on Men and Masculinity,* edited by M. S. Kimmel. Newbury Park, CA: Sage.

Mahay, Jenna and Edward O. Laumann. 2004. "Neighborhoods as Sex Markets." In *The Sexual Organization of the City,* edited by E. O. Laumann, S. Ellingson, J. Mahay, A. Paik, and Y. Youm. Chicago: University of Chicago Press.

Martin, Patricia Yancey. 2001. "'Mobilizing Mascu-linities': Women's Experiences of Men at Work." *Organization* 8(4):587–618.

Martin, Patricia Yancey and Robert A. Hummer. 1989. "Fraternities and Rape on Campus." *Gender & Society* 3(4):457–73.

Maurer, David W. 1940. *The Big Con: The Story of the Confidence Man.* New York: Bobbs-Merrill.

Max, Tucker. 2006. *I Hope They Serve Beer in Hell.* New York: Citadel. "Maxim's Wingman Training Manual." 2003. *Maxim,* May.

McLeod, Kembrew. 1999. "Authenticity within Hip-Hop and Other Cultures Threatened with Assim-ilation." *Journal of Communication* 49(4):134–50.

Messner, Michael A. 2002. *Taking the Field: Women, Men, and Sports.* Minneapolis: University of Min-nesota Press.

Michael, Robert T., John H. Gagnon, Edward O. Laumann, and Gina Kolata. 1995. *Sex in America: A Definitive Survey.* New York: Warner Books.

Mishkind, Marc, Judith Rodin, Lisa R. Silberstein, and Ruth H. Striegel-Moore. 1986. "The Embodi-ment of Masculinity." *American Behavioral Scien-tist* 29(5):545–62.

Owen, Frank. 2003. *Clubland: The Fabulous Rise and Murderous Fall of Club Culture.* New York: Broadway.

Paules, Greta Foff. 1991. *Dishing It Out: Power and Resistance among Waitresses in a New Jersey Res-taurant.* Philadelphia: Temple University Press.

Polk, Kenneth. 1994. "Masculinity, Honor, and Con-frontational Homicide." In *Just Boys Doing Busi-ness? Men, Masculinities, and Crime,* edited by T. Newburn and E. A. Stanko. London: Routledge.

Quinn, Beth A. 2002. "Sexual Harassment and Masculinity: The Power and Meaning of 'Girl Watching.'" *Gender & Society* 16(3):386–402.

Rostand, Edmond. 1897. *Cyrano de Bergerac.*

Rupp, Leila and Verta Taylor. 2003. *Drag Queens at the 801 Cabaret.* Chicago: University of Chicago Press.

Sanday, Peggy Reeves. 1990. *Fraternity Gang Rape: Sex, Brotherhood, and Privilege on Campus.* New York: New York University Press.

Schwalbe, Michael, Sandra Goodwin, Daphne Holden, Douglas Schrock, Shealy Thompson, and Michele Wolkomir. 2000. "Generic Processes in the Reproduction of Inequality: An Inter-actionist Analysis." *Social Forces* 79 (2):419–52.

Snow, David A., Cherylon Robinson, and Patricia L. McCall. 1991. "'Cooling Out' Men in Singles Bars and Nightclubs: Observations on the Interpersonal Survival Strategies of Women in Public Places." *Journal of Contemporary Ethnography* 19(4):423–49.

Spradley, James P. and Brenda J. Mann. 1975. *The Cocktail Waitress: Woman's Work in a Man's World.* New York: Wiley.

Strauss, Neil. 2005. *The Game: Penetrating the Secret Society of Pickup Artists.* New York: Regan Books.

Swidler, Ann. 2001. *Talk of Love: How Culture Mat-ters.* Chicago: University of Chicago Press.

Thorne, Barrie and Zella Luria. 1986. "Sexuality and Gender in Children's Daily Worlds." *Social Problems* 33(3):176–90.

U.S. News and World Report. 2005.

Waller, Willard. 1937. "The Rating and Dating Com-plex." *American Sociological Review* 2(5):727–34.

West, Candace and Don H. Zimmerman. 1987. "Doing Gender." *Gender & Society* 1(2): 125–51.

Whyte, William H. 1988. *City: Rediscovering the Cen-ter.* New York: Doubleday.

Williams, Alex. 2005. "Casual Relationships, Yes. Casual Sex, Not Really." *New York Times,* April 3, pp. 1, 12.

Wright, Robert. 1995. *The Moral Animal: Evolutionary Psychology and Everyday Life.* New York: Vintage.

Questions

1. According to Grazian, what is the *primary* goal of "girl hunting"?

2. What does Grazian mean by "normative" masculinity?

3. How does girl hunting help reproduce social inequality between men and women?

4. Grazian suggests that girl hunting leads to men suppressing their empathy for women. How does this work?

14

THE PRESENTATION OF SELF IN EVERYDAY LIFE

Erving Goffman

In this 1959 reading, Erving Goffman introduces what has come to be called the *dramaturgical* approach to the study of social interaction (so called because, in effect, it views social life as theater). Goffman's focus is on what happens when people are in the presence of others, on how they play their roles. As you will see, from Goffman's point of view, routine social interaction is a cooperative effort between the social actor and his or her audience. The actor may play a role, but frequently he or she must be helped along by the complicity of the audience.

When an individual enters the presence of others, they commonly seek to acquire information about him or to bring into play information about him already possessed. They will be interested in his general socioeconomic status, his conception of self, his attitude toward them, his competence, his trustworthiness, etc. Although some of this information seems to be sought almost as an end in itself, there are usually quite practical reasons for acquiring it. Information about the individual helps to define the situation, enabling others to know in advance what he will expect of them and what they may expect of him. Informed in these

ways, the others will know how best to act in order to call forth a desired response from him.

For those present, many sources of information become accessible and many carriers (or "sign-vehicles") become available for conveying this information. If unacquainted with the individual, observers can glean clues from his conduct and appearance which allow them to apply their previous experience with individuals roughly similar to the one before them or, more important, to apply untested stereotypes to him. They can also assume from past experience that only individuals of a particular kind are likely to be found in a given social setting. They can rely on what the individual says about himself or on documentary evidence he provides as to who and what he is. If they know, or know of, the individual by virtue of experience prior to the interaction, they can rely on assumptions as to the persistence and generality of psychological traits as a means of predicting his present and future behavior.

However, during the period in which the individual is in the immediate presence of the others, few events may occur which directly provide the others with the conclusive information they will need if they are to direct wisely their own activity. Many crucial facts lie beyond the time and place of interaction or lie concealed with it. For example, the "true" or "real" attitudes, beliefs, and emotions of the individual can be ascertained only indirectly, through his avowals or through what appears to be involuntary expressive behavior. Similarly, if the individual offers the others a product or service, they will often find that during the interaction there will be no time and place immediately available for eating the pudding—that the proof can be found in. They will be forced to accept some events as conventional or natural signs of something not directly available to the senses. In other terms, the individual will have to act so that he intentionally or unintentionally *expresses* himself, and the others will in turn have to be *impressed* in some way by him (Ichheiser 1949, 6–7).

The expressiveness of the individual (and therefore his capacity to give impressions) appears to involve two radically different kinds of sign activity: the expression that he *gives,* and the expression that he *gives off.* The first involves verbal symbols or their substitutes which he uses admittedly and solely to convey the information that he and the others are known to attach to these symbols. This is communication in the traditional and narrow sense. The second involves a wide range of action that others can treat as symptomatic of the actor, the expectation being that the action was performed for reasons other than the information conveyed in this way. As we shall have to see, this distinction has only an initial validity. The individual does of course intentionally convey misinformation by means of both of these types of communication, the first involving deceit, the second feigning.

Taking communication in both its narrow and broad sense, one finds that when the individual is in the immediate presence of others, his activity will have a promissory character. The others are likely to find that they must accept the individual on faith, offering him a just return while he is present before them in exchange for something whose true value will not be established until after he has left their presence. (Of course, the others also live by inference in their dealings with the physical world, but it is only in the world of social interaction that the objects about which they make inferences will purposely facilitate and hinder this inferential process.) The security that they justifiably feel in making inferences about the individual will vary, of course, depending on such factors as the amount of information they already possess about him, but no amount of such past evidence can entirely obviate the necessity of acting on the basis of inferences. As William I. Thomas suggested:

infer
guess

> It is also highly important for us to realize that we do not as a matter of fact lead our lives, make our decisions, and reach our goals in everyday life either statistically or scientifically. We live in inference. I am, let us say, your guest. You do not know, you cannot determine scientifically, that I will not steal your money or your spoons. But inferentially I will not, and inferentially you have me as a guest. (quoted in Volkart 1951, 5)

Let us now turn from the others to the point of view of the individual who presents himself before them. He may wish them to think highly of him, or to think that he thinks highly of them, or to perceive how in fact he feels toward them, or to obtain no clear-cut impression; he may wish to ensure sufficient harmony so that the interaction can be sustained, or to defraud, get rid of, confuse, mislead, antagonize, or insult them. Regardless of the particular objective which the individual has in mind and of his motive for having this objective, it will be in his interests to control the conduct of the others, especially their responsive treatment of him. This control is achieved largely by influencing the definition

2 different expressions

of the situation which the others come to formulate, and he can influence this definition by expressing himself in such a way as to give them the kind of impression that will lead them to act voluntarily in accordance with his own plan. Thus, when an individual appears in the presence of others, there will usually be some reason for him to mobilize his activity so that it will convey an impression to others which it is in his interests to convey. Since a girl's dormitory mates will glean evidence of her popularity from the calls she receives on the phone, we can suspect that some girls will arrange for calls to be made, and Willard Waller's (n.d., 730) finding can be anticipated.

> It has been reported by many observers that a girl who is called to the telephone in the dormitories will often allow herself to be called several times, in order to give all the other girls ample opportunity to hear her paged.

Of the two kinds of communication—expressions given and expressions given off—this report will be primarily concerned with the latter, with the more theatrical and contextual kind, the non-verbal, presumably unintentional kind, whether this communication be purposely engineered or not. As an example of what we must try to examine, I would like to cite at length a novelistic incident in which Preedy, a vacationing Englishman, makes his first appearance on the beach of his summer hotel in Spain:

> But in any case he took care to avoid catching anyone's eye. First of all, he had to make it clear to those potential companions of his holiday that they were of no concern to him whatsoever. He stared through them, round them, over them—eyes lost in space. The beach might have been empty. If by chance a ball was thrown his way, he looked surprised; then let a smile of amusement lighten his face (Kindly Preedy), looked round dazed to see that there *were* people on the beach, tossed it back with a smile to himself and not a smile *at* the people, and then resumed carelessly his nonchalant survey of space.

But it was time to institute a little parade, the parade of the Ideal Preedy. By devious handlings he gave any who wanted to look a chance to see the title of his book—a Spanish translation of Homer, classic thus, but not daring, cosmopolitan too—and then gathered together his beach-wrap and bag into a neat sand-resistant pile (Methodical and Sensible Preedy), rose slowly to stretch at ease his huge frame (Big-Cat Preedy), and tossed aside his sandals (Carefree Preedy, after all).

The marriage of Preedy and the sea! There were alternative rituals. The first involved the stroll that turns into a run and a dive straight into the water, thereafter smoothing into a strong splashless crawl towards the horizon. But of course not really to the horizon. Quite suddenly he would turn on to his back and thrash great white splashes with his legs, somehow thus showing that he could have swum further had he wanted to, and then would stand up a quarter out of water for all to see who it was.

The alternative course was simpler, it avoided the cold-water shock and it avoided the risk of appearing too high-spirited. The point was to appear to be so used to the sea, the Mediterranean, and this particular beach, that one might as well be in the sea as out of it. It involved a slow stroll down and into the edge of the water—not even noticing his toes were wet, land and water all the same to *him!*—with his eyes up at the sky gravely surveying portents, invisible to others, of the weather (Local Fisherman Preedy). (Sansom 1956, 230–232)

The novelist means us to see that Preedy is improperly concerned with the extensive impressions he feels his sheer bodily action is giving off to those around him. We can malign Preedy further by assuming that he has acted merely in order to give a particular impression, that this is a false impression, and that the others present receive either no impression at all, or, worse still, the impression that Preedy is affectedly trying to cause them to receive this particular impression. But the important point for us here is that the kind of impression

Preedy thinks he is making is in fact the kind of impression that others correctly and incorrectly glean from someone in their midst.

I have said that when an individual appears before others his actions will influence the definition of the situation which they come to have. Sometimes the individual will act in a thoroughly calculating manner, expressing himself in a given way solely in order to give the kind of impression to others that is likely to evoke from them a specific response he is concerned to obtain. Sometimes the individual will be calculating in his activity but be relatively unaware that this is the case. Sometimes he will intentionally and consciously express himself in a particular way, but chiefly because the tradition of his group or social status requires this kind of expression and not because of any particular response (other than vague acceptance or approval) that is likely to be evoked from those impressed by the expression. Sometimes the traditions of an individual's role will lead him to give a well-designed impression of a particular kind and yet he may be neither consciously nor unconsciously disposed to create such an impression. The others, in their turn, may be suitably impressed by the individual's efforts to convey something, or may misunderstand the situation and come to conclusions that are warranted neither by the individual's intent nor by the facts. In any case, in so far as the others act *as if* the individual had conveyed a particular impression, we may take a functional or pragmatic view and say that the individual has "effectively" projected a given definition of the situation and "effectively" fostered the understanding that a given state of affairs obtains.

There is one aspect of the others' response that bears special comment here. Knowing that the individual is likely to present himself in a light that is favorable to him, the others may divide what they witness into two parts: a part that is relatively easy for the individual to manipulate at will, being chiefly his verbal assertions, and a part in regard to which he

seems to have little concern or control, being chiefly derived from the expressions he gives off. The others may then use what are considered to be the ungovernable aspects of his expressive behavior as a check upon the validity of what is conveyed by the governable aspects. In this a fundamental asymmetry is demonstrated in the communication process, the individual presumably being aware of only one stream of his communication, the witnesses of this stream and one other. For example, in Shetland Isle one crofter's wife, in serving native dishes to a visitor from the mainland of Britain, would listen with a polite smile to his polite claims of liking what he is eating; at the same time she would take note of the rapidity with which the visitor lifted his fork or spoon to his mouth, the eagerness with which he passed food into his mouth, and the gusto expressed in chewing the food, using these signs as a check on the stated feelings of the eater. The same woman, in order to discover what one acquaintance (A) "actually" thought of another acquaintance (B), would wait until B was in the presence of A but engaged in conversation with still another person (C). She would then covertly examine the facial expressions of A as he regarded B in conversation with C. Not being in conversation with B, and not being directly observed by him, A would sometimes relax usual constraints and tactful deceptions, and freely express what he was "actually" feeling about B. This Shetlander, in short, would observe the unobserved observer.

Now given the fact that others are likely to check up on the more controllable aspects of behavior by means of the less controllable, one can expect that sometimes the individual will try to exploit this very possibility, guiding the impression he makes through behavior felt to be reliably informing. For example, in gaining admission to a tight social circle, the participant observer may not only wear an accepting look while listening to an informant, but may also be careful to wear the same look when observing the informant talking to others; observers of the observer will then not as easily discover where he actually stands. A specific illustration may be cited from Shetland Isle. When a neighbor dropped in to have a cup of tea, he would ordinarily wear at least a hint of an expectant warm smile as he passed through the door into the cottage. Since lack of physical obstructions outside the cottage and lack of light within it usually made it possible to observe the visitor unobserved as he approached the house, islanders sometimes took pleasure in watching the visitor drop whatever expression he was manifesting and replace it with a sociable one just before reaching the door. However, some visitors, in appreciating that this examination was occurring, would blindly adopt a social face a long distance from the house, thus ensuring the projection of a constant image.

This kind of control upon the part of the individual reinstates the symmetry of the communication process, and sets the stage for a kind of information game—a potentially infinite cycle of concealment, discovery, false revelation, and rediscovery. It should be added that since the others are likely to be relatively unsuspicious of the presumably unguided aspect of the individual's conduct, he can gain much by controlling it. The others of course may sense that the individual is manipulating the presumably spontaneous aspects of his behavior, and seek in this very act of manipulation some shading of conduct that the individual has not managed to control. This again provides a check upon the individual's behavior, this time his presumably uncalculated behavior, thus re-establishing the asymmetry of the communication process. Here I would like only to add the suggestion that the arts of piercing an individual's effort at calculated unintentionality seem better developed than our capacity to manipulate our own behavior, so that regardless of how many steps have occurred in the information game, the witness is likely to have the advantage over the actor, and the initial asymmetry of the communication process is likely to be retained.

When we allow that the individual projects a definition of the situation when he appears before others, we must also see that the others, however passive their role may seem to be, will themselves effectively project a definition of the situation by virtue of their response to the individual and by virtue of any lines of action they initiate to him. Ordinarily the definitions of the situation projected by the several different participants are sufficiently attuned to one another so that open contradiction will not occur. I do not mean that there will be the kind of consensus that arises when each individual present candidly expresses what he really feels and honestly agrees with the expressed feelings of the others present. This kind of harmony is an optimistic ideal and in any case not necessary for the smooth working of society. Rather, each participant is expected to suppress his immediate heartfelt feelings, conveying a view of the situation which he feels the others will be able to find at least temporarily acceptable. The maintenance of this surface of agreement, this veneer of consensus, is facilitated by each participant concealing his own wants behind statements which assert values to which everyone present feels obliged to give lip service. Further, there is usually a kind of division of definitional labor. Each participant is allowed to establish the tentative official ruling regarding matters which are vital to him but not immediately important to others, e.g., the rationalizations and justifications by which he accounts for his past activity. In exchange for this courtesy he remains silent or noncommittal on matters important to others but not immediately important to him. We have then a kind of interactional *modus vivendi*.[1]

---

[1]*Modus vivendi* is Latin and can be literally translated as "a way of living." But generally it refers to "a way of acting" so that people who might not feel positively toward one another can nonetheless get along.—Ed.

Together the participants contribute to a single over-all definition of the situation which involves not so much a real agreement as to what exists but rather a real agreement as to whose claims concerning what issues will be temporarily honored. Real agreement will also exist concerning the desirability of avoiding an open conflict of definitions of the situation.[2] I will refer to this level of agreement as a "working consensus." It is to be understood that the working consensus established in one interaction setting will be quite different in content from the working consensus established in a different type of setting. Thus, between two friends at lunch, a reciprocal show of affection, respect, and concern for the other is maintained. In service occupations, on the other hand, the specialist often maintains an image of disinterested involvement in the problem of the client, while the client responds with a show of respect for the competence and integrity of the specialist. Regardless of such differences in content, however, the general form of these working arrangements is the same.

In noting the tendency for a participant to accept the definitional claims made by the others present, we can appreciate the crucial importance of the information that the individual *initially* possesses or acquires concerning his fellow participants, for it is on the basis of this initial information that the individual starts to define the situation and starts to build up lines of responsive action. The individual's initial projection commits him to what he is proposing to be and requires him to drop all pretenses of being other things. As the interaction among the participants progresses, additions and modifications in this initial informational state will of course occur, but it is essential that these later developments be related without contradiction to, and even built up from, the initial positions taken by several participants. It would seem that an individual can more easily make a choice as to what line of treatment to demand from and extend to the others present at the beginning of an encounter than he can alter the line of treatment that is being pursued once the interaction is underway.

In everyday life, of course, there is a clear understanding that first impressions are important. Thus, the work adjustment of those in service occupations will often hinge upon a capacity to seize and hold the initiative in the service relation, a capacity that will require subtle aggressiveness on the part of the server when he is of lower socio-economic status than his client. W. F. Whyte (1946, 132–133) suggests the waitress as an example:

> The first point that stands out is that the waitress who bears up under pressure does not simply respond to her customers. She acts with some skill to control their behavior. The first question to ask when we look at the customer relationship is, "Does the waitress get the jump on the customers, or does the customer get the jump on the waitress?" The skilled waitress realizes the crucial nature of this question. . . .
>
> The skilled waitress tackles the customer with confidence and without hesitation. For example, she may find that a new customer has seated himself before she could clear off the dirty dishes and change the cloth. He is now leaning on the table studying the menu. She greets him, says, "May I change the cover, please?" and, without waiting for an answer, takes his menu away from him so that he moves back from the table, and she goes about her work. The relationship is handled politely but firmly, and there is never any question as to who is in charge.

---

[2]An interaction can be purposely set up as a time and place for voicing differences in opinion, but in such cases participants must be careful to agree not to disagree on the proper tone of voice, vocabulary, and degree of seriousness in which all arguments are to be phrased, and upon the mutual respect which disagreeing participants must carefully continue to express toward one another. This debaters' or academic definition of the situation may also be invoked suddenly and judiciously as a way of translating a serious conflict of views into one that can be handled within a framework acceptable to all present.

When the interaction that is initiated by "first impressions" is itself merely the initial interaction in an extended series of interactions involving the same participants, we speak of "getting off on the right foot" and feel that it is crucial that we do so. Thus, one learns that some teachers take the following view:

> "You can't ever let them get the upper hand on you or you're through. So I start out tough. The first day I get a new class in, I let them know who's boss. . . . You've got to start off tough, then you can ease up as you go along. If you start out easy-going, when you try to get tough, they'll just look at you and laugh." (quoted in Becker n.d., 459)

Similarly, attendants in mental institutions may feel that if the new patient is sharply put in his place the first day on the ward and made to see who is boss, much future difficulty will be prevented (Taxel 1953).

Given the fact that the individual effectively projects a definition of the situation when he enters the presence of others, we can assume that events may occur within the interaction which contradict, discredit, or otherwise throw doubt upon this projection. When these disruptive events occur, the interaction itself may come to a confused and embarrassed halt. Some of the assumptions upon which the responses of the participants had been predicated become untenable, and the participants find themselves lodged in an interaction for which the situation has been wrongly defined and is now no longer defined. At such moments the individual whose presentation has been discredited may feel ashamed while the others present may feel hostile, and all the participants may come to feel ill at ease, nonplussed, out of countenance, embarrassed, experiencing the kind of anomy that is generated when the minute social system of face-to-face interaction breaks down.

In stressing the fact that the initial definition of the situation projected by an individual tends to provide a plan for the cooperative activity that follows—in stressing this action point of view—we must not overlook the crucial fact that any projected definition of the situation also has a distinctive moral character. It is this moral character of projections that will chiefly concern us in this report. Society is organized on the principle that any individual who possesses certain social characteristics has a moral right to expect that others will value and treat him in an appropriate way. Connected with this principle is a second, namely that an individual who implicitly or explicitly signifies that he has certain social characteristics ought in fact to be what he claims he is. In consequence, when an individual projects a definition of the situation and thereby makes an implicit or explicit claim to be a person of a particular kind, he automatically exerts a moral demand upon the others, obliging them to value and treat him in the manner that persons of his kind have a right to expect. He also implicitly forgoes all claims to be things he does not appear to be and hence forgoes the treatment that would be appropriate for such individuals. The others find, then, that the individual has informed them as to what is and as to what they *ought* to see as the "is."

One cannot judge the importance of definitional disruptions by the frequency with which they occur, for apparently they would occur more frequently were not constant precautions taken. We find that preventive practices are constantly employed to avoid these embarrassments and that corrective practices are constantly employed to compensate for discrediting occurrences that have not been successfully avoided. When the individual employs these strategies and tactics to protect his own projections, we may refer to them as "defensive practices"; when a participant employs them to save the definition of the situation projected by another, we speak of "protective practices" or "tact." Together, defensive and protective practices comprise the techniques employed to safeguard the impression fostered by an individual during his presence before others. It should be added that while we may be ready to see that no fostered impression would survive if defensive practices were not employed, we are less ready perhaps to see that few impressions could survive if those who received the impression did not exert tact in their reception of it.

In addition to the fact that precautions are taken to prevent disruption of projected definitions, we may also note that an intense interest in these disruptions comes to play a significant role in the social life of the group. Practical jokes and social games are played in which embarrassments which are to be taken unseriously are purposely engineered. Fantasies are created in which devastating exposures occur. Anecdotes from the past—real, embroidered, or fictitious—are told and retold, detailing disruptions which occurred, almost occurred, or occurred and were admirably resolved. There seems to be no grouping which does not have a ready supply of these games, reveries, and cautionary tales, to be used as a source of humor, a catharsis for anxieties, and a sanction for inducing individuals to be modest in their claims and reasonable in their projected expectations. The individual may tell himself through dreams of getting into impossible positions. Families tell of the time a guest got his dates mixed and arrived when neither the house nor anyone in it was ready for him. Journalists tell of times when an all-too-meaningful misprint occurred, and the paper's assumption of objectivity or decorum was humorously discredited. Public servants tell of times a client ridiculously misunderstood form instructions, giving answers which implied an unanticipated and bizarre definition of the situation (Blau n.d., 127–129). Seamen, whose home away from home is

rigorously he-man, tell stories of coming back home and inadvertently asking mother to "pass the fucking butter" (Beattie 1950, 35). Diplomats tell of the time a nearsighted queen asked a republican ambassador about the health of his king (Ponsonby 1952, 46). . . .

It will be convenient to end this introduction with some definitions that are implied in what has gone before and required for what is to follow. For the purpose of this report, interaction (that is, face-to-face interaction) may be roughly defined as the reciprocal influence of individuals upon one another's actions when in one another's immediate physical presence. *An* interaction may be defined as all the interaction which occurs throughout any one occasion when a given set of individuals are in one another's continuous presence; the term "an encounter" would do as well. A "performance" may be defined as all the activity of a given participant on a given occasion which serves to influence in any way any of the other participants. Taking a particular participant and his performance as a basic point of reference, we may refer to those who contribute the other performances as the audience, observers, or co-participants. The pre-established pattern of action which is unfolded during a performance and which may be presented or played through on other occasions may be called a "part" or "routine." These situational terms can easily be related to conventional structural ones. When an individual or performer plays the same part to the same audience on different occasions, a social relationship is likely to arise. Defining social role as the enactment of rights and duties attached to a given status, we can say that a social role will involve one or more parts and that each of these different parts may be presented by the performer on a series of occasions to the same kinds of audience or to an audience of the same persons.

References

Beattie, Walter M., Jr. 1950. "The Merchant Seaman." Unpublished M. A. report, Department of Sociology, University of Chicago.

Becker, Howard S. n.d. "Social Class Variations in the Teacher–Pupil Relationship." *Journal of Educational Sociology* 25.

Blau, Peter. n.d. "Dynamics of Bureaucracy." Ph.D. dissertation, Department of Sociology, Columbia University.

Ichheiser, Gustav. 1949. "Misunderstandings in Human Relations." Supplement to *The American Journal of Sociology* 55 (September).

Ponsonby, Sir Frederick. 1952. *Recollections of Three Reigns.* New York: Dutton.

Sansom, William. 1956. *A Contest of Ladies.* London: Hogarth.

Taxel, Harold. 1953. "Authority Structure in a Mental Hospital Ward." Unpublished M.A. thesis, Department of Sociology, University of Chicago.

Volkart, E. H. (ed.). 1951. "Contributions of W. I. Thomas to Theory and Social Research." In *Social Behavior and Personality.* New York: Social Science Research Council.

Waller, Willard. n.d. "The Rating and Dating Complex." *American Sociological Review* 2.

Whyte, W. F. 1946. "When Workers and Customers Meet." Chap. 7 in W. F. Whyte (ed.), *Industry and Society.* New York: McGraw-Hill.

Questions

1. What is Goffman's distinction between expressions that one gives and expressions that one gives off?

2. Suppose you are about to visit your professor to ask a question about the upcoming exam. Besides information gathering, you would like to influence your professor's definition of the situation such that he or she infers that you are a smart student. How might you do this (in terms of both expressions you give and expressions you give off)?

   Now suppose you are preparing for a date that you've been looking forward to for several days. Your goal this time is to have fun and to influence your date's definition of the situation so that he or she infers that you are a cool person. How might you do this?

   Is there a difference between how you would act in each situation? Which is the "real" you?

3. Think of a time in which you exercised "tact." Using that situation as an example, how did you (as Goffman would say) employ this projective technique in order to save the definition of the situation projected by another?

15
THE PATHOLOGY OF IMPRISONMENT

Philip G. Zimbardo

When I was a kid in school, I was very shy. I rarely volunteered answers to questions posed by my teachers, and I cringed whenever I was asked to do an arithmetic problem on the chalkboard. That wasn't the best way to fulfill my role as a student, but it was an acceptable way. Now I am a professor, and I am the one who not only asks questions but makes scholarly pronouncements that I expect everyone in the room to write down. My first-grade teacher, who regarded my shyness with despair, would be shocked to see that I actually seem to do these professorial things comfortably. Has my personality changed? Not really. I'm still shy. But the role expectations of a professor evoke a different side of me, one that's "outgoing" and even extroverted. As you will read in this 1972 article by Philip Zimbardo, roles—the social scripts that are attached to the statuses people occupy—are powerfully evocative. They can bring out parts of someone's "personality" that the individual never knew existed.

I was recently released from solitary confinement after being held therein for 37 months [months!]. A silent system was imposed upon me and to even whisper to the man in the next cell resulted in being beaten by guards, sprayed with chemical mace, black-jacked, stomped and thrown into a strip-cell naked to sleep on a concrete floor without bedding, covering, wash basin or even a toilet. The floor served as toilet and bed, and even there the silent system was enforced. To let a moan escape your lips because of the pain and discomfort . . . resulted in another beating. I spent not days, but months there during my 37 months in solitary. . . . I have filed every writ possible against the administrative acts of brutality. The state courts have all denied the petitions. Because of my refusal to let the things die down and forget all

that happened during my 37 months in solitary . . . I am the most hated prisoner in [this] penitentiary, and called a "hard-core incorrigible."

Maybe I am an incorrigible, but if true, it's because I would rather die than to accept being treated as less than a human being. I have never complained of my prison sentence as being unjustified except through legal means of appeals. I have never put a knife on a guard's throat and demanded my release. I know that thieves must be punished and I don't justify stealing, even though I am a thief myself. But now I don't think I will be a thief when I am released. No, I'm not rehabilitated. It's just that I no longer think of becoming wealthy by stealing. I now only think of killing—killing those who have beaten me and treated me as if I were a dog. I hope and pray for the sake of my own soul and future life of freedom that I am able to overcome the bitterness and hatred which eats daily at my soul, but I know to overcome it will not be easy.

Philip G. Zimbardo, "The Pathology of Imprisonment" from *Society* (April 1972). Copyright © 1972 by Transaction Publishers. Reprinted with kind permission from Springer Science+Business Media and Philip G. Zimbardo Inc.

This eloquent plea for prison reform—for humane treatment of human beings, for the basic dignity that is the right of every American—came to me secretly in a letter from a prisoner who cannot be identified because he is still in a state correctional institution. He sent it to me because he read of an experiment I recently conducted at Stanford University. In an attempt to understand just what it means psychologically to be a prisoner or a prison guard, Craig Haney, Curt Banks, Dave Jaffe and I created our own prison. We carefully screened over 70 volunteers who answered an ad in a Palo Alto city newspaper and ended up with about two dozen young men who were selected to be part of this study. They were mature, emotionally stable, normal, intelligent college students from middle-class homes throughout the United States and Canada. They appeared to represent the cream of the crop of this generation. None had any criminal record and all were relatively homogeneous on many dimensions initially.

Half were arbitrarily designated as prisoners by a flip of a coin, the others as guards. These were the roles they were to play in our simulated prison. The guards were made aware of the potential seriousness and danger of the situation and their own vulnerability. They made up their own formal rules for maintaining law, order and respect, and were generally free to improvise new ones during their eight-hour, three-man shifts. The prisoners were unexpectedly picked up at their homes by a city policeman in a squad car, searched, handcuffed, fingerprinted, booked at the Palo Alto station house and taken blindfolded to our jail. There they were stripped, deloused, put into a uniform, given a number and put into a cell with two other prisoners where they expected to live for the next two weeks. The pay was good ($15 a day) and their motivation was to make money.

We observed and recorded on videotape the events that occurred in the prison, and we interviewed and tested the prisoners and guards at various points throughout the study. Some of the videotapes of the actual encounters between the prisoners and guards were seen on the NBC News feature "Chronolog" on November 26, 1971.

At the end of only six days we had to close down our mock prison because what we saw was frightening. It was no longer apparent to most of the subjects (or to us) where reality ended and their roles began. The majority had indeed become prisoners or guards, no longer able to clearly differentiate between role playing and self. There were dramatic changes in virtually every aspect of their behavior, thinking and feeling. In less than a week the experience of imprisonment undid (temporarily) a lifetime of learning; human values were suspended, self-concepts were challenged and the ugliest, most base, pathological side of human nature surfaced. We were horrified because we saw some boys (guards) treat others as if they were despicable animals, taking pleasure in cruelty, while other boys (prisoners) became servile, dehumanized robots who thought only of escape, of their own individual survival and of their mounting hatred for the guards.

We had to release three prisoners in the first four days because they had such acute situational traumatic reactions as hysterical crying, confusion in thinking and severe depression. Others begged to be paroled, and all but three were willing to forfeit all the money they had earned if they could be paroled. By then (the fifth day) they had been so programmed to think of themselves as prisoners that when their request for parole was denied, they returned docilely to their cells. Now, had they been thinking as college students acting in an oppressive experiment, they would have quit once they no longer wanted the $15 a day we used as our only incentive. However, the reality was not quitting an experiment but "being paroled by the parole board from the Stanford

County Jail." By the last days, the earlier solidarity among the prisoners (systematically broken by the guards) dissolved into "each man for himself." Finally, when one of their fellows was put in solitary confinement (a small closet) for refusing to eat, the prisoners were given a choice by one of the guards: give up their blankets and the incorrigible prisoner would be let out, or keep their blankets and he would be kept in all night. They voted to keep their blankets and to abandon their brother.

About a third of the guards became tyrannical in their arbitrary use of power, in enjoying their control over other people. They were corrupted by the power of their roles and became quite inventive in their techniques of breaking the spirit of the prisoners and making them feel they were worthless. Some of the guards merely did their jobs as tough but fair correctional officers, and several were good guards from the prisoners' point of view since they did them small favors and were friendly. However, no good guard ever interfered with a command by any of the bad guards; they never intervened on the side of the prisoners, they never told the others to ease off because it was only an experiment, and they never even came to me as prison superintendent or experimenter in charge to complain. In part, they were good because the others were bad; they needed the others to help establish their own egos in a positive light. In a sense, the good guards perpetuated the prison more than the other guards because their own needs to be liked prevented them from disobeying or violating the implicit guards' code. At the same time, the act of befriending the prisoners created a social reality which made the prisoners less likely to rebel.

By the end of the week the experiment had become a reality, as if it were a Pirandello[1] play directed by Kafka[2] that just keeps going after the audience has left. The consultant for our prison, Carlo Prescott, an ex-convict with 16 years of imprisonment in California's jails, would get so depressed and furious each time he visited our prison, because of its psychological similarity to his experiences, that he would have to leave. A Catholic priest who was a former prison chaplain in Washington, D.C., talked to our prisoners after four days and said they were just like the other first-timers he had seen.

But in the end, I called off the experiment not because of the horror I saw out there in the prison yard, but because of the horror of realizing that I could have easily traded places with the most brutal guard or become the weakest prisoner full of hatred at being so powerless that I could not eat, sleep or go to the toilet without permission of the authorities. *I* could have become Calley at My Lai, George Jackson at San Quentin, one of the men at Attica or the prisoner quoted at the beginning of this article.

Individual behavior is largely under the control of social forces and environmental contingencies rather than personality traits, character, will power or other empirically unvalidated constructs. Thus we create an illusion of freedom by attributing more internal control to ourselves, to the individual, than actually exists. We thus underestimate the power and pervasiveness of situational controls over behavior because (a) they are often non-obvious and subtle, (b) we can often avoid entering situations where we might be so controlled, (c) we label as "weak" or

---

[1]Luigi Pirandello (1867–1936) was a Sicilian author. He won the 1934 Nobel Prize for literature. His fame is primarily owing to his grimly humorous plays dealing with the confusions of illusions and reality (for example, *Six Characters in Search of an Author*).—Ed.

[2]The writer Franz Kafka (1883–1924) was born in Prague of Jewish parents. In his novels and short stories, Kafka painted a world that was steeped in illusion and contradiction. His characters suffered from feelings of guilt, anxiety, and despair and an overwhelming sense of futility as they struggled to cope with rigid bureaucracies and totalitarian regimes. Today, similarly tortured visions of society are often referred to as "Kafkaesque."—Ed.

"deviant" people in those situations who do behave differently from how we believe we would.

Each of us carries around in our heads a favorable self-image in which we are essentially just, fair, humane and understanding. For example, we could not imagine inflicting pain on others without much provocation or hurting people who had done nothing to us, who in fact were even liked by us. However, there is a growing body of social psychological research which underscores the conclusion derived from this prison study. Many people, perhaps the majority, can be made to do almost anything when put into psychologically compelling situations—regardless of their morals, ethics, values, attitudes, beliefs or personal convictions. My colleague, Stanley Milgram, has shown that more than 60 percent of the population will deliver what they think is a series of painful electric shocks to another person even after the victim cries for mercy, begs them to stop and then apparently passes out. The subjects complained that they did not want to inflict more pain but blindly obeyed the command of the authority figure (the experimenter) who said that they must go on. In my own research on violence, I have seen mild-mannered coeds repeatedly give shocks (which they thought were causing pain) to

another girl, a stranger whom they had rated very favorably, simply by being made to feel anonymous and put in a situation where they were expected to engage in this activity.

Observers of these and similar experimental situations never predict their outcomes and estimate that it is unlikely that they themselves would behave similarly. They can be so confident only when they are outside the situation. However, since the majority of people in these studies do act in non-rational, non-obvious ways, it follows that the majority of observers would also succumb to the social psychological forces in the situation.

With regard to prisons, we can state that the mere act of assigning labels to people and putting them into a situation where those labels acquire validity and meaning is sufficient to elicit pathological behavior. This pathology is not predictable from any available diagnostic indicators we have in the social sciences, and is extreme enough to modify in very significant ways fundamental attitudes and behavior. The prison situation, as presently arranged, is guaranteed to generate severe enough pathological reactions in both guards and prisoners as to debase their humanity, lower their feelings of self-worth and make it difficult for them to be part of a society outside of their prison. . . .

Questions

1. What are the similarities between Zimbardo's findings and Milgram's (see reading 7)?

2. Zimbardo's experiment cemented sociologists' conviction that the roles people play have a lot of power to elicit particular behaviors from them. Sociologists refer to the process by which people take on socially constructed roles and carry them out as "role-taking." The men chosen to be prisoners and to be guards were, for all intents and purposes, the same until they took on their respective roles; it was taking on and playing the roles that "changed" them (or elicited new behaviors from them).

   Role-taking is a part of everyday life. When an individual reaches adulthood (or possibly sooner!), he or she may take the status and role of married person—husband or wife. As many women and men have found in recent decades, it is hard to change those roles to fit new understandings of, for example, gender roles. But sociologists are aware that all people, in all cases, do not simply take on conventional roles, that people do not simply do role-taking. In some cases, people adapt the roles to themselves rather than the other way around. Sociologists call that "role-making." It isn't easy; when you do not act the way people expect you to act, you can expect some sort of response—often, informal negative sanctions. Think of the young man who wishes, for example, to study ballet rather than football. He wants to make the role of young man fit his own proclivities.

Consider how you play the role of student. What things do you do that an observer would judge to be role-taking? What do you do that an observer would judge to be role-making?

16

"GETTING" AND "MAKING" A TIP

Greta Foff Paules

In this 1991 article, Greta Foff Paules, who received a PhD in cultural anthropology from Princeton University, takes us into the world of the waitress. If you've never waited on tables, you might naturally assume that waitresses (and waiters, for that matter) are there to serve the customers. But as Paules discovered through participant observation, there is a lot more to the customer–waitress relationship than meets the eye. You decide who has what kind of power in this relationship.

The waitress can't help feeling a sense of personal failure and public censure when she is "stiffed."

—William F. Whyte,
"When Workers and Customers Meet"

They're rude, they're ignorant, they're obnoxious, they're inconsiderate. . . . Half of these people don't deserve to come out and eat, let alone try and tip a waitress.

—Route waitress

Making a Tip at Route

A common feature of past research is that the worker's control over the tipping system is evaluated in terms of her efforts to con, coerce, compel, or otherwise manipulate a customer into relinquishing a bigger tip. Because these efforts have for the most part proven futile, the worker has been seen as having little defense against the financial vicissitudes of the tipping system. What these studies have overlooked is that an employee can increase her tip income

by controlling the number as well as the size of tips she receives. This oversight has arisen from the tendency of researchers to concentrate narrowly on the relationship between server and served, while failing to take into account the broader organizational context in which this relationship takes place.

Like service workers observed in earlier studies, waitresses at Route strive to boost the amount of individual gratuities by rendering special services and being especially friendly. As one waitress put it, "I'll sell you the world if you're in my station." In general though, waitresses at Route Restaurant seek to boost their tip income, not by increasing the amount of individual gratuities, but by increasing the number of customers they serve. They accomplish this (a) by securing the largest or busiest stations and working the most lucrative shifts; (b) by "turning" their tables quickly; and (c) by controlling the flow of customers within the restaurant.

Technically, stations at Route are assigned on a rotating basis so that all waitresses, including rookies, work fast and slow stations equally. Station assignments are listed on the work schedule that is posted in the office window where it can be examined by all workers on all shifts, precluding the possibility of blatant favoritism or discrimination. Yet a number of methods exist whereby experienced waitresses are able to circumvent the formal rotation system and secure the more lucrative stations for themselves. A waitress can trade assignments with a rookie who is uncertain of her ability to handle a fast station; she can volunteer to take over a large station when a *call-out* necessitates reorganization of station assignments; or she can establish herself as the only waitress capable of handling a particularly large or chaotic station. Changes in station assignments tend not to be formally recorded, so inconsistencies in the rotation system often do not show up on the schedule. Waitresses on the same shift may notice of course that a co-worker has managed to avoid an especially slow station for many days, or has somehow ended up in the busiest station two weekends in a row, but the waitresses' code of noninterference . . . inhibits them from openly objecting to such irregularities.

A waitress can also increase her tip income by working the more lucrative shifts. Because day is the busiest and therefore most profitable shift at Route, it attracts experienced, professional waitresses who are most concerned and best able to maximize their tip earnings. There are exceptions: some competent, senior-ranking waitresses are unable to work during the day due to time constraints of family or second jobs. Others choose not to work during the day despite the potential monetary rewards, because they are unwilling to endure the intensely competitive atmosphere for which day shift is infamous.

The acutely competitive environment that characterizes day shift arises from the aggregate striving of each waitress to maximize her tip income by serving the greatest possible number of customers. Two strategies are enlisted to this end. First, each waitress attempts to turn her tables as quickly as possible. Briefly stated, this means she takes the order, delivers the food, clears and resets a table, and begins serving the next party as rapidly as customer lingering and the speed of the kitchen allow. A seven-year veteran of Route describes the strategy and its rewards:

> What I do is I prebus my tables. When the people get up and go all I got is glasses and cups, pull off, wipe, set, and I do the table turnover. But see that's from day shift. See the girls on graveyard . . . don't understand the more times you turn that table the more money you make. You could have three tables and still make a hundred dollars. If you turn them tables.

As the waitress indicates, a large part of turning tables involves getting the table cleared and set for the next customer. During a rush, swing and grave waitresses tend to leave dirty tables standing, partly because they are less experienced and therefore less efficient, partly to avoid being given parties, or *sat*, when they are already behind. In contrast, day waitresses assign high priority to keeping their tables cleared and ready for customers. The difference in method reflects increased skill and growing awareness of and concern with money-making strategies.

A waitress can further increase her customer count by controlling the flow of customers within the restaurant. Ideally the hostess or manager running the front house rotates customers among stations, just as stations are rotated among waitresses. Each waitress is given, or *sat*, one party at a time in turn so that all waitresses have comparable customer counts at the close of a shift. When no hostess is on duty, or both she and the manager are detained and customers are waiting to be seated, waitresses will typically seat incoming parties.

Whether or not a formal hostess is on duty, day waitresses are notorious for bypassing

---

[1] A call-out (which more logically might be termed a "call-in") occurs when an employee calls in sick or with some other reason why he or she can't make it to work that day.—Ed.

the rotation system by racing to the door and directing incoming customers to their own tables. A sense of the urgency with which this strategy is pursued is conveyed in the comment of one five-year veteran, "They'll run you down to get that person at the door, to seat them in their station." The competition for customers is so intense during the day that some waitresses claim they cannot afford to leave the floor (even to use the restroom) lest they return to find a co-worker's station filled at their expense. "In the daytime, honey," remarks an eight-year Route waitress, "in the daytime it's like pulling teeth. You got to stay on the floor to survive. To survive." It is in part because they do not want to lose customers and tips to their co-workers that waitresses do not take formal breaks. Instead, they rest and eat between waiting tables or during lulls in business, returning to the floor intermittently to check on parties in progress and seat customers in their stations.

The fast pace and chaotic nature of restaurant work provide a cover for the waitress's aggressive pursuit of customers, since it is difficult for other servers to monitor closely the allocation of parties in the bustle and confusion of a rush. Still, it is not uncommon for waitresses to grumble to management and co-workers if they notice an obvious imbalance in customer distribution. Here again, the waitress refrains from directly criticizing her fellow servers, voicing her displeasure by commenting on the paucity of customers in her own station, rather than the overabundance of customers in the stations of certain co-waitresses. In response to these grumblings, other waitresses may moderate somewhat their efforts to appropriate new parties, and management may make a special effort to seat the disgruntled server favorably.

A waitress can also exert pressure on the manager or hostess to keep her station filled. She may, for instance, threaten to leave if she is not seated enough customers.

I said, "Innes [a manager], I'm in [station] one and two. If one and two is not filled at all times from now until three, I'm getting my coat, my pocketbook, and I'm leaving." And one and two was filled, and I made ninety-five dollars.

Alternatively, she can make it more convenient for the manager or hostess to seat her rather than her co-workers, either by keeping her tables open (as described), or by taking extra tables. If customers are waiting to be seated, a waitress may offer to pick up parties in a station that is closed or, occasionally, to pick up parties in another waitress's station. In attempting either strategy, but especially the latter, the waitress must be adept not only at waiting tables, but in interpersonal restaurant politics. Autonomy and possession are of central concern to waitresses, and a waitress who offers to pick up tables outside her station must select her words carefully if she is to avoid being accused of invading her co-workers' territory. Accordingly, she may choose to present her bid for extra parties as an offer to help—the manager, another waitress, the restaurant, customers—rather than as a request.

The waitress who seeks to increase her tip income by maximizing the number of customers she serves may endeavor to cut her losses by refusing to serve parties that have stiffed her in the past. If she is a low-ranking waitress, her refusal is likely to be overturned by the manager. If she is an experienced and valuable waitress, the manager may ask someone else to take the party, assure the waitress he will take care of her (that is, pad the bill and give her the difference), or even pick up the party himself. Though the practice is far from common, a waitress may go so far as to demand a tip from a customer who has been known to stiff in the past.

This party of two guys come in and they order thirty to forty dollars worth of food . . . and they stiff us. Every time. So Kaddie told them, "If you don't tip us, we're not going to wait

[handwritten: Story of tipping]

on you." They said, "We'll tip you." So Kaddie waited on them, and they tipped her. The next night they came in, I waited on them and they didn't tip me. The third time they came in [the manager] put them in my station and I told [the manager] straight up, "I'm not waiting on them. . . ." So he made Hailey pick them up. And they stiffed Hailey. So when they came in the next night . . . [they] said, "Are you going to give us a table?" I said, "You going to tip me? I'm not going to wait on you. You got all that money, you sell all that crack on the streets and you come here and you can't even leave me a couple of bucks?" . . . So they left me a dollar. So when they come in Tuesday night, I'm telling them a dollar ain't enough.

The tactics employed by waitresses, and particularly day-shift waitresses, to increase their customer count and thereby boost their tip earnings have earned them a resounding notoriety among their less competitive co-workers. Day (and some swing) waitresses are described as "money hungry," "sneaky little bitches," "self-centered," "aggressive," "back-stabbing bitches," and "cutthroats over tables." The following remarks of two Route waitresses, however, indicate that those who employ these tactics see them as defensive, not aggressive measures. A sense of the waitress's preoccupation with autonomy and with protecting what is hers also emerges from these comments.

[handwritten: Competitive name calling]

> You have to be like that. Because if you don't be like that, people step on you. You know, like as far as getting customers. I mean, you know, I'm sorry everybody says I'm greedy. I guess that's why I've survived this long at Route. Cause I am greedy. . . . *I want what's mine,* and if it comes down to me cleaning your table or my table, I'm going to clean my table. Because see I went through all that stage where I would do your table. To be fair. And you would walk home with seventy dollars, and I'd have twenty-five, cause I was being fair all night. (emphasis added)

> If the customer comes in the door and I'm there getting that door, don't expect me to cover

your backside while you in the back smoking a cigarette and I'm here working for myself. You're not out there working for me. . . . When I go to the door and get the customers, when I keep my tables clean and your tables are dirty, and you wonder why you only got one person . . . then that's just tough shit. . . . You're damn right my station is filled. *I'm not here for you.* (emphasis added)

Whether the waitress who keeps her station filled with customers is acting aggressively or defensively, her tactics are effective. It is commonly accepted that determined day waitresses make better money than less competitive co-workers even when working swing or grave. Moreover Nera, the waitress most infamous for her relentless use of "money-hungry tactics," is at the same time most famous for her consistently high daily takes. While other waitresses jingle change in their aprons, Nera is forced to store wads of bills in her shoes and in paper bags to prevent tips from overflowing her pockets. She claims to make a minimum of five hundred dollars a week in tip earnings; her record for one day's work exceeds two hundred dollars and is undoubtedly the record for the restaurant.

[handwritten: $200 a day in tip]

Inverting the Symbolism of Tipping

It may already be apparent that the waitress views the customer—not as a master to pamper and appease—but as a substance to be processed as quickly and in as large a quantity as possible. The difference in perspective is expressed in the objectifying terminology of waitresses: a customer or party is referred to as a *table,* or by table number, as *table five* or simply *five*; serving successive parties at a table is referred to as *turning the table*; taking an order is also known as *picking up a table*; and to serve water, coffee, or other beverages is to *water, coffee,* or *beverage* a table, number, or customer. Even personal acquaintances assume the status of inanimate matter, or tip-bearing plants, in the language of the server:

> I got my fifth-grade teacher [as a customer] one time. . . . I kept her coffeed. I kept her boyfriend coked all night. Sodaed. . . . And I kept them filled up.

If the customer is perceived as material that is processed, the goal of this processing is the production or extraction of a finished product: the tip. This image too is conveyed in the language of the floor. A waitress may comment that she "got a good tip" or "gets good tips," but she is more likely to say that she "made" or "makes good tips." She may also say that she "got five bucks out of" a customer, or complain that some customers "don't want to give up on" their money. She may accuse a waitress who stays over into her shift of "tapping on" her money, or warn an aspiring waitress against family restaurants on the grounds that "there's no money in there." In all these comments (and all are actual), the waitress might as easily be talking about mining for coal or drilling for oil as serving customers.

Predictably, the waitress's view of the customer as substance to be processed influences her perception of the meaning of tips, and especially substandard tips. At Route, low tips and stiffs are not interpreted as a negative reflection on the waitress's personal qualities or social status. Rather, they are felt to reveal the refractory nature or poor quality of the raw material from which the tip is extracted, produced, or fashioned. In less metaphorical terms, a low tip or stiff is thought to reflect the negative qualities and low status of the customer who is too cheap, too poor, too ignorant, or too coarse to leave an appropriate gratuity. In this context, it is interesting to note that *stiff*, the term used in restaurants to refer to incidents of nontipping or to someone who does not tip, has also been used to refer to a wastrel

or penniless man, a hobo, tramp, vagabond, deadbeat, and a moocher (Wentworth and Flexner 1975).

Evidence that waitresses assign blame for poor tips to the tipper is found in their reaction to being undertipped or stiffed. Rather than breaking down in tears and lamenting her "personal failure," the Route waitress responds to a stiff by announcing the event to her co-workers and managers in a tone of angry disbelief. Co-workers and managers echo the waitress's indignation and typically ask her to identify the party (by table number and physical description), or if she has already done so, to be more specific. This identification is crucial for it allows sympathizers to join the waitress in analyzing the cause of the stiff, which is assumed a priori[2] to arise from some shortcoming of the party, not the waitress. The waitress and her co-workers may conclude that the customers in question were rude, troublemakers, or bums, or they may explain their behavior by identifying them as members of a particular category of customers. It might be revealed, for instance, that the offending party was a church group: church groups are invariably tightfisted. It might be resolved that the offenders were senior citizens, Southerners, or businesspeople: all well-known cheapskates. If the customers were European, the stiff will be attributed to ignorance of the American tipping system; if they were young, to immaturity; if they had children, to lack of funds.

These classifications and their attendant explanations are neither fixed nor trustworthy. New categories are invented to explain otherwise puzzling incidents, and all categories are subject to exception. Though undependable as predictive devices, customer typologies serve a crucial function: they divert blame for stiffs and low tips from the waitress to the characteristics of the customer. It is for

---

[2]*A priori* is Latin for "from what comes before," or reasoning from what is already known.—Ed.

this reason that it is "important" for workers to distinguish between different categories of customers, despite the fact that such distinctions are based on "unreliable verbal and appearance clues." In fact, it is precisely the unreliability, or more appropriately the flexibility, of customer typologies that makes them valuable to waitresses. When categories can be constructed and dissolved on demand, there is no danger that an incident will fall outside the existing system of classification and hence be inexplicable.

While waitresses view the customer as something to be processed and the tip as the product of this processing, they are aware that the public does not share their understanding of the waitress–diner–tip relationship. Waitresses at Route recognize that many customers perceive them as needy creatures willing to commit great feats of service and absorb high doses of abuse in their anxiety to secure a favorable gratuity or protect their jobs. They are also aware that some customers leave small tips with the intent to insult the server and that others undertip on the assumption that for a Route waitress even fifty cents will be appreciated. One waitress indicated that prior to being employed in a restaurant, she herself subscribed to the stereotype of the down-and-out waitress "because you see stuff on television, you see these wives or single ladies who waitress and they live in slummy apartments or slummy houses and they dress in rags)." It is these images of neediness and desperation, which run so strongly against the waitress's perception of herself and her position, that she attacks when strained relations erupt into open conflict.

Five rowdy black guys walked in the door and they went to seat themselves at table seven. I said, "Excuse me. You all got to wait to be seated." "We ain't got to do *shit*. We here to eat. . . ." So they went and sat down. And I turned around and just looked at them. And they said, "Well, I hope you ain't our waitress, cause you

blew your tip. Cause you ain't getting nothing from us." And I turned around and I said, "You need it more than I do, baby."

This waitress's desire to confront the customer's assumption of her destitution is widely shared among service workers whose status as tipped employees marks them as needy in the eyes of their customers. Davis (1959, 162–163) reports that among cabdrivers "a forever repeated story is of the annoyed driver, who, after a grueling trip with a Lady Shopper, hands the coin back, telling her, 'Lady, keep your lousy dime. You need it more than I do.'" Mars and Nicod (1984, 75) report a hotel waitress's claim that "if she had served a large family with children for one or two weeks, and then was given a 10p piece,[3] she would give the money back, saying, 'It's all right, thank you, I've got enough change for my bus fare home.'" In an incident I observed (not at Route), a waitress followed two male customers out of a restaurant calling, "Excuse me! You forgot this!" and holding up the coins they had left as a tip. The customers appeared embarrassed, motioned for her to keep the money, and continued down the sidewalk. The waitress, now standing in the outdoor seating area of the restaurant and observed by curious diners, threw the money after the retreating men and returned to her work. Episodes such as these allow the worker to repudiate openly the evaluation of her financial status that is implied in an offensively small gratuity, and permit her to articulate her own understanding of what a small tip says and about whom. If customers can only afford to leave a dime, or feel a 10p piece is adequate compensation for two weeks' service, they must be very hard up or very ignorant indeed.

In the following incident the waitress interjects a denial of her neediness into an altercation

---

[3]Until it converts to the Eurodollar, the British monetary unit is the pound sterling (£). One pound is worth about $1.65 in U.S. currency. There are 100 pence to the pound. So, 10p (pronounced "10 pea") is worth about 17 cents.—Ed.

that is not related to tipping, demonstrating that the customer's perception of her financial status is a prominent and persistent concern for her.

> She [a customer] wanted a California Burger with mayonnaise. And when I got the mayonnaise, the mayonnaise had a little brown on it. . . . So this girl said to me, she said, "What the fuck is this you giving me?" And I turned around, I thought, "Maybe she's talking to somebody else in the booth with her." And I turned around and I said, "Excuse me?" She said, "You hear what I said. I said, 'What the fuck are you giving me?" And I turned around, I said, "I don't know if you're referring your information to *me*," I said, "but if you're referring your information to *me*," I said, "I don't *need* your bullshit." I said, "I'm not going to even take it. . . . Furthermore, I could care less if you eat or *don't* eat. . . . And you see this?" And I took her check and I ripped it apart. . . . And I took the California Burger and I says, "You don't have a problem anymore now, right?" She went up to the manager. And she says, "That black waitress"—I says, "Oh. By the way, what is my name? I don't have a name, [using the words] 'that black waitress'. . . . My name happens to be Nera. . . . That's N-E-R-A. . . . And I don't need your bullshit, sweetheart. . . . People like you I can walk on, because you don't know how to talk to human beings." And I said, "I don't need you. I don't need your quarters. I don't need your nickels. I don't need your dimes. So if you want service, be my guest. Don't you *ever* sit in my station, cause I won't wait on you." The manager said, "Nera, please. Would you wait in the back?" I said, "No. I don't take back seats no more for nobody."

In each of these cases, the waitress challenges the customer's definition of the relationship in which tipping occurs. By speaking out, by confronting the customer, she demonstrates that she is not subservient or in fear of losing her job; that she is not compelled by financial need or a sense of social hierarchy to accept abuse from customers; that she does not, in Nera's words, "take back seats no more for nobody." At the same time, she reverses the symbolic force of the low tip, converting a statement on her social status or work skills into a statement on the tipper's cheapness or lack of savoir faire.[4] . . .

References

Davis, Fred. 1959. "The Cabdriver and His Fare: Facets of a Fleeting Relationship." *American Journal of Sociology* 65(2): 158–165.

Mars, Gerald, and Michael Nicod. 1984. *The World of Waiters*. London: Allen & Unwin.

Wentworth, Harold, and Stuart Berg Flexner (eds. and comps.). 1975. *Dictionary of American Slang*. 2nd supplemental ed. New York: Crowell.

---

[4]*Savoir faire* is French and means literally "knowing how to do." Generally the phrase is used to mean "a knowledge of how to get around in the world," or simply, tact.—Ed.

Questions

1. You've just been out to dinner at a nice restaurant. Your waitress presented you with a tab for $72.50. Assuming the service was fine, how much did you tip her? How much do you think she might have expected? Where did you learn the appropriate amount to tip?

2. Have you ever tried to send a "message" to a waitperson by leaving no tip or a very small one? What was that message? Whether you've ever sent such a message, based on what you've read in Paules's article, do you think the message was received?

3. One of the techniques for understanding how people interact within a social structure is to look at "role sets"—that is, the set of statuses with which one interacts in carrying out one's role. In the accompanying diagram, I've sketched my role set as a professor. Try your hand at this by sketching the role set of the waitress.

   Generally, people within a particular role set have a similar understanding of one another's role—that is, their rights and duties as incumbents in a particular status. As Paules tells it, however, the customer has a different understanding of the waitress's role than the waitress does. To what sorts of complications might this lead? What would be the effect on the relationship if both customer and waitress understood the waitress's role from the waitress's point of view? From the customer's point of view?

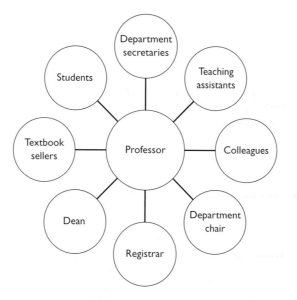

Professor's Role Set

17

COMMANDING THE ROOM IN SHORT SKIRTS

Cheering as the Embodiment of Ideal Girlhood

Natalie Adams and Pamela Bettis

Cheerleading isn't what it used to be. A generation ago, no one thought of cheerleading as a sport; the idea of cheerleader conjured up images of pompoms, short skirts, and pep. Today, it's different; cheerleading requires an athleticism that rivals that displayed by the players on the field. But, as Professors Adams and Bettis discover, cheerleaders have it tougher than other athletes—they have to smile when they get hurt and they aren't allowed to burp or fart.

Cheerleaders | popular | pretty...

In the United States, the cheerleader is a cultural icon, on one hand, symbolizing "youthful prestige, wholesome attractiveness, peer leadership and popularity," while simultaneously representing "mindless enthusiasm, shallow boosterism, objectified sexuality, and promiscuous availability" (Hanson 1995, 2). A staple of American life and popular culture, the cheerleader has received little scholarly attention. When discussed at all in academic research, as illustrated in the following quote, cheerleading is typically presented as an activity that exploits and demeans girls: "The function of the cheerleader is to encourage the worship of the men—the prettiest, nicest and most lively are selected to show and encourage adoration" (Weis 1997, 83).

In this article, we challenge such trivialization of cheerleading in academic research and argue that a feminist poststructuralist reading of cheerleading offers a unique opportunity to theorize this role in ways that honor the concrete realities of girls' lives. We follow Walkerdine's (1993, 15) suggestion to problematize traditional approaches to studying girls, as found in developmental psychology and socialization theories, by carrying out research that

> understand[s] the social world as constituted materially and discursively and replete with fantasies and fictions which shore up power in all its many guises. To understand the constitution of girls within this means that we understand girlhood as constituted in and through the discursive practices that make up the social world.

Drawing on an ethnographic study of a Midwestern middle school, we discuss cheerleading as a socially sanctioned space for a few girls to create multiple gendered subject positions that accommodate the shifting and often contradictory meanings of normative adolescent femininity. Our intent is to offer an examination of cheerleading that acknowledges the multiple meanings embedded in this cultural institution. We argue that cheerleading

Natalie Adams and Pamela Bettis, "Commanding the Room in Short Skirts: Cheering the Embodiment of Ideal Girlhood" from *Gender & Society* 17, no. 1 (February 2003): 73–91.

represents a liberating shift in normative femininity while simultaneously perpetuating a norm that does not threaten dominant social values and expectations about the role of girls and women. . . .

The Changing Face of Cheerleading: A Historical Overview

- Cheerleading vs sport. men

Originally, cheerleading was an exclusively male activity representing normative masculinity. During the mid- to late 1800s and the early 1900s, cheerleading was an idealized activity for privileged males and was seen as both an athletic and an aesthetic endeavor, as reported by the editors of *The Nation* (Organized cheering 1911, 6), who argued that organized cheering was a noble activity for undergraduates (i.e., males), and

> the reputation of having been a valiant "cheerleader" is one of the most valuable things a boy can take away from college. As a title to promotion in professional or public life, it ranks hardly second to that of having been a quarterback.

1920 girls started

Girls began entering collegiate organized cheering in small numbers in the late 1920s and early 1930s, but as late as the 1930s, cheerleading was still considered to be a male activity, associated with masculine characteristics of athleticism and leadership (Hanson 1995).

By the 1940s, more than 30,000 American high schools and colleges had cheerleaders, many of whom were girls. The trend to include girls in this previously masculine activity was precipitated in part by World War II. As young men fought in the war, girls were offered entrance into spaces once relegated solely for males. Cheerleading was one of those spaces (Hanson 1995). However, as men returned from the war, they sought to reclaim their place in the public spheres, including cheerleading squads. Thus, by the 1950s, several

colleges (e.g., the University of Tennessee) and high schools began to ban girls from the cheering squad (Gonzales 1956).

Despite the ban on women cheerleaders in some squads and the number of men still participating in cheerleading at the collegiate level, by the 1950s, cheerleading was becoming more and more feminized, as illuminated in a 1955 published list of desirable traits for high school cheerleaders. Gymnastics ability was not included; rather, the important traits were manners, cheerfulness, and good disposition—traits traditionally associated with women and girls (Kutz 1955, 310). Noting the transformation of cheerleading by the 1960s from a masculine activity to a highly feminized activity, McElroy (1999, 15) asserted,

> Cheerleading in the sixties consisted of pompoms, cutesy chants, big smiles and revealing uniforms. There were no gymnastic tumbling runs. No complicated stunting. Never any injuries. About the most athletic thing sixties cheerleaders did was a cartwheel followed by the splits.

However, in the aftermath of the second wave of feminist activism and theorizing in the 1960s, and the passage of title IX in 1972, the cultural scripts for ideal femininity began to change. The new ideal woman was one who did not relegate her needs to the needs of men. She sought to enter spheres once reserved only for men (e.g., occupations, sports). As the signifier of normative femininity began to change, so too did notions of the ideal girl, who, of course, had to be prepared for taking on a new role in adult society. As gendered identity began to be rethought, cheerleading began to be shaped by different discursive practices with different aims than before.

Recognizing the potential of losing profits due to an outdated image of cheerleading, national cheerleading organizations actively sought to reshape this activity as congruent with the newer ideals of normative femininity

(Woodmansee 1993). As Argetsinger (1999, A-1) asserted, "in post–Title IX, cheerleading might have vanished but it harnessed the spirit of the time, evolving into a melange of highflying acrobatics and show-biz flair that required more athleticism than before." Tight athletic motions, difficult jumps, and pyramid building began to be emphasized in the hundreds of cheerleading camps offered throughout the country. These new cheerleading techniques required girls who not only were strong but also were agile, were well-coordinated, and possessed athletic prowess.

Part of the transformation of cheerleading centered on the introduction of national, state, and regional competitions. Cheerleaders suddenly moved from the sidelines where they were motivational spectators to become the competitors themselves. In 1981, the first national high school cheerleading competition was held, and in 1983, ESPN televised the event (Hanson 1995). With the introduction and proliferation of national competitions, demands on cheerleading squads increased, with many squads practicing 12 months a year, often two or three times a day. Special coaches were often hired to teach squads difficult and often dangerous routines for competition (Argetsinger 1999).

By the 1990s, competitive cheerleading squads (called All-Star) were being formed throughout the United States. These competitive cheerleading squads were not affiliated with schools or any sports teams but competed for themselves (Argetsinger 1999; Brenner 1999; McElroy 1999). According to the National Federation of State High Schools, in the 1997–1998 school year, approximately 59,000 girls participated in competitive cheerleading—an increase of approximately 25,000 since 1995–1996 (Deardorff 1999).

As illuminated in this brief overview of the evolution of cheerleading, the discursive practices of this activity have changed to accommodate the changing nature of gender roles and normative gendered behavior in our society. From the late 1800s to the 1930s, cheerleading squads comprised primarily men, and cheerleading signified ideal masculinity. However, by the mid-1950s, cheerleading had changed significantly from an activity representing normative masculinity to one representing ideal femininity. In discussing the shift from a masculine activity to a naturalized feminine activity during this time period, Davis (1990, 155) pointed out that cheerleaders came to symbolize "dominant ideology about how females should look and act in our society." That is, women/cheerleaders were to be pretty, were to possess appealing figures, were to play a secondary role to males, and were not to be taken too seriously. In the aftermath of title IX and the second wave of women's rights, notions of the appropriate role and behavior of women in society began to shift; thus, cheerleading had to change to reflect new ideals about normative femininity and ideal girlhood. This study illuminates those changes.

Data Collection

In August 1998, along with two other researchers,[1] we began a study focusing on girls and leadership at Powhaton Middle School, a sixth- and seventh-grade school located in a Midwestern town of 26,000.[2] The racial composition of the student body was 75 percent white, 14 percent Native American, 8.3 percent Hispanic, 4.5 percent African American, and 0.8 percent Asian. During the initial interviews with 61 seventh-grade girls, and throughout our field notes, cheerleaders were frequently mentioned as leaders in the school. Therefore, beginning in January 1999, we began five

---

[1]Drs. Deb Jordan and Diane Montgomery, along with the authors, collected the data for the larger study on girls and leadership.

[2]Pseudonyms are used for all people and places in this study.

months of weekly observations of two cheer-leading classes the school had instituted to prepare girls for the March cheerleading try-outs. The details leading to the creation of this class are complicated and are discussed else-where (Adams and Bettis in press). However, for the purposes of this article, it is sufficient to explain that the Powhaton school district implemented a cheerleading preparation class at two schools as one way to meet the demands of the Office of Civil Rights after a grievance was filed against the district in 1994. These cheerleading preparation classes were intended to level the playing field by offering any girl the opportunity to enroll in the class as a physical education elective. The purpose of the class, according to the school board's minutes, was to "provide an elective physi-cal education class to teach skills needed in cheerleading and drill teams to grades 7–9." At Powhaton Middle School, this class was referred to as the cheer prep class.

The two cheer prep classes were scheduled back to back to meet the schedule of the part-time instructor who was the cheerleader spon-sor for the junior varsity cheerleading squad at the local high school. Typically, we situated ourselves along the gym wall and took copi-ous field notes while the girls participated in the various activities Louise Stone, the teacher, planned for helping them prepare for tryouts.[3] We also observed the cheerleading clinic held after school to teach the girls the tryout rou-tines, the mock tryouts (held the night before the real tryouts, which were closed to the public), and a cheerleading camp for those who were selected for the team during the fol-lowing summer. We conducted initial inter-views before the tryouts with 22 of the 64 girls enrolled in the class. These 22 girls were all part of the larger study on girls and leader-ship and had been previously interviewed about their perceptions of leadership. A second round of interviews with 18 of the 22 was con-ducted following tryouts.

Of the 20 girls ultimately chosen for the squad, 19 were white, and 1 was Native Amer-ican.[4] The racial composition of the girls we initially interviewed consisted of 14 whites, 5 Native Americans, and 3 African Americans: 13 of the 20 girls chosen for the squad were among those we interviewed. In addition, 9 other girls who did not make the squad or who decided not to try out, but who were in the cheer preparation class, were interviewed. The two formal interviews were semistructured and conducted in a variety of locations dur-ing the cheer preparation class while informal interviews took place at lunch and before and after classes. The cheer preparation teacher, Ms. Stone, was also interviewed. Documents pertinent to the study, including handouts disseminated to students and parents about tryouts, local newspaper articles featuring the cheerleaders, and Powhaton School Board minutes, were also studied. . . .

---

[3]In our larger study of cheerleading (Adams and Bettis in press), we found that a majority of cheerleading sponsors are former cheerleaders, and they have great passion for the activity. In this sense, Ms. Stone, as a former high school and junior college cheerleader, represents a fairly typical cheerleading sponsor. She is somewhat atypical in that there is a high turnover rate among cheerleader sponsors, but Ms. Stone has been a cheerleader sponsor in this school district for more than 10 years.

[4]As we discuss elsewhere (Adams and Bettis in press), despite the Office of Civil Rights's involvement, five years later, the cheerleading squads continued to be white and middle class. The school board policies were not fully implemented. Social class continued to be a major factor in who made the squad. Only those girls who could afford the hefty fees at private gyms learned advanced tumbling skills, which greatly enhanced one's chances of being selected. More important, many of the working-class white, Native American, and African American girls contested certain facets of normative femininity found in the cheerleading identity of this middle school while many of the middle-class white girls who were also members of a dominant group called the preps embraced the requirements of achieving this identity.

Data: Cheerleading and the Ideal Girl

I am not arrogant.
I am confident.
I am not a daredevil.
I am daring.
I am not a beauty queen.
I am an athlete.
I am not a stereotype.
I am my own person.
I am not interested in the past.
I am living for the future.
I am not afraid of success.
I am afraid of nothing.
I am not another face in the crowd.
I am the ones others wish they could be.
I am not just any cheerleader.
I am the one in the Varsity uniform.
　　　　　　　—Varsity Spirit Corporation (1999, 1)

As is evident in the above poem from the 1999 Varsity Cheerleading catalog, the cheerleader has been reconstructed to represent new ideals of normative femininity, which include confidence, rationality, risk taking, athleticism, independence, and fearlessness. In this section, we demonstrate how the girls in our study take up these signifiers of ideal girlhood to create their own version of femininity, one that allows them to dabble with the traditional markers of masculinity without having to give up those feminine characteristics they deem enjoyable and desirable. We argue that while they are playing an active role in constituting their own gendered identity within the discursive practice of cheerleading, they are also "constrained by larger material practices, structures and discourses that shape and coerce as well as potentiate individual action" (Davies 1989, xi). By doing so, we hope to demonstrate how girls are both productions of and producers of their own gendered subjectivities.

MASCULINITY AND THE CHEERLEADER ATHLETE:
DISCIPLINE, RISK TAKING, AND POWER
IN THE PHYSICAL

In the cheerleading preparation classes we observed at Powhaton Middle School, cheerleading as an athletic endeavor was emphasized repeatedly. In preparation for trying out in front of three judges, the cheerleader sponsor continuously instructed the girls to show off their muscular bodies: "All right, girls, make your muscles tight so the judges can see them. Tight across the shoulders. Tomorrow you should hurt. Legs are tight. This is a great time to show off your muscles." In addition to having a muscular, fit body, the ability to tumble and maintain tight motion technique—rigid body movements that some would characterize as almost militaristic in style—were also critical to making the squad. Lisa, a petite blonde who scored the highest number of points at tryouts, explained the importance of being tight:

> Like when you cheer, your arms have to be tight, and your emotions are like aggressive, not like to where you're going to punch someone, just like when they're tight. Like when I get up there, I'm like [hard snapping noise] push my arms down and slap them.

This aggressive attitude was encouraged by Ms. Stone, whose language during practices was replete with militaristic jargon. "Command the room" was a phrase she frequently used to motivate the girls into maintaining an aggressive attitude toward the judges and audience. In teaching proper motion techniques, she would instruct them, "Punch forward—don't swing your arms. Keep everything close to your body. Think close. Tight, tight, tight." Much like a drill sergeant, while working with the girls on motion technique, Ms. Stone would yell,

> Chins up, shoulders back, smiles. Hit the motion. Hit. Hit. Hit. 1, 2, 3, hit. 1, 2, 3, hit. When I say Hit, do a V. When I say, Hit, do a down V. Hit L; Hit V; Hit Down V.

At one point, she advised the girls, "Don't be afraid to push through the floor. Smash—power off your toes." At another time, she told the girls, "Attack those jumps even if you don't like the side we're doing." In addition to the girls' using robotic, tight motions, cheers were to be yelled in a deep, masculine voice.

Disciplining the body is an integral part of cheerleading. Preparation for cheerleading at Powhaton means that one must work long hours to master the movements, techniques, and tumbling required to be a serious contender for the cheerleading squad. Two of the criteria judges use at Powhaton to select the girls for the junior high squad are jumps (e.g., herkies, toe touches) and tumbling (back handsprings, back tucks), both of which require practice, perseverance, and athletic prowess. Every girl we interviewed who eventually was selected cheerleader either participated in tumbling classes at one of the local gyms or paid money to individuals to help them in mastering the requisite cheerleading skills. Although Ms. Stone would often tell the girls that tumbling was not an absolute requirement for making the squad, the reality was, as Patti, eventually selected cocaptain of the squad, noted, "all of us can do a back handspring."

Part of disciplining the cheerleader body entailed assuming a stance of invulnerability to pain. Embodying the image of the fierce athlete who is able to overcome pain to emerge the triumphant victor, Lisa recounted the harrowing events of tryouts, which eventually led to her obtaining the number 1 spot on the cheerleading squad:

> On the day of tryouts, I had 104 degrees fever; I had pneumonia. I had been sick for days and lost six pounds before tryouts. At tryouts, I fell on my head during my back handspring. It was like my wrists just collapsed. But I scored number 1. I couldn't even come to school the next day because I was so sick. My dad said he was proud of me because I showed determination.

During the cheer prep class, Leslie tore a ligament and had to be sent to the emergency room. Michelle suffered a severe sprain and was on crutches for two weeks. Neither saw these injuries as a deterrent to their trying out.

In describing the typical cheerleader, Julie, who was selected to be an eighth-grade cheerleader, said, "They are really peppy and hyper and just jump all over the place all the time." Sharon, also selected cheerleader, stated that she wanted to be a cheerleader because she was "always hyper." The reality is that cheering is not a spontaneous emotional activity. Rather, cheerleaders are to practice rationality and discipline. Indeed, unbridled emotion and spontaneity is appropriate only on the sidelines of sports events and only in certain contexts (e.g., a football player intercepts the ball and runs for a 60-yard touchdown). At all other times, cheerleading is a very controlled, organized, and disciplined activity. Cheers are orchestrated with complex tumbling moves, pyramid building, and partner stunts; dances are choreographed with precision; and chants often sound like military yells. There is little room for individual creativity in cheerleading at Powhaton.

Part of controlling one's emotion means the girls were to act in a way that on the surface seemed inauthentic. As preparation for tryouts, Ms. Stone repeatedly told the girls, "Pretend that you are having the time of your life. Show it in your faces, in your smiles." The ability to assume an inauthentic stance was most readily visible in the edicts to the girls to always have a smile on their face. More than any other quality, the ability to smile at all times seemed to be the most prized cheerleading attribute. Yet smiling in this context is not a spontaneous emotional response; rather, the ability to plaster a smile on one's face at a moment's notice was a very disciplined activity requiring a particular mind-set and lots of practice, as illustrated in the following comments:

> You have to have a cheerleading personality, you know, smile all the time. Like Ms. Stone

told me, "I don't care if it's a fake smile or not, just smile." (Terry, selected cheerleader)

You have to smile to look good, so everyone will think you're having a wonderful time. (Allison, selected cheerleader)

When you see a cheerleader, she's always smiling. But I can't smile if I don't feel like smiling. (Tamara, member of the cheer prep class, did not try out)

You've got to have fake smiles all the time. You know, cheesey. It takes practice to smile without it looking fake. I practice all the time in front of my mirror. It's hard work. (Lisa, selected cheerleader)

You have to be a prep to become a cheerleader because they got that fake happy look about them. I can't get that. I have to really be happy to look happy. (Daneka, member of cheer prep class, did not try out)

The ability to execute tight movements and complicated jumps and tumbling feats was a source of confidence for the girls selected cheerleader, as explained by Lisa—"It just gives you confidence, makes you feel good when you know you can make your body do these really hard things"—and Allison—"the prep girls will make it because they have confidence; they can jump, tumble, and do tight motions. They have it all." Karla, who tried out but was not selected, probably because of her lack of tumbling ability, noted,

When you can tumble, the judges think of you as more flexible. Like you can do things better than everybody else. It gives them confidence. If you mess up, they don't just sit there. They get back up and do it again.

Clearly, for some girls, cheerleading offers a space for them to gain confidence in their bodies and themselves.

The desired female body is continuously rethought and reshaped through disciplining and normalizing practices that reflect both contemporary and historical understandings of what constitutes ideal femininity. Unlike the ideal female body of yesteryear that was prized because of its inertness, delicacy, and helplessness, the revered female body today is that of the hard-muscled, sleek athlete, and girls today are being taught that it is not only appropriate but desirable to run, jump, tumble, act boldly, and move daringly (Bordo 1993). Cheerleading offers a safe space for girls to do just this, that is, to revel and delight in the physicality of their bodies. This is one of the main reasons why cheerleading, despite feminist critiques, continues to grow and attract large numbers of girls. With the assumption of many of the discursive practices once associated primarily with men and sports (e.g., musculature, strength, athletic prowess, fear of danger, and risk taking), cheerleading offers a space for some girls to embody the masculine look of the athlete and the concomitant values of self-discipline, aggressiveness, and self-mastery, thus entering a sphere once relegated to only boys and men.

FEMININITY AND GIRLIE GIRLS DIVERTING THE GAZE: PLEASURE AND SEXUALIZED SUBJECTIVITY IN CHEERLEADING

Most of us want to be cheerleaders because we are more into being a girlie girl. (Lisa)

The girls selected cheerleader at Powhaton embraced the public nature of cheerleading, which allowed them to demonstrate to the world that they were confident, assertive, competitive, and athletic. However, the appeal of cheerleading went beyond simply the opportunity to prove they were athletes. In fact, the majority of the girls selected cheerleader were already known at their school as accomplished athletes; many of them had to juggle track and basketball practice with the mandatory cheerleading preparation clinic. This number is in line with recent data from a poll of 2,500 cheerleaders conducted by the Universal Cheerleaders Association, which found that more than 50 percent of girls who cheer also participate in other athletic activities at their school (Roenigk 2002). Cheerleading was appealing to these girls because it also offered them a space to revel in what they called being a girlie girl. Unlike other athletes, these girls are participating in an activity that remains firmly entrenched within a feminine discourse; thus, they do not have to veil their masculinity nor worry, like other athletes, about being stigmatized as too masculine or as lesbians. These girls embrace cheerleading as a way to have it all—to flirt with the masculine without ever questioning or having someone else question their femininity or their sexual identity.

Traditionally, cheerleading has been constructed as an activity that valorizes stereotypical feminine virtues such as nurturance, selflessness, subservience, and loyalty. Cheerleading as a stereotypical feminine discourse was certainly evident at Powhaton, particularly as enacted in the values and beliefs of Ms. Stone, who explains the purpose of cheerleading as follows:

> My school spirit comes from the heart, and these young women need to learn how to be loyal. They need to learn how to take the eyes off of themselves. We're there for other people; we're not there for ourselves. . . . If it weren't for the athletes in the building, there would be no reason for us; we're to give of ourselves; we are serving our athletes.

The Powhaton Cheerleading Constitution, which all cheerleaders must sign, clearly situates cheerleaders in a supportive role: "The primary purpose of cheerleading is to promote unity, sportsmanship, and school spirit at school and school events. . . . The primary function of a cheerleading program is to support interscholastic athletics."

Interestingly, none of the girls interviewed indicated that the purpose of cheerleading was to demonstrate loyalty to their school. Most of them, like Nan, wanted to

be a cheerleader "because all my friends are doing it and you get to cheer in front of people and have lots of fun." The cheerleaders in this study do not view themselves as passive girls on the sidelines, and they certainly do not intend, as Ms. Stone suggested, to take the "eyes off of themselves," as explained by Lisa, Julie, and Patti:

> I thought cheerleading's just neat 'cause you get to tumble and you get to be some of the stars of the game. . . . It's just you want to be one of the main focuses of the game instead of the players. And you want to get people's attention. (Lisa)
>
> I like getting up in front of people and, like, being the one in charge. I like showing off and being with the guys. (Julie)
>
> Most of us are loud, and we like to cheer because we like to draw attention to ourselves. (Patti)

For the girls in this study, one of the primary joys of being a cheerleader derived from the knowledge that cheerleaders are the object of everyone's gaze—not just males. Most of the girls who were selected cheerleader told stories of how they, as early as four years old, envied and wanted to emulate the cheerleaders they saw from their view in the stands. Lisa explained,

> There are so many people who aren't into basketball or football and all they do is watch the cheerleaders and say, "Wow! I want to do that!" And they think of them as a role model, like, Yeah, mom there's a cheerleader. I want to be that when I grow up. That's what I did.

Being the center of attention, being the one "others wish they could be," offered these girls a form of power and pleasure not experienced in other activities, such as playing basketball or being in the school orchestra. Milea, the only Native American chosen for the squad, explained the difference between cheerleading and other sports: "Cheerleading is a sport you can have fun at. Sports were invented so that people could have fun, but most sports have turned into work, not fun. But not cheer-leading. It's just fun!" The cheerleaders in this study saw themselves as central to the sporting event being observed and believed they had the power to control how the crowd and the players respond to the game on the field or the court, as illuminated in the following quotes:

> Cheerleaders are supposed to cheer the players on so they feel like they're doing good even when everyone knows they stink. (Allison)

> Cheerleaders are supposed to, like, even if your team's not that good, show them that, like, to try hard and motivate them. (Suzi)

> During a game, you'd be out there and you'd be leading a cheer, like, to help the team players, you know, make them feel confident that they can do it. (Terry)

> Cheerleaders are leaders because if the team is losing, they'll get those big old smiles on and get all perky and they're able to get everybody back into the game. (Sharon)

In conveying her implicit understanding of the ideal woman as one who is heterosexual, a wife, and a mother, Ms. Stone explicated how cheerleading prepares girls for adult womanhood:

> Cheerleaders are still very feminine, and we work on those characteristics. We have rules, no burping, no farting. You are young ladies. But we build, we jump, we try to get a balance because cheerleading does prepare them for later on in life. They've got to be strong. They've got to bear pain to have children. . . . They've got to be able to stand on their feet and make decisions when it may be mom, or dad, or husband, who's laid out there and you've got to do what is the right thing to do. You've got to support. You've got to lift up. That's the whole role of being an adult woman.

Undoubtedly, cheerleading can still be read as a discourse that affirms heterosexualized femininity in which a woman's most basic desire is to be affiliated with a man. Although none of the girls expressed the sentiment that cheer-leading was excellent preparation for being a wife and mother, many of the girls trying out for cheerleader at Powhaton expressed the belief that cheerleading made one more popular, thus increasing one's likelihood of gaining a boyfriend, a high-status marker for adolescent girls at this school. For example, Milea pointed out, "Boys like cheerleaders so that makes you popular. I want more boys to like me." Shanna, who was in the cheer prep class but did not try out, explained, "Some girls think the boys will like you if you're a cheerleader 'cause boys like the cheeriest people." Daneka, who did not try out for cheerleader although she participated in the cheer prep class, stated that "girls want to be cheerleaders because they believe that guys will like them more—they will see them as cute women in short skirts."

Daneka's use of "girls" and "women" in the same sentence reflects a primary attraction of cheerleading for many girls: It allows girls to try on a womanly (i.e., sexualized) identity in a school-sanctioned space. Walkerdine (1993) argued that in most accounts about girls' experiences in schools, the schoolgirl typified is the one who follows rules and is deferential, is loyal, is quiet, and works hard. This image of the schoolgirl, Walkerdine (1993, 20) asserted, has been constructed as a "defence against being the object of male fantasies. The erotic is displaced [in school accounts] as too dangerous. But it re-enters, it enters in the spaces that are outlawed in the primary school: popular culture." Cheerleading does allow the erotic to enter into school spaces; in fact, cheerleading at Powhaton Middle School offered the only school-sanctioned space for girls simultaneously to play with or to try on the identity of the all-American nice girl next door and the sexually provocative woman. Cheerleaders are allowed to wear short skirts and tight-fitting vests, which violate school dress codes, while performing sexually provocative dance moves (e.g., pelvic thrusts) on the school stage to popular music typically not allowed elsewhere in school. For many of the girls, such as Julie, this opportunity to play with a sexualized identity was a primary reason cheerleading was so appealing. She explained, "I'm in it for the short skirts, the guys, getting in front of everybody, and making a total fool of myself."

Yet at the same time, cheerleaders at Powhaton were viewed as leaders who serve the interests of the school and community, symbolizing values and traditions deemed positive in American culture (Eckert 1989). As mentioned earlier, cheerleaders were cited as school leaders by almost all of the 61 girls interviewed in the larger study. The girls selected to be cheerleaders took this role seriously and recognized that being a cheerleader meant they would be role models for others. Suzi offered this explanation of the responsibility of cheerleading:

> It's not like it used to be, like popularity and stuff. Now you have to like have what it takes to be a cheerleader. You can't just like get up there and just smile. You have to have tight motions. You have to know what you're supposed to be doing, and you have big responsibility now. You have to be at cheerleading practice on time. If you have to have the tape for the dance, you have to remember to bring it. You have to be responsible. You're going to have a lot of people looking up to you, and so you're going to have lots of responsibility to do right things.

Undeniably, the sexualized nature of cheerleading, which situates girls as objects of desire—clad in short skirts and tight-fitting vests—was part of the discourse of cheerleading at Powhaton. While performing tight, militaristic movements and using a deep voice, the girls were also instructed to look at the judges in a sexy way. "When you make that turn," instructed Ms. Stone, "give the judges a sexy look." She further instructed them, "You should be oozing out cheerleading stuff.

Dazzle me, smile, give me goosebumps. I want to be dazzled." The last advice Ms. Stone gave the girls before the day of tryouts was to "put Vaseline on your teeth and put on a little extra makeup, but not too much. Don't come looking like someone who could stand on the street."

Conclusion

Operating at the juncture of all-American good looks, traditional femininity, and sportslike athleticism, contemporary cheerleading provides a culturally sanctioned space for performing the requisite traits of the ideal girl in the new millennium. Quite literally, cheerleading is a performative act—one that has been traditionally understood as girls performing for the pleasure of others, particularly men. Many would argue, as in the film *American Beauty*, that this performance situates the girl body as the object of the masculine gaze and male fantasy. As Kurman (1986, 58) noted, "the cheerleader is a disturbing erotic icon. . . . She incarnates, in a word, a basic male-voyeuristic fantasy." Yet Kenway et al. (1994, 205), in discussing their work with adolescent girls and gender reform in Australia, offered a different reading of the performance metaphor:

> The performance metaphor allows the girls to feel a sense of control over different performance genres, to pick up, discard, play and take risks within them, and even to go beyond them through improvisation, collage, and carnival. Femininity can then become a source of power and pleasure rather than a source of control.

We found ample evidence in our study to suggest that cheerleading offers a critical space for certain girls to take risks, to try on different personas, to delight in the physicality of their bodies, and to control and revel in their own power and desire. In other words, cheerleading offers some girls the opportunity to perform ideal girlhood without being located in a disabling discourse of femininity that equates femininity with exploitation and oppression. In many ways, these girls have embraced cheerleading as a way of accommodating the contradictions of constructing oneself as a feminine subject. Thus, any reading of cheerleading and the new girl order must acknowledge that girls themselves play an active role in reconstituting ideal femininity as they resist, rethink, and re-envision for themselves who they want to be as gendered individuals.

Although the girls in this study took up multiple gendered subjectivities within the discursive practices of cheerleading, they are not free to construct any gender identity they desire. As feminist poststructuralists (Davies 1989; Walkerdine 1993; Weedon 1987) have pointed out, constructing a gendered identity is always constrained by larger material practices, structures, and discourses. This study shows how these shape and influence the ways in which girls negotiate a gendered identity within a patriarchal society that continues to define ideal girlhood very narrowly. Hence, we are reminded how powerful certain discourses are despite the changing landscape for normative masculinity and femininity. As several researchers of girl culture have pointed out (Brumberg 1997; Inness 1998; Johnson, Roberts, and Worell 1999), growing up female is not an easy task, particularly in a time when the signifiers of masculinity and femininity seem to be always in flux. As ideal femininity has shifted, girls in the twenty-first century are faced with the problem of how far they can go in displaying femininity and masculinity, in what contexts such displays are appropriate, and to what degree. This study reveals how these contradictions play out in the discursive practices associated with contemporary cheerleading and sports. For example, cheerleaders dressed in short skirts and tight vests often cheer for female basketball players dressed in baggy shorts and shirts. Through

their uniforms, the cheerleaders accentuate their femininity while the basketball players hide theirs. The cheerleaders try to play up their masculinity, not through their clothing but through their stunts and tumbling, while the female basketball players often play up their femininity off court to become the "heterosexy" athlete (Griffin 1992), thus gaining acceptance and avoiding the lesbian label.[5]

Obviously, cheerleading is but one avenue for girls to contest stereotypical images of the docile, unathletic female body. Girls now have opportunities, although much more limited, to engage in ice hockey, football, boxing, and bodybuilding. However, as Inness (1999) and Lowe (1998) pointed out, despite the gains women have made in many areas once relegated solely for men, in the twenty-first century, we still do not exactly know what to do with women who box, women bodybuilders, and women who want to play professional football and ice hockey. When women enter a masculine discourse and assume masculine signifiers, mainstream society is threatened, and when a woman steps over the boundaries of acceptable feminine behavior, she is typically viewed as gender deviant (Adams 1999; Inness 1999). Similar to the All-American Girls Baseball League begun in the 1940s and disbanded in the 1950s, cheerleaders, as personifications of the ideal girl, merely flirt with the masculine. As Candice Berry, coach of the Greenup County High cheerleading squad in Kentucky, one of the top cheerleading squads in the country, stated, "cheerleading offers budding young women something that girls' basketball, track, soccer, softball can't offer: lessons in how to be a *lady,* how to be tough without imitating men" (McElroy 1999, 119). Cheerleaders, for all their athleticism, toughness, and risk taking, do

---

[5]We would like to thank one of the reviewers for this helpful insight.

not disrupt twenty-first-century, taken-for-granted notions of normative femininity and masculinity. In other words, they ultimately do not challenge the status quo by transgressing gendered boundaries.

References

Adams, Natalie. 1999. "Fighting to Be Somebody: The Discursive Practices of Adolescent Girls Fighting." *Educational Studies* 30: 115–39.

Adams, Natalie, and Pamela Bettis. 2005. *Cheerleader: An American Icon.* New York: Palgrave Press.

Argetsinger, Amy. 1999. "When Cheerleaders Are the Main Event: For Private Teams, Victory Is Their Own." *Washington Post,* July 10, Al.

Bordo, Susan. 1993. "Unbearable Weight: Feminism, Western Culture, and the Body." Berkeley: University of California Press.

Brenner, Elsa. 1999. "Cheerleading Changes as Boys Join Sidelines: Stereotypes Slip Away, Attitudes Shift and a Sport Calls for More Acrobatics." *New York Times,* 2 May, Section 14, 1, 4–5.

Brumberg, Joan. 1997. *The Body Project: An Intimate History of American Girls.* New York: Random House.

Davies, Bronwyn. 1989. *Frogs and Snails and Feminist Tales.* Sydney, Australia: Allen and Unwin.

———. 1993. *Shards of Glass: Children Reading and Writing Beyond Gendered Identity.* Cresskill, NJ: Hampton Press.

Davis, L. 1990. "Male Cheerleaders and the Naturalization of Gender." In Michael Messner and Don Sabo (eds.), *Sports, Men and the Gender Order.* Champaign, IL: Human Kinetics Books.

Deardorff, Julie. 1999. "Cheerleaders Want R-E-S-P-E-C-T: Competitions Take Pep Squads Beyond Old Sis-Boom Bah." *Chicago Tribune,* 30 May, 1, 3.

Eckert, Penelope. 1989. *Jocks and Burnouts.* New York: Teachers College Press.

Gonzales, Arturo. 1956. "The First College Cheer." *American Mercury* 83: 100–104.

Griffin, Pat. 1992. "Changing the Game: Homophobia, Sexism, and Lesbians In Sport." *Quest* 44: 251–65.

Hanson, Mary Ellen. 1995. *Go! Fight! Win! Cheerleading In American Culture.* Bowling Green, OH: Bowling Green University Press.

Inness, Sherrie. 1998. *Millennium Girls: Today's Girls Around the World.* Lanham, MD: Rowman & Littlefield.

———. 1999. *Tough Girls: Women Warriors and Wonder Women in Popular Culture.* Philadelphia: University of Pennsylvania Press.

Johnson, Norine, Michael Roberts, and Judith Worell. 1999. *Beyond Appearance: A New Look at Adolescent Girls.* Washington, DC: American Psychological Association.

Kenway, Jane, Sue Willis, Jill Blackmore, and Leonia Rennie. 1994. "Making 'Hope Practical' Rather Than 'Despair convincing': Feminist Poststructuralism, Gender Reform and Educational change." *British Journal of Sociology of Education* 15: 187–210.

Kurman, George. 1986. "What Does Girls' Cheerleading Communicate?" *Journal of Popular Culture* 20: 57–64.

Kutz, F. B. 1955. "Cheerleading Rules, Desirable Traits and Qualifications." *School Activities* 26: 310.

Lowe, Maria. 1998. *Women of Steel: Female Body Builders and the Struggle for Self-Definition.* New York: New York University Press.

McElroy, James. 1999. *We've Got Spirit: The Life and Times of America's Greatest Cheerleading Team.* New York: Simon & Schuster.

Organized cheering. 1911. *Nation* 92: 5–6.

Roenigk, Alyssa. 2002. "Cheer Safety: Setting the Record Straight." *American Cheerleader* 8: 46–48.

Varsity Spirit Corporation. 1999. *Varsity.* Memphis, TN: Varsity Spirit Corporation.

Walkerdine, Valerie. 1990. *Schoolgirl Fictions.* London: Verso.

———. 1993. "Girlhood Through the Looking Glass." In Marion de Ras and Mieke Lunenberg (eds.), *Girls, Girlhood and Girls' Studies in Transition.* Amsterdam: Het Spinhuis.

Weedon, Chris. 1987. *Feminism Practice and Poststructuralist Theory.* Oxford, UK: Basil Books.

Weis, Lois. 1997. "Gender and the Reports: The Case of the Missing Piece." In Catherine Marshall (ed.), *Feminist critical policy analysis: A Perspective from Primary and Secondary Schooling.* London: Falmer.

Woodmansee, Ken. 1993. "Cheers! Jeff Webb's Multicolored World Wide Spirit Machine." *Memphis Business* 3: 14–19.

Questions

1. The authors of this article assert that cheerleading operates "at the juncture . . . of traditional femininity and sports-like athleticism." How does the modern cheerleader combine these traits?

2. Female athletes are frequently regarded with suspicion in American society—for example, many athletic women may be suspected of being lesbians. How is it that female cheerleaders manage to avoid this sort of suspicion?

3. At Powhaton Middle School, any girl was allowed to take classes to learn the skills needed to be a cheerleader. As it turns out, however, other skills (e.g., tumbling) are needed to be selected as a cheerleader. How do the girls acquire these additional skills? What are the implications of this for the composition of the cheerleading squad—does everyone have an equal chance?

4. Historically, cheerleading was a male domain and, according to one commentator cited in the article,

   > the reputation of having been a valiant "cheer-leader" is one of the most valuable things a boy can take away from college. As a title to promotion in professional or public ranks, it ranks hardly second to that of having been a quarterback.

   There still are male cheerleaders, of course, but does the fact of having been a valiant cheerleader still have the same positive impact on a man's career? Why or why not? What is its impact on a woman's career?

18

ORTHODOX AND INCLUSIVE MASCULINITY: COMPETING MASCULINITIES AMONG MALE CHEERLEADERS

*Eric Anderson**

For most people, the word *cheerleader* evokes the image of a peppy, smiling girl in a short skirt. Cheerleaders are enthusiastic, feminine and cute. Or, to the less charitable, cheerleaders are snobs and ditzy airheads. Positive or negative, the stereotypic cheerleader is female. This stereotype is so pervasive that the idea of a male cheerleader seems unnatural. And yet, cheerleading began in the late 19th century as a male activity; women were excluded from cheer squads premised on such "facts" as men's low voices would be more easily heard by the crowd and because cheerleading took a lot of strength. It was not until the 1940s when men disappeared from college campuses to fight in the war that women were allowed to become cheerleaders. Once the war was over, there were attempts to once again exclude women from cheering, but the women would not be moved.

Cheerleading is now so dominated by females that "male cheerleaders" are frequently regarded as somehow less than truly masculine. In 2012, for example, you might remember the "scandal" that ensued when presidential candidate Mitt Romney was accused of being a bully in high school when he organized a group assault on a boy who was acting gay. A few days later, a reporter from another paper followed up with another article: "The Real Romney Prep-School Scandal: He Was A Cheerleader."

Nonetheless, it is no longer rare to see males participate in cheerleading—especially at the collegiate level. In this article, Eric Anderson describes the results of his research into how male cheerleaders deal with the problems of being masculine in a "feminized terrain."

This research uses sixty-eight in-depth interviews of collegiate male cheerleaders and

* Direct all correspondence to: Eric Anderson, Department of Education, University of Bath, Bath, BA2 7AY, United Kingdom; *e-mail:* E.Anderson@bath.ac.uk

Eric Anderson, "Orthodox and Inclusive Masculinity: Competing Masculinities among Male Cheerleaders," *Sociological Perspectives*, Vol. 48, no. 3 (Fall 2005): 337–355. Original title "Orthodox and Inclusive Masculinity: Competing Masculinities among Heterosexual Men in a Feminized Terrain." University of California Press. Used by permission.

participant observation from four selected cheerleading teams to examine the construction of masculinity among heterosexual men in a feminized terrain. Previous studies maintain that a hegemonic process of masculine dominance and submission (Connell 1987, 1995) influences most heterosexual men in feminized arenas to bolster their masculinity through the approximation of orthodox masculine requisites, including the expression of homophobic and antifeminine-acting attitudes (Davis 1990; Majors 1990; Messner 1992; Sargent 2001; Williams 1989, 1993, 1995). This research shows, however, that men in collegiate cheerleading today exhibit two contrasting and competing forms of normative masculinity, each supported by organizational and institutional culture and each with near-equal membership.

The first category of masculine performance is labeled as *orthodox*. The men categorized into this group are shown to perform masculinity in a manner consistent with previous studies of men in feminized terrain: they attempt to approximate the hegemonic form of masculinity, largely by devaluing women and gay men (Adams 1993; Davis 1990; Hanson 1995; Sargent 2001; Williams 1993, 1995). The performance of masculinity among men in this group is influenced by a number of factors, including the institutional culture of one of the two major cheerleading governing bodies, the "Orthodox Cheerleading Association."

The second category of masculine performance is labeled as *inclusive*. The men in this group view orthodox masculinity as undesirable and do not aspire to many of its tenets. Particularly important to the study of men in feminized terrain, this research shows that inclusive masculinity is based less on homophobia and antifemininity than orthodox masculinity. Men in this group willingly embrace the feminized underpinnings of their sport and largely value their gay teammates. Notably, the construction of inclusive masculinity is influenced by the institutional culture of the other major governing cheerleading body, the "Inclusive Cheerleading Association."

Whereas previous studies of heterosexual men in feminized terrain found that men almost unanimously attempt to align themselves with orthodox masculinity, this research finds that heterosexual men in collegiate cheerleading are nearly evenly split between these two normative forms of masculine expression. The emergence of a more inclusive form of masculinity is attributed to many factors, including the structure of the sport; the reduction of cultural, institutional, and organizational homophobia; and the resocialization of men into a gender-integrated sport.

Background

David and Brannon (1976:12) have categorized four basic tenets that "seem to comprise the core requirements" of American masculinity. These include: (1) no sissy stuff, (2) be a big wheel, (3) be a sturdy oak, and (4) give 'em hell. Although all four rules are important in understanding the construction and stratification of masculine power and privilege, this research is mostly concerned with the "no sissy stuff" principle because of a durable sociological understanding that contemporary masculinity largely exists in opposition to femininity (Bourdieu 2001; Chodorow 1978; Connell 1987; David and Brannon 1976; Dellinger 2004; Frye 1983; Gilmore 1990; Kimmel 1996, 2004; Lorber 1994; Lucal 1999; West and Zimmerman 1987). Kimmel (2004:97) says, "While different groups of men may disagree about other traits and their significance in gender definitions, the antifemininity component of masculinity is perhaps the single dominant and universal characteristic."

The marginalization of men in feminine fields has been shown effective in deterring heterosexual men from engaging in these settings (Adams 1993; Davis 1990; Sargent 2001; Williams 1993, 1995), perhaps because men who enter these fields find their sexuality publicly scrutinized (Martin and Collinson 1999). Accordingly, it has also been shown that North American masculinity is based in a disassociation from homosexuality (Chauncey 1985; Gorer 1964; Halperin 1989; Humphreys 1975; Kimmel 1994; Lancaster 1988; Plummer 2001; Pollack 1998), something particularly true to athletic settings (Adams 1993; Anderson 2005; Pronger 1990). When one adds homophobia to David and Brannon's (1976) tenets, it produces an orthodox form of masculinity. Orthodox masculinity is reflected in and reproduced through an institutionalized, gender-segregated, and highly competitive sporting culture in North America (Anderson 2005; Burstyn 1999).

Previous investigations into the social construction of masculinities have shown a relationship between the dominant form of masculine expression and subordinate forms (Anderson 2002; Connell 1987, 1995; Gramsci 1971; Messner 1992). Connell (1995:77) has described hegemonic masculinity as a social process in which one form of institutionalized masculinity is "culturally exalted" above all others. Key to understanding the operation of hegemony[1] in relationship to masculinity, Connell (1987, 1995) maintains that most men exhibiting a subordinate form of masculinity actually desire to obtain the hegemonic form. Essentially, the process of hegemony influences the oppressed to maintain the rightfulness or naturalization of their oppression. Indeed, it is this aspiration that makes the process hegemonic (Gramsci 1971). Thus, if hegemony applies to masculinity, one would expect most who transgress masculine-defined boundaries to preserve, if not inflate, their position by adopting as many tenets of orthodox masculinity as possible. These identity management techniques might include: (1) being homophobic, (2) devaluing femininity, (3) increasing masculine bravado, and (4) claiming masculine space within the larger feminized arena.

Examinations of feminized terrain have consistently shown men to approximate orthodox masculinity and to justify their transgression as consistent with hegemonic expectations of masculinity (Adams 1993; Anderson 2002; Davis 1990; Klein 1993; Majors 1990; Williams 1993, 1995). For example, men who occupy feminized space are quick to defend their transgressions as consistent within normative boundaries of orthodox masculinity, maintaining that they have not transgressed masculine acceptability, rather that the space has been inappropriately gendered. Or, if men do acknowledge the feminine underpinnings of their field, they attempt to select a particular role within that space and define it as masculine (Davis 1990; McGuffey and Rich 1999; Sargent 2001; Williams 1993, 1995). Accordingly, heterosexual male cheerleaders have been shown to emphasize that certain tasks within cheerleading (such as lifting women above their heads) are masculine, believing women lack the strength to perform these tasks as well as men. Conversely, they designate other tasks (such as erotic dancing) to be exclusively feminine (Davis 1990; Hanson 1995).

Although the types of identity management techniques exhibited by men in feminized terrain are considered to be a reflection of the social process of hegemonic masculinity (Connell 1987, 1995), it is important to clarify that hegemonic masculinity is not an archetype.[2] "It is, rather, the masculinity that occupies the hegemonic position in a given pattern of gender relations, a position always contestable" (Connell 1995:76). And although Connell does describe the contemporary form of hegemonic masculinity as including the tenets of homophobia and antifemininity, she does

---

[1]Hegemony is from the Greek word for dominance. In the United States, the word is pronounced *heh-jem-o-nee* (accent on the second syllable) or *hedge-o-mon-ee* (accent on the first syllable). In Britain, hegemony is pronounced *heh-gem-o-nee* (accent on second syllable)—Ed.

[2]From Greek words for origin and forms or patterns. Psychiatrist Carl Gustav Jung (1875-1961) used archetype (or primordial image) to refer to the basic types of personalities (the Innocent, the Hero, the Caregiver, the Rebel, etc.). More generally, an archetype a perfect example of something; an example that contains all the essentials of the thing. Mohammed Ali is the archtypal boxer; Yoda is the archtypal wise man; apple pie is the archtypal American food, Harry Potter is the archtypal hero.—Ed.

not assign a categorical label to this group. This makes it easy to erroneously conflate the process of hegemonic masculinity with an archetype of masculinity. This study refrains from using "hegemonic masculinity" as a categorical label; instead, the term is used to describe a social process of subordination and stratification. In this research, the difference between an archetype and a social process of dominance is understood by delineating the traditionally hegemonic category of masculinity as *orthodox masculinity*. Thus, traditionally marginalized masculinities (such as gay, nonathletic, or feminine-acting men) occupy the lower rungs of the hierarchy based in defiance to orthodox masculinity (Anderson 2005; Messner 1992, 2002).

Methods

This research uses in-depth interviews and participant observations to examine how heterosexual men in collegiate cheerleading construct masculinity through micro and macro social processes (Dellinger 2004). Because cheerleading is commonly understood to be a feminized terrain, this research also examines the relationship between hegemonic processes of masculine dominance and individual agency[3] (Dilorio 1989; Glaser and Strauss 1967) in the social construction of gendered identities. Considering that previous investigations of masculine construction in cheerleading were conducted more than a decade ago (Davis 1990; Hanson 1995), this research might also capture the effect of decreasing homophobia in recent years.

The informants are sixty-eight self-identified heterosexual men who used to play high school football but became collegiate cheerleaders

---

[3]"Agency" here refers to an individual's ability to change the conditions of his or her situation (as opposed to being at the mercy of social factors).—Ed.

because they were unable to make their university football teams. Although a self-selection process cannot be ruled out (i.e., it is possible that men most affected by the masculinization process of football do not become cheerleaders), most of the informants reported that upon entering cheerleading, they held orthodox notions of masculinity, including sexist views and overt homophobia. The men, between eighteen and twenty-three years of age, come from diverse regions from throughout the United States, but 80 percent of the informants were white, middle-class men, so generalizations can only be made for this group.

My orientation into the culture of collegiate cheerleading began with informal discussions with friends who were collegiate male cheerleaders and through the analysis of cheerleading Web pages. Next, twelve collegiate male cheerleaders were contacted for interviews by using the member profile search on America Online, which provides a search engine for accessing the stated interests of AOL's 33 million subscribers. After communicating with these cheerleaders through instant messaging, I asked them for in-depth, taped telephone interviews. Snowball and theoretical sampling techniques (Corbin and Strauss 1990) were used with these initial informants to obtain an additional twelve interviews. The forty-four other informant interviews were obtained randomly at cheerleading competitions by asking potential informants if they were willing to participate in academic research. In total, sixty-eight interviews with self-identified heterosexual male cheerleaders were transcribed and coded.

The interviews began by asking informants to discuss their life history in sports and the process by which they came into cheerleading. Informants were then asked about their views on homosexuality and feminine expression among men as well as their perceptions of women's athleticism and leadership qualities. They were also asked to discuss how they maintained a heterosexual identity in cheerleading and how their identity, or identity management techniques, might vary from when they were in football. In addition to these coded and transcribed interviews, twelve informal group interviews (60 to 120 minutes) were conducted on coed cheerleading teams throughout the United States, some of which included women, coaches, and gay men. Men in these groups were asked about their relationships with women and gay men and about the gendered underpinnings of cheerleading.

In addition to these interviews, 300 hours of participant observation were conducted on four selected coed teams. These teams were solicited in advance of a major competition, and each agreed to be observed and interviewed over three- to four-day competitions, but observations also took place at practices in their home states and while they socialized away from the athletic arena. Field notes (with either a microrecorder or a pocket-sized memo pad) were recorded outside their direct presence. The teams' willingness to be observed was due in part to my experience as a coach. Knowledge of kinesiology[4] and sport psychology enabled me to speak their language and help with their athletic endeavors. During the analysis of this research, I maintained relationships with several heterosexual male cheerleaders (from both cheerleading institutions), who were used as key informants for understanding the complexities of cheerleading rules, maneuvers, and cultural practices.

Categorizing informants as belonging to one form of masculinity or the other was based largely on an informant's perceptions of how men and women should act and what tasks men should or should not perform within

the sport of cheer-leading. Categorization was also influenced by the informant's views on homosexuality and feminine-acting men. For example, athletes who expressed dislike of gay men or held antifeminine or misogynistic attitudes were grouped as orthodox cheerleaders, whereas those expressing support for gay men and femininity among men were classified as inclusive. Men who stigmatized the performance of certain roles within coed cheerleading as strictly feminine (such as erotic dancing or being thrown into the air) were classified as orthodox, and men who comfortably performed these feminine-coded roles were grouped as inclusive.

It is important to understand that there are two major competing associations that control the world of cheerleading. This research, however, analyzes these associations only as far as they relate to collegiate cheerleading. This is not an analysis of high school or professional cheerleading. Each cheerleading association is a profit-oriented corporation that markets cheerleading instruction, merchandise, and training camps. At the collegiate level, each of these two associations maintains near-equal university membership, and each organizes a series of competitions leading to a national meet that draws hundreds of college teams. To protect their identity, the names of these associations have been changed in this article to the Inclusive Cheerleading Association and the Orthodox Cheerleading Association. Because these two cheerleading associations maintain different institutionalized perspectives on gender (in collegiate cheerleading), data collection was evenly split between them.

It is also important to understand that the given names of the two cheerleading associations are intentionally conflated with the categorized forms of masculine expression found in this study. This is primarily for simplicity but also because, as one might expect, the informants of each association largely reflect the institutional creed of their governing body.

---

[4]Kinesiology or human or animal kinetics is the science of movement of humans or animals.—Ed.

Men who belonged to the Orthodox Cheerleading Association largely displayed and valued the tenets of orthodox masculinity. The men in the Inclusive Cheerleading Association largely displayed and valued the tenets of inclusive masculinity. During the coding of the research, however, men were classified as belonging to one group of men or the other, independent of their organizational (university) or cheerleading association affiliation.

Results

Cheerleading has evolved from the days of simply cheering for the victory of athletic teams. Cheerleading squads today compete against each other in complex athletic performances in which contestants dance, cheer, perform stunts, and tumble to rhythmically synchronized, high-energy music. Higher, faster, and more complicated are the hallmarks of winning squads, and these qualities demand cheerleaders of both sexes to be fearless acrobats who perform dangerously complicated maneuvers.

Research on cheerleading, however, shows that despite the evolution of cheerleading from the sidelines to the main stage, the sport has largely maintained its cultural ascription of femininity (Adams and Bettis 2003). Hanson says, "The overriding contemporary perception that cheerleader equals girl is reinforced by popular culture which defines it strictly in feminized terms" (1995:116). Adams and Bettis have even shown that young women who play masculinized sports often participate in cheerleading as a way to counter stereotypes of their masculinization, reporting that cheerleading offers young women "a space to revel in what they called being a 'girlie girl'" (2003:84).

Men who cheer in college, however, have been shown to view themselves as being far from "girlie men." Previous studies of these men have found that they maintain themselves to be "real men": daring, heterosexual, and strong enough to hold a woman (or two) above their heads, while still agile enough to perform gymnastic feats (Davis 1990; Hanson 1995). Despite the fact that the entire field is culturally feminized, many cheerleaders of both sexes maintain that certain tasks within the sport are actually highly masculinized activities, even if women perform the same tasks in the all-women's division of cheerleading.

Gendering certain tasks as masculine has been credited with paving the way for more men to join cheerleading (Hanson 1995). Still, because not enough men cheer in high school, most collegiate teams competing in the coed division must recruit men who have no experience in cheerleading. They often look to football players, believing them well suited for the complexities of competitive cheerleading because they are strong, used to rigorous training, and value self-sacrifice in the pursuit of victory. But because football players have been socialized into a highly sexist and homophobic arena (Anderson 2005; Messner 1992; Pronger 1990) and because cheerleading is culturally defined as a feminine activity (Adams and Bettis 2003; Davis 1990; Hanson 1995), convincing men to *give up* football is not effective. After all, football players occupy a space described to accrue social power, prestige, and privilege (Anderson 2005; Bissinger 1990; Connell 1987, 1995; Messner 1992, 2002; Miracle and Rees 1994; Pronger 1990). Football, however, is also a highly competitive sport, and there are a large number of former high school football players who do not make their university teams during tryouts. It is these men that become the recruitment targets for cheerleading squads.

Threatened by a disengagement from their previous athletic identity (Messner 1987) and desiring an association with the highly masculinized ethos attributed to men in team sports, former football players report a desire to join other competitive athletic teams. However, they are generally not trained in the rigors of other team sports (such as baseball or basketball), which also maintain a competitive selection process. Thus, cheerleading becomes a common avenue for "getting back into the game."

While having lunch with a group of male cheerleaders, I asked, "How many of you would rather be on the football team?" All six resoundingly answered, "I would." After indicating a fondness for the cultural power that came to him as a football player, Richie said, "Yeah, I wish I could have made the football team; I really miss football." He added, "But I wasn't going to make any other team, so cheerleading was a way of getting back into the game. Well, as close as I could anyhow." This was the leitmotif[5] among men who were recruited into cheerleading after playing football. To these men, cheerleading became an acceptable last effort to return to sport. For them, being in a feminized athletic arena was judged to be better than being outside it altogether.

PERFORMING ORTHODOX MASCULINITY

During the first day of cheerleading, Randy (a college senior) instructed the younger men:

> It is really important for you guys to give these women a lot of respect. . . . You are going to be putting your hands in certain places, and catching them when they fall, so be sure to be respectful. . . . Remember that we do things better; we pick up on things faster than women do, so don't rub that in by telling them, "We are better than you." Be respectful of the fact that guys are better. Just as important, when you are out in the field you have to portray a masculine image. When you are on the field, you must be the king of masculinity. We don't care what your sexual orientation is; that is none of our business. What you are at home is none of our business. But when you are here you have to be

masculine. And if anyone gives you shit, and says you are gay or whatever, remind them that while they are out there playing with guys, you are out here with all these beautiful women.

Randy's talk illustrates the institutional and cultural attitudes of masculinity, homophobia, and sexism among men categorized as belonging to the orthodox group. This speech, in some variation, is traditional for veteran male cheerleaders to give to new men in the Orthodox Cheerleading Association. It is something they call "guy talk," and it best exemplifies orthodox masculinity because it maintains that men should strictly avoid activities culturally determined to be feminine and portrays women as less intelligent and less athletic than men. The form of masculinity promoted in Randy's speech also subjugates homosexuality and sends a message to gay men that to be accepted they must downplay their sexuality and act in accordance with dominant notions of orthodox masculinity (Anderson 2002, 2005; Messner 2002). Thus, similar to previous investigations of men in feminized terrain—and synonymous with the findings of marginalized men in masculinized terrain—this study found that the orthodox group of men in collegiate cheerleading attempted to mitigate and justify their transgression into feminized terrain (Anderson 2002; Davis 1990; Majors 1990; Messner 1992; Williams 1989, 1993, 1995).

Those who valued orthodox masculinity often relied on the same identity management techniques discussed in previous investigations of collegiate cheerleading (Davis 1990; Hanson 1995). Namely, they maintained that their role within the sport was consistent with orthodox expectations of masculinity and that the feminized nature of their terrain was falsely attributed. Daren said, "I know that people don't think that this is a masculine sport, but I challenge them to throw a girl up in the air and then catch her as she falls. Besides, the original cheerleaders *were* men." Daren, like many men in cheerleading, postulates that not only is

---

[5]*Leitmotif* from German, "lending motive," is a term of art in musical studies; it refers to a specific melody or musical phrase that is associated (for example) with a particular character's arrival on the scene. More generally, leitmotif refers to a theme.—Ed.

cheerleading a sport in which men and women are polarized into masculine and feminine roles, but that it is also a sport that requires men to be "really" masculine. "Yeah, most of the guys are *really* masculine. . . . We aren't a bunch of fairies out here dancing in skirts."

There was variance about attitudes toward women among those belonging to the orthodox group. Although some held misogynistic attitudes, viewing women as purely sex objects, most maintained that they respected women as athletes but usually considered them to be inferior to men in their athleticism. Patrick agreed:

> I was asked to be on the team because the women needed me to help them do their routines better. They just can't throw girls as high as guys can. I'm not saying that they can't throw girls, but I am saying that the best cheerleading comes from the coed squads, and that's because we give them a better show. We can do what women can't.

In addition to the maintenance of sexist attitudes, many of the men categorized as belonging to the orthodox group also expressed varying degrees of homophobia. Although this was sometimes found in overt expressions, it was most often expressed covertly. Perhaps much of this group's homophobic and/or heterosexist sentiment was used to challenge cultural assumptions that male cheerleaders are gay. Indeed, it is common for heterosexual men to confront (or displace) accusations of homosexuality with homophobia (Anderson 2002, 2005; Martin and Collinson 1999; McGuffey and Rich 1999; Messner 1992; Plummer 1999, 2001; Smith 1998), and these men certainly found themselves inundated with homosexual suspicion. In fact, the suspicion of homosexuality may be even more prominent among male cheerleaders today than among male cheerleaders of yesteryear.

Loftus (2001) used General Social Survey data to show that homosexuality was not as visible two decades ago as it is today, and Ibson (2002) has shown that the mere awareness that

homosexuality exists is enough to alter men's behaviors. Furthermore, Pronger (1990) suggests that homosexuality in the 1980s was largely thought incompatible with athletic men, but recently it has been shown that athleticism no longer provides the same veneer of heterosexuality (Anderson 2005). Finally, the reduction of cultural homophobia in recent years may also have encouraged a larger percentage of male cheerleaders to come out of the closet, and this might place the heterosexuality of other male cheerleaders under suspicion through a guilt-by-association process (Anderson 2000, 2005). Therefore, heterosexual men who cheered a decade or more ago may not have had to prove their heterosexuality in the same manner heterosexual cheerleaders do today.

However, the reduction of cultural homophobia and the increased presence of openly gay men seems to have made the expression of homophobia somewhat outmoded, even among many members of the orthodox group. The expression of homophobia is therefore largely accomplished through covert mechanisms of heterosexism. One such manner comes in the form of *defensive heterosexuality.*

Defensive heterosexuality is characterized by the expressive signaling of heterosexuality through a variety of repeated mechanisms. For example, the most common narrative heterosexual male cheerleaders used to explain their transgression into feminized space was a well crafted and collectively constructed story about men lusting for their female teammates. One male cheerleader said, "Yeah, there are all these hot chicks in cheerleading. That is why I came out for the team." Another said, "Who wouldn't want to be out here with all these beautiful women?" The story was common: so compelled to be around hot women, heterosexual male cheerleaders were sexually drawn to the feminized arena of cheerleading.

These heterosexist and objectifying remarks even dominated the Orthodox Cheerleading Association's Web site. In one discussion forum, the question was asked, "How do I get more guys to cheer in high school?" Fifteen of nineteen responses included the "tell them about the girls" pitch. It was also common for men classified in the orthodox group to make heterosexualized and/or objectifying comments about women, often talking about whom they slept with or would like to sleep with. One night, five heterosexual male cheerleaders were sitting in a hotel room when one said, "Let's order a prostitute." The men then talked about this for the better part of an hour. It was doubtful this would happen, however, for they had had the same conversation the previous night.

For the orthodox men in this study, masculinity is constructed within well-established feminist findings (Chodorow 1978; David and Brannon 1976; Frye 1983; Kimmel 1994; Lorber 1994; Lucal 1999; Plummer 1999, 2001; Pronger 1990; Smith 1998): namely, that to be a "real man," one must not be like a woman and one must not be gay. Most of the men in the orthodox group stressed their athleticism and their masculinity, and they attempted to distance themselves from acting feminine or being perceived as gay. They justified their transgression into feminized terrain by challenging the feminine attributes of the arena and by claiming that their particular tasks (e.g., holding women above their heads) were inappropriately labeled as feminine.

In contrast to previous studies of masculine construction in cheerleading, however, only about half of these men in collegiate cheerleading were categorized as subscribing to the orthodox form of masculinity. The other half were shown to perform masculinity in a surprising, fascinating, and theoretically important manner.

PERFORMING INCLUSIVE MASCULINITY

With their competition finished, dinner eaten, and the movie over, a group of seven men (five straight and two gay) walked back to their hotel. Howie said, "Time for some drinking games. I've invited over the guys from Lincoln." When asked if he was worried that the cheerleaders from the other team might think him gay because he was not only sharing a room with a gay man, but also sharing a bed, he responded, "No. Why would I?"

After an hour of drinking games, one of the heterosexual men said, "Hey guys, do you want to see if coach will drive us to a club?" Howie responded, "You guys know of any around here?" To which his best friend, Steve, answered, "There is Gold Diggers, the Slush House, and then of course there is the Phoenix; it's a gay club." Howie interrupted, "Let's go there," and the others agreed. When asked why they would rather go to a gay club than a straight one, Howie answered, "The vibe is better, the music is better, and there are still good-looking women, so why wouldn't we want to go there?" When asked, "Aren't you worried about being thought gay?," the five heterosexual men shook their heads no and Howie asked, "Why would we?" They rounded up more teammates, piled into two vans, and headed for the club. Once there, heterosexual men danced with both women *and* gay men, two heterosexual men even "freaked" each other (a term used by these men to describe two people dancing with their groins together).

Although there was not a universal position on homosexuality among men in the inclusive group (just as there was not in the orthodox group), these men had few inhibitions about homosexuality. Their attitudes ran from tolerant to celebratory. Typical comments included, "I don't care what people think of me" to "Why is it necessary to have a label?" One male cheerleader even said, "I used to go to gay clubs all the time, and then I actually got a job at a gay club. I got hit on all the time. It was flattering." Still another said, "Why should I care? Why should people care if I'm straight?"

These attitudes are particularly unusual given that these men previously played high school football. "I used to hate gays," one inclusive cheerleader told me. "But now I don't care. I've gotten over it." His teammate added, "Yeah, most of my teammates used to just hate gays. I mean, what football player doesn't?" Perhaps most telling, another cheerleader said, "To be honest with you, I used to be homophobic. I used to be one of the guys calling the cheerleaders on my high school team fags." He continued, "Now, I'm on the other side. I mean, I'm not gay, but others sometimes think I am because I cheer, and if that's what they want to think, I don't bother to try to tell them different."

Data suggests that this shift in attitude from homophobic to gay-friendly might be made possible for several reasons. First, gay male cheerleaders seem to have strong support from female and older male teammates. For example, Dan said, "Oh yeah, you learn not to be homophobic real quick. I mean, you can't be. The women and coaches in cheer would never stand for that." Another said, "I made some homophobic comment when I first joined, and one of the guys pulled me to the side and schooled me on it." Second, heterosexual men generally befriended at least one gay male teammate. Jeffrey, a fourth-year cheerleader, said,

> I grew up in a town of 2,000. I never met a gay person. In my town, you were just taught to hate them, even though we didn't know who it was we were supposed to hate. So I did . . . until I met Jaime [who was the only openly gay member on his team]. I mean, I used to call guys fags all the time, but I'd never call him that. He was a real cool guy, and now I think that gay people are just really cool people.

A third possible reason for the shift in attitude is that institutional support has helped in shaping a new understanding of homosexuality. Whereas overt homophobia was generally replaced with heterosexism in the Orthodox Cheerleading Association, homosexuality and femininity among men was institutionally supported in the Inclusive Cheerleading Association. This has led many gay men who

cheered in high school to self-select into colleges that compete for the Inclusive Cheerleading Association. Thus, there are more openly gay athletes in this association, and this makes it easier for closeted men to come out.

The heterosexual men classified as belonging to the inclusive group were not only less concerned with mitigating homosexual suspicion through homophobia and heterosexism, but they were also less concerned about associating with femininity. That is to say, men who subscribed to inclusive masculinity were far less concerned with the expression of femininity among other men. In fact, discussions of what behaviors were considered feminine or masculine often suggested a great deal of thought and critical thinking as to the nature of gender performance in the sport. Men in this group were willing, often eager, to participate in role-reversal activities otherwise stigmatized by men in the orthodox group. Some men in the inclusive group agreed that certain behaviors were understood to be feminine but displayed irreverence for such essentialist thinking. Other men questioned the usefulness of categorizing things as gendered. Men from one inclusive squad even wore sleeveless shirts that zipped up the back (something associated with women's uniforms in this sport). In this respect, the gendered perspectives of many men in this group might best be understood from a queer theory perspective (Jargose 1996; Kosofsky 1993; Seidman 1996).

For example, Jeff, a heterosexual cheerleader, practiced with another male teammate for nearly half an hour, trying to put a female into the air with perfect form. But after growing bored he said, "My turn." The athletes switched positions, and Jeff stood atop the hands of a male and a female. According to those with an orthodox understanding of masculinity, this position is one of the most feminine things a man can do in cheerleading. Jeff, however, was unconcerned. He willingly embraced the coded femininity of such tasks. In this respect, men in this group were shown to be less concerned about performing consistently with some of the tenets of traditional masculinity, challenging the bifurcation of gender.

When men in this group were asked about their masculine identities, many indicated that they considered themselves to be "metrosexual," a recent pop-culture term they understand to describe a gay-friendly heterosexual male who presents himself with the style-conscious behaviors otherwise attributed to gay men (Cashmore and Parker 2003; Flocker 2004; Hyman 2004). Thus, just as "guy talk" was a useful defining construct for men in the orthodox group, the term "metrosexual" was useful for men in the inclusive group.

It is important to note that in the collegiate cheerleading arena, it would be inappropriate to describe the men belonging to the inclusive group as maintaining a subordinate form of masculinity. That label does not work for these men because (like hegemonic masculinity) subordination describes a social process, not an archetype. Specifically, Connell (1987, 1995) describes subordinate masculinity in relation to a dominant (and hegemonic) form of masculinity. But because these men construct a hierarchy that esteems inclusivity and stigmatizes orthodox masculinity, it would be hard to say they are subordinate. Furthermore, Connell describes subordinate masculinity as existing *only* in relationship to a dominant *institutionalized* form of masculinity, and in the Inclusive Cheerleading Association, it is inclusive masculinity that is institutionalized, not orthodox masculinity. This highlights that the process of gender construction in collegiate cheerleading is a product of individuals, organizations, and institutions.

STRUCTURE AND AGENCY IN CONSTRUCTING MASCULINITY

Individuals are not free to construct simply any version of identity that they desire; identity construction is influenced and constrained

by a number of micro and macro social processes (Acker 1990; Connell 1987; Messner 2002; Walkerdine 1993; West and Zimmerman 1987). To understand how cultural scripts and organizational rules institutionalize gender in collegiate cheerleading, Acker's (1990) theory of gendered institutions was employed—the same theory used in other investigations of men in feminized terrain (Davis 1990; Williams 1993, 1995).

Acker views organizational hierarchies, job descriptions, and informal workplace practices as containing deeply gendered assumptions that eventually become naturalized. In this manner, gender is institutionalized by employing hegemonic processes that reify gender myths and stigmatize those who do not follow institutional norms. Within the same institution, however, there can be variances in gender expression, suggesting that organizational culture and individual agency also maintain influence in the process of gender construction (Dellinger 2004).

The Orthodox Cheerleading Association institutionalizes masculinity along the lines of other masculinized team sports. It values a bifurcation of gender and views homosexuality as a threat to this polarization. In the maintenance of orthodox masculinity, this cheerleading association uses covert and overt techniques to police masculine behaviors. For example, cultural norms stigmatize men (or entire teams) that perform in ways contrary to orthodox masculine perspectives. Men who dance complicated or erotic choreography (similar to women) find that their showmanship lowers their team's score. Because of this, men move in a rigid fashion, leaving the hip-swinging and erotic choreography exclusively to women.

In the Inclusive Cheerleading Association, however, men are expected to dance as competently and erotically as women. Men often take center stage, thrusting their pelvises and caressing their bodies to the thunderous approval of the audience, while their female teammates wait on the side. In the Inclusive Cheerleading Association, men even throw other men into the air, the strictest taboo in the Orthodox Cheerleading Association. Although this does not happen with regular frequency (largely because it is more difficult to throw and catch a 180-pound man than a 100-pound woman), one squad concluded their national championship routine in the Inclusive Cheerleading Association by having a man fly over a two-person high pyramid and land safely into the arms of four other men. This finale brought cheers of deafening approval that carried on longer than is customary. Because of this kind of activity, the Inclusive Cheerleading Association's competitions are widely recognized as being more dynamic and daring than those of the Orthodox Cheerleading Association, whose members, in turn, feel that they uphold the traditional form of cheerleading.

The institutional variance of gender roles between these two associations is fiercely contested and politically charged. The Orthodox Cheerleading Association even bans (for three years) any collegiate team that participates in an Inclusive Cheerleading Association event. In this manner, the Orthodox Cheerleading Association relies on traditional tools of marginalization, stigmatization, and institutional punishment for associating with femininity. The Inclusive Cheerleading Association makes no such demands of its participants.

The two leading cheerleading associations also maintain near-opposite perspectives on homosexuality. Highlighting the institutional perspective on homosexuality in the Orthodox Cheerleading Association, men who are out or who act in less than masculinized ways are equated with being unprofessional. Accordingly, it was harder to find openly gay cheerleaders in the Orthodox Cheerleading Association. Similar to the "don't ask, don't tell" policy found among openly gay athletes in highly masculinized team sports (Anderson 2005), their status was often privately recognized but not publicly discussed. Conversely, in many cases, gay members of the Inclusive Cheerleading Association talked more freely about their sexuality.

But just because a cheerleading association sanctions a particular version of masculinity does not imply that all the cheerleaders who belong to that governing body agree with this perspective. Some individuals and, in some cases, entire teams publicly protested their association's gender paradigm.

The best example of organizational contestation in reformulating representations of institutionalized masculinity comes from participant observations of the Troubadours. Unlike the coaches of most teams of the Orthodox Cheerleading Association, the Troubadours' coaches made a decision to challenge the tough-guy image that their governing body esteems. One of the coaches told me, "Oh, I say to hell with all that macho stuff. We are just here to have fun, and if others don't like us for who we are, to hell with them." One of his athletes agreed, "Everyone here is like 'that's just stupid, acting so macho and stuff.'" His comments were supported by participant observations, which showed a great deal of physical intimacy (hugging and holding) between men on the Troubadours team. In a restaurant after one competition, one heterosexual man even kissed another on the cheek in an expression of his friendship.

The Troubadours have also taken a political stand against the conservative nature of the Orthodox Cheerleading Association. The coach reflected, "I remember one year, well I knew we would be dinged points for it, but I had this male flyer (one who is thrown into the air) that was just amazing. So I took a chance. I figured why not? I put a guy into the air." When asked if this wasn't the most feminine movement possible in a cheerleading routine, he answered, "Of course, and we were dinged points for it, too. But I didn't care."

The gender rebellion the Troubadours exhibited in the Orthodox Cheerleading Association made them highly ostracized by other Orthodox Cheerleading Association teams. One coach raised his eyebrow even at the mention of the Troubadours, saying, "Oh, you don't want to talk to them. They are not what cheerleading is all about," despite the fact that the Troubadours hold five consecutive national championship titles in their division. Furthermore, the Orthodox Cheerleading Association has recently responded to the Troubadours' embracement of femininity and homosexuality by removing points for the dance portion of cheer-leading routines. One coach told me that this was a direct response to the fact that *some* judges had ceased to demerit the Troubadours for dancing in other-than-masculinized ways, suggesting that the institutional creed of this organization is contested by individuals as well as organizations.

Likewise, not all teams that belonged to the Inclusive Cheerleading Association reflected an inclusive form of masculinity. Several teams competed in the style of the Orthodox Cheerleading Association, even interrupting their high-energy and dynamic performances to yell cheers such as "go! fight! win!" to the crowd (something considered taboo in this association). Upon finishing an orthodox-styled performance at the Inclusive Cheerleading Association's National Championship meet, one team even handed out Bibles to other teams. When asked why, one of the male cheerleaders said, "So others can see God's word." When asked, "See God's word on what?," he answered, "Well, like on homosexuality."

Discussion

Previous investigations of masculine construction among men in feminized terrain have shown that hegemonic processes serve to stigmatize the expression of masculinity in ways that do not meet orthodox perspectives (Davis 1990; Williams 1995). This is attributable to

the hegemonic understandings of masculine construction that requires cultural and institutional punishment for those who fail to meet the mandates of the dominant form, in whichever form it currently exists. The hegemonic privileging of one form of masculine expression and the subordination of all others are particularly salient among men in feminized terrain because these arenas have been shown to be more permissive of marginalized men than masculinized arenas (Connell 1995). Thus, there is a greater variance of masculinities exhibited among men in feminized terrain than among men in highly masculinized fields (Anderson 2005).

The presence of feminized, gay, or otherwise marginalized men in feminized terrain has not, however, been shown to influence a significant number of men to challenge the dominant form of masculinity. In fact, just the opposite has been shown to occur. Previous investigations of heterosexual men in feminized occupational and/or recreational terrain find that orthodox masculinity retains its hegemonic position. Men in these terrains have been shown to distance themselves from subordinate status by aligning themselves with orthodox masculinity (Adams 1993; Anderson 2002, 2005: Davis 1990; Hanson 1995; Sargent 2001; Williams 1993, 1995). Thus, men in feminized spaces have been shown to preserve and/or inflate their masculine identities by being homophobic, devaluing femininity, and claiming their space to be erroneously labeled as feminized.

In this study, male cheerleaders who ascribed to orthodox understandings of masculinity also relied on these identity-management techniques. Men in this group were shown to inflate their masculine worth, distance themselves from acting feminine, and use "guy talk" to socialize new cheerleaders into their gendered perspective. Men in this group also reproduced heterosexism by classifying gay male cheerleaders who discussed their sexuality as "unprofessional" and sexism by stressing that they are athletically superior to women. In other words, most men within the orthodox category devalued and distanced themselves from homosexuality and femininity.

Additionally, this research found that, similar to the fashion in which men must prove and reprove their masculinity (Kimmel 2004), male cheerleaders who desire a public image of heterosexuality had to prove and reprove their heterosexuality. Most heterosexual men in the orthodox group signaled their heterosexuality through a variety of overt and covert methods. One method of doing this was found in the display of defensive heterosexuality, which included overt sexualization of women and, for those who did not desire to be thought overtly homophobic, prefacing many statements with, "I'm not gay, but . . ."

Conversely, those who subscribed to inclusive masculinity were shown to behave in effeminate ways without experiencing social stigma. This group largely chose not to value whether people perceived them as gay or straight, masculine or feminine. In this respect, they were less (or not at all) defensive about their heterosexuality, and they regularly stated support for homosexuality. Because these men had a culturally positive association with homosexuality, homophobia ceased to be a tool of masculine marginalization. Conversely, homophobic expression was stigmatized among men in this group. In fact, the inclusive form of masculinity proposed by this group was the near-antithesis of orthodox masculinity. Many self-identified heterosexual men in this (equally large) group found the label "metro-sexual" useful for self-identification of their modified masculine perspective.

Men in the inclusive group also participated in tasks traditionally defined as feminine and supported women who performed tasks traditionally defined as masculine. This included allowing themselves to be tossed into the air (flying), standing atop the shoulders of others, wearing clothing defined as feminine, and dancing in the same erotic fashion as their female teammates. With the performance of these tasks these men challenge the utility of binary thinking. Thus, about half the men in the world of collegiate cheerleading contested the masculine/feminine binary that previous studies have shown to be intensely policed.

To be clear, the existence of marginalized men in feminized terrain is not new. What is significant with these findings, however, is that about half the heterosexual men in collegiate cheerleading were found to align themselves politically away from the orthodox form of masculinity. They responded differently to their transgression than previous investigations of men in feminized terrain. In fact, they resisted many of the tenets of orthodox masculinity and constructed a normative form of masculinity based on inclusiveness. What is also new is that their inclusive definition of masculinity was institutionally supported by one of the two dominating cheerleading associations, as there was found to be a variance in the institutionalization of masculinity between the two dominating cheerleading associations that govern the sport.

The Orthodox Cheerleading Association was shown to codify orthodox masculine behaviors by penalizing those who perform in ways it deems feminine, while the Inclusive Cheerleading Association merited behaviors that break the traditional mode. Foucault (1984) suggests that power must be understood as a multiplicity of factors emanating from individuals, organizations, and institutions. In this manner, men are not merely subject to institutional modeling on masculinity, they are simultaneously active in shaping institutional perspectives through their complacency or protest. Foucault's analysis of power seems fitting in describing gender construction in these cheerleading associations because, despite attempts toward universal solidarity, both associations experienced internal dissension from both individuals and organizations (teams).

I suggest that the emergence of inclusive masculinity characterizing a group with an institutionalized power and membership equal to those of orthodox masculinity is the product of a number of influences. First, the increasing structural demands for originality and innovation in cheerleading routines has compelled the Inclusive Cheerleading Association to replace the "go, fight, win" mantra of yesteryear's cheerleading (Hanson 1995) with a choreographic philosophy of "higher, faster, and more complicated." But this is not the sole or even the primary impetus for the creation of an inclusive form of masculinity. If this were the case, one might expect to see men dance in feminized ways and then, when away from competition, return to orthodox prescriptions of masculinity. This did not occur. Observations confirm that men who exhibited inclusive masculinity during competition also expressed it while socializing away from competition. These men also self-reported a reconstructed understanding of homophobia and sexism in other social spaces (family, school, work), although these self-reports were not confirmed with observations.

Second, the research design provides evidence of a strong institutional influence on the construction of gender within collegiate cheerleading. Although virtually all informants mentioned that as football players they displayed orthodox notions of masculinity, those who attended a university with membership in the Inclusive Cheerleading Association substantially reformulated their masculine perspectives compared to men who attended a university belonging to the Orthodox Cheerleading Association. Men who ended up at universities belonging to the Inclusive Cheerleading Association also exhibited a greater openness to homosexuality and feminine-acting men than men from teams belonging to the Orthodox Cheerleading Association.

Because orthodox masculinity is largely predicated on homophobia, this study also suggests the emergence of inclusive masculinity to be a product of the rapidly decreasing levels of cultural homophobia in American society (Laumann et al. 2004; Loftus 2001; Persell, Green, and Gurevich 2001; Widmer, Treas, and Newcomb 1998). It is reasonable to suspect that if masculinity is based largely on homophobia, then as homophobia declines there might also be a change in the way masculinity is constructed and valued (Carillo 2003; Guttman 2003). Accordingly, even men in the orthodox group reported they were *less* homophobic than they had been as football players.

Finally, the emergence of inclusive masculinity in this feminized arena might also be influenced by the athletes' introduction to the narratives and experiences of women and gay men as teammates. Men in cheerleading, from both associations, reported that their relationships with women and gay men had helped them reconstruct their views on homosexuality and femininity among men, a finding that has implications for the sex-segregated manner in which competitive, institutionalized team sports are currently structured in North American society.

Acknowledgments: The author would like to thank Don Barrett for his guidance in this article.

References

Acker, Joan. 1990. "Hierarchies, Jobs, Bodies: A Theory of Gendered Organizations." *Gender & Society* 4:139–58.

Adams, Marie Louise. 1993. "To Be an Ordinary Hero: Male Figure Skaters and the Ideology of Gender." Pp. 93–110 in *Men and Masculinities*, edited by T. Haddad. Toronto: Canadian School Press.

Adams, Natalie, and Pamela Bettis. 2003. "Commanding the Room in Short Skirts: Cheering as the Embodiment of Ideal Girlhood." *Gender & Society* 17(1):73–91.

Anderson, Eric. 2000. *Trailblazing: The True story of America's First Openly Gay Track Coach.* Hollywood: Alyson Publications.

———. 2002. "Openly Gay Athletes: Contesting Hegemonic Masculinity in a Homophobic Environment." *Gender & Society* 16(6):860–77.

———. 2005. *In the Game: Gay Athletes and the Cult of Masculinity.* New York: State University of New York Press.

Berger, Peter, and Thomas Luckmann. 1966. *The Social Construction of Reality.* Garden City, NY: Doubleday.

Bissinger, H. G. 1990. *Friday Night Lights: A Town, a Team, and a Dream.* Reading, MA: Addison-Wesley.

Bourdieu, Pierre. 2001. *Masculine Domination.* Translated by Richard Nice. Stanford, CA: Stanford University Press.

Burstyn, Varda. 1999. *The Rites of Men: Manhood, Politics, and the Culture of Sport.* Toronto: University of Toronto Press.

Carillo, Hector. 2003. "Helping Lift Machismo." Pp. 351–68 in *Changing Men and Masculinities in Latin America,* edited by M. Gutman. London: Duke University Press.

Cashmore, Ellis, and Andrew Parker. 2003. "One David Beckham: Celebrity, Masculinity, and the Soccerati." *Sociology of Sport Journal* 20(3):214–31.

Chauncey, George. 1985. "Christian Brotherhood or Sexual Perversion? Homosexual Identities and the Construction of Sexual Boundaries in the World War One Era." *Journal of Social History* 19:189–211.

Chodorow, Nancy. 1978. *The Reproduction of Mothering.* Berkeley: University of California Press.

Connell, Robert. 1987. *Gender and Power.* Stanford, CA: Stanford University Press.

———. 1995. *Masculinities.* Berkeley: University of California Press.

Corbin, Juliet, and Anselm Strauss. 1990. "Grounded Theory Research: Procedures, Canon, and Evaluative Criteria." *Qualitative Sociology* 13(1):3–21.

David, Deborah, and Robert Brannon. 1976. *The Forty Nine Percent Majority: The Male Sex Role.* Reading, MA: Addison-Wesley.

Davis, Laurel. 1990. "Male Cheerleaders and the Naturalization of Gender." Pp. 153–61 in *Sport,*

Men and the Gender Order, edited by M. Messner and D. Sabo. Champaign, IL: Human Kinetics.

Dellinger, Kirsten. 2004. "Masculinities in 'Safe' and 'Embattled' Organizations: Accounting for Pornographic and Feminist Magazines." *Gender & Society* 18(5):545–66.

Dilorio, Judith 1989. "Feminism, Gender, and the Ethnographic Study of Sport." *Arena Review* 13(1):49–59.

Flocker, Michael. 2004. *The Metrosexual Guide to Style: A Handbook for the Modern Man.* New York: DaCapo Press.

Foucault, Michel. 1984. *The History of Sexuality, Volume 1: An Introduction.* Translated by Robert Hurley. New York: Vintage Press.

Frye, Marilyn. 1983. *The Politics of Reality: Essays in Feminist Theory.* Berkeley, CA: Crossing Press.

Gilmore, David. 1990. *Manhood in the Making: Cultural Concepts of Masculinity.* New Haven, CT: Yale University Press.

Glaser, Barney, and Anselm Strauss. 1967. *The Discovery of Grounded Theory: Strategies for Qualitative Research.* New York: Aldine de Gruyter.

Gorer, Geoffrey. 1964. *The American People: A Study in National Character.* New York: Norton.

Gramsci, Antonio. 1971. *Selections from Prison Notebooks.* London: New Left Books.

Gutman, Matthew. 2003. *Changing Men and Masculinities in Latin America.* London: Duke University Press.

Halperin, David. 1989. *One Hundred Years of Homosexuality: And Other Essays on Greek Love.* New York: Routledge.

Hanson, Mary Ellen. 1995. *Go! Fight! Win! Cheerleading in American Culture.* Bowling Green, OH: Bowling Green State University Popular Press.

Humphreys, Laud. 1975. *Tearoom Trade: Impersonal Sex in Public Places.* New York: Aldine De Gruyter.

Hyman, Peter. 2004. *The Reluctant Metrosexual: Dispatches from an Almost Hip Life.* New York: Villard.

Ibson, John. 2002. *A Century of Male Relationships in Everyday American Photography.* Washington, DC: Smithsonian Books:

Jargose, Annamarie. 1996. *Queer Theory: An Introduction.* New York: New York University Press.

Kimmel, Michael. 1994. "Homophobia as Masculinity: Fear, Shame and Silence in the Construction of Gender Identity." Pp. 119–11 in

Theorizing Masculinities, edited by H. Brod and M. Kaufman. Thousand Oaks, CA: Sage.

———. 1996. *Manhood in America: A Cultural History.* New York: Free Press.

———. 2004. *The Gendered Society: Sociological Perspective on Sex and Gender.* London: Oxford University Press.

Klein, Alan. 1993. *Little Big Men: Bodybuilding Subculture and Gender Construction.* New York: State University of New York Press.

Kosofsky, Sedgwick. 1993. *Tendencies.* Durham, NC: Duke University Press.

Lancaster, Roger. 1988. "Subject Honor and Object Shame: The Construction of Male Homosexuality and Stigma in Nicaragua." *Ethnomethodology* 27(2):111–25.

Laumann, Edward, Stephen Ellingson, Jenna Mahay, Anthony Paik, and Yoosik Youm. 2004. *The Sexual Organization of the City.* Chicago: University of Chicago Press.

Lorber, Judith. 1994. *Paradoxes of Gender.* New Haven, CT: Yale University Press.

Loftus, Jeni. 2001. "America's Liberalization in Attitudes toward Homosexuality, 1973 to 1998." *American Sociological Review* 66(5):762–82.

Lucal, Betsy. 1999. "What It Means to Be Gendered Me: Life on the Boundaries of a Dichotomous Gender System." *Gender & Society* 13:781–97.

Majors, Richard. 1990. "Cool Pose: Black Masculinity and Sport." Pp. 109–14 in *Sport, Men and the Gender Order,* edited by M. Messner and D. Sabo. Champaign, IL: Human Kinetics.

Martin, Patricia Yancey, and David Collinson. 1999. "Gender and Sexuality in Organizations." Pp. 285–310 in *Revisioning Gender,* edited by M. M. Ferree, J. Lorber, and B. B. Hess. Thousand Oaks, CA: Sage.

McGuffey, Shawn, and Lindsey Rich. 1999. "Playing in the Gender Transgression Zone: Race, Class, and Hegemonic Masculinity in Middle Childhood." *Gender & Society* 13(5): 608–10.

Messner, Michael. 1987. "The Meaning of Success: The Athletic Experience and the Development of Identity." Pp. 193–209 in *The Making of Masculinities: The New Men's Studies,* edited by H. Brod. Boston: Allen and Unwin.

———. 1992. *Power at Play: Sports and the Problem of Masculinity.* Boston: Beacon.

———. 2002. *Taking the Field: Women, Men and Sports.* Minneapolis: University of Minnesota Press.

Miracle, Andrew and Roger Rees. 1994. *Lessons of the Locker Room: The Myth of School Sports.* New York: Prometheus Books.

Persell, Caroline, Adam Green, and Liena Gurevich. 2001. "Civil Society, Economic Distress, and Social Tolerance." *Sociological Forum* 16:203–30.

Plummer, David. 1999. *One of the Boys: Masculinity, Homophobia and Modern Manhood.* New York: Harrington Park Press.

———. 2001. "Policing Manhood: New Theories about the Social Significance of Homophobia." Pp. 60–75 in *Sexual Positions,* edited by C. Wood. Melbourne: Hill of Content.

Pollack, William. 1998. *Real Boys: Rescuing Our Sons from the Myth of Boyhood.* New York: Henry Holt.

Pronger, Brian. 1990. *The Arena of Masculinity: Sports, Homosexuality, and the Meaning of Sex.* New York: St. Martin's Press.

Sargent, Paul. 2001. *Real Men or Real Teachers: Contradictions in the Lives of Men Elementary School Teachers.* Harriman, TN: Men's Studies Press.

Seidman, Steven. 1996. *Queer Theory Sociology.* Oxford, UK: Blackwell.

Smith, George. 1998. "The Ideology of Fag: The School Experience of Gay Students." *Sociological Quarterly* (39)2:309–35.

Walkerdine, Valerie. 1993. "Girlhood through the Looking Glass." Pp. 9–25 in *Girls, Girlhood and Girls' Studies in Transition,* edited by M. de Ras and M. Lunenberg. Amsterdam: Het Spinhuis.

West, Candice, and Don Zimmerman. 1987. "Doing Gender." *Gender & Society* 1(2):125–51.

Widmer, Eric D, Judith Treas, and Robert Newcomb. 1998. "Attitudes toward Nonmarital Sex in 24 Countries." *Journal of Sex Research* 35(4):349–58.

Williams, Christine L. 1989. *Gender Differences at Work.* Berkeley: University of California Press.

———. 1993. (ed.) *Doing "Women's Work": Men in Nontraditional Occupations.* Newbury Park, CA: Sage.

———. 1995. *Still a Man's World: Men Who Do "Women's Work."* Berkeley: University of California Press.

Questions

1. Besides cheerleading, what are some other examples of "feminized terrains"?

2. What is "defensive heterosexuality"? Have you ever witnessed this behavior?

3. Anderson asserts that "individuals are not free to construct simply any version of identity that they desire; identity construction is influenced and constrained by a number of micro and macro social processes." Describe some of the factors that Anderson found influenced and constrained the identity of male cheerleaders.

4. Anderson seems to imply that football players tend to be homophobic. In your judgment is this connection owing to the fact that there is something about the men who become football players OR something about the football itself that influences men to be homophobic?

19

THE REST ROOM AND EQUAL OPPORTUNITY*

Harvey Molotch

On the face of it, this article is about the degree to which Western society provides men and women with equal opportunities to pee. Now, while few would argue that having a place to pee is a trivial matter, this would hardly seem to be a topic worthy of inclusion in a book of sociological readings. If you read this article carefully, however, you will discover that Professor Molotch is making a larger point: Structure affects behavior as well as opportunities. Yes, people make choices, but their choices are influenced by pre-existing social arrangements. And, given all of the relevant facts, structures that seem equal may not be.

At the risk of appearing disrespectful, let me say that the best way to understand equal opportunity is to use the public toilet. Sometimes a gross approach can best clarify a subtle issue. Through the example of how society is organized to provide men and women with the capacity to relieve themselves, we can understand what it takes, as a more general matter, to provide members of different social groups with authentic equal opportunity.

In many public buildings, the amount of floor area dedicated for the men's room and the women's room is the same. The prevailing public bathroom doctrine in the U.S. is one of segregation among the genders, but with equality the guiding ideology. In some jurisdictions, this square footage equality is enshrined in law. Such an arrangement follows the dictum that equality can be achieved only by policies that are "gender-blind" (or "color-blind" or "ethnic-blind") in the allocation of a public resource. To give less to women (or blacks or Hispanics) would be discrimination; to give more would be "reverse discrimination." Women and men have the same proportion of a building to use as rest rooms. Presumably this should provide members of both genders with equal opportunity for dealing with their bodily needs in a timely and convenient way.

The trouble with this sort of equality is that, being blind, it fails to recognize differences between men as a group and women as a group. These differences are not amenable to easy change. Part of women's demand for bathrooms cannot exist for men because only women menstruate. Women make trips to the rest room to secure hygienic and socially appropriate adaptations to this physical fact. And because men's physiology suits them for the use of urinals, a large number of men can be serviced by a relatively small physical space. Women in our society use toilets to urinate, and toilets require a larger area than urinals. By creating men's and women's rooms

*Encouragement and assistance was provided by Howard Becker, Gayle Binion, and Beth Schneider.

Harvey Molotch, "The Rest Room and Equal Opportunity" from *Sociological Forum* 3, no. 1 (Winter 1988). Reprinted with the permission of Blackwell Publishing Ltd.

Women need bigger bathrooms

Woman should squat!? ← stupid idea

of the same size, society guarantees that *individual* women will be worse off than individual men. By distributing a resource equally, an unequal result is structurally guaranteed.

The consequences are easily visible at intermission time whenever men and women congregate in theater lobbies. When the house is full, the women form a waiting line in front of the bathroom while the men do their business without delay. Women experience discomfort and are excluded from conversations that occur under more salutary conditions elsewhere in the lobby. If toward the rear of the line, women may experience anxiety that they will miss the curtain rise. Indeed, they may arrive too late to be seated for the opening scene, dance routine, or orchestral movement. Their late arrival is easily taken by others (particularly men) as evidence of characterological slowness or preoccupation with primping and powder room gossip. All these difficulties are built into the structure of the situation. Equality of square feet to the genders delivers women special burdens of physical discomfort, social disadvantage, psychological anxiety, compromised access to the full product (the performance), and public ridicule.

woman foel

An obvious solution, one I'll call the "liberal" policy, is to make women's rooms larger than men's. Women's bathrooms need to be big enough to get women in and out as quickly as men's bathrooms get men in and out. No more and no less. A little applied sociological research in various types of settings would establish the appropriate ratios needed to accomplish such gender equality.

Liberal

An alternative solution, one I'll call "conservative," would be for women to change the way they do things, rather than for society to change the structuring of rest room space. There is no need to overturn the principle of equality of square footage among the genders. Instead, women need to use their allotted square footage more efficiently. If women truly want to relieve themselves as efficiently as men, they

conservative

can take some initiative. Options do exist short of biological alteration. While women may not be capable of adapting to urinals, they could relieve themselves by squatting over a common trough. This would save some space—perhaps enough to achieve efficiency parity with men. Women are not physically bound to use up so many square feet. It is a cultural issue, and in this case the problem derives from a faulty element of women's culture. It is not physiologically given that each woman should have her own cubicle, much less her own toilet, or that she should sit rather than squat.

This joins the issue well. Should women be forced to change or should the burden be placed on men who may have to give up some of their own square footage so that women might have more? The response from the liberal camp is that even if women's spatial needs are cultural, these needs should be recognized and indulged. Cultural notions of privacy and modes of using toilets were not arrived at by women in isolation from men. Men's conceptions of "decency"—at least as much as women's—encourage women to be physically modest and demure. Men's recurring violence toward women encourages bathroom segregation in the first instance because segregation makes it easier for potential assailants to be spotted as "out of place." Providing women with latched cubicles provides a further bit of security in a world made less secure by men. Thus, prescriptions of dignity and protections from assault come from the common culture produced by women and men. Whatever their origins, these cultural imperatives have become a real force and are sustained by continuing pressures on women's lives. Until this common culture is itself transformed, U.S. women cannot become as efficient as Tiwi women in their capacity to urinate in public settings, regardless of the efficiency advantages. On the other hand, altering the spatial allocations for men's and women's bathrooms is relatively simple and inexpensive.

It becomes harder to be a liberal as the weight of cultural imperative seems to lighten. Suppose, for example, that *a part* of the reason for the line in front of the ladies' room is, in fact, a tendency for women to primp longer than men or to gossip among one another at the sinks (although the lines in front of *toilet stalls* would belie such an assumption). Should vanity and sociability be subsidized at the expense of the larger community? But here again, the culture that men and women have produced in common becomes relevant. Perhaps women "take a powder" to escape the oppression of men, using the rest room as a refuge from social conditions imposed by the dominant gender? Perhaps the need to look lovely, every moment and in every way, is created by men's need to display a public companion whose make-up is flawless, whose head has every hair in place, and whose body is perfectly scented. Women are driven to decorate themselves as men's commodities and the consequence is bathroom demand. Should men pay for this "service" through sacrificing their own square footage or should women adjust by waiting in line and climbing all over one another for a patch of the vanity mirror?

Again it turns on who should change what. The conservative answer might be for women to give up primping, but that would fly in the face of the demand (also championed by conservatives) that women's cultural role is to be beautiful for their men. Although not because they wished to increase rest room efficiency, radical feminists have argued that women should ease up on their beauty treatments, precisely because it ratifies their subservience to men and deflects them from success in occupational and other realms. But again the liberal view holds appeal: at least until the transition to feminism, the existing *cultural arrangement* necessitates an asymmetric distribution of space to provide equality of opportunity among the genders.

feminists

As the issues become subtle, reasonable people come to disagree on who should do what and what community expense should be incurred to achieve parity. Such controversy stems from the effort to provide equal opportunity for individuals by taking into account differences among groups. The same problem arises no matter what the issue and no matter what the group. If people commonly get their job leads by word-of-mouth through friends and neighbors, then black people—excluded from the neighborhoods of employers and of those employed in expanding job sectors—will be at a labor market disadvantage. Black people's chronically higher unemployment rate stands as evidence of disadvantage: their longer queue for jobs is analogous to the longer line in front of the women's rest room. Blacks can be told to work harder, to use their meager resources more efficiently, to rearrange their lives and cultures to better their job qualifications. Alternatively, their present plight can be understood as *structural*—stemming from a history of enslavement, Jim Crow segregation, and white prejudice that now results in concrete arrangements that hinder individual life changes. One must be color-sighted, rather than color-blind, to deal with these differences. But this is no reverse racism: it rests on perception of social structural locations, not upon inherent inferiority attributed to group membership. Such government mandated policies as open job-searches, ethnic hiring targets, and preference for minority vendors and subcontractors can counteract structural biases that hold down opportunities of women, blacks, and other minorities. Affirmative action programs should be conceived as compensatory efforts to overcome such structured disadvantage (although the legal interpretation of the statutes is usually drawn more narrowly).

Equality is not a matter of arithmetic division, but of social accounting. Figuring out what is equal treatment necessitates—in every instance—a sociological analysis of exactly *blaming victim*

how it is that structures operate on people's lives. Besides rejecting the conservatives' penchant for blaming the victim, liberal policies need a concrete analytic basis that goes beyond good-hearted sympathy for the downtrodden. As in the rest room case, we need to specify how current patterns of "equal" treatment of groups yield unequal opportunities to individuals. We then should determine exactly what it would take (e.g., square feet to gender ratios) to redress the inequality.

Besides careful analysis, equality also involves a decision as to who is going to change and in what way. These decisions will often take from some and give to others. Thus we have the two-pronged essence of action on behalf of equal opportunity: sociological analysis and political struggle.

Questions

1. Briefly summarize the author's point: Under what circumstances does equality of space to pee not mean equality of opportunity to pee? Do you agree or disagree with his analysis?

2. At one point, Professor Molotch offers two possibilities for creating more equality between men and women. One of these options he labels as "liberal"; the other he labels as "conservative." Summarize (briefly) each option. Which option seems (to you) to be more fair? Why?

3. Here's a difficult question: Why does the author use the labels "liberal" and "conservative" to describe the options for change?

20

CADAVER STORIES AND THE EMOTIONAL SOCIALIZATION OF MEDICAL STUDENTS

Frederic W. Hafferty

Surviving "Gross Anatomy" has traditionally been a rite of passage for medical students—it's the class in which the students meet their first patient—one who cannot complain and to whom they can do no harm because he or she is dead. Although students are urged to approach their body with reverence, it is just as likely that they approach with anxiety. In this article, the author discusses the nature of "cadaver stories" told by students to one another. As you read, think about why Hafferty concludes that the telling of these stories is an important part of medical students' socialization.

undergrad med ed

Sociological studies of medical education and of the socialization of health care providers occupy a prominent position in the medical sociological literature. Beginning with the classic studies by Merton, Reader, and Kendall (1957) and Becker, Geer, Hughes, and Strauss (1961), a number of studies have focused on undergraduate medical education (Bloom 1973, Broadhead 1983, Haas and Shaffir 1987), nursing (Olesen and Whittacker 1968,

Acknowledgments: I wish to thank Arnold Arluke, Mary Zimmerman, Irving Zola, the reviewers, the editor and the special editor, for their comments on earlier versions of this paper. Address correspondence to Frederic W. Hafferty, Department of Behavioral Sciences, Duluth School of Medicine, University of Minnesota, Duluth, MN 55812.

Frederic W. Hafferty, "Cadaver Stories and the Emotional Socialization of Medical Students," *Journal of Health and Social Behavior*, Vol. 29, no. 4, Theme: Continuities in the Sociology of Medical Education (Dec. 1988): 344–356. Reprinted with the permission of the American Sociological Association.

Simpson 1979), and graduate medical training (Bosk 1979, Bucher and Stelling 1977, Light 1980, Mizrahi 1986, Mumford 1970). Within this literature, several themes and trends are important for our purposes. First, researchers tend to focus on the clinical rather than the preclinical years of medical training. In some cases this emphasis reflects little more than the numerical dominance of the clinical training years (including clerkship and residency training) over that of basic science coursework. In other cases, this preference is based more on the belief that the locus of socialization is best studied in the patient-centered years of clinical training (Konner 1987, Light 1983). Work in the "clinic" also appears infinitely more dramatic and more exciting than work in the classroom. Whatever the cause or the constellation of causes, the outcome is a relative neglect of earlier but formatively important stages in the socialization process (Conrad 1986). This paper seeks to address this bias and argues that the anticipation of, approach toward, and early involvement in the medical school subculture is a critically important phase of the socialization of physicians. Furthermore, this paper will argue that a fundamental ingredient in early medical socialization is the transmission and internalization of rules about feelings and emotions.

A second theme is the important role of oral culture in this transition from the lay world to the world of medicine. As initiates face the uncertainties of the admissions process and the unknowns of medical training, they tell each other stories or tales highlighting issues of common concern or anxiety. Conrad's (1986) insights into the myth of cut-throats[1] among premedical students is one example. Another is Haas and Shaffir's (1987) analysis of how medical student hopefuls craft an acceptable applications package and admissions interview. Cadaver stories are a third type of oral culture. Each of these three types of oral culture (stories about tricks played by admissions interviewers on students, about sabotaged organic lab experiments, and about the emotionally vulnerable being victimized in anatomy lab) plays a pivotal role in transmitting group culture to newcomers, establishing orienting principles, defining areas and elements of social control, and setting up lines of demarcation, particularly in differentiating insiders from outsiders and marking one's progress from one camp to the other.

In addition to serving as critically important sources of information, these stories also provide storytellers and their audience with an opportunity to demonstrate an awareness of, and commitment to, the underlying norms and traditions of this new and highly

desired (medical) culture. This body of oral culture both anticipates and mirrors a number of other oral traditions in medicine which function at later stages of training and practice. Leiderman and Grisso's (1985) discussion of the 'gomer phenomenon'[2] is one example. Others are Dingwall's (1977) analysis of "atrocity stories" told by British public health nurses about social service workers and Stimson and Webb's (1975) similar examination of stories told by patients about physicians. "Horror stories" also circulate among physicians about medical mistakes, the management of error, and the structure of occupational rituals designed to cope with uncertainty in medicine (Arluke 1977; Bosk 1979). Friedson (1975) notes the use of hearsay, stories, and gossip among physicians as a form of social control. An oral tradition also can be found in "rescue" stories, which circulate among animal lab caretakers engaged in biomedical research (Arluke 1988). Nonmedical accounts of oral culture include typification stories of tenants by janitors (Gold 1952), storytelling among jazz musicians (Becker 1963), and corporate culture in high-tech computer companies (Kelly 1985).

A third theme in the medical socialization literature is the role of emotional socialization within the overall process of professional training. Socialization in medicine involves more than the transmission of technical skills and knowledge about diagnosis and treatment and the internalization of attitudes, values, and outlooks with respect to such skills and knowledge (Merton et al. 1957). Socialization also involves one's feelings about that work, and in particular how one manages one's emotions and expresses one's feelings in and around troublesome areas of work (Bosk 1986). In this regard Parsons (1951) developed the concept of

---

[1]Cut-throats refers to students who are excessively competitive and not above using underhanded tactics to make sure that other students don't shine by stealing important reference materials, ruining other's lab work.—Ed.

[2]Gomer, as used here, is a negative term applied by doctors-in-training (e.g., residents in hospitals) to patients who are difficult to diagnose or difficult to treat because of mental or other issues. Sometimes, it is used to refer to unwelcome patients in the emergency room, as in "Get Out of My Emergency Room." —Ed.

"affective neutrality." Fox (1979a, 1979b) prefers the term "detached concern." Whatever the label, it is important to differentiate between the transmission of technical skills and knowledge and the transmission of rules regarding the experience and expression of feelings. Bosk (1986), for example, differentiates between "public" and "private" curricula. The former involves the mastery of cognitive knowledge and technical skills. The latter deals more with existential problems centering around uncertainty, limitations, and emotions. Bosk argues that for the technical demands of work, controls are external, formal, and explicit. In contrast, the moral or normative dimensions of medical work involve controls that are internal, informal, and implicit. Most important, Bosk maintains that these latter norms often are transmitted by allusion, parables, or mock or ironic jokes. Further- more, Bosk, along with such observers as Fox (1957, 1979a, 1979b, 1980) and Light (1979, 1983), links the problems of uncertainty, limits, and emotions to educational settings that are distinctly medical, namely the anatomy lab and the autopsy.

A number of other individuals, including Knight (1973), Coombs (1978), and Finkelstein (1986), have identified a variety of stressful stimuli associated with anatomy lab and/or the autopsy, including the particularly anxiety-provoking perception of the cadaver as a human reference. Finally, many of these authors also note the use of gallows humor (Obrdlik 1942) as a routinized coping mechanism in times of stress, particularly in situations or settings involving death and dying. Thus we may view cadaver stories not only as a descriptive source of information (both for ourselves and for medical student initiates) about one such type of stressful situation, but also as a vehicle for normative rules that mandate gallows humor as an appropriate coping device. Inasmuch as cadaver stories function to tell medical students how to "deal with" rendering whole and dead human beings into largely unidentifiable pieces of tissue and bone, they function as a source of "feeling rules" (Hochschild 1979, 1983) in a process that Shott (1979) terms "emotional socialization."

This paper has three goals: first, to delineate some of the structural characteristics of cadaver stories and to locate their telling as an important part of the oral tradition of medical training; second, to establish the role of these stories in the early emotional socialization of medical students; and third, to highlight the importance of humor in this process.

Methods

The data for this paper have been collected over a 14-year period. I first encountered cadaver stories during a study of exposures to death and dying in the first year of medical school (Hafferty 1976). The basic methodology of this study was participant observation, supplemented by semistructured interviews. Directly before the beginning of the anatomy lab phase of this study, I was approached independently by several students who proceeded to tell me stories about jokes played by medical students on unsuspecting victims via the manipulation of cadavers and cadaver parts. All of these stories were told to me as faithful accounts of true events that had taken place at some other medical school, and they were told with knowing smiles and laughter. As I listened, I had the distinct impression that I was supposed to find them humorous, and that my ability to share an insider's frame of reference was being tested. Curious about the circulation of these stories, I added several questions about cadaver stories to my interview schedule. I wanted to know more about students' familiarity with such stories, their content, the circumstances around their telling, and what reaction(s) the students had on hearing them. Thus more than 100 students were questioned formally about cadaver stories.

Additional recountings or mentions of cadaver stories also were collected in the field (in lab).

After completing this study, I continued to collect cadaver stories as a part of several other investigations. These subsequent studies included an investigation of fourth-year students taking an elective in anatomical dissection and a study of medical residents rotating through an elective in pathology. In addition, over a four-year period I drew on the topic of cadaver stories in classroom discussions during a required medical sociology course for first-year medical students. All the members of one of these classes were interviewed formally about the role and place of humor in lab, including their familiarity with cadaver stories. Also during this 14-year period, but in a much more informal manner, I asked practicing physicians, including a few retired physicians, whether they could recall hearing or telling cadaver stories when they were in medical school.

All told, the data for this paper are drawn from nearly 200 formal interviews and an equal number of informal interviews and conversations held during this 14-year period. Two of the medical schools at which data were collected are private the first and the third; two are public. The four schools are in different parts of the country: the East Coast, the West Coast, the Midwest, and the south central region. In all four of these schools, anatomy lab is scheduled in the first semester of the first year.

All data, both field-generated and interview-based, were gathered when either the lab or morgue was in session. The amount of detail gathered about any given cadaver story was guided by the "saturation" methodology outlined by Glaser and Strauss (1967). As might be expected in any oral tradition, I found that no two stories were told in exactly the same manner or with exactly the same details. As also is true in oral culture (Dingwall 1977), the detail needed to convey the information contained in these stories was found to diminish as initiates became more involved in the culture. For these reasons, I did not make a literal count of the "different" cadaver stories. Instead, I developed a rough typology as I encountered new stories and as I established the fundamental structure of these stories.

The Structure and Types of Cadaver Stories

"You hear about those guys at Columbia?" said Harry. "It was in the papers. They went to a subway change maker and when he gave them the token they put an amputated hand underneath the glass to pick it up. But as soon as he saw it, the guy had a heart attack and died." . . .

"So they were kicked out?" . . .

Claudia's and my eyes met over the cadaver. A chill went between us. Could that really take place . . . actually handed over to the outside world, never to return? . . . all that careful preparation of one's mind, to be wasted because of the accidental demise of someone who had nothing to do with medicine at all, who was just . . . just a token collector? What could juries of outside people understand of Lineweaver-Burk plots and membrane potentials and three-factor crosses, all the colossal volumes of facts we absorb in bulk at such great cost to our daily lives? No, no—that kind of thing just wouldn't be allowed to happen . . . (LeBaron 1981, p. 190).

This quote, abstracted from Charles LeBaron's autobiographical account of his first year at Harvard Medical School, is telling for two reasons. First, it is a rare example of a cadaver story in print. Second, the cadaver story itself is embedded in another dialogue about anatomy lab and the culture of medical school. In this second exchange we witness a conversation between two medical students and find, in their reflections on a distant and nonunderstanding lay culture, how far they have traveled from an identity and a frame of reference (lay) that recently was theirs.

Cadaver stories are composed of four basic elements: medical student perpetrators, unwilling, unwitting, and emotionally vulnerable victims, cadavers, either whole or represented by particular body parts, and a storytelling device that I call "reality anchors." This device is composed of references to "real" people, places, and things, and is used to convey a specific setting or context to the story. Examples include references to locations "at Columbia University"), printed sources ("the newspaper"), people ("*my* cousin told me that . . ."), and time ("last fall"). Most cadaver stories contain multiple reality anchors. Cadaver stories can be characterized further by whether the victims are lay people or other medical students. In this paper the stories with lay victims will be referred to as "out-of-lab" stories, and the stories with medical student victims, "in-lab" stories.

There are at least five different types of cadaver stories. In one commonly told type, medical students carry whole bodies or body parts out of lab in order to shock lay victims. LeBaron's story is an example of this type. The variations are endless. The body part may be a hand, a leg, an ear, or a sexual organ. The setting (if we are dealing with toll collectors) might be the subway (in New York City), a specific bridge (in San Francisco), or a toll road. Other variations include organs sent by mail to "friends," fingers dropped in shopping bags, and legs or arms placed in public toilets. Regardless of the body part or the victim, the punch line centers around the victim's shocked reaction upon encountering the severed body part. In contrast, the medical student perpetrators, rolling with laughter, almost always escape unencumbered either by the body part or by any feelings of guilt, remorse, or empathy with their victim.

A second type of cadaver story centers around the manipulation or mutilation of sexual organs; these are told most often as in-lab stories. Here the victim is an emotionally weak and vulnerable (and thus laylike) medical student. In an almost legendary story of this type, a group of male medical students cut off the penis

of their cadaver and insert it into the vagina of a nearby cadaver. The emotional coup de grace comes when the unsuspecting victim enters lab, undrapes that cadaver, and screams or faints at the sight. A variation on this basic story line describes how medical students link two whole cadavers in a sexual embrace. In another story a cadaver's penis is fitted with a condom and again is left to provoke the emotional reaction of some unsuspecting and vulnerable victim.

A third and similar story type describes incidents in which cadavers or cadaver parts appear to be, or become, more alive or lifelike. In these stories, cadavers are dressed up by students or otherwise manipulated to appear more alive. In one of these "resurrection" stories, medical students dress up their cadaver and take "it"[3] to the homecoming football game. The victim might be someone in the stands or an unsuspecting hot dog vendor. A frequently told in-lab version of a resurrection story describes how a medical student takes the place of a cadaver under the wrappings and sits up abruptly as the "body" is undraped. The victim, of course, is both startled and shocked, and usually faints or rushes from the lab.[4] In another frequently told story, students pump up a cadaver's penis to make it appear erect and turgid.

In a fourth type of story, cadavers are portrayed as food. There are two basic types of cadaver-as-food stories. One type is decidedly cannibalistic, and depicts medical students engaged in eating cadaver flesh or body organs. In a variant of this story type, the student perpetrators only pretend to eat such body parts. In both cases the victims are unsuspecting observers who experience great shock and revulsion upon witnessing a peer engaged in such an activity. The second type

---

[3]The gender of the cadaver is usually not identified or otherwise referred to in cadaver stories except in those stories describing the manipulation or mutilation of sexual organs.

[4]I have also heard a version of this story told by undertakers, in which the body unexpectedly sits up in the casket during a viewing.

food / Dead per

of cadaver-as-food story depicts the cadaver (or cadaver parts) as a receptacle for food. Candy, potato chips, or other types of food are hidden in body cavities, ready to be hauled out and consumed in front of unsuspecting viewers. Both of these types of cadaver-as-food stories appear most frequently as in-lab stories. In one story students transform an eviscerated abdomen into a gigantic lunchtime salad bowl. The abdomen is lined with aluminum foil and the cavity is filled with greens, vegetables, and other salad fixings, all of which the students consumed with great relish. An out-of-lab variation on this basic story line portrays a medical student (with a nonmedical student roommate) taking a skull cap home to be used as a soup bowl.

A fifth story type portrays the cadaver as a recently deceased relative or friend.[5] This type deserves special notice not only for its frequency of telling but also because of its fundamentally unique content. In this type of story, a student uncovers his or her cadaver's face for the first time only to discover that the cadaver is a recently deceased parent, sibling, friend, or other relative. Usually the setting is the first day of lab. In one variation the discovery takes place at the end of lab, when "nothing was left to do except the head and neck dissection." In this version the student's shock is compounded because he "hacked his mother to pieces" before discovering who the cadaver "really was." In these cadaver-as-relative stories the unwitting transgressors are always profoundly shocked; many become physically ill. Some must leave lab or even drop out of school. Frequently (but not always), this type of story ends with the statement that the student eventually returns to school and to the anatomy lab, having "worked through" his

or her upset. Stories that depict the cadaver as a loved one are unique in that they contain victims, but no perpetrators.[6] In addition, the action described is accidental, not purposeful or manipulated. As a class, these stories are the only ones that routinely feature male medical students as victims and therefore as emotion- ally vulnerable individuals. They are also the only type in which a shocked emotional response by medical students is presented as both warranted and appropriate.

Two additional characteristics of cadaver stories are worthy of note. First, although it may seem rather odd that medical students can horrify, maim, and even shock their victims to death with impunity, the inclusion of such a consequential ending is actually quite rare (LeBaron's story is an exception rather than the rule).[7] This type of finale appears frequently in stories told by gross anatomy or other medical school faculty members who wish to warn students indirectly about what they would consider inappropriate lab behavior. Stories that cite a medical faculty member as one of the reality anchors ("I had a friend whose anatomy professor told him . . .") are also more likely to end on such a consequential note. The theme of punishment or consequences always appears as an epilogue, and therefore can function only in conjunction with one of the five basic story themes.

Second, protagonists are not only characterized as emotionally detached and "cool" but also are scripted to appear as "fun-loving" members of a closely knit cohort of peers. In contrast, victims are portrayed as isolated outsiders

---

[5]I have never heard similar stories in which the cadaver was a deceased enemy or hated other, that is, with the element of revenge embedded in the story framework. My thanks to Arnold Arluke for raising this issue.

[6]We might hypothesize that the cadaver, as a future self, is the perpetrator. In this case the cadaver-as-relative stories, including the portrayal of a personal relationship between the cadaver and the student, involve an ironic twist in which the initial aggressor (student) becomes the actual victim (see "Issues of Gender" for a further development of this theme).

[7]Perhaps this element of consequences must be present because the story does appear in a printed form and is readily available to lay eyes, and thus to lay criticisms.

as well as emotionally weak. Although out-of-lab stories occasionally might depict a solitary medical student acting to shock a lay victim or a group of lay victims, in lab stories virtually always portray protagonists as a group of like-minded peers aligned against a solitary and thus doubly vulnerable classmate.

Storytellers and Settings

Cadaver stories circulate most freely and most frequently among and within two groups of individuals: medical student aspirants and medical student initiates. Correspondingly, cadaver stories are encountered most readily in three settings: the undergraduate "premed" college setting, the medical school setting directly before lab, and during lab itself, particularly during the first few weeks.

Most medical students first encounter cadaver stories as college undergraduates. As students begin to identify themselves and others as medical school aspirants, and as they become involved in the application process and begin to anticipate what it means to be a medical student, a fertile medium develops for the growth and circulation of these stories. One's identification as a pre-med is important to the circulation of cadaver stories. Medical students who report a nontraditional background, including applying late or from the work force, or even students who say that they keep their medical aspirations largely secret are less likely to report having heard cadaver stories before entering medical school. Consequently, fellow pre-med students are the most frequent source of the stories heard during this period. Older medical student friends or medical student siblings are reported as additional sources. Less frequently a story is attributed to a professor or teaching assistant. Because virtually all stories are accompanied by reality anchors, a story's source often is embedded in the story line itself.

The telling of cadaver stories is particularly endemic in that period directly before and during the first few weeks of lab. Stories can be interjected into virtually any conversation about anatomy lab. Although the setting sometimes is related to the story line (cadaver-as-food stories told during lunch, for example), there appears to be little association between the type of story told and the setting or time period. Cadaver stories appear to circulate more freely and more frequently among male medical students, but certain story lines were found to be more current among female cohorts (see "Issues of Gender" below). It was not uncommon, however, to encounter stories that had circulated among members of both sexes. After the students' initial adjustment to lab, the circulation of cadaver stories enters a dormant phase. They reappear subsequently and briefly, but usually only during times in lab that students find most anxiety-producing (dissection of the sexual organs and the face, and the hemisection of the body). In these situations, the story line or theme appears to be attached more directly to the general source of the stressful stimuli. The "salad bowl" story, for example, was told as one group of students wrestled with a particularly foul and smelly abdomen. Stories of sexual organ mutilation or manipulation also were heard more frequently during the pelvic dissections.

Once lab ends, cadaver stories disappear, but they are not forgotten. In later years a particular story might be told to a colleague ("Remember when. . . .") to the son (rarely the daughter) of a colleague who is applying to medical school or to a sociologist friend who the physician hears is doing research on "anatomy labs." These stories are rarely told to outsiders, however. Even so, the demise of this particular type of oral culture does not mark the end of storytelling among students. Cadaver stories are replaced by other types of stories which revolve around other sources of stress in medical training or practice situations.

mistakes

Second-year students tell horror stories about "dog lab" or National Boards. Clerkship students or residents, in turn, circulate stories about undesirable patients, diagnostic and treatment mistakes, and uncertainties in medical practice.

In sum, the act of telling cadaver stories (as well as their content) marks the anxious anticipation of anatomy lab, the initial adjustment to lab, and those periods in lab when the cadaver is most likely to appear as a human referent. During the application process, cadaver stories function alongside pre-med atrocity stories (Conrad 1986) and admission interview stories (Haas and Shaffir 1987) as a major source of oral culture. Cadaver stories differ from the other two types of story in that they focus much more clearly (both in telling and in content) on the transition between the lay and the medical cultures, and on the normative expectation that initiates should distance themselves from former lay attitudes and emotions in their quest for a new and more "medical" identity. The three story types are similar in that they can depict an environment (medical school or the process of getting into medical school) which is hostile, combative, and emotionally dangerous.

The Function of Cadaver Stories

For both tellers and listeners, cadaver stories serve as a highly developed form of communication about the anatomy lab experience. These stories present versions of what it is like to dissect human cadavers, and how students should act and feel in that experience. They also reflect a primordial fear held by many students, namely that cadavers can horrify, cripple emotionally, and perhaps even "kill" those who are emotionally weak and vulnerable. For most prospective and entering students, anatomy lab is a place of mystery, a normative void, and the one medical school

course that clearly differentiates their undergraduate college curriculum from that of medical school (Fox, 1979b, Reilly 1987). Anatomy lab is special; what transpires within its walls is not simply an extension of everyday life (Klass 1987). In fact, much of what occurs in anatomy lab is the antithesis of everyday social existence. Within the subculture of medical school, anatomy lab constitutes a right of passage, a unique emotional test whose successful negotiation signifies the ability to handle the presence of disease, decay, disfigurement, disability, and death which marks the world of medicine.

In their exposure to cadaver stories, initiates are asked to identify with the emotionally tough, cool protagonists at the expense of the emotionally weak, vulnerable victims. With the exception of cadaver-as-relative stories, all cadaver stories center around the interaction between these two stereotypical character types. The victim is scripted to display the more taboo emotions of fear, disgust, and revulsion, and is cast in turn as the solitary and tormented pawn in a highly stylized drama. Protagonists, on the other hand, appear as happy, fun-loving, in-group members whose emotional equilibrium has transcended the horrors of lab.

Within this dichotomy of emotional repertoires, cadaver stories contain two different levels of feeling rules. These two levels are similar to what Hochschild (1979, 1983) calls surface and deep acting, and what Bosk (1986) defines as public and private curricula.

First of all, cadaver stories convey norms governing the public expression of emotions in and around lab. Behaviors that indicate the presence of anxiety, fear, and revulsion are characterized in these stories as both inappropriate and sanctionable. Conversely, behaviors reflecting humor and "good-natured" camaraderie are characterized as both appropriate and functional. Cadaver stories stress that within the culture of medicine, the cadaver should exist as a learning tool and an object for manipulation rather than as a formerly living human being. In these stories, students who fail to behave accordingly, and thus threaten the emotional equilibrium of lab, are held up to ridicule and to the possibility of further torment at the hands of their peers. More deeply buried within these stories is the additional message that those who are unable to control their emotional behavior in public may court academic disaster as well. Those who must flee lab, or who remain unable to gaze upon their cadaver's face with at least the appearance of equanimity, are considered to be not only undesirable lab partners, unable to carry their own weight, but also individuals who will be unable to master the expected amount of anatomical material presented in lab.

In addition, cadaver stories convey feeling rules that govern the experience of lab. These rules operate on a more personal and more private level; they also represent the ultimate in one's affective adjustment to lab. In cadaver stories, perpetrators represent an ideal in emotional competence. This competence is derived from something more than an ability to maintain a public mask of scientific indifference, oblivious to the cadaver as a human referent. Rather it is grounded in the protagonist's ability to recognize the cadaver as a fundamentally ambiguous entity and to manipulate that ambiguity for his or her own benefit and amusement. The very essence of the cadaver story as a joke requires that the perpetrators view the cadaver *both* as a human referent and as a learning tool or object for manipulation. Indeed, if protagonists (and, not incidentally, storytellers and listeners) were unable to conceive of the cadaver as a formerly living human being, there could be no planning of the joke and no anticipation of their intended victims' emotional reactions.

In summary, the surface and deep feeling rules embedded in cadaver stories operate in concert both to posit a primary definition of the cadaver and to define how the medical gaze is to operate in the face of decay, death, and dismemberment. In addition, the surface feeling rules function to set a basic, minimal, and public standard for behavior in lab, which condemns the presence of disruptive emotional behavior while it establishes the preferred presence of camaraderie through humor. Perhaps even more important. cadaver stories serve to transmit the message that emotional competence is a necessary precursor to what is described often as the principal task of preclinical education, namely the mastery of technical information. In the absence of emotional equanimity, these stories suggest that little can or will be learned in lab, whether by the individual affected directly or by his or her lab mates, who find themselves faced with an emotionally distraught lab partner and a countervailing image of their cadaver.

The fact that protagonists use the cadaver's fundamentally ambiguous nature (both as a human referent and as a learning tool) to torment their victims highlights a particularly important dimension of the deep feeling rules conveyed in these stories. In cadaver stories, perpetrators are depicted as identifying neither with the cadaver (as a future me) nor with the victim (as a former me). In this way cadaver stories explicitly define emotional competence as involving both a requisite lack of empathy (entering into) and sympathy (suffering with) for those either unable or unwilling to adopt a medical frame of reference (outsiders). In cadaver stories, victims are not portrayed simply as different from real medical students; they are also presented as deserving objects of derision and abuse.

The abuse and antipathy portrayed in cadaver stories is obscured somewhat by the presence of humor both as a story theme and as a storytelling device. Protagonists are not portrayed as intending to hurt their victims; they only wish to have a little fun. If serious harm befalls the victim, it does so accidentally, and not through any direct or malicious intent by the perpetrator. In fact, any harm is really the victim's own fault, the result of an emotional weakness residing in the victim. Nonetheless, the stereotypical characterization of protagonists and victims contains the message that empathy and sympathy are decidedly dysfunctional emotions in the world of medicine.

The effectiveness of cadaver stories as sources of feeling rules and emotion work is grounded in the fact that they are told as true, and that the story characters themselves are first-year medical students. Both out-of-lab stories and in-lab stories are populated by students who are not much farther along in their training than the medical students and students-to-be who are telling and listening to these stories. Lay victims represent an emotional identity that initiates wish to leave behind. The protagonists represent the triumph of the medical gaze over baser laylike emotions. The emotionally vulnerable medical student, in turn, represents those who have not yet escaped their former lay selves.

Finally, the omnipresent cadaver-as-relative stories function as an important source of balance within this genre. This type of cadaver story depicts a set of circumstances in which the experience and the public reactions of shock and fear are appropriate and to be expected. Thus cadaver-as-relative stories function as a safety valve. This story type shows that the presence of "negative" emotions in lab is not totally outlawed. As noted earlier, this type of story is the only one in which male students are portrayed as emotionally vulnerable. More important, these stories tell how medical students can overcome even the most shocking situations. It would be difficult to imagine anatomy lab without the presence of cadaver stories; it would be equally difficult to imagine the genre of cadaver stories without the counterbalancing messages of the cadaver-as-relative stories.

Although it is not critical to this analysis, it is important to point out that the literal accuracy of "trueness" of these stories lies not in the events depicted but in the symbolic transformation of the actual fears and concerns held by medical students as they approach, and thus begin to experience, lab. Medical students do not dissect their mothers, uncles, or fourth-grade teachers, nor are they required to do so. They do fear, however, that their cadaver will remind them of someone—if not someone in particular, then the human form in general. Similarly, lab does not transform students into gastronomes with a fetish for cadavers, but many students find themselves associating cadaver flesh with uncooked meat. Some experience revulsion (even to the point of gagging) at meals following lab. Medical students also do not battle strong necrophiliac tendencies in lab, but many are disturbed by the sight (or anticipated sight) of so much nakedness, not to mention the sight of so many penises, vaginas, breasts, and nipples permanently shorn of their sensuality by death. In short, cadaver stories take those concerns which medical student initiates and aspirants harbor and transform them into something much more horrible and more grotesque. In this way students gain distance from that which is truly troubling by offering themselves something even more grotesque as a normative source of humor. These stories contain a dual layer of humor; most are told as humorous tales with the expectation that they will evoke humor, and the story line itself depicts protagonists experiencing humor at their victim's distress. The humor provides students with several sources of emotional distance. First, the presence of humor in these stories functions to shield the students from the basic content of the stories and from the normative messages contained therein. Without the normative presence of humor, these stories, told as true, would be a striking indictment both of the medical education system and of medical students. Second, the humor embedded in cadaver stories serves to distance medical students from the dominating symbolic presence of the cadaver as a human referent. Third, the presence of humor provides listeners with an alternative and sanctioned source of emotions in lab. In all three instances, the distance is accompanied by a sense of situational control and by a growing identity within the culture of medicine.

Issues of Gender

In addition to their stereotypical differentiation between emotional competence and emotional weakness, most cadaver stories are sexist in content. Traditionally, cadaver stories depict males as the emotionally transcendent and detached perpetrators, and cast women most often (particularly in the case of in-lab stories) in the role of the emotionally vulnerable victim. If a story depicts a medical student eating cadaver flesh, mutilating a cadaver's sexual organs, or hiding in a body bag, the protagonist is virtually always male (mind) and the intended victim is almost always female (heart). In this sense notations of gender serve a metaphorical purpose in cadaver stories. Cadaver stories reflect not only a culture (medicine) which has been (and in many respects still is) dominated by male values, attitudes, and stereotypes (many of which are decidedly antifemale), but also the broader lay culture in which many of these sexist orientations remain firmly entrenched.

One most illuminating aspect of this research has been the opportunity to follow changes in cadaver stories over time, particularly with respect to issues of gender. During the period covered by this research, not only has the proportion of women entering medical school increased appreciably, but there has also been a broader movement toward gender equality in the workplace and other arenas of social life. Changes in cadaver stories reflect these broader social events, however insignificant. When I began to collect these stories, the solitary exception to the protagonist-male, victim-female dichotomy was found in the cadaver-as-relative stories. More recently, however, newer versions of some traditional story lines have emerged in which women are more likely to be portrayed, if not as equals, then at least as less than passive and pliant victims. The following two stories illustrate this shift. One story opens (on a traditional note) with a male medical student taking the place of the cadaver inside a body bag. The unsuspecting female medical student unzips the bag and screams (as expected). This time, however, instead of fainting or fleeing (the more traditional ending), she "instinctively" lashes out as her "cadaver" begins to sit up. Unfortunately for the male perpetrator, the female medical student is holding a scalpel, and the male student is killed. Here the concept of role playing and the theme of consequence take on a dually ironic twist as the perpetrator-playing-cadaver becomes not only the victim but a cadaver as well. In a similar variation on another traditional story line, the female victim does not faint with shock when she discovers a penis stuck in her cadaver's vagina. Instead she masterfully escapes the intended victim status by turning to the expectant male audience with a cavalier, "I see one of you pulled out too quickly last night."

These two stories, as well as similar variations, were told to this investigator by women. Stories of this type also were reported to circulate more among female students than among male students, with little cross-gender recitation (except as a comeback to male students who were overheard telling one of the more traditional male-dominant varieties of cadaver stories). This theme of turning the tables has great appeal for many female medical students, perhaps even more so than the portrayal of women as perpetrators. The most fascinating aspect of these newer stories[8] is their clearly evolutionary character. They were constructed by grafting new and ironic endings onto more traditional story lines rather than through the construction of altogether new story types. In these updated versions, women are portrayed not only as less victimlike but also as the match for any male medical student who fails to recognize that women in general, and female medical students in particular, are no longer emotional foils or ready victims of emotional abuse.

In many respects, however, the sexist nature of cadaver stories has not changed fundamentally during the study period. Cadaver-as-food stories, for example, continue to circulate today just as they did decades ago, with males continuing to populate the ranks of the perpetrators. Similarly, I have not encountered stories in which women are portrayed specifically as eating body parts, nor have I found women shocking unsuspecting toll collectors to death. In regard to content, women have yet to be accorded the status of the cold and unfeeling perpetrator. At best, cadaver stories have become more gender-neutral in that the perpetrators' sexual identity simply is not mentioned, but once again, this is more the exception than the rule. Even when women are portrayed as triumphant nonvictims, the telling (and thus the presence) of such stories still represent a minority of the cadaver stories told. The telling and the content of cadaver stories remain largely a male province.

Conclusions and Implications

Cadaver stories function as an important vehicle in the social construction of anatomy lab. By telling and listening to cadaver

stories, medical student aspirants and initiates construct an experience which is both a source of horror and an emotional rite of passage. The highly stereotypical presentation of perpetrators and victims and the presence of the cadaver as an ambiguous entity identify problematic aspects not only of medical training but also in the construction of medical identities. In turn, the feeling rules conveyed in these stories cover not only the behavioral manifestations but also the subjective experience of feelings. Cadaver stories also suggest more appropriate and more functional feelings and behaviors. Thus telling, listening to, and even thinking about cadaver stories (however fleetingly) all constitute an important source of emotion work in which the feeling rules of emotional detachment are initially encountered and internalized in medicine. Cadaver stories also function to validate and perpetuate the traditional gender-based power relations in medicine.

One issue raised by this paper, but not yet addressed, is how might the phenomena of oral culture function as a source of data about situations or settings that otherwise would prove resistant to routine sociological inquiry? In the case of cadaver stories, we have found that such stories convey feeling rules which mandate that information about the affective dimensions of medical work be hidden not only from lay outsiders but also from peers and even from oneself. How, then, are we to gather information from respondents in the face of such normative barriers? What if potential respondents are willing to talk to us but find our questions unintelligible or irrelevant, in view of the consequential presence of deep feeling rules? Goffman's (1961) frontstage-backstage dichotomy is applicable in the case of surface feeling rules, and field researchers have developed strategies for tapping information under such circumstances. When "information about" is restricted to a few insiders, the investigator might seek an

---

[8]I do not imply that these stories were nonexistent 14 years ago, but only that their telling was sufficiently restricted or controlled to escape the notice of this (male) investigator.

informant or might attempt to establish more of an insider status via the role of the participant observer. But what strategies are appropriate in the face of deep feeling rules? Here the situation becomes more complex; our potential respondents are not so much unwilling as possibly unable to describe, reflect on, or otherwise shed much light on that which we consider interesting. Their perspectives may have changed. They may no longer see, feel, or otherwise react to things as they did in the past. Furthermore, the effective deployment of deep feeling rules requires that those so changed see nothing problematic or unusual in any such change.

This dilemma is very much at the heart of earlier studies, which reported that anatomy lab and the dissection of the cadaver were of no particular emotional importance to medical students. What do we do with the medical student who insists that his cadaver is "nothing more than a slab of meat" or "a learning tool"? How are we to determine whether such an assertion is the product of feeling rules internalized over time, or of something else? On the one hand, we might accept the assertion at face value, but then we would have accepted a one-sided and ultimately distorted view of the cadaver. On the other hand, we might suggest that our respondent is lying, but this course of action is both sociologically awkward and ultimately an insufficient resolution to our problem.

The use of oral culture as a potentially countervailing source of data can represent one possible, if partial, resolution to such issues. To return to the example cited above, what if this student also had told us some cadaver stories? Now a distinctly contradictory element has been introduced into the picture. On the one hand, our student maintains that the cadaver is "nothing more than a tool." On the other hand, he or she has told us a story which requires that both protagonists and victims view the cadaver as a formerly living human being. Furthermore, the normative presence of

humor in the telling of this story requires that both the storyteller and the audience also recognize the cadaver in this light. Although this issue of data validity is far too complicated to be addressed adequately here, one finding of this study is that the study of oral culture may offer a rich, and often alternative, source of data in situations dominated by feeling rules.

A second issue important to the study of feeling rules is the distinction between short term benefits and the potential for longer term dysfunctional outcomes. However adaptive cadaver stories might be to those anxiously awaiting lab and actually dissecting human cadavers, the feeling rules promulgated in cadaver stories may promote maladaptive coping strategies in clinical settings. Cadaver stories are one of the earliest forms of oral culture that students encounter in their medical training. The feeling rules introduced in these stories, particularly as they deal with the issue of affect and the social control of empathy, are built on continually in a number of other oral traditions and in a variety of subsequent settings. The very feeling rules that operate to distance initiates from the emotional consequences of dissecting human cadavers, performing autopsies, or killing animals in physiology lab (Fox 1979b) also may distance practitioners from their patients. In addition, feeling rules may come to be generalized to (or to bleed into) other settings or situations (family or interpersonal relationships, for example) quite distinct and separate from their original focus.

Finally, we should continue to think of cadaver stories as dynamic rather than static sources of oral culture. In this study we have found that the content of cadaver stories does change with changes in the broader culture. This observation raises the possibility of further changes in both the form and the content of these stories, and thus introduces the prospect of gathering additional information about this rather private aspect of medical training. It is exciting to consider the possibility that we may continue to learn about the themes of social control and gender relationships in medicine through this source.

References

Arluke, Arnold. 1977. "Social Control Rituals in Medicine: The Case of Death Rounds." Pp. 108–25 in *Health Care and Health Knowledge*, edited by Robert Dingwall, Christian Heath, Margaret Reid, and Margaret Stacey. New York: Prodist.

———. 1988. "Guilt and Its Management among Biomedical Animal Care Technicians." Unpublished paper.

Becker, Howard S. 1963. *Outsiders.* New York: Free Press.

Becker, Howard S., Blanche Geer, Everett C. Hughes, and Anselm L. Strauss. 1961. *Boys in White: Student Culture in Medical School.* Chicago: University of Chicago Press.

Bloom, Samuel W. 1973. *Power and Dissent in Medical School.* New York. Free Press.

Bosk, Charles L. 1979. *Forgive and Remember: Managing Medical Failure.* Chicago: University of Chicago Press.

———. 1986. "Professional Responsibility and Medical Error." Pp. 460–77 in *Applications of Social Science and Health Policy*, edited by Linda H. Aiken and David Mechanic. New Brunswick, NJ: Rutgers University Press.

Broadhead, Robert S. 1983. *The Private Lives and Professional Identity of Medical Students.* New Brunswick, NJ: Transaction.

Bucher, Rue and Joan G. Stelling. 1977. *Becoming Professional.* Beverly Hills: Sage.

Conrad, Peter. 1986. "The Myth of Cut-Throats among Premedical Students: On the Role of Stereotypes in Justifying Failure and Success." *Journal of Health and Social Behavior* 27:150–60.

Coombs, Robert H. 1978. *Mastering Medicine: Professional Socialization in Medical School.* New York: Free Press.

Dingwall, Robert. 1977. "'Atrocity Stories' and Professional Relationships." *Sociology of Work and Occupations* 4:371–96.

Finkelstein, Peter. 1986. "Studies in Anatomy Laboratory: A Portrait of Individual and Collective Defense." Pp. 22–42 in *Inside Doctoring: Stages and Outcomes in the Professional Development of Physicians,* edited by Robert H. Coombs, D. Scott May, and Gary W. Small. New York: Praeger.

Fox, Renee C. 1957. "Training for Uncertainty." Pp. 204–41 in *The Student Physician,* edited by Robert K. Merton, George Reader, and Patricia Kendall. Cambridge, MA: Harvard University Press.

———. 1979a. *Essays In Medical Sociology: Journeys into the Field.* New York: Wiley.

———. 1979b. "The Human Condition of Health Professionals." Lecture delivered at the University of New Hampshire.

———. 1980. "The Evolution of Medical Uncertainty." *Milbank Memorial Fund Quarterly* 58:1–49.

Freidson, Eliot. 1975. *Doctoring Together: A Study of Professional Social Control.* Chicago: University of Chicago Press.

Glaser, Barney and Anselm Strauss. 1967. *The Discovery of Grounded Theory.* Chicago: Aldine.

Goffman, Erving. 1961. *Asylums.* Garden City, NJ: Doubleday Anchor.

Gold, R. 1952. "Janitors versus Tenants: a Status-Income Dilemma." *American Journal of Sociology* 57:486–93.

Haas, Jack and William Shaffir. 1987. *Becoming Doctors: The Adoption of a Cloak of Competence.* Greenwich, CT: JAI.

Hafferty, Frederic W. 1976. "Exposure to Death and Dying in the First Year of Medical School: An Examination of Content and Consequences." Unpublished dissertation, Yale University.

Hochschild, Arlie Russell. 1979. "Emotion Work, Feeling Rules, and Social Structure." *American Journal of Sociology* 85:551–75.

———. 1983. *The Managed Heart: Commercialization of Human Feeling.* Berkeley: University of California Press.

Kelly, Jan W. 1985. "Storytelling in High Tech Organizations: A Medium for Sharing Culture." *Journal of Applied Communications Research* 13:45–88.

Klass, Perri. 1987. *A Not Entirely Benign Procedure: Four Years as a Medical Student.* New York: Putnum.

Knight, James A. 1973. *Doctor-To-Be: Coping with the Trials and Triumphs of Medical School.* New York: Appleton-Century-Crofts.

Konner, Melvin. 1987. *Becoming A Doctor: A Journey of Initiation in Medical School.* New York: Viking.

LeBaron, Charles. 1986. *Gentle Vengeance.* New York: Marek.

Leiderman, Deborah B. and Jean-Anne Grisso. 1985. "The Gomer Phenomenon." *Journal of Health and Social Behavior* 26:222–32.

Lief, Harold I. and Renee C. Fox. 1963. "Training for 'Detached Concern' in Medical Students." Pp. 12–35 in *The Psychological Basis of Medical Practice*, edited by Harold I. Lief, and N.R. Lief. New York: Harper &Row.

Light, Donald Jr. 1979. "Uncertainty and Control in Professional Training." *Journal of Health and Social Behavior* 20:310–22.

———. 1980. *Becoming Psychiatrists: The Professional Transformation of Self.* New York: Norton.

———. 1983. "Medical and Nursing Education: Surface Behavior and Deep Structure." Pp. 455–78 in *Handbook of Health, Health Care, and the Health Professions*, edited by D. Mechanic. New York: Free Press.

Merton, Robert K. , George Reader, and Patricia L. Kendall. 1957. *The Student-Physician: Introductory Studies in the Sociology of Medical Education.* Cambridge, MA: Harvard University Press.

Mizrahi, Terry. 1986. *Getting Rid of Patients: Contradictions in the Socialization of Physicians.* New Brunswick, NJ: Rutgers University Press.

Mumford, Emily. 1970. *Interns: From Students to Physicians.* Cambridge, MA: Harvard University Press.

Obrdlik, Antonin J. 1942. "Humor, A Sociological Phenomenon." *American Journal of Sociology* 47:709–16.

Olesen, Virginia and Elvi W. Whittacker. 1968. *The Silent Dialogue: A Study of the Social-Psychology of Professional Socialization.* San Francisco: Jossey-Bass.

Parsons, Talcott. 1951. *The Social System.* New York: Free Press.

Reilly, Phillip. 1987. *To Do No Harm: A Journey through Medical School.* Dover, MA: Auburn House.

Shott, Susan. 1979. "Emotions and Social Life." *American Journal of Sociology* 84:1317–34.

Simpson, Ida Harper. 1979. *From Student to Nurse: A Longitudinal Study of Socialization.* Cambridge, UK: Cambridge University Press.

Stimson, Gerry V. and Barbara Webb. 1975. *Going to See the Doctor.* London: Routledge

Questions

1. The author of this article says that cadaver stories are part of the "emotional socialization" of medical students. Based on what you read in this article, what sort of emotional socialization do medical students need?

2. According to Professor Hafferty, cadaver stories are rarely told to outsiders. Why do you think that is?

3. Some medical schools have reduced (or abandoned) their reliance on having the students dissect cadavers, and replaced hands-on dissection with such on-line resources as the U.S. National Library's, Visible Human Project®—a digital database of "complete human male cadavers in MRI, CT and anatomical modes." Given what the author says is the function of cadaver stories, what impact might "virtual" dissection have on medical students' attitudes toward the human body?

21

ANYBODY'S SON WILL DO

Gwynne Dyer

Ordinary people would be loathe to do the sorts of things that soldiers may be called upon to do—but societies seem to need soldiers. As Dyer explains in this chapter excerpted from his 1985 book *War,* the means of socializing men out of the civilian role and into the soldier/killer role has become institutionalized as a result of centuries of experience.

. . . All soldiers belong to the same profession, no matter what country they serve, and it makes them different from everybody else. They have to be different, for their job is ultimately about killing and dying, and those things are not a natural vocation for any human being. Yet all soldiers are born civilians. The method for turning young men into soldiers—people who kill other people and expose themselves to death—is basic training. It's essentially the same all over the world, and it always has been, because young men everywhere are pretty much alike.

Human beings are fairly malleable, especially when they are young, and in every young man there are attitudes for any army to work with: the inherited values and postures, more or less dimly recalled, of the tribal warriors who were once the model for every young boy to emulate. Civilization did not involve a sudden clean break in the way people behave, but merely the progressive distortion and redirection of all the ways in which people in the old tribal societies used to behave, and modern definitions of maleness still contain a great deal of the old warrior ethic. The anarchic machismo of the primitive warrior is not what modern armies really need in their soldiers, but it does provide them with promising raw material for the transformation they must work in their recruits.

Just how this transformation is wrought varies from time to time and from country to country. In totally militarized societies—ancient Sparta, the samurai class of medieval Japan, the areas controlled by organizations like the Eritrean People's Liberation Front today[1]—it begins at puberty or before, when the young boy is immersed in a disciplined society in which only the military values are allowed to penetrate. In more sophisticated modern societies, the process is briefer and more concentrated, and the way it works is much more visible. It is, essentially, a conversion process in an almost religious sense—and as in all conversion phenomena, the emotions are far more important than the specific ideas. . . .

> When I was going to school, we used to have to recite the Pledge of Allegiance every day. They don't do that now. You know, we've got kids that come in here now, when they first get here, they don't know the Pledge of Allegiance

[1]Eritrea, an Italian colony from 1885 to 1941, was annexed by Ethiopia in 1962. After a 30-year civil war, Eritrea gained its independence in 1992.—Ed.

to the flag. And that's something—that's like a cardinal sin. . . . My daughter will know that stuff by the time she's three; she's two now and she's working on it. . . . You know, you've got to have your basics, the groundwork where you can start to build a child's brain from. . . .

—USMC drill instructors,
Parris Island recruit training depot, 1981

That is what the rhetoric of military patriotism sounds like, in every country and at every level—and it is virtually irrelevant so far as the actual job of soldiering is concerned. Soldiers are not just robots; they are ordinary human beings with national and personal loyalties, and many of them do feel the need for some patriotic or ideological justification for what they do. But which nation, which ideology, does not matter: men will fight as well and die as bravely for the Khmer Rouge as for "God, King, and Country." Soldiers are the instruments of politicians and priests, ideologues and strategists, who may have high national or moral purposes in mind, but the men down in the trenches fight for more basic motives. The closer you get to the front line, the fewer abstract nouns you hear.

Armies know this. It is their business to get men to fight, and they have had a long time to work out the best way of doing it. All of them pay lip service to the symbols and slogans of their political masters, though the amount of time they must devote to this activity varies from country to country. It is less in the United States than in the Soviet Union, and it is still less in a country like Israel, which actually fights frequent wars. Nor should it be thought that the armies are hypocritical—most of their members really do believe in their particular national symbols and slogans. But their secret is that they know these are not the things that sustain men in combat.

What really enables men to fight is their own self-respect, and a special kind of love that has nothing to do with sex or idealism. Very few men have died in battle, when the moment actually arrived, for the United States of America or for the sacred cause of Communism, or even for their homes and families; if they had any choice in the matter at all, they chose to die for each other and for their own vision of themselves. . . .

The way armies produce this sense of brotherhood in a peacetime environment is basic training: a feat of psychological manipulation on the grand scale which has been so consistently successful and so universal that we fail to notice it as remarkable. In countries where the army must extract its recruits in their late teens, whether voluntarily or by conscription, from a civilian environment that does not share the military values, basic training involves a brief but intense period of indoctrination whose purpose is not really to teach the recruits basic military skills, but rather to change their values and their loyalties. "I guess you could say we brainwash them a little bit," admitted a U.S. Marine drill instructor, "but you know they're good people." . . .

It's easier if you catch them young. You can train older men to be soldiers; it's done in every major war. But you can never get them to believe that they like it, which is the major reason armies try to get their recruits before they are twenty. There are other reasons too, of course, like the physical fitness, lack of dependents, and economic dispensability of teenagers, that make armies prefer them, but the most important qualities teenagers bring to basic training are enthusiasm and naiveté. Many of them actively want the discipline and the closely structured environment that the armed forces will provide, so there is no need for the recruiters to deceive the kids about what will happen to them after they join.

There is discipline. There is drill. . . . When you are relying on your mates and they are relying on you, there's no room for slackness or sloppiness. If you're not prepared to accept the rules, you're better off where you are.

—British army recruiting advertisement, 1976

People are not born soldiers, they become soldiers. . . . And it should not begin at the moment when a new recruit is enlisted into the ranks, but rather much earlier, at the time of the first signs of maturity, during the time of adolescent dreams.

—*Red Star* (Soviet army newspaper), 1973

Young civilians who have volunteered and have been accepted by the Marine Corps[2] arrive at Parris Island, the Corps's East Coast facility for basic training, in a state of considerable excitement and apprehension: most are aware that they are about to undergo an extraordinary and very difficult experience. But they do not make their own way to the base; rather, they trickle in to Charleston airport on various flights throughout the day on which their training platoon is due to form, and are held there, in a state of suppressed but mounting nervous tension, until late in the evening. When the buses finally come to carry them the seventy-six miles to Parris Island, it is often after midnight—and this is not an administrative oversight. The shock treatment they are about to receive will work most efficiently if they are worn out and somewhat disoriented when they arrive.

The basic training organization is a machine, processing several thousand young men every month, and every facet and gear of it has been designed with the sole purpose of turning civilians into Marines as efficiently as possible. Provided it can have total control over their bodies and their environment for approximately three months, it can practically guarantee converts. Parris Island provides that controlled environment, and the recruits do not set foot outside it again until they graduate as Marine privates eleven weeks later.

They're allowed to call home, so long as it doesn't get out of hand—every three weeks or so they can call home and make sure everything's all right, if they haven't gotten a letter or there's a particular set of circumstances. If it's a case of an emergency call coming in, then they're allowed to accept that call; if not, one of my staff will take the message. . . .

In some cases I'll get calls from parents who haven't quite gotten adjusted to the idea that their son had cut the strings—and in a lot of cases that's what they're doing. The military provides them with an opportunity to leave home but they're still in a rather secure environment.

—Captain Brassington, USMC

For the young recruits, basic training is the closest thing their society can offer to a formal rite of passage,[3] and the institution probably stands in an unbroken line of descent from the lengthy ordeals by which young males in pre-civilized groups were initiated into the adult community of warriors. But in civilized societies it is a highly functional institution whose product is not anarchic warriors, but trained soldiers.

Basic training is not really about teaching people skills; it's about changing them, so that they can do things they wouldn't have dreamt of otherwise. It works by applying enormous physical and mental pressure to men who have been isolated from their normal civilian environment and placed in one where the only right way to think and behave is the way the Marine Corps wants them to. The key word the men who run the machine use to describe this process is *motivation.*

I can motivate a recruit and in third phase, if I tell him to jump off the third deck, he'll jump off the third deck. Like I said before, it's a captive audience and I can train that guy; I can get him to do anything I want him to do. . . . They're good kids and they're out to do the right thing.

[handwritten margin note: Shouted at drills]

We get some bad kids, but you know, we weed those out. But as far as motivation—here, we can motivate them to do anything you want, in recruit training.

—USMC drill instructor, Parris Island

The first three days the raw recruits spend at Parris Island are actually relatively easy, though they are hustled and shouted at continuously. It is during this time that they are documented and inoculated, receive uniforms, and learn the basic orders of drill that will enable young Americans (who are not very accustomed to this aspect of life) to do everything simultaneously in large groups. But the most important thing that happens in "forming" is the surrender of the recruits' own clothes, their hair—all the physical evidence of their individual civilian identities.

During a period of only seventy-two hours, in which they are allowed little sleep, the recruits lay aside their former lives in a series of hasty rituals (like being shaven to the scalp) whose symbolic significance is quite clear to them even though they are quite deliberately given absolutely no time for reflection, or any hint that they might have the option of turning back from their commitment. The men in charge of them know how delicate a tightrope they are walking, though, because at this stage the recruits are still newly caught civilians who have not yet made their ultimate inward submission to the discipline of the Corps.

Forming Day One makes me nervous. You've got a whole new mob of recruits, you know, sixty or seventy depending, and they don't know anything. You don't know what kind of a reaction you're going to get from the stress you're going to lay on them, and it just worries me the first day.

Things could happen, I'm not going to lie to you. Something might happen. A recruit might decide he doesn't want any part of this stuff and maybe take a poke at you or something like that. In a situation like that it's going to be a spur-of-the-moment thing and that worries me.

—USMC drill instructor

But it rarely happens. The frantic bustle of forming is designed to give the recruit no time to think about resisting what is happening to him. And so the recruits emerge from their initiation into the system, stripped of their civilian clothes, shorn of their hair, and deprived of whatever confidence in their own identity they may previously have had as eighteen-year-olds, like so many blanks ready to have the Marine identity impressed upon them.

The first stage in any conversion process is the destruction of an individual's former beliefs and confidence, and his reduction to a position of helplessness and need. It isn't really as drastic as all that, of course, for three days cannot cancel out eighteen years; the inner thoughts and the basic character are not erased. But the recruits have already learned that the only acceptable behavior is to repress any unorthodox thoughts and to mimic the character the Marine Corps wants. Nor are they, on the whole, reluctant to do so, for they *want* to be Marines. From the moment they arrive at Parris Island, the vague notion that has been passed down for a thousand generations that masculinity means being a warrior becomes an explicit article of faith, relentlessly preached: to be a man means to be a Marine.

There are very few eighteen-year-old boys who do not have highly romanticized ideas of what it means to be a man, so the Marine Corps has plenty of buttons to push. And it starts pushing them on the first day of real training: the officer in charge of the formation appears before them for the first time, in full dress uniform with medals, and tells them how to become men.

The United States Marine Corps has 205 years of illustrious history to speak for itself. You have made the most important decision in your life . . . by signing your name, your life, your pledge to the Government of the United States, and even more importantly, to the United States Marine Corps—a brotherhood, an elite unit. In 10.3 weeks you are going to become a member of that history, those traditions, this organization—if you have what it takes.

All of you want to do that by virtue of your signing your name as a man. The Marine Corps says that we build men. Well, I'll go a little bit further. We develop the tools that you have—and everybody has those tools to a certain extent right now. We're going to give you the blueprints, and we are going to show you how to build a Marine. *You've* got to build a Marine—you understand?

—Captain Pingree, USMC

The recruits, gazing at him with awe and adoration, shout in unison, "Yes sir!" just as they have been taught. They do it willingly, because they are volunteers—but even conscripts tend to have the romantic fervor of volunteers if they are only eighteen years old. Basic training, whatever its hardships, is a quick way to become a man among men, with an undeniable status, and beyond the initial consent to undergo it, it doesn't even require any decisions.

I had just dropped out of high school and I wasn't doing much on the street except hanging out, as most teenagers would be doing. So they gave me an opportunity—a recruiter picked me up, gave me a good line, and said that I could make it in the Marines, that I have a future ahead of me. And since I was living with my parents, I figured that I could start my own life here and grow up a little.

—USMC recruit, 1982

I like the hand-to-hand combat and . . . things like that. It's a little rough going on me, and since I have a small frame I would like to become deadly, as I would put it. I like to have them words, especially the way they've been teaching me here.

—USMC recruit (from Brooklyn), Parris Island, 1982

The training, when it starts, seems impossibly demanding physically for most of the recruits—and then it gets harder week by week. There is a constant barrage of abuse and insults aimed at the recruits, with the deliberate purpose of breaking down their pride and so destroying their ability to resist the transformation of values and attitudes that the Corps intends them to undergo. At the same time the demands for constant alertness and for instant obedience are continuously stepped up, and the standards by which the dress and behavior of the recruits are judged become steadily more unforgiving. But it is all carefully calculated by the men who run the machine, who think and talk in terms of the stress they are placing on the recruits: "We take so many c.c.'s of stress and we administer it to each man—they should be a little bit scared and they should be unsure, but they're adjusting." The aim is to keep the training arduous but just within most of the recruits' capability to withstand. One of the most striking achievements of the drill instructors is to create and maintain the illusion that basic training is an extraordinary challenge, one that will set those who graduate apart from others, when in fact almost everyone can succeed.

There has been some preliminary weeding out of potential recruits even before they begin training, to eliminate the obviously unsuitable minority, and some people do "fail" basic training and get sent home, at least in peacetime. The standards of acceptable performance in the U.S. armed forces, for example, tend to rise and fall in inverse proportion to the number and quality of recruits available to fill the forces to the authorized manpower levels. (In 1980, about 15 percent of Marine recruits did not graduate from basic training.) But there are very few young men who cannot be turned into passable soldiers if the forces are willing to invest enough effort in it.

Not even physical violence is necessary to effect the transformation, though it has been used by most armies at most times.

It's not what it was fifteen years ago down here. The Marine Corps still occupies the position of a tool which the society uses when it feels like that is a resort that they have to fall to.

Our society changes as all societies do, and our society felt that through enlightened training methods we could still produce the same product—and when you examine it, they're right. . . . Our 100 c.c.'s of stress is really all we need, not two gallons of it, which is what used to be.[4] . . . In some cases with some of the younger drill instructors it was more an initiation than it was an acute test, and so we introduced extra officers and we select our drill instructors to "fine-tune" it.

—Captain Brassington, USMC

There is, indeed, a good deal of fine-tuning in the roles that the men in charge of training any specific group of recruits assume. At the simplest level, there is a sort of "good cop–bad cop" manipulation of the recruits' attitudes toward those applying the stress. The three younger drill instructors with a particular serial are quite close to them in age and unremittingly harsh in their demands for ever higher performance, but the senior drill instructor, a man almost old enough to be their father, plays a more benevolent and understanding part and is available for individual counseling. And generally offstage, but always looming in the background, is the company commander, an impossibly austere and almost godlike personage.

At least these are the images conveyed to the recruits, although of course all these men cooperate closely with an identical goal in view. It works: in the end they become not just role models and authority figures, but the focus of the recruits' developing loyalty to the organization.

I imagine there's some fear, especially in the beginning, because they don't know what to expect. . . . I think they hate you at first, at least for a week or two, but it turns to respect. . . . They're seeking discipline, they're seeking someone to take charge, 'cause at home they

never got it. . . . They're looking to be told what to do and then someone is standing there enforcing what they tell them to do, and it's kind of like the father-and-son game, all the way through. They form a fatherly image of the DI[5] whether they want to or not.

—Sergeant Carrington, USMC

Just the sheer physical exercise, administered in massive doses, soon has the recruits feeling stronger and more competent than ever before. Inspections, often several times daily, quickly build up their ability to wear the uniform and carry themselves like real Marines, which is a considerable source of pride. The inspections also help to set up the pattern in the recruits of unquestioning submission to military authority: standing stock-still, staring straight ahead, while somebody else examines you closely for faults is about as extreme a ritual act of submission as you can make with your clothes on.

But they are not submitting themselves merely to the abusive sergeant making unpleasant remarks about the hair in their nostrils. All around them are deliberate reminders—the flags and insignia displayed on parade, the military music, the marching formations and drill instructors' cadenced calls—of the idealized organization, the "brotherhood" to which they will be admitted as full members if they submit and conform. Nowhere in the armed forces are the military courtesies so elaborately observed, the staffs' uniforms so immaculate (some DIs change several times a day), and the ritual aspects of military life so highly visible as on a basic training establishment.

Even the seeming inanity of close-order drill has a practical role in the conversion process. It has been over a century since mass formations of men were of any use on the battlefield, but every army in the world still drills its troops, especially during basic training, because marching in formation, with

---

[4]As a point of information, there are 4 c.c.'s in a teaspoon.—Ed.

[5]Drill instructor.—Ed.

every man moving his body in the same way at the same moment, is a direct physical way of learning two things a soldier must believe: that orders have to be obeyed automatically and instantly, and that you are no longer an individual, but part of a group.

The recruits' total identification with the other members of their unit is the most important lesson of all, and everything possible is done to foster it. They spend almost every waking moment together—a recruit alone is an anomaly to be looked into at once—and during most of that time they are enduring shared hardships. They also undergo collective punishments, often for the misdeed or omission of a single individual (talking in the ranks, a bed not swept under during barracks inspection), which is a highly effective way of suppressing any tendencies toward individualism. And, of course, the DIs place relentless emphasis on competition with other "serials" in training: there may be something infinitely pathetic to outsiders about a marching group of anonymous recruits chanting, "Lift your heads and hold them high, 3313 is a-passin' by," but it doesn't seem like that to the men in the ranks.

Nothing is quite so effective in building up a group's morale and solidarity, though, as a steady diet of small triumphs. Quite early in basic training, the recruits begin to do things that seem, at first sight, quite dangerous: descend by ropes from fifty-foot towers, cross yawning gaps hand-over-hand on high wires (known as the Slide for Life, of course), and the like. The common denominator is that these activities are daunting but not really dangerous: the ropes will prevent anyone from falling to his death off the rappelling tower, and there is a pond of just the right depth—deep enough to cushion a falling man, but not deep enough that he is likely to drown—under the Slide for Life. The goal is not to kill recruits, but to build up their confidence as individuals and as a group by allowing them to overcome apparently frightening obstacles.

You have an enemy here at Parris Island. The enemy that you're going to have at Parris Island is in every one of us. It's in the form of cowardice. The most rewarding experience you're going to have in recruit training is standing on line every evening, and you'll be able to look into each other's eyes, and you'll be able to say to each other with your eyes: "By God, we've made it one more day! We've defeated the coward."

—Captain Pingree, USMC

Number on deck, sir, forty-five . . . highly motivated, truly dedicated, rompin', stompin', bloodthirsty, kill-crazy United States Marine Corps recruits, SIR!

—Marine chant, Parris Island, 1982

If somebody does fail a particular test, he tends to be alone, for the hurdles are deliberately set low enough that most recruits can clear them if they try. In any large group of people there is usually a goat: someone whose intelligence or manner or lack of physical stamina marks him for failure and contempt. The competent drill instructor, without deliberately setting up this unfortunate individual for disgrace, will use his failure to strengthen the solidarity and confidence of the rest. When one hapless young man fell off the Slide for Life into the pond, for example, his drill instructor shouted the usual invective—"Well, get out of the water. Don't contaminate it all day"—and then delivered the payoff line: "Go back and change your clothes. You're useless to your unit now."

"Useless to your unit" is the key phrase, and all the recruits know that what it means is "useless *in battle*." The Marine drill instructors at Parris Island know exactly what they are doing to the recruits, and why. They are not rear-echelon people filling comfortable jobs, but the most dedicated and intelligent NCOs[6] the Marine Corps can find: even now, many of them have combat experience. The Corps has

6Noncommissioned officers.—Ed.

a clear-eyed understanding of precisely what it is training its recruits for—combat—and it ensures that those who do the training keep that objective constantly in sight.

The DIs "stress" the recruits, feed them their daily ration of synthetic triumphs over apparent obstacles, and bear in mind all the time that the goal is to instill the foundations for the instinctive, selfless reactions and the fierce group loyalty that is what the recruits will need if they ever see combat. They are arch-manipulators, fully conscious of it, and utterly unashamed. These kids have signed up as Marines, and they could well see combat; this is the way they have to think if they want to live. . . .

Combat is the ultimate reality that Marines—or any other soldiers, under any flag—have to deal with. Physical fitness, weapons training, battle drills, are all indispensable elements of basic training, and it is absolutely essential that the recruits learn the attitudes of group loyalty and interdependency which will be their sole hope of survival and success in combat. The training inculcates or fosters all of those things, and even by the halfway point in the eleven-week course, the recruits are generally responding with enthusiasm to their tasks.

But there is nothing in all this (except the weapons drill) that would not be found in the training camp of a professional football team. What sets soldiers apart is their willingness to kill. But it is not a willingness that comes easily to most men—even young men who have been provided with uniforms, guns, and official approval to kill those whom their government has designated as enemies. They will, it is true, fall very readily into the stereotypes of the tribal warrior group. Indeed, most of them have had at least a glancing acquaintance in their early teens with gangs (more or less violent, depending on, among other things, the neighborhood), the modern relic of that ancient institution.

And in many ways what basic training produces is the uniformed equivalent of a modern street gang: a bunch of tough, confident kids full of bloodthirsty talk. But gangs don't actually kill each other in large numbers. If they behaved the way armies do, you'd need trucks to clean the bodies off the streets every morning. They're held back by the civilian belief—the normal human belief—that killing another person is an awesome act with huge consequences.

There is aggression in all of us—men, women, children, babies. Armies don't have to create it, and they can't even increase it. But most of us learn to put limits on our aggression, especially physical aggression, as we grow up. . . .

There is such a thing as a "natural soldier": the kind of man who derives his greatest satisfaction from male companionship, from excitement, and from the conquering of physical and psychological obstacles. He doesn't necessarily want to kill people as such, but he will have no objections if it occurs within a moral framework that gives him a justification—like war—and if it is the price of gaining admission to the kind of environment he craves. Whether such men are born or made, I do not know, but most of them end up in armies (and many move on again to become mercenaries, because regular army life in peacetime is too routine and boring).

But armies are not full of such men. They are so rare that they form only a modest fraction even of small professional armies, mostly congregating in the commando-type special forces. In large conscript armies they virtually disappear beneath the weight of numbers of more ordinary men. And it is these ordinary men, who do not like combat at all, that the armies must persuade to kill. Until only a generation ago, they did not even realize how bad a job they were doing.

Armies had always assumed that, given the proper rifle training, the average man would kill in combat with no further incentive than the knowledge that it was the only way to defend his own life. After all, there are no historical records of Roman legionnaires refusing to use their swords, or Marlborough's infantrymen[7] refusing to fire their muskets against the enemy. But then dispersion hit the battlefield, removing each rifleman from the direct observation of his companions—and when U.S. Army Colonel S. L. A. Marshall finally took the trouble to inquire into what they were doing in 1943–45, he found that on average only 15 percent of trained combat riflemen fired their weapons at all in battle. The rest did not flee, but they would not kill—even when their own position was under attack and their lives were in immediate danger.

> The thing is simply this, that out of an average one hundred men along the line of fire during the period of an encounter, only fifteen men on average would take any part with the weapons. This was true whether the action was spread over a day, or two days or three. . . . In the most aggressive infantry companies, under the most intense local pressure, the figure rarely rose above 25% of total strength from the opening to the close of an action.
>
> —Col. S. L. A. Marshall

Marshall conducted both individual interviews and mass interviews with over four hundred infantry companies, both in Europe and in the Central Pacific, immediately after they had been in close combat with German or Japanese troops, and the results were the same each time. They were, moreover, as astonishing to the company officers and the troops themselves as they were to Marshall; each man who hadn't fired his rifle thought he had been alone in his defection from duty.

Even more indicative of what was going on was the fact that almost all the crew-served weapons had been fired. Every man had been trained to kill and knew it was his duty to kill,

and so long as he was in the presence of other soldiers who could see his actions, he went ahead and did it. But the great majority of the riflemen, each unobserved by the others in his individual foxhole, had chosen not to kill, even though it increased the likelihood of his own death. . . .

But the question naturally arises: if the great majority of men are not instinctive killers, and if most military killing these days is in any case done by weapons operating from a distance at which the question of killing scarcely troubles the operators—then why is combat an exclusively male occupation? The great majority of women, everyone would agree, are not instinctive killers either, but so what? If the remote circumstances in which the killing is done or the deliberate conditioning supplied by the military enable most men to kill, why should it be any different for women?

My own guess would be that it probably wouldn't be different; it just hasn't been tried very extensively. But it is an important question, because it has to do with the causes and possible cure of war. If men fight wars because that is an intrinsic part of the male character, then nothing can abolish the institution of warfare short of abolishing the male half of the human race (or at least, as one feminist suggested, disfranchising it for a hundred years).

If, on the other hand, wars are a means of allocating power between civilized human groups, in which the actual soldiers have always been male simply because men were more suited to it by their greater physical strength and their freedom from the burden of childbearing, then what we are discussing is not Original Sin, but simply a mode of social behavior. The fact that almost every living male for thousands of generations has imbibed some of the warrior mystique is no proof of a genetic predisposition to be warlike. The cultural continuity is quite enough to transmit such attitudes, and men were

---

[7]John Churchill (1650–1722), first Duke of Marlborough, British general, supreme commander of the British forces in the War of the Spanish Succession.—Ed.

specialized in the hunting and warrior functions for the same physical reasons long before civilized war was invented.

It was undoubtedly men, the "hunting" specialists, who invented civilized war, just as it was probably women, specializing in the "gathering" part of the primitive economy, who invented agriculture. That has no necessary relevance today: we all eat vegetables, and we can all die in war. It is a more serious allegation against males to say that all existing forms of political power have been shaped predominantly by men, so that even if wars are about power and not about the darker side of the masculine psyche, war is still a male problem. That has unquestionably been true through all of history (although it remains to be proven that women exercising power respond very differently to its temptations and obsessions). But there is no need to settle that argument: if war and masculinity are not inseparable, then we have already moved onto negotiable ground. For the forms of political power, unlike psyches, are always negotiable.

Unfortunately there is little direct support for this optimistic hypothesis in the prevailing current of opinion among soldiers generally, where war and maleness are indeed seen as inseparable. To say that the combat branches of the armed forces are sexist is like remarking that gravity generally pulls downward, and nowhere is the contempt for women greater than at a recruit training base like Parris Island. The DIs are quite ruthless in exploiting every prejudice and pushing every button that will persuade the recruits to accept the value system they are selling, and one of those buttons (quite a large one) is the conviction of young males—or at least the desire to be convinced—that they are superior to young females. (After all, even recruits want to feel superior to somebody, and it certainly isn't going to be anybody in their immediate vicinity at Parris Island.)

When it's all boys together, especially among the younger men, Marine Corps slang for any woman who isn't the wife, mother, or daughter of anyone present is "Suzie." It is short for "Suzie Rottencrotch"—and Suzie crops up a lot in basic training. Even when the topic of instruction is hand and arm signals in combat.

> Privates, if you don't have a little Suzie now, maybe you're going to find one when you get home. You bet. You'll find the first cheap slut you can get back home. What do you mean, "No"? You're a Marine, you're going to do it.
>
> If we get home with little Suzie . . . we're in a nice companionship with little Suzie and here you are getting hot and heavy and then you're getting ready to go down there and make that dive, privates, and Suzie says . . . Suzie says it's the wrong time of the month. Privates, if you don't want to get back home and indulge in this little adventure, you can show your girlfriend the hand and arm signal for "close it up."
>
> And you want her to close up those nasty little thighs of hers, do you not, privates? The hand and arm signal: the arms are laterally shoulder height, the fingers are extended, and the palms are facing toward the front. This is the starting position for "close it up" [tighten up the formation]: just like closing it up, bring the arms together just like that.
>
> Privates, in addition, I want you to dedicate all this training to one very special person. Can anyone tell me who that is, privates?
>
> (Voice) The Senior Drill Instructor, sir?
>
> No, not your Senior Drill Instructor. You're going to dedicate all this training, privates, to your enemy . . . to your enemy. To your enemy: the reason being, so *he* can die for *his* country. So who are we going to dedicate all this training to, privates?
>
> —lecture on hand and arm signals, Parris Island, 1982

And they shouted enthusiastically: "The enemy, sir! The enemy, sir!" It would not be instantly clear to the disinterested observer from Mars, however, why these spotty-faced male eighteen-year-olds are uniquely qualified to kill the enemy, while their equally spotty-faced female counterparts get to admire them from afar (or so the supposition goes), and get called Suzie Rottencrotch for their trouble.

Interestingly, it isn't entirely clear either to the senior military and civilian officials whose responsibility it is to keep the organization filled up with warm bodies capable of doing the job. Women are not employed in combat roles in the regular armed forces of any country (though increasing numbers of women have been admitted to the noncombat military jobs in the course of this century). But in the last decade the final barrier has come under serious consideration. It was, unsurprisingly, in the United States, where the problems of getting enough recruits for the all-volunteer armed forces converged with the changes of attitude flowing from the women's liberation movement, that the first serious proposals to send women into combat were entertained, during the latter years of the Carter administration.

> There is no question but that women could do a lot of things in the military. So could men in wheelchairs. But you couldn't expect the services to want a whole company of people in wheelchairs.
>
> —Gen. Lewis B. Hershey,
> former director, Selective Service System, 1978

> If for no other reason than because women are the bearers of children, they should not be in combat. Imagine your daughter as a ground soldier sleeping in the fields and expected to do all the things that soldiers do. It represents to me an absolute horror.
>
> —Gen. Jacqueline Cochran, U.S. Air Force

Despite the anguished cries of military conservatives, both male and female, the reaction of younger officers in the combat branches (all male, of course) was cautious but not entirely negative. The more intelligent ones dismissed at once arguments about strength and stamina—the average American woman, one pointed out, is bigger than the average Vietnamese man—and were as little impressed by the alleged special problems arising from the fact that female soldiers may become pregnant. In the noncombat branches, the army loses less time from its women soldiers due to pregnancy than it loses from desertion, drug abuse, and alcoholism in its male soldiers.

More important, few of the male officers involved in the experimental programs giving combat training to women recruits in the late 1970s had any doubt that the women would function effectively in combat. Neither did the women themselves. Despite their lack of the traditional male notions about the warrior stereotype, the training did its job. As one female trainee remarked: "I don't like the idea of killing anything . . . [and] I may not at this moment go into combat. But knowing that I can fire as well as I can fire now, knowing that today, I'd go in. I believe in my country . . . I'd fight to keep it."

The one major reservation the male officers training the "infantrywomen" had was about how the presence of women in combat would affect the men. The basic combat unit, a small group of men bound together by strong male ties of loyalty and trust, was a time-tested system that worked, and they were reluctant to tamper with it by adding an additional, unknown factor to the equation.

In the end a more conservative administration canceled the idea of introducing women to American combat units, and it may be some years yet before there are female soldiers in the infantry of any regular army. But it is manifestly sheer social conservatism that is retarding this development. Hundreds of thousands, if not millions, of women have fought in combat as irregular infantry in the past half-century, from the Yugoslav and Soviet partisans of World War II to Nicaragua in 1978–79. They performed quite satisfactorily, and so did the mixed units of which they were members. There are numerous differences of detail between guerrilla and regular army units, but none of them is of the sort to suggest that women would not fight just as well in a regular infantry battalion, or that the battalion would function less well if women were present.

The point of all this is not that women should be allowed (or indeed compelled) to take their fair share of the risks in combat. It is rather that war has moved a very long way from its undeniably warrior male origins, and that human behavior, male or female, is extremely malleable. Combat of the sort we know today, even at the infantryman's level—let alone the fighter pilot's—simply could not occur unless military organizations put immense effort into reshaping the behavior of individuals to fit their unusual and exacting requirements. The military institution, for all its imposing presence, is a highly artificial structure that is maintained only by constant endeavor. And if ordinary people's behavior is malleable in the direction the armed forces require, it is equally open to change in other directions. . . .

Questions

1. Why did Dyer title his article "*Anybody's* Son Will Do"?

2. "To be a man means to be a Marine"—or so recruits are taught. In what ways does the success of basic training seem to rely on the additional idea that if one cannot perform as a Marine, one is no better than a woman? How might the presence of female Marines in boot camp complicate the job of socializing males into their soldier role?

3. Erving Goffman, in *Asylums* (1961), defined "total institution" as "a place of residence and work where a large number of like-situated individuals, cut off from the wider society for an appreciable period of time, together lead an enclosed, formally administered round of life." Imagine that you've been put in charge of creating a total institution that has the goal of radically changing people's behavior. Military boot camp is one of the most successful types of total institutions. Based on what you've learned from Dyer's description of the way this total institution resocializes men, what sorts of procedures would you institute in your total institution to help ensure its success? For example, what sorts of things would you do to your "recruits" when they first arrive at your total institution?

22

SUSPENDED IDENTITY

Identity Transformation in a Maximum Security Prison

Thomas J. Schmid and Richard S. Jones

Schmid and Jones look closely at the resocialization process that new prison inmates undergo—but from the point of view of the prisoner and his concerns about his identity. As you read this 1991 article, consider how experiences in this sort of total institution differ from those undergone by men in boot camp.

prison

A prison sentence constitutes a "massive assault" on the identity of those imprisoned (Berger 1963, 100–101). This assault is especially severe on first-time inmates, and we might expect radical identity changes to ensue from their imprisonment. At the same time, a prisoner's awareness of the challenge to his identity affords some measure of protection against it. As part of an ethnographic analysis of the prison experiences of first-time, short-term inmates, this article presents an identity transformation model that differs both from the gradual transformation processes that characterize most adult identity changes and from such radical transformation processes as brainwashing or conversion.

Data for the study are derived principally from ten months of participant observation at a maximum security prison for men in the upper midwest of the United States. One of the authors was an inmate serving a felony sentence for one year and one day, while the other participated in the study as an outside observer. Relying on traditional ethnographic data collection and analysis techniques, this approach offered us general observations of hundreds of prisoners, and extensive field-notes that were based on repeated, often daily, contacts with about fifty inmates, as well as on personal relationships established with a smaller number of inmates. We subsequently returned to the prison to conduct focused interviews with other prisoners; using information provided by prison officials, we were able to identify and interview twenty additional first-time inmates who were serving sentences of two years or less. See Schmid and Jones (1987) for further description of this study.

Three interrelated research questions guided our analysis: How do first-time, short-term inmates define the prison world, and how do their definitions change during their prison careers? How do these inmates adapt to the prison world, and how do their adaptation strategies change during their prison careers? How do their self-definitions change during their prison careers? Our analyses of the first

adapt to jail

ANTICIPATORY IMAGE ⟶ **ANTICIPATORY SURVIVAL STRATEGY**

Outsider's perspective: violence; uncertainty; fear

Protective resolutions: to avoid unnecessary contacts with inmates; to avoid unnecessary contacts with guards; not to be changed in prison; to disregard questionable information; to avoid all hostilities; to engage in self-defense if hostilities arise

SURVIVAL STRATEGY

Territorial caution; selective interaction with inmates; impression management with inmates; partnership with another inmate; redefinition of prison violence as "explained" rather than random events

MID-CAREER IMAGE ⟶ **ADAPTATION STRATEGY**

Insider's perspective: boredom

Legal and illegal diversions; suppression of thoughts about outside world; minimization of outside contacts; impression management with inmates and outsiders; partnership

CONCLUDING IMAGE ⟷ **DISSIPATION OF ADAPTATION STRATEGY**

Synthetic perspective: revision of prison image and reformulation of outside image

Continued diversions; decreasing impression management; decreasing suppression of outside thoughts; disassociation with partner; formulation of outside plan

Figure 1 Prison Images and Strategies of New Inmates

two questions are presented in detail elsewhere (Schmid and Jones 1987, 1990); an abbreviated outline of these analyses, to which we will allude throughout this article, is presented in Figure 1. The identity transformation model presented here, based on our analysis of the third question, is outlined in Figure 2.

Preprison Identity

Our data suggest that the inmates we studied have little in common before their arrival at prison, except their conventionality. Although convicted of felonies, most do not possess "criminal" identities (cf. Irwin 1970, 29–34).

They begin their sentences with only a vague, incomplete image (Boulding 1961) of what prison is like, but an image that nonetheless stands in contrast to how they view their own social worlds. Their prison image is dominated by the theme of violence: they see prison inmates as violent, hostile, alien human beings, with whom they have nothing in common. They have several specific fears about what will happen to them in prison, including fears of assault, rape, and death. They are also concerned about their identities, fearing that—if they survive prison at all—they are in danger of changing in prison, either through the intentional efforts of rehabilitation personnel or through the unavoidable hardening effects

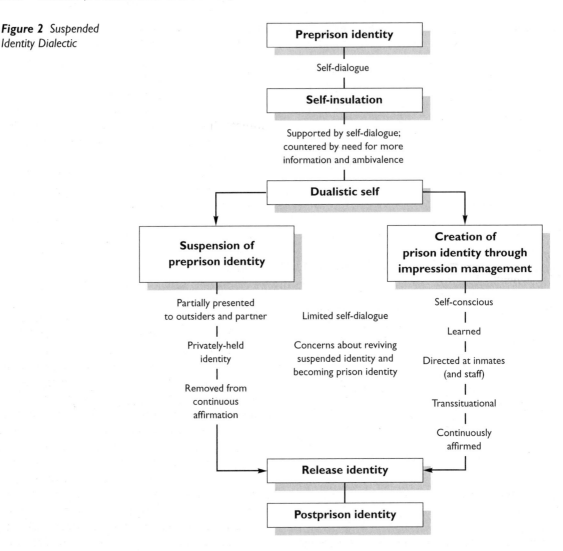

Figure 2 *Suspended Identity Dialectic*

of the prison environment. Acting on this imagery (Blumer 1969)—or, more precisely, on the inconsonance of their self-images with this prison image—they develop an anticipatory survival strategy (see Figure 1) that consists primarily of protective resolutions: a resolve to avoid all hostilities; a resolve to avoid all non-essential contacts with inmates and guards; a resolve to defend themselves in any way possible; and a resolve not to change, or to be changed, in prison.

A felon's image and strategy are formulated through a running self-dialogue, a heightened state of reflexive awareness (Lewis 1979) through which he ruminates about his past behavior and motives, and imaginatively projects himself into the prison world. This self-dialogue begins shortly after his arrest, continues intermittently during his trial or court hearings, and becomes especially intense at the time of his transfer to prison.

You start taking a review—it's almost like your life is passing before your eyes. You wonder how in the heck you got to this point and, you know, what are—what's your family gonna think about it—your friends, all the talk, and how are you going to deal with that—and the kids, you know, how are they gonna react to it? . . . All those things run through your head. . . . The total loss of control—the first time in my life that some other people were controlling my life.

• • •

My first night in the joint was spent mainly on kicking myself in the butt for putting myself in the joint. It was a very emotional evening. I thought a lot about all my friends and family, the good-byes, the things we did the last couple of months, how good they had been to me, sticking by me. I also thought about my fears: Am I going to go crazy? Will I end up fighting for my life? How am I going to survive in here for a year? Will I change? Will things be the same when I get out?

His self-dialogue is also typically the most extensive self-assessment he has ever conducted; thus, at the same time that he is resolving not to change, he is also initiating the kind of introspective analysis that is essential to any identity transformation process.

Self-Insulation

A felon's self-dialogue continues during the initial weeks and months of his sentence, and it remains a solitary activity, each inmate struggling to come to grips with the inconsonance of his established (preprison) identity and his present predicament. Despite the differences in their preprison identities, however, inmates now share a common situation that affects their identities. With few exceptions, their self-dialogues involve feelings of vulnerability, discontinuity, and differentiation from other inmates, emotions that reflect both the degradations and deprivations of institutional life (cf. Garfinkel 1956; Goffman 1961; and

Sykes 1958) and their continuing outsiders' perspective on the prison world. These feelings are obviously the result of everything that has happened to the inmates, but they are something else as well: they are the conditions in which every first-time, short-term inmate finds himself. They might even be called the common attributes of the inmates' selves-in-prison, for the irrelevance of their preprison identities within the prison world reduces their self-definitions, temporarily, to the level of pure emotion. These feelings, and a consequent emphasis on the "physical self" (Zurcher 1977, 176), also constitute the essential motivation for the inmates' self-insulation strategies.[1]

An inmate cannot remain wholly insulated within the prison world, for a number of reasons. He simply spends too much of his time in the presence of others to avoid all interaction with them. He also recognizes that his prison image is based on incomplete and inadequate information, and that he must interact with others in order to acquire first-hand information about the prison world. His behavior in prison, moreover, is guided not only by his prison image but by a fundamental ambivalence he feels about his situation, resulting from his marginality between the prison and outside social worlds (Schmid and Jones 1987). His ambivalence has several manifestations throughout his prison career, but the most important is his conflicting desires for self-insulation and for human communication.

---

[1]There are four principal components to the survival strategies of the inmates we studied, in the early months of their prison sentences. "Selective interaction" and "territorial caution" are essentially precautionary guidelines that allow inmates to increase their understanding of the prison world while minimizing danger to themselves. "Partnership" is a special friendship bond between two inmates, typically based on common backgrounds and interests (including a shared uncertainty about prison life) and strengthened by the inmates' mutual exploration of a hostile prison world. The fourth component of their strategies, impression management, is discussed in subsequent sections of this article.

Managing a Dualistic Self

An inmate is able to express both directions of his ambivalence (and to address his need for more information about the prison) by drawing a distinction between his "true" identity (i.e., his outside, preprison identity) and a "false" identity he creates for the prison world. For most of a new inmate's prison career, his preprison identity remains a "subjective" or "personal" identity while his prison identity serves as his "objective" or "social" basis for interaction in prison (see Goffman 1963; Weigert 1986). This bifurcation of his self (Figure 2) is not a conscious decision made at a single point in time, but it does represent two conscious and interdependent identity-preservation tactics, formulated through self-dialogue and refined through tentative interaction with others.

First, after coming to believe that he cannot "be himself" in prison because he would be too vulnerable, he decides to "suspend" his preprison identity for the duration of his sentence. He retains his resolve not to let prison change him, protecting himself by choosing not to reveal himself (his "true" self) to others. Expressions of a suspension of identity emerged repeatedly and consistently in both the fieldwork and interview phases of our research through such statements as

> I was reserved. . . . I wouldn't be very communicative, you know. I'd try to keep conversation to a minimum. . . . I wasn't interested in getting close to anybody . . . or asking a lot of questions. You know, try to cut the conversation short . . . go my own way back to my cell or go to the library or do something.
>
> • • •
>
> I didn't want nobody to know too much about me. That was part of the act.

An inmate's decision to suspend his preprison identity emanates directly from his feelings of vulnerability, discontinuity, and differentiation from other inmates. These emotions foster

something like a "proto-sociological attitude" (Weigert, 1986, 173; see also Zurcher 1977), in which new inmates find it necessary to step outside their taken-for-granted preprison identities. Rather than viewing these identities and the everyday life experience in which they are grounded as social constructions, however, inmates see the *prison* world as an artificial construction, and judge their "naturally occurring" preprison identities to be out of place within this construction. By attempting to suspend his preprison identity for the time that he spends in prison, an inmate believes that he will again "be his old self" after his release.

While he is in confinement, an inmate's decision to suspend his identity leaves him with little or no basis for interaction. His second identity tactic, then, is the creation of an identity that allows him to interact, however cautiously, with others. This tactic consists of his increasingly sophisticated impression management skills (Goffman 1959;[2] Schlenker 1980), which are initially designed simply to hide his vulnerability, but which gradually evolve into an alternative identity felt to be more suitable to the prison world. The character of the presented identity is remarkably similar from inmate to inmate:

> Well, I learned that you can't act like—you can't get the attitude where you are better than they are. Even where you might be better than them, you can't strut around like you are. Basically, you can't stick out. You don't stare at people and things like that. I knew a lot of these things from talking to people and I figured them out by myself. I sat down and figured out just what kind of attitude I'm going to have to take.
>
> • • •
>
> Most people out here learn to be tough, whether they can back it up or not. If you don't learn to be tough, you will definitely pay for it.

---

[2]Recall from reading 14 Goffman's concepts of expressions given and expressions given off—these are important components of impression management.—Ed.

This toughness can be demonstrated through a mean look, tough language, or an extremely big build. . . . One important thing is never to let your guard down.

An inmate's prison identity, as an inauthentic presentation of self, is not in itself a form of identity transformation but is rather a form of identity construction. His prison identity is simply who he must pretend to be while he is in prison. It is a false identity created for survival in an artificial world. But this identity nonetheless emerges in the same manner as any other identity: it is learned from others, and it must be presented to, negotiated with, and validated by others. A new inmate arrives at prison with a general image of what prisoners are like, and he begins to flesh out this image from the day of his arrival, warily observing others just as they are observing him. Through watching others, through eavesdropping, through cautious conversation and selective interaction, a new inmate refines his understanding of what maximum security prisoners look like, how they talk, how they move, how they act. Despite his belief that he is different from these other prisoners, he knows that he cannot appear to be too different from them, if he is to hide his vulnerability. His initial image of other prisoners, his early observations, and his concern over how he appears to others thus provide a foundation for the identity he gradually creates through impression management.

Impression management skills, of course, are not exclusive to the prison world; a new inmate, like anyone else, has had experience in presenting a "front" to others, and he draws upon his experience in the creation of his prison identity. He has undoubtedly even had experience in projecting the very attributes— strength, stoicism, aplomb—required by his prison identity. Impression management in prison differs, however, in the totality with which it governs interactions and in the perceived costs of failure: humiliation, assault, or death. For these reasons the entire impression management process becomes a more highly conscious endeavor. When presenting himself before others, a new inmate pays close attention to such minute details of his front as eye contact, posture, and manner of walking:

> I finally got out of orientation. I was going out with the main population, going down to get my meals and things. The main thing is not to stare at a bunch of people, you know. I tried to just look ahead, you know, not stare at people. 'Cause I didn't really know; I just had to learn a little at a time.

> • • •

> The way you look seems to be very important. The feeling is you shouldn't smile, that a frown is much more appropriate. The eyes are very important. You should never look away; it is considered a sign of weakness. Either stare straight ahead, look around, or look the person dead in the eyes. The way you walk is important. You shouldn't walk too fast; they might think you were scared and in a hurry to get away.

To create an appropriate embodiment (Stone 1962; Weigert 1986) of their prison identities, some new inmates devote long hours to weightlifting or other body-building exercises, and virtually all of them relinquish their civilian clothes—which might express their pre-prison identities—in favor of the standard issue clothing that most inmates wear. Whenever a new inmate is open to the view of other inmates, in fact, he is likely to relinquish most overt symbols of his individuality, in favor of a standard issue "prison inmate" appearance.

By acting self-consciously, of course, a new inmate runs the risk of exposing the fact that he *is* acting. But he sees no alternative to playing his part better; he cannot "not act" because that too would expose the vulnerability of his "true" identity. He thus sees every new prison experience, every new territory that he is allowed to explore, as a test of his impression management skills. Every nonconfrontive encounter with another inmate symbolizes his success at these skills, but it is also a social validation of his prison identity. Eventually he comes to see that many, perhaps most, inmates are engaging in the same kind of inauthentic presentations of self (cf. Glaser and Strauss 1964). Their identities are as "false" as his, and their validations of his identity may be equally false. But he realizes that he is powerless to change this state of affairs, and that he must continue to present his prison identity for as long as he remains in prison.

A first-time inmate enters prison as an outsider, and it is from an outsider's perspective that he initially creates his prison identity. In contrast to this suspended preprison identity, his prison identity is a *shared* identity, because it is modeled on his observations of other inmates. Like those of more experienced prisoners, his prison identity is tied directly to the social role of "prison inmate" (cf. Scheff 1970; Solomon 1970); because he is an outsider, however, his prison identity is also severely limited by his narrow understanding of that role. It is based on an outsider's stereotype of who a maximum security inmate is and what he acts like. It is, nonetheless, a *structural* identity (Weigert 1968), created to address his outsider's institutional problems of social isolation and inadequate information about the prison world.

By the middle of his sentence, a new inmate comes to adopt what is essentially an insider's perspective on the prison world. His prison image has evolved to the point where it is dominated by the theme of boredom rather than violence. (The possibility of violence is still acknowledged and feared, but those violent incidents that do occur have been redefined as the consequences of prison norm violations rather than as random predatory acts; see Schmid and Jones 1990.) His survival strategy, although still extant, has been supplemented by such general adaptation techniques as legal and illegal diversionary activities and conscious efforts to suppress his thoughts about the outside world (Figure 1). His

impression management tactics have become second nature rather than self-conscious, as he routinely interacts with others in terms of his prison identity.

An inmate's suspension of his preprison identity, of course, is never absolute, and the separation between his suspended identity and his prison identity is never complete. He continues to interact with his visitors at least partially in terms of his preprison identity, and he is likely to have acquired at least one inmate "partner" with whom he interacts in terms of his preprison as well as his prison identity. During times of introspection, however—which take place less frequently but do not disappear—he generally continues to think of himself as being the same person he was before he came to prison. But it is also during these periods of self-dialogue that he begins to have doubts about his ability to revive his suspended identity.

> That's what I worry about a lot. Because I didn't want to change. . . . I'm still fighting it, 'cause from what I understood, before, I wasn't that bad—I wasn't even violent. But I have people say stuff to me now, before I used to say "O.k., o.k."—but now it seems like I got to eye them back, you know.
>
> • • •
>
> I don't know, but I may be losing touch with the outside. I am feeling real strange during visits, very uncomfortable. I just can't seem to be myself, although I am not really sure what myself is all about. My mind really seems to be glued to the inside of these walls. I can't even really comprehend the outside. I haven't even been here three months, and I feel like I'm starting to lose it. Maybe I'm just paranoid. But during these visits I really feel like I'm acting. I'm groping for the right words, always trying to keep the conversation going. Maybe I'm just trying to present a picture that will relieve the minds of my visitors, I just don't know.
>
> • • •
>
> I realized that strength is going to be an important factor whether I'm going to turn into

a cold person or whether I'm going to keep my humanitarian point of view. I know it is going to be an internal war. It's going to take a lot of energy to do that. . . . I just keep telling myself that you gotta do it and sometimes you get to the point where you don't care anymore. You just kinda lose it and you get so full of hate, so full of frustration, it gets wound up in your head a lot.

At this point, both the inmate's suspended preprison identity and his created prison identity are part of his "performance consciousness" (Schechner 1985), although they are not given equal value. His preprison identity is grounded primarily in the memory of his biography (Weigert 1986) rather than in self-performance. His concern, during the middle of his sentence, is that he has become so accustomed to dealing with others in terms of his prison identity—that he has been presenting and receiving affirmation of this identity for so long—that it is becoming his "true" identity.[3]

An inmate's fear that he is becoming the character he has been presenting is not unfounded. All of his interactions within the prison world indicate the strong likelihood of a "role-person merger" (Turner 1978). An inmate views his presentation of his prison identity as a necessary expression of his inmate status. Unlike situational identities presented through impression management in the outside world, performance of the inmate role is transsituational and continuous. For a new inmate, prison consists almost exclusively of front regions, in which he must remain in

_____
[3]Clemmer (1958, 299) has defined "prisonization" as the "taking on in greater or less degree of the folkways, mores, customs, and general culture of the penitentiary." Yet new inmates begin to "take on" these things almost immediately, as part of the impression they are attempting to present to other inmates. Thus, we would argue instead that prisonization (meaning assimilation to the prison world) begins to occur for these inmates when their prison identities become second nature—when their expressions of prison norms and customs are no longer based on self-conscious acting. A new inmate's identity concerns, during the middle of his sentence, are essentially a recognition of this assimilation.

character. As long as he is in the maximum security institution, he remains in at least partial view of the audience for which his prison identity is intended: other prison inmates. Moreover, because the stakes of his performance are so high, there is little room for self-mockery or other forms of role distance (Coser 1966; Ungar 1984) from his prison identity, and there is little possibility that an inmate's performance will be "punctured" (Adler and Adler 1989) by his partner or other prison acquaintances. And because his presentation of his prison identity is continuous, he also receives continuous affirmation of his identity from others—affirmation that becomes more significant in light of the fact that he also remains removed from day-to-day reaffirmation of his preprison identity by his associates in the outside world. The inauthenticity of the process is beside the point: Stone's (1962, 93) observation that "one's identity is established when others *place* him as a social object by assigning him the same words of identity that he appropriates for himself or *announces*" remains sound even when both the announcements and the placements are recognized as false.

Standing against these various forms of support for an inmate's prison identity are the inmate's resolve not to be changed in prison, the fact that his sentence is relatively brief (though many new inmates lose sight of this brevity during the middle of their careers) and the limited reaffirmation of his preprison identity that he receives from outsiders and from his partner. These are not insubstantial resources, but nor do they guarantee an inmate's future ability to discard his prison identity and revive the one he has suspended.

Identity Dialectic

When an inmate's concerns about his identity first emerge, there is little that he can do about them. He recognizes that he has no choice but to present his prison identity so, following the insider's perspective he has now adopted, he consciously attempts to suppress his concerns. Eventually, however, he must begin to consider seriously his capacity to revive his suspended identity: his identity concerns, and his belief that he must deal with them, become particularly acute if he is transferred to the minimum security unit of the prison for the final months of his sentence.[4] At the conclusion of his prison career, an inmate shifts back toward an outsider's perspective on the prison world (see Figure 1); this shift involves the dissipation of his maximum security adaptation strategy, further revision of his prison image, reconstruction of an image of the outside world, and the initial development of an outside plan.[5] The inmate's efforts to revive his suspended identity are part of his shift in perspectives.

It is primarily through a renewed self-dialogue that the inmate struggles to revive his suspended identity—a struggle that amounts to a dialectic between his suspended identity and his prison identity. Through self-dialogue he recognizes, and tries to confront, the extent to which these two identities really do differ. He again tries to differentiate himself from maximum security inmates.

> There seems to be a concern with the inmates here to be able to distinguish . . . themselves from the other inmates. That is—they feel

they are above the others. . . . Although they may associate with each other, it still seems important to degrade the majority here.

And he does have some success in freeing himself from his prison identity.

> Well, I think I am starting to soften up a little bit. I believe the identity I picked up in the prison is starting to leave me now that I have left the world of the [maximum security] joint. I find myself becoming more and more involved with the happenings of the outside world. I am even getting anxious to go out and see the sights, just to get away from this place.

But he recognizes that he *has* changed in prison, and that these changes run deeper than the mask he has been presenting to others. He has not returned to his "old self" simply because his impression management skills are used less frequently in minimum security. He raises the question—though he cannot answer it—of how permanent these changes are. He wonders how much his family and friends will see him as having changed. As stated by one of our interview respondents:

> I know I've changed a little bit. I just want to realize how the people I know are going to see it, because they [will] be able to see it more than I can see it. . . . Sometimes I just want to go somewhere and hide.

He speculates about how much the outside world—especially his own network of outside relationships—has changed in his absence. (It is his life, not those of his family and friends, that has been suspended during his prison sentence; he knows that changes have occurred in the outside world, and he suspects that some of these changes may have been withheld from him, intentionally or otherwise.) He has questions, if not serious doubts, about his ability to "make it" on the outside, especially concerning his relationships with others; he knows, in any case, that he cannot simply return to the outside world

---

[4]Not all prisoners participate in this unit; inmates must apply for transfer to the unit, and their acceptance depends both on the crimes for which they were sentenced and staff evaluation of their potential for success in the unit. Our analysis focuses on those inmates who are transferred.

[5]There are three features of the minimum security unit that facilitate this shift in perspectives: a more open physical and social environment; the fact that the unit lies just outside the prison wall (so that an inmate who is transferred is also physically removed from the maximum security prison); and greater opportunity for direct contact with the outside world, through greater access to telephones, an unrestricted visitor list, unrestricted visiting hours and, eventually, weekend furloughs.

as if nothing has happened. Above all, he repeatedly confronts the question of who he is, and who he will be in the outside world.

An inmate's struggle with these questions, like his self-dialogue at the beginning of his prison career, is necessarily a solitary activity. The identity he claims at the time of his release, in contrast to his prison identity, cannot be learned from other inmates. Also like his earlier periods of self-dialogue, the questions he considers are not approached in a rational systematic manner. The process is more one of rumination—of pondering one question until another replaces it, and then contemplating the new question until it is replaced by still another, or suppressed from his thoughts. There is, then, no final resolution to any of the inmate's identity questions. Each inmate confronts these questions in his own way, and each arrives at his own understanding of who he is, based on this unfinished, unresolved self-dialogue. In every case, however, an inmate's release identity is a synthesis of his suspended preprison identity and his prison identity.[6]

Postprison Identity

Because each inmate's release identity is the outcome of his own identity dialectic, we cannot provide a profile of the "typical" release identity. But our data do allow us to specify some of the conditions that affect this outcome. Reaffirmations of his preprison identity by outsiders—visits and furloughs during which others interact with him as if he has not changed—provide powerful support for his efforts to revive his suspended identity. These efforts are also promoted by an inmate's recollection of his preprison identity (i.e., his

---

[6]This is an important parallel with our analysis of the inmate's changing prison definitions: his concluding prison image is a synthesis of the image he formulates before coming to prison and the image he holds at the middle of his prison career; see Schmid and Jones, 1990.

attempts, through self-dialogue, to assess who he was before he came to prison), by his desire to abandon his prison identity, and by his general shift back toward an outsider's perspective. But there are also several factors that favor his prison identity, including his continued use of diversionary activities; his continued periodic efforts to suppress thoughts about the outside world; his continued ability to use prison impression management skills; and his continuing sense of injustice about the treatment he has received. Strained or cautious interactions with outsiders, or unfulfilled furlough expectations, inhibit the revival of his preprison identity. And he faces direct, experiential evidence that he has changed: when a minimum security resident recognizes that he is now completely unaffected by reports of violent incidents in maximum security, he acknowledges that he is no longer the same person that he was when he entered prison. Turner (1978, 1) has suggested three criteria for role-person merger: "failure of role compartmentalization, resistance to abandoning a role in the face of advantageous alternative roles, and the acquisition of role-appropriate attitudes"; at the time of their release from prison, the inmates we studied had already accrued some experience with each of these criteria.

Just as we cannot define a typical release identity, we cannot predict these inmates' future, postprison identities, not only because we have restricted our analysis to their prison experiences but because each inmate's future identity is inherently unpredictable. What effect an ex-inmate's prison experience has on his identity depends on how he, in interaction with others, defines this experience. Some of the men we have studied will be returned to prison in the future; others will not. But all will have been changed by their prison experiences. They entered the prison world fearing for their lives; they depart with the knowledge that they have survived. On the one hand, these men are undoubtedly stronger persons by virtue of this accomplishment. On the other hand, the same tactics that enabled them to survive the prison world can be called upon, appropriately or not, in difficult situations in the outside world. To the extent that these men draw upon their prison survival tactics to cope with the hardships of the outside world—to the extent that their prison behavior becomes a meaningful part of their "role repertoire" (Turner 1978) in their everyday lives—their prison identities will have become inseparable from their "true" identities. . . .

References

Adler, Patricia A., and Peter Adler. 1989. "The Gloried Self: The Aggrandizement and the Construction of Self." *Social Psychology Quarterly* 52: 299–310.

Berger, Peter L. 1963. *Invitation to Sociology: A Humanistic Perspective*. Garden City, NY: Doubleday Anchor Books.

Blumer, Herbert. 1972. "Action vs. Interaction: Review of *Relations in Public* by Erving Goffman." *Transaction* 9: 50–53.

———. 1969. *Symbolic Interactionism: Perspective and Method*. Englewood Cliffs, NJ: Prentice-Hall.

Boulding, Kenneth. 1961. *The Image*. Ann Arbor: University of Michigan Press.

Clemmer, Donald. 1958. *The Prison Community*. New York: Holt, Rinehart & Winston.

Coser, R. 1966. "Role Distance, Sociological Ambivalence and Traditional Status Systems." *American Journal of Sociology* 72: 173–187.

Garfinkel, Harold. 1956. "Conditions of Successful Degradation Ceremonies." *American Journal of Sociology* 61: 420–424.

Glaser, Barney, and Anselm Strauss. 1964. "Awareness Contexts and Social Interaction." *American Sociological Review* 29: 669–679.

Goffman, Erving. 1961. *Asylums*. Garden City, NY: Doubleday Anchor Books.

———. 1959. *The Presentation of Self in Everyday Life*. Garden City, NY: Doubleday Anchor Books.

———. 1963. *Stigma: Notes on the Management of Spoiled Identity*. Englewood Cliffs, NJ: Prentice-Hall.

Irwin, John. 1970. *The Felon*. Englewood Cliffs, NJ: Prentice-Hall.

Lewis, David J. 1979. "A Social Behaviorist Interpretation of the Median I." *American Journal of Sociology* 84: 261–287.

Schechner, Richard. 1985. *Between Theater and Anthropology*. Philadelphia: University of Pennsylvania Press.

Scheff, Thomas. 1970. "On the Concepts of Identity and Social Relationships." Pp. 193–207 in T. Shibutani (ed.), *Human Nature and Collective Behavior*. Englewood Cliffs, NJ: Prentice-Hall.

Schlenker, B. 1980. *Impression Management: The Self Concept, Social Identity and Interpersonal Relations*. Belmont, CA: Wadsworth.

Schmid, Thomas, and Richard Jones. 1987. "Ambivalent Actions: Prison Adaptation Strategies of New Inmates." American Society of Criminology, annual meetings, Montreal, Quebec.

Schmid, Thomas, and Richard Jones. 1990. "Experiential Orientations to the Prison Experience: The Case of First-Time, Short-Term Inmates." Pp. 189–210 in Gale Miller and James A. Holstein (eds.), *Perspectives on Social Problems*. Greenwich, CT: JAI Press.

Solomon, David N. 1970. "Role and Self-Conception: Adaptation and Change in Occupations." Pp. 286–300 in T. Shibutani (ed.), *Human Nature and Collective Behavior*. Englewood Cliffs, NJ: Prentice-Hall.

Stone, Gregory P. 1962. "Appearance and the Self." Pp. 86–118 in Arnold Rose (ed.), *Human Behavior and Social Processes*. Boston: Houghton Mifflin.

Sykes, Gresham. 1958. *The Society of Captives: A Study of a Maximum Security Prison*. Princeton, NJ: Princeton University Press.

Turner, Ralph H. 1978. "The Role and the Person." *American Journal of Sociology* 84: 1–23.

Ungar, Sheldon. 1984. "Self-Mockery: An Alternative Form of Self-Presentation." *Symbolic Interaction* 7: 121–133.

Weigert, Andrew J. 1986. "The Social Production of Identity: Metatheoretical Foundations." *Sociological Quarterly* 27: 165–183.

Zurcher, Louis A. 1977. *The Mutable Self*. Beverly Hills, CA: Sage.

Questions

1. Define the following terms, as used by Schmid and Jones in the article.
   a. rumination
   b. inauthentic presentation of self
   c. performance consciousness
   d. identity dialectic
   e. proto-sociological attitude

2. How do Schmid and Jones distinguish between "identity transformation" and "identity construction"?

3. In what ways, if any, do you think prison might have a different effect on women's identity than on men's identity? Explain.

4. Identify the parallels between identity transformation in prison and the implicit identity transformation undergone by kids as they are introduced to street culture (as described by Anderson in reading 12).

23

HOW WOMEN RESHAPE
THE PRISON GUARD ROLE

Lynn Zimmer

As Professor Zimmer observes, sociologists have traditionally assumed that personal behavior is very much shaped by the social arrangements in which an individual finds him- or herself. For example, as you read in reading 16, college men altered their behavior when put into the role of prison guard.

Yet what happens when one set of social arrangements (i.e., socially prescribed gender rules) come face to face with another (i.e., the socially prescribed role of prison guard)? Professor Zimmer finds that in such cases, becoming a prison guard isn't just "role-taking"; it requires innovating and "role-making."

Today, few people would question the ability of women to perform successfully in most occupations in which the workers are predominantly men; however, a number of jobs, such as soldier, police officer, and prison guard, retain their male identification, and a decade or more of women's presence in these jobs has not eliminated speculation regarding women's ability to perform them. Both during and after conducting research on women guards who work in men's prisons (Zimmer 1986), the question constantly asked of me was, "Can women really do the job?" Since the job requirements of prison guards seem to be in direct contrast to the traditional norms for women's behavior, the question is not surprising. Expectations for women have changed over the past two decades, to be sure, but not so much that women's ability to perform in jobs traditionally held by men goes

unquestioned, especially if the job entails the exercise of power and authority.

What is generally meant when people ask whether women can perform as prison guards is whether their performance is similar to that of their male counterparts. It is assumed that jobs, especially those at the lower ranks, exist as predetermined slots waiting to be filled by workers. Weber (1964) suggests that the efficient bureaucracy breeds conformity and that individual workers become dispensable, replaceable, and interchangeable. More recently, Hall (1977) has claimed that because the same occupational role constraints operate on each worker, organizational behavior is not dependent on the characteristics of individuals:

> When a new member enters the organization, he is confronted with a social structure . . . and a set of expectations for . . . behavior. It does not matter who the particular individual is; the organization has established a system of norms and expectations to be followed regardless of who its personnel happen to be. (p. 26)

Nieva and Gutek (1981) similarly suggest that when women workers enter jobs traditionally

Lynn Zimmer, "How Women Reshape the Prison Guard Role" from *Gender & Society* 1, no. 4 (December 1987): 415–431. Copyright © 2002 by Sociologists for Women in Society. Reprinted with the permission of Sage Publications, Inc.

held by men, they will generally not be able to alter work roles so as to reduce the conflict between occupational norms and gender-role norms. Instead, they will have to alter their own behavior:

> Although individuals will always retain some latitude in deciding how to act, social structures heavily shape the options and tools available to them. Individual behaviors adapt to their environment. (p. 132)

Rosabeth Kanter (1977) agrees: "To a very large degree, organizations make their workers into who they are. Adults change to fit the system" (p. 263).

If occupational role restraints are strong in all work organizations, they might be expected to be particularly strong in highly structured, paramilitary organizations like prisons. E. Johnson (1981) describes the rigidity of the guard's job:

> The prison guard must follow the rules and their interpretations made by his superiors; the guard is not free to act toward inmates—either sentimentally or punitively—as he would personally prefer. (p. 82)

Research by Haney et al. (1973), in which student subjects assigned as guards in a mock prison quickly assumed fairly typical guard behaviors, further suggests that the guard's role requirements overshadow any individual characteristics or predispositions.

The work behavior of women prison guards calls these assumptions regarding the rigidity of work roles into question. Based on unstructured interviews with 70 women guards working in men's prisons in New York and Rhode Island, as well as with a high-level personnel in the central administrative offices, midlevel supervisors at the prisons, men guards, and men prisoners,[1] this study explores the ways women have reshaped the guard role and how their presence has an impact on the prisons and the job of guarding. The data indicate that workers, even in highly regulated environments like prisons, can develop innovative and successful ways to perform the job when they find established work roles inadequate or find they are blocked from achieving success using predetermined definitions of appropriate work behavior. Employment roles, like other social roles, offer opportunity for role making as well as role taking (Turner 1962), and women working as guards in men's prisons have, out of both choice and necessity, acted upon this opportunity, creating new ways to do an old job. This pattern of role making may be typical of women in other traditionally male occupations as well. To find out, researchers need to examine more closely the various ways women perform jobs and evaluate their performance on its own terms rather than how closely it resembles that of men.

The Job of Prison Guard

The prison guard is, according to Hawkins (1976), "the key figure in the penal equation, the man on whom the whole edifice of the penitentiary system depends" (p. 105). Because prisons are, in effect, separate societies, guards must perform a wide range of diverse tasks to keep the prison operating, but the most important ones center around their custody and control functions—keeping prisoners inside the walls and following the rules and regulations for inmate behavior that have been established by prison administrators.

The primary mechanism through which guards maintain control in prisons is the constant regulation of inmate movement. On a normal day, most prisoners are released from their cells for meals, work detail, school, medical care, recreation, and visits, but they will constantly be monitored by guards who are

---

[1]For a more detailed description of the research methodology used in this analysis, see Appendix in Zimmer (1986).

stationed throughout the prison. Many guards spend their day checking inmate passes, frisking inmates as they move from one area to another, and unlocking and then relocking gates as inmates pass through. Several times a day, all prisoners are ordered to their cells, allowing guards to take "the count" and make sure no prisoners have escaped.

Guards are also responsible for enforcing the extensive rules that govern inmate behavior. In addition to rules similar to the laws outside of prison—rules that forbid assault, rape, theft, and the like, there are many rules specific to prison life that, for example, prohibit profanity and gambling, regulate smoking, establish grooming and clothing standards, and dictate the items considered contraband. There may also be very general rules for inmate conduct, requiring them to obey direct orders of guards and treat guards with appropriate respect. Not all of the rules are equally important to the maintenance of internal order, and many guards are willing to overlook violation of some petty rules, but for both the guards' own safety and the security of the institution, it is important that most inmates obey most of the rules most of the time. Given the low guard-to-inmate ratio in prisons, there is always the potential for mass violence. Because guards have limited ability to control inmate behavior during a riot or takeover, they must prevent such situations from occurring by controlling inmate movement and obtaining inmate compliance to the most critical rules.

One way guards may obtain inmate compliance with prison rules is through the threat of institutionalized punishment: segregation, loss of privileges (such as commissary, recreation, visitation), and loss of good-time credits. Guards generally cannot implement these punishments themselves, but can write reports to be reviewed by a special disciplinary committee, which may then order appropriate penalties. This threat of formal punishment is

an important management tool, and guards use it frequently. However, since this process is time consuming and removes punishment from the immediate situation, guards often supplement the formal system with an informal system of rewards and punishments over which they have more direct control.

Prisoners are dependent on guards to provide a wide range of services for them, and although Crouch (1980a) points out that inmate dependency has been reduced by the recent increase in prisoners' legal rights, guards still have the potential to increase substantially the "pains of imprisonment" (Sykes 1958) that accompany incarceration. For example, the inmate who too frequently disobeys the rules may find that he or she is always the last to receive mail or that a written request to make a phone call has been "lost" in the pile of paperwork that cell-block guards accumulate. Guards can also manipulate rewards, and the compliant inmate may be able to obtain a favorable work assignment, a roomier cell, or more freedom of movement. Even small privileges are important to prisoners and, knowing this, guards can grant or withhold privileges as a way of encouraging compliant behavior.

Guards may also obtain inmate cooperation with regard to important rules by agreeing to ignore prisoners' minor infractions, in what Sykes (1956) calls "corruptions of the guard's authority." Such arrangements are potentially dangerous because prisoners may try to "up the ante," asking for even greater concessions from guards for the same amount of compliance. In spite of this danger, most guards do find it advantageous to engage in such mutual accommodations with prisoners; as long as they are used only to supplement and not replace other techniques of control, such "corruption" seems to present no serious threat to prison security.

Finally, guards may use the threat of physical force to control prison behavior; being unarmed and outnumbered, guards cannot use force to control the prison population on a regular basis, but force may be used to punish particular unruly or disrespectful inmates and serve as an example to others (Marquart 1986).

There are many techniques of control, then, that have become part of the guard role as it has traditionally been performed by men. Individual guards may differ in the degree to which they stress some techniques over others, but the overriding strategy is to remain in a position of control vis-à-vis inmates. Concessions and accommodations may be granted, but only if they add to rather than compromise the guards' position of superiority. Crouch (1980b), a noted authority on the guard role, compares guard-inmate interaction to a contest in which the two parties remain in constant competition, each trying to establish dominance. To emerge victorious, the guard must project an image of personal, physical dominance:

> All officers, to maintain some respect and authority, must project some degree of physical competence. Regardless of duty assignment, the man who cannot muster some version of this masculine image before both inmates and peers is in for trouble. For example, one rather obese young man I worked with . . . had never been able to gain respect from either [inmates or other officers]. . . . His appearance and behavior did not fit with the informal expectations of this masculine world. (p. 219)

Physical strength, but more important, an image of masculinity and dominance, are crucial characteristics of the traditional guard role. They are characteristics that women entering this profession do not generally possess. To survive on this job, then, it has been necessary for women to redefine the guard role in a way that eliminates the competitive atmosphere and instead utilizes the skills, characteristics, and patterns of interaction that women are likely to bring to the job.

Women in the Guard Role

Most of the women who work as guards in men's prisons have neither the desire nor the capacity to perform the job as it has been traditionally performed by men. Perhaps many of the women have experienced the type of role conflict that Hughes (1944, 1958) suggests occurs when sexual status and occupational status are incongruent. If they have, women guards have not resolved that conflict by embracing one set of role expectations over the other, as researchers have found of women in other occupations (Kanter 1977; Martin 1980; Nieva and Gutek 1981; Rustad 1982). Instead, women guards, like the women police officers studied by Hunt (1986), have integrated certain aspects of the traditional female gender role into a traditional male occupational role to create new ways of performing the job. Jurik's (1985a) research shows that women and men guards do not differ substantially in their attitudes toward crime and punishment, but my research shows that men and women do behave differently on the job. Not all women guards perform the job alike, but they do, by and large, use strategies different from those used by men.[2]

Women guards who work in direct contact with prisoners[3] use many of the control

---

[2]There are some women guards who try to perform the job "by the book," but even this is different from the way men generally perform the job. These women have adopted what I call the "institutional role" (Zimmer 1986), hoping that a strict adherence to the rules will provide solutions to all job-related problems and insulate them from any criticism by male coworkers and supervisors. Male guards are much more likely to "bend the rules" when the formal rules seem to them to be inappropriate.

[3]There are a number of women guards who do not regularly work in direct contact with men prisoners because they have managed to receive a job assignment in an area of the prison where such contact is minimal (e.g., administrative offices, mailroom, visiting room). These women perform a "modified role" in the prison and, because they have so little contact with inmates, have not developed a style of guarding consistent with that outlined in this article (see Zimmer 1986).

techniques that are part of the traditional guard role; they maintain control through regulation of inmate movement and use of the formal system of punishment for rule violation. Women guards can also implement informal rewards and punishments, but because they lack the support and cooperation of most of the men guards in the prison (Fox 1982; Peterson 1982; Zimmer 1986), such efforts may be undermined. Women guards have complained, for example, that male coworkers sometimes reverse their decisions, taking away privileges they had granted to inmates or punishing inmates for actions they had approved.

Like the men, women guards can also engage in mutual accommodations with inmates, ignoring some rules in return for inmate compliance to others, a control technique that women find particularly useful. Although not all women guards can be counted on to ignore minor rule violations, inmates often report that the women who guard them are more willing than the men to overlook what inmates consider the petty rules related to clothing and grooming. In return, prisoners agree to comply with the rules that are more critical to prison security.

While utilizing many traditional guard techniques, women guards also use a strategy that is seldom used by men: the development of friendly, pleasant relationships with prisoners as a way of generating prisoners' voluntary compliance. Some women play a mothering, nurturing role vis-à-vis inmates, a role that is in direct contrast to the macho, competitive role typical of men guards. Women guards are also more likely to have a social worker's orientation toward the job and to spend a great deal of time listening to inmate problems, discussing their family relationships, assisting them in letter writing, and helping them make plans for their release. Prison administrators are uneasy about the development of friendly bonds between inmates and guards, especially women guards, fearing that the guard's

allegiance could shift from the prison to the prisoner and jeopardize security. Many prisons, in fact, have specific rules that prohibit undue familiarity between guards and inmates (May 1981); Toch's (1981) research suggests that when men guards violate these rules, they risk the disapproval not only of administrators but also of their colleagues, many of whom define prisoners as the enemy (Duffee 1974). Because women seldom have the approval of men guards to begin with, they may be freer to use friendship-oriented strategies for gaining inmate compliance with prison rules.

Men prisoners, for the most part, respond positively to women's style of guarding. They follow the daily routine under women's supervision and comply with women's direct orders. Moreover, prisoners tend to behave better in women's presence by, for example, refraining from extensive use of vulgar language. Some men prisoners try to help the women by taking responsibility for control of the more troublesome inmates; in a few instances, men prisoners have even protected women against physical attack.

This style of guarding successfully incorporates aspects of women's traditional behavior into the guard role; as one woman guard put it, "to survive on this job, women have to do what they know best." At the same time, of course, this strategy is successful only because many men prisoners are willing to accept and contribute to the development of friendly, cooperative relationships with the women who guard them. Their motivations in doing so may be complex, and almost certainly contain a large component of self-interest, but it is also the case that men prisoners come into the prison with their own traditional patterns of interacting differently with women and men. No matter how women guards perform the job, most men prisoners will respond to them in gender-specific ways. Many of the women who succeed in this job have found ways of using male responses to their advantage.

Guarding techniques typical of the women, like those of the men, are far from foolproof, and inmate rule violation, sometimes of a serious nature, is common in prisons. Nonetheless, the women's techniques do represent a viable strategy that has allowed many women to remain on a job that they would find difficult to perform in a more traditional, male-defined way. Like the women who broke into the professions at the turn of the century, women guards have used "every creative strategy that could serve their larger purposes of building meaningful careers" (Glazer and Slater 1987).

There are a number of explanations for why most women do not perform the job of prison guard as it is generally performed by men. For one thing, women often fail to receive adequate socialization during the on-the-job training phase of their employment; their trainers are generally men guards, most of whom do not want the women there. They may actively undermine women's ability to succeed on the job by denying them information about both formal and informal techniques for handling inmates. The training assignments of men and women may also differ, so that at the end of their probationary period, many women have had only limited experience in dealing directly with inmates, especially in emergencies. As women continue on the job, they face persistent opposition and sexual harassment from male guards; many women remain skeptical about men's willingness to assist them if needed. In short, women do not receive the kind of support from coworkers that is important to success on any job (Feldman 1976; Terborg et al. 1982; Van Maanen and Schein 1979); without that support, many women find it useful to develop alliances with inmates who will then voluntarily comply with women's orders and even offer to protect women when potentially dangerous situations erupt.

While it is true that women face many obstacles in performing the job like men, it is not at all clear that these obstacles alone are the cause of women's occupational behavior or that the removal of those obstacles would lead women to choose a job performance strategy identical to that of men. There are, of course, many individual differences among women guards and the kind of skills and abilities they bring to the job, but it is important to remember that the women who become guards today have been socialized in a society in which expectations for women are only gradually changing. Women guards therefore tend to bring to this job a set of experiences and, to some extent, a mind-set quite different from men. For most men, growing up in this society has prepared them for confrontational situations; most men who work as prison guards have had considerable experience in competitive exchanges with other men, and they are used to vying for control. Most women who work as prison guards have not had these kinds of experiences and, even if they have, find it difficult to replicate them in the prison, where their ability to compete physically with inmates for control is questionable. So instead, women rely on the qualities and characteristics that have served them well in their relationships outside of prison: skills of communication and persuasion and the ability to generate voluntary cooperation from others.

Finally, it is important to see women guards' job behavior as, in some ways, reflective of male-female interactive patterns outside of prison. If women's style of guarding were based solely on what they bring to the job with them—skills and abilities somewhat different from men—then we would expect women guards to behave the same whether working among men or women prisoners. They do not. Pollock's (1986) research indicates that both women and men change their style of guarding as the sex of the inmate population changes and that each of the four combinations (male guard–male inmate; male guard–female inmate; female guard–female inmate;

female guard–male inmate) produces different strategies for managing inmates. Some of the strategies used by women who guard men incorporate role behaviors more typical of women interacting with men than of guards interacting with prisoners (e.g., being friendly, understanding, and supportive). This works for women because most prisoners are willing, in turn, to respond with typically male role behaviors (e.g., being protective). These interactive patterns do not replace those of guard and inmate but are interwoven into them in a way that allows women guards to perform the basic requirements of the job and allows men prisoners to feel comfortable having women in official positions of authority over them.[4]

Impact of Women in Prisons and on the Job of Guarding

Women have shown their ability to perform the job of guarding on a day-to-day basis while remaining less intimidating, less competitive, and less physical than most men guards, but there are some occasions in the prison when intimidation, confrontation, and physical force are needed. In even the best-run prison, fights between inmates are common, inmate attacks against guards occur, and there is always the potential for mass violence should a riot take place; it is guards who must bring these situations under control and, in doing so, may find it necessary to use force and violence themselves. Male administrators and male guards feel that the women working as guards are extremely reluctant to respond to situations in which physical force may be necessary and that they are inadequately

prepared to perform this aspect of the job. In their eyes, the presence of women presents a danger to prison security.

In actuality, there has been no reported decrease in prison security or internal order in the decade or more since women began working in men's prisons. Women, of course, do remain a small proportion of the staff in men's prisons, and it is impossible to predict the impact of many more women guards, but current levels do not appear to pose a security risk. An even greater proportion of women might be easily accommodated if prison administrators followed the suggestions of a 1981 American Correctional Association report that special tactical teams be trained and made available in all prisons for response to emergency situations. Rank-and-file men guards may, in fact, act too aggressively in such situations and produce an escalation of violence by those they are trying to control (Attica 1972; Stotland 1976; Toch 1977). The presence of women at the site of erupting violence might do more to reduce aggression by all parties than would any actual physical intervention by them. Several researchers have reported that women workers have a calming effect on men prisoners (Becker 1975; Biemer 1977; Cormier 1975; Flynn 1982; Graham 1981), perhaps because women are less likely to engage in competitive relationships with inmates and do not encourage the "ego-showdowns" that may, themselves, set the stage for violence between inmates and guards.

At some point, the presence of women guards who use different strategies for handling inmates may have an impact on the occupational role itself. Already some men guards use strategies that stress relationship building with prisoners (R. Johnson 1977; Toch 1981), but certainly not to the extent advocated over the years by prison reformers (Bennett 1976; Glaser 1964; Hawkins 1976; Morris and Morris 1980; Schrag 1961). Most men guards have vehemently rejected these suggestions

---

[4]Different methods for handling a situation in which gender status is inconsistent with occupational role requirements are outlined by Whyte (1946). He found that the physical environment in the restaurant could be altered to soften the effect of male-female interactions that conflicted with the norm.

and have, instead, insisted that they need more direct control over inmates to perform the job effectively (Fox 1982). Women's ability to perform the job without reliance on coercive control lends support to reformers' suggestions that the job of guarding itself can be transformed. There is, perhaps, much to be learned from women's adaptations to this job; the guard role may not be as rigid as men guards or some researchers (Haney et al. 1973) have maintained. And as the job is redesigned by women's presence, women entering prison work in the future may find it easier to adjust to the job and to gain the acceptance of their coworkers.

Women in Traditional Men's Jobs

As women have moved into traditional men's jobs, they have usually been evaluated on the basis of how closely their performance approximates that of men. These job roles were originally designed and shaped by men, presumably to fit their own particular skills and abilities, but once created, they have been assumed to be neutral positions that qualified women as well as men should be able to fill. When women have not succeeded (i.e., they have not reproduced men's occupational behavior), coworkers and supervisors, usually men, have felt justified in calling for their removal. Researchers, on the other hand, have often pointed to the structural obstacles in their way, implying that when such barriers are removed, women's work behavior will be more similar to that of men (Jurik 1985b; Kanter 1977; Martin 1980; Rustad 1982). Others have focused on how gender-role socialization has left women unprepared for "men's work" (Hennig and Jardim 1977) and suggest that women themselves need to change— to act, talk, dress, and think like men (Carr-Ruffino 1982; Harley and Koff 1980; Mirides and Cote 1980; Smith and Grenier

1982) or learn to play "the games mother never taught you" (Harrigan 1978).

This study of women guards suggests that there is more than discrimination and structural barriers to prevent most women from performing jobs like men. These factors are important determinants of women's occupational behavior and need to be given serious attention, but also important is the different approach that many women themselves bring to the job. This study also indicates that women need not change themselves nor copy men's behavior to perform traditional men's jobs successfully.

Other research on women working in male-dominated occupations leads to the same conclusion. Loden (1985) claims that a "feminine leadership style," typical of many (but not all) women managers, is just as successful in managing subordinates as is the traditional masculine style and may be more productive under some circumstances. Ramey (1981) finds that women, in general, approach scientific problems differently from men and maintains that the approaches of women scientists should be valued for their difference, because the more varied approaches brought to scientific problems, the more likely it is solutions will be found. Goffee and Scase's (1985) research on women entrepreneurs identifies their successful adaptations to business, some of which successfully incorporate traditional gender roles.

Research on women in policing, an occupation—like guarding—identified with men, has been equivocal. Gross (1981) and Berg and Budnick (1986) have found "defeminized" women officers, displaying "pseudo-masculinity," to be more successful on the job and more accepted by their peers. But others have found women officers with less aggressive personalities to be more successful in defusing potentially violent situations and decreasing the chance of injury to all participants (Bell 1982; Block and Anderson 1974; Remmington 1981; Sherman 1975).

The main reason for such disparity in the evaluation of women police officers is the lack of clear criteria for what constitutes good job performance. Public sector, service-oriented occupations present special difficulties in establishing evaluation criteria (Wholey et al. 1986), and policing, an occupation in which professionals themselves argue over the most important role requirements (Whitaker et al. 1982), is particularly problematic. Morash and Greene (1986) show that most evaluation studies of the police stress the attributes and tasks that are biased toward men and do little more than measure officers' conformity to stereotypical men's behavior. This is true of evaluations of prison guards as well, and such gender-typed evaluations probably occur to some degree in all occupations in which the workers are predominantly men or women.

The evaluation of women (and men) workers, then, by their peers, supervisors, and even outside researchers, continues to contain a great deal of gender bias. When women are evaluated according to occupational standards created for men, many women fail to make the grade. When women do perform like men, they are still not evaluated positively (West 1982). Nor do women receive positive evaluations when they find ways to produce results without duplicating typical men's strategies. Auster (1987) shows that occupational gender bias is particularly prevalent when tasks are unpredictable, complex, or difficult to measure; in the prisons, where accomplishments like reducing tension, de-escalating conflict, and averting riots cannot be quantified, or even observed, the opportunity for bias against women guards is enormous.

Conclusions

This article has focused on the subtle but insidious form of bias against women in the devaluation of their different approaches to their work. This bias occurs in many different social contexts—when women think, act, or approach problems differently from men, the women's approach tends to be undercut and devalued (French 1985; Gilligan 1982; Keller 1985; Oakley 1981).

This article argues that it would be beneficial to women's efforts to achieve equality, and ultimately beneficial to the organizations in which women work, if the different approaches used by women were valued precisely because they are different. If, at some point in the future, there is less distinction between what it means to be a man and what it means to be a woman, some of the differences in how women and men perform jobs may disappear. In the meantime, gender equality may best be achieved through an equal valuing of current differences, both in and out of the workplace. A truly nonsexist society is not only one in which structural barriers and gender discrimination are removed but also one in which women and men have the opportunity to change and reshape the roles they fill.

References

American Correctional Association. 1981. *Riots and Disturbances in Correctional Institutions.* College Park, MD: American Correctional Association.

Attica. 1972. *Official Report of the New York State Commission on Attica.* New York: Bantam Books.

Auster, Ellen. 1987. "Task Characteristics as a Bridge Between Macro and Micro Research on Male-Female Wage Differences." Paper presented at Academy of Management Meetings, New Orleans, LA.

Becker, Arlene. 1975. "Women in Corrections: A Process of Change." *Resolutions* 1: 19–21.

Bell, Daniel J. 1982. "Policewomen: Myths and Reality." *Journal of Police Science and Administration* 10: 112–20.

Bennett, Lawrence. 1976. "A Study of Violence in California Prisons: A Review with Policy Implications." Pp. 149–68 in A. Cohen et al. (eds.), *Prison Violence.* Lexington, MA: Lexington Books.

Berg, Bruce, and Kimberly Budnick. 1986. "Defemi-nization of Women in Law Enforcement: A New Twist on the Traditional Police Personality." *Journal of Police Science and Administration* 14: 314–19.

Biemer, Carol. 1977. "The Role of the Female Mental Health Professional in a Male Correctional Setting." *Journal of Sociology and Social Welfare* 4: 882–87.

Block, Peter, and Deborah Anderson. 1974. *Police-women on Patrol: Final Report*. Washington, DC: Police Foundation.

Carr-Ruffino, Norma. 1982. *The Promotable Woman*. New York: Van Nostrand.

Cormier, Bruno. 1975. *The Watcher and the Watched*. Plattsburgh, NY: Tundra Books.

Crouch, Ben M. 1980a. "The Guard in a Changing Prison World." Pp. 5–45 in B. Crouch (ed.), *The Keepers*. Springfield, IL: Charles C Thomas.

———. 1980b. "The Book vs. the Boot: Two Styles of Guarding in a Southern Prison." Pp. 207–23 in B. Crouch (ed.), *The Keepers*. Springfield, IL: Charles C Thomas.

Duffee, David. 1974. "The Correction Officer Sub-culture and Organizational Change." *Journal of Research in Crime and Delinquency* 11: 155–72.

Feldman, D. C. 1976. "A Contingency Theory of Socialization." *Administrative Science Quarterly* 21: 433–52.

Flynn, Edith Elisabeth. 1982. "Women as Criminal Justice Professionals: A Challenge to Change Tradition." Pp. 305–40 in N. Rafter and E. Stanko (eds.), *Judge, Lawyer, Victim, Thief*. Boston: North-eastern University Press.

Fox, James. 1982. *Organizational and Racial Conflict in Maximum-Security Prisons*. Lexington, MA: Lexington Books.

French, Marilyn. 1985. *Beyond Power: On Women, Men, and Morals*. New York: Ballantine Books.

Gilligan, Carol. 1982. *In a Different Voice*. Cambridge, MA: Harvard University Press.

Glaser, Daniel. 1964. *The Effectiveness of a Prison and Parole System*. New York: Bobbs-Merrill.

Glazer, Penina, and Miriam Slater. 1987. *Unequal Colleagues: The Entrance of Women into the Profes-sions, 1890–1940*. New Brunswick, NJ: Rutgers University Press.

Goffee, Robert, and Richard Scase. 1985. *The Expe-riences of Female Entrepreneurs*. London: George Allen and Unwin.

Graham, Camille. 1981. "Women Are Succeeding in Male Institutions." *American Correctional Associa-tion Monographs* 1: 27–36.

Gross, S. 1981. "Socialization in Law Enforcement: The Female Police Recruit." Final Report for the Southeast Institute of Criminal Justice, Miami, FL.

Hall, Richard. 1977. *Organizations: Structure and Process* (revised edition). Englewood Cliffs, NJ: Prentice-Hall.

Haney, Craig et al. 1973. "Interpersonal Dynamics in a Simulated Prison." *International Journal of Criminology* 1: 69–97.

Harley, Joan, and Lois Koff. 1980. "Prepare Women for Tomorrow's Managerial Challenge." *The Per-sonnel Administrator* 25: 41–42.

Harrigan, Betty. 1978. *Games Mother Never Taught You*. New York: Warner Books.

Hawkins, Gordon. 1976. *The Prison—Policy and Practice*. Chicago: University of Chicago Press.

Hennig, Margaret, and Ann Jardim. 1977. *The Mana-gerial Woman*. New York: Doubleday.

Hughes, Everett. 1944. "Dilemmas and Contradic-tions of Status." *American Journal of Sociology* 50: 353–59.

———. 1958. *Men and Their Work*. Glencoe, IL: Fret Press.

Hunt, Jennifer. 1986. "The Logic of Sexism Among Police." Paper presented at American Sociologi-cal Association Annual Meeting, New York, NY.

Johnson, Elmer. 1981. "Changing World of the Correctional Officer." Pp. 77–85 in R. Ross (ed.), *Prison Guard/Correctional Officer*. Toronto: Butterworths.

Johnson, Robert. 1977. "Ameliorating Prison Stress: Some Helping Roles for Custodial Personnel." *International Journal of Criminology and Penology* 5: 263–73.

Jurik, Nancy. 1985a. "Individual and Organiza-tional Determinants of Correctional Officer Atti-tudes Toward Inmates." *Criminology* 23: 523–40.

———. 1985b. "An Officer and a Lady: Organiza-tional Barriers to Women Working as Correc-tional Officers in Men's Prisons." *Social Problems* 32: 373–88.

Kanter, Rosabeth. 1977. *Men and Women of the Corpo-ration*. New York: Basic Books.

Keller, Evelyn Fox. 1985. *Reflections on Gender and Science*. New Haven, CT: Yale University Press.

Loden, Marilyn. 1985. *Feminine Leadership.* New York: Time Books.

Marquart, James. 1986. "Prison Guards and the Use of Physical Coercion as a Mechanism of Prisoner Control." *Criminology* 24: 347–66.

Martin, Susan. 1980. *Breaking and Entering: Policewomen on Patrol.* Berkeley: University of California Press.

May, Edgar. 1981. "Prison Guards in America—The Inside Story." Pp. 19–40 in R. Ross (ed.), *Prison Guard/Correctional Officer.* Toronto: Butterworths.

Mirides, Ellyn, and Andre Cote. 1980. "Women in Management: The Obstacles and Opportunities They Face." *Personnel Administrator* 25: 25–28, 48.

Morash, Merry, and Jack Greene. 1986. "Evaluating Women on Patrol: A Critique of Contemporary Wisdom." *Evaluation Review* 10: 230–55.

Morris, Terrance, and Pauline Morris. 1980. "Where Staff and Prisoners Meet." Pp. 247–68 in B. Crouch (ed.), *The Keepers: Prison Guards and Contemporary Corrections.* Springfield, IL: Charles C Thomas.

Nieva, Veronica, and Barbara Gutek. 1981. *Women and Work: A Psychological Perspective.* New York: Praeger.

Oakley, Ann. 1981. *Subject Women.* New York: Pantheon Books.

Peterson, Cheryl Bowser. 1982. "Doing Time with the Boys: An Analysis of Women Correctional Officers in All-Male Facilities." Pp. 437–60 in B. Price and N. Sokoloff (eds.), *The Criminal Justice System and Women.* New York: Clark Boardman.

Pollock, Joycelyn. 1986. *Sex and Supervision: Guarding Male and Female Inmates.* New York: Greenwood Press.

Ramey, Estelle (in interview with Barbara Goldman). 1981. "Different Is Not Lesser: Women in Science." Pp. 42–54 in B. Forisha and B. Goldman (eds.), *Outsiders on the Inside.* Englewood Cliffs, NJ: Prentice-Hall.

Remmington, Patricia. 1981. *Policing: The Occupation and the Introduction of Female Officers.* Washington, DC: University Press of America.

Rustad, Michael. 1982. *Women in Khaki.* New York: Praeger.

Schrag, Clarence. 1961. "Some Foundations for a Theory of Correction." Pp. 309–57 in D. Cressey (ed.), *The Prison: Studies in Institutional Organization and Change.* New York: Holt, Rinehart, & Winston.

Sherman, Lawrence. 1975. "Evaluation of Police-Women on Patrol in a Suburban Police Department." *Journal of Police Science and Administration* 3: 434–38.

Smith, Howard L., and Mary Grenier. 1982. "Sources of Organizational Power for Women: Overcoming Structural Obstacles." *Sex Roles* 8: 733–46.

Stotland, Ezra. 1976. "Self-Esteem and Violence by Guards and State Troopers at Attica." *Criminal Justice and Behavior* 3: 85–96.

Sykes, Gresham. 1956. "The Corruption of Authority and Rehabilitation." *Social Forces* 34: 157–62.

———. 1958. *The Society of Captives.* Princeton, NJ: Princeton University Press.

Terborg, James et al. 1982. "Socialization Experiences of Women and Men Graduate Students in Male Sex-Typed Career Fields." Pp. 124–55 in H. J. Bernardin (ed.), *Women in the Workforce.* New York: Praeger.

Toch, Hans. 1977. *Police, Prisons, and the Problem of Violence.* Washington, DC: U.S. Government Printing Office.

———. 1981. "Is a 'Correctional Officer' by Any Other Name, a 'Screw?'" Pp. 87–104 in R. Ross (ed.), *Prison Guard/Correctional Officer.* Toronto: Butterworths.

Turner, Ralph. 1962. "Role Taking: Process Versus Conformity." Pp. 20–40 in A. Rose (ed.), *Human Behavior and Social Processes.* Boston: Houghton Mifflin.

Van Maanen, John, and E. H. Schein. 1979. "Towards a Theory of Organizational Socialization." *Research in Organizational Behavior* 1: 209–64.

Weber, Max (translated by A. M. Henderson and T. Parsons). 1964. *The Theory of Social and Economic Organization.* New York: Free Press.

West, Candace. 1982. "Why Can't a Woman Be More Like a Man?" *Work and Occupations* 9: 5–29.

Whitaker, G. P. et al. 1982. *Basic Issues in Police Performance.* Washington, DC: National Institute of Justice.

Wholey, Joseph et al. 1986. *Performance and Credibility: Developing Excellence in Public and Nonprofit Organizations.* Lexington, MA: Lexington Books.

Whyte, William Foote. 1946. *Industry and Society.* New York: McGraw-Hill.

Zimmer, Lynn. 1986. *Women Guarding Men.* Chicago: University of Chicago Press.

Questions

1. Zimmer (and others) have suggested that women don't fare well when the quality of a woman's performance is judged on the basis of whether she does her job the same way her male colleagues do. Yet, how else should people's job performances be evaluated in traditionally male-dominated occupations?

2. According to Zimmer's research, who responds best to the strategies used by women guards: male guards or male prisoners?

3. Imagine that Zimbardo and his colleagues (reading 16) had used women students to guard male prisoners in the Stanford Prison Experiment. Based on what Zimmer discovered, how would the behavior of female guards have differed from the behavior of the male guards studied by Zimbardo?

24

NOT JUST BODIES: STRATEGIES FOR DESEXUALIZING THE PHYSICAL EXAMINATION OF PATIENTS

Patti A. Giuffre and Christine L. Williams

The role of a health care practitioner requires one to maintain what sociologist Talcott Parsons called "affective neutrality": one must keep a tight grip on one's affect (emotions). At no time is the need for affective neutrality more important than during the physical exam. Patients are comforted by their belief that the sight of a naked body is routine to physicians and nurses; they trust that not only will their health care practitioner not comment on the size or shape of their body parts, but that he or she does not even notice them except in medically relevant ways. As Giuffre and Williams point out, however, affective neutrality does not come easily to practitioners.

Physicians and nurses routinely examine naked bodies and discuss intimate, sexual issues with their patients. Yet, these health care professionals are expected to avoid or deny personal sexual feelings and ignore the expression of any sexual desire from their patients. How do they do it? That is, how do they desexualize the physical exam?

Health care professionals are guided in this task in several ways. First, formal organizational policies and professional ethics govern

Patti Giuffre and Christine L. Williams, "Not Just Bodies: Strategies for Desexualizing the Physical Examination of Patients" from *Gender & Society* 14, no. 4 (June 2000): 457–482. Copyright © 2000 by Sociologists for Women in Society. Reprinted with the permission of Sage Publications, Inc.

AUTHORS' NOTE: *We would like to thank Kirsten Dellinger, Dana Britton, Martin Button, Ellen Slaten, Edith Elwood, Beth Schneider, and the reviewers for comments on this article. We would also like to thank Teresa Sullivan, Ronald Angel, Charles Bonjean, Sue Hoppe, and Janice Beyer, who supervised the original research.*

doctors' and nurses' interactions with patients. Health care providers are usually prohibited from engaging in sexual relationships with patients, particularly when patients are under their direct care. Second, the medical school curriculum socializes students to desexualize the human body. Medical students are trained to hide their feelings and avoid emotional involvement with their patients. Students are taught to use scientific, biomedical language for the human body, rather than colloquial terms, which may encourage students to approach the human body in a less personal, more abstract way. Medical students often devise their own strategies for managing inappropriate feelings, for example, engaging in sick humor with other students and mentally transforming their patients into inanimate objects.

Interaction rituals also may help to desexualize the physical examination of patients. For example, some physicians engage in casual conversation with the fully clothed patient prior to the actual exam, leave the room and allow the nurse to enter and instruct the patient about the exam, insist on the presence of a nurse to chaperone the exam, or use draping sheets to expose only specific parts of the body. By adhering closely to scripted performances such as these, physicians may be better able to control the interaction and repress the arousal of sexual feelings and interpretations.

Because social definitions of appropriate—and inappropriate—sexual behavior are linked to gender, it is likely that men and women use different desexualization strategies, but researchers have yet to examine this possibility. In this article, we address the following questions: Do male and female health care professionals rely on different strategies for desexualizing the physical exam? Are male and female patients subjected to different strategies? Are there differences in how doctors and nurses examine the bodies of male and female patients?

To address these questions, we conducted in-depth interviews with nurses and physicians who routinely conduct physical examinations of patients. Our overall goal is to investigate how the enactment of the physical examination is based on, and reproduces assumptions about, gender differences. We do not make claims about the average or typical behavior of men and women (an impossible goal in a qualitative study such as this). Rather, we describe and analyze the gendered meanings in the logic used by men and women health care providers who are trying to desexualize the physical examination of their patients. How does the gender of the doctor or nurse, and the gender of their patients, figure into their choices of which strategies to use? We are less interested in the effectiveness of these strategies and more interested in understanding what logic compels male and female health care providers to use different strategies. We also seek to understand why

nurses and physicians might choose different strategies for desexualizing the physical exam of male and female patients.

Method

Semistructured in-depth interviews were conducted with 36 nurses (licensed vocational nurses and registered nurses) and 34 doctors, most of whom were employed in one teaching hospital. To protect the anonymity of the respondents and to generate a more racially diverse sample, doctors and nurses from two surrounding cities who did not work in this teaching hospital were also interviewed. Four of the nurses were faculty members at the nursing school; the others were hospital staff nurses. The sample of doctors includes men and women from a variety of clinical specialties, including family practice, several surgical specialties, and internal medicine. Excluded were specialties that did not require physical examinations of patients while they are partially or fully unclothed, such as psychiatry and ophthalmology.

Only one respondent (a physician) said during the interview that he was gay. Several nurses and physicians noted that it was difficult for their gay and lesbian coworkers to be "out" in the hospital with patients and among colleagues.

The sample was generated by using "snowball" techniques. An original list of contacts was obtained from colleagues in the teaching hospital and through personal acquaintances. This group were sent letters describing the study and inviting their participation. At the close of each interview, respondents were asked for names of other doctors or nurses who might be willing to be interviewed, who were also sent letters. In total, 81 letters were sent. Fifty-four of the 81 people who received letters agreed to do the interview. (Two people refused to participate, and 27 never responded to the letter.) An additional 16 respondents were contacted by telephone or in person, and all agreed to participate, making the total response rate 72 percent.

Findings

With few exceptions, the men and women in this study reported that they were uncomfortable performing physical examinations in the early part of their training but that they became more comfortable as they progressed through their careers. Several physicians and nurses noted that they "see 20 patients a day and everybody looks the same" and that they "have been doing this for so long" that they never get uncomfortable. All of the respondents, however, had developed strategies to desexualize the physical exam so that their patients would not interpret the interaction as sexual and to repress any feelings of sexual attraction that they might have toward their patients.

Three of the strategies mentioned were general ones, used by both men and women health care providers, regardless of the patient's characteristics. To make patients feel more comfortable, some doctors and nurses engaged them in casual conversation or nonsexual joking ("Try on our designer gown"). Some physicians insisted on meeting their patients fully clothed prior to the exam to decrease patients' feelings of vulnerability. Finally, two physicians mentioned using medical terms instead of colloquial terms, which helped to define the interaction as a scientific, diagnostic encounter instead of a sexual and personal one.

However, six strategies were used more selectively. The respondent either indicated that there was a special condition for the use of these strategies or the strategy emerged from the analysis as one that was mentioned primarily by men or women. In the discussion that follows, we describe each of these "gendered strategies" and explore the organizational logic and individual interests that underlie them.

USING A CHAPERONE

Nineteen physicians (13 men and 6 women) and two nurses (both men) insisted on the presence of a chaperone during physical exams. Two of the women used chaperones for both male and female patients, but all of the others who mentioned this strategy used chaperones only for their female patients. And with only one exception, the chaperone was always a woman.

The men and women who mentioned this strategy used it for a variety of reasons. Some believed that having a chaperone present helped to comfort their female patients:

> I always use chaperones for gynecological examinations and breast examinations. Part of it is a medical-legal issue, and part of it is that it's a big comfort to the patient. There's been a situation where I've only had a male nurse, and I won't or I guess I can't use a male nurse for chaperones with female patients . . . I don't think women would be comfortable with two men in the room. A female needs to be physically present. (Latino family practitioner)

Why are only female patients offered the comfort of a female chaperone? When directly asked, most physicians could not explain why they did not use chaperones for male patients, noting that they "have just never thought about it." One of the four male physicians who did not use chaperones explained that his reason was because all of his patients were men, and "male patients are comfortable with a male physician." Another doctor explained why she did not use chaperones with men:

> I can't have a woman in the room with me when I'm examining a man. Plus I think it would be worse to have another guy in there for the guy . . . I just think it's embarrassing enough for him already. I think it would be even more embarrassing if there was another guy in there. . . . I have male help, so theoretically I could have someone else in there with me but it would be embarrassing for them. (white female physician in internal medicine)

This physician believes that her physical presence during the exam is "embarrassing enough" to male patients; adding a chaperone to the scene potentially would worsen his embarrassment.

Thus, female patients are protected by chaperones, but men must be protected from chaperones. Men's vulnerability during the physical exam is defined differently from women's. Perhaps, as Cassell (1998) argues, the comfort provided by a female surgeon's body elicits feelings of childish dependency. While such feelings may be considered acceptable in female patients, they may be considered emasculating in male patients. A woman physically examining a man may be "embarrassing enough" because this is an affront to a man's sense of mastery and self-control. The presence of a witness to this emasculation—either a man or a woman—could exacerbate his feelings of powerlessness.

A second interpretation of this asymmetry is that in our society women are more readily defined as victims than men are; thus, female patients are considered to be in greater need of a chaperone to comfort and protect them. In a male doctor/female patient situation, the female chaperone equalizes the female power of the weaker member of the encounter (the female patient). The presence of the second man as a chaperone would be more threatening and could lead to suggestions of multiple men abusing a woman. In contrast, a man is assumed to have sufficient resources to protect himself, and this appears to be true even when he is a patient in a doctor-patient encounter. The presence of a chaperone would tip the scales in favor of the physician's power and thus make the male patient a potential "victim." Using any chaperone might also imply that any given man is unable to protect himself, which could be interpreted as an affront to his masculinity. Thus, the gender differences in the use of chaperones reflect assumptions about the relative power and powerlessness of men and women in social interactions.

Some health care providers claim that they use chaperones for *their* protection and not their patients. Respondents mentioned three ways that chaperones protected them. First, chaperones provide legal protection in cases where patients falsely accuse doctors of sexual misconduct. One male physician referred to chaperones as "cheap insurance" against such charges. This rationale for using chaperones was given by both male and female physicians, as well as by two male nurses. Because "sexual allegations usually come from women," as one female doctor put it, most believed they only needed this legal protection from female patients.

The women who used chaperones did not articulate any fears about false accusations from lesbian patients in particular, but this may have been a contributing factor in their practice. A nurse claimed that a complaint of sexual misconduct from a lesbian patient about a female physician prompted some women in the teaching hospital to start using chaperones for their female patients. On the other hand, female physicians may feel the need to protect themselves from accusations that they harbor lesbian desires toward their patients. Although none of these female doctors articulated this concern, it is commonly assumed that women in nontraditional occupations are lesbian, and granted the intimate nature of their work, some may feel especially vulnerable to such charges.

A second form of protection provided by chaperones is protection from sexual advances by patients. This rationale was mentioned by one female doctor, a urologist, which is a specialty composed of only 2 percent women (Randolph, Seidman, and Pasko 1996). She claimed that many men, especially her Hispanic patients, are often embarrassed to be treated by her because they are "really macho" and uneasy with women "in a position of authority." She discussed a variety of strategies she uses to make her male patients feel comfortable during invasive procedures such as the rectal exam, but she did not mention chaperones until she was asked (in a follow-up question), "Has a male patient ever tried to fondle you or anything?" In direct response, she said, "I have a chaperone in the room with me any time I examine a patient. Male or female. I have a male chaperone with men, and a female with women." The context of the interview suggests that her purpose for using a chaperone is physical protection from sexual harassment or assault.

Several other female health care providers we interviewed experienced sexual harassment by patients, but they did not use chaperones to protect themselves. This urologist was unique in using this strategy. Instead, as we will discuss later, female doctors and nurses typically relied on more informal strategies for dealing with the problem of sexual harassment and assault from patients.

The third form of protection that chaperones offer, according to the respondents, is protection from the doctor's own sexual feelings. Four men in this study gave this rationale for using a chaperone. A surgeon explained,

> One time I had a patient . . . [and] there were times I couldn't even examine her. I don't know if she and I were flirting with each other. It really unsettled me. She was gorgeous. I knew then that if I ever got in that situation again, I needed to use a chaperone. A chaperone not for her comfort but for mine. (white male orthopedic surgeon)

For this physician the presence of a chaperone helps him control his own sexual desires.

Some female health care professionals admitted that they sometimes experienced unwanted sexual feelings when examining an attractive man, but they never used chaperones to control themselves or diffuse this sexual tension. The women who were interviewed seemed more concerned about controlling their male patients' sexual desire. Several respondents perceive that men are expected to act on their sexual desires and women are not. One nurse suggested that this social expectation limits the roles of male nurses:

> Younger teenage girls, I would rather just female nurses take care of them. I think we kind of discourage male nurses from taking care of teenage girls. You don't want anybody to get the wrong idea. Teenage boys are very uncomfortable with me, so I try to distract them, talk to them, try to make them more comfortable. (Latina nurse)

Although this nurse admits that teenage boys may be uncomfortable with her, she does not believe that a man should be called in to replace her because this discomfort is unlikely to result in the "wrong idea," that is, that the nurse is not in control of her sexual feelings and might sexually assault the boys. However, this is the assumption made of male nurses, and it is compelling enough for her to dissuade men from administering care to teenage girls. Again, this asymmetry reflects certain hegemonic beliefs regarding gender and sexuality. Just as women are more likely to be cast in the role of "victim," so are men likely to be seen as sexual aggressors. These beliefs are internalized by some health care providers and institutionalized in the patterns of chaperone use.

Nurses typically do not have the organizational authority to call in a chaperone, but as the above example illustrates, on occasion a male or a female nurse may be specifically requested to administer certain invasive procedures. One nurse recalled that in her training, women were not allowed to catheterize male patients. Today this rule is no longer in place, but occasionally male patients will request a male nurse for this procedure. This practice seems intended to lessen the discomfort and embarrassment of the patient, more than to protect them from sexual assault by female nurses. She said, "If a male patient wants a male, that's fine. Some male patients are hesitant about anyone catheterizing them. They feel their pride. They feel embarrassed. They usually feel okay if men do it" (white female nurse). On the other hand, some male patients prefer female nurses to perform such intimate procedures because they are uncomfortable with men. One nurse claimed that "some men are homophobic. They think their male nurses are homosexual" and thus prefer female nurses. Again, the unstated assumption is that men will act on their sexual desires; women will not.

Using a chaperone is a complex gendered strategy for desexualizing the physical exam. According to the organization's logic, female patients are comforted by the presence of a female chaperone, but male patients are likely to be embarrassed by one. Some doctors and nurses consider chaperones necessary when examining female patients to protect them from false accusations of sexual misconduct, but they assume that male patients will not falsely accuse them: Male patients are perceived to be better able to protect themselves from such misconduct. One doctor uses a chaperone to protect her from sexual harassment or assault from her patients. Some male doctors use chaperones to help them control their sexual feelings toward their female patients. Male nurses are almost never chosen as chaperones; in fact, some male nurses are expected to use chaperones (or to refrain from performing certain procedures altogether) for the same reasons that male physicians use chaperones. It is critical in most instances that the chaperone is a woman: A man in this role might make female patients feel even more victimized and vulnerable, and might be emasculating for male patients.

This complex strategy to desexualize the physical exam is grounded on assumptions about men's and women's sexuality. Men are

sexually powerful; women are sexually vulnerable. Women's bodies are comforting and soothing, but they also elicit feelings of childish vulnerability, which is an acceptable feeling in women but not in men. Men act on their sexual desires; women do not. These gender and sex stereotypes are bolstered through the organizational practice of using chaperones to desexualize the physical exam.

OBJECTIFYING THE PATIENT

Eight of the physicians and nurses reported that viewing their patients as something other than a person helped them to cope with the sexual nature of their work. This finding is consistent with previous research indicating that medical students and residents deal with uncomfortable feelings about patient nudity and examinations by objectifying their patients' bodies. Smith and Kleinman (1989) noted that students referred to examining patients as analogous to "looking under the hood of a car." The medical curriculum encourages students to dehumanize their patients' bodies because it focuses on the biological disease process and its cure ("lung in room 5") (Todd 1989). In contrast, the nursing school curriculum with its focus on "caring" and not "curing" emphasizes a more humane and holistic approach to treating patients. Fisher (1995) suggests that the nursing profession's focus on empathy discourages nurses from dehumanizing their patients in an extreme manner.

We found that both men and women objectify patients, but we noticed that the men and women interviewed used different metaphors in the process. The four women who mentioned using this strategy referred to their patients as "just another body" and did so for male and female patients. The four men who mentioned using this strategy referred to their patient as something other than a human being, usually a car. Moreover, these men only used this strategy with female patients.

A white female nurse described her training:

[The nursing faculty] tried to tell us like, "Don't think about it. Treat it like just another body." Usually, you've already messed with cadavers by the time you get to the hospital. So it's just another body. The hardest thing is trying to convince your patients of that . . . that it doesn't bother you.

Because she dissected cadavers in nursing school, this nurse was better able to view her patients as "just another body" and thus desexualize her own view of the patient. And according to a physician:

I'm never uncomfortable now. . . . You forget that students get uncomfortable. It's almost humorous, when you see how uncomfortable they are and you remember how uncomfortable it was at first. I tell them that it is just a body. If you get embarrassed, then your patient is going to be embarrassed. . . . If you're a professional, then they'll think it's a matter of course. (white female neurologist)

Many women provide care for their children and other relatives. If women routinely manage bodies in their personal lives, they may be more comfortable than men examining naked bodies in their professional lives, without thinking of them in a sexual way. One nurse explained that she thought of her patients as family members to make herself more comfortable with the physical exam:

I've never been nervous. My husband sometimes asks me about it. I tell him, "I can't even tell you what size a man was. I don't look at their bodies in that way." . . . You focus on a certain part of their body, and it's just a body. Nothing else. They stressed in school that we should preserve dignity and privacy. Treat the patient like they were one of your family members. Put yourself in their place. (African American female nurse)

While this nurse refers to her patients as "just a body," she also empathizes with them, thinking of them as family members. Referring to

patients as bodies does not seem to imply that these women lose compassion or empathy for their patients as human beings.

In contrast, the four male practitioners who claimed to dehumanize their patients as a strategy to desexualize the physical exam compared them to machines, and they did so only for their female patients. For example, a nurse said that examining female patients was no different from "checking the oil." Similarly, a physician described examining female patients:

When you're doing an examination, the genital examination, it's so routine and mundane. . . . You're looking at the body and trying to identify other things that are going on, like a pathology. . . . Sometimes I use the analogy of the car. . . . What you're focusing on is under the hood. You step back and say, "This is a nice car." But I'm not looking at the car. I'm checking the spark plugs. . . . It's part of my job. They are there because their car is misfiring. . . . You're not looking at it on a personal level or a sexual excitement level . . . it's not a turn on. (Latino physician in family practice)

This physician is not uncomfortable examining female patients because he is not looking at their bodies for his own personal sexual enjoyment. From his point of view, examining a patient "on a personal level" might provoke "sexual excitement." Thinking of his female patients as inanimate objects enables him to desexualize the exam.

Some physicians report they are most uncomfortable examining people they know. Having a personal relationship with someone clouds professional judgment according to one physician: "It's harder to take care of patients you know very well, and they're in a dangerous situation. I still treat them, but I'm more nervous about it compared to patients who I've just met" (white male cardiologist).

In the operating room, the patient may be more anonymous, and even unconscious, making the encounter less personal and unsettling for this physician. Having a personal relationship with a patient who is being examined is more difficult for him. This contrasts with the nurse, quoted above, who attributed family status to her patients to ensure the top quality of care.

Similarly, some physicians said they managed to maintain their composure around nude patients when the patient is passively lying down on an examination table, but they are more vulnerable to embarrassment if the patient is not so passive:

> I can walk into an exam room and see a lady in the wide-open-legs position, and examine her, and do a breast exam and pelvic exam, and that doesn't bother me at all. That's so clinical. But if I walk in, and you're getting dressed or undressed, I lose it. I get flabbergasted. I turn red and I have to walk out. That's the weird thing. I can see you totally buck naked and it doesn't bother me, but if you're getting dressed or undressed, that's it. . . . It's like when you're undressed and you have a gown on, and you're on the table, you're an auto engine. You're not really, but . . . I'm here to do a job, to make a diagnosis and do a treatment, and there are certain things I have to look for so it becomes mechanical. (white male urologist)

This physician is less able to dehumanize his patients like "an auto engine" when he sees female patients in a stage of dressing. Witnessing the transition between the clothed and the unclothed states disturbs his fantasy that the human being is an inanimate machine. Three other male physicians and nurses reported that they were only uncomfortable during physical exams if they saw a female patient dressing or undressing. None of the women reported that this made them uncomfortable.

The men who were interviewed only mentioned this strategy when describing exams of female patients. They did not describe dehumanizing their male patients in this way, perhaps because these heterosexual men only fear sexual arousal with their female patients. They may not have to dehumanize their male

patients as cars because they perceive no danger of sexual attraction.

Dehumanization seems to help these health care professionals deal with the sexual nature of their work. This strategy sheds new light on complaints that doctors do not care enough about their patients. Health care professionals are taught that they should have some level of detachment to deal rationally with their patients' problems. For some physicians and nurses, objectifying their patients might also help them to cope with the sexual nature of their work. Our interviews suggest further that this may be a gendered strategy, with men more likely than women to feel the need to distance themselves from their female patients to provide a high level of care.

EMPATHIZING WITH THE PATIENT AND PROTECTING PRIVACY

Some health care providers used the opposite strategy to objectification: to diffuse sexual tension and to make their patients feel more comfortable during the physical exam, they said they empathized with them. Some said that this empathy was combined with their efforts to protect the patient's privacy, by draping or covering the patient, exposing only the small area in need of attention, or drawing privacy curtains around the patient's bed. We combined empathy and protecting privacy in tallying up the strategies since the rationale given by the respondents was similar in both cases. In sum, 6 men and 27 women reported using one or both of these strategies to desexualize the physical exam.

For example, to make her patients feel more comfortable during the exam, one nurse follows these guidelines:

> First, explain what's going to happen and that privacy will be maintained as much as possible. The door will be shut and the curtains will be drawn or whatever. Let them know that you understand how uncomfortable it can be. Empathize. (white female nurse)

This practice of empathizing with the patient, and protecting their privacy, seems more characteristic of nursing than medicine. Seven of the physicians and 15 of the nurses said that they always covered their patients.

Whereas several nurses explained that they were taught in nursing school to empathize with their patients' needs for privacy, the opposite lesson was stressed in the medical training of some of the physicians who were interviewed. One doctor reported that a former professor required students to physically examine him in front of the class:

> He tried to show that there's nothing to be uncomfortable about during the exam. Every year it escalated, and it got to the point where he completely disrobed and insisted that all parts of the exam be performed on him in front of this huge group of people. I don't know how effective it was. I thought it was embarrassing. (white male internist)

Students even administered a rectal exam on this professor in front of the class. In contrast to nursing education, which stresses patient dignity and privacy, the goal here seems to be to desensitize medical students and to disregard the personal and physical boundaries of patients.

Other physicians mentioned aspects of their education that seem intended to violate their own physical integrity and sense of personal boundaries. One medical student intern described a former professor who forced some of the male students to be physically examined in front of the class, an experience he described as sexual harassment. Female students were not called upon to submit to these public examinations; the organization almost certainly would have considered that an illegal and harmful practice. At the medical school where most of this study was conducted, students had been required to conduct full examinations of each other, but when the students collectively rebelled against this practice, the school changed to its current practice of employing people from the community to help students practice their exam skills.

Nurses also are required to examine each other in training and even to give each other bed baths, but unlike these examples from medical schools, nursing students are explicitly taught how to conduct these invasive procedures while maintaining personal boundaries. One nurse recalled how she was taught to "be gentle and handle conversation carefully":

> Conversation shouldn't be about what you see on their body. It should be about the weather or the game that was on last night, or finding something in common with your patient. You should be able to converse with all people, from the retired professional to the laborer who can't read. I feel like we were trained well. (white female nurse)

In this way, sensitivity to the patients' needs for privacy and dignity is emphasized as part of the standard nursing curriculum.

In contrast, some doctors are subjected to insensitivity training. One doctor recalled being shown "desensitization tapes" as preparation for dealing with patients' sexuality:

> You're not supposed to be judgmental [as a doctor]. They showed us a bunch of tapes, like on sexual counseling. It's supposed to desensitize us to sexual things and to help us acknowledge our own sexual feelings and deal with them. They were generally kind of like gross porno-like films. Not porno films, but everybody made a lot of fun of them. In medical school, some people were offended by them, by the nudity in them. So they began showing them at night. Of course, the students were still uncomfortable. There were still jokes, but everybody was uncomfortable watching naked people and sexual acts. This was stuff we had never seen outside of porno films. (white female gynecologist)

Empathy and modesty, which are values built into nursing education, appear to be actively suppressed in physician education.

This difference reflects a gendered organizational logic: Since most nursing students are women, and until recently, women have been vastly underrepresented among medical students, the expectations of appropriate professional behavior that are embedded in physician and nurse education reflect and reinforce gender stereotypes. To be a good nurse/woman means to be empathetic and modest; to be a good physician/man means to be unflappable, detached, and powerful. The hidden curriculum of health care education is thus a gendered and, to some extent, sexualized curriculum.

JOKING ABOUT SEX

Joking about sex might seem incongruent with attempts to desexualize interactions with patients, but eight men and women engaged in sexual banter with their patients as a strategy to make themselves or the patient more comfortable with intimate topics, such as the sexual history. The interviews indicate, however, that this strategy was used selectively: With a few exceptions, the men and women interviewed only joked with opposite-sex patients or older patients.

A male urologist said he occasionally jokes about sex with his female patients:

There is innuendo. Like yesterday there was a 23-year-old girl in, who had recurrent urinary tract infections. . . . It seemed to be with her new partner that she got a lot of infections . . . I said, "Well, what you're going to need to do is take an antibiotic tablet after you have intercourse . . . every time after you have intercourse. For some women, that means you have to take one everyday." She looked at me and said, "Everyday?" I said, "There was a time in my life where I would have had to take one everyday. It didn't last very long but. . . ."So that's about as risqué as it gets. . . . Men are more uncomfortable being messed with, with their bodies than women. Women pretty much recognize that they have to go get

a pap smear, and when they've had babies, everyone is sticking their fingers up there. So women, from an early age are pretty much, for lack of a better word, resigned to it. Men . . . don't like it. You know, we see a lot of men for impotence. . . . That's . . . getting into intimate details, broaching subjects that . . . many men find very difficult to talk about . . . there's not that much joking with the men. . . . When they're talking about difficulty getting an erection, I don't think they want a locker room discussion. (white male urologist)

While he is cautious about engaging in sexual banter with women, he assumes that women are more comfortable joking about these personal matters. He perceives men's exams and histories as more sensitive than women's. He therefore avoids sexual joking with men; he does not think the examining room is the proper context for a "locker room discussion." Because the joking that does take place in locker rooms and other all-male contexts typically involves the ritual exchange of sexual insults—about sexual practices, the women they date, and the size of a man's penis (Lyman 1987)—it is inappropriate in the examining room, where the unclothed patient is in an especially passive and vulnerable position, unable to return the banter or to maintain his composure. Moreover, in the context of the exam, any sexual innuendo made to another man might be interpreted as sexual harassment.

The other physicians who mentioned this strategy engaged in joking with patients of the opposite sex to make patients more comfortable. A female general surgeon describes how she occasionally jokes about sex:

I remember one time . . . this guy had a hernia. . . . His wife was with him. He had been coming to see us for several weeks, once a week, so we kind of had a relationship going. I walked in the room and said, "Drop your pants." He said, "Oh, I love it when women talk dirty." We all stood around laughing. It's not something you would do with everybody, but

I felt comfortable in this situation. I think most patients respond well to humor, when they know it's humor. (white female surgeon)

Joking about sex with this patient seems to diffuse any hint of sexual interest. Their sexual banter plays on the absurdity of sexual interest between a female doctor and a male patient, thus dispelling any concerns the patient's wife might have.

This function of sexual humor was most apparent when some of the men and women discussed ways to avoid false allegations. A female nurse described how she avoided false allegations from patients:

> Well, really I don't worry because I use a lot of joking and kidding and get to know my patients a little bit before I have to do anything to them. I have a patient now, and the first thing this guy said was, "You just want to peek at me, don't you? You just want to take a look at me?" I said, "Sure, that's going to be the thrill of my day. I've seen 9 million of these things honey." (white female nurse)

This nurse uses joking to assure her male patient that this exam is not intended to have sexual overtones, even though he initiates the banter. These interviews suggest that joking about sex is a way to let the patient know that the physician or nurse is not sexually attracted to them, and that any hint of sexual attraction is both outrageous and taboo. As Fine (1976, 135) observes, sexual joking often functions this way: "By describing behavior considered sexually improper (and thus comical), [sexual humor] reveals by implication the correct forms of sexual interaction."

Men and women also engaged in sexual joking with older patients. A male nurse described how he made older patients more comfortable during physical exams:

> I joke about sex with some of the male patients. Once in a while I might say something to a female. . . . One woman that we're rendering care to right now is 93 years old. When you go

to visit her, the first thing she wants to know is why hasn't she died. . . . One day I said, "I think it's because you need to find a man. You haven't done that yet." She laughed, but I don't think I would go more than that. With male patients, we joke pretty openly. Like a diabetic patient in his middle seventies, who also had a little bit of cancer of the prostate, asked me if he should be involved in sex. . . . He wanted to know about protection with respect to AIDS. . . . Well, I seriously doubt he was going to get any, pardon my language (laughs). . . . With younger males, it's easy. I even joke with homosexuals a little bit, but not about homosexuals. I tell homosexuals heterosexual jokes. They know I'm straight pretty soon. (white male nurse)

This nurse engages in sexual joking with older patients and some young men as a way to set them at ease. But significantly, the strategy is used very selectively. He makes the ageist assumption that joking with older patients is safe because these individuals are neither active sexually nor do they have sexual interests. This reaffirms the hegemonic belief that only young people are sexual. His joking with young men appears to be a strategy designed to let them know that he is straight. Male nurses often face stereotypes that they are gay (Williams 1995), and this may be one way to dispel this suspicion among his patients.

Sexual banter with patients is a strategy that might fail if the patient is gay or lesbian, and the physician or nurse is heterosexual. Stevens (1996) conducted a study of lesbians' experiences with physicians during physical exams and found that physicians engaged in sexual innuendo with the respondents. The respondents noted that physicians seemed uncomfortable and unsure how to proceed if they "came out" during the physical examination. For example, one woman noted that her physician "didn't seem to know how to make conversation with a female client except through heterosexual jokes" (Stevens 1996, 34). Stevens' research suggests that joking about sex was based on the assumption of heterosexuality of the doctor and patient, and it might be used more often in heterosocial encounters in the intimate context of the physical exam.

Joking reaffirms the legitimacy and normalcy of some sexual behaviors, and the taboo nature of others. But it does this by inverting the normal and the taboo. Often what makes a joke funny is the absurdity and impossibility of the situations it describes. Thus, some of the health care workers who were interviewed felt comfortable joking about sex with opposite-sex patients and elderly patients. By pointing out what is absurd, it affirms what is normal and expected. Sexual joking is also a means through which men establish intimacy, although typically this involves challenging each other's masculinity and sexual prowess. Male joking of this type requires that participants appear invulnerable to these attacks (Lyman 1987), a situation impossible to maintain in the context of a medical examination. Consequently, this type of joking is absent from the accounts of our respondents, except in the case of the male nurse who uses joking to demonstrate his heterosexuality to his male patients. Finally, joking can decrease the social distance between patients and their health care providers, and hence it can be used to help comfort and empathize with patients. Even so, it is used selectively, often only with elderly patients, reflecting the ageist assumption that old people are asexual. Several health care providers did acknowledge that sexual joking is potentially dangerous in heterosocial encounters in the examining room because of its sexualized overtones: Consequently, most of the doctors and nurses interviewed said they assiduously avoid any such joking because they fear it will be misconstrued as a sexual interest.

THREATENING THE PATIENT

Four female physicians and nurses encountered problems desexualizing the physical examination of their patients because they experienced unwanted sexual advances from male patients. To control such patients, they threatened to physically or verbally punish them. Some men also reported sexual harassment from patients, but they never threatened them to control their behaviors. Seven physicians (5 of them were women) and 11 nurses (9 of them women) said they experienced sexual harassment from patients, ranging from male patients who attempted to fondle or grab them, to engage in sexual innuendo, and/or to expose themselves. Some of these behaviors were experienced as threatening; others were seen as "nothing to get upset about" and "a part of the job."

Recent studies indicate that sexual harassment affects many women in the health care industry. Phillips and Schneider (1993) found that 75 percent of female doctors surveyed reported sexual harassment from patients, most of whom were male. Grieco (1987) found that 76 percent of nurses surveyed experienced sexual harassment from both physicians and patients. Foner's (1994) study of a nursing home indicates that some female health care workers actually may be required to tolerate these behaviors as part of their jobs.

A nurse described her experience of sexual harassment:

> I had a patient try to pull me into bed with him. I hit him. . . . I reached down to take his pulse, and he yanked my hand. I had a foreigner grab my hand and shove it down his pants. . . . At first I thought, "Well, he's just a foreigner. He can't speak English. He's used to having women serve all of his needs." He wasn't speaking so I assumed that he didn't speak English. He was pretty dark. I thought he was Middle Eastern. He took my hand like he was trying to tell me something. So I was saying, "What's the matter? What are you trying to tell me?" He grabbed my hand, pulled it down his pants and he had a hard-on. That was very scary . . . I got very angry. I yelled at him, "I don't care if you speak English or not! You don't do that again! I'll tie you to the

bed!" I went back and got mad at the other nurses for not telling me about him. They were like, "Whoops. We forgot he did that to young women." I said, "He's done this before?!" They said, "You can give him up if you want to." I said, "No. I can handle it." He would say, "Will you help me?" I said, "Nope. Don't you touch me." I was rude. (white female nurse)

The fact that her coworkers "forgot" to tell her that this patient sexually harassed other women suggests that sexual harassment is a routine and expected part of their job, which is managed through informal "warnings" about patients who instigate unwanted sexual advances. To desexualize the exam and control this patient, she gets "rude" and threatens to tie his hands.

None of the physicians or nurses interviewed had received formal or informal training about handling unwanted sexual advances from patients. The women who were interviewed had to devise their own strategies to control behaviors of male patients. According to one nurse:

Oh yeah. [Sexual harassment from male patients] happens all the time. Oh yeah (laughs). . . . Last week, this one guy exposed himself to me every time I walked in the room, or he'd grab himself and leer at me. I've had them proposition me, grab my boobs, my butt. It's been a wild time (laughs). . . . The guy who was exposing himself and grabbing himself just had an infected left hand. There was nothing wrong up here [points to her forehead] . . . I said to him, "Are you having trouble keeping your gown down, buddy?" I talk to them real stern. With my size, they tend to do what I say. . . . I've had to report a couple of guys who wouldn't keep their hands to themselves. I went to their doctor. The doctors are always real supportive about that. I tell them, "I'm having trouble with this guy," and the doctor goes in and says, "That's not acceptable. You leave the nurses alone." (white female nurse)

Even though she feels protected because of her size (she is more than six feet tall),

ultimately this nurse must call on physicians to control the unacceptable sexual behavior of some of her patients. Three other nurses noted that they threaten to call the police if male patients "got out of hand." This strategy thus perpetuates gendered beliefs about women (nurses) as victims and men (police/doctors) as protectors.

One female physician changed specialties from internal medicine to obstetrics-gynecology to avoid sexual harassment by male patients:

When I was in internal medicine—I remember one guy in the ER had a heart attack. I was listening to his heart beating and he reaches around and grabs my butt. I said, "I don't think you understand. You have had a heart attack. I'm your doctor. If I were you, I don't think I'd piss me off." He was drunk as a skunk. Out dancing with a woman who wasn't his wife. I said, "Would you like for me to call your wife and explain the situation to your family? Okay. We understand each other." . . . I was [in] internal medicine for about four months. I found [the male patients] unpleasant and went into ob-gyn. (white female physician in obstetrics-gynecology)

In order to control the sexual behavior of her patient, this physician had to assert her professional status and threaten to expose his sexual infidelity to his family. After she changed specialties to obstetrics-gynecology, she treated only female patients. In this way, sexual harassment may contribute to internal occupational segregation in the health care professions. In fact, research shows that women in professional, nontraditional occupations suffer high rates of sexual harassment, often the "hostile work environment" type that punishes women for entering traditionally male environments (DiTomaso 1989; Konrad and Gutek 1986; Schultz 1998).

Physicians are often criticized today for their domineering and controlling attitudes toward patients. Our study suggests that for at least some female physicians, asserting power may be a means to overcome sexual harassment. According to Phillips and Schneider (1993, 1939),

> At a time when physicians are criticized for magnifying the inevitable differences in power that separate them from their patients, it is ironic that female doctors see the reinforcement of a physician's power as a means of protection. Despite this power, female doctors are treated primarily as women, not as physicians, by many of their male patients. The vulnerability inherent in their sex seems in many cases to override their power as doctors, leaving female physicians open to sexual harassment.

Female physicians and nurses may be forced to draw on their institutional power and authority to desexualize the physical exam, in response to unwanted sexual advances from their male patients.

LOOKING PROFESSIONAL

Four female nurses and doctors in this study attempted to control the sexual desires of their patients and diffuse the sexual meanings of the physical exam by emphasizing their professionalism. This was usually accomplished by dressing in a particular way:

> The way you dress is important. I think it's really important for women. I don't go to work with tight pants or short skirts. I wear business attire so the patient gets the idea that you're there to take care of them and nothing else. It's also important how the other people in the clinic dress. We have the nurses dress in scrubs or uniforms, and the secretaries also don't dress like they're going out to the disco (laughs). (Latina internist)

The importance of dressing to suppress sexual feelings was also emphasized by this physician:

> Some female physicians have their hair all made up, and lots of makeup and they look like a Barbie doll. I like to dress nicely but I don't wear excessive jewelry. I don't wear excessive makeup. I'm not too ornate. I don't try to look like a Barbie doll because I can see where it would be difficult for the patient to keep in mind that you're their physician, you know? (Asian American female in general medicine)

The conventional markers of femininity (styled hair, makeup, jewelry) are incompatible with "looking professional" because they sexualize the female health care provider and thus potentially arouse sexual feelings in patients. It is telling that none of the male health care providers mentioned the importance of dress for controlling patients' sexuality. Men may have an easier time than women looking the part of a professional. According to Dellinger and Williams (1997), the fact that men do not have to strategize their appearance reinforces the idea that women are the ones who bring "gender" and "sexuality" to the workplace.

Certain institutional practices exacerbate the problems women face "looking professional." Three of the female surgeons who occasionally worked at the same hospital mentioned that they were unhappy with the uniforms made available to them there. Two types of scrub suits were worn in the operating room: the typical green scrubs, which they preferred, and flowery scrubs with longer sleeves and tops intended to be worn by the female nurses. These physicians did not like the flowery scrubs because they claimed it was harder to do surgery in them, and because they did not want to be mistaken for nurses, yet they were typically the only type available in the women's changing room (which was shared by doctors and nurses). The administration ignored their complaints that the flowery scrubs undermined their efforts to look professional and garner the respect they felt they deserved. One said she often had to go into the doctors' dressing room (which was used by men only) to retrieve a set of green scrubs to wear:

> In some hospitals that don't have separate female surgeons' dressing rooms, there are no male scrubs available. So I just knock on the

door to the male dressing room, and I walk in and get some scrubs. If there's men in there and they're naked, I don't care. I just walk in. I say, "If you don't like me doing this, then complain to so-and-so, and get us a female physicians' dressing room." But they don't care. The men don't care. It's kind of a joke. They kind of laugh about it. It's another form of insidious discrimination . . . to not provide female physicians with the same clothes that they provide the male physicians. (white female urologist)

In addition to having the right clothes, having the right body shape also helps to "look professional," according to another physician. When asked if she had ever been sexually harassed, she said,

Younger guys have said something suggestive over the years but it's never been a big problem [for me]. Again, I think it helps that I am tall with dark hair. I think there are ways of being friendly, yet clearly professional, and that's hard to teach. I know some women have had more of a problem. I'm not very buxom either, and I think that makes a difference. I really think these things are things that women have no control over, but they make a huge difference. There are also clothes I wouldn't wear to see patients, like no short skirts. I dress conservatively. It shouldn't make a difference, but it does. (white female internist)

Women's bodies arouse sexual feelings, according to this physician, making it more difficult for women to achieve professional recognition. Some women's bodies may be especially incompatible with professional status. This is another example of how organizations are gendered and sexualized: The image of professionalism in the hospital is a masculine one. Women's bodies must be desexualized to achieve the same level of respect that men are accorded automatically. Having the wrong kind of body can be a formidable impediment to success.

Conclusion

Health care professionals are expected to manage their personal feelings during the physical examination of patients. This article describes how physicians and nurses control their own sexual feelings and the sexual behaviors of their patients. The men and women interviewed devised strategies to desexualize the exam, several of which were used selectively, depending on the gender and other characteristics of the patient and the health care worker. The interviews with doctors and nurses indicate that the choice to use certain strategies is shaped by, and reinforces, stereotypes about gender and sexuality.

The findings in this article are based on a small, nonrandom sample; hence, it is difficult to generalize to the entire population of doctors and nurses. Health care practitioners in other settings, such as private practices, may manage sexuality differently, compared with the physicians and nurses in teaching hospitals. The management of sexuality may also be specialty specific. Surgeons, pediatricians, urologists, and family practitioners may desexualize the exam differently.

This study suggests that desexualizing the exam is a gendered process. Men and women confront different obstacles to desexualizing the physical examination of patients. Male physicians and nurses are subject to assumptions that they are out of control of their sexuality. The use of female chaperones during their examination of female patients is based, in part, on this belief. Some men actually do fear sexual arousal, especially in their gynecological examinations of young, attractive women. Some men are also uncomfortable when they examine women they know or when they witness female patients undressing. Having a personal relationship with women is conflated with sexual meanings for some. Some endeavor to dehumanize their patient as a car to help them control their physical attraction.

In contrast, the women who were interviewed were less concerned about controlling their own sexual desire and more concerned about controlling the sexual desire of their male patients. Many of the female physicians and nurses in this study reported that sexual harassment from patients was "a part of their job." To protect themselves from sexual harassment, the female health care providers changed specialties, threatened their male patients, and dressed in ways to minimize their femininity and sexual attractiveness.

It is interesting how stereotypes about male and female patients' behavior provoke different institutional responses. Some doctors (both men and women) and male nurses fear that female patients will falsely accuse them of sexual assault, so they take measures to protect their reputations, including the institutionalized use of female chaperones. On the other hand, some female health care providers (both doctors and nurses) fear that they will be sexually harassed or assaulted by their male patients. But chaperones typically are not used to prevent these behaviors because chaperones might "embarrass" the male patient. Consequently, female health care providers must devise personal solutions to this problem without institutionalized support.

The professions of medicine and nursing, like many occupations, are profoundly gendered. Doctors are assumed to possess characteristics conventionally associated with masculinity (mastery, control, objectivity), while nurses are expected to display putatively feminine characteristics (empathy, modesty). The different training they receive in professional schools bolsters these expectations, with physicians focused on "curing" the disease and nurses learning to "care" for the whole patient. These gendered expectations are reflected in the strategies that men/doctors and women/nurses use to desexualize the exam. Women/nurses manage the relationship (empathize/protect privacy) between the provider and the patient, reflecting women's widely emphasized interactional and communication skills. The men/doctors do not stress managing the relationship; they just bring in another person (the chaperone) to control and to monitor the situation. Because female doctors and male nurses have to negotiate conflicting sets of gender expectations, they use some strategies not common to their professional colleagues of the opposite sex. Thus, female doctors stress the importance of looking professional, and male nurses sometimes call in chaperones.

This study of desexualization strategies reveals how gender is embedded in the informal organization and daily interactions with patients in the hospital. It is difficult to imagine how an embodied procedure such as a physical exam could ever escape gendered meanings. But recognizing how cultural assumptions about gender and sexuality shape this experience is a critical first step toward eventually reconfiguring those expectations in more just and liberating ways.

References

Cassell, J. 1998. *The Woman in the Surgeon's Body.* Cambridge, MA: Harvard University Press.

Dellinger, K. A., and C. L. Williams, 1997. "Makeup at Work: Negotiating Appearance Rules in the Workplace." *Gender & Society* 11: 151–77.

DiTomaso, N. 1989. "Sexuality in the Workplace: Discrimination and Harassment." In J. Hearn, D. L. Sheppard, P. Tancred-Sheriff, and G. Burrell (eds.), *The Sexuality of Organization.* London: Sage.

Fine, G. A. 1976. "Obscene Joking Across Cultures." *Journal of Communication* 26: 134–40.

Fisher, S. 1995. *Nursing Wounds: Nurse Practitioners/Doctors/Women Patients/and the Negotiation of Meaning.* New Brunswick, NJ: Rutgers University Press.

Foner, N. 1994. *The Caregiving Dilemma: Work in an American Nursing Home.* Berkeley: University of California Press.

Grieco, A. 1987. "Scope and Nature of Sexual Harassment in Nursing." *Journal of Sex Research* 23: 261–66.

Konrad, A. M., and B. A. Gutek. 1986. "Impact of Work Experiences on Attitudes Toward Sexual Harassment." *Administrative Science Quarterly* 31: 422–38.

Lyman, P. 1987. "The Fraternal Bond as a Joking Relationship: A Case Study of the Role of Sexist Jokes in Male Group Bonding." In M. S. Kimmel (ed.), *Changing Men: New Directions in Research on Men and Masculinity*. Newbury Park, CA: Sage.

Phillips, S. P., and M. S. Schneider. 1993. "Sexual Harassment of Doctors by Patients." *New England Journal of Medicine* 329: 1936–39.

Randolph, L., B. Seidman, and T. Pasko. 1996. *Physician Characteristics and Distribution in the U.S.* Chicago: American Medical Association.

Schultz, V. 1998. "Reconceptualizing Sexual Harassment." *Yale Law Journal* 107: 1683–1805.

Smith, A. C., and S. Kleinman. 1989. "Managing Emotions in Medical School: Students' Contact with the Living and the Dead." *Social Psychology Quarterly* 52: 56–69.

Stevens, P. E. 1996. "Lesbians and Doctors: Experiences of Solidarity and Domination in Health Care Settings." *Gender & Society* 10: 24–41.

Todd, A. D. 1989. *Intimate Adversaries: Cultural Conflict Between Doctors and Women Patients.* Philadelphia: University of Pennsylvania Press.

Williams, C. L. 1995. *Still a Man's World: Men Who Do "Women's Work."* Berkeley: University of California Press.

Questions

1. What do the authors mean when they say that the physical exam must be "desexualized"?

2. According to professors Giuffre and Williams, desexualizing physical exams is done in a gendered way. What strategies are primarily employed by women practitioners? What strategies are primarily employed by male practitioners?

3. The authors argue that "female patients are protected by chaperones, but men must be protected from chaperones." What do they mean?

4. This article focuses mostly on what practitioners do to desexualize physical exams. In your experience, what role does the patient play in desexualizing physical exams? Is the patient's response gendered? (That is, do men play their role as patients during the physical exam differently than women do?)

25

THE NORMALITY OF CRIME

Émile Durkheim

The following excerpt is from Émile Durkheim's 1895 essay *Rules of the Sociological Method*. The excerpt is brief but (like much of what people wrote in the nineteenth century) fairly complex. Durkheim begins by pointing out that crime—or acts that offend the collective conscience—is normal in every society. In other words, every society can expect some of its members occasionally to do things that offend that society's shared values and beliefs. According to Durkheim's analysis, the only way to completely do away with murder, for example, would be for every single person in the society to develop intense respect for all other members. If that happened, Durkheim points out, then the crime of murder might disappear, but previously minor offenses would then seem more serious. In a society of saints, he says, the crime of murder would not be a problem, but perhaps the "crime" of insulting others would be.

Here we are, then, in the presence of a conclusion in appearance quite paradoxical. Let us make no mistake. To classify crime among the phenomena of normal sociology is not to say merely that it is an inevitable, although regrettable phenomenon, due to the incorrigible wickedness of men; it is to affirm that it is a factor in public health, an integral part of all healthy societies. This result is, at first glance, surprising enough to have puzzled even ourselves for a long time. Once this first surprise

has been overcome, however, it is not difficult to find reasons explaining this normality and at the same time confirming it.

In the first place crime is normal because a society exempt from it is utterly impossible. Crime, we have shown elsewhere, consists of an act that offends certain very strong collective sentiments. In a society in which criminal acts are no longer committed, the sentiments they offend would have to be found without exception in all individual consciousnesses, and they must be found to exist with the same degree as sentiments contrary to them. Assuming that this condition could actually be realized, crime would not thereby disappear; it would only change its form, for the very cause which would thus dry up the sources of criminality would immediately open up new ones.

Indeed, for the collective sentiments which are protected by the penal law[1] of a people at a specific moment of its history to take possession of the public conscience or for them to acquire a stronger hold where they have an insufficient grip, they must acquire an intensity greater than that which they had hitherto had. The community as a whole must experience them more vividly, for it can acquire from no other source the greater force necessary to control these individuals who formerly were the most refractory. For murderers to disappear, the horror of bloodshed must become greater in those social strata from which murderers are recruited; but, first it must become greater throughout the entire society. Moreover, the very absence of crime would directly contribute to produce this horror; because any sentiment seems much more respectable when it is always and uniformly respected.

One easily overlooks the consideration that these strong states of the common consciousness cannot be thus reinforced without reinforcing at the same time the more feeble states, whose violation previously gave birth to mere infraction of convention—since the weaker ones are only the prolongation, the attenuated form, of the stronger. Thus robbery and simple bad taste injure the same single altruistic sentiment, the respect for that which is another's. However, this same sentiment is less grievously offended by bad taste than by robbery; and since, in addition, the average consciousness has not sufficient intensity to react keenly to the bad taste, it is treated with greater

tolerance. That is why the person guilty of bad taste is merely blamed, whereas the thief is punished. But, if this sentiment grows stronger, to the point of silencing in all consciousnesses the inclination which disposes man to steal, he will become more sensitive to the offenses which, until then, touched him but lightly. He will react against them, then, with more energy; they will be the object of greater opprobrium, which will transform certain of them from the simple moral faults that they were and give them the quality of crimes. For example, improper contracts, or contracts improperly executed, which only incur public blame or civil damages, will become offenses in law.

Imagine a society of saints, a perfect cloister of exemplary individuals. Crimes, properly so called, will there be unknown; but faults which appear venial to the layman will create there the same scandal that the ordinary offense does in ordinary consciousnesses. If, then, this society has the power to judge and punish, it will define these acts as criminal and will treat them as such. For the same reason, the perfect and upright man judges his smallest failings with a severity that the majority reserve for acts more truly in the nature of an offense. Formerly, acts of violence against persons were more frequent than they are today, because respect for individual dignity was less strong. As this has increased, these crimes have become more rare; and also, many acts violating this sentiment have been introduced into the penal law which were not included there in primitive times. . . .

Questions

1. Durkheim argues that crime is "normal." What does he mean by this?

2. Does Durkheim believe that it is either possible or desirable for a society to exist in which there is no crime? Why or why not?

[1]Penal law is criminal law.—Ed.

26

THE SAINTS AND THE ROUGHNECKS

William J. Chambliss

Robert K. Merton was inspired by the "Thomas theorem"—the notion (from W. I. Thomas) that if people "define situations as real, they are real in their consequences." Merton observed that Thomas was pointing out that people "not only respond to the objective features of a situation" but to the "meaning this situation has for them." One implication of the Thomas theorem was something that Merton called the "self-fulfilling prophecy": "The self-fulfilling prophecy is, in the beginning, a *false* definition of the situation evoking a new behavior which makes the originally false conception come *true*." For example, if a rumor circulates that the town bank is about to fail, that rumor, even if initially false, can come true simply because it's there. That is, the rumor may worry people sufficiently that they hurry to the bank and withdraw their funds. Ultimately, the bank *does* fail. Then, the rumormonger can say, "See, I told you the bank was going to fail."[1]

The following 1972 article by William Chambliss explores some of the ways in which public definitions of a situation come into being with respect to two small groups of high school kids. As you read this article, look for examples of how the ways in which people define the situation have real consequences for the people involved.

Eight promising young men—children of good, stable, white upper-middle-class families, active in school affairs, good precollege students—were some of the most delinquent boys at Hanibal High School. While community residents and parents knew that these boys occasionally sowed a few wild oats, they were totally unaware that sowing wild oats completely occupied the daily routine of these young men. The Saints were constantly occupied with truancy, drinking, wild driving, petty theft and vandalism. Yet not one was officially arrested for any misdeed during the two years I observed them.

[1]From Robert Merton, *Social Theory and Social Structure* (New York: Free Press, 1968), p. 477.—Ed.

William J. Chambliss, "The Saints and the Roughnecks" from *Society* (November/December 1973). Copyright © 1973 by Transaction Publishers. Reprinted with kind permission from Springer Science+Business Media.

This record was particularly surprising in light of my observations during the same two years of another gang of Hanibal High School students, six lower-class white boys known as the Roughnecks. The Roughnecks were constantly in trouble with police and community even though their rate of delinquency was about equal with that of the Saints. What was the cause of this disparity? The result? The following consideration of the activities, social class and community perceptions of both gangs may provide some answers.

The Saints from Monday to Friday

The Saints' principal daily concern was with getting out of school as early as possible. The boys managed to get out of school with minimum danger that they would be accused of

265

class early
Get out of playing hookey through an elaborate procedure for obtaining legitimate release from class. The most common procedure was for one boy to obtain the release of another by fabricating a meeting of some committee, program or recognized club. Charles might raise his hand in his 9:00 chemistry class and ask to be excused—a euphemism for going to the bathroom. Charles would go to Ed's math class and inform the teacher that Ed was needed for a 9:30 rehearsal of the drama club play. The math teacher would recognize Ed and Charles as "good students" involved in numerous school activities and would permit Ed to leave at 9:30. Charles would return to his class, and Ed would go to Tom's English class to obtain his release. Tom would engineer Charles' escape. The strategy would continue until as many of the Saints as possible were freed. After a stealthy trip to the car (which had been parked in a strategic spot), the boys were off for a day of fun.

help each other leave class

Over the two years I observed the Saints, this pattern was repeated nearly every day. There were variations on the theme, but in one form or another, the boys used this procedure for getting out of class and then off the school grounds. Rarely did all eight of the Saints manage to leave school at the same time. The average number avoiding school on the days I observed them was five.

Having escaped from the concrete corridors the boys usually went either to a pool hall on the other (lower-class) side of town or to a cafe in the suburbs. Both places were out of the way of people the boys were likely to know (family or school officials), and both provided a source of entertainment. The pool hall entertainment was the generally rough atmosphere, the occasional hustler, the sometimes drunk proprietor and, of course, the game of pool. The cafe's entertainment was provided by the owner. The boys would "accidentally" knock a glass on the floor or spill cola on the counter—not all the time, but enough to be

secret places

sporting. They would also bend spoons, put salt in sugar bowls and generally tease whoever was working in the cafe. The owner had opened the cafe recently and was dependent on the boys' business which was, in fact, substantial since between the horsing around and the teasing they bought food and drinks.

The Saints on Weekends

On weekends the automobile was even more critical than during the week, for on weekends the Saints went to Big Town—a large city with a population of over a million 25 miles from Hanibal. Every Friday and Saturday night most of the Saints would meet between 8:00 and 8:30 and would go into Big Town. Big Town activities included drinking heavily in taverns or nightclubs, driving drunkenly through the streets, and committing acts of vandalism and playing pranks.

By midnight on Fridays and Saturdays the Saints were usually thoroughly high, and one or two of them were often so drunk they had to be carried to the cars. Then the boys drove around town, calling obscenities to women and girls; occasionally trying (unsuccessfully so far as I could tell) to pick girls up; and driving recklessly through red lights and at high speeds with their lights out. Occasionally they played "chicken." One boy would climb out the back window of the car and across the roof to the driver's side of the car while the car was moving at high speed (between 40 and 50 miles an hour); then the driver would move over and the boy who had just crawled across the car roof would take the driver's seat.

Searching for "fair game" for a prank was the boys' principal activity after they left the tavern. The boys would drive alongside a foot patrolman and ask directions to some street. If the policeman leaned on the car in the course of answering the question, the driver would speed away, causing him to lose his balance.

The Saints were careful to play this prank only in an area where they were not going to spend much time and where they could quickly disappear around a corner to avoid having their license plate number taken.

Construction sites and road repair areas were the special province of the Saints' mischief. A soon-to-be-repaired hole in the road inevitably invited the Saints to remove lanterns and wooden barricades and put them in the car, leaving the hole unprotected. The boys would find a safe vantage point and wait for an unsuspecting motorist to drive into the hole. Often, though not always, the boys would go up to the motorist and commiserate with him about the dreadful way the city protected its citizenry.

Leaving the scene of the open hole and the motorist, the boys would then go searching for an appropriate place to erect the stolen barricade. An "appropriate place" was often a spot on a highway near a curve in the road where the barricade would not be seen by an oncoming motorist. The boys would wait to watch an unsuspecting motorist attempt to stop and (usually) crash into the wooden barricade. With saintly bearing the boys might offer help and understanding.

A stolen lantern might well find its way onto the back of a police car or hang from a street lamp. Once a lantern served as a prop for a reenactment of the "midnight ride of Paul Revere" until the "play," which was taking place at 2:00 A.M. in the center of a main street of Big Town, was interrupted by a police car several blocks away. The boys ran, leaving the lanterns on the street, and managed to avoid being apprehended.

Abandoned houses, especially if they were located in out-of-the-way places, were fair game for destruction and spontaneous vandalism. The boys would break windows, remove furniture to the yard and tear it apart, urinate on the walls and scrawl obscenities inside.

Through all the pranks, drinking and reckless driving the boys managed miraculously to avoid being stopped by police. Only twice in two years was I aware that they had been stopped by a Big City policeman. Once was for speeding (which they did every time they drove whether they were drunk or sober), and the driver managed to convince the policeman that it was simply an error. The second time they were stopped they had just left a nightclub and were walking through an alley. Aaron stopped to urinate and the boys began making obscene remarks. A foot patrolman came into the alley, lectured the boys and sent them home. Before the boys got to the car one began talking in a loud voice again. The policeman, who had followed them down the alley, arrested this boy for disturbing the peace and took him to the police station where the other Saints gathered. After paying a $5.00 fine, and with the assurance that there would be no permanent record of the arrest, the boy was released.

The boys had a spirit of frivolity and fun about their escapades. They did not view what they were engaged in as "delinquency," though it surely was by any reasonable definition of that word. They simply viewed themselves as having a little fun and who, they would ask, was really hurt by it? The answer had to be no one, although this fact remains one of the most difficult things to explain about the gang's behavior. Unlikely though it seems, in two years of drinking, driving, carousing and vandalism no one was seriously injured as a result of the Saints' activities.

The Saints in School

The Saints were highly successful in school. The average grade for the group was "B," with two of the boys having close to a straight "A" average. Almost all of the boys were popular and many of them held offices in the school. One of the boys was vice president of the student body one year. Six of the boys played on athletic teams.

At the end of their senior year, the student body selected ten seniors for special recognition as the "school wheels"; four of the ten were Saints. Teachers and school officials saw no problem with any of these boys and anticipated that they would all "make something of themselves."

How the boys managed to maintain this impression is surprising in view of their actual behavior while in school. Their technique for covering truancy was so successful that teachers did not even realize that the boys were absent from school much of the time. Occasionally, of course, the system would backfire and then the boy was on his own. A boy who was caught would be most contrite, would plead guilty and ask for mercy. He inevitably got the mercy he sought.

Cheating on examinations was rampant, even to the point of orally communicating answers to exams as well as looking at one another's papers. Since none of the group studied, and since they were primarily dependent on one another for help, it is surprising that grades were so high. Teachers contributed to the deception in their admitted inclination to give these boys (and presumably others like them) the benefit of the doubt. When asked how the boys did in school, and when pressed on specific examinations, teachers might admit that they were disappointed in John's performance, but would quickly add that they "knew that he was capable of doing better," so John was given a higher grade than he had actually earned. How often this happened is impossible to know. During the time that I observed the group, I never saw any of the boys take homework home. Teachers may have been "understanding" very regularly.

One exception to the gang's generally good performance was Jerry, who had a "C" average

in his junior year, experienced disaster the next year and failed to graduate. Jerry had always been a little more nonchalant than the others about the liberties he took in school. Rather than wait for someone to come get him from class, he would offer his own excuse and leave. Although he probably did not miss any more classes than most of the others in the group, he did not take the requisite pains to cover his absences. Jerry was the only Saint whom I ever heard talk back to a teacher. Although teachers often called him a "cut up" or a "smart kid," they never referred to him as a troublemaker or as a kid headed for trouble. It seems likely, then, that Jerry's failure his senior year and his mediocre performance his junior year were consequences of his not playing the game the proper way (possibly because he was disturbed by his parents' divorce). His teachers regarded him as "immature" and not quite ready to get out of high school.

The Police and the Saints

The local police saw the Saints as good boys who were among the leaders of the youth in the community. Rarely, the boys might be stopped in town for speeding or for running a stop sign. When this happened the boys were always polite, contrite and pled for mercy. As in school, they received the mercy they asked for. None ever received a ticket or was taken into the precinct by the local police.

The situation in Big City, where the boys engaged in most of their delinquency, was only slightly different. The police there did not know the boys at all, although occasionally the boys were stopped by a patrolman. Once they were caught taking a lantern from a construction site. Another time they were stopped for running a stop sign, and on several occasions they were stopped for speeding. Their behavior was as before:

contrite, polite and penitent. The urban police, like the local police, accepted their demeanor as sincere. More important, the urban police were convinced that these were good boys just out for a lark.

The Roughnecks

Hanibal townspeople never perceived the Saints' high level of delinquency. The Saints were good boys who just went in for an occasional prank. After all, they were well dressed, well mannered and had nice cars. The Roughnecks were a different story. Although the two gangs of boys were the same age, and both groups engaged in an equal amount of wild-oat sowing, everyone agreed that the not-so-well-dressed, not-so-well-mannered, not-so-rich boys were heading for trouble. Townspeople would say, "You can see the gang members at the drugstore, night after night, leaning against the storefront (sometimes drunk) or slouching around inside buying cokes, reading magazines, and probably stealing old Mr. Wall blind. When they are outside and girls walk by, even respectable girls, these boys make suggestive remarks. Sometimes their remarks are downright lewd."

From the community's viewpoint, the real indication that these kids were in for trouble was that they were constantly involved with the police. Some of them had been picked up for stealing, mostly small stuff, of course, "but still it's stealing small stuff that leads to big time crimes." "Too bad," people said. "Too bad that these boys couldn't behave like the other kids in town; stay out of trouble, be polite to adults, and look to their future."

The community's impression of the degree to which this group of six boys (ranging in age from 16 to 19) engaged in delinquency was somewhat distorted. In some ways the gang was more delinquent than the community thought; in other ways they were less.

The fighting activities of the group were fairly readily and accurately perceived by almost everyone. At least once a month, the boys would get into some sort of fight, although most fights were scraps between members of the group or involved only one member of the group and some peripheral hanger-on. Only three times in the period of observation did the group fight together: once against a gang from across town, once against two blacks and once against a group of boys from another school. For the first two fights the group went out "looking for trouble"— and they found it both times. The third fight followed a football game and began spontaneously with an argument on the football field between one of the Roughnecks and a member of the opposition's football team.

Jack had a particular propensity for fighting and was involved in most of the brawls. He was a prime mover of the escalation of arguments into fights.

More serious than fighting, had the community been aware of it, was theft. Although almost everyone was aware that the boys occasionally stole things, they did not realize the extent of the activity. Petty stealing was a frequent event for the Roughnecks. Sometimes they stole as a group and coordinated their efforts; other times they stole in pairs. Rarely did they steal alone.

The thefts ranged from very small things like paperback books, comics and ballpoint pens to expensive items like watches. The nature of the thefts varied from time to time. The gang would go through a period of systematically shoplifting items from automobiles or school lockers. Types of thievery varied with the whim of the gang. Some forms of thievery were more profitable than others, but all thefts were for profit, not just thrills.

Roughnecks siphoned gasoline from cars as often as they had access to an automobile, which was not very often. Unlike the Saints, who owned their own cars, the Roughnecks would have to borrow their parents' cars, an event which occurred only eight or nine times a year. The boys claimed to have stolen cars for joy rides from time to time.

Ron committed the most serious of the group's offenses. With an unidentified associate the boy attempted to burglarize a gasoline station. Although this station had been robbed twice previously in the same month, Ron denied any involvement in either of the other thefts. When Ron and his accomplice approached the station, the owner was hiding in the bushes beside the station. He fired both barrels of a double-barreled shotgun at the boys. Ron was severely injured; the other boy ran away and was never caught. Though he remained in critical condition for several months, Ron finally recovered and served six months of the following year in reform school. Upon release from reform school, Ron was put back a grade in school, and began running around with a different gang of boys. The Roughnecks considered the new gang less delinquent than themselves, and during the following year Ron had no more trouble with the police.

The Roughnecks, then, engaged mainly in three types of delinquency: theft, drinking and fighting. Although community members perceived that this gang of kids was delinquent, they mistakenly believed that their illegal activities were primarily drinking, fighting and being a nuisance to passersby. Drinking was limited among the gang members, although it did occur, and theft was much more prevalent than anyone realized.

Drinking would doubtless have been more prevalent had the boys had ready access to liquor. Since they rarely had automobiles at their disposal, they could not travel very far, and the bars in town would not serve them. Most of the boys had little money, and this, too, inhibited their purchase of alcohol. Their major source of liquor was a local drunk who would buy them a fifth if they would give him

enough extra to buy himself a pint of whiskey or a bottle of wine.

The community's perception of drinking as prevalent stemmed from the fact that it was the most obvious delinquency the boys engaged in. When one of the boys had been drinking, even a casual observer seeing him on the corner would suspect that he was high.

There was a high level of mutual distrust and dislike between the Roughnecks and the police. The boys felt very strongly that the police were unfair and corrupt. Some evidence existed that the boys were correct in their perception.

The main source of the boys' dislike for the police undoubtedly stemmed from the fact that the police would sporadically harass the group. From the standpoint of the boys, these acts of occasional enforcement of the law were whimsical and uncalled for. It made no sense to them, for example, that the police would come to the corner occasionally and threaten them with arrest for loitering when the night before the boys had been out siphoning gasoline from cars and the police had been nowhere in sight. To the boys, the police were stupid on the one hand, for not being where they should have been and catching the boys in a serious offense, and unfair on the other hand, for trumping up "loitering" charges against them.

From the viewpoint of the police, the situation was quite different. They knew, with all the confidence necessary to be a policeman, that these boys were engaged in criminal activities. They knew this partly from occasionally catching them, mostly from circumstantial evidence ("the boys were around when those tires were slashed"), and partly because the police shared the view of the community in general that this was a bad bunch of boys. The best the police could hope to do was to be sensitive to the fact that these boys were engaged in illegal acts and arrest them whenever there was some evidence that they had been involved. Whether or not the boys had in fact committed a particular act in a particular way was not especially important. The police had a broader view: their job was to stamp out these kids' crimes; the tactics were not as important as the end result.

Over the period that the group was under observation, each member was arrested at least once. Several of the boys were arrested a number of times and spent at least one night in jail. While most were never taken to court, two of the boys were sentenced to six months' incarceration in boys' schools.

The Roughnecks in School

The Roughnecks' behavior in school was not particularly disruptive. During school hours they did not all hang around together, but tended instead to spend most of their time with one or two other members of the gang who were their special buddies. Although every member of the gang attempted to avoid school as much as possible, they were not particularly successful and most of them attended school with surprising regularity. They considered school a burden—something to be gotten through with a minimum of conflict. If they were "bugged" by a particular teacher, it could lead to trouble. One of the boys, Al, once threatened to beat up a teacher and, according to the other boys, the teacher hid under a desk to escape him.

Teachers saw the boys the way the general community did, as heading for trouble, as being uninterested in making something of themselves. Some were also seen as being incapable of meeting the academic standards of the school. Most of the teachers expressed concern for this group of boys and were willing to pass them despite poor performance, in the belief that failing them would only aggravate the problem.

The group of boys had a grade point average just slightly above "C." No one in the group failed either grade, and no one had better than a "C" average. They were consistent in their achievement or, at least, the teachers were consistent in their perception of the boys' achievement.

Two of the boys were good football players. Herb was acknowledged to be the best player in the school and Jack was almost as good. Both boys were criticized for their failure to abide by training rules, for refusing to come to practice as often as they should, and for not playing their best during practice. What they lacked in sportsmanship they made up for in skill, apparently, and played every game no matter how poorly they had performed in practice or how many practice sessions they had missed.

Two Questions

Why did the community, the school and the police react to the Saints as though they were good, upstanding, nondelinquent youths with bright futures but to the Roughnecks as though they were tough, young criminals who were headed for trouble? Why did the Roughnecks and the Saints in fact have quite different careers after high school—careers which, by and large, lived up to the expectations of the community?

The most obvious explanation for the differences in the community's and law enforcement agencies' reactions to the two gangs is that one group of boys was "more delinquent" than the other. Which group was more delinquent? The answer to this question will determine in part how we explain the differential responses to these groups by the members of the community and, particularly, by law enforcement and school officials.

In sheer number of illegal acts, the Saints were the more delinquent. They were truant from school for at least part of the day almost every day of the week. In addition, their drinking and vandalism occurred with surprising regularity. The Roughnecks, in contrast, engaged sporadically in delinquent episodes. While these episodes were frequent, they certainly did not occur on a daily or even a weekly basis.

The difference in frequency of offenses was probably caused by the Roughnecks' inability to obtain liquor and to manipulate legitimate excuses from school. Since the Roughnecks had less money than the Saints, and teachers carefully supervised their school activities, the Roughnecks' hearts may have been as black as the Saints', but their misdeeds were not nearly as frequent.

There are really no clear-cut criteria by which to measure qualitative differences in antisocial behavior. The most important dimension of the difference is generally referred to as the "seriousness" of the offenses.

If seriousness encompasses the relative economic costs of delinquent acts, then some assessment can be made. The Roughnecks probably stole an average of about $5.00 worth of goods a week. Some weeks the figure was considerably higher, but these times must be balanced against long periods when almost nothing was stolen.

The Saints were more continuously engaged in delinquency but their acts were not for the most part costly to property. Only their vandalism and occasional theft of gasoline would so qualify. Perhaps once or twice a month they would siphon a tankful of gas. The other costly items were street signs, construction lanterns and the like. All of these acts combined probably did not quite average $5.00 a week, partly because much of the stolen equipment was abandoned and presumably could be recovered. The difference in cost of stolen property between the two groups was trivial, but the Roughnecks probably had a slightly more expensive set of activities than did the Saints.

Another meaning of seriousness is the potential threat of physical harm to members of the community and to the boys themselves. The Roughnecks were more prone to physical violence; they not only welcomed an opportunity to fight; they went seeking it. In addition, they fought among themselves frequently. Although the fighting never included deadly weapons, it was still a menace, however minor, to the physical safety of those involved.

The Saints never fought. They avoided physical conflict both inside and outside the group. At the same time, though, the Saints frequently endangered their own and other people's lives. They did so almost every time they drove a car, especially if they had been drinking. Sober, their driving was risky; under the influence of alcohol it was horrendous. In addition, the Saints endangered the lives of others with their pranks. Street excavations left unmarked were a very serious hazard.

Evaluating the relative seriousness of the two gangs' activities is difficult. The community reacted as though the behavior of the Roughnecks was a problem, and they reacted as though the behavior of the Saints was not. But the members of the community were ignorant of the array of delinquent acts that characterized the Saints' behavior. Although concerned citizens were unaware of much of the Roughnecks' behavior as well, they were much better informed about the Roughnecks' involvement in delinquency than they were about the Saints'.

Visibility

Differential treatment of the two gangs results in part because one gang was infinitely more visible than the other. This differential visibility was a direct function of the economic standing of the families. The Saints had access to automobiles and were able to remove themselves from the sight of the community. In as routine a decision as to where to go to have a milkshake after school, the Saints stayed away from the mainstream of community life. Lacking transportation, the Roughnecks could not make it to the edge of town. The center of town was the only practical place for them to meet since their homes were scattered throughout the town and any noncentral meeting place put an undue hardship on some members. Through necessity the Roughnecks congregated in a crowded area where everyone in the community passed frequently, including teachers and law enforcement officers. They could easily see the Roughnecks hanging around the drugstore.

The Roughnecks, of course, made themselves even more visible by making remarks to passersby and by occasionally getting into fights on the corner. Meanwhile, just as regularly, the Saints were either at the cafe on one edge of town or in the pool hall at the other edge of town. Without any particular realization that they were making themselves inconspicuous, the Saints were able to hide their time-wasting. Not only were they removed from the mainstream of traffic, but they were almost always inside a building.

On their escapades the Saints were also relatively invisible, since they left Hanibal and travelled to Big City. Here, too, they were mobile, roaming the city, rarely going to the same area twice.

Demeanor

To the notion of visibility must be added the difference in the responses of group members to outside intervention with their activities. If one of the Saints was confronted with an accusing policeman, even if he felt he was truly innocent of a wrongdoing, his demeanor was apologetic and penitent. A Roughneck's attitude was almost the polar opposite. When confronted with a threatening adult authority,

even one who tried to be pleasant, the Roughneck's hostility and disdain were clearly observable. Sometimes he might attempt to put up a veneer of respect, but it was thin and was not accepted as sincere by the authority.

School was no different from the community at large. The Saints could manipulate the system by feigning compliance with the school norms. The availability of cars at school meant that once free from the immediate sight of the teacher, the boys could disappear rapidly. And this escape was well enough planned that no administrator or teacher was nearby when the boys left. A Roughneck who wished to escape for a few hours was in a bind. If it were possible to get free from class, downtown was still a mile away, and even if he arrived there, he was still very visible. Truancy for the Roughnecks meant almost certain detection, while the Saints enjoyed almost complete immunity from sanctions.

Bias

Community members were not aware of the transgressions of the Saints. Even if the Saints had been less discreet, their favorite delinquencies would have been perceived as less serious than those of the Roughnecks.

In the eyes of the police and school officials, a boy who drinks in an alley and stands intoxicated on the street corner is committing a more serious offense than is a boy who drinks to inebriation in a nightclub or a tavern and drives around afterwards in a car. Similarly, a boy who steals a wallet from a store will be viewed as having committed a more serious offense than a boy who steals a lantern from a construction site.

Perceptual bias also operates with respect to the demeanor of the boys in the two groups when they are confronted by adults. It is not simply that adults dislike the posture affected by boys of the Roughneck ilk; more important is the conviction that the posture adopted by the Roughnecks is an indication of their devotion and commitment to deviance as a way of life. The posture becomes a cue, just as the type of the offense is a cue, to the degree to which the known transgressions are indicators of the youths' potential for other problems.

Visibility, demeanor and bias are surface variables which explain the day-to-day operations of the police. Why do these surface variables operate as they do? Why did the police choose to disregard the Saints' delinquencies while breathing down the backs of the Roughnecks?

The answer lies in the class structure of American society and the control of legal institutions by those at the top of the class structure. Obviously, no representative of the upper class drew up the operational chart for the police which led them to look in the ghettoes and on streetcorners—which led them to see the demeanor of lower-class youth as troublesome and that of upper-middle-class youth as tolerable. Rather, the procedures simply developed from experience—experience with irate and influential upper-middle-class parents insisting that their son's vandalism was simply a prank and his drunkenness only a momentary "sowing of wild oats"—experience with cooperative or indifferent, powerless, lower-class parents who acquiesced to the law's definition of their son's behavior.

Adult Careers of the Saints and the Roughnecks

The community's confidence in the potential of the Saints and the Roughnecks apparently was justified. If anything, the community members underestimated the degree to which these youngsters would turn out "good" or "bad."

Seven of the eight members of the Saints went on to college immediately after high school. Five of the boys graduated from college in four years. The sixth one finished college after two years in the army, and the seventh spent fours years in the air force before returning to college and receiving a B.A. degree. Of these seven college graduates, three went on for advanced degrees. One finished law school and is now active in state politics, one finished medical school and is practicing near Hanibal, and one boy is now working for a Ph.D. The other four college graduates entered submanagerial, managerial or executive training positions with larger firms.

The only Saint who did not complete college was Jerry. Jerry had failed to graduate from high school with the other Saints. During his second senior year, after the other Saints had gone on to college, Jerry began to hang around with what several teachers described as a "rough crowd"—the gang that was heir apparent to the Roughnecks. At the end of his second senior year, when he did graduate from high school, Jerry took a job as a used-car salesman, got married and quickly had a child. Although he made several abortive attempts to go to college by attending night school, when I last saw him (ten years after high school) Jerry was unemployed and had been living on unemployment for almost a year. His wife worked as a waitress.

Some of the Roughnecks have lived up to community expectations. A number of them were headed for trouble. A few were not.

Jack and Herb were the athletes among the Roughnecks and their athletic prowess paid off handsomely. Both boys received unsolicited athletic scholarships to college. After Herb received his scholarship (near the end of his senior year), he apparently did an about-face. His demeanor became very similar to that of the Saints. Although he remained a member in good standing of the Roughnecks, he stopped participating in most activities and did not hang on the corner as often.

Jack did not change. If anything, he became more prone to fighting. He even made excuses for accepting the scholarship. He told the gang members that the school had guaranteed him a "C" average if he would come to play football—an idea that seems far-fetched, even in this day of highly competitive recruiting.

During the summer after graduation from high school, Jack attempted suicide by jumping from a tall building. The jump would certainly have killed most people trying it, but Jack survived. He entered college in the fall and played four years of football. He and Herb graduated in four years, and both are teaching and coaching in high schools. They are married and have stable families. If anything, Jack appears to have a more prestigious position in the community than does Herb, though both are well respected and secure in their positions.

Two of the boys never finished high school. Tommy left at the end of his junior year and went to another state. That summer he was arrested and placed on probation on a manslaughter charge. Three years later he was arrested for murder; he pleaded guilty to second degree murder and is serving a 30-year sentence in the state penitentiary.

Al, the other boy who did not finish high school, also left the state in his senior year. He is serving a life sentence in a state penitentiary for first degree murder.

Wes is a small-time gambler. He finished high school and "bummed around." After several years he made contact with a bookmaker who employed him as runner. Later he acquired his own area and has been working it ever since. His position among the bookmakers is almost identical to the position he had in the gang; he is always around but no one is really aware of him. He makes no trouble and he does not get into any. Steady, reliable, capable of keeping his mouth closed, he plays the game by the rules, even though the game is an illegal one.

That leaves only Ron. Some of his former friends reported that they had heard he was "driving a truck up north," but no one could provide any concrete information.

Reinforcement

The community responded to the Roughnecks as boys in trouble, and the boys agreed with that perception. Their pattern of deviancy was reinforced, and breaking away from it became increasingly unlikely. Once the boys acquired an image of themselves as deviants, they selected new friends who affirmed that self-image. As that self-conception became more firmly entrenched, they also became willing to try new and more extreme deviances. With their growing alienation came freer expression of disrespect and hostility for representatives of the legitimate society. This disrespect increased the community's negativism, perpetuating the entire process of commitment to deviance. Lack of a commitment to deviance works the same way. In either case, the process will perpetuate itself unless some event (like a scholarship to college or a sudden failure) external to the established relationship intervenes. For two of the Roughnecks (Herb and Jack), receiving college athletic scholarships created new relations and culminated in a break with the established pattern of deviance. In the case of one of the Saints (Jerry), his parents' divorce and his failing to graduate from high school changed some of his other relations. Being held back in school for a year and losing his place among the Saints had sufficient impact on Jerry to alter his self-image and virtually to assure that he would not go on to college as his peers did. Although the experiments of life can rarely be reversed, it seems likely in view of the behavior of the other boys who did not enjoy this special treatment by the school that Jerry, too, would have "become something" had he graduated as anticipated. For Herb and Jack outside intervention worked to their advantage; for Jerry it was his undoing.

Selective perception and labelling—finding, processing and punishing some kinds of criminality and not others—means that visible, poor, nonmobile, outspoken, undiplomatic "tough" kids will be noticed, whether their actions are seriously delinquent or not. Other kids, who have established a reputation for being bright (even though underachieving), disciplined and involved in respectable activities, who are mobile and monied, will be invisible when they deviate from sanctioned activities. They'll sow their wild oats—perhaps even wider and thicker than their lower-class cohorts—but they won't be noticed. When it's time to leave adolescence most will follow the expected path, settling into the ways of the middle class, remembering fondly the delinquent but unnoticed fling of their youth. The Roughnecks and others like them may turn around, too. It is more likely that their noticeable deviance will have been so reinforced by police and community that their lives will be effectively channelled into careers consistent with their adolescent background.

Questions

1. Why were the Saints seen as good boys and the Roughnecks seen as bad boys?

2. The conventional wisdom is that criminals are different from noncriminals, that bad things are done by bad people. To what extent does the information presented in Chambliss's article contradict the conventional wisdom?

3. In what specific way did differences in social class (for example, economic resources and cultural capital) contribute to the community's different treatment of and regard for the Saints and the Roughnecks?

4. What evidence do you find in this article that supports Merton's ideas about the self-fulfilling prophecy? What evidence seems to contradict it?

27

ON BEING SANE IN INSANE PLACES

D. L. Rosenhan

Although the following selection was written by a professor of psychology and law at Stanford University, it seems that everyone who publishes a reader for introductory sociology students includes this 1973 article (obviously, including me). There's a reason. Rosenhan's exploration of what happens to sane people in mental hospitals contains some important lessons about the impact of people's definition of the situation—especially the impact of the definitions of people in authority.

If sanity and insanity exist, how shall we know them?

The question is neither capricious nor itself insane. However much we may be personally convinced that we can tell the normal from the abnormal, the evidence is simply not compelling. It is commonplace, for example, to read about murder trials wherein eminent psychiatrists for the defense are contradicted by equally eminent psychiatrists for the prosecution on the matter of the defendant's sanity. More generally, there are a great deal of conflicting data on the reliability, utility, and meaning of such terms as "sanity," "insanity," "mental illness," and "schizophrenia." Finally, as early as 1934, Benedict suggested that normality and abnormality are not universal. What is viewed as normal in one culture may be seen as quite aberrant in another. Thus, notions of normality and abnormality may not be quite as accurate as people believe they are.

To raise questions regarding normality and abnormality is in no way to question the fact that some behaviors are deviant or odd.

Murder is deviant. So, too, are hallucinations. Nor does raising such questions deny the existence of the personal anguish that is often associated with "mental illness." Anxiety and depression exist. Psychological suffering exists. But normality and abnormality, sanity and insanity, and the diagnoses that flow from them may be less substantive than many believe them to be.

At its heart, the question of whether the sane can be distinguished from the insane (and whether degrees of insanity can be distinguished from each other) is a simple matter: do the salient characteristics that lead to diagnoses reside in the patients themselves or in the environments and contexts in which observers find them? From Bleuler[1] through

---

[1]Paul Eugen Bleuler (1857–1939) was a Swiss psychiatrist who, in 1911, introduced the term *schizophrenia* (from the Greek *shizo*, "split or cleave," and *phren*, "mind") to refer to a form of dementia (madness). Today, schizophrenia refers to a general pathology characterized by disturbance of thinking, mood, and behavior (including inappropriate emotional responses and lack of empathy), and sometimes hallucinations and delusions. It is thought to afflict more than 2 million Americans, and "about half of the available hospital beds for the mentally ill (or about one-quarter of available beds in all U.S. hospitals) are occupied by patients diagnosed as schizophrenic" (Philip M. Groves and George V. Rebec, *Introduction to Biological Psychology*. [Dubuque, IA: Brown, 1988], p. 479).—Ed.

the formulators of the recently revised *Diagnostic and Statistical Manual* of the American Psychiatric Association, the belief has been strong that patients present symptoms, that those symptoms can be categorized, and, implicitly, that the sane are distinguishable from the insane. More recently, however, this belief has been questioned. Based in part on theoretical and anthropological considerations, but also on philosophical, legal, and therapeutic ones, the view has grown that psychological categorization of mental illness is useless at best and downright harmful, misleading, and pejorative at worst. Psychiatric diagnoses, in this view, are in the minds of the observers and are not valid summaries of characteristics displayed by the observed.

Gains can be made in deciding which of these is more nearly accurate by getting normal people (that is, people who do not have, and have never suffered, symptoms of serious psychiatric disorders) admitted to psychiatric hospitals and then determining whether they were discovered to be sane and, if so, how. If the sanity of such pseudopatients were always detected, there would be prima facie[2] evidence that a sane individual can be distinguished from the insane context in which he is found. Normality (and presumably abnormality) is distinct enough that it can be recognized wherever it occurs, for it is carried within the person. If, on the other hand, the sanity of the pseudopatients were never discovered, serious difficulties would arise for those who support traditional modes of psychiatric diagnosis. Given that the hospital staff was not incompetent, that the pseudopatient had been behaving as sanely as he had been outside of the hospital, and that it had never been previously suggested that he belonged in a psychiatric hospital, such an unlikely outcome

would support the view that psychiatric diagnosis betrays little about the patient but much about the environment in which an observer finds him.

This article describes such an experiment. Eight sane people gained secret admission to 12 different hospitals. . . .

Pseudopatients and Their Settings

The eight pseudopatients were a varied group. One was a psychology graduate student in his 20's. The remaining seven were older and "established." Among them were three psychologists, a pediatrician, a psychiatrist, a painter, and a housewife. Three pseudopatients were women, five were men. All of them employed pseudonyms, lest their alleged diagnoses embarrass them later. Those who were in mental health professions alleged another occupation in order to avoid the special attentions that might be accorded by staff, as a matter of courtesy or caution, to ailing colleagues. With the exception of myself (I was the first pseudopatient and my presence was known to the hospital administrator and chief psychologist and, so far as I can tell, to them alone), the presence of pseudopatients and the nature of the research program was not known to the hospital staffs.

The settings were similarly varied. In order to generalize the findings, admission into a variety of hospitals was sought. The 12 hospitals in the sample were located in five different states on the East and West coasts. Some were old and shabby, some were quite new. Some were research-oriented, others not. Some had good staff–patient ratios, others were quite understaffed. Only one was a strictly private hospital. All of the others were supported by state or federal funds or, in one instance, by university funds.

After calling the hospital for an appointment, the pseudopatient arrived at the

---

[2]*Prima facie,* from the Latin, means "at first sight." Prima facie evidence of something is regarded as apparently valid evidence.—Ed.

admissions office complaining that he had been hearing voices. Asked what the voices said, he replied that they were often unclear, but as far as he could tell they said "empty," "hollow," and "thud." The voices were unfamiliar and were of the same sex as the pseudopatient. The choice of these symptoms was occasioned by their apparent similarity to existential symptoms. Such symptoms are alleged to arise from painful concerns about the perceived meaninglessness of one's life. It is as if the hallucinating person were saying, "My life is empty and hollow." The choice of these symptoms was also determined by the *absence* of a single report of existential psychoses in the literature.

Beyond alleging the symptoms and falsifying name, vocation, and employment, no further alterations of person, history, or circumstances were made. The significant events of the pseudopatient's life history were presented as they had actually occurred. Relationships with parents and siblings, with spouse and children, with people at work and in school, consistent with the aforementioned exceptions, were described as they were or had been. Frustrations and upsets were described along with joys and satisfactions. These facts are important to remember. If anything, they strongly biased the subsequent results in favor of detecting sanity, since none of their histories or current behaviors were seriously pathological in any way.

Immediately upon admission to the psychiatric ward, the pseudopatient ceased simulating *any* symptoms of abnormality. In some cases, there was a brief period of mild nervousness and anxiety, since none of the pseudopatients really believed that they would be admitted so easily. Indeed, their shared fear was that they would be immediately exposed as frauds and greatly embarrassed. Moreover, many of them had never visited a psychiatric ward; even those who had, nevertheless had some genuine fears about what might happen

to them. Their nervousness, then, was quite appropriate to the novelty of the hospital setting, and it abated rapidly.

Apart from that short-lived nervousness, the pseudopatient behaved on the ward as he "normally" behaved. The pseudopatient spoke to patients and staff as he might ordinarily. Because there is uncommonly little to do on a psychiatric ward, he attempted to engage others in conversation. When asked by staff how he was feeling, he indicated that he was fine, that he no longer experienced symptoms. He responded to instructions from attendants, to calls for medication (which was not swallowed),[3] and to dining-hall instructions. Beyond such activities as were available to him on the admissions ward, he spent his time writing down his observations about the ward, its patients, and the staff. Initially these notes were written "secretly," but as it soon became clear that no one much cared, they were subsequently written on standard tablets of paper in such public places as the dayroom. No secret was made of these activities.

The pseudopatient, very much as a true psychiatric patient, entered a hospital with no fore-knowledge of when he would be discharged. Each was told that he would have to get out by his own devices, essentially by convincing the staff that he was sane. The psychological stresses associated with hospitalization

---

[3]In part of the article not included in this excerpt, Rosenhan notes that over the course of their hospitalization, "the pseudopatients were administered nearly 2100 pills, including Elavil, Stelazine, Compazine, and Thorazine, to name a few. (That such a variety of medications should have been administered to patients presenting identical symptoms is itself worthy of note.) Only two were swallowed. The rest were either pocketed or deposited in the toilet. The pseudopatients were not alone in this. Although I have no precise records on how many patients rejected their medications, the pseudopatients frequently found the medications of other patients in the toilets before they deposited their own. As long as they were cooperative, their behavior and the pseudopatients' own in this matter, as in other important matters, went unnoticed throughout."—Ed.

were considerable, and all but one of the pseudopatients desired to be discharged almost immediately after being admitted. They were, therefore, motivated not only to behave sanely, but to be paragons of cooperation. That their behavior was in no way disruptive is confirmed by nursing reports, which have been obtained on most of the patients. These reports uniformly indicate that the patients were "friendly," "cooperative," and "exhibited no abnormal indications."

The Normal Are Not Detectably Sane

Despite their public "show" of sanity, the pseudopatients were never detected. Admitted, except in one case, with a diagnosis of schizophrenia, each was discharged with a diagnosis of schizophrenia "in remission." The label "in remission" should in no way be dismissed as a formality, for at no time during any hospitalization had any question been raised about any pseudopatient's simulation. Nor are there any indications in the hospital records that the pseudopatient's status was suspect. Rather, the evidence is strong that, once labeled schizophrenic, the pseudopatient was stuck with that label. If the pseudopatient was to be discharged, he must naturally be "in remission"; but he was not sane, nor, in the institution's view, had he ever been sane.

The uniform failure to recognize sanity cannot be attributed to the quality of the hospitals, for, although there were considerable variations among them, several are considered excellent. Nor can it be alleged that there was simply not enough time to observe the pseudopatients. Length of hospitalization ranged from 7 to 52 days, with an average of 19 days. The pseudopatients were not, in fact, carefully observed, but this failure clearly speaks more to traditions within psychiatric hospitals than to lack of opportunity.

Finally, it cannot be said that the failure to recognize the pseudopatients' sanity was due to the fact that they were not behaving sanely. While there was clearly some tension present in all of them, their daily visitors could detect no serious behavioral consequences—nor, indeed, could other patients. It was quite common for the patients to "detect" the pseudopatients' sanity. During the first three hospitalizations, when accurate counts were kept, 35 of a total of 118 patients on the admissions ward voiced their suspicions, some vigorously. "You're not crazy. You're a journalist, or a professor [referring to the continual notetaking]. You're checking up on the hospital." While most of the patients were reassured by the pseudopatient's insistence that he had been sick before he came in but was fine now, some continued to believe that the pseudopatient was sane throughout his hospitalization. The fact that the patients often recognized normality when staff did not raises important questions.

Failure to detect sanity during the course of hospitalization may be due to the fact that physicians . . . are more inclined to call a healthy person sick (a false positive) than a sick person healthy (a false negative). The reasons for this are not hard to find: it is clearly more dangerous to misdiagnose illness than health. Better to err on the side of caution, to suspect illness even among the healthy.

But what holds for medicine does not hold equally well for psychiatry. Medical illnesses, while unfortunate, are not commonly pejorative. Psychiatric diagnoses, on the contrary, carry with them personal, legal, and social stigmas. It was therefore important to see whether the tendency toward diagnosing the sane insane could be reversed. The following experiment was arranged at a research and teaching hospital whose staff had heard these findings but doubted that such an error could occur in their hospital. The staff was informed that at some time during the following

3 months, one or more pseudopatients would attempt to be admitted into the psychiatric hospital. Each staff member was asked to rate each patient who presented himself at admissions or on the ward according to the likelihood that the patient was a pseudopatient. A 10-point scale was used, with a 1 and 2 reflecting high confidence that the patient was a pseudopatient.

Judgments were obtained on 193 patients who were admitted for psychiatric treatment. All staff who had had sustained contact with or primary responsibility for the patient—attendants, nurses, psychiatrists, physicians, and psychologists—were asked to make judgments. Forty-one patients were alleged, with high confidence, to be pseudopatients by at least one member of the staff. Twenty-three were considered suspect by at least one psychiatrist. Nineteen were suspected by one psychiatrist *and* one other staff member. Actually, no genuine pseudopatient (at least from my group) presented himself during this period.

The experiment is instructive. It indicates that the tendency to designate sane people as insane can be reversed when the stakes (in this case, prestige and diagnostic acumen) are high. But what can be said of the 19 people who were suspected of being "sane" by one psychiatrist and another staff member? Were these people truly "sane," or was it rather the case that in the course of avoiding the false positive error the staff tended to make more errors of the false negative sort—calling the crazy "sane"? There is no way of knowing. But one thing is certain: any diagnostic process that lends itself so readily to massive errors of this sort cannot be a very reliable one.

The Stickiness of Psychodiagnostic Labels

Beyond the tendency to call the healthy sick—a tendency that accounts better for diagnostic behavior on admission than it does for such behavior after a lengthy period of exposure—the data speak to the massive role of labeling in psychiatric assessment. Having once been labeled schizophrenic, there is nothing the pseudopatient can do to overcome the tag. The tag profoundly colors others' perceptions of him and his behavior.

From one viewpoint, these data are hardly surprising, for it has long been known that elements are given meaning by the context in which they occur. Gestalt psychology made this point vigorously, and Asch demonstrated that there are "central" personality traits (such as "warm" versus "cold") which are so powerful that they markedly color the meaning of other information in forming an impression of a given personality. "Insane," "schizophrenic," "manic-depressive," and "crazy" are probably among the most powerful of such central traits. Once a person is designated abnormal, all of his other behaviors and characteristics are colored by that label. Indeed, that label is so powerful that many of the pseudopatients' normal behaviors were overlooked entirely or profoundly misinterpreted. Some examples may clarify this issue.

Earlier I indicated that there were no changes in the pseudopatient's personal history and current status beyond those of name, employment, and, where necessary, vocation. Otherwise, a veridical description of personal history and circumstances was offered. Those circumstances were not psychotic. How were they made consonant with the diagnosis of psychosis? Or were those diagnoses modified in such a way as to bring them into accord with the circumstances of the pseudopatient's life, as described by him?

As far as I can determine, diagnoses were in no way affected by the relative health of the circumstances of a pseudopatient's life. Rather, the reverse occurred: the perception of his circumstances was shaped entirely by the diagnosis. A clear example of such translation is found in the case of a pseudopatient who had had a close relationship with his mother but was rather remote from his father during his early childhood. During adolescence and beyond, however, his father became a close friend, while his relationship with his mother cooled. His present relationship with his wife was characteristically close and warm. Apart from occasional angry exchanges, friction was minimal. The children had rarely been spanked. Surely there is nothing especially pathological about such a history. Indeed, many readers may see a similar pattern in their own experiences with no markedly deleterious consequences. Observe, however, how such a history was translated in the psychopathological context, this from the case summary prepared after the patient was discharged.

> This white 39-year-old male . . . manifests a long history of considerable ambivalence in close relationships, which begins in early childhood. A warm relationship with his mother cools during his adolescence. A distant relationship to his father is described as becoming very intense. Affective[4] stability is absent. His attempts to control emotionality with his wife and children are punctuated by angry outbursts and, in the case of the children, spankings. And while he says that he has several good friends, one senses considerable ambivalence embedded in those relationships also. . . .

The facts of the case were unintentionally distorted by the staff to achieve consistency with a popular theory of the dynamics of a schizophrenic reaction. Nothing of an ambivalent nature had been described in relations with parents, spouse, or friends. To the extent that ambivalence could be inferred, it was probably not greater than is found in all human relationships. It is true the pseudopatient's relationships with his parents changed over time, but in the ordinary context that would hardly be remarkable—indeed, it might very well be

expected. Clearly, the meaning ascribed to his verbalizations (that is, ambivalence, affective instability) was determined by the diagnosis: schizophrenia. An entirely different meaning would have been ascribed if it were known that the man was "normal."

All pseudopatients took extensive notes publicly. Under ordinary circumstances, such behavior would have raised questions in the minds of observers, as, in fact, it did among patients. Indeed, it seemed so certain that the notes would elicit suspicion that elaborate precautions were taken to remove them from the ward each day. But the precautions proved needless. The closest any staff member came to questioning these notes occurred when one pseudopatient asked his physician what kind of medication he was receiving and began to write down the response. "You needn't write it," he was told gently. "If you have trouble remembering, just ask me again."

If no questions were asked of the pseudopatients, how was their writing interpreted? Nursing records for three patients indicate that the writing was seen as an aspect of their pathological behavior. "Patient engages in writing behavior" was the daily nursing comment on one of the pseudopatients who was never questioned about his writing. Given that the patient is in the hospital, he must be psychologically disturbed. And given that he is disturbed, continuous writing must be a behavioral manifestation of that disturbance, perhaps a subset of the compulsive behaviors that are sometimes correlated with schizophrenia.

One tacit characteristic of psychiatric diagnosis is that it locates the sources of aberration within the individual and only rarely within the complex of stimuli that surrounds him. Consequently, behaviors that are stimulated by the environment are commonly misattributed to the patient's disorder. For example, one kindly nurse found a pseudopatient pacing the long hospital corridors. "Nervous, Mr. X?" she asked. "No, bored," he said.

---

[4]*Affective* means "emotional."—Ed.

The notes kept by pseudopatients are full of patient behaviors that were misinterpreted by well-intentioned staff. Often enough, a patient would go "berserk" because he had, wittingly or unwittingly, been mistreated by, say, an attendant. A nurse coming upon the scene would rarely inquire even cursorily into the environmental stimuli of the patient's behavior. Rather, she assumed that his upset derived from his pathology, not from his present interactions with other staff members. Occasionally, the staff might assume that the patient's family (especially when they had recently visited) or other patients had stimulated the outburst. But never were the staff found to assume that one of themselves or the structure of the hospital had anything to do with a patient's behavior. One psychiatrist pointed to a group of patients who were sitting outside the cafeteria entrance half an hour before lunchtime. To a group of young residents he indicated that such behavior was characteristic of the oral-acquisitive nature of the syndrome. It seemed not to occur to him that there were very few things to anticipate in a psychiatric hospital besides eating.

A psychiatric label has a life and an influence of its own. Once the impression has been formed that the patient is schizophrenic, the expectation is that he will continue to be schizophrenic. When a sufficient amount of time has passed, during which the patient has done nothing bizarre, he is considered to be in remission and available for discharge. But the label endures beyond discharge, with the unconfirmed expectation that he will behave as a schizophrenic again. Such labels, conferred by mental health professionals, are as influential on the patient as they are on his relatives and friends, and it should not surprise anyone that the diagnosis acts on all of them as a self-fulfilling prophecy.[5] Eventually, the patient himself accepts the diagnosis, with all of its surplus meanings and expectations, and behaves accordingly.

The inferences to be made from these matters are quite simple. Much as Zigler and Phillips have demonstrated that there is enormous overlap in the symptoms presented by patients who have been variously diagnosed, so there is enormous overlap in the behaviors of the sane and the insane. The sane are not "sane" all of the time. We lose our tempers "for no good reason." We are occasionally depressed or anxious, again for no good reason. And we may find it difficult to get along with one or another person—again for no reason that we can specify. Similarly, the insane are not always insane. Indeed, it was the impression of the pseudopatients while living with them that they were sane for long periods of time—that the bizarre behaviors upon which their diagnoses were allegedly predicated constituted only a small fraction of their total behavior. . . .

The Consequences of Labeling and Depersonalization

Whenever the ratio of what is known to what needs to be known approaches zero, we tend to invent "knowledge" and assume that we understand more than we actually do. We seem unable to acknowledge that we simply don't know. The needs for diagnosis and remediation of behavioral and emotional problems are enormous. But rather than acknowledge that we are just embarking on understanding, we continue to label patients "schizophrenic," "manic-depressive," and "insane," as if in those words we had captured the essence of understanding. The facts of the matter are that we have known for a long time that diagnoses are often not useful or reliable, but we have nevertheless continued to use them. We now know that we cannot distinguish insanity

---

[5]See the introductory notes to reading 27, "The Saints and the Roughnecks," for an explanation of this concept.—Ed.

from sanity. It is depressing to consider how that information will be used.

Not merely depressing, but frightening. How many people, one wonders, are sane but not recognized as such in our psychiatric institutions? How many have been needlessly stripped of their privileges of citizenship, from the right to vote and drive to that of handling their own accounts? How many have feigned insanity in order to avoid the criminal consequences of their behavior, and, conversely, how many would rather stand trial than live interminably in a psychiatric hospital—but are wrongly thought to be mentally ill? How many have been stigmatized by well-intentioned, but nevertheless erroneous, diagnoses? On the last point, recall again that a false positive error in psychiatric diagnosis does not have the same consequences it does in medical diagnosis. A diagnosis of cancer that has been found to be in error is cause for celebration. But psychiatric diagnoses are rarely found to be in error. The label sticks, a mark of inadequacy forever. . . .

Questions

1. With which of the following statements would Rosenhan agree, and why?
   a. In this study, the symptoms observed by the psychiatric staff led to the diagnosis.
   b. In this study, the diagnosis led to the symptoms observed by the psychiatric staff.

2. What might be the significance of the fact that many *patients* managed to detect pseudopatients while none of the staff did?

3. Why does a false diagnosis of mental illness generally have more serious repercussions than a false diagnosis of physical illness?

28

POWER, STATUS, AND ABUSE AT WORK

General and Sexual Harassment

Steven H. Lopez, Randy Hodson,
and Vincent J. Roscigno*

As norms and values change over time, so too does the nature of deviance. Behaviors that were once tolerated (slavery, child abuse, smoking) may become subject to negative sanctions. In this article the authors investigated the nature of a behavior that only recently has come to be seen as deviant harassment in the workplace. Their focus, however, is not on the individuals who harass, but on how certain kinds of organizational structures may encourage or discourage "incivility" in the workplace.

Workplace harassment can be devastating, seriously harming individuals *and* organizations by undermining norms of civility and mutual respect (Ashforth 1994). In legal terms, such injuries are termed *dignitary harm* (Kleinschmidt 2005), and studies report that between 10 and 20 percent of employees are subjected to it each year (Rayner, Hoel, and Cooper 2002:23; Zapf et al. 2003:105–108). Moreover, the resulting shame and despair often last long after the harassment has ended (Hodson 2001; Vaez, Ekberg, and LaFlamme 2004).

The workplace is an arena rife with power differentials that are at the core of many forms of abusive workplace behavior (Walker and Zelditch 1993). Yet, various types of workplace harassment are, more often than not, examined separately rather than comparatively, and

within distinct, nonoverlapping literatures. Consequently, how unique forms of workplace harassment relate to one another is not well understood. In particular, not enough is known about the extent to which different kinds of workplace harassment stem from the same or unique underlying causes—a question with important implications for prevention.

In this article, we address the aforementioned question and extend the literature by comparing *general workplace harassment* with *workplace sexual harassment*. We adapt the "routine activities" model of deviance to organizational contexts, and then estimate the resulting model with content-coded data from the population of workplace ethnographies. We conclude by discussing the implications of our integrated approach for understanding workplace harassment and in its various forms.

General and Sexual Harassment

Many scholars explicitly note commonalities between workplace bullying and on-the-job sexual harassment, both in terms of the

*Direct all correspondence to Steven H. Lopez, Department of Sociology, Ohio State University, Columbus, OH 43210; e-mail: Lopez.137@sociology.osu.edu

Steven H. Lopez, Randy Hodson, and Vincent J. Roscigno, "Power, Status, and Abuse At Work: General and Sexual Harassment," *The Sociological Quarterly* Vol. 50, Issue 1 (2009): 3–27 © 2009 Midwest Sociological Society. Reprinted by permission of John Wiley & Sons, Inc.

constituent behaviors and in terms of emotional, health, and employment consequences. At the same time, however, these can be experienced as distinctly different forms of victimization. How can we disentangle these phenomena? On one hand, cross-national differences in harassment law help to explain why people articulate and act on claims of sexual harassment in some contexts and general harassment in others. In some countries, such as the United States, sexual harassment has a clear legal definition it is a civil offense and the employer is potentially liable while general harassment is not illegal.[1] In other countries, both categories of behavior are against the law. In France, for example, sexual harassment is defined narrowly (in terms of the use of coercion by a superior to obtain sexual favors), and it is a criminal matter. In fact, if convicted, an offender may face fines and even jail time while the employer is nonliable (Saguy 2000, 2003). On the other hand, general harassment is a civil offense in France, for which the employer *is* liable. Thus, employees seeking damages may be more likely to frame and pursue claims of sexual harassment in the United States and general harassment in France.

Assessing these kinds of differences is important, but in this article, we take a different approach. While we recognize that what is considered general or sexual harassment is socially constructed and may vary from place to place, we seek to define and explore general and sexual harassment as analytically distinct varieties of workplace harassment, based on detailed empirical descriptions of actual behaviors rather than legal claimsmaking.

GENERAL WORKPLACE HARASSMENT

General workplace harassment is typically defined as expressions of disrespect and hostility that are intended to harm the target (Skarlicki and Kulik 2005). Such behaviors range from staring, dirty looks, belittling statements, ostracism, and ridicule, up to threats and physical violence (Ehrenreich 1999). It does not involve targeting victims because of their gender but rather emerges out of the hierarchical power relations and struggles for power in the workplace.

Interpersonal conflict in organizations, of course, is not new and was a central concern among the earliest sociological theorists. Marx's ([1844] 1964) critique of capitalism conveys much of its moral power through examples of interpersonal abuse and demeaning of workers by individual owners. Similarly, Weber's (1968) writings on bureaucracy are underwritten by his concern for legitimate versus illegitimate power. Contemporary sociological theory and industrial sociology includes a running commentary on conflict and the abuse of interpersonal power in organizations (see Perrow 1986; Jacoby 2004). Classic writings in this tradition include Blau (1955) on government clerks, Gouldner (1964) on management in a gypsum plant, Walker, Guest, and Turner (1956) on middle managers, Van Maanen (1977) on policing, and Morrill (1995) on executives.

Emerging analytic interest in general harassment, or bullying, adds to this body of work by focusing on the reification of formal and informal status hierarchies through the humiliation and even annihilation of victims—victims who are, more often than not, already occupying structurally or socially weak positions. Job insecurity and organizational chaos, in particular, have been implicated as organizational conditions leading to a heightened likelihood of supervisory bullying and general harassment. Job insecurity can lead to general harassment through a shortened shadow of the future that reduces the consequences of current actions. Chaos can create an environment in which bullying is substituted for coherent work procedures.

SEXUAL HARASSMENT

Although there is cross-national variation in the legal definition, sexual harassment is generally defined as behavior that violates, derogates, demeans, or humiliates an individual based on sex or gender. It is not simply an organic outgrowth of hierarchical organizational power relations but rather is connected to a larger gender stratification project.

Researchers interested in sexual harassment have developed three major theories attempting to explain this phenomenon: male dominance, gender-role spillover, and sex ratio theories. Theories that stress *male dominance* argue that men use sexual harassment to maintain their own power in the workplace. Sexualizing relations with female coworkers, for example, reduces them to sexual objects and diminishes their role as colleagues, thus reinforcing male power and privilege (Acker 1990; Gruber 1998; Uggen and Blackstone 2004). Alternatively, the maintenance of male power and dominance may lead men to harass other men as when they delegitimate male coworkers by "feminizing" them or by coercively enforcing dominant gender norms (see, e.g., Sallaz 2002).

Gender-role spillover theories suggest that men harass women because they are accustomed to dealing with women in a subordinate role in the domestic and social spheres and this behavior carries over into the workplace. Thus, the subordinate feminine role, defined originally and principally in the home, carries over into the workplace and creates scripts for both men and women about how they should interact scripts that allow or even facilitate sexual harassment.

A third approach to sexual harassment is based on the observation that workplaces vary greatly in the ratio of men to women. Numeric dominance theories suggest that sex ratios heavily skewed in either direction can produce greater sexual harassment because

gender becomes more visible in such settings (Gruber 1998). In heavily female occupational settings, such as secretarial work or waitressing, the femininity of the incumbents becomes highlighted, leading to a greater potential for sexual harassment. Conversely, in heavily male occupational settings, such as construction or law, female entrants may be visible and harassed because of the potential threat they bring to male jobs and occupational identities (DiTomaso 1989).

COMMONALITIES AND DIFFERENCES

Perhaps the most important commonality between generalized and sexual harassment is that each rests on the defense of power (Walker and Zelditch 1993). Both also involve a process of demeaning the dignity of the other in order to protect or elevate one's own status and identity (Molm 1997). Both capture processes of status hierarchy maintenance. And sadly, the consequences are also similar. Both generalized harassment and sexual harassment can result in devastating emotional, psychological, and even health consequences for those victimized (Berdahl 2007). But what are the differences, and are the same organizational factors associated with each? Below, we present a routine activities model of organizational behavior that offers a useful framework for articulating these questions systematically.

Routine Activities in Organizations

The possibility that general and sexual harassment emerge in specific organizational contexts suggests the need for clearer conceptualization of the links between organizational structures, on the one hand, and patterns of incivility on the other. The "routine activities" model a perspective originally developed for studies of criminal deviance provides a useful heuristic, denoting how interpersonal crime, deviance, or abuse occurs when motivated offenders converge with suitable targets, especially in the absence of capable guardians (Cohen and Felson 1979). The term "routine activities" references the idea that the everyday activities of victims, perpetrators, and potential guardians serve as a starting point for understanding opportunities for deviance, or harassment in the current case.

A routine activities model brings theoretical leverage to the analysis of workplace harassment by simultaneously highlighting (1) organizational factors leading to the identification of potential victims, (2) organizational factors encouraging potential perpetrators. Perhaps more importantly, it also moves beyond victims and perpetrators to also consider, and (3) the role of potential guardians in this case organizational actors or structures that can act to prevent, disrupt, or otherwise block emerging patterns of incivility and harassment.[2]

VICTIMS

A range of social theories suggest that powerlessness and low relative status are core determinants of victimization and general assaults on one's dignity at work (Blau 1964; Jacoby 2004). *Job insecurity,* an important aspect of powerlessness in the workplace, may be influential. Indeed, a commonly cited cause for the reported upswing in bullying is the increasingly insecure job environment brought about by corporate restructuring and outsourcing (Hearn and Parkin 2001). In this environment, top management bullies middle management to implement aggressive cost cutting and middle management passes on the abuse to frontline workers (Vaez et al. 2004). Job insecurity may also create a "shortened shadow of the future" under which people feel less constrained to act civilly because of

reduced expectations of having a relationship in the future. One question our analysis below explores, therefore, is whether job insecurity predicts both general and sexual harassment, or whether it is more strongly associated with one or the other.

Minority workforces may also be more vulnerable to general workplace harassment (Salin 2003)—quite apart from *racially motivated harassment* (an analysis of which is beyond the scope of the current article). To the extent that minority workers are less powerful than white workers, they make especially vulnerable targets for *general* harassment (Williams and O'Reilly 1998; Zapf et al. 2003). General harassment may be easier to commit against minority workers because these employees already face a certain degree of social isolation and exclusion (Tsui and Gutek 1999). But this also raises the question: is sexual harassment more severe in the context of minority female workforces? In other words, are minority workforces equally vulnerable to general and sexual harassment?

PERPETRATORS

Many aspects of organizational structure and culture may well act as important facilitators of incivility and harassment. We focus on two such organizational features that can create motivations for potential perpetrators: *chaotic organizational procedures* and the *physicality* of the work.

An important potential source of harassment is *chaos in workplace* procedures. Coherent organizational procedures are essential for organizational effectiveness and for the maintenance of civility and mutual respect in the workplace (Hegtvedt and Johnson 2000). Employees generally want to do their jobs well for a variety of reasons, including pride in work, a sense of accomplishment, and personal career advancement. Chaotic workplaces and mismanagement interfere with these important goals. Ambiguity (Zapf et al. 2003), weak supervisors (Vartia 1996), and mismanagement (Hodson 2001; Skarlicki and Kulik 2005) have all been identified as potentially underwriting abusive behavior in organizations. In contexts without clear protocols and procedures, supervisory discretion complete with subjective biases and informal efforts at bolstering individual status and power—can come to prevail, and effective management can quickly be overtaken by yelling and abuse (Walker and Zelditch 1993; Molm 1997). It is thus clear how organizational chaos might contribute to general harassment but what about sexual harassment? Might not organizational chaos also provide cover, or opportunities, for this form of harassment?

A second dimension of work that may contribute to incivility is the normative character of work life in settings defined by *physically demanding work.* Difficult manual work in traditional male work environments is often associated with a culture of male solidarity and pride (Welsh 1999). In such contexts, female employees may be perceived as threats to men's masculine work identity (Berdahl 2007), resulting in efforts toward social closure including, but not limited to, sexual harassment and abuse (DiTomaso 1989). The sexual harassment literature also suggests that an emphasis on physical prowess and the body can highlight sexuality, further encouraging sexual harassment (Ragins and Scandura 1995). But one can also ask whether physical work and masculine work cultures might not also encourage general harassment as part of a culture of machismo and personal confrontation.

Chaotic procedures and highly physical work can thus create organizational environments that allow or even encourage potential harassers. A core question, which our analyses tackle, is whether organizational chaos and physical work are equally facilitative of general and sexual harassment.

GUARDIANS

Organizational attributes, such as those mentioned previously, may be conducive to workplace incivility and abuse, but it is equally important to recognize the possibility of deterrence effects in contexts where a "capable guardian" is present. The literature on "organizational justice" has recently begun to recognize and investigate the role of such third parties in the pursuit of workplace fairness (see Skarlicki and Kulik 2005). Two of the most important protective mechanisms in this regard, relative to the employment context, are *grievance procedures* and *workteams.*

The existence of in-place *grievance procedures* may deter incivility by providing an outside authority to exercise preventative social control. Such deterrence may be particularly important for limiting sexual harassment because of the existence of laws and regulations specifically outlawing it. Workplaces with grievance procedures may also regulate and control the behavior among employees more extensively. As such, grievance procedures may mitigate general as well as sexual harassment. Evidence on this possibility, however, is mixed. Indeed, some research suggests that grievance procedures may simply be "window dressing" to circumvent organizational culpability in lawsuits (Kalev, Dobbin, and Kelly 2006) or may actually work against victims and organizational whistle-blowers (Edelman 1990, 1992, 2002; Edelman, Fuller, and Mara-Drieta 2001).

A second organizational mechanism with the potential to provide guardianship against harassment is the *work team.* Employees are increasingly organized into work teams with significant components of self-management (Vallas 2006). The new rights and obligations given to these teams can translate into significantly changed interpersonal relations at work, generating both greater job satisfaction and greater stress (Smith 2001). The overall impact of teams on workplace harassment, however, has not been systematically investigated. It seems reasonable, however, to suspect that greater accountability and transparency associated with teams could produce pressures on members to not engage in either general or sexual harassment. Having to work closely with one another over time may, in fact, heighten the interpersonal costs of both kinds of harassment.

The conception offered previously helps us to move beyond the psychological characteristics of individual victims and toward identifying organizational structures that allow or facilitate harassment. Moreover, novel research questions are generated about the possibly distinct relationships between those structures and general and sexual harassment. Finally, the model also facilitates the investigation of workplace structures that may act as guardians to protect potential victims and preempt general and sexual harassment.

Data and Methods

Our analysis is based on content-coded qualitative data representing the full population of book-length organizational ethnographies. These data and our analyses are an attempt to meet organizational researchers' call for analytic techniques that combine the insights of quantitative and qualitative traditions for studying complex workplace issues and problems (see Tsui and Gutek 1999). Such methods are especially important for the study of sensitive organizational topics, such as interpersonal harassment, because survey or interview data are especially vulnerable to self-censorship, given fears of potential reprisals. Accordingly, direct observation and ethnographic techniques built on establishing a greater rapport are especially important for the study of sensitive organizational topics (see Mouly and Sankaran 1997).

ORGANIZATIONAL ETHNOGRAPHIES AS DATA: FROM NARRATIVE TO NUMBERS

Appropriate ethnographies were selected in a two-part procedure. First, the population of workplace ethnographies was identified via computer-assisted searches of archives and examination of the bibliographies of located ethnographies. The search ended when no new titles were generated for review. We also utilized a team of 20 experts to review our lists and suggest new titles.

The second phase of selection involved examining each book in detail. The final pool selected for coding conformed to three criteria: (1) data collection extending over a period of at least six months, (2) a focus on a single organizational setting, and (3) a focus on at least one clearly identifiable occupational group. The result is a set of cases with basic coverage of organizational, managerial, worker, and labor force characteristics for a particular work group in a particular organization. Of the books examined in detail, 158 met these criteria and were retained for analysis. Twenty-six books allowed the coding of multiple cases generating 204 ethnographic cases from the 158 published books.[3] The current analysis focuses on the subset of cases with data on both the dependent variables of interest general and sexual harassment. We *did not* assume that cases that did not discuss harassment explicitly were devoid of harassment. Rather, we choose the more conservative option of treating the data as missing and excluded such cases from the analysis. The sample for the current analysis is thus based on 110 ethnographies with good data on both general and sexual harassment.

A team of four researchers developed the coding instrument for the ethnographies. First, a list of variables and preliminary response categories representing core concepts in the workplace literature was generated. Second, each of the four team members individually read and coded a common selected ethnography, and then met to discuss consistencies and inconsistencies in their respective codings, the retention or removal of items, and the refinement of variables, response categories, and coding protocols. This process of reading, coding, and refinement was repeated for eight representative ethnographies. The goal was to create an instrument that trained coders could complete for each of the ethnographies with maximum reliability.

Once the coding instrument was finalized, the full set of ethnographies were read and coded by the same initial team of four researchers, participants in a yearlong graduate research practicum, and additional graduate research assistants supported through a National Science Foundation grant. All coders were trained to use a common protocol. Coders worked individually, documenting their conclusions with page numbers, and then met together to review each case in detail and to resolve questions. Where coders found contradictory information for particular variables, they discussed relevant passages with the team, which determined as a group how to code the item. To evaluate the reliability of the content-coding process, 13 percent of cases were coded a second time. The average intercorrelation between codings was .79, indicating a relatively high degree of intercoder agreement.[4]

MEASUREMENT

One of the benefits of analyzing content-coded narrative data is the ability to return to the original passages to illustrate the meanings of the concepts and the manner in which they are coded. A pattern of frequent *general harassment* of subordinate employees is reported in an ethnography of a Japanese apparel factory:

> There used to be a lot of malicious teasing. I cried a lot. . . . It was a supervisor a woman who was the mean one. . . . She yelled at us for brushing against the clothes that were hanging up in the changing room. . . . And if you were sewing labels on garments and you asked for some more, she would take a bunch and throw them at you, so they'd fall all over the place, and then you'd have to pick them up. It takes time to pick them up, and then you'd have to rush like crazy to catch up to your quota. I cried a lot. (Roberts 1994:61)

Sexual harassment is coded as a four-level variable: none, patronizing, taunting, and predatory. It is noteworthy that although the mean of sexual harassment is 2.15, the largest single category is "none." In 43 of the ethnographies (39 percent of cases), the ethnographic report clearly suggested that sexual harassment was absent or atypical. Although indications of the absence of a phenomenon must often be inferred indirectly, it was often possible to make such an inference from information provided on gender relations in the workplace. As an example, we interpreted the following description of relations between men and women in a counseling center as suggesting that sexual harassment would have been atypical. The ethnographer obviously could not be everywhere at all times, but for the period observed, the nature of workplace relations seems inconsistent with a pattern of widespread sexual harassment.

The staff at Helpline had made distinct efforts to see that the women in the organization had as much power as the men. The men on the staff had become self-conscious about interrupting when women were talking at meetings and not expecting women to become fund raisers or coordinators. . . . [Women] were as likely as the men to be chosen as someone whose judgment another would respect on an issue relating to Helpline (Mansbridge 1980:191–92).

Given the ethnographer's attention to gender relations, the absence of any reports of sexual harassment in this case suggest that it was not a widespread pattern.

Table 1 Variable Definitions (Organizational Ethnographies, N = 110)

Variable	Definition
Workplace incivility	
General harassment	(1) never, (2) rarely, (3) sometimes, (4) frequently, and (5) constantly
Sexual harassment	(1) none, (2) patronizing, (3) taunting, and (4) predatory
Victim characteristics	4 variable standardized scale
Job insecurity	1st and 2nd eigenvalues = 1.72 and .75; alpha = .61
Job security (r)	(1) none, (2) some, (3) average, and (4) high
Layoffs (r)	(1) never, (2) seldom, (3) sometimes, and (4) frequent
Firings	(0) no and (1) yes
Female percent	Percentage of female employees in work group
Minority percent	Percentage of minority employees in work group
Organizational context Chaos	4 variable standardized scale 1st and 2nd eigenvalues = 2.42 and .72; alpha = .78
Bad organization	(1) exceptional, (2) good, (3) adequate, (4) marginal, and (5) catastrophic
Communication	(1) good, (2) average, and (3) poor
Poor leadership	(1) exceptional, (2) good, (3) adequate, (4) marginal, and (5) catastrophic
Ill repair	(1) good repair, (2) average, and (3) poor
Physicality	(1) easy, (2) average, (3) difficult, and (4) brutal
Guardian characteristics Grievance system	(0) none and (1) union or company grievance committee
Team control	(0) no and (1) yes

Patronizing sexual harassment was reported in an ethnography of a British apparel factory: "As women, they were exposed to constant sexist patronization. . . . 'Hey gorgeous', 'Do us a favour, love', 'Come here sexy'—all are familiar addresses for most women" (Pollert 1981:142). Repeated episodes of *taunting* sexual harassment were observed in an ethnography of car sales. For example:

> So they invited me to a sales meeting . . . first time ever! And I felt like I had really made it. I go to this back room and all the guys are sitting around laughing. The local prostitute is up on the table doing a strip, shaking her ass, and they're looking at me for my reaction. (Lawson 2000:3)

The highest level of sexual harassment— *predatory*—was observed in 22 of the 110 ethnographies coded. A graphic example is provided by an ethnography of prison guards:

> Everyone here knows about Captain X. At first he tries his "come on," as if he's God's gift to women. If that fails, he threatens you with what he'll do if you don't cooperate. (Zimmer 1986:93)

The independent variables measuring victim characteristics, organization context, and guardian characteristics can also be illustrated using the passages that underlie their coding. For instance, *job insecurity* is measured as a scale based on job insecurity, frequent layoffs, and capricious firings. Frequent layoffs are illustrated in the following passage from an ethnography of an outsourcing plant in the home products industry:

> Factory owners cut costs by dramatically decreasing their labor force to minimum in the off-season. . . . One assembly factory had completely shut down its operation. The glass, box body, hardware, and other assembly factories only kept their insiders. Mr. Li's factory continued to operate with less than 40 percent of its peak-season labor force, having excluded all the outsiders. . . . It is by drastically cutting labor costs in this way that the owners can generate maximum profits. (Hsiung 1996:84)

The organizational factors that we hypothesize as supporting the emergence of perpetrators are organizational chaos and work that is physically demanding. *Chaos* is measured as a scale based on disorganization, poor communication, poor leadership, and disrepair. Poor repair, and the resulting disorganization, is illustrated in the following quote from an ethnography of a restaurant in the American Midwest:

> Cooks become frustrated when management forces them to work with poor-quality equipment, complicating their job, limiting what they can prepare, and lowering the esteem that others have of them. . . . The knobs on the stove burners do not turn properly; the only way to light a burner is to toss a match at it. . . . "It's terrible. We have the worst equipment." (Fine 1996:84)

We also hypothesize that extremely *physically demanding work* may contribute to an environment conducive to bullying and especially to sexual harassment. An example of physically demanding work is provided by an ethnography of firefighters:

> As firefighters are fond of saying, "We run into burning buildings while other people are running out." [Firefighting] requires an interior attack, in which firefighters actually enter the building, often forcibly, to face enormous heat, smoke, darkness, and flames in order to search for possible victims and to locate the seat of the fire and put it out. (Chetkovich 1997:21)

Organizational characteristics that can serve the role of providing third-party review and guardianship against harassment include the existence of a grievance procedure and organization of work into self-managing teams. The measurement of these characteristics is reasonably straightforward and was routinely reported in the ethnographies.

General and Sexual Harassment: Correspondence and Divergence

The correlation between general and sexual harassment is .342 (significant at the .001 level), suggesting that general and sexual harassment do indeed co-occur in organizations. This lends support to arguments that both phenomena are triggered by an underlying culture of incivility with at least some common organizational roots. At the same time, however, a correlation of .342 also implies less than a full identity between general and sexual harassment and the possibility of both common and distinct causes.

> We test the proposition of common versus distinct causes by estimating two competing structural equation models one assuming that both forms of harassment reduce to a single underlying phenomenon, and one in which general and sexual harassment are assumed to be distinct. The statistical results clearly support the two-factor model of distinct causes.

[The data] suggest that both general harassment *and* sexual harassment are more likely where the work is highly physical, lending support to the image of a masculine work culture as a foundation for multiple forms of workplace incivility. Minority workforces, too, are more vulnerable to both general and sexual harassment.

In terms of distinct causes, general harassment is more common in workplaces where workers are more vulnerable because of job insecurity. Importantly, job insecurity does not appear to be a significant predictor of sexual harassment. High female work group composition increases the likelihood of sexual harassment, but not general harassment. Organizational chaos and disorganization, conversely, are associated with general harassment but not with sexual harassment. Interestingly, neither of the organizational guardian characteristics—grievance machinery and team organizations of work—act to protect workers from general harassment (a finding consistent with the absence of protective legislation against general harassment). Both, however, do act to mitigate sexual harassment.

What mechanisms produce these patterns and relationships? By returning to the original narrative accounts, we can garner a better sense of the underlying processes. We address first the unique causes of general and sexual harassment and then their common causes.

UNIQUE CAUSES OF GENERAL HARASSMENT AT WORK

General harassment is particularly prevalent in organizational contexts characterized by job insecurity and organizational chaos. For instance, in a large legal firm, the work for paralegals is routinely chaotic because of the personalized and idiosyncratic demands of lawyers (Pierce 1995:155) and because of the unbridled nature of their personalities (p. 148). This chaos contributes to an environment were paralegals are routinely abused and bullied (coded 4 "frequent"):

> Whether a lawyer is angry about X, Y, or Z, the paralegal is liable to suffer the consequences. . . . For example, Greg, a paralegal, had brought a client into his office to wait until the attorney, Chris (a woman), got off the phone. Greg had been specifically instructed to sit with the client

rather than leaving him out in the lobby to wait. While they were waiting, Greg received an important and long-awaited call about the client's case. Rather than discuss the business in front of the client, he forwarded the call to a more private line and retreated to a nearby, empty conference room. In his absence, the impatient client began to wander the halls and happened into the attorney's office. The attorney immediately got off the phone, welcomed the client, and commenced their business. After the client left, Chris yelled at the paralegal for leaving the client by himself. Greg explained what had happened. Rather than apologizing for her outburst, the attorney angrily replied: "Well, I just had to yell at someone, and you were there" (Pierce 1995:91–2).

Sexual harassment, however, while certainly present in this setting, does not appear to be significantly aggravated by the chaos.

A typical episode follows: "Daniel, for example, complimented the personal appearance of his secretary Janice *only* when she was wearing a short skirt" (Pierce 1995:34). Thus, bosses yell aggressively at workers in chaotic settings, but such situations do not appear to contribute to increased sexual harassment. Sexual harassment appears to emerge out of more stable power imbalances in the workplace (as discussed in the next section).

Job insecurity also leads to increased levels of general harassment, but again does not have an aggravating effect on sexual harassment. In an automobile parts supply plant, where variability in orders results in frequent layoffs of up to 50 percent of the workers, abuse is commonplace (coded 4 "frequent"):

> [Bobby] was originally called to make a small adjustment on the depth of the machine's applicator. It was a simple adjustment accomplished by loosening a single screw. In a normally equipped shop it would have been a five-minute job, but Bobby could not find the proper screwdriver. We searched all the toolboxes, but the screwdrivers were either too large or had been ground at the ends. Bobby asked Carroll [the boss] if he could buy

a screwdriver at the hardware store down the street. Carroll refused and told him to grind one of the ones we had. Bobby tried, but ended up stripping the screwhead so badly that nothing could get it out. Then Carroll came to the floor and in typical fashion chewed Bobby out in front of everybody. (Juravich 1985:136)

Sexual harassment, while not unknown in this setting, is not rampant or aggravated, and is largely restricted to condescending attitudes as in the following example:

Carroll [the foreman] often commented on how inflexible the girls were, and implied that his solutions would be perfectly good if the "girls" were not so set in their ways. . . . "You can't trust some of those girls to do anything. I don't know how some of them walk around without bumping into things." (Juravich 1985:105–106)

Last, like Roscigno (2007) and others, we find that grievance procedures and work teams do not reduce general harassment. A typical example of the limited efficacy of organizational structures in reducing general harassment is embodied in the abhorrent behavior a widely hated manager in a setting with both a fully developed team organization of work and a visible grievance program:

Ted Meadows . . . was said, for example, to be "unthinking and absolutely uncaring about the people aspects of management; numbers of people had resigned because of him" [He was frequently] "abusive, insulting and nasty" and "the foulness of his language—aimed right at you as the total effing prat he made you out to be—was his nearest idea to motivating people." (Watson 1994:175)

This finding thus suggests that grievance procedures and other potential organizational protections often function as window dressing rather than as substantive protections. The finding on work teams also supports a significant strand in the literature, which finds teams to be yet another mechanism of intensified control under which workers exert control on each other laterally (see Vallas [2003] for a review).

UNIQUE CAUSES OF SEXUAL HARASSMENT

The unique influences on sexual harassment are its activation in situations with high female work composition (i.e., feminized settings) and its suppression where there are active grievance mechanisms and team organizations of work. The vulnerability of women in feminized workplaces is consistent with findings reported in the sexual harassment literature on the negative effects of gender-typing of occupations (DiTomaso 1989; Gruber 1998).

The newer findings are those of the suppression of sexual harassment under certain organizational conditions. An example of the protective effects of an in-place grievance system is provided by work in a textile factory in the South China industrial boom region adjacent to Hong Kong. In this setting, the local Labor Management Bureaua—holdover from the Communist era—provides a mechanism for third-party review for factory workers, ameliorating some, but not all abuses. Sexual harassment, in particular, is limited to the use of condescending terms for the young female workers: "This terminology (*buk-mui* [northern women] or *dagong méi* [women workers in bosses' factories]) carried the connotation of young, immature, ignorant, and single women" (Lee 1998:128). However, more generalized harassment and abuse was rampant and unchecked:

Because absenteeism was heavily penalized and fined, Chi-ying came to work even when she was sick. Many times, she had seen line girls suffering from fever or menstrual pain clinging to the line, sobbing or cursing. Overtime shifts were frequent and mandatory. In busy seasons, work lasted until eleven at night. If workers refused to do overtime work, they would first be fined and later dismissed if they repeatedly refused. . . . Constant arguments, tears, and fights abound. (Lee 1998:6, 9)

Team organizations of work are also associated with reduced sexual harassment, although (as we saw previously) not with reduced general harassment. An example of such a case is provided by a telecommunications company with a significant history of team organization used to promote productivity. Here, only patronizing attitudes were in evidence (coded 2 "condescending"):

> There's something patronizing in their tone—"Thank you, my dear". . . . It's the way they keep at it, always reminding you of your place with this "dearie" stuff. . . . There is one manager who calls me "little girl." It's his style: "you do this, little one." (Watson 1994:198)

In this setting, the increased visibility and accountability of groups helped to prevent more obvious and aggressive forms of harassment. Forms of behavior that would have been regarded as taboo—such as serious forms of sexual harassment—were clearly off-limits even to abusive managers such as the one quoted in a previous quote.

COMMON CAUSES: PHYSICALITY AND MINORITY CONCENTRATION

As well as having unique causes, generalized and sexual harassment have common causes as well. Investigating these common causes— the physicality of work and predominantly minority work groups—allows us to see the extent to which common *processes* are indeed involved in the emergence of both general and sexual harassment. We investigate these causes by returning to the original ethnographic accounts.

Physicality We consider first the role of physically demanding work as underwriting both general and sexual harassment. We explore three typical cases involving hard physical work—construction, firefighting, and automobile assembly—and find that each has somewhat different implications for general and sexual harassment. The *construction* case involves setting concrete—work that is

extremely physical and demanding (coded 4 "brutal"):

> Physical strength and stamina play a large part in determining construction workers' self-respect. It is associated with their ideas about maleness and manliness. . . . Construction men must develop the stamina to persevere through very adverse conditions—extreme cold; arm-weary shoveling; leg-weary sloshing through mud; the chilling effect of high winds; the backstraining pushing and lifting of heavy weights. Men who must do this work are proud of their physical capabilities. (Applebaum 1981:32–3)

> At one work site, a woman is hired to drive a large dump truck. At least initially, she is the object of repeated jokes and harassment (coded 2 "taunting"): "For a while, after Mary came to the job, she was the subject of many salacious jokes. One day one of the men remarked, 'Hey, Mary's all dressed up today, she's wearing a bra'" (Applebaum 1981:131).

While such hazing is certainly unpleasant, the men thought of it as being in good humor. The rationale for this pattern of aggressive joking and hazing seems to be a defense of masculine identity tied to the job. However, neither the general nor the sexual harassment in this admittedly physically demanding setting reach the same intensity and meanness that they do in the next setting.

In *firefighting*, the work is also physically demanding, dangerous, and a source of male identity and bonding. In this setting, however, Equal Opportunity mandates have generated pressures for the employment of women that create a sense of significant job threat for male job incumbents. As a result, the harassment is decidedly more pointed and seems to go well beyond defense of mere identity to include direct attempts to make the job unpleasant enough to force out new female recruits:

> Jane Macey didn't think of herself as a puritanical woman, but she came to find the constant references to sexuality and the presence of pornographic material disturbing,

particularly when they seemed to reflect an overt hostility toward women.

. . . This man kept a collection of pornographic photos posted in his locker, which was sometimes left open. When Jane saw them for the first time, she was shocked. "He's got Polaroid pictures of women in very vulnerable positions. . . . I mean, I've watched porn films and stuff, but when I saw those pictures I was kind of blown away."

Talk could also feel threatening. "We get sexual innuendos a lot—and . . . some of 'em aren't even innuendos. . . . There's nothing subtle about it. One night an officer . . . was talkin' about how he knew a guy who put cigarette butts out on women's tits. And I'm just sitting there, just like I can't believe my ears." (Chetkovich 1997:76)

New male recruits in this setting are similarly subjected to abuse that also seems aggravated by a desire to protect the positions of senior employees. For no apparent reason, a longtime veteran yells at a recruit, who then blows up:

That was it . . . I'd had my limit. I just looked at him, I said, "Who the fuck are you talking to?" . . . And then he came, just steamin' out, and like runnin' at me like he wanted to fight. . . . And he's just yellin' and screamin', "You blank blank new kids! I got ten years on this job! I tell you what to do, you do it." (Chetkovich 1997:136)

In this contentious setting, sexual harassment and general harassment take on a decidedly meaner tone as the defense of employment and position come to the fore.

In an *automobile assembly plant* in the Midwest, the defense of masculine identity and the defense of jobs become intermingled in the following episode, which evidences both significant general and sexual harassment. The episode grows out of long-standing problems with carpel tunnel syndrome in the plant, which affects many workers, but especially women.

At first, a majority of workers with hand and wrist injuries seemed to be women; however,

men soon experienced the same injuries. Nevertheless, since women appeared to be afflicted sooner and more often than men, a form of sexual harassment emerged which threatened to interfere further with safety. For example, in Paint, one of the men who operated a hand sprayer wore splints. Some of his male fellow workers in Paint said that he had "Corporal Klinger's disease," implying that the man was faking a woman's disease in order to get out of work. . . . [Joan] said that Mary (her teammate) has carpal tunnel and [her supervisor] makes fun of her for having it. Joan said that no matter how bad her hands ever hurt, she will not go to the doctor because of him. (Graham 1995:65, 91)

The physically demanding nature of the work, the significant entry of women into the industry, and the long, slow decline of jobs in the "rustbelt" combine in this setting to produce incivility that combines the mocking of women as "easy targets" for abuse and harassment with employment pressures that are felt by everyone.

A close look at these three cases thus suggests that physically demanding work encourages general and sexual harassment as a mechanism for defending both masculine identities and privileged access to jobs and advancement (see DiTomaso 1989). The intensity of this process escalates as threats to job security increase. Where manly identity is at stake—as in the construction example—harassment and bullying have a milder tone, even masquerading as friendly teasing and joking. Where jobs are at risk, as in the fire-fighting and automobile assembly examples, harassment and bullying take a decidedly meaner turn as current job incumbents create abusive and potentially threatening situations for novices as they struggle to integrate into a new setting.

Minority Concentration. The second common cause of generalized and sexual harassment is minority concentration. Close examination of the ethnographies with more than 50 percent minority workforces reveals two distinct patterns of association between minority concentration and general harassment. In some settings, this association results at least partly from the fact that minorities are concentrated in workplaces with large power differentials between employers and workers and fewer protections against abuse. For example, an ethnography of domestic work illustrates how employers of domestics may use nonverbal intimidation to discourage domestics from taking breaks to which they are legally entitled:

> It was 12:30 and I, weary and hungry, decided to take a short break and have lunch later. Since he [a fifty-five-year-old psychiatrist] was on the phone in the kitchen, I sat in the dining area, ate an apple I had brought and read a magazine. He could hear me but not see me. As soon as he got off the phone, he walked a roundabout route to go upstairs, apparently so he could see what I was doing. Walking by slowly, he literally glared at me. I smiled slightly; he did not return the smile, seeming to want to make it clear he was checking me out and disapproved of my not working. He glared, said nothing, continued upstairs. (Rollins 1985:67–8)

In this context, the unrationalized nature of work, in particular the absence of regularized procedures, creates some discretion for the worker and simultaneously makes the employer suspicious of, and hostile to, any break-taking at all (since he has no real procedures in place for regulating it). It is not possible to tell for certain from this account exactly how much, if any, of the employer's hostility can be traced to the race of the employee, but it does seem clear that this particular organizational setting is rife with possibilities for harassment.

The ethnography also notes a preference by white employers for black domestics, for whom social difference along the multiple dimensions of race and class helps justify treatment of the domestic worker as a servant. The master–servant relationship between white employers and black domestic workers, Rollins finds, reinforces employers' race and class identities by confirming, for them, their own superiority and the inferiority of blacks and the working class (pp. 197–203). Thus, part of the powerlessness of domestic workers, beyond the structure of the organizational setting itself, may lie precisely in the additional permission white employers feel to treat black domestics as their natural social inferiors.

This latter interpretation is amplified by a second pattern underlying the relationship between minority concentration and generalized harassment, in which minority workers are in fact singled out for abuses from which their white counterparts are largely spared. This pattern was visible in a number of the ethnographies. For example, an ethnography of a meatpacking plant reports that the plant's largely non-English-speaking Asian immigrant workers are treated by management (and by white coworkers) as a shadow population of nameless, interchangeable faces, that they are driven more harshly by management than are the white workers, that they are concentrated in the most dismal jobs and work areas, that their safety conditions are more neglected, and that they are subject to abrupt discipline or dismissal, ostensibly in order to set an example to their fellow ethnics (Fink 1998).

These two distinct patterns, both clearly visible in the ethnographies, put flesh on the bones of the statistical relationship between minority concentration and generalized harassment. In some kinds of situations, the association between harassment and minority workforce may be a consequence of minority workers' concentration in bad jobs, but in other settings, it is clear that harassment of minority workers serves white identity and job-protection functions in much the same way as general and sexual harassment serve male identity and job protection.

The process through which minority concentration translates into sexual harassment remains somewhat unclear because the available ethnographic discussions of sexual harassment almost universally fail to engage with questions of race. The ethnographers in our population treat the victims of sexual harassment simply as women, making it all but impossible from their accounts to shed further light on the statistical association between minority concentration in the work group and sexual harassment. In short, the ethnographers simply do not tell us if the harassed women in high minority concentration work groups are minority or white.

Two points can be gleaned from this impasse. First, future workplace ethnographies should attempt to be more aware of the racial dimensions of sexual harassment than they have been to date and should not avoid reporting this dimension. Second, this finding underscores the value of examining a population of ethnographies as a collected body of work. The conclusion that minority workforce is associated with sexual harassment would be difficult to draw from any of the ethnographies individually—simply reading these ethnographies would not yield this insight because the ethnographers do not highlight it. This finding only emerges from systematic analysis of the entire population of organizational ethnographies.

Discussion

Our results suggest that sexual harassment and general harassment have statistically distinct patterns of causation and yet share common causes as well. By returning to the original ethnographic accounts, we have been able to better understand some of the processes beneath these common causes. For both

general and sexual harassment, the underlying dynamics involve processes of social closure.

In jobs defined by their *physicality*, both general and sexual harassment processes are often motivated by defense of a masculine job identity—although a return to the passages describing particular episodes of harassment suggest that physicality most typically results in *relatively* milder forms of general and sexual harassment. Where job security is at risk, harassment processes quickly take a meaner turn as incumbents create barriers for novices in an effort to make their lives miserable or even pressure them out. The sexual harassment literature has frequently debated whether harassment serves to protect masculine identities or men's privileged access to jobs. By returning to the original accounts of a range of harassment episodes, we are able see that *both* identity defense and job defense are involved in harassment and in an escalating manner. Where job security is an issue, however, harassment becomes much more mean-spirited and threatening.

The study of general and sexual harassment has important implications for material inequality as well as for emotional well-being. For those who are the victims of exclusion and closure processes, the consequences are not confined to distress and the erosion of dignity at work. Harassment can also be successful in forcing people out of jobs with direct and immediate implications for their material as well as emotional well-being. Similarly, part of the reason that *minority workforces* are more likely to experience general harassment seems to be that they are more likely than whites to find themselves in highly unequal power relationships with their employers.

Several organizational policy implications emerge from our findings. First, and perhaps most obvious, jobs with high physical demands and large minority workforces provide environments conducive to both general and sexual harassment and deserve special scrutiny for anti-bullying and anti-harassment training. In this policy arena, there can be a dovetailing of efforts to curtail sexual harassment and more generalized incivility (see also Lim and Cortina 2005:494). We have also seen that grievance procedures curtail at least some forms of sexual harassment. The expansion of more general grievance mechanisms could also be an effective strategy in curtailing general harassment.

Our findings support the emerging consensus that a serious treatment of the problem of bullying and incivility in the workplace requires legislation parallel to that outlawing sexual harassment (Ehrenreich 1999). With a similar legal structure in place, anti-harassment and anti-bullying policies have the opportunity to dovetail programs of training and accountability leading to mutually supporting gains and hopefully to greater returns to policy efforts (Kleinschmidt 2005).

Conclusions

Our unified model of general and sexual harassment suggests that although these two behaviors are statistically distinct, they have both unique and shared organizational causes. We have used a routine activities model to highlight key organizational features that may be implicated in generating victims, encouraging perpetrators, or providing guardianship. This model suggests that job insecurity and organizational chaos are key factors creating vulnerabilities to general harassment, that grievance mechanisms and team organization act to modestly curtail sexual harassment, and that general and sexual harassment are both more likely where the work is highly physically demanding and where it involves a minority workforce.

Our findings support the use of a routine activities model as a way to conceptualize

organizational features that may lead to malfeasance in the workplace and support the further elaboration of this model for studying a range of negative workplace behaviors (see Williams 1997). This model, as useful as it is for identifying the organizational features implicated in general and sexual harassment, nevertheless leaves unanswered the larger question of why people harass. The answer, which is revealed by our qualitative reimmersion into the ethnographic materials themselves, is that generalized harassment and sexual harassment are often elements in a larger process of social exclusion and closure. In this process of closure, mocking, barriers, and sometimes blatant threats are used to exclude certain groups (even potentially forcing them out of the workplace), or to keep members of these groups "in their place." These processes involve both the defense of identity and the defense of jobs. The intensity and ugliness of the harassment increases, it appears, with the movement toward the defense of jobs and material interests. *This process—the defense of identity and the defense of position—is at the heart of general and sexual harassment and serves as their common unifying base.*

The most obvious limitation of our analysis derives from its reliance on available ethnographic studies of the workplace—the cases analyzed are not a representative sample of all organizations. Thus, generalization from these data to the population of all organizations must be made with caution. Still, these data represent the population of available ethnographic evidence on harassment within work organizations. And unlike much prior qualitative and quantitative work based on single or limited cases, there is significant organizational heterogeneity in our data that supports a meaningful analysis of organizational contexts. We hope that these findings will stimulate further research into the commonalities between various forms of incivility in the workplace. An important goal in that research will be further refinement of a unified model and theory capable of shedding light on the full range of workplace incivilities. The current research suggests that concepts of routine organizational activities and social closure and exclusion may provide potential building blocks toward such a theory.

Acknowledgments

We would like to thank Pamela Paxton, Lindsey Chamberlain, Martha Crowley, and Daniel Tope for their insightful comments on the ideas and analyses presented here. This material is based on work supported by the National Science Foundation, Innovation and Organizational Change and Sociology Programs under Grant 0112434. Any opinions, findings, and conclusions or recommendations expressed in this material are those of the authors and do not necessarily reflect the views of the National Science Foundation.

Notes

1. Title VII of the 1964 Civil Rights Act prohibits discrimination on the basis of race, color, religion, national origin, or sex.
2. See De Coster, Estes, and Mueller (1999) for an application of the routine activities model to sexual harassment.
3. A list of the ethnographies included and those considered but excluded is available from the author on request and at http://www.sociology.ohio-state.edu/rdh/Workplace-EthnographyProject.html.
4. The code sheet, coding protocol, and data are available at http://www.sociology.ohio-state.edu/rdh/Workplace-Ethnography-Project.html. As with any content-analysis project, we may have made errors in the interpretation of the texts or in the coding of the data. The data, however, are available for public scrutiny and reanalysis and we welcome suggestions, criticisms, and alternative views on the recorded data.

References

Acker, Joan. 1990. "Hierarchies, Jobs, Bodies: A Theory of Gendered Organizations." *Gender and Society* 4:139–58.

Applebaum, Herbert. 1981. *Royal Blue: The Culture of Construction Workers.* New York: Holt.

Ashforth, Blake. 1994. "Petty Tyranny in Organizations." *Human Relations* 47:755–78.

Berdahl, Jennifer L. 2007. "Harassment Based on Sex: Protecting Social Status in the Context of Gender Hierarchy." *Academy of Management Review* 32:641–58.

Blau, Peter. 1955. *The Dynamics of Bureaucracy.* Chicago, IL: University of Chicago Press.

Blau, Peter M. 1964. *Exchange and Power in Social Life.* New York: Wiley.

Chetkovich, Carol. 1997. *Real Heat: Gender and Race in the Urban Fire Service.* New Brunswick, NJ: Rutgers University Press.

Cohen, Lawrence E. and Marcus Felson. 1979. "Social Change and Crime Rate Trends: A Routine Activity Approach." *American Sociological Review* 44:588–608.

De Coster, S., S. B. Estes, and C. W. Mueller. 1999. "Routine Activities and Sexual Harassment in the Workplace." *Work and Occupations* 26:21–49.

DiTomaso, Nancy. 1989. "Sexuality in the Workplace: Discrimination and Harassment." Pp. 71–90 in *The Sexuality of Organization,* edited by Jeff Hearn, Deborah Sheppard, Peta Tancred-Sheriff, and Gibson Burrell. London, England: Sage.

Edelman, Lauren B. 1990. "Legal Environments and Organizational Governance: The Expansion of Due Process in the American Workplace." *American Journal of Sociology* 95:1401–40.

———. 1992. "Legal Ambiguity and Symbolic Structures: Organizational Mediation of Civil Rights Law." *American Journal of Sociology* 97:1531–76.

———. 2002. "Legality and the Endogeneity of Law." Pp. 187–202 in *Legality and Community: On the Intellectual Legacy of Philip Selznick,* edited by Robert A. Kagan, Martin Krygier, and Kenneth Winston. Lanham, MD: Rowman & Littlefield; Berkeley, CA: Berkeley Public Policy Press.

Edelman, Lauren B., Sally Riggs Fuller, and Iona Mara-Drieta. 2001. "Diversity Rhetoric and the Managerialization of Law." *American Journal of Sociology* 106:1589–641.

Ehrenreich, Rosa. 1999. "Dignity and Discrimination: Toward a Pluralistic Understanding of Workplace Harassment." *Georgetown Law Review* 88:1–47.

Fine, Gary Alan. 1996. *Kitchens: The Culture of Restaurant Work.* Berkeley: University of California Press.

Fink, Deborah 1998. *Cutting into the Meatpacking Line: Workers and Change in the Rural Midwest.* Chapel Hill: University of North Carolina Press.

Gouldner, Alvin W. 1964. *Patterns of Industrial Bureaucracy.* New York: Free Press.

Graham, Laurie. 1995. *On the Line at Subaru-Isuzu.* Ithaca, NY: Industrial and Labor Relations Press.

Gruber, James E. 1998. "The Impact of Male Work Environments and Organizational Policies on Women's Experiences of Sexual Harassment." *Gender and Society* 12:301–20.

Hearn, Jeff and Wendy Parkin. 2001. *Gender, Sexuality and Violence in Organizations: The Unspoken Forms of Organizational Violations.* London, England: Sage.

Hegtvedt, Karen A. and Cathryn Johnson. 2000. "Justice beyond the Individual: A Future for Legitimation." *Social Psychology Quarterly* 63:298–311.

Hodson, Randy. 2001. *Dignity at Work.* Cambridge, England: Cambridge University Press.

Hsiung, Ping-Chun. 1996. *Living Rooms as Factories: Class, Gender and the Satellite Factory System in Taiwan.* Philadelphia, PA: Temple University Press.

Jacoby, Sanford. 2004. *Employing Bureaucracy: Managers, Unions, and the Transformation of Work in the 20th Century.* Mahwah, NJ: Lawrence Erlbaum.

Juravich, Tom. 1985. *Chaos on the Shop Floor: A Worker's View of Quality, Productivity, and Management.* Philadelphia, PA: Temple University Press.

Kalev, Alexandra, Frank Dobbin, and Erin Kelly. 2006. "Best Practices or Best Guesses? Assessing the Efficiency of Corporate Affirmative Action and Diversity Policies." *American Sociological Review* 71:589–617.

Kleinschmidt, Heather L. 2005. "Reconsidering Severe or Pervasive: Aligning the Standard in Sexual Harassment and Racial Harassment Causes of Action." *Indiana Law Journal* 80:1119.

Lawson, Helene M. 2000. *Ladies on the Lot: Women, Car Sales and the Pursuit of the American Dream.* Lanham, MD: Rowman & Littlefield.

Lee, Ching Kwan. 1998. *Gender and the South China Miracle: Two Worlds of Factory Women.* Berkeley: University of California Press.

Lim, Sandy and Lilia M. Cortina. 2005. "Interpersonal Mistreatment in the Workplace: The Interface and Impact of General Incivility and Sexual Harassment." *Journal of Applied Psychology* 90:483–96.

Mansbridge, Jane. 1980. *Beyond Adversary Democracy.* New York: Basic.

Marx, Karl. [1844] 1964. *Economic and Philosophic Manuscripts of 1844.* Translated by Martin Mulligan. New York: International Publishers.

Molm, Linda D. 1997. *Coercive Power in Social Exchange.* New York: Cambridge University Press.

Morrill, Calvin. 1995. *The Executive Way: Conflict Management in Corporations.* Chicago, IL: University of Chicago Press.

Mouly, V. Suchitra and Jayaram K. Sankaran. 1997. "On the Study of Settings Marked by Severe Superior-Subordinate Conflict." *Organization Studies* 18:175–92.

Perrow, Charles. 1986. *Complex Organizations: A Critical Essay,* 3rd ed. Glenview, IL: Scott, Foresman.

Pierce, Jennifer L. 1995. *Gender Trials: Emotional Lives in Contemporary Law Firms.* Berkeley: University of California Press.

Pollert, Anna. 1981. *Girls, Wives, Factory Lives.* London, England: Macmillan.

Ragins, B. R. and T. A. Scandura. 1995. "Antecedents and Work-Related Correlates of Reported Sexual Harassment." *Sex Roles* 32:429–55.

Rayner, Charlotte, Helge Hoel, and Cary L. Cooper. 2002. *Workplace Bullying.* London, England: Taylor & Francis.

Roberts, Glenda S. 1994. *Staying on the Line: Blue-Collar Women in Contemporary Japan.* Honolulu: University of Hawaii Press.

Rollins, Judith. 1985. *Between Women: Domestics and Their Employers.* Philadelphia, PA: Temple University Press.

Roscigno, Vincent J. 2007. *The Face of Discrimination: How Race and Sex Impact Work and Residential Lives.* New York: Rowman & Littlefield.

Saguy, Abigail. 2000. "Employment Discrimination or Sexual Violence? Defining Sexual Harassment in American, and French Law." *Law and Society Review* 34(4):1091–128.

——. 2003. *What Is Sexual Harassment? From Capitol Hill to the Sorbonne.* Berkeley: University of California Press.

Salin, Denise. 2003. "Ways of Explaining Bullying." *Human Relations* 56:1213–32.

Sallaz, Jeff. 2002. "Manufacturing Concessions: Attritionary Outsourcing at General Motors' Lordstown, USA Assembly Plant." *Work, Employment and Society* 18(4):687–708.

Skarlicki, D. P. and C. T. Kulik. 2005. "Third-Party Reactions to Employee (Mis)treatment: A Justice Perspective." *Research in Organizational Behavior* 26:183–226.

Smith, Vicki. 2001. *Crossing the Great Divide: Worker Risk and Opportunity in the New Economy.* Ithaca, NY: Cornell University Press.

Tsui, Anne S. and Barbara A. Gutek. 1999. *Demographic Differences in Organizations: Current Research and Future Directions.* New York: Lexington.

Uggen, Christopher and Amy Blackstone. 2004. "Sexual Harassment as a Gendered Expression of Power." *American Sociological Review* 69:64–92.

Vaez, Marjan, Kerstin Ekberg, and Lucie LaFlamme. 2004. "Abusive Events at Work among Young Working Adults." *Relations Industrielles/Industrial Relations* 59:569–84.

Vartia, Maarit. 1996. "The Sources of Bullying." *European Journal of Work and Organizational Psychology* 5:203–14.

Vallas, Steven P. 2003. "The Adventures of Managerial Hegemony: Teamwork, Ideology, and Worker Resistance." *Social Problems* 50:204–25.

——. 2006. "Empowerment Redux: Structure, Agency, and the Remaking of Managerial Authority." *American Journal of Sociology* 111:1677–717.

Van Maanen, John. 1977. *Organizational Careers.* London, England: Wiley.

Walker, Charles R., Robert H. Guest, and Arthur N. Turner. 1956. *The Foreman on the Assembly Line.* Cambridge, MA: Harvard University Press.

Walker, Henry A. and Morris Zelditch, Jr. 1993. "Power, Legitimacy, and the Stability of Authority." Pp. 364–84 in *Theoretical Research Programs,* edited by Joseph Berger and Morris Zelditch, Jr. Stanford, CA: Stanford University Press.

Watson, Tony. 1994. *In Search of Management.* London, England: Routledge.

Weber, Max. 1968. *Economy and Society.* Edited by Guenther Roth and Claus Wittich. New York: Bedminster.

Welsh, Sandy. 1999. "Gender and Sexual Harassment." *Annual Review of Sociology* 25:169–90.

Williams, Christine. 1997. "Sexual Harassment in Organizations: A Critique of Current Research and Policy." *Sexuality and Culture* 1:19–43.

Williams, K. Y. and C. A. O'Reilly. 1998. "Demography and Diversity in Organizations: A Review of Forty Years of Research." Pp. 77–140 in *Research in Organizational Behavior,* vol. 20, edited by B. Staw and R. Sutton. Stamford, CT: JAI.

Zapf, Dieter, Stale Einarsen, Helge Hoel, and Maarit Vartia. 2003. "Empirical Findings on Bullying in the Workplace." Pp. 103–27 in *Bullying and Emotional Abuse in the Workplace,* edited by Stale Einarsen, Helge Hoel, Dieter Zapf, and Cary L. Cooper. London, England: Taylor & Francis.

Zimmer, Lynn. 1986. *Women Guarding Men.* Chicago, IL: University of Chicago Press.

Questions

1. In your judgment, at what point does mere "incivility" become "harassment"?

2. According to the article, in what ways do "chaos in the workplace" and "physically demanding work" facilitate harassment?

3. Assume that you owned a business and discovered that general harassment was occurring in your workplace. Given what you have learned in this article, what steps would you take to ameliorate the situation? What if you needed to deal with sexual harassment?

29

SITUATIONAL ETHICS AND COLLEGE STUDENT CHEATING

Emily E. LaBeff, Robert E. Clark, Valerie J. Haines, and George M. Diekhoff

In this 1990 article, Professor LaBeff and her colleagues explore the ways in which students who have cheated avoid guilt by finding excuses for their wrongdoing. In other words, the authors explore how students "neutralize" their actions.

Introduction

Studies have shown that cheating in college is epidemic, and some analysts of this problem estimate that fifty percent of college students may engage in such behavior. . . . Such studies have examined demographic and social characteristics of students such as age, sex, academic standing, major, classification, extracurricular activity, level of test anxiety, degree of sanctioned threat, and internal social control. Each of these factors has been found to be related, to some extent, to cheating although the relationship of these factors varies considerably from study to study. . . .

In our freshman classes, we often informally ask students to discuss whether they have cheated in college and, if so, how. Some students have almost bragged about which of their methods have proven most effective including writing notes on shoes and caps and on the backs of calculators. Rolling up a tiny cheat sheet into a pen cap was mentioned. And one student said he had "incredibly gifted

eyes" which allowed him to see the answers of a smart student four rows in front of him. One female student talked about rummaging through the dumpsters at night close to final examination time looking for test dittos. She did find at least one examination. A sorority member informed us that two of her term papers in her freshman year were sent from a sister chapter of the sorority at another university, retyped and submitted to the course professor. Further, many of these students saw nothing wrong with what they were doing, although they verbally agreed with the statement that cheating was unethical.

It appears that students hold qualified guidelines for behavior which are situationally determined. As such, the concept of situational ethics might well describe this college cheating in that rules for behavior may not be considered rigid but depend on the circumstances involved (Norris and Dodder 1979, 545). Joseph Fletcher, in his well-known philosophical treatise, *Situation Ethics: The New Morality* (1966), argues that this position is based on the notion that any action may be considered good or bad depending on the social circumstances. In other words, what is wrong in most situations might be considered right or acceptable if the end is defined as appropriate. This concept focuses

Emily E. LaBeff, Robert E. Clark, Valerie J. Haines, and George M. Diekhoff, "Situational Ethics and College Student Cheating" from *Sociological Inquiry* 60, no. 2 (May 1990): 190–197. Copyright © 1990 by The University of Texas Press. Reprinted with the permission of Blackwell Publishing Ltd.

on contextual appropriateness, not necessarily what is good or right, but what is viewed as fitting, given the circumstances. Central to this process is the idea that situations alter cases, thus altering the rules and principles guiding behavior (Edwards 1967).

Of particular relevance to the present study is the work of Gresham Sykes and David Matza (1957) who first developed the concept of neutralization to explain delinquent behavior. Neutralization theory in the study of delinquency expresses the process of situationally defining deviant behavior. In this view, deviance is based upon ". . . an unrecognized extension of defenses to crimes, in the form of justifications . . . seen as valid by the delinquent but not by . . . society at large" (Sykes and Matza 1957, 666). Through neutralization individuals justify violation of accepted behavior. This provides protection ". . . from self blame and the blame of others . . ." (Sykes and Matza 1957, 666). They do this before, during, and after the act. Such techniques of neutralization are separated into five categories: denial of responsibility, condemnation of condemners, appeal to higher loyalties, denial of victim, and denial of injury. In each case, individuals profess a conviction about a particular law but argue that special circumstances exist which cause them to violate the rules in a particular instance. However, in recent research, only Liska (1978) and Haines et al. (1986) found neutralization to be an important factor in college student cheating.

Methodology

The present analysis is based on a larger project conducted during the 1983–1984 academic year when a 49-item questionnaire about cheating was administered to students at a small southwestern university. The student body (N = 4950) was evenly distributed

throughout the university's programs with a disproportionate number (27%) majoring in business administration. In order to achieve a representative sample from a cross-section of the university student body, the questionnaire was administered to students enrolled in courses classified as a part of the university's core curriculum. Freshmen and sophomores were overrepresented (84% of the sample versus 60% of the university population). Females were also overrepresented (62% of the sample versus 55% of the university population).

There are obvious disadvantages associated with the use of self-administered questionnaires for data-gathering purposes. One such problem is the acceptance of student responses without benefit of contest. To maximize the return rate, questionnaires were administered during regularly scheduled class periods. Participation was on a voluntary basis. In order to establish the validity of responses, students were guaranteed anonymity. Students were also instructed to limit their responses regarding whether they had cheated to the current academic year.

. . . The present analysis is intended to assess the narrative responses to the incidence of cheating in three forms, namely on major examinations, quizzes, and class assignments, as well as the perceptions of and attitudes held by students toward cheating and the effectiveness of deterrents to cheating. Students recorded their experiences in their own words. Most students (87%) responded to the open-ended portion of the questionnaire.

Results

Of the 380 undergraduate students who participated in the spring survey, 54% indicated they had cheated during the previous six-month period. Students were requested to indicate whether cheating involved examination, weekly quizzes, and/or homework assignments. Much cheating took the form of looking on someone else's paper, copying homework, and either buying term papers or getting friends to write papers for them. Only five of the 205 students who admitted cheating reported being caught by the professor. However, 7% (n = 27) of the students reported cheating more than five times during the preceding six-month period. Twenty percent (n = 76) indicated that most students openly approved of cheating. Only seventeen students reported they would inform the instructor if they saw another student cheating. Many students, especially older students, indicated they felt resentment toward cheaters, but most also noted that they would not do anything about it (i.e., inform the instructor).

To more fully explore the ways in which students neutralize their behavior, narrative data from admitted student cheaters were examined (n = 149). The narrative responses were easily classified into three of the five techniques described by Sykes and Matza (1957).

DENIAL OF RESPONSIBILITY

Denial of responsibility was the most often identified response. This technique involves a declaration by the offenders that, in light of circumstances beyond their control, they cannot be held accountable for their actions. Rather than identifying the behavior as "accidental," they attribute wrongdoing to the influence of outside forces. In some instances, students expressed an inability to withstand peer pressure to cheat. Responses show a recognition of cheating as an unacceptable behavior, implying that under different circumstances cheating would not have occurred. One student commented:

> I was working forty plus hours a week and we had a lot to read for that day. I just couldn't get it all in. . . . I'm not saying cheating is okay, sometimes you just have to.

Another student explained her behavior in the following statement:

> . . . I had the flu the week before . . . had to miss several classes so I had no way of knowing what was going to be on the exam. My grades were good up to that point and I hadn't cheated. . . . I just couldn't risk it.

It is noteworthy that these statements indicate the recognition that cheating is wrong under normal circumstances.

Other responses demonstrate the attempt by students to succeed through legitimate means (e.g., taking notes and studying) only to experience failure. Accordingly, they were left with no alternative but to cheat. One student commented:

> . . . even though I've studied in the past, I've failed the exam so I cheated on my last test hoping to bring a better grade.

Another student explained his behavior in the following manner:

> I studied for the exam and I studied hard but the material on the test was different from what I expected. . . . I had to make a good grade.

In some accounts, students present a unique approach to the denial of responsibility. Upon entering the examination setting, these students had no intention of cheating, but the opportunity presented itself. The following statement by one student provides a clear illustration of this point:

> . . . I was taking the test and someone in another part of the room was telling someone else an answer. I heard it and just couldn't not write it down.

Although viewing such behavior as dishonest, the blame for any wrongdoing is quickly transferred to those who provide the answers. Another student justified her action in the following manner:

> . . . I didn't mean to cheat but once you get the right answer it's hard, no impossible, not

to. How could you ignore an answer that you knew was right?

In addition, some students reported accidentally seeing other students' test papers. In such instances, the cheaters chastised classmates for not covering up their answer sheets. As one student wrote, such temptation simply cannot be overcome:

> I studied hard for the exam and needed an A. I just happened to look up and there was my neighbor's paper uncovered. I found myself checking my answers against his through the whole test.

APPEAL TO HIGHER LOYALTIES

Conflict also arises between peer group expectations and the normative expectations of the larger society. When this occurs, the individual may choose to sacrifice responsibility, thereby maintaining the interest of peers. Such allegiance allows these individuals to supersede moral obligations when special circumstances arise.

Students who invoke this technique of neutralization frequently described their behavior as an attempt to help another. One student stated:

> I only cheated because my friend had been sick and she needed help. . . . It (cheating) wouldn't have happened any other time.

Another student denied any wrongdoing on her part as the following statement illustrates:

> I personally have never cheated. I've had friends who asked for help so I let them see my test. Maybe some would consider that to be cheating.

These students recognize the act of cheating is wrong. However, their statements also suggest that in some situations cheating can be overlooked. Loyalty to a friend in need takes precedence over honesty in the classroom.

Another student described his situation in the following manner:

> I was tutoring this girl but she just couldn't understand the material. . . . I felt I had to help her on the test.

CONDEMNATION OF CONDEMNERS

Cheaters using this technique of neutralization attempt to shift attention from their own actions to the actions of others, most often authority figures. By criticizing those in authority as being unfair or unethical, the behavior of the offender seems less consequential by comparison. Therefore, dishonest behavior occurs in reaction to the perceived dishonesty of the authority figure. Students who utilize this technique wrote about uncaring, unprofessional instructors with negative attitudes who were negligent in their behavior. These incidents were said to be a precursor to their cheating behavior. The following response illustrates this view:

> The teachers here are boring and I dislike this school. The majority of teachers here don't care about the students and are rude when you ask them for help.

In other instances, students cite unfair teaching practices which they perceive to be the reason for their behavior. One student stated:

> Major exams are very important to your grade and it seems that the majority of instructors make up the exams to try and trick you instead of testing your knowledge.

In this case, the instructor is thought to engage in a deliberate attempt to fail the students by making the examinations difficult. Also within this category were student accounts which frequently express a complaint of being overworked. As one student wrote:

> One instructor assigns more work than anyone could possibly handle . . . at least I know I can't, so sometimes cheating is the answer.

Another student described his situation as follows:

> Sometimes it seems like these instructors get together and plan to make it difficult. . . . I had three major tests in one day and very little time to study. . . .

Although less frequently mentioned, perceived parental pressure also serves as a neutralizing factor for dishonesty. One student stated:

> During my early years at school my parents constantly pressured me for good grades. . . . They would have withheld money if grades were bad.

Another student blamed the larger society for his cheating:

> In America, we're taught that results aren't achieved through beneficial means, but through the easiest means.

Another stated:

> Ted Kennedy has been a modeling example for many of us. . . . This society teaches us to survive, to rationalize. . . . It is built on injustice and expediency.

This student went on to say that he cheated throughout a difficult science course so he could spend more time studying for major courses which he enjoyed.

DENIAL OF INJURY AND DENIAL OF THE VICTIM

Denial of injury and denial of the victim do not appear in the student accounts of their cheating. In denial of injury, the wrongdoer states that no one was harmed or implies that accusations of injury are grossly exaggerated. In the second case, denial of the victim, those who violate norms often portray their targets as legitimate. Due to certain factors such as the societal role, personal characteristics, or lifestyle of the victim, the wrongdoer felt the victim "had it coming."

It is unlikely that students will either deny injury or deny the victim since there are no real targets in cheating. However, attempts to deny injury are possible when the one who is cheating argues that cheating is a personal matter rather than a public one. It is also possible that some students are cognizant of the effect their cheating activities have upon the educational system as a whole and, therefore, choose to neutralize their behavior in ways which allow them to focus on the act rather than the consequences of cheating. By observing their actions from a myopic viewpoint, such students avoid the larger issues of morality.

Conclusion

The purpose of this report was to analyze student responses to cheating in their college coursework. Using Sykes and Matza's model of techniques of neutralization, we found that students rationalized their cheating behavior and do so without challenging the norm of honesty. Student responses fit three of the five techniques of neutralization. The most common technique is a denial of responsibility. Second, students tend to "condemn the condemners," blaming faculty and testing procedures. Finally, students "appeal to higher loyalties" by arguing that it is more important to help a friend than to avoid cheating. The use of these techniques of neutralization conveys the message that students recognize and accept cheating as an undesirable behavior which, nonetheless, can be excused under certain circumstances. Such findings reflect the prevalence of situational ethics.

The situation appears to be one in which students are not caught and disciplined by instructors. Additionally, students who cheat do not concern themselves with overt negative sanctions from other students. In some groups, cheating is planned, expected, and often rewarded in that students may receive better grades. That leaves a student's ethical, internalized control as a barrier to cheating. However, the neutralizing attitude allows students to sidestep issues of ethics and guilt by placing the blame for their behavior elsewhere. Neutralization allows them to state their belief that in general cheating is wrong, but in some special circumstances cheating is acceptable, even necessary.

Given such widespread acceptance of cheating in the university setting, it may be useful to further test the salience of neutralization and other such factors in more diverse university environments. This study is limited to a small state university. It is important also to extend the research to a wider range of institutions including prestigious private colleges, large state universities, and church-related schools.

Cross-cultural studies of cheating may also prove useful for identifying broader social and cultural forces which underlie situational ethics and cheating behavior. In this regard, the process involved in learning neutralizing attitudes could be integrated with work in the field of deviance in order to expand our understanding of the rule breakers along a continuum of minor to major forms of deviance.

References

Edwards, Paul. 1967. *The Encyclopedia of Philosophy*, Vol. 3, edited by Paul Edwards. New York: Macmillan Company and Free Press.

Fletcher, Joseph. 1966. *Situation Ethics: The New Morality*. Philadelphia: The Westminster Press.

Haines, Valerie J., George Diekhoff, Emily LaBeff, and Robert Clark. 1986. "College Cheating: Immaturity, Lack of Commitment, and the Neutralizing Attitude." *Research in Higher Education* 25: 342–354.

Liska, Allen. 1978. "Deviant Involvement, Associations, and Attitudes: Specifying the Underlying Causal Structures." *Sociology and Social Research* 63: 73–88.

Norris, Terry D., and Richard A. Dodder. 1979. "A Behavioral Continuum Synthesizing Neutralization Theory, Situational Ethics and Juvenile Delinquency." *Adolescence* 55: 545–555.

Sykes, Gresham, and David Matza. 1957. "Techniques of Neutralization: A Theory of Delinquency." *American Sociological Review* 22: 664–670.

Questions

1. Explain what the authors mean by "neutralization."

2. List the five major categories of neutralization techniques. According to LaBeff and her colleagues, what do these techniques have in common?

3. Review the kinds of excuses given by student cheaters in this study. Then, assume that you are a college professor who has just caught some students cheating. Which kinds of excuses would seem the most compelling to you? Would any of these lead you to treat the students' behavior as acceptable (i.e., not take any action against them for cheating)? Which kinds of excuses would seem the most lame to you? Why?

30
DENYING THE GUILTY MIND

Accounting for Involvement in a White-Collar Crime

Michael L. Benson

In this 1985 article, Michael Benson reports on the results of conversations he had with thirty men convicted of white-collar crime. The term *white-collar crime* was coined by criminologist Edwin Sutherland in 1949 to refer to any "crime committed by a person of respectability and high social status in the course of his occupation."

Benson encouraged each convict to talk about how he felt about his involvement with the justice system. One interesting finding: None of the men said he felt he was a "criminal."

Denying the Guilty Mind

Adjudication as a criminal is, to use Garfinkel's (1956) classic term, a degradation ceremony.[1] The focus of this article is on how offenders attempt to defeat the success of this ceremony and deny their own criminality through the use of accounts. However, in the interest of showing in as much detail as possible all sides of the experience undergone by these offenders, it is necessary to treat first the guilt and inner anguish that is felt by many white-collar offenders even though they deny being criminals. This is best accomplished by beginning with a description of a unique feature of the prosecution of white-collar crimes.

In white-collar criminal cases, the issue is likely to be *why* something was done, rather than *who* did it (Edelhertz 1970, 47). There is often relatively little disagreement as to what happened. In the words of one Assistant U.S. Attorney interviewed for the study:

> If you actually had a movie playing, neither side would dispute that a person moved in this way and handled this piece of paper, etc. What it comes down to is, did they have the criminal intent?

If the prosecution is to proceed past the investigatory stages, the prosecutor must infer from the pattern of events that conscious criminal intent was present and believe that sufficient evidence exists to convince a jury of this interpretation of the situation. As Katz (1979, 445–446) has noted, making this inference can be difficult because of the way in which white-collar illegalities are integrated into ordinary occupational routines. Thus, prosecutors in conducting trials, grand jury hearings, or plea negotiations spend a great

---

[1]A degradation ceremony is a public ritual in which the individual is stripped of his or her identity as a member of respectable society and formally labeled as an outsider or even as something less than human.—Ed.

Michael L. Benson, "Denying the Guilty Mind: Accounting for Involvement in White-Collar Crime" from *Criminology* 23, no. 4 (1985): 583–607. Reprinted with the permission of the American Society of Criminology.

deal of effort establishing that the defendant did indeed have the necessary criminal intent. By concentrating on the offender's motives, the prosecutor attacks the very essence of the white-collar offender's public and personal image as an upstanding member of the community. The offender is portrayed as someone with a guilty mind.

Not surprisingly, therefore, the most consistent and recurrent pattern in the interviews, though not present in all of them, was denial of criminal intent, as opposed to the outright denial of any criminal behavior whatsoever. Most offenders acknowledged that their behavior probably could be construed as falling within the conduct proscribed by statute, but they uniformly denied that their actions were motivated by a guilty mind. This is not to say, however, that offenders *felt* no guilt or shame as a result of conviction. On the contrary, indictment, prosecution, and conviction provoke a variety of emotions among offenders.

The enormous reality of the offender's lived emotion (Denzin 1984) in admitting guilt is perhaps best illustrated by one offender's description of his feelings during the hearing at which he pled guilty.

> You know (the plea's) what really hurt. I didn't even know I had feet. I felt numb. My head was just floating. There was no feeling, except a state of suspended animation. . . . For a brief moment, I almost hesitated. I almost said not guilty. If I had been alone, I would have fought, but my family. . . .

The traumatic nature of this moment lies, in part, in the offender's feeling that only one aspect of his life is being considered. From the offender's point of view his crime represents only one small part of his life. It does not typify his inner self, and to judge him solely on the basis of this one event seems an atrocious injustice to the offender.

For some the memory of the event is so painful that they want to obliterate it entirely, as the two following quotations illustrate.

> I want quiet. I want to forget. I want to cut with the past.
>
>   I've already divorced myself from the problem.
>   I don't even want to hear the names of certain people ever again. It brings me pain.

For others, rage rather than embarrassment seemed to be the dominant emotion.

> I never really felt any embarrassment over the whole thing. I felt rage and it wasn't false or self-serving. It was really (something) to see this thing in action and recognize what the whole legal system has come to through its development, and the abuse of the grand jury system and the abuse of the indictment system. . . .

The role of the news media in the process of punishment and stigmatization should not be overlooked. All offenders whose cases were reported on by the news media were either embarrassed or embittered or both by the public exposure.

> The only one I am bitter at is the newspapers, as many people are. They are unfair because you can't get even. They can say things that are untrue, and let me say this to you. They wrote an article on me that was so blasphemous, that was so horrible. They painted me as an insidious miserable creature, wringing out the last penny. . . .

Offenders whose cases were not reported on by the news media expressed relief at having avoided that kind of embarrassment, sometimes saying that greater publicity would have been worse than any sentence they could have received.

In court, defense lawyers are fond of presenting white-collar offenders as having suffered enough by virtue of the humiliation of public adjudication as criminals. On the other hand, prosecutors present them as cavalier individuals who arrogantly ignore the law and brush off its weak efforts to stigmatize them as criminals. Neither of these stereotypes is entirely accurate. The subjective effects of conviction on white-collar offenders are varied and complex. One suspects that this is true of all offenders, not only white-collar offenders.

The emotional responses of offenders to conviction have not been the subject of extensive research. However, insofar as an individual's emotional response to adjudication may influence the deterrent or crime-reinforcing impact of punishment on him or her, further study might reveal why some offenders stop their criminal behavior while others go on to careers in crime (Casper 1978, 80).

Although the offenders displayed a variety of different emotions with respect to their experiences, they were nearly unanimous in denying basic criminality. To see how white-collar offenders justify and excuse their crimes, we turn to their accounts. The small number of cases rules out the use of any elaborate classification techniques. Nonetheless, it is useful to group offenders by offense when presenting their interpretations.

ANTITRUST VIOLATORS[2]

Four of the offenders have been convicted of antitrust violations, all in the same case involving the building and contracting industry. Four major themes characterized their accounts. First, antitrust offenders focused on the everyday character and historical continuity of their offenses.

> It was a way of doing business before we even got into the business. So it was like why do you brush your teeth in the morning or something.
> . . . It was part of the everyday. . . . It was a method of survival.

The offenders argued that they were merely following established and necessary industry practices. These practices were presented as being necessary for the well-being of the industry as a whole, not to mention their own companies. Further, they argued that cooperation among competitors was either allowed or actively promoted by the government in other industries and professions.

The second theme emphasized by the offenders was the characterization of their actions as blameless. They admitted talking to competitors and admitted submitting intentionally noncompetitive bids. However, they presented these practices as being done not for the purpose of rigging prices nor to make exorbitant profits. Rather, the everyday practices of the industry required them to occasionally submit bids on projects they really did not want to have. To avoid the effort and expense of preparing full-fledged bids, they would call a competitor to get a price to use. Such a situation might arise, for example, when a company already had enough work for the time being, but was asked by a valued customer to submit a bid anyway.

> All you want to do is show a bid, so that in some cases it was for as small a reason as getting your deposit back on the plans and specs. So you just simply have no interest in getting the job and just call to see if you can find someone to give you a price to use, so that you didn't have to go through the expense of an entire bid preparation. Now that is looked on very unfavorably, and it is a technical violation, but it was strictly an opportunity to keep your name in front of a desired customer. Or you may find yourself in a situation where somebody is doing work for a customer, has done work for many, many years and is totally acceptable, totally fair. There is no problem. But suddenly they (the customer) get an idea that they ought to have a few tentative figures, and you're called in, and you are in a moral dilemma. There's really no reason for you to attempt to compete in that circumstance. And so there was a way to back out.

---

[2]Antitrust laws date back to the end of the nineteenth century. They are intended to promote fair business practices. For example, it is a violation of antitrust laws for business leaders to get together (or "collude") to fix consumer prices at artificially high levels.—Ed.

Managed in this way, an action that appears on the surface to be a straightforward and conscious violation of antitrust regulations becomes merely a harmless business practice that happens to be a "technical violation." The offender can then refer to his personal history to verify his claim that, despite technical violations, he is in reality a law-abiding person. In the words of one offender, "Having been in the business for 33 years, you don't just automatically become a criminal overnight."

Third, offenders were very critical of the motives and tactics of prosecutors. Prosecutors were accused of being motivated solely by the opportunity for personal advancement presented by winning a big case. Further, they were accused of employing prosecution selectively and using tactics that allowed the most culpable offenders to go free. The Department of Justice was painted as using antitrust prosecutions for political purposes.

The fourth theme emphasized by the antitrust offenders involved a comparison between their crimes and the crimes of street criminals. Antitrust offenses differ in their mechanics from street crimes in that they are not committed in one place and at one time. Rather, they are spatially and temporally diffuse and are intermingled with legitimate behavior. In addition, the victims of antitrust offenses tend not to be identifiable individuals, as is the case with most street crimes. These characteristics are used by antitrust violators to contrast their own behavior with that of common stereotypes of criminality. Real crimes are pictured as discrete events that have beginnings and ends and involve individuals who directly and purposely victimize someone else in a particular place and at a particular time.

> It certainly wasn't a premeditated type of thing in our cases as far as I can see. . . . To me it's different than—and I sitting down and we plan, well, we're going to rob this bank tomorrow and premeditatedly go in there. . . . That wasn't the case at all. . . . It wasn't like sitting down

and planning I'm going to rob this bank type of thing. . . . It was just a common everyday way of doing business and surviving.

A consistent thread running through all of the interviews was the necessity for antitrust-like practices, given the realities of the business world. Offenders seemed to define the situation in such a manner that two sets of rules could be seen to apply. On the one hand, there are the legislatively determined rules—laws—which govern how one is to conduct one's business affairs. On the other hand, there is a higher set of rules based on the concepts of profit and survival, which are taken to define what it means to be in business in a capitalistic society. These rules do not just regulate behavior; rather, they constitute or create the behavior in question. If one is not trying to make a profit or trying to keep one's business going, then one is not really "in business." Following Searle (1969, 33–41), the former type of rule can be called a regulative rule and the latter type a constitutive rule. In certain situations, one may have to violate a regulative rule in order to conform to the more basic constitutive rule of the activity in which one is engaged.

This point can best be illustrated through the use of an analogy involving competitive games. Trying to win is a constitutive rule of competitive games in the sense that if one is not trying to win, one is not really playing the game. In competitive games, situations may arise where a player deliberately breaks the rules even though he knows or expects he will be caught. In the game of basketball, for example, a player may deliberately foul an opponent to prevent him from making a sure basket. In this instance, one would understand that the fouler was trying to win by gambling that the opponent would not make the free throws. The player violates the rule against fouling in order to follow the higher rule of trying to win.

Trying to make a profit or survive in business can be thought of as a constitutive rule of capitalist economies. The laws that govern *how* one is allowed to make a profit are regulative rules, which can understandably be subordinated to the rules of trying to survive and profit. From the offender's point of view, he is doing what businessmen in our society are supposed to do—that is, stay in business and make a profit. Thus, an individual who violates society's laws or regulations in certain situations may actually conceive of himself as thereby acting more in accord with the central ethos of his society than if he had been a strict observer of its law. One might suggest, following Denzin (1977), that for businessmen in the building and contracting industry, an informal structure exists below the articulated legal structure, one which frequently supersedes the legal structure. The informal structure may define as moral and "legal" certain actions that the formal legal structure defines as immoral and "illegal."

TAX VIOLATORS

Six of the offenders interviewed were convicted of income tax violations. Like antitrust violators, tax violators can rely upon the complexity of the tax laws and an historical tradition in which cheating on taxes is not really criminal. Tax offenders would claim that everybody cheats somehow on their taxes and present themselves as victims of an unlucky break, because they got caught.

> Everybody cheats on their income tax, 95% of the people. Even if it's for ten dollars it's the same principle. I didn't cheat. I just didn't know how to report it.

The widespread belief that cheating on taxes is endemic helps to lend credence to the offender's claim to have been singled out and to be no more guilty than most people.

Tax offenders were more likely to have acted as individuals rather than as part of a group and, as a result, were more prone to account for their offenses by referring to them as either mistakes or the product of special circumstances. Violations were presented as simple errors which resulted from ignorance and poor recordkeeping. Deliberate intention to steal from the government for personal benefit was denied.

> I didn't take the money. I have no bank account to show for all this money, where all this money is at that I was supposed to have. They never found the money, ever. There is no Swiss bank account, believe me.
>
> My records were strictly one big mess. That's all it was. If only I had an accountant, this wouldn't even of happened. No way in God's creation would this ever have happened.

Other offenders would justify their actions by admitting that they were wrong while painting their motives as altruistic rather than criminal. Criminality was denied because they did not set out to deliberately cheat the government for their own personal gain. Like the antitrust offenders discussed above, one tax violator distinguished between his own crime and the crimes of real criminals.

> I'm not a criminal. That is, I'm not a criminal from the standpoint of taking a gun and doing this and that. I'm a criminal from the standpoint of making a mistake, a serious mistake. . . . The thing that really got me involved in it is my feeling for the employees here, certain employees that are my right hand. In order to save them a certain amount of taxes and things like that, I'd extend money to them in cash, and the money came from these sources that I took it from. You know, cash sales and things of that nature, but practically all of it was turned over to the employees, because of my feeling for them.

All of the tax violators pointed out that they had no intention of deliberately victimizing the government. None of them denied the legitimacy of the tax laws, nor did they claim that they cheated because the government is not representative of the people

(Conklin 1977, 99). Rather, as a result of ignorance or for altruistic reasons, they made decisions which turned out to be criminal when viewed from the perspective of the law. While they acknowledged the technical criminality of their actions, they tried to show that what they did was not criminally motivated.

VIOLATIONS OF FINANCIAL TRUST

Four offenders were involved in violations of financial trust. Three were banking officers who embezzled or misapplied funds, and the fourth was a union official who embezzled from a union pension fund.[3] Perhaps because embezzlement is one crime in this sample that can be considered *mala in se,* these offenders were much more forthright about their crimes. Like the other offenders, the embezzlers would not go so far as to say "I am a criminal," but they did say "What I did was wrong, was criminal, and I knew it was." Thus, the embezzlers were unusual in that they explicitly admitted responsibility for their crimes. . . .

Unlike tax evasion, which can be excused by reference to the complex nature of tax regulations or antitrust violations, which can be justified as for the good of the organization as a whole, embezzlement requires deliberate action on the part of the offender and is almost inevitably committed for personal reasons. The crime of embezzlement, therefore, cannot be accounted for by using the same techniques that tax violators or antitrust violators do. The act itself can only be explained by showing that one was under extraordinary circumstances which explain one's uncharacteristic behavior. Three of the

offenders referred explicitly to extraordinary circumstances and presented the offense as an aberration in their life history. For example, one offender described his situation in this manner:

> As a kid, I never even—you know kids will sometimes shoplift from the dime store— I never even did that. I had never stolen a thing in my life and that was what was so unbelievable about the whole thing, but there were some psychological and personal questions that I wasn't dealing with very well. I wasn't terribly happily married. I was married to a very strong-willed woman and it just wasn't working out.

The offender in this instance goes on to explain how, in an effort to impress his wife, he lived beyond his means and fell into debt.

A structural characteristic of embezzlement also helps the offender demonstrate his essential lack of criminality. Embezzlement is integrated into ordinary occupational routines. The illegal action does not stand out clearly against the surrounding set of legal actions. Rather, there is a high degree of surface correspondence, the offender must exercise some restraint when committing his crime. The embezzler must be discreet in his stealing; he cannot take all of the money available to him without at the same time revealing crime. Once exposed, the offender can point to this restraint on his part as evidence that he is not really a criminal. That is, he can compare what happened with what could have happened in order to show how much more serious the offense could have been if he was really a criminal at heart.

> What I could have done if I had truly had a devious criminal mind and perhaps if I had been a little smarter—and I am not saying that with any degree of pride or any degree of modesty whatever, [as] it's being smarter in a bad, an evil way—I could have pulled this off on a grander scale and I might still be doing it.

[3]Embezzlement is not just theft. Embezzlement is theft from someone who has entrusted his or her money or property to you.—Ed.

Even though the offender is forthright about admitting his guilt, he makes a distinction between himself and someone with a truly "devious criminal mind."

Contrary to Cressey's (1953, 57–66) findings, none of the embezzlers claimed that their offenses were justified because they were underpaid or badly treated by their employers. Rather, attention was focused on the unusual circumstances surrounding the offense and its atypical character when compared to the rest of the offender's life. This strategy is for the most part determined by the mechanics and organizational format of the offense itself. Embezzlement occurs within the organization but not for the organization. It cannot be committed accidentally or out of ignorance. It can be accounted for only by showing that the actor "was not himself" at the time of the offense or was under such extraordinary circumstances that embezzlement was an understandable response to an unfortunate situation. This may explain the finding that embezzlers tend to produce accounts that are viewed as more sufficient by the justice system than those produced by other offenders (Rothman and Gandossy 1982). The only plausible option open to a convicted embezzler trying to explain his offense is to admit responsibility while justifying the action, an approach that apparently strikes a responsive chord with judges.

FRAUD AND FALSE STATEMENTS

Ten offenders were convicted of some form of fraud or false statements charge. Unlike embezzlers, tax violators, or antitrust violators, these offenders were much more likely to deny committing any crime at all. Seven of the ten claimed that they, personally, were innocent of any crime, although each admitted that fraud had occurred. Typically, they claimed to have been set up by associates and to have been wrongfully convicted by the U.S. Attorney handling the case. One might call this the scapegoat strategy. Rather than admitting technical wrongdoing and then justifying or excusing it, the offender attempts to paint himself as a victim by shifting the blame entirely to another party. Prosecutors were presented as being either ignorant or politically motivated.

The outright denial of any crime whatsoever is unusual compared to the other types of offenders studied here. It may result from the nature of the crime of fraud. By definition, fraud involves a conscious attempt on the part of one or more persons to mislead others. While it is theoretically possible to accidentally violate the antitrust and tax laws, or to violate them for altruistic reasons, it is difficult to imagine how one could accidentally mislead someone else for his or her own good. Furthermore, in many instances, fraud is an aggressively acquisitive crime. The offender develops a scheme to bilk other people out of money or property, and does this not because of some personal problem but because the scheme is an easy way to get rich. Stock swindles, fraudulent loan scams, and so on are often so large and complicated that they cannot possibly be excused as foolish and desperate solutions to personal problems. Thus, those involved in large-scale frauds do not have the option open to most embezzlers of presenting themselves as persons responding defensively to difficult personal circumstances.

Furthermore, because fraud involves a deliberate attempt to mislead another, the offender who fails to remove himself from the scheme runs the risk of being shown to have a guilty mind. That is, he is shown to possess the most essential element of modern conceptions of criminality: an intent to harm another. His inner self would in this case be exposed as something other than what it has been presented as, and all of his previous actions would be subject to reinterpretation in light of his new perspective. For this reason, defrauders are most prone to denying any crime at all. The cooperative and conspiratorial nature of many fraudulent schemes makes it possible to put the blame on someone else and to present oneself as a scapegoat. Typically, this is done by claiming to have been duped by others.

Two illustrations of this strategy are presented below.

> I figured I wasn't guilty, so it wouldn't be that hard to disprove it, until, as I say, I went to court and all of a sudden they start bringing in these guys out of the woodwork implicating me that I never saw. Lot of it could be proved that I never saw.
>
> Inwardly, I personally felt that the only crime that I committed was not telling on these guys. Not that I deliberately, intentionally committed a crime against the system. My only crime was that I should have had the guts to tell on these guys, what they were doing, rather than putting up with it and then trying to gradually get out of the system without hurting them or without them thinking I was going to snitch on them.

Of the three offenders who admitted committing crimes, two acted alone and the third acted with only one other person. Their accounts were similar to the others presented earlier and tended to focus on either the harmless nature of their violations or on the unusual circumstances that drove them to commit their crimes. One claimed that his violations were only technical and that no one besides himself had been harmed.

> First of all, no money was stolen or anything of that nature. The bank didn't lose any money. . . . What I did was a technical violation. I made a mistake. There's no question about that, but the bank lost no money.

Another offender who directly admitted his guilt was involved in a check-kiting scheme. In a manner similar to embezzlers, he argued that his actions were motivated by exceptional circumstances.

> I was faced with the choice of all of a sudden, and I mean now, closing the doors or doing

something else to keep that business open. . . . I'm not going to tell you that this wouldn't have happened if I'd had time to think it over, because I think it probably would have. You're sitting there with a dying patient. You are going to try to keep him alive.

In the other fraud cases more individuals were involved, and it was possible and perhaps necessary for each offender to claim that he was not really the culprit.

Discussion: Offenses, Accounts, and Degradation Ceremonies

The investigation, prosecution, and conviction of a white-collar offender involves him in a very undesirable status passage (Glaser and Strauss 1971). The entire process can be viewed as a long and drawn-out degradation ceremony with the prosecutor as the chief denouncer and the offender's family and friends as the chief witnesses. The offender is moved from the status of law-abiding citizen to that of convicted felon. Accounts are developed to defeat the process of identity transformation that is the object of a degradation ceremony. They represent the offender's attempt to diminish the effect of his legal transformation and to prevent its becoming a publicly validated label. It can be suggested that the accounts developed by white-collar offenders take the forms that they do for two reasons: (1) the forms are required to defeat the success of the degradation ceremony, and (2) the specific forms used are the ones available given the mechanics, history, and organizational context of the offenses.

Three general patterns in accounting strategies stand out in the data. Each can be characterized by the subject matter on which it focuses: the event (offense), the perpetrator (offender), or the denouncer (prosecutor). These are the natural subjects of accounts in that to be successful, a degradation ceremony requires each of these elements to be presented in a particular manner (Garfinkel 1956). If an account giver can undermine the presentation of one or more of the elements, then the effect of the ceremony can be reduced. Although there are overlaps in the accounting strategies used by the various types of offenders, and while any given offender may use more than one strategy, it appears that accounting strategies and offenses correlate. . . .

References

Casper, Jonathan D. 1978. *Criminal Courts: The Defendant's Perspective.* Washington, DC: U.S. Department of Justice.

Conklin, John E. 1977. *Illegal But Not Criminal: Business Crime in America.* Englewood Cliffs, NJ: Prentice-Hall.

Cressey, Donald. 1953. *Other People's Money.* New York: Free Press.

Denzin, Norman K. 1977. "Notes on the Criminogenic Hypothesis: A Case Study of the American Liquor Industry." *American Sociological Review* 42: 905–920.

Denzin, Norman K. 1984. *On Understanding Emotion.* San Francisco: Jossey-Bass.

Edelhertz, Herbert. 1970. *The Nature, Impact, and Prosecution of White Collar Crime.* Washington, DC: U.S. Government Printing Office.

Garfinkel, Harold. 1956. "Conditions of Successful Degradation Ceremonies." *American Journal of Sociology* 61: 420–424.

Glaser, Barney G., and Anselm L. Strauss. 1971. *Status Passage.* Chicago: Aldine.

Katz, Jack. 1979. "Legality and Equality: Plea Bargaining in the Prosecution of White-Collar Crimes." *Law and Society Review* 13: 431–460.

Rothman, Martin, and Robert F. Gandossy. 1982. "Sad Tales: The Accounts of White-Collar Defendants and the Decision to Sanction." *Pacific Sociological Review* 4: 449–473.

Searle, John R. 1969. *Speech Acts.* Cambridge: Cambridge University Press.

Questions

1. Look back at the list of "techniques of neutralization" that you made in response to the first question following reading 29 about student cheating. Which of the explanations offered by white-collar criminals interviewed by Benson used any of the techniques of neutralization?

2. A single white-collar criminal may steal as much money as a whole host of burglars. Why, then, do white-collar offenders deny that they are as bad as street criminals? In your judgment, who is more criminal—the thief who steals $50 from a convenience store or the thief who steals $100,000 from an insurance company?

3. Consider the student cheater who says that "cheating is the only way to get through all the ridiculous demands that teachers place on us" and the insurance executive who says that "breaking the law is the only way to do business in this country." What, if anything, do they have in common?

31

THE LAND OF OPPORTUNITY

James Loewen

Many of us who teach sociology in U.S. colleges are frequently puzzled and even stunned by students' reactions to the subject of social inequality. If we blithely explain the extent and consequences of social inequality in the United States, we find our students regarding us as if we are sadly misinformed or (less charitably) have simply gone mad: "What do you mean America is not the land of equal opportunity?" Sometimes students' responses are downright hostile.

Still, if there is one thing sociologists know, it is that there is a great deal of inequality in the United States. The question is: Why does this fact come as such a big surprise to students? Perhaps James Loewen has the answer. He says that students graduate from high school as "terrible sociologists." As you will read in this 1995 piece, he puts part of the blame for this situation on the content of those social studies and history texts to which students were subjected in elementary, middle, and high school. Loewen is confident that he is right. He explains:

> For several years I have been lugging around twelve [history] textbooks, taking them seriously as works of history and ideology, studying what they say and don't say, and trying to figure out why. I chose the twelve as representing the range of textbooks available for history courses. . . . These twelve textbooks have been my window into the world of what high school students carry home, read, memorize, and forget. In addition, I have spent many hours observing high school history classes in Mississippi, Vermont, and the Washington, DC, metropolitan area, and more hours interviewing high school history teachers.

High school students have eyes, ears, and television sets (all too many have their own TV sets), so they know a lot about relative privilege in America. They measure their family's social position against that of other families,

Excerpt from *Lies My Teacher Told Me: Everything Your American History Textbook Got Wrong.* Copyright © 1995, 2007 by James W. Loewen. Reprinted by permission of The New Press. www.thenewpress.com

and their community's position against other communities. Middle-class students, especially, know little about how the American class structure works, however, and nothing at all about how it has changed over time. These students do not leave high school merely ignorant of the workings of the class structure; they come out as terrible sociologists. "Why are people poor?" I have asked first-year college students. Or, if their own class position is one of relative privilege, "Why is your family well off?" The answers I've received, to characterize them charitably, are half-formed and naive. The students blame the poor for not being successful. They have no understanding of the ways that opportunity is not equal in America and no notion that social structure pushes people around, influencing the ideas they hold and the lives they fashion.

High school history textbooks can take some of the credit for this state of affairs. Some textbooks cover certain high points of labor history, such as the 1894 Pullman strike near Chicago that President Cleveland broke with federal troops,[1] or the 1911 Triangle Shirtwaist fire that killed 146 women in New York City,[2] but the most recent event mentioned in most books is the Taft-Hartley Act of fifty years ago.[3] No book mentions the Hormel meat-packers' strike in the mid-1980s or the air traffic controllers' strike broken by President Reagan. Nor do textbooks describe any continuing issues facing labor, such as the growth of multinational corporations and their exporting of jobs overseas. With such omissions, textbook authors can construe labor history as something that happened long ago, like slavery,

and that, like slavery, was corrected long ago. It logically follows that unions appear anachronistic. The idea that they might be necessary in order for workers to have a voice in the workplace goes unstated.

Textbooks' treatments of events in labor history are never anchored in any analysis of social class. This amounts to delivering the footnotes instead of the lecture! Six of the dozen high school American history textbooks I examined contain no index listing at all for "social class," "social stratification," "class structure," "income distribution," "inequality," or any conceivably related topic. Not one book lists "upper class," "working class," or "lower class." Two of the textbooks list "middle class," but only to assure students that America is a middle-class country. "Except for slaves, most of the colonists were members of the 'middling ranks,'" says Land of Promise, and nails home the point that we are a middle-class country by asking students to "Describe three 'middle-class' values that united free Americans of all classes." Several of the textbooks note the explosion of middle-class suburbs after World War II. Talking about the middle class is hardly equivalent to discussing social stratification, however; in fact, as Gregory Mantsios (1988) has pointed out, "such references appear to be acceptable precisely because they mute class differences."

Stressing how middle-class we all are is particularly problematic today, because the proportion of households earning between 75 percent and 125 percent of the median income has fallen steadily since 1967. The Reagan-Bush administrations accelerated this shrinkage of the middle class, and most families who left its ranks fell rather than rose. This is the kind of historical trend one would think history books would take as appropriate subject matter, but only four of the twelve books in my sample provide any analysis of social stratification in the United States. Even these fragmentary analyses are set mostly in colonial

[1]The trouble started when George M. Pullman, owner of the Pullman Palace Car Company, refused even to discuss his employees' grievances (for example, deep wage cuts) with them. The workers' cause was taken up by the American Railway Union, which started a boycott against all Pullman train cars. Because Pullman cars were used on nearly every train running, the boycott brought the entire U.S. rail system to a standstill. President Cleveland called in federal troops to break the strike (Cleveland justified his intervention by claiming that the boycott was interfering with the U.S. mail).—Ed.

[2]The fire broke out on Saturday, March 25. Smoke was first seen on the eighth floor of the building where some 500 people—mostly female—were working. Escape was nearly impossible because the owners of the factory had locked the doors in order to keep their employees at work. Many women and girls jumped to their deaths from the windows of the building rather than face death in fire.—Ed.

[3]The Taft-Hartley Act of 1947 placed serious restrictions on union activities, including the requirement that union leaders swear under oath that they weren't communists.—Ed.

America. *Land of Promise* lives up to its reassuring title by heading its discussion of social class "Social Mobility." "One great difference between colonial and European society was that the colonists had more social mobility," echoes *The American Tradition.* "In contrast with contemporary Europe, eighteenth-century America was a shining land of equality and opportunity—with the notorious exception of slavery," chimes in *The American Pageant.* Although *The Challenge of Freedom* identifies three social classes—upper, middle, and lower—among whites in colonial society, compared to Europe "there was greater *social mobility.*"

Never mind that the most violent class conflicts in American history—Bacon's Rebellion and Shays's Rebellion[4]—took place in and just after colonial times. Textbooks still say that colonial society was relatively classless and marked by upward mobility. And things have gotten rosier since. "By 1815," *The Challenge of Freedom* assures us, two classes had withered away and "America was a country of middle class people and of middle class goals." This book returns repeatedly, at intervals of every fifty years or so, to the theme of how open opportunity is in America. "In the years after 1945, *social mobility*—movement from one social class to another—became more widespread in America," *Challenge* concludes. "This meant that people had a better chance to move upward in society." The stress on upward mobility is striking. There is almost nothing in any of these textbooks about class inequalities or barriers of any kind to social mobility. "What conditions made it possible for poor white immigrants to become richer in the colonies?"

---

[4]Bacon's Rebellion (1676) involved a bloody dispute between settlers and colonial authorities. The settlers' complaints included the fact that the authorities were not providing protection against hostile Native Americans. Shays's Rebellion (1786–1787) resulted from the refusal of Massachusetts legislators to assist debt-ridden farmers who were facing foreclosures.—Ed.

Land of Promise asks, "What conditions made/make it difficult?" goes unasked. Textbook authors thus present an America in which, as preachers were fond of saying in the nineteenth century, men start from "humble origins" and attain "the most elevated positions."

Social class is probably the single most important variable in society. From womb to tomb, it correlates with almost all other social characteristics of people that we can measure. Affluent expectant mothers are more likely to get prenatal care, receive current medical advice, and enjoy general health, fitness, and nutrition. Many poor and working-class mothers-to-be first contact the medical profession in the last month, sometimes the last hours, of their pregnancies. Rich babies come out healthier and weighing more than poor babies. The infants go home to very different situations. Poor babies are more likely to have high levels of poisonous lead in their environments and their bodies. Rich babies get more time and verbal interaction with their parents and higher quality day care when not with their parents. When they enter kindergarten, and through the twelve years that follow, rich children benefit from suburban schools that spend two to three times as much money per student as schools in inner cities or impoverished rural areas. Poor children are taught in classes that are often 50 percent larger than the classes of affluent children. Differences such as these help account for the higher school-dropout rate among poor children.

Even when poor children are fortunate enough to attend the same school as rich children, they encounter teachers who expect only children of affluent families to know the right answers. Social science research shows that teachers are often surprised and even distressed when poor children excel. Teachers and counselors believe they can predict who is "college material." Since many working-class children give off the wrong signals, even in first grade, they end up in the "general education" track

Rich better School a century

in high school. "If you are the child of low-income parents, the chances are good that you will receive limited and often careless attention from adults in your high school," in the words of Theodore Sizer's best-selling study of American high schools, *Horace's Compromise.* "If you are the child of upper-middle-income parents, the chances are good that you will receive substantial and careful attention" (quoted in Karp 1985, 73). Researcher Reba Page (1987) has provided vivid accounts of how high school American history courses use rote learning to turn off lower-class students. Thus schools have put into practice Woodrow Wilson's recommendation: "We want one class of persons to have a liberal education, and we want another class of persons, a very much larger class of necessity in every society, to forgo the privilege of a liberal education[5] and fit themselves to perform specific difficult manual tasks" (quoted in Lapham 1991).

As if this unequal home and school life were not enough, rich teenagers then enroll in the Princeton Review or other coaching sessions for the Scholastic Aptitude Test. Even without coaching, affluent children are advantaged because their background is similar to that of the test-makers, so they are comfortable with the vocabulary and subtle subcultural assumptions of the test. To no one's surprise, social class correlates strongly with SAT scores.

All these are among the reasons why social class predicts the rate of college attendance and the type of college chosen more effectively than does any other factor, including intellectual ability, however measured. After college, most affluent children get white-collar jobs, most working-class children get blue-collar jobs, and the class differences continue. As adults, rich people are more likely to have

hired an attorney and to be a member of formal organizations that increase their civic power. Poor people are more likely to watch TV. Because affluent families can save some money while poor families must spend what they make, wealth differences are ten times larger than income differences. Therefore most poor and working-class families cannot accumulate the down payment required to buy a house, which in turn shuts them out from our most important tax shelter, the writeoff of home mortgage interest. Working-class parents cannot afford to live in elite subdivisions or hire high-quality day care, so the process of educational inequality replicates itself in the next generation. Finally, affluent Americans also have longer life expectancies than lower- and working-class people, the largest single cause of which is better access to health care. Echoing the results of Helen Keller's study of blindness, research has determined that poor health is not distributed randomly about the social structure but is concentrated in the lower class. Social Security then becomes a huge transfer system, using monies contributed by all Americans to pay benefits disproportionately to longer-lived affluent Americans.

Ultimately, social class determines how people think about social class. When asked if poverty in America is the fault of the poor or the fault of the system, 57 percent of business leaders blamed the poor; just 9 percent blamed the system. Labor leaders showed sharply reversed choices: only 15 percent said the poor were at fault while 56 percent blamed the system. (Some replied "don't know" or chose a middle position.) The largest single difference between our two main political parties lies in how their members think about social class: 55 percent of Republicans blamed the poor for their poverty, while only 13 percent blamed the system for it; 68 percent of Democrats, on the other hand, blamed the system, while only 5 percent blamed the poor (Verba and Orren 1985, 72–75).

---

[5]"Liberal education," by definition, is education suited for the free (or liberated) citizen. The contrasting form of education is not "conservative education," but "vocational training."—Ed.

Few of these statements are news, I know, which is why I have not documented most of them, but the majority of high school students do not know or understand these ideas. Moreover, the processes have changed over time, for the class structure in America today is not the same as it was in 1890, let alone in colonial America. Yet in *Land of Promise*, for example, social class goes unmentioned after 1670.

Many teachers compound the problem by avoiding talking about social class. Recent interviews with teachers "revealed that they had a much broader knowledge of the economy, both academically and experientially, than they admitted in class." Teachers "expressed fear that students might find out about the injustices and inadequacies of their economic and political institutions" (McNeil 1983, 116). . . .

Historically, social class is intertwined with all kinds of events and processes in our past. Our governing system was established by rich men, following theories that emphasized government as a bulwark of the propertied class. Although rich himself, James Madison worried about social inequality and wrote *The Federalist #10* to explain how the proposed government would not succumb to the influence of the affluent. Madison did not fully succeed, according to Edward Pessen, who examined the social-class backgrounds of all American presidents through Reagan. Pessen found that more than 40 percent hailed from the upper class, mostly from the upper fringes of that elite group, and another 15 percent originated in families located between the upper and upper-middle classes. More than 25 percent came from a solid upper-middle-class background, leaving just six presidents, or 15 percent, to come from the middle and lower-middle classes and just one, Andrew Johnson, representing any part of the lower class. For good reason, Pessen (1984) titled his book *The Log Cabin Myth.* While it was sad when the great ship *Titanic* went down, as the old song refrain

goes, it was saddest for the lower classes: among women, only 4 of 143 first-class passengers were lost, while 15 of 93 second-class passengers drowned, along with 81 of 179 third-class women and girls. The crew ordered third-class passengers to remain below deck, holding some of them there at gunpoint (Hollingshead and Redlich 1958). More recently, social class played a major role in determining who fought in the Vietnam War: sons of the affluent won educational and medical deferments through most of the conflict (Baskir and Strauss 1986). Textbooks and teachers ignore all this.

Teachers may avoid social class out of a laudable desire not to embarrass their charges. If so, their concern is misguided. When my students from nonaffluent backgrounds learn about the class system, they find the experience liberating. Once they see the social processes that have helped keep their families poor, they can let go of their negative self-image about being poor. If to understand is to pardon, for working-class children to understand how stratification works is to pardon *themselves* and their families. Knowledge of the social-class system also reduces the tendency of Americans from other social classes to blame the victim for being poor. Pedagogically, stratification provides a gripping learning experience. Students are fascinated to discover how the upper class wields disproportionate power relating to everything from energy bills in Congress to zoning decisions in small towns.

Consider a white ninth-grade student taking American history in a predominantly middle-class town in Vermont. Her father tapes Sheet-rock, earning an income that in slow construction seasons leaves the family quite poor. Her mother helps out by driving a school bus part-time, in addition to taking care of her two younger siblings. The girl lives with her family in a small house, a winterized former summer cabin, while most of her classmates live in large suburban homes. How is this girl to understand her poverty? Since history textbooks present the American past as 390 years of progress and portray our society as a land of opportunity in which folks get what they deserve and deserve what they get, the failures of working-class Americans to transcend their class origin inevitably get laid at their own doorsteps.

Within the white working-class community the girl will probably find few resources—teachers, church parishioners, family members—who can tell her of heroes or struggles among people of her background, for, except in pockets of continuing class conflict, the working class usually forgets its own history. More than any other group, white working-class students believe that they deserve their low status. A subculture of shame results. This negative self-image is foremost among what Richard Sennett and Jonathan Cobb have called "the hidden injuries of class" (1972). Several years ago, two students of mine provided a demonstration: they drove around Burlington, Vermont, in a big, nearly new, shiny black American car (probably a Lexus would be more appropriate today) and then in a battered ten-year-old subcompact. In each vehicle, when they reached a stoplight and it turned green, they waited until they were honked at before driving on. Motorists averaged less than seven seconds to honk at them in the subcompact, but in the luxury car the students enjoyed 13.2 seconds before anyone honked. Besides providing a good reason to buy a luxury car, this experiment shows how Americans unconsciously grant respect to the educated and successful. Since motorists of all social stations honked at the subcompact more readily, working-class drivers were in a sense disrespecting themselves while deferring to their betters. The biting quip "If you're so smart, why aren't you rich?" conveys the injury done to the self-image of the poor when the idea that America is a meritocracy goes unchallenged in school.

Part of the problem is that American history textbooks describe American education itself as meritocratic. A huge body of research

confirms that education is dominated by the class structure and operates to replicate that structure in the next generation. Meanwhile, history textbooks blithely tell of such federal largesse to education as the Elementary and Secondary Education Act, passed under President Lyndon Johnson. Not one textbook offers any data on or analysis of inequality within educational institutions. None mentions how school districts in low-income areas labor under financial constraints so shocking that Jonathan Kozol (1991) calls them "savage inequalities." No textbook ever suggests that students might research the history of their own school and the population it serves. The only two textbooks that relate education to the class system at all see it as a remedy! Schooling "was a key to upward mobility in postwar America," in the words of *The Challenge of Freedom*.

The tendency of teachers and textbooks to avoid social class as if it were a dirty little secret only reinforces the reluctance of working-class families to talk about it. Paul Cowan has told of interviewing the children of Italian immigrant workers involved in the famous 1912 Lawrence, Massachusetts, mill strike. He spoke with the daughter of one of the Lawrence workers who testified at a Washington congressional hearing investigating the strike. The worker, Camella Teoli, then thirteen years old, had been scalped by a cotton-twisting machine just before the strike and had been hospitalized for several months. Her testimony "became front-page news all over America." But Teoli's daughter, interviewed in 1976 after her mother's death, could not help Cowan. Her mother had told her nothing of the incident, nothing of her trip to Washington, nothing about her impact on America's conscience—even though almost every day, the daughter "had combed her mother's hair into a bun that disguised the bald spot" (Gutman 1987, 386–390). A professional of working-class origin told me a similar story about being ashamed of her uncle "for being a steelworker." A certain defensiveness is built into working-class culture; even its successful acts of working-class resistance, like the Lawrence strike, necessarily presuppose lower status and income, hence connote a certain inferiority. If the larger community is so good, as textbooks tell us it is, then celebrating or even passing on the memory of conflict with it seems somehow disloyal.

Textbooks do present immigrant history. Around the turn of the century immigrants dominated the American urban working class, even in cities as distant from seacoasts as Des Moines and Louisville. When more than 70 percent of the white population was native stock, less than 10 percent of the urban working class was (Gutman 1987, 386–390). But when textbooks tell the immigrant story, they emphasize Joseph Pulitzer, Andrew Carnegie, and their ilk—immigrants who made super-good. Several textbooks apply the phrases *rags to riches* or *land of opportunity* to the immigrant experience. Such legendary successes were achieved, to be sure, but they were the exceptions, not the rule. Ninety-five percent of the executives and financiers in America around the turn of the century came from upper-class or upper-middle-class backgrounds. Fewer than 3 percent started as poor immigrants or farm children. Throughout the nineteenth century, just 2 percent of American industrialists came from working-class origins (Miller 1962, 326–328). By concentrating on the inspiring exceptions, textbooks present immigrant history as another heartening confirmation of America as the land of unparalleled opportunity.

Again and again, textbooks emphasize how America has differed from Europe in having less class stratification and more economic and social mobility. This is another aspect of the archetype of American exceptionalism: our society has been uniquely fair. It would never occur to historians in, say, France or Australia, to claim that their society was exceptionally equalitarian. Does this treatment of the United States prepare students for reality? It certainly does not accurately describe our country today. Social scientists have on many occasions compared the degree of economic equality in the United States with that in other industrial nations. Depending on the measure used, the United States has ranked sixth of six, seventh of seven, ninth of twelve, or fourteenth of fourteen (Verba and Orren 1985, 10). In the United States the richest fifth of the population earns eleven times as much income as the poorest fifth, one of the highest ratios in the industrialized world; in Great Britain the ratio is seven to one, in Japan just four to one (Mantsios 1988, 59). In Japan the average chief executive officer in an automobile-manufacturing firm makes 20 times as much as the average worker in an automobile assembly plant; in the United States he (and it is not she) makes 192 times as much (*Harper's* 1990, 19). The Jeffersonian conceit of a nation of independent farmers and merchants is also long gone: only one working American in thirteen is self-employed, compared to one in eight in Western Europe (*Harper's* 1993, 19). Thus not only do we have far fewer independent entrepreneurs compared to two hundred years ago, we have fewer compared to Europe today.

Since textbooks claim that colonial America was radically less stratified than Europe, they should tell their readers when inequality set in. It surely was not a recent development. By 1910 the top 1 percent of the United States population received more than a third of all personal income, while the bottom fifth got less than one-eighth (Tyack and Hansot 1981). This level of inequality was on a par with that in Germany or Great Britain (Williamson and Lindert 1980). If textbooks acknowledged inequality, then they could describe the changes in our class structure over time, which would introduce their students to fascinating historical debate.

For example, some historians argue that wealth in colonial society was more equally distributed than it is today and that economic inequality increased during the presidency of Andrew Jackson—a period known, ironically, as the age of the common man. Others believe that the flowering of the large corporation in the late nineteenth century made the class structure more rigid. Walter Dean Burnham has argued that the Republican presidential victory in 1896 (McKinley over Bryan) brought about a sweeping political realignment that changed "a fairly democratic regime into a rather broadly based oligarchy,"[6] so by the 1920s business controlled public policy (1965, 23–25). Clearly the gap between rich and poor, like the distance between blacks and whites, was greater at the end of the Progressive Era in 1920 than at its beginning around 1890 (Schwartz 1991, 94). The story is not all one of increasing stratification, for between the depression and the end of World War II income and wealth in America gradually became more equal. Distributions of income then remained reasonably constant until President Reagan took office in 1981, when inequality began to grow. Still other scholars think that little change has occurred since the Revolution. Lee Soltow (1989), for example, finds "surprising inequality of wealth and income" in America in 1798. At least for Boston, Stephan Thernstrom (1973) concludes that inequalities in life chances owing to social class show an eerie continuity. All this is part of American history. But it is not part of American history as taught in high school.

To social scientists, the level of inequality is a portentous thing to know about a society. When we rank countries by this variable, we find Scandinavian nations at the top, the most equal, and agricultural societies like Colombia and India near the bottom. The policies of the Reagan and Bush administrations, which openly favored the rich, abetted a trend already in motion, causing inequality to increase measurably between 1981 and 1992. For the United States to move perceptibly toward Colombia in social inequality is a development of no small

import (Danziger and Gottschalf 1993; Kohn 1990; Macrobert 1984). Surely high school students would be interested to learn that in 1950 physicians made two and a half times what unionized industrial workers made but now make six times as much. Surely they need to understand that top managers of clothing firms, who used to earn fifty times what their American employees made, now make 1,500 times what their Malaysian workers earn. Surely it is wrong for our history textbooks and teachers to withhold the historical information that might prompt and inform discussion of these trends.

Why might they commit such a blunder? First and foremost, publisher censorship of textbook authors. "You always run the risk, if you talk about social class, of being labeled Marxist," the editor for social studies and history at one of the biggest publishing houses told me. This editor communicates the taboo, formally or subtly, to every writer she works with, and she implied that most other editors do too.

Publisher pressure derives in part from textbook adoption boards and committees in states and school districts. These are subject in turn to pressure from organized groups and individuals who appear before them. Perhaps the most robust such lobby is Educational Research Analysts, led by Mel Gabler of Texas. Gabler's stable of right-wing critics regards even alleging that a textbook contains some class analysis as a devastating criticism. As one writer has put it, "Formulating issues in terms of class is unacceptable, perhaps even un-American" (Mantsios 1988). Fear of not winning adoption in Texas is a prime source of publisher angst, and might help explain why *Life and Liberty* limits its social-class analysis to colonial times in *England!* By contrast, "the colonies were places of great opportunity," even back then. Some Texans cannot easily be placated, however. Deborah L. Brezina, a Gabler ally, complained to the Texas textbook board that *Life and Liberty* describes America "as an unjust society," unfair to lower

---

[6]*Oligarchy* means "rule by a few"—as opposed to *aristocracy*, which means, technically, "rule by the best few."—Ed.

economic groups, and therefore should not be approved. Such pressure is hardly new. Harold Rugg's *Introduction to Problems of American Culture* and his popular history textbook, written during the depression, included some class analysis. In the early 1940s, according to Frances FitzGerald, the National Association of Manufacturers attacked Rugg's books, partly for this feature, and "brought to an end" social and economic analysis in American history textbooks (1979).

More often the influence of the upper class is less direct. The most potent rationale for class privilege in American history has been Social Darwinism,[7] an archetype that still has great power in American culture. The notion that people rise and fall in a survival of the fittest may not conform to the data on intergenerational mobility in the United States, but that has hardly caused the archetype to fade away from American education, particularly from American history classes (Tyack and Hansot 1981). Facts that do not fit with the archetype, such as the entire literature of social stratification, simply get left out. . . .

But isn't it nice simply to believe that America is equal? Maybe the "land of opportunity" archetype is an empowering myth— maybe believing in it might even help make it come true. For if students *think* the sky is the limit, they may reach for the sky, while if they don't, they won't.

The analogy of gender points to the problem with this line of thought. How could high school girls understand their place in American history if their textbooks told them that, from colonial America to the present, women have had equal opportunity for upward mobility and political participation? How could they then explain why no woman has been president? Girls would have to infer, perhaps unconsciously,

that it has been their own gender's fault, a conclusion that is hardly empowering.

Textbooks do tell how women were denied the right to vote in many states until 1920 and faced other barriers to upward mobility. Textbooks also tell of barriers confronting racial minorities. The final question *Land of Promise* asks students following its "Social Mobility" section is "What social barriers prevented blacks, Indians, and women from competing on an equal basis with white male colonists?" After its passage extolling upward mobility, *The Challenge of Freedom* notes, "Not all people, however, enjoyed equal rights or an equal chance to improve their way of life," and goes on to address the issues of sexism and racism. But neither here nor anywhere else do *Promise* or *Challenge* (or most other textbooks) hint that opportunity might not be equal today for white Americans of the lower and working classes. Perhaps as a result, even business leaders and Republicans, the respondents statistically most likely to engage in what sociologists call "blaming the victim," blame the social system rather than African Americans for black poverty and blame the system rather than women for the latter's unequal achievement in the workplace. In sum, affluent Americans, like their textbooks, are willing to credit racial discrimination as the cause of poverty among blacks and Indians and sex discrimination as the cause of women's inequality but don't see class discrimination as the cause of poverty in general (Verba and Orren 1985, 72–75).

More than math or science, more even than American literature, courses in American history hold the promise of telling high school students how they and their parents, their communities, and their society came to be as they are. One way things are is unequal by social class. Although poor and working-class children usually cannot identify the cause of their alienation, history often turns them off because it justifies rather than explains the present. When these students react by dropping out, intellectually if not physically, their poor school

---

[7]For a discussion of this concept, see chapter 1 in *The Practical Skeptic: Core Concepts in Sociology.*—Ed.

performance helps convince them as well as their peers in the faster tracks that the system is meritocratic and that they themselves lack merit. In the end, the absence of social-class analysis in American history courses amounts to one more way that education in America is rigged against the working class.

References

Baskir, L., and W. Strauss. 1986. *Chance and Circumstance.* New York: Random House.

Bowles, S., and H. Gintis. 1976. *Schooling in Capitalist America.* New York: Basic Books.

Brezina, D. L. 1993. "Critique of *Life and Liberty*," distributed by Mel Gabler's Educational Research Analysts.

Burnham, W. D. 1965. "The Changing Shape of the American Political University." *American Political Science Review* 59: 23–25.

Danziger, S., and P. Gottschalf. 1993. *Uneven Tides.* New York: Sage.

FitzGerald, F. 1979. *America Revised.* New York: Vintage Books.

Gutman, H. 1987. *Power and Culture.* New York: Pantheon Books.

Harper's. 1990. "Index" (citing data from the United Automobile Workers; Chrysler Corp; "Notice of Annual Meeting of Stockholders"). April 1.

Harper's. 1993. "Index" (citing the Organization for Economic Cooperation and Development). January 19.

Hollingshead, A., and F. C. Redlich. 1958. *Social Class and Mental Illness.* New York: Wiley.

Karp, Walter. 1985. "Why Johnny Can't Think." *Harper's,* June, p. 73.

Kohn, A. 1990. *You Know What They Say. . . .* New York: HarperCollins.

Kozol, J. 1991. *Savage Inequalities.* New York: Crown.

Lapham, Lewis. 1991. "Notebook." *Harper's,* July, p. 10.

Macrobert, A. 1984. "The Unfairness of It All." *Vermont Vanguard Press,* September 30, pp. 12–13.

Mantsios, Gregory. 1988. "Class in America: Myths and Realities." In Paula S. Rothenberg (ed.), *Racism and Sexism: An Integrated Study.* New York: St. Martin's Press.

McNeil, Linda. 1983. "Teaching and Classroom Control." In M. W. Apple and L. Weis (eds.), *Ideology and Practice in Schooling.* Philadelphia: Temple University Press.

Miller, W. 1962. "American Historians and the Business Elite." In W. Miller (ed.), *Men in Business.* New York: Harper & Row.

Page, Reba. 1987. *The Lower-track Students' View of Curriculum.* Washington, DC: American Education Research Association.

Pessen, E. 1984. *The Log Cabin Myth.* New Haven, CT: Yale University Press.

Schwartz, B. 1991. "The Reconstruction of Abraham Lincoln," in D. Middleton and D. Edwards (eds.), *Collective Remembering.* London: Sage.

Sennett, R., and J. Cobb. 1972. *The Hidden Injuries of Class.* New York: Knopf.

Soltow, L. 1989. *Distribution of Wealth and Income in the United States in 1798.* Pittsburgh: University of Pittsburgh Press.

Thernstrom, S. 1973. *The Other Bostonians.* Cambridge, MA: Harvard University Press.

Tyack, D., and E. Hansot. 1981. "Conflict and Consensus in American Public Education." *Daedalus* 110: 11–12.

Verba, S., and G. Orren. 1985. *Equality in America.* Cambridge, MA: Harvard University Press.

Williamson, J., and P. Lindert. 1980. *American Inequality: A Macroeconomic History.* New York: Academic Press.

Questions

1. Loewen asserts that high school students graduate as "terrible sociologists." To what extent do you agree or disagree with this assessment? Why?

2. Assuming that Loewen is correct about the "mythical" quality of the information given in high school history textbooks, what might be the function of these myths in American society? What might be the dysfunctions?

32

NICKEL AND DIMED

On (Not) Getting By in America

Barbara Ehrenreich

This article, published in 1999, eventually became the first chapter in Ehrenreich's book by the same title; it's an interesting but thoroughly depressing account of what it takes to survive on the proceeds of a minimum-wage job. In the introduction to her book, Ehrenreich stresses the fact that her experience represented the *best* case scenario: "A person with every advantage that ethnicity and education, health and motivation can confer attempting, in a time of exuberant prosperity, to survive in the economy's lowest depths."

At the beginning of June 1998 I leave behind everything that normally soothes the ego and sustains the body—home, career, companion, reputation, ATM card—for a plunge into the low-wage workforce. There, I become another, occupationally much diminished "Barbara Ehrenreich"—depicted on job-application forms as a divorced homemaker whose sole work experience consists of housekeeping in a few private homes, I am terrified, at the beginning, of being unmasked for what I am: a middle-class journalist setting out to explore the world that welfare mothers are entering, at the rate of approximately 50,000 a month, as welfare reform kicks in. Happily, though, my fears turn out to be entirely unwarranted: during a month of poverty and toil, my name goes unnoticed and for the most part unuttered. In this parallel universe where my father never got out of the mines and I never got through college, I am "baby," "honey," "blondie," and, most commonly, "girl."

My first task is to find a place to live. I figure that if I can earn $7 an hour—which, from the want ads, seems doable—I can afford to spend $500 on rent, or maybe, with severe economies, $600. In the Key West area, where I live, this pretty much confines me to flophouses and trailer homes—like the one, a pleasing fifteen-minute drive from town, that has no air-conditioning, no screens, no fans, no television, and, by way of diversion, only the challenge of evading the landlord's Doberman pinscher. The big problem with this place, though, is the rent, which at $675 a month is well beyond my reach. All right, Key West is expensive. But so is New York City, or the Bay Area, or Jackson Hole, or Telluride, or Boston, or any other place where tourists and the wealthy compete for living space with the people who clean their toilets and fry their hash browns.[1] Still, it is a

---

[1] According to the Department of Housing and Urban Development, the "fair-market rent" for an efficiency is $551 here in Monroe County, Florida. A comparable rent in the five boroughs of New York City is $704; in San Francisco, $713; and in the heart of Silicon Valley, $808. The fair-market rent for an area is defined as the amount that would be needed to pay rent plus utilities for "privately owned, decent, safe, and sanitary rental housing of a modest (non-luxury) nature with suitable amenities."

shock to realize that "trailer trash" has become, for me, a demographic category to aspire to.

So I decide to make the common trade-off between affordability and convenience, and go for a $500-a-month efficiency thirty miles up a two-lane highway from the employment opportunities of Key West, meaning forty-five minutes if there's no road construction and I don't get caught behind some sun-dazed Canadian tourists. I hate the drive, along a roadside studded with white crosses commemorating the more effective head-on collisions, but it's a sweet little place—a cabin, more or less, set in the swampy back yard of the converted mobile home where my landlord, an affable TV repairman, lives with his bartender girlfriend.

No, this is a purely objective, scientific sort of mission. The humanitarian rationale for welfare reform—as opposed to the more punitive and stingy impulses that may actually have motivated it—is that work will lift poor women out of poverty while simultaneously inflating their self-esteem and hence their future value in the labor market. Thus, whatever the hassles involved in finding child care, transportation, etc., the transition from welfare to work will end happily, in greater prosperity for all. Now there are many problems with this comforting prediction, such as the fact that the economy will inevitably undergo a downturn, eliminating many jobs. Even without a downturn, the influx of a million former welfare recipients into the low-wage labor market could depress wages by as much as 11.9 percent, according to the Economic Policy Institute (EPI) in Washington, D.C.

But is it really possible to make a living on the kinds of jobs currently available to unskilled people? Mathematically, the answer is no, as can be shown by taking $6 to $7 an hour, perhaps subtracting a dollar or two an hour for child care, multiplying by 160 hours a month, and comparing the result to the prevailing rents. According to the National Coalition for the Homeless, for example, in 1998 it took, on average nationwide, an hourly wage of $8.89 to afford a one-bedroom apartment, and the Preamble Center for Public Policy estimates that the odds against a typical welfare recipient's landing a job at such a "living wage" are about 97 to 1. If these numbers are right, low-wage work is not a solution to poverty and possibly not even to homelessness.

It may seem excessive to put this proposition to an experimental test. As certain family members keep unhelpfully reminding me, the viability of low-wage work could be tested, after a fashion, without ever leaving my study. I could just pay myself $7 an hour for eight hours a day, charge myself for room and board, and total up the numbers after a month. Why leave the people and work that I love? But I am an experimental scientist by training. In that business, you don't just sit at a desk and theorize; you plunge into the everyday chaos of nature, where surprises lurk in the most mundane measurements. Maybe, when I got into it, I would discover some hidden economies in the world of the low-wage worker. After all, if 30 percent of the workforce toils for less than $8 an hour, according to the EPI, they may have found some tricks as yet unknown to me. Maybe—who knows?— I would even be able to detect in myself the bracing psychological effects of getting out of the house, as promised by the welfare wonks at places like the Heritage Foundation. Or, on the other hand, maybe there would be unexpected costs—physical, mental, or financial—to throw off all my calculations. Ideally, I should do this with two small children in tow, that being the welfare average, but mine are grown and no one is willing to lend me theirs for a month-long vacation in penury. So this is not the perfect experiment, just a test of the best possible case: an unencumbered woman, smart and even strong, attempting to live more or less off the land.

On the morning of my first full day of job searching, I take a red pen to the want ads, which are auspiciously numerous. Everyone in Key West's booming "hospitality industry" seems to be looking for someone like me—trainable, flexible, and with suitably humble expectations as to pay. I know I possess certain traits that might be advantageous—I'm white and, I like to think, well-spoken and poised—but I decide on two rules: One, I cannot use any skills derived from my education or usual work—not that there are a lot of want ads for satirical essayists anyway. Two, I have to take the best-paid job that is offered me and of course do my best to hold it; no Marxist rants or sneaking off to read novels in the ladies' room. In addition, I rule out various occupations for one reason or another: Hotel front-desk clerk, for example, which to my surprise is regarded as unskilled and pays around $7 an hour, gets eliminated because it involves standing in one spot for eight hours a day. Waitressing is similarly something I'd like to avoid, because I remember it leaving me bone tired when I was eighteen, and I'm decades of varicosities and back pain beyond that now. Telemarketing, one of the first refuges of the suddenly indigent, can be dismissed on grounds of personality. This leaves certain supermarket jobs, such as deli clerk, or housekeeping in Key West's thousands of hotel and guest rooms. Housekeeping is especially appealing, for reasons both atavistic and practical: it's what my mother did before I came along, and it can't be too different from what I've been doing part-time, in my own home, all my life.

So I put on what I take to be a respectful-looking outfit of ironed Bermuda shorts and scooped-neck T-shirt and set out for a tour of the local hotels and supermarkets. Best Western, Econo Lodge, and HoJo's all let me fill out application forms, and these are, to my relief, interested in little more than whether I am a legal resident of the United States and have

committed any felonies. My next stop is Winn-Dixie, the supermarket, which turns out to have a particularly onerous application process, featuring a fifteen-minute "interview" by computer since, apparently, no human on the premises is deemed capable of representing the corporate point of view. I am conducted to a large room decorated with posters illustrating how to look "professional" (it helps to be white and, if female, permed) and warning of the slick promises that union organizers might try to tempt me with. The interview is multiple choice: Do I have anything, such as child-care problems, that might make it hard for me to get to work on time? Do I think safety on the job is the responsibility of management? Then, popping up cunningly out of the blue: How many dollars' worth of stolen goods have I purchased in the last year? Would I turn in a fellow employee if I caught him stealing? Finally, "Are you an honest person?"

Apparently, I ace the interview, because I am told that all I have to do is show up in some doctor's office tomorrow for a urine test. This seems to be a fairly general rule: if you want to stack Cheerio boxes or vacuum hotel rooms in chemically fascist America, you have to be willing to squat down and pee in front of some health worker (who has no doubt had to do the same thing herself). The wages Winn-Dixie is offering—$6 and a couple of dimes to start with—are not enough, I decide, to compensate for this indignity.[2]

---

[2] According to the *Monthly Labor Review* (November 1996), 28 percent of work sites surveyed in the service industry conduct drug tests (corporate workplaces have much higher rates), and the incidence of testing has risen markedly since the Eighties. The rate of testing is highest in the South (56 percent of work sites polled), with the Midwest in second place (50 percent). The drug most likely to be detected—marijuana, which can be detected in urine for weeks—is also the most innocuous, while heroin and cocaine are generally undetectable three days after use. Prospective employees sometimes try to cheat the tests by consuming excessive amounts of liquids and taking diuretics and even masking substances available through the Internet.

I lunch at Wendy's where $4.99 gets you unlimited refills at the Mexican part of the Superbar, a comforting surfeit of refried beans and "cheese sauce." A teenage employee, seeing me studying the want ads, kindly offers me an application form, which I fill out, though here, too, the pay is just $6 and change an hour. Then it's off for a round of the locally owned inns and guesthouses. At "The Palms," let's call it, a bouncy manager actually takes me around to see the rooms and meet the existing housekeepers, who, I note with satisfaction, look pretty much like me—faded exhippie types in shorts with long hair pulled back in braids. Mostly, though, no one speaks to me or even looks at me except to proffer an application form. At my last stop, a palatial B&B, I wait twenty minutes to meet "Max," only to be told that there are no jobs now but there should be one soon, since "nobody lasts more than a couple weeks." (Because none of the people I talked to knew I was a reporter, I have changed their names to protect their privacy and, in some cases perhaps, their jobs.)

Three days go by like this, and, to my chagrin, no one out of the approximately twenty places I've applied calls me for an interview. I had been vain enough to worry about coming across as too educated for the jobs I sought, but no one even seems interested in finding out how overqualified I am. Only later will I realize that the want ads are not a reliable measure of the actual jobs available at any particular time. They are, as I should have guessed from Max's comment, the employers' insurance policy against the relentless turnover of the low-wage workforce. Most of the big hotels run ads almost continually, just to build a supply of applicants to replace the current workers as they drift away or are fired, so finding a job is just a matter of being at the right place at the right time and flexible enough to take whatever is being offered that day. This finally happens to me at one of the big discount hotel chains, where I go, as usual, for housekeeping

and am sent, instead, to try out as a waitress at the attached "family restaurant," a dismal spot with a counter and about thirty tables that looks out on a parking garage and features such tempting fare as "Pollish [sic] sausage and BBQ sauce" on 95-degree days. Phillip, the dapper young West Indian who introduces himself as the manager, interviews me with about as much enthusiasm as if he were a clerk processing me for Medicare, the principal questions being what shifts can I work and when can I start. I mutter something about being woefully out of practice as a waitress, but he's already on to the uniform: I'm to show up tomorrow wearing black slacks and black shoes; he'll provide the rust-colored polo shirt with HEARTH-SIDE embroidered on it, though I might want to wear my own shirt to get to work, ha ha. At the word "tomorrow," something between fear and indignation rises in my chest. I want to say, "Thank you for your time, sir, but this is just an experiment, you know, not my actual life."

So begins my career at the Hearthside, I shall call it, one small profit center within a global discount hotel chain, where for two weeks I work from 2:00 P.M. till 10:00 P.M. for $2.43 an hour plus tips.[3] In some futile bid for gentility, the management has barred employees from using the front door, so my first day I enter through the kitchen, where a red-faced man with shoulder-length blond hair is throwing frozen steaks against the wall and yelling, "Fuck this shit!" "That's just Jack," explains Gail, the wiry middle-aged waitress who is assigned to train me. "He's on the rag again"—a condition occasioned, in this instance, by the fact that the cook on the morning shift had

---

[3]According to the Fair Labor Standards Act, employers are not required to pay "tipped employees," such as restaurant servers, more than $2.13 an hour in direct wages. However, if the sum of tips plus $2.13 an hour falls below the minimum wage, or $5.15 an hour, the employer is required to make up the difference. This fact was not mentioned by managers or otherwise publicized at either of the restaurants where I worked.

forgotten to thaw out the steaks. For the next eight hours, I run after the agile Gail, absorbing bits of instruction along with fragments of personal tragedy. All food must be trayed, and the reason she's so tired today is that she woke up in a cold sweat thinking of her boyfriend, who killed himself recently in an upstate prison. No refills on lemonade. And the reason he was in prison is that a few DUIs caught up with him, that's all, could have happened to anyone. Carry the creamers to the table in a monkey bowl, never in your hand. And after he was gone she spent several months living in her truck, peeing in a plastic pee bottle and reading by candlelight at night, but you can't live in a truck in the summer, since you need to have the windows down, which means anything can get in, from mosquitoes on up.

At least Gail puts to rest any fears I had of appearing overqualified. From the first day on, I find that of all the things I have left behind, such as home and identity, what I miss the most is competence. Not that I have ever felt utterly competent in the writing business, in which one day's success augurs nothing at all for the next. But in my writing life, I at least have some notion of procedure: do the research, make the outline, rough out a draft, etc. As a server, though, I am beset by requests like bees: more iced tea here, ketchup over there, a to-go box for table fourteen, and where are the high chairs, anyway? Of the twenty-seven tables, up to six are usually mine at any time, though on slow afternoons or if Gail is off, I sometimes have the whole place to myself. There is the touch-screen computer-ordering system to master, which is, I suppose, meant to minimize server-cook contact, but in practice requires constant verbal fine-tuning: "That's gravy on the mashed, okay? None on the meatloaf," and so forth—while the cook scowls as if I were inventing these refinements just to torment him. Plus, something I had forgotten in the years since I was eighteen: about a third of a server's job is "side work" that's invisible to customers—sweeping, scrubbing, slicing, refilling, and restocking. If it isn't all done, every little bit of it, you're going to face the 6:00 P.M. dinner rush defenseless and probably go down in flames. I screw up dozens of times at the beginning, sustained in my shame entirely by Gail's support—"It's okay, baby, everyone does that sometime"—because, to my total surprise and despite the scientific detachment I am doing my best to maintain, I care.

The whole thing would be a lot easier if I could just skate through it as Lily Tomlin in one of her waitress skits, but I was raised by the absurd Booker T. Washingtonian precept that says: If you're going to do something, do it well. In fact, "well" isn't good enough by half. Do it better than anyone has ever done it before. Or so said my father, who must have known what he was talking about because he managed to pull himself, and us with him, up from the mile-deep copper mines of Butte to the leafy suburbs of the Northeast, ascending from boilermakers to martinis before booze beat out ambition. As in most endeavors I have encountered in my life, doing it "better than anyone" is not a reasonable goal. Still, when I wake up at 4:00 A.M. in my own cold sweat, I am not thinking about the writing deadlines I'm neglecting; I'm thinking about the table whose order I screwed up so that one of the boys didn't get his kiddie meal until the rest of the family had moved on to their Key Lime pies. That's the other powerful motivation I hadn't expected—the customers, or "patients," as I can't help thinking of them on account of the mysterious vulnerability that seems to have left them temporarily unable to feed themselves. After a few days at the Hearthside, I feel the service ethic kick in like a shot of oxytocin, the nurturance hormone. The plurality of my customers are hard-working locals—truck drivers, construction workers, even housekeepers from the attached hotel—and I want them to have the closest to a "fine dining" experience that the grubby circumstances will allow. No "you guys" for me; everyone over twelve is "sir" or "ma'am." I ply them with iced tea and coffee refills; I return, mid-meal, to inquire how everything is; I doll up their salads with chopped raw mushrooms, summer squash slices, or whatever bits of produce I can find that have survived their sojourn in the cold-storage room mold-free.

Sometimes I play with the fantasy that I am a princess who, in penance for some tiny transgression, has undertaken to feed each of her subjects by hand. But the non-princesses working with me are just as indulgent, even when this means flouting management rules—concerning, for example, the number of croutons that can go on a salad (six). "Put on all you want," Gail whispers, "as long as Stu isn't looking." She dips into her own tip money to buy biscuits and gravy for an out-of-work mechanic who's used up all his money on dental surgery, inspiring me to pick up the tab for his milk and pie. Maybe the same high levels of agape can be found throughout the "hospitality industry." I remember the poster decorating one of the apartments I looked at, which said "If you seek happiness for yourself you will never find it. Only when you seek happiness for others will it come to you," or words to that effect—an odd sentiment, it seemed to me at the time, to find in the dank one-room basement apartment of a bellhop at the Best Western. At the Hearthside, we utilize whatever bits of autonomy we have to ply our customers with the illicit calories that signal our love. It is our job as servers to assemble the salads and desserts, pouring the dressings and squirting the whipped cream. We also control the number of butter patties our customers get and the amount of sour cream on their baked potatoes. So if you wonder why Americans are so obese, consider the fact that waitresses both express their humanity and earn their tips through the covert distribution of fats.

Ten days into it, this is beginning to look like a livable lifestyle. I like Gail, who is "looking at fifty" but moves so fast she can alight in one place and then another without apparently being anywhere between them. I clown around with Lionel, the teenage Haitian busboy, and catch a few fragments of conversation with Joan, the svelte fortyish hostess and militant feminist who is the only one of us who dares to tell Jack to shut the fuck up. I even warm up to Jack when, on a slow night and to make up for a particularly unwarranted attack on my abilities, or so I imagine, he tells me about his glory days as a young man at "coronary school"—or do you say "culinary"?—in Brooklyn, where he dated a knock-out Puerto Rican chick and learned everything there is to know about food. I finish up at 10:00 or 10:30, depending on how much side work I've been able to get done during the shift, and cruise home to the tapes I snatched up at random when I left my real home—Marianne Faithfull, Tracy Chapman, Enigma, King Sunny Ade, the Violent Femmes—just drained enough for the music to set my cranium resonating but hardly dead. Midnight snack is Wheat Thins and Monterey Jack, accompanied by cheap white wine on ice and whatever AMC has to offer. To bed by 1:30 or 2:00, up at 9:00 or 10:00, read for an hour while my uniform whirls around in the landlord's washing machine, and then it's another eight hours spent following Mao's central instruction, as laid out in the Little Red Book, which was: Serve the people.

I could drift along like this, in some dreamy proletarian idyll, except for two things. One is management. If I have kept this subject on the margins thus far it is because I still flinch to think that I spent all those weeks under the surveillance of men (and later women) whose job it was to monitor my behavior for signs of sloth, theft, drug abuse, or worse. Not that managers and especially "assistant managers" in low-wage settings like this are exactly the class enemy. In the restaurant business, they are mostly former cooks or servers, still capable of pinch-hitting in the kitchen or on the floor, just as in hotels they are likely to be former clerks, and paid a salary of only about $400 a week. But everyone knows they have crossed over to the other side, which is, crudely put, corporate as opposed to human. Cooks want to prepare tasty meals; servers want to serve them graciously; but managers are there for only one reason—to make sure that money is made for some theoretical entity that exists far away in Chicago or New York, if a corporation can be said to have a physical existence at all. Reflecting on her career, Gail tells me ruefully that she had sworn, years ago, never to work for a corporation again. "They don't cut you no slack. You give and you give, and they take."

Managers can sit—for hours at a time if they want—but it's their job to see that no one else ever does, even when there's nothing to do, and this is why, for servers, slow times can be as exhausting as rushes. You start dragging out each little chore, because if the manager on duty catches you in an idle moment, he will give you something far nastier to do. So I wipe, I clean, I consolidate ketchup bottles and recheck the cheesecake supply, even tour the tables to make sure the customer evaluation forms are all standing perkily in their places—wondering all the time how many calories I burn in these strictly theatrical exercises. When, on a particularly dead afternoon, Stu finds me glancing at a *USA Today* a customer has left behind, he assigns me to vacuum the entire floor with the broken vacuum cleaner that has a handle only two feet long, and the only way to do that without incurring orthopedic damage is to proceed from spot to spot on your knees.

On my first Friday at the Hearthside there is a "mandatory meeting for all restaurant employees," which I attend, eager for insight into our overall marketing strategy and the niche (your basic Ohio cuisine with a tropical twist?) we aim to inhabit. But there is no "we"

at this meeting. Phillip, our top manager except for an occasional "consultant" sent out by corporate headquarters, opens it with a sneer: "The break room—it's disgusting. Butts in the ashtrays, newspapers lying around, crumbs." This windowless little room, which also houses the time clock for the entire hotel, is where we stash our bags and civilian clothes and take our half-hour meal breaks. But a break room is not a right, he tells us. It can be taken away. We should also know that the lockers in the break room and whatever is in them can be searched at any time. Then comes gossip; there has been gossip; gossip (which seems to mean employees talking among themselves) must stop. Off-duty employees are henceforth barred from eating at the restaurant, because "other servers gather around them and gossip." When Phillip has exhausted his agenda of rebukes, Joan complains about the condition of the ladies' room and I throw in my two bits about the vacuum cleaner. But I don't see any backup coming from my fellow servers, each of whom has subsided into her own personal funk; Gail, my role model, stares sorrowfully at a point six inches from her nose. The meeting ends when Andy, one of the cooks, gets up, muttering about breaking up his day off for this almighty bullshit.

Just four days later we are suddenly summoned into the kitchen at 3:30 P.M., even though there are live tables on the floor. We all—about ten of us—stand around Phillip, who announces grimly that there has been a report of some "drug activity" on the night shift and that, as a result, we are now to be a "drug-free" work-place, meaning that all new hires will be tested, as will possibly current employees on a random basis. I am glad that this part of the kitchen is so dark, because I find myself blushing as hard as if I had been caught toking up in the ladies' room myself: I haven't been treated this way—lined up in the corridor, threatened with locker searches, peppered with carelessly aimed accusations—since junior high school. Back on the floor, Joan cracks, "Next they'll be telling us we can't have sex on the job." When I ask Stu what happened to inspire the crackdown, he just mutters about "management decisions" and takes the opportunity to upbraid Gail and me for being too generous with the rolls. From now on there's to be only one per customer, and it goes out with the dinner, not with the salad. He's also been riding the cooks, prompting Andy to come out of the kitchen and observe—with the serenity of a man whose customary implement is a butcher knife—that "Stu has a death wish today."

Later in the evening, the gossip crystallizes around the theory that Stu is himself the drug culprit, that he uses the restaurant phone to order up marijuana and sends one of the late servers out to fetch it for him. The server was caught, and she may have ratted Stu out or at least said enough to cast some suspicion on him, thus accounting for his pissy behavior. Who knows? Lionel, the busboy, entertains us for the rest of the shift by standing just behind Stu's back and sucking deliriously on an imaginary joint.

The other problem, in addition to the less-than-nurturing management style, is that this job shows no sign of being financially viable. You might imagine, from a comfortable distance, that people who live, year in and year out, on $6 to $10 an hour have discovered some survival stratagems unknown to the middle class. But no. It's not hard to get my co-workers to talk about their living situations, because housing, in almost every case, is the principal source of disruption in their lives, the first thing they fill you in on when they arrive for their shifts. After a week, I have compiled the following survey:

- Gail is sharing a room in a well-known downtown flophouse for which she and a roommate pay about $250 a week. Her roommate, a male friend, has begun hitting on her, driving her nuts, but the rent would be impossible alone.

- Claude, the Haitian cook, is desperate to get out of the two-room apartment he shares with his girlfriend and two other, unrelated, people. As far as I can determine, the other Haitian men (most of whom only speak Creole) live in similarly crowded situations.

- Annette, a twenty-year-old server who is six months pregnant and has been abandoned by her boyfriend, lives with her mother, a postal clerk.

- Marianne and her boyfriend are paying $170 a week for a one-person trailer.

- Jack, who is, at $10 an hour, the wealthiest of us, lives in the trailer he owns, paying only the $400-a-month lot fee.

- The other white cook, Andy, lives on his dry-docked boat, which, as far as I can tell from his loving descriptions, can't be more than twenty feet long. He offers to take me out on it, once it's repaired, but the offer comes with inquiries as to my marital status, so I do not follow up on it.

- Tina and her husband are paying $60 a night for a double room in a Days Inn. This is because they have no car and the Days Inn is within walking distance of the Hearthside. When Marianne, one of the breakfast servers, is tossed out of her trailer for subletting (which is against the trailer-park rules), she leaves her boyfriend and moves in with Tina and her husband.

- Joan, who had fooled me with her numerous and tasteful outfits (hostesses wear their own clothes), lives in a van she parks behind a shopping center at night and showers in Tina's motel room. The clothes are from thrift shops.[4]

---

[4]I could find no statistics on the number of employed people living in cars or vans, but according to the National Coalition for the Homeless's 1997 report "Myths and Facts About Homelessness," nearly one in five homeless people (in twenty-nine cities across the nation) is employed in a full- or part-time job.

It strikes me, in my middle-class solipsism, that there is gross improvidence in some of these arrangements.[5] When Gail and I are wrapping silverware in napkins—the only task for which we are permitted to sit—she tells me she is thinking of escaping from her roommate by moving into the Days Inn herself. I am astounded: How can she even think of paying between $40 and $60 a day? But if I was afraid of sounding like a social worker, I come out just sounding like a fool. She squints at me in disbelief, "And where am I supposed to get a month's rent and a month's deposit for an apartment?" I'd been feeling pretty smug about my $500 efficiency, but of course it was made possible only by the $1,300 I had allotted myself for start-up costs when I began my low-wage life: $1,000 for the first month's rent and deposit, $100 for initial groceries and cash in my pocket, $200 stuffed away for emergencies. In poverty, as in certain propositions in physics, starting conditions are everything.

There are no secret economies that nourish the poor; on the contrary, there are a host of special costs. If you can't put up the two months' rent you need to secure an apartment, you end up paying through the nose for a room by the week. If you have only a room, with a hot plate at best, you can't save by cooking up huge lentil stews that can be frozen for the week ahead. You eat fast food, or the hot dogs and styrofoam cups of soup that can be microwaved in a convenience store. If you have no money for health insurance—and the Hearthside's niggardly plan kicks in only after three months—you go without routine care or prescription drugs and end up paying the price. Gail, for example, was

fine until she ran out of money for estrogen pills. She is supposed to be on the company plan by now, but they claim to have lost her application form and need to begin the paperwork all over again. So she spends $9 per migraine pill to control the headaches she wouldn't have, she insists, if her estrogen supplements were covered. Similarly, Marianne's boyfriend lost his job as a roofer because he missed so much time after getting a cut on his foot for which he couldn't afford the prescribed antibiotic.

My own situation, when I sit down to assess it after two weeks of work, would not be much better if this were my actual life. The seductive thing about waitressing is that you don't have to wait for payday to feel a few bills in your pocket, and my tips usually cover meals and gas, plus something left over to stuff into the kitchen drawer I use as a bank. But as the tourist business slows in the summer heat, I sometimes leave work with only $20 in tips (the gross is higher, but servers share about 15 percent of their tips with the busboys and bartenders). With wages included, this amounts to about the minimum wage of $5.15 an hour. Although the sum in the drawer is piling up, at the present rate of accumulation it will be more than a hundred dollars short of my rent when the end of the month comes around. Nor can I see any expenses to cut. True, I haven't gone the lentil-stew route yet, but that's because I don't have a large cooking pot, pot holders, or a ladle to stir with (which cost about $30 at Kmart, less at thrift stores), not to mention onions, carrots, and the indispensable bay leaf. I do make my lunch almost every day—usually some slow-burning, high-protein combo like frozen chicken patties with melted cheese on top and canned pinto beans on the side. Dinner is at the Hearthside, which offers its employees a choice of BLT, fish sandwich, or hamburger for only $2. The burger lasts longest, especially if it's heaped with gut-puckering jalapeños, but by midnight my stomach is growling again.

So unless I want to start using my car as a residence, I have to find a second, or alternative, job.

---

[5]Solipsism is a tricky concept—even if you are a philosophy major. It comes from the Latin *solus* (alone) and *ipse* (self); literally it means "only-oneself-ism." The extreme form of solipsism holds that there is no reality outside of one's mind. In this case, Ehrenreich is using the term loosely to suggest that her thinking was limited to the middle-class reasoning that holds it is improvident to spend $1200–$1800 a month for a motel room as long as there are apartments to be had for half that amount.

I call all the hotels where I filled out housekeeping applications weeks ago—the Hyatt, Holiday Inn, Econo Lodge, HoJo's, Best Western, plus a half dozen or so locally run guesthouses. Nothing. Then I start making the rounds again, wasting whole mornings waiting for some assistant manager to show up, even dipping into places so creepy that the front-desk clerk greets you from behind bullet-proof glass and sells pints of liquor over the counter. But either someone has exposed my real-life housekeeping habits—which are, shall we say, mellow—or I am at the wrong end of some infallible ethnic equation: most, but by no means all, of the working housekeepers I see on my job searches are African Americans, Spanish-speaking, or immigrants from the Central European post-Communist world, whereas servers are almost invariably white and monolingually English-speaking. When I finally get a positive response, I have been identified once again as server material. Jerry's, which is part of a well-known national family restaurant chain and physically attached here to another budget hotel chain, is ready to use me at once. The prospect is both exciting and terrifying, because, with about the same number of tables and counter seats, Jerry's attracts three or four times the volume of customers as the gloomy old Hearthside.

Picture a fat person's hell, and I don't mean a place with no food. Instead there is everything you might eat if eating had no bodily consequences—cheese fries, chicken-fried steaks, fudge-laden desserts—only here every bite must be paid for, one way or another, in human discomfort. The kitchen is a cavern, a stomach leading to the lower intestine that is the garbage and dishwashing area, from which issue bizarre smells combining the edible and the offal: creamy carrion, pizza barf, and that unique and enigmatic Jerry's scent—citrus fart. The floor is slick with spills, forcing us to walk through the kitchen with tiny steps, like Susan McDougal in leg irons. Sinks everywhere are clogged with scraps of lettuce, decomposing lemon wedges, waterlogged toast crusts. Put your hand down on any counter and you risk being stuck to it by the film of ancient syrup spills, and this is unfortunate, because hands are utensils here, used for scooping up lettuce onto salad plates, lifting out pie slices, and even moving hash browns from one plate to another. The regulation poster in the single unisex restroom admonishes us to wash our hands thoroughly and even offers instructions for doing so, but there is always some vital substance missing—soap, paper towels, toilet paper—and I never find all three at once. You learn to stuff your pockets with napkins before going in there; and too bad about the customers, who must eat, though they don't realize this, almost literally out of our hands.

The break room typifies the whole situation: there is none, because there are no breaks at Jerry's. For six to eight hours in a row, you never sit except to pee. Actually, there are three folding chairs at a table immediately adjacent to the bathroom, but hardly anyone ever sits here, in the very rectum of the gastro-architectural system. Rather, the function of the peritoilet area is to house the ashtrays in which servers and dishwashers leave their cigarettes burning at all times, like votive candles, so that they don't have to waste time lighting up again when they dash back for a puff. Almost everyone smokes as if his or her pulmonary well-being depended on it—the multinational mélange of cooks, the Czech dishwashers, the servers, who are all American natives—creating an atmosphere in which oxygen is only an occasional pollutant. My first morning at Jerry's, when the hypoglycemic shakes set in, I complain to one of my fellow servers that I don't understand how she can go so long without food. "Well, I don't understand how you can go so long without a cigarette," she responds in a tone of reproach—because work is what you do for others; smoking is what you do for yourself. I don't know why the antismoking crusaders have never grasped the element of defiant self-nurturance that makes the habit so endearing to its victims—as if, in the American workplace, the only thing people have to call their own is the tumors they are nourishing and the spare moments they devote to feeding them.

Now, the Industrial Revolution is not an easy transition, especially when you have to zip through it in just a couple of days. I have gone from craft work straight into the factory, from the air-conditioned morgue of the Hearthside directly into the flames. Customers arrive in human waves, sometimes disgorged fifty at a time from their tour buses, peckish and whiny. Instead of two "girls" on the floor at once, there can be as many as six of us running around in our brilliant pink-and-orange Hawaiian shirts. Conversations, either with customers or fellow employees, seldom last more than twenty seconds at a time. On my first day, in fact, I am hurt by my sister servers' coldness. My mentor for the day is an emotionally uninflected twenty-three-year-old, and the others, who gossip a little among themselves about the real reason someone is out sick today and the size of the bail bond someone else has had to pay, ignore me completely. On my second day, I find out why. "Well, it's good to see you again," one of them says in greeting. "Hardly anyone comes back after the first day." I feel powerfully vindicated—a survivor—but it would take a long time, probably months, before I could hope to be accepted into this sorority.

I start out with the beautiful, heroic idea of handling the two jobs at once, and for two days I almost do it: the breakfast/lunch shift at Jerry's, which goes till 2:00 P.M., arriving at the Hearthside at 2:10 P.M., and attempting to hold out until 10:00 P.M. In the ten minutes between jobs, I pick up a spicy chicken sandwich at the Wendy's drive-through window, gobble it down in the car, and change from khaki slacks to black, from Hawaiian to rust polo. There is a problem, though. When during the 3:00 P.M. to 4:00 P.M. dead time I finally sit down to wrap

silver, my flesh seems to bond to the seat. I try to refuel with a purloined cup of soup, as I've seen Gail and Joan do dozens of times, but a manager catches me and hisses "No eating!" though there's not a customer around to be offended by the sight of food making contact with a server's lips. So I tell Gail I'm going to quit, and she hugs me and says she might just follow me to Jerry's herself.

But the chances of this are minuscule. She has left the flophouse and her annoying roommate and is back to living in her beat-up old truck. But guess what? she reports to me excitedly later that evening: Phillip has given her permission to park overnight in the hotel parking lot, as long as she keeps out of sight, and the parking lot should be totally safe, since it's patrolled by a hotel security guard! With the Hearthside offering benefits like that, how could anyone think of leaving?

Gail would have triumphed at Jerry's, I'm sure, but for me it's a crash course in exhaustion management. Years ago, the kindly fry cook who trained me to waitress at a Los Angeles truck stop used to say: Never make an unnecessary trip; if you don't have to walk fast, walk slow; if you don't have to walk, stand. But at Jerry's the effort of distinguishing necessary from unnecessary and urgent from whenever would itself be too much of an energy drain. The only thing to do is to treat each shift as a one-time-only emergency: you've got fifty starving people out there, lying scattered on the battlefield, so get out there and feed them! Forget that you will have to do this again tomorrow, forget that you will have to be alert enough to dodge the drunks on the drive home tonight—just burn, burn, burn! Ideally, at some point you enter what servers call "a rhythm" and psychologists term a "flow state," in which signals pass from the sense organs directly to the muscles, bypassing the cerebral cortex, and a Zen-like emptiness sets in. A male server from the Hearthside's morning shift tells me about the time he "pulled a triple"—three shifts in a row, all the way around the clock—and then got off and had a drink and met this girl, and maybe he shouldn't tell me this, but they had sex right then and there, and it was like, beautiful.

But there's another capacity of the neuro-muscular system, which is pain. I start tossing back drugstore-brand ibuprofen pills as if they were vitamin C, four before each shift, because an old mouse-related repetitive-stress injury in my upper back has come back to full-spasm strength, thanks to the tray carrying. In my ordinary life, this level of disability might justify a day of ice packs and stretching. Here I comfort myself with the Aleve commercial in which the cute blue-collar guy asks: If you quit after working four hours, what would your boss say? And the not-so-cute blue-collar guy, who's lugging a metal beam on his back, answers: He'd fire me, that's what. But fortunately, the commercial tells us, we workers can exert the same kind of authority over our pain-killers that our bosses exert over us. If Tylenol doesn't want to work for more than four hours, you just fire its ass and switch to Aleve.

Management at Jerry's is generally calmer and more "professional" than at the Hearth-side, with two exceptions. One is Joy, a plump, blowsy woman in her early thirties, who once kindly devoted several minutes to instructing me in the correct one-handed method of carrying trays but whose moods change disconcert-ingly from shift to shift and even within one. Then there's B.J., a.k.a. B.J.-the-bitch, whose contribution is to stand by the kitchen counter and yell, "Nita, your order's up, move it!" or, "Barbara, didn't you see you've got another table out there? Come on, girl!" Among other things, she is hated for having replaced the whipped-cream squirt cans with big plastic whipped-cream-filled baggies that have to be squeezed with both hands—because, report-edly, she saw or thought she saw employees trying to inhale the propellant gas from the squirt cans, in the hope that it might be nitrous

oxide. On my third night, she pulls me aside abruptly and brings her face so close that it looks as if she's planning to butt me with her forehead. But instead of saying, "You're fired," she says, "You're doing fine." The only trouble is I'm spending time chatting with custom-ers: "That's how they're getting you." Fur-thermore I am letting them "run me," which means harassment by sequential demands: you bring the ketchup and they decide they want extra Thousand Island; you bring that and they announce they now need a side of fries; and so on into distraction. Finally she tells me not to take her wrong. She tries to say things in a nice way, but you get into a mode, you know, because everything has to move so fast.[6]

I mumble thanks for the advice, feeling like I've just been stripped naked by the crazed enforcer of some ancient sumptuary law.[7] No chatting for you, girl. No fancy service ethic allowed for the serfs. Chatting with custom-ers is for the beautiful young college-educated servers in the downtown carpaccio joints, the kids who can make $70 to $100 a night. What had I been thinking? My job is to move orders from tables to kitchen and then trays from kitchen to tables. Customers are, in fact, the major obstacle to the smooth transforma-tion of information into food and food into

---

[6]In *Workers in a Lean World: Unions in the International Economy* (Verso, 1997), Kim Moody cites studies finding an increase in stress-related workplace injuries and illness between the mid-1980s and the early 1990s. He argues that rising stress levels reflect a new system of "management by stress," in which workers in a variety of industries are being squeezed to extract maximum productivity, to the detriment of their health.

[7]Sumptuary laws (from Latin *sumptus*, or expense, and *sumere*, or to take, use, or consume) were quite common in England, European countries, and even colonial America through the seventeenth century. Sumptuary laws prohibited consumers from spending their money "foolishly" to purchase luxury or extravagant clothing, food, and so forth. The Constitution of the United States would seem to forbid sumptuary laws except in cases where the government seeks to protect the health of its citizens. Many regard the prohibition of alcohol sales in the early twentieth century as the last real example of a sumptuary law in the United States.—Ed.

money—they are, in short, the enemy. And the painful thing is that I'm beginning to see it this way myself. There are the traditional asshole types—frat boys who down multiple Buds and then make a fuss because the steaks are so emaciated and the fries so sparse—as well as the variously impaired—due to age, diabetes, or literacy issues—who require patient nutritional counseling. The worst, for some reason, are the Visible Christians—like the ten-person table, all jolly and sanctified after Sunday-night service, who run me mercilessly and then leave me $1 on a $92 bill. Or the guy with the crucifixion T-shirt (SOMEONE TO LOOK UP TO) who complains that his baked potato is too hard and his iced tea too icy (I cheerfully fix both) and leaves no tip. As a general rule, people wearing crosses or WWJD? (What Would Jèsus Do?) buttons look at us disapprovingly no matter what we do, as if they were confusing waitressing with Mary Magdalene's original profession.

I make friends, over time, with the other "girls" who work my shift: Nita, the tattooed twenty-something who taunts us by going around saying brightly, "Have we started making money yet?" Ellen, whose teenage son cooks on the graveyard shift and who once managed a restaurant in Massachusetts but won't try out for management here because she prefers being a "common worker" and not "ordering people around." Easy-going fiftyish Lucy, with the raucous laugh, who limps toward the end of the shift because of something that has gone wrong with her leg, the exact nature of which cannot be determined without health insurance. We talk about the usual girl things—men, children, and the sinister allure of Jerry's chocolate peanut-butter cream pie—though no one, I notice, ever brings up anything potentially expensive, like shopping or movies. As at the Hearthside, the only recreation ever referred to is partying, which requires little more than some beer, a joint, and a few close friends. Still, no one here is homeless, or cops to it anyway, thanks usually to a working husband or boyfriend. All in all, we

form a reliable mutual-support group: If one of us is feeling sick or overwhelmed, another one will "bev" a table or even carry trays for her. If one of us is off sneaking a cigarette or a pee,[8] the others will do their best to conceal her absence from the enforcers of corporate rationality.

But my saving human connection—my oxytocin receptor, as it were—is George, the nineteen-year-old, fresh-off-the-boat Czech dishwasher. We get to talking when he asks me, tortuously, how much cigarettes cost at Jerry's. I do my best to explain that they cost over a dollar more here than at a regular store and suggest that he just take one from the half-filled packs that are always lying around on the break table. But that would be unthinkable. Except for the one tiny earring signaling his allegiance to some vaguely alternative point of view, George is a perfect straight arrow—crew-cut, hardworking, and hungry for eye contact. "Czech Republic," I ask, "or Slovakia?" and he seems delighted that I know the difference. "Václav Havel," I try. "Velvet Revolution, Frank Zappa?" "Yes, yes, 1989," he says, and I realize we are talking about history.

I make the decision to move closer to Key West. First, because of the drive. Second and third, also because of the drive: gas is eating up $4 to $5 a day, and although Jerry's is as high-volume as you can get, the tips average only

---

[8]Until April 1998, there was no federally mandated right to bathroom breaks. According to Marc Linder and Ingrid Nygaard, authors of *Void Where Prohibited: Rest Breaks and the Right to Urinate on Company Time* (Cornell University Press, 1997), "The right to rest and void at work is not high on the list of social or political causes supported by professional or executive employees, who enjoy personal workplace liberties that millions of factory workers can only daydream about.... While we were dismayed to discover that workers lacked an acknowledged legal right to void at work, [the workers] were amazed by outsiders' naive belief that their employers would permit them to perform this basic bodily function when necessary.... A factory worker, not allowed a break for six-hour stretches, voided into pads worn inside her uniform; and a kindergarten teacher in a school without aides had to take all twenty children with her to the bathroom and line them up outside the stall door when she voided."

10 percent, and not just for a newbie like me. Between the base pay of $2.15 an hour and the obligation to share tips with the busboys and dishwashers, we're averaging only about $7.50 an hour. Then there is the $30 I had to spend on the regulation tan slacks worn by Jerry's servers—a setback it could take weeks to absorb. (I had combed the town's two down-scale department stores hoping for something cheaper but decided in the end that these marked-down Dockers, originally $49, were more likely to survive a daily washing.) Of my fellow servers, everyone who lacks a working husband or boyfriend seems to have a second job: Nita does something at a computer eight hours a day; another welds. Without the forty-five–minute commute, I can picture myself working two jobs and having the time to shower between them.

So I take the $500 deposit I have coming from my landlord, the $400 I have earned toward the next month's rent, plus the $200 reserved for emergencies, and use the $1,100 to pay the rent and deposit on trailer number 46 in the Overseas Trailer Park, a mile from the cluster of budget hotels that constitute Key West's version of an industrial park. Number 46 is about eight feet in width and shaped like a barbell inside, with a narrow region—because of the sink and the stove—separating the bedroom from what might optimistically be called the "living" area, with its two-person table and half-sized couch. The bathroom is so small my knees rub against the shower stall when I sit on the toilet, and you can't just leap out of the bed, you have to climb down to the foot of it in order to find a patch of floor space to stand on. Outside, I am within a few yards of a liquor store, a bar that advertises "free beer tomorrow," a convenience store, and a Burger King—but no supermarket or, alas, laundromat. By reputation, the Overseas park is a nest of crime and crack, and I am hoping at least for some vibrant, multicultural street life. But desolation rules night and day, except for a thin stream of pedestrian traffic heading for their jobs at the

Sheraton or 7-Eleven. There are not exactly people here but what amounts to canned labor, being preserved from the heat between shifts.

In line with my reduced living conditions, a new form of ugliness arises at Jerry's. The next day, when I go for straws, for the first time I find the dry-storage room locked. Ted, the portly assistant manager who opens it for me, explains that he caught one of the dishwashers attempting to steal something, and, unfortunately, the miscreant will be with us until a replacement can be found—hence the locked door. I neglect to ask what he had been trying to steal, but Ted tells me who he is— the kid with the buzz cut and the earring. You know, he's back there right now.

I wish I could say I rushed back and confronted George to get his side of the story. I wish I could say I stood up to Ted and insisted that George be given a translator and allowed to defend himself, or announced that I'd find a lawyer who'd handle the case pro bono. The mystery to me is that there's not much worth stealing in the dry-storage room, at least not in any fenceable quantity: "Is Gyorgi here, and am having 200—maybe 250—ketchup packets. What do you say?" My guess is that he had taken—if he had taken anything at all— some Saltines or a can of cherry-pie mix, and that the motive for taking it was hunger.

So why didn't I intervene? Certainly not because I was held back by the kind of moral paralysis that can pass as journalistic objectivity. On the contrary, something new—something loathsome and servile—had infected me, along with the kitchen odors that I could still sniff on my bra when I finally undressed at night. In real life I am moderately brave, but plenty of brave people shed their courage in concentration camps, and maybe something similar goes on in the infinitely more congenial milieu of the low-wage American workplace. Maybe, in a month or two more at Jerry's, I might have regained my crusading spirit. Then again, in a month or two I might have turned into a different person altogether—say, the kind of person who would have turned George in.

But this is not something I am slated to find out. When my month-long plunge into poverty is almost over, I finally land my dream job—housekeeping. I do this by walking into the personnel office of the only place I figure I might have some credibility, the hotel attached to Jerry's, and confiding urgently that I have to have a second job if I am to pay my rent and, no, it couldn't be front-desk clerk. "All right," the personnel lady fairly spits, "So it's housekeeping," and she marches me back to meet Maria, the housekeeping manager, a tiny, frenetic Hispanic woman who greets me as "babe" and hands me a pamphlet emphasizing the need for a positive attitude. The hours are nine in the morning till whenever, the pay is $6.10 an hour, and there's one week of vacation a year. I don't have to ask about health insurance once I meet Carlotta, the middle-aged African American woman who will be training me. Carla, as she tells me to call her, is missing all of her top front teeth.

On that first day of housekeeping and last day of my entire project—although I don't yet know it's the last—Carla is in a foul mood. We have been given nineteen rooms to clean, most of them "checkouts," as opposed to "stay-overs," that require the whole enchilada of bed-stripping, vacuuming, and bathroom-scrubbing. When one of the rooms that had been listed as a stay-over turns out to be a checkout, Carla calls Maria to complain, but of course to no avail. "So make up the motherfucker," Carla orders me, and I do the beds while she sloshes around the bathroom. For four hours without a break I strip and remake beds, taking about four and a half minutes per queen-sized bed, which I could get down to three if there were any reason to. We try to avoid vacuuming by picking up the larger specks by hand, but often there is nothing to do but drag the monstrous vacuum cleaner—it weighs about thirty pounds—off our cart and

try to wrestle it around the floor. Sometimes Carla hands me the squirt bottle of "BAM" (an acronym for something that begins, ominously, with "butyric"; the rest has been worn off the label) and lets me do the bathrooms. No service ethic challenges me here to new heights of performance. I just concentrate on removing the pubic hairs from the bathtubs, or at least the dark ones that I can see.

I had looked forward to the breaking-and-entering aspect of cleaning the stay-overs, the chance to examine the secret, physical existence of strangers. But the contents of the rooms are always banal and surprisingly neat—zipped up shaving kits, shoes lined up against the wall (there are no closets), flyers for snorkeling trips, maybe an empty wine bottle or two. It is the TV that keeps us going, from *Jerry* to *Sally* to *Hawaii Five-O* and then on to the soaps. If there's something especially arresting, like "Won't Take No for Answer" on *Jerry,* we sit down on the edge of a bed and giggle for a moment as if this were a pajama party instead of a terminally dead-end job. The soaps are the best, and Carla turns the volume up full blast so that she won't miss anything from the bathroom or while the vacuum is on. In room 503, Marcia confronts Jeff about Lauren. In 505, Lauren taunts poor cuckolded Marcia. In 511, Helen offers Amanda $10,000 to stop seeing Eric, prompting Carla to emerge from the bathroom to study Amanda's troubled face. "You take it, girl," she advises. "I would for sure."

The tourists' rooms that we clean and, beyond them, the far more expensively appointed interiors in the soaps, begin after a while to merge. We have entered a better world—a world of comfort where every day is a day off, waiting to be filled up with sexual intrigue. We, however, are only gatecrashers in this fantasy, forced to pay for our presence with backaches and perpetual thirst. The mirrors, and there are far too many of them in hotel rooms, contain the kind of person you would normally find pushing a shopping cart down a city street—bedraggled, dressed in a damp hotel polo shirt two sizes too large, and with sweat dribbling down her chin like drool. I am enormously relieved when Carla announces a half-hour meal break, but my appetite fades when I see that the bag of hot-dog rolls she has been carrying around on our cart is not trash salvaged from a checkout but what she has brought for her lunch.

When I request permission to leave at about 3:30, another housekeeper warns me that no one has so far succeeded in combining housekeeping at the hotel with serving at Jerry's: "Some kid did it once for five days, and you're no kid." With that helpful information in mind, I rush back to number 46, down four Advils (the name brand this time), shower, stooping to fit into the stall, and attempt to compose myself for the on-coming shift. So much for what Marx termed the "reproduction of labor power," meaning the things a worker has to do just so she'll be ready to work again. The only unforeseen obstacle to the smooth transition from job to job is that my tan Jerry's slacks, which had looked reasonably clean by 40-watt bulb last night when I handwashed my Hawaiian shirt, prove by daylight to be mottled with ketchup and ranch-dressing stains. I spend most of my hour-long break between jobs attempting to remove the edible portions with a sponge and then drying the slacks over the hood of my car in the sun.

I can do this two-job thing, is my theory, if I can drink enough caffeine and avoid getting distracted by George's ever more obvious suffering.[9] The first few days after being caught he seemed not to understand the trouble he

was in, and our chirpy little conversations had continued. But the last couple of shifts he's been listless and unshaven, and tonight he looks like the ghost we all know him to be, with dark half-moons hanging from his eyes. At one point, when I am briefly immobilized by the task of filling little paper cups with sour cream for baked potatoes, he comes over and looks as if he'd like to explore the limits of our shared vocabulary, but I am called to the floor for a table. I resolve to give him all my tips that night and to hell with the experiment in low-wage money management. At eight, Ellen and I grab a snack together standing at the mephitic[10] end of the kitchen counter, but I can only manage two or three mozzarella sticks and lunch had been a mere handful of McNuggets. I am not tired at all, I assure myself, though it may be that there is simply no more "I" left to do the tiredness monitoring. What I would see, if I were more alert to the situation, is that the forces of destruction are already massing against me. There is only one cook on duty, a young man named Jesus ("Hay-Sue," that is) and he is new to the job. And there is Joy, who shows up to take over in the middle of the shift, wearing high heels and a long, clingy white dress and fuming as if she'd just been stood up in some cocktail bar.

Then it comes, the perfect storm. Four of my tables fill up at once. Four tables is nothing for me now, but only so long as they are obligingly staggered. As I bev table 27, tables 25, 28, and 24 are watching enviously. As I bev 25, 24 glowers because their bevs haven't even been ordered. Twenty-eight is four yuppyish types, meaning everything on the side and agonizing instructions as to the chicken Caesars. Twenty-five is a middle-aged black couple, who complain, with some justice, that the iced tea isn't fresh and the

---

[9]In 1996, the number of persons holding two or more jobs averaged 7.8 million, or 6.2 percent of the workforce. It was about the same rate for men and for women (6.1 versus 6.2), though the kinds of jobs differ by gender. About two thirds of multiple jobholders work one job full-time and the other part-time. Only a heroic minority—4 percent of men and 2 percent of women—work two full-time jobs simultaneously. (From John F. Stinson Jr., "New Data on Multiple Jobholding Available from the CPS," in the *Monthly Labor Review*, March 1997.)

[10]I confess, I have never encountered the word "mephitic" in anything written later than the nineteenth century. A thing is mephitic if it has an offensive or noxious smell (hence, the term "mephitic weasel" was once used to refer to what we call skunks).—Ed.

tabletop is sticky. But table 24 is the meteorological event of the century: ten British tourists who seem to have made the decision to absorb the American experience entirely by mouth. Here everyone has at least two drinks—iced tea and milk shake, Michelob and water (with lemon slice, please)—and a huge promiscuous orgy of breakfast specials, mozzarella sticks, chicken strips, quesadillas, burgers with cheese and without, sides of hash browns with cheddar, with onions, with gravy, seasoned fries, plain fries, banana splits. Poor Jesus! Poor me! Because when I arrive with their first tray of food—after three prior trips just to refill bevs—Princess Di refuses to eat her chicken strips with her pancake-and-sausage special, since, as she now reveals, the strips were meant to be an appetizer. Maybe the others would have accepted their meals, but Di, who is deep into her third Michelob, insists that everything else go back while they work on their "starters." Meanwhile, the yuppies are waving me down for more decaf and the black couple looks ready to summon the NAACP.

Much of what happened next is lost in the fog of war. Jesus starts going under. The little printer on the counter in front of him is spewing out orders faster than he can rip them off, much less produce the meals. Even the invincible Ellen is ashen from stress. I bring table 24 their reheated main courses, which they immediately reject as either too cold or fossilized by the microwave. When I return to the kitchen with their trays (three trays in three trips), Joy confronts me with arms akimbo: "What is this?" She means the food—the plates of rejected pancakes, hash browns in assorted flavors, toasts, burgers, sausages, eggs. "Uh, scrambled with cheddar," I try, "and that's . . ." "NO,"she screams in my face. "Is it a traditional, a super-scramble, an eye-opener?" I pretend to study my check for a clue, but entropy has been up to its tricks, not only on the plates but in my head, and I have to admit that the original order is beyond reconstruction. "You don't know an eye-opener

from a traditional?" she demands in outrage. All I know, in fact, is that my legs have lost interest in the current venture and have announced their intention to fold. I am saved by a yuppie (mercifully not one of mine) who chooses this moment to charge into the kitchen to bellow that his food is twenty-five minutes late. Joy screams at him to get the hell out of her kitchen, please, and then turns on Jesus in a fury, hurling an empty tray across the room for emphasis.

I leave. I don't walk out, I just leave. I don't finish my side work or pick up my credit-card tips, if any, at the cash register or, of course, ask Joy's permission to go. And the surprising thing is that you can walk out without permission, that the door opens, that the thick tropical night air parts to let me pass, that my car is still parked where I left it. There is no vindication in this exit, no fuck-you surge of relief, just an overwhelming, dank sense of failure pressing down on me and the entire parking lot. I had gone into this venture in the spirit of science, to test a mathematical proposition, but somewhere along the line, in the tunnel vision imposed by long shifts and relentless concentration, it became a test of myself, and clearly I have failed. Not only had I flamed out as a housekeeper/server, I had even forgotten to give George my tips, and, for reasons perhaps best known to hardworking, generous people like Gail and Ellen, this hurts. I don't cry, but I am in a position to realize, for the first time in many years, that the tear ducts are still there, and still capable of doing their job.

When I moved out of the trailer park, I gave the key to number 46 to Gail and arranged for my deposit to be transferred to her. She told me that Joan is still living in her van and that Stu had been fired from the Hearthside. I never found out what happened to George.

In one month, I had earned approximately $1,040 and spent $517 on food, gas, toiletries, laundry, phone, and utilities. If I had remained in my $500 efficiency, I would have been able to pay the rent and have $22 left over (which is

$78 less than the cash I had in my pocket at the start of the month). During this time I bought no clothing except for the required slacks and no prescription drugs or medical care (I did finally buy some vitamin B to compensate for the lack of vegetables in my diet). Perhaps I could have saved a little on food if I had gotten to a supermarket more often, instead of convenience stores, but it should be noted that I lost almost four pounds in four weeks, on a diet weighted heavily toward burgers and fries.

How former welfare recipients and single mothers will (and do) survive in the low-wage workforce, I cannot imagine. Maybe they will figure out how to condense their lives—including child-raising, laundry, romance, and meals—into the couple of hours between full-time jobs. Maybe they will take up residence in their vehicles, if they have one. All I know is that I couldn't hold two jobs and I couldn't make enough money to live on with one. And I had advantages unthinkable to many of the long-term poor—health, stamina, a working car, and no children to care for and support. Certainly nothing in my experience contradicts the conclusion of Kathryn Edin and Laura Lein, in their recent book *Making Ends*

Meet: How Single Mothers Survive Welfare and Low-Wage Work that low-wage work actually involves more hardship and deprivation than life at the mercy of the welfare state. In the coming months and years, economic conditions for the working poor are bound to worsen, even without the almost inevitable recession. As mentioned earlier, the influx of former welfare recipients into the low-skilled workforce will have a depressing effect on both wages and the number of jobs available. A general economic downturn will only enhance these effects, and the working poor will of course be facing it without the slight, but nonetheless often saving, protection of welfare as a backup.

The thinking behind welfare reform was that even the humblest jobs are morally uplifting and psychologically buoying. In reality they are likely to be fraught with insult and stress. But I did discover one redeeming feature of the most abject low-wage work—the camaraderie of people who are, in almost all cases, far too smart and funny and caring for the work they do and the wages they're paid. The hope, of course, is that someday these people will come to know what they're worth, and take appropriate action.

Questions

1. Compare Ehrenreich's story of life as a waitress to Paules' account (reading 16) of being a waitress. Given that both studied similar subjects, one would expect there to be several similarities. However, did you spot important differences? Paules interviewed women working as waitresses while Ehrenreich lived the life. To what extent might this difference in methods explain the differences in their findings?

2. Imagine that tomorrow you had to postpone finishing college and survive in the "real world." How difficult would it be for you to put together enough money to get started out there? (Consider such things as transportation, housing [including first and last months' rent and security deposit], the cost of uniforms, etc.) (If your instructor assigns you to answer this question on paper and turn it in, take care not to reveal any details that are too personal!) Do you think that your parents or others would be happy to help you get started? What do you think happens to people whose relatives can't (or won't) help them out financially?

33
THE JOB GHETTO

Katherine Newman and Chauncy Lennon

One of my students expressed the conventional "wisdom" this way: "If people want to bad enough, they can get a job and make something of themselves. It might not be a great job, but at least it's a job. No one has to be poor in this society." In this 1995 article, Katherine Newman and Chauncy Lennon challenge such widely held assumptions about the availability of employment in our society.

To fix the welfare mess, conservatives say, we should stop making life on the dole so comfortable, cut benefits, and force overindulged welfare moms to go out and find honest jobs. Unskilled foreigners can find work, so why can't AFDC[1] recipients? With unemployment rates down, these expectations sound reasonable, particularly to middle-class Americans with stagnating incomes. The premise that jobs are available for those willing to take them is a great comfort to politicians with budget axes in hand and to conservative commentators calling on them to slash benefits. After all, they can claim they're not really casting poor women and children into the streets; they're just upholding the American work ethic.

But can just any warm body find a job? For the past two years, we have studied the low-wage labor market in Harlem, focusing on minimum-wage jobs in the fast-food industry, which are typical of the employment opportunities many reformers have in mind for welfare recipients. After all, these jobs presumably demand little skill, education, or prior work experience—or so the public believes.

The fast-food industry is growing more rapidly than almost any other service business and now employs more than 2.3 million workers. One in 15 Americans working today found their first job at McDonald's—not including Burger King and the rest. As a gateway to employment, fast-food establishments are gaining on the armed forces, which have long functioned as a national job-training factory. No wonder the average citizen believes these jobs are wide open! Yet, in inner cities, the picture looks different. With manufacturing gone, fast-food jobs have become the object of fierce competition.

Downward Pressures

Between 1992 and 1994, we tracked the work histories of 200 people working in fast-food restaurants in central Harlem, where according to official data about 18 percent of the population are unemployed and about 40 percent live below the poverty line. These numbers are typical of the communities where many long-term recipients of public assistance will have to look for work if their benefits are cut off. Some 29 percent of the households in Harlem receive public assistance.

---

[1] Aid to Families with Dependent Children, a form of welfare.—Ed.

Katherine D. Newman and Chauncy Lennon, "The Job Ghetto" from *The American Prospect* (June 23, 1995), http://www.prospect.org. Reprinted with permission from *The American Prospect*, 1710 Rhode Island Avenue NW, 12th floor, Washington, DC 20036. All rights reserved.

Although the 200 workers in our study receive only the minimum wage, they are actually the victors in an intense competition to find work in a community with relatively few jobs to offer. At the restaurants where they work, the ratio of applicants to hires is approximately 14 to 1. Among those people who applied but were rejected for fast-food work in early 1993, 73 percent had not found work of any kind a year later, despite considerable effort. Even the youngest job hunters in our study (16- to 18-year-olds) had applied for four or five positions before they came looking for these fast-food jobs. The oldest applicants (over 25) had applied for an average of seven or eight jobs.

The oversupply of job seekers causes a creeping credentialism in the ghetto's low-wage service industries. Older workers in their twenties, who are more often high school graduates, now dominate jobs once taken by school dropouts or other young people first starting out. Long-term welfare recipients will have a tough time beating out their competition even for these low-wage jobs. They will be joining an inner-city labor market that is already saturated with better educated and more experienced workers who are preferred by employers.

Winners and Losers

We tracked nearly 100 people who applied for these minimum-wage jobs but were turned down, and compared them to the fortunate ones who got jobs. The comparison is instructive. Even in Harlem, African Americans are at a disadvantage in hiring compared to Latinos and others. Employers, including black employers, favor applicants who are not African American. Blacks are not shut out of the low-wage labor market; indeed, they represent about 70 percent of the new hires in these jobs. But they are rejected at a much higher rate than applicants from other ethnic groups with the same educational qualifications.

Employers also seem to favor job applicants who commute from more distant neighborhoods. The rejection rate for local applicants is higher than the rate for similarly educated individuals who live farther away. This pattern holds even for people of the same race, sex, and age. Other studies in the warehouse and dockyard industries report the same results. These findings suggest that residents of poor neighborhoods such as central Harlem are at a distinct disadvantage in finding minimum-wage jobs near home.

Mothers of young children face particular problems if they can't find jobs close to home. The costs and logistical complexities of commuting (and paying for longer child care hours to accommodate it) are a big burden.

In searching for jobs, "who you know" makes a big difference. Friends and family members who already have jobs help people get work even in the fast-food industry; those isolated from such networks are less likely to get hired. Personal contacts have long been recognized as crucial for getting higher-skilled employment. This research suggests that contacts are important at the bottom of the job ladder, too.

Native-born applicants are at a disadvantage compared to legal immigrants in securing entry-level work. In fact, even though central Harlem residents are nearly all African American, recent immigrants have a higher probability of being hired for Harlem's fast-food jobs than anyone else. Interviews with employers suggest that they believe immigrants are easier to manage in part because they come from countries where $4.25 an hour represents a king's ransom. Whether or not employers are right about the tractability of immigrants, such attitudes make it harder for the native-born to obtain low-wage jobs.

The people who succeed in getting these minimum-wage jobs are not new to the labor market. More than half of the new hires over the age of 18 found their first jobs when they

Blacks in Harlem

were younger than 15 years of age. Even the people rejected for the minimum-wage positions had some prior job experience. Half of them also began working before they were 15 years old. Welfare recipients with no prior job experience, or no recent job experience, are going to be at a disadvantage in the competition.

"They Expect Too Much"

One explanation often advanced for low employment in poor communities is that the poor have unrealistic expectations. In this view, they are reluctant to seek (or take) jobs that fall below a "reservation wage," which is supposedly far above the minimum. We asked job seekers who were refused these entry-level jobs what they were hoping for and what wages they would accept. Their desires were modest: $4.59 per hour on average, which is quite close to the minimum wage. The younger the job-seeker, the lower was the expectation.

These job seekers were willing to accept even more modest wages. On average the lowest they would take was $4.17 per hour, which is less than the minimum level legally permitted for adult workers. It is striking that many applicants previously had higher salaries; the average wage for the best job they had ever held was $6.79 per hour. Many of central Harlem's job hunters are suffering from downward mobility, falling into the minimum-wage market even though they have done better in the past.

Comparing job seekers to jobholders shows the intensity of employment competition in the inner city, but it doesn't tell us how welfare recipients will fare. What assets do welfare recipients bring to the competition compared to other job hunters? The news is grim.

Nationally, one-third of the long-term welfare recipients have received high school diplomas. Recently hired fast-food workers in central Harlem have completed high school at a higher rate—54 percent. Almost 40 percent of welfare recipients have not held jobs in the year preceding their enrollment in welfare. Yet even the central Harlem applicants rejected for fast-food jobs have had more job experience. They have held an average of more than three jobs before applying for these positions.

In short, it is simply not the case that anyone who wants a low-wage job can get one. As is true for almost any glutted labor market, there is a queue of applicants, and employers can be fairly choosy. When conservatives point to the success of immigrants as proof that jobs are available for welfare moms, they are ignoring the realities of the inner city. Ethnic minorities of all kinds are already locked into a fierce struggle for scarce opportunities at the bottom.

When they go looking for jobs, welfare recipients go to the back of a long line. Policymakers should neither fool nor comfort themselves with the notion that welfare mothers can simply go out and get jobs. Investment in public employment and tax incentives for private employers will be needed on a massive scale if anything like that rosy scenario is to come about. Even then, the competitive hurdles facing the very poor will be high and many better-qualified people will be out there looking to leap over them.

Questions

1. According to Newman and Lennon's research, what sorts of factors distinguish jobholders and job seekers in Harlem?

2. How likely do Newman and Lennon think it is that welfare moms will be able to get off welfare and find jobs in the near future? Explain.

34

RACISM

Joe R. Feagin

If ever there comes a time that I want absolute silence in my classroom, I will simply announce, "Today, we are going to talk about racism."

It is hard to talk about race, let alone racism, in a public setting. White students confide that black students are "too sensitive" and "will think I'm a racist if I say anything." Black students mostly just say that white students "just don't get it," and "don't *want* to get it."

In his book, *Racist America: Roots, Current Realities, and Future Reparations,* Professor Feagin, one of today's most respected sociologists, offers us insight into why conversations about racism are so difficult. Whites and blacks, he has found, have very different understandings of the importance of race in U.S. society. Blacks experience racist behavior in schoolrooms, on the streets, in shops, at work, and even in health care settings. As Feagin notes, "being black in U.S. society means always having to be prepared for antiblack actions by whites—in most places and at most times of the day, week, month, or year." For black men and women, racism is an unfortunately large part of the present.

On the other hand, as far as most whites are concerned, "racism is a thing of the past"; thus, "black Americans who complain of it are paranoid or confused. There is a common saying among whites that a black person is 'playing the race card,' a comment generally used to suggest that person is making an illegitimate demand [or complaint] because antiblack racism is no longer thought of as a serious obstacle in the United States."

What follows is an excerpt from *Racist America,* in which Feagin explores the disjunction between race as it's seen by white and black Americans.

Soon after the 1960s civil rights movement declined in intensity, most whites were moving toward the view that racial discrimination is no longer an important problem for the nation. In a 1976 survey, for example, most (71 percent) whites agreed that "blacks and other minorities no longer face unfair employment conditions. In fact they are favored in

many training and job programs." A meager 12 percent of whites agreed with the statement that "discrimination affects all black people. The only way to handle it is for blacks to organize together and demand rights for all." In a 1980 survey respondents were asked, "How much discrimination do you feel there is against blacks and other minorities in any area of life that limits their chances to get ahead?" Just over half of blacks replied "a lot" compared to only a quarter of whites. In these surveys only a minority of whites viewed discrimination as a major hurdle (Kluegel and Smith 1986).

Joe R. Feagin, excerpts from *Racist America: Roots, Current Realities, and Future Reparations.* Copyright © 2000. Reprinted with the permission of Taylor & Francis Group LLC via Copyright Clearance Center.

In more recent surveys, black and white Americans still differ dramatically in how they view discrimination. A 1990 NORC survey question asked why blacks have worse jobs, income, and housing than whites. Choosing among alternative explanations, two-thirds of black respondents said that it was "mainly due to discrimination," compared to only 35 percent of whites. Similarly, in a mid-1990s Pennsylvania survey researchers found that eight in ten black respondents thought inequality in jobs, housing, and income stemmed mostly from discrimination, while the majority of whites viewed this inequality as resulting from blacks' lack of motivation. Respondents were asked whether the quality of life for black Americans had gotten better in the last decade. Nearly six in ten whites said it had gotten better, compared to less than a third of black respondents (Smith 1996). Recent national polls have shown the same pattern. A 1997 ABC/*Washington Post* poll found that only 17 percent of the white respondents felt there was a lot of racial discrimination, compared to nearly half the blacks polled. In addition, several other surveys have found that on questions dealing with specific institutional areas such as housing, education, and jobs less than a majority of whites believe that blacks currently face discrimination (Blendon et al. 1986).

Several recent surveys have found that many whites think blacks are as well off as or are better off than whites in regard to education, health care, and jobs. For example, a Massachusetts survey found a majority of the white respondents saying that African Americans, Asian Americans, and Latino Americans now have *equality* in life chances with whites (Lehigh 1998). However, government statistical data indicate that such views are very much in error. Perhaps because of erroneous or misleading media reports, most whites do not understand just how much worse off blacks actually are than

whites in most areas of political and economic life (Feagin and Feagin 1999).

"I AM NOT A RACIST": DENYING INDIVIDUAL RACISM

Clearly, a majority of whites do not see the United States as a nation that has a problem of serious and widespread racial discrimination. Apparently, most whites also do not view themselves as significantly racist in thought or action, often asserting "I am not a racist." In recent years many whites have also made such statements as "my family never owned slaves" or "my family did not segregate lunch counters." Many will say to black Americans something like, "Slavery happened hundreds of years ago—get over it." They do not know, or pretend they do not, that official slavery ended less than 140 years or so prior to their statements. In addition, whites making such assertions usually do not admit that they and their families have benefited greatly from slavery, segregation, and present-day discrimination.[1]

Many whites seem to mix negative views of black Americans with images of white innocence, thereby giving specific expression to elements of a broader racial ideology. Take this example of a white college student's reply to a question about her first experience with black Americans, in this case children: "I switched from a private school which had no blacks to a public school, and I was thrown in the middle of a bunch of apes,

---

[1]Elsewhere in his book, Feagin observes that "slaveholders were not the only beneficiaries of the slavery system; those who bought and sold products of plantations were also major beneficiaries. This latter group included merchants and consumers in many nations. In addition, many white workers in Britain and other parts of Europe owed their livelihood directly or indirectly to the slaves and plantation products. It seems unlikely that British and other European economic development would have occurred when it did without the very substantial capital generated by the slavery system" (51).—Ed.

no I'm just kidding. . . . And I don't know, my parents have always instilled in me that blacks aren't equal, because we are from [the Deep South]." In her interview she continues in this vein, making several negative comments about African Americans. Then at the end of her interview, she adds, "I don't consider myself racist. I, when I think of the word racist, I think of KKK, people in white robes burning black people on crosses and stuff, or I think of the Skinheads or some exaggerated form of racism" (Feagin and Vera 1995). We see here the imaging of the white self in positive terms.

It seems that most whites can assert that they are "not racist" because they see racism as something that *other* whites do. That is, they know other whites who are much more racist in thought or action than they are, and thus they see themselves as already beyond that racism. Jerome Culp has said, "To many white people, not being racist means having less racial animosity than their parents (something almost all can at least claim); having less racial animosity than someone they know (something all can claim); or not belonging to a white supremacist group. . . . For many white people, unless they believe overwhelmingly in the inferiority of black people, they are not collaborators with racism and are not racist" (Culp 1993). As we saw in white views of athletes and actors on "The Cosby Show," many whites hold some more or less positive images of selected black men or women. However, these usually superficial positive views reduce the ability of whites to see their own culpability in personal and institutional racism. Indeed, many a white person has a false consciousness that occurs when a white "believes he or she is identifying with a person of color, but in fact is doing so only in a slight, superficial way" (Delgado 1996). It is possible to hold that black Americans can be good entertainers, musicians, or sports figures, yet also believe

that most are inferior to whites in character, morality, or intelligence.[2]

Historical changes in racism have also been misperceived by whites. When the legal segregation era came to an end with the passage of civil rights laws in the 1960s, most whites apparently concluded that serious racism was being rapidly extinguished. Today, most whites, like the young woman interviewed above, seem to view what racism remains as a matter of isolated Klan-type bigotry and not as a system of racism cutting across U.S. institutions. As a result, they do not see their own racism. Moreover, the level at which racist attitudes are held can vary in degree of consciousness. Psychologist Patricia Devine has suggested that whites who reject overtly prejudiced views can still hold less consciously prejudiced thoughts that stem from prior socialization. For many whites this attitudinal racism is a persisting bad habit that keeps coming up in everyday thought and behavior. One reason for this is the fact that human beings are characterized by automatic information processing, which involves the unintentional activation of previously socialized attitudes such as racist stereotypes and prejudices (Devine 1989). Racist attitudes can thus be conscious, half-conscious, or even subconscious.

---

[2]Feagin introduced the racist stereotype of lazy black men and women earlier in the book and argued that it persists today: "A recent NORC national survey asked whites to evaluate on a scale just how work-oriented blacks are. Only a small percentage, 16 percent, ranked blacks at the hardworking end; just under half put blacks at the lazy end of the spectrum. . . ." Notions of laziness are so strong as to overcome countering evidence. Researchers Justin Lewis and Sut Jhally had white subjects watch 'The Cosby Show,' a popular television show from the 1980s and 1990s that is still seen in reruns across the globe. Whites generally like the black Huxtable family portrayed on the show, yet many processed the images in a way that fit in with preexisting attitudes. They saw the success of the Huxtables as evidence that any black person could succeed if he or she would just work harder. As Lewis and Jhally concluded about white views, "The Huxtables proved that black people can succeed; yet in so doing they also prove the inferiority of black people in general (who have, in comparison with whites, failed)" (111).—Ed.

White Views on Government Action Against Discrimination

If antiblack discrimination is no longer regarded as a serious problem, then it is not surprising that most whites see less need, or no need, for strong antidiscrimination efforts by governments. From this perspective blacks pressing for continuing or enhanced antidiscrimination programs, such as aggressive affirmative action, are seen as making illegitimate demands. David Wellman has suggested that "the concrete problem facing white people is how to come to grips with the demands made by blacks while at the same time *avoiding* the possibility of institutional change and reorganization that might affect them" (Wellman 1977).

SYMBOLIC AND LAISSEZ-FAIRE RACISM

Some researchers have described a contemporary white perspective called *symbolic racism*. Whites often combine the notion of declining or eradicated blatant racism with the idea that blacks are making illegitimate demands for societal changes. As these researchers see the current situation, a majority of whites have shifted away from old-fashioned racist ideas and have accepted modest desegregation while strongly resisting aggressive government action for large-scale desegregation. This symbolic racism is grounded in white resistance to substantial changes in the status quo. Central to white concerns is a fear whites have of losing status and power because of black attempts to bring change. Deep-lying antiblack views—especially views of blacks violating traditional American work values—are still present, but white resentment of pressures for substantial change is central to the current racist ideology (Sears 1988). This symbolic racism perspective has been criticized by some scholars as playing down old-fashioned racism, when the latter still

exists among whites and is directly connected to negative views of programs to eradicate discrimination.

Lawrence Bobo, James Kluegel, and Ryan Smith have suggested a more historical approach. Since the 1950s, and shaped by structural changes in the society, they say white attitudes have shifted from an accent on strict segregation and overt bigotry to "laissez-faire racism,"[3] by which they mean whites' continuing stereotyping of blacks and blaming of blacks for their problems. Most ordinary whites have given up a commitment to compulsory racial segregation. Yet, they still strive to maintain white privilege and position. Survey data since the 1960s indicate a substantial discrepancy between white views on the *principle* of desegregation versus white views on the *implementation* of desegregation by government. While surveys in the mid-1960s indicated that nearly two-thirds of whites accepted integrated schooling in principle, just 38 percent accepted a role for government in pressing for more integration. By the mid-1980s white support for the principle of school integration had grown to 93 percent, while endorsement of government intervention had declined to 26 percent (Bobo et al. 1997). The survey data indicate similar discrepancies in white views of job and housing integration. Acceptance of the principle of racial integration does not mean that whites wish to see government intervene aggressively, or to personally have more contact with blacks. Whites maintain a positive sense of self and their claims to

---

[3]*Laissez-faire* (French, "let alone, don't interfere"). Laissez-faire capitalism thus is based on the premise that capitalism will work best if the government doesn't interfere by regulating. By extension, laissez-faire racism is racism that will continue and even flourish as long as the government does not attempt to push antiracist laws and policies (e.g., affirmative action).—Ed.

greater privileges and resources while fending off what whites see as illegitimate black demands for a fair share of those resources.

VIEWS ON AFFIRMATIVE ACTION

Affirmative action is a major example of a remedial program to deal with racial discrimination. Yet most whites, including most white leaders, have been opposed to *aggressive* affirmative action since at least the 1970s. In one 1977 survey of mostly white and male local and national leaders in business, farming, unions, the media, and academia, *most were* overwhelmingly opposed to affirmative-action quotas for black Americans in school admissions and jobs. Only 10 to 22 percent of the several leadership groups favored strong remedial quotas (Verba and Orren 1985). In addition, the overwhelming majority of these elites thought that equality of opportunity, not equality of results, was the best way to eradicate disparities. The white public seems to share this view.

Earlier we noted mid-1970s surveys suggesting that the white majority views blacks as no longer facing serious job discrimination and expresses opposition to an expanded effort for civil rights. Recent data show the same pattern: more than half of whites do not believe that government or private agencies should be making aggressive remedial efforts on behalf of black Americans or other Americans of color. In an ABC News/*Washington Post* survey only a quarter of whites thought minorities should receive some preferences in jobs and college admissions (Ladd 1995). And a late-1990s Gallup poll found that 70 percent of Republicans, a heavily white group, felt the federal government should not make special efforts to help Americans of color, because they should help themselves (Blendon et al. 1986). A majority of whites took the same position in a late-1990s survey in Massachusetts (Lehigh 1998). Most national surveys have shown the same pattern of white opposition

to strong programs with special preferences or quotas as a means of aggressively remedying past discrimination. (Milder remedial programs may sometimes be acceptable.) Indeed, today many whites believe that they are likely to be the victims of governmental policies helping black Americans. One recent Pennsylvania survey asked a question as to how likely it would be that a white worker might lose a job or a promotion to a less qualified black worker. Most black respondents (57 percent) thought this was unlikely, while most whites (80 percent) thought it was likely (Smith 1996). National polls using such a question have gotten similar responses: The majority of whites seem convinced that antiwhite discrimination is now commonplace.

White elites have periodically expended substantial effort to shape the public's views of remedial programs. Researcher Robert Entman has examined trends in mass media reports of the controversy over affirmative action that recurred periodically in the 1980s and 1990s. He found significant peaking in media attention to affirmative action during the years 1987, 1991, and 1995—years that preceded presidential elections. This pattern suggests elite manipulation of the affirmative action issue for political purposes. The media elites and their white-collar employees tended to present the issue of affirmative action in white-framed ways or in terms of national controversy, using such phrases as the "tide of white anger" or the "growing white backlash." Entman concludes that "journalists, it seems, built their frame on claims by elite sources with an interest in promoting the impression of white arousal, filtered through the conflict norm that shapes story construction" (Entman 1997). The media attention accelerated concerns about affirmative action in the white public.

Related to opposition to strong affirmative action programs is the old individualistic ethic, especially the blame-the-victim version. Today, as in the past, many whites comment about the problems of blacks with such statements as, "Why can't they be like us?" The notion here is that if "they" will work harder and improve their personal and family values, then the normal assimilation processes will enable them to have greater socioeconomic mobility. One recent survey asked whether respondents agreed with this statement: "The Irish, Italians, and many other groups overcame prejudice and worked their way up, African Americans and other minorities should do the same without any special help from the government." Most whites (69 percent) agreed (Blendon et al. 1986). Most seem to perceive the black experience in terms of an individualistic mobility model. Black Americans, from this viewpoint, are little different from white immigrant groups, such as the southern and eastern European immigrants of the early 1900s. Like those immigrants, who are seen as having encountered discrimination, black Americans should be able to work themselves up the social ladder. If they do not make it, it is mostly their own fault.

Imaging the White Self

The racist ideas and attitudes of white Americans encompass *much more* than their anti-black views. Among these racist attitudes are positive views of white superiority and merit. Generally, the broad white-racist ideology sees white history as meritorious. Indeed, in the United States, group merit and individual merit are judged by standards created by the white majority. [Earlier in the book] we noted the images of white superiority and virtue in many Hollywood films. From the first years of movie-making to the present, when racial matters have been portrayed, whites as a group have almost always been portrayed as morally superior, intellectually superior, or otherwise meritorious. In these movies—including more recent television movies—there may be a

few white individuals who are racist bigots, but the society as a whole is not portrayed as racist. Some white person is typically a central hero, even in movies mostly about black Americans (for example, *Glory*).

Among elites and in the general public, whites have developed numerous sincere fictions that reproduce aspects of the broad racist ideology at an everyday level. Such fictions may describe whites as "not racist" and as "good people" even as the same whites take part in racist actions or express racist ideas. This moral privileging of whiteness may be conscious or it can be half-conscious or unconscious. Ruth Frankenberg found evidence of this unconsciousness in her research on white women: whiteness, she noted, is "difficult for white people to name. . . . Those who are securely housed within its borders usually do not examine it" (Frankenberg 1993). The sense of whiteness is often hidden deeply in individual psyches and practices. Being white, one might say, means rarely or never having to think about it. Whiteness is the national norm, and thus the white majority's views, practices, and culture are generally seen as normal.

Examining commentaries on racial inequality written by white students, Joyce King found that most were "unaware of how their own subjective identities reflect an uncritical identification with the existing social order." Only one student out of fifty-seven linked persisting racial inequality to the larger system of racial oppression (King 1991). Thus, while whites get many substantial advantages from systemic racism, they do pay a subtle and hidden price. This may include a lack of conscious awareness about certain critical aspects of social reality. Many have an uncritical mind that accepts the existing racial order with little questioning.

Perhaps most amazing is that a majority of whites today do not see the centuries of slavery and segregation as bringing whites substantial socioeconomic benefit. One survey found that nearly two-thirds of white respondents did *not* think that whites as a group had benefited from past and present discrimination against black Americans. Nor did they think whites should take significant action to remedy continuing discrimination (Blendon et al. 1991). Moreover, as we have seen, many whites have asserted their innocence with a torrent of comments such as "my family never owned slaves." This white guiltlessness is professed at all class levels, even by presidential candidates. Clearly, much work has gone into reframing the American history of racial oppression so that white Americans can appear blameless for the brutality and carnage they and their ancestors created.

Fostering and Learning Racist Attitudes

THE ROLE OF ELITES

[Elsewhere in this book] we examined how elites have fostered a racist ideology rationalizing the realities of unjust impoverishment and enrichment. This effort is a major source of the racist ideology and its associated attitudes that are held in the nonelite part of the white population. Through various means the white elites have manipulated ordinary white Americans to accept the racist ideology and its component parts. Moreover, after the elements of an era's racist ideology and structural arrangements are in place, ordinary whites need less manipulation, for they generally understand what is in their group interest. Indeed, groups of ordinary people often generate new permutations on old racist ideas, innovations that in their turn reinforce and reproduce the racist ideology.

The often hidden power of the elite works through propagating the racist ideology and its associated beliefs and images by means of the mass media and the educational system, as well as in workplaces and churches. Increasingly, the mass media are as important as family or school in creating and propagating racist images

and attitudes. When blacks encounter whites in a broad array of contemporary settings, they often meet negative beliefs about their abilities, values, and orientations. Racial barriers persist today because a substantial majority of whites harbor antiblack sentiments, images, and beliefs and because a large minority are very negative in their perspectives. When most whites interact with black Americans at work, in restaurants, on the street, at school, or in the media they tend to think about the latter, either consciously or unconsciously, in terms of racist stereotypes inherited from the past and constantly reiterated and reinforced in the present.

The translation of antiblack attitudes into actual discrimination is shaped not only by these attitudes but also by subjective norms, such as what other people might think, and by perceived behavioral controls, such as what the response to discrimination will be. Most discrimination is thereby contextualized. Routinized discrimination in housing, employment, politics, and public accommodations is carried out by whites acting alone or in groups. Whites are usually implementing shared racist attitudes and norms of their families and other important social networks. The social norms guiding discrimination can be formal or legal, but most today are unwritten and informal. Moreover, much antiblack action is not sporadic but is carried out repeatedly and routinely by numerous dominant-group members influenced by the norms of their social networks. Whites have the power to discriminate as individuals, but much of their power to harm comes from membership in traditionally white networks and organizations.

EVERYDAY RACISM: SUBTLE, COVERT, AND BLATANT

The character of discrimination varies. Whites may actively persecute blacks, or they may engage in an array of avoidance behaviors. Discrimination can be self-consciously motivated, or it can be half-conscious or unconscious and deeply imbedded in an actor's core beliefs. At the level of everyday interaction with black Americans, most whites can create racial tensions and barriers even without conscious awareness they are doing so. Examples of this include when white men lock their car doors as a black man walks by on the street or when white women step out or pull their purses close to them when a black man comes into an elevator they are on.[4] Stereotyped images of black men as criminals probably motivate this and similar types of defensive action. Such practices represent, according to Philomena Essed, the "integration of racism into everyday situations" (Essed 1991). Systemic racism is thus a system of oppression made up of many thousands of everyday acts of mistreatment of black Americans by white Americans, incidents that range from the subtle and hard to observe to the blatant and easy to notice. These acts of mistreatment can be nonverbal or verbal, nonviolent or violent. Moreover, many racist actions that crash in on everyday life are, from the victim's viewpoint, unpredictable and sporadic. Such actions are commonplace, recurring, and cumulative in their negative impact. They are, as one retired black American in her eighties put it, "little murders" that happen every day (Feagin and Sikes 1994).

In a specific setting, such as an employment setting, a white person in authority may select another white person over an equally or better qualified black person because of a preconceived notion that whites are more competent or because of discomfort with people perceived as somehow different. This latter type of subtle discrimination includes, in John Calmore's words, "the unconscious failure to extend to a minority the same recognition of humanity, and hence the same sympathy and care, given as a matter of course to one's own group." The selectivity results "often unconsciously—from our tendency to sympathize most readily with those who seem most like ourselves" (Calmore 1989). Yet oppression is not less serious because it is more subtle.

The racist system is made even more complex by its reinforcement in many other aspects of the everyday behavior of white Americans. When whites make racist comments to other whites, or when they think or say racist things when watching television by themselves or with their families, they also reinforce and maintain the white-racist system, even though no blacks are present. Racism is systemic because it infiltrates most aspects of life.

WHO DOES THE DISCRIMINATING?

Antiblack discrimination comes from all levels and categories of white Americans. Most whites are involved in some way in creating, reinforcing, or maintaining the racist reality of U.S. society. Depending on the situation and the opportunity to discriminate, very large numbers of whites can and do discriminate. Judging from housing audit studies[5], perhaps half of all whites are inclined to discriminate in some fashion, whether subtly or blatantly,

[4]Elsewhere in the book, Professor Feagin notes the irony of this situation: "Federal surveys of white victims of violent crime have found that about 17 percent of these attackers are black, while about three-quarters are white. Most violent crime affecting whites is carried out by *white* criminals. Yet most whites do not take similar precautions when they are in the presence of those whites—disproportionately white men—who perpetrate most of the violent crime suffered by whites. The reason for this is that they do not see themselves as being in the presence of someone likely to commit a violent crime when they are around those socially defined as white" (114).—Ed.

[5]Audit studies are used to test the degree to which discrimination exists in a particular social arena. In a housing audit study, a white couple and a black couple might (separately) visit rental agencies to inquire about the availability of rentals. If antiblack discrimination exists, the study will show that black couples were more likely to be told that no appropriate rentals are currently available, whereas the white couple may discover that several rentals just happen to be available.—Ed.

in situations where they have housing to rent or sell to black individuals or families. It may well be that whites discriminate at similarly high levels in other major institutional arenas.

There are actively antiracist whites scattered across the nation. They consistently and regularly speak out against white racism, even to the point of risking personal injury, friendships, and jobs. However, in regard to racist practice, most whites seem to fall into three other categories of action. One large group of whites regularly engage in overtly racist behavior; some of these whites are greatly consumed by their racist hatreds, as can be seen in lynchings and hate crimes. A second, much larger, group of whites discriminate against blacks in a variety of ways, as the occasion arises, but they frequently discriminate in less overt or more subtle ways and may often not be consciously aware of their discrimination. A third group of whites are consistently bystanders, engaging in less direct discrimination but knowingly providing support for those who do. Whites in the latter two groups often reject the type of blatant discrimination in which some in the first group engage, and may speak out against it, even as they themselves are engaging in more subtle or covert types of discrimination. Most whites in these three groups routinely think in white-oriented terms when choosing mates, neighborhoods, schools, and business partners. The racist system is thereby reinforced in daily interactions among whites. A sense of white superiority, however dim, seems to be part of the consciousness of most whites, including those who are relatively liberal on racial matters.

Interestingly, when issues of racism are discussed in the mass media, it is often working-class whites, the Archie Bunkers of television fame, who get tagged as the serious racists by the news and other media programs. Blue-collar violence against black Americans often does get significant news attention. Yet elite and middle-class whites are less frequently the focus of attention in media discussions of racial problems, and media discussions of discrimination that do involve a few middle class or elite discriminators usually avoid making connections to broader issues of systemic racism. Indeed, most elite and middle class whites vigorously deny that they are racist.

The portrait of discriminatory practice that emerges from research is quite different. Judging from hundreds of interviews that I and my colleagues have conducted with black and white Americans over the last decade, as well as from numerous other field studies of discrimination in housing, employment, and public accommodations, the majority of whites who do the serious discriminating are those with some power to bring harm, such as white employers, managers, teachers, social workers, real estate agents, lenders, landlords and apartment managers, and police officers (Feagin and Sikes 1994; Feagin, Vera, and Imani 1996; St. Jean and Feagin 1998). Middle-income and upper-income men and women are heavily implicated in racial oppression, though it is likely that in most major institutional areas, such as corporate promotions and urban policing, white men account for the lion's share of discriminatory actions. Generally speaking, these middle-income and upper-income whites are the ones in a position to most significantly affect black lives. Certainly, whites with less social or economic power also discriminate against black Americans in all income categories. Blue-collar employees frequently harass black workers in the work-place, and blue-collar bigots may yell racist epithets or hurl beer cans at a black man, woman, or child on the street. And working-class whites do seem to predominate as perpetrators in violent attacks on blacks in public places.

Given the right circumstances, most whites in all income groups have the ability to put black Americans "in their place," to frustrate or sabotage their lives for racist reasons. However, the patterns of discrimination vary.

Many in the employer class, for instance, may be most interested in the exploitation of black workers, whose lowest-paid members constitute a reserve army of workers. In contrast, those in the white working and middle classes may be more concerned about housing or educational competition with black Americans, and they appear to be the most likely to discriminate in these latter areas.

Facing Lifetimes of Racial Discrimination

Whether subtle, covert, or blatant, racist practices are commonplace and recurring in a great variety of settings, ranging from public accommodations to educational facilities, business arenas, workplaces, and neighborhoods. How frequent is the discrimination faced by black Americans? What forms does this discrimination take? We do not yet have full answers to these questions, but recent surveys are helpful.

Researchers Nancy Krieger and Stephen Sidney gave some 2,000 black respondents a list of seven settings, such as the workplace, where one can face discrimination. Seventy percent of the female and 84 percent of the male respondents reported encountering discrimination in at least one area. The majority reported discrimination in at least three settings (Krieger and Sidney 1996). Similarly, a survey in the Detroit area asked black respondents about facing discrimination in six situations. Thirty-two percent reported discrimination recently in at least one of the situations, and four in ten reported facing at least one form of discrimination frequently (Forman, Williams, and Jackson 1997). In addition, a recent Gallup survey inquired of black respondents if they had experienced discrimination in five areas (work, dining out, shopping, with police, in public transportation) during the last month. Just under half reported discrimination in one

or more of these areas, including 70 percent of black men under the age of 35 (Gallup 1977). Many black Americans frequently face racist barriers in an array of societal arenas.

Even these substantial data are likely to be serious underestimates of the frequency of racist obstacles. Short survey questions do not explore the great range of discrimination faced by black Americans in everyday life. Indeed, survey research on the black experience with discrimination is relatively recent and remarkably limited. Survey questions are usually brief and customarily deal with only a few of the many types of racial mistreatment in the society. Indeed, a few survey researchers have suggested that more detailed questioning would reveal a more substantial portrait of discrimination (Sigelman and Welch 1991).

There are other reasons why the existing survey data do not adequately describe the reality of everyday racism. Most black and white Americans are taught as children to focus on individual reasons for personal barriers or failures. Most are taught that blaming others, however legitimate that may seem, is generally not appropriate. The reasoning behind such socialization seems to be that a system-blame orientation makes a person seem weak to those she or he respects. Some black Americans who suffer from discrimination may thus feel that talking too much about racist barriers suggests that they as individuals are not capable of dealing with these difficulties. However, this reluctance to report to survey researchers some of the discrimination they experience does not mean that the discrimination is not harmful in the respondent's life.

In addition, the terminology used in most surveys leads to underestimates. The term "discrimination" itself is used by some black Americans only for very serious abuse by whites. Lesser forms of mistreatment, because they are so commonplace, may not be characterized as discrimination. For example, a young black college professor recently explained to me that he does not ordinarily think of certain everyday examples of differential treatment—such as white cashiers not putting money in his hand because they do not want to touch a black person—as "racial discrimination." It is the more serious incidents of racism that he would recall if asked a question by a pollster about having encountered racial discrimination recently. Racial obstacles are so much a part of black lives that they generally become a part of the societal woodwork. This "everydayness" of racist barriers means that for many black Americans a survey researcher's brief question about discrimination will bring quickly to mind primarily the more serious incidents that stay at the front of the mind—and sometimes not the many intrusions of more subtle racism that occur in one's life. A failure to recall some incidents with whites when questioned briefly does not mean these encounters are of little consequence. In order to survive in a racist society, black Americans cannot attend consciously to all the racist incidents that intrude on their lives. The personal and family cost of too-close attention to much discrimination is too great.

To my knowledge, there is no research on the frequency of the incidents and events of discrimination faced by individual black Americans over their lifetimes. In a few exploratory interviews with black respondents, I have asked a question about frequency and gotten large estimates in response. For example, I asked a retired printer from New York City how often he has faced discrimination over the course of his life. After some careful reflection, this man estimated that he confronts at least 250 significant incidents of discrimination from whites each year, if he only includes the incidents that he consciously notices and records. Blatant and subtle mistreatment by white clerks in stores and restaurants are examples he had in mind. Judging from my own field studies using

in-depth interviews with black Americans, this man's experience seems representative. Over the course of a lifetime, a typical black man or woman likely faces *thousands* of instances of blatant, covert, or subtle discrimination at the hands of whites. Today, this omnipresent and routinized discrimination remains a key mechanism in the social reproduction of systemic racism.

Racial Discrimination in Public Places

Racial oppression has a distinctive spatial dimension, and its character can vary as a black person travels from the private home site to more public spaces. In one study that interviewed a large number of middle-class black Americans, a professor at a major university noted the stress that comes from dealing with whites in public places:

> If I'm in those areas that are fairly protected, within gatherings of my own group, other African Americans, or if I'm in the university where my status as a professor mediates against the way I might be perceived, mediates against the hostile perception, then it's fairly comfortable. . . . When I divide my life into encounters with the outside world, and of course that's ninety percent of my life, it's fairly consistently unpleasant at those sites where there's nothing that mediates between my race and what I have to do. For example, if I'm in a grocery store, if I'm in my car, which is a 1970 Chevrolet, a real old ugly car, all those things—being in a grocery store in casual clothes, or being in the car—sort of advertises something that doesn't have anything to do with my status as far as people I run into are concerned. (Feagin and Sikes 1994)

The increase in unpleasant encounters that comes as this professor moves from her home into public arenas such as stores is attributed to the absence of mediating factors such as whites knowing that she is a professor. Much antiblack discrimination occurs outside social contexts where there are family or friends or symbols of status that may reduce the likelihood of discrimination. On the way to work or school there can be unpleasant contacts with white police officers, white clerks who will not touch your hand, white teenagers at a traffic light, or white customers in stores who are rude. These racist practices are not limited to one setting but rather take place across many public arenas.

DISCRIMINATION IN PUBLIC PLACES

Psychological researchers have staged situations of possible discrimination in public places, and have discovered that white bystanders will often not respond to a black person's call for help in a staged emergency situation. In contrast, whites are much more likely to respond to calls for help from a white person (Dovidio 1993). One study found that when a black woman drops a bag of groceries in a public setting, a white person is less likely to help her than to help a white woman who has the same mishap (Crosby et al. 1980). The racial identity of the person needing help strongly affects white responses. Overt dislike of black people is one likely reason. One analyst has suggested yet another possible reason for the white reactions: The more whites see of black people suffering, such as in the media, the more they come to see that condition as normal, and the less sympathy they have for blacks in difficulty (Delgado 1996).

In a recent Gallup survey asking black respondents about discrimination in various settings in the preceding month, retail shopping was the area in which the largest percentage (30 percent) of the sample reported racial mistreatment. Indeed, 45 percent of the young men in this sample reported such discrimination. Twenty-one percent of the sample (and 32 percent of young men) also reported

discrimination when dining out. Discrimination in dining includes very poor service that seems racially motivated and often being seated in an undesirable place, such as at the back of the restaurant near the kitchen. Discrimination in retail stores encompasses the extra surveillance often faced by black shoppers and other discrimination by white sales clerks. In this survey, moreover, those black respondents with higher incomes reported encountering more discrimination than those with lower incomes (Gallup 1997). Leanita McClain, a prize-winning black columnist for the *Chicago Tribune,* once suggested an important difference between contemporary racist practices and the old segregationist practices: "The old racism wouldn't let blacks into some stores; the new racism assumes that any black person, no matter how well dressed, in a store is probably there to steal, not to buy." Undoubtedly drawing on her own experience, she added that the old racism "didn't have to address black people; the new racism is left speechless when a black, approached condescendingly, has an eloquent comeback" (McClain 1986).

Black customers face discrimination in the buying process. One major Chicago study examined more than 180 buyer-salesperson negotiations at ninety car dealerships. Black and white testers, with similar economic characteristics and bargaining scripts, posed as car buyers. White male testers got much better prices from the salespeople than did white women or black men and women. Compared to the markup given to white men, black men paid twice the markup and black women paid more than three times the markup. The average dealer profit in the final offers to each category of tester was as follows: white men, $362; white women, $504; black men, $783; and black women, $1237. In another study the researchers used thirty-eight testers who bargained for some 400 cars at 242 dealers. Again, black testers were quoted much higher prices than white men, though this time black men were quoted the highest prices. In some cases racist language was used by salespeople, but the researchers concluded that the more serious problem was stereotyping about how much black customers will pay. The cost of this commonplace discrimination is high. Given that black customers pay two to three times the markup offered to white men—if this holds across the nation—then black customers "annually would pay $150 million more for new cars than do white males" (Ayres 1991).

Discrimination has also been found in professional services. Recently, one group of researchers used actors to portray black and white patients with certain coronary disease symptoms. A total of 720 physicians were asked to look at these recorded interviews and other patient data, to assess the probability of coronary artery disease, and to suggest treatment. The researchers found differences in proposed treatment: blacks, and especially black women, were less likely to be recommended for cardiac catheterization, compared to whites with the same dress, occupations, and medical histories (Schulman et al. 1999; Bach et al. 1999). Another recent study reported in the *New England Journal of Medicine* found that black patients with lung cancer were less likely to receive the best surgical treatment than white patients. The reasons for these patterns of differential medical treatment along racial lines are yet to be delineated, but they may include not only traditional racial stereotypes but also specific stereotypes shared by some white medical practitioners, such as the notion that black patients who get special or expensive treatments are not as likely as whites to take proper care of themselves after treatment. The explanation for differences in surgery may also include the reluctance on the part of some black patients to trust the recommendations of white physicians. More research remains to be done, but there is no reason to expect that the racism of the larger society does not extend into the medical professions.

References

Ayres, Ian. 1991. "Fair Driving: Gender and Race Discrimination in Retail Car Negotiations." *Harvard Law Review* 104 (February).

Bach, Peter B. et al. 1999. "Racial Differences in the Treatment of Early-Stage Lung Cancer." *New England Journal of Medicine* (October 14).

Blendon, Robert J. et al. 1998. "The Public and the President's Commission on Race." *The Public Perspective*, February.

Bobo, Lawrence. 1988. "Group Conflict, Prejudice and the Paradox of Contemporary Racial Attitudes." In Phyllis A. Katz and Dalmas A. Taylor (eds.), *Eliminating Racism*. New York: Plenum.

Bobo, Lawrence, James R. Kluegel, and Ryan A. Smith. 1997. "Laissez-faire Racism: The Crystallization of a Kinder, Gentler, Antiblack Ideology." In Steven A. Tuch and Jack K. Martin (eds.), *Racial Attitudes in the 1990s: Continuity and Change*. Westport, CT: Praeger.

Calmore, John O. 1989. "To Make Wrong Right: The Necessary and Proper Aspirations of Fair Housing." In *The State of Black America 1989*. New York: The National Urban League.

Crosby, Faye et al. 1980. "Recent Unobtrusive Studies of Black and White Discrimination and Prejudice: A Literature Review." *Psychological Bulletin* 87.

Culp, Jerome M., Jr. 1993. "Water Buffalo and Diversity: Naming Names and Reclaiming the Racial Discourse." *Connecticut Law Review* 26 (Fall).

Delgado, Richard. 1996. *The Coming Race War?* New York: New York University Press.

Devine, Patricia G. 1989. "Stereotypes and Prejudice: Their Automatic and Controlled Components." *Journal of Personality and Social Psychology* 56: 15–16.

Dovidio, John F. 1993. "The Subtlety of Racism." *Training and Development*, April.

Entman, Robert M. 1997. "Manufacturing Discord: Media in the Affirmative Action Debate." *Press/Politics* 2.

Essed, Philomena. 1991. *Understanding Everyday Racism*. Newbury Park, CA: Sage.

Feagin, Joe R., and Clairece B. Feagin. 1999. *Racial and Ethnic Relations*. 6th ed. Upper Saddle River, NJ: Prentice-Hall.

Feagin, Joe R., and Melvin P. Sikes. 1994. *Living with Racism: The Black Middle-Class Experience*. Boston: Beacon Press.

Feagin, Joe R., and Hernan Vera. 1995. *White Racism: The Basics*. New York: Routledge.

Feagin, Joe R., Hernan Vera, and Nikitah Imani. 1996. *The Agony of Education: Black Students at White Colleges and Universities*. New York: Routledge.

Forman, Tyrone, David R. Williams, and James S. Jackson. 1997. "Race, Place, and Discrimination." In Carol Brooks Gardner (ed.), *Perspectives on Social Problems*. Stamford, CT: JAI Press.

Frankenberg, Ruth. 1993. *White Women, Race Matters*. Minneapolis: University of Minnesota Press.

Gallup Organization. 1997. *Black/White Relations in the United States*. Princeton, NJ: Gallup Organization.

Hughes, Michael. 1997. "Symbolic Racism, Old-fashioned Racism, and Whites' Opposition to Affirmative Action." In Steven A. Tuch and Jack K. Martin (eds.), *Racial Attitudes in the 1990s: Continuity and Change*. Westport, CT: Praeger.

Jhally, Sut, and Justin Lewis. 1992. *Enlightened Racism*. Boulder, CO: Westview Press.

King, Joyce E. 1991. "Dysconscious Racism: Ideology, Identity, and the Miseducation of Teachers." *Journal of Negro Education* 60.

Kluegel, James R., and Eliot R. Smith. 1986. *Beliefs about Inequality*. New York: Aldine de Gruyter.

Krieger, Nancy, and Stephen Sidney. 1996. "Racial Discrimination and Blood Pressure." *American Journal of Public Health* 86.

Ladd, Everett C. 1995. "Rethinking the Sixties." *The American Enterprise*, May/June.

Lehigh, Scott. 1998. "Conflicting Views of Massachusetts; Poll Shows a Sharp Racial Divide over the State of Equality." *Boston Globe*, June 14.

McClain, Leanita. 1986. "The Insidious New Racism." In Clarence Page (ed.), *A Foot in Each World*. Evanston, IL: Northwestern University Press.

NORC. 1990. *General Social Survey*. Chicago, IL: National Opinion Research Center.

Schulman, Kevin A., et al. 1999. "The Effect of Race and Sex on Physicians' Recommendations for Cardiac Catheterization." *New England Journal of Medicine*, February.

Sears, David O. 1988. "Symbolic Racism." In Phyllis A. Katz and Dalmas A. Taylor (eds.), *Eliminating Racism*. New York: Plenum.

Sigelman, Lee, and Susan Welch. 1991. *Black Americans' Views of Racial Inequality: The Dream Deferred*. Cambridge: Cambridge University Press.

Smith, Matthew P. 1996. "Bridging the Gulf Between Blacks and Whites." *Pittsburgh Post Gazette*, April 7.

St. Jean, Yanick, and Joe R. Feagin. 1998. *Double Burden: Black Women and Everyday Racism*. New York: M. E. Sharpe.

Verba, Sidney, and Gary R. Orren. 1985. *Equality in America: The View from the Top*. Cambridge, MA: Harvard University Press.

Wellman, David. 1977. *Portraits of White Racism*. Cambridge: Cambridge University Press.

Questions

1. Make a list of the varieties of antiblack racist acts that were described by black people in Feagin's article. Assume that these kinds of discriminatory acts are familiar to just about every black person in the United States. Which discriminatory acts on your list are of the sort that the average white person is likely to have many opportunities to personally observe and understand as racist?

2. It has been claimed that subtle bias can be as harmful as overt bids. Does Feagin's work tend to support this claim? Explain why or why not. Then, are there any circumstances under which subtle bias is even more harmful than overt bias?

35

"RACE DOESN'T MATTER, BUT . . ."

The Effect of Race on College Professors' Experiences and Emotion Management in the Undergraduate College Classroom

Roxanna Harlow

I hate to admit it, but as a college student I gave little thought to the difficulties of being a professor. Indeed, it seemed to me to be a pretty cushy job. Not surprisingly, I've since changed my mind. However, as a white college professor, it's clear that my job is easier than my colleagues of color. Professor Harlow discusses how the experience of being a college professor varies depending upon one's race.

Anyone who has taught at the college level probably can tell numerous stories about the rewards and exhilaration as well as the challenges and frustrations of teaching undergraduates. Many scholars have studied and discussed the college classroom in various ways (see, for example, Gallop 1997; Hendrix 1998; Jacobs 1999; Statham, Richardson, and Cook 1991); few, however, talk about it, other than anecdotally, as an emotional space where professors' multiple status characteristics shape their affective experiences in the classroom as they negotiate roles, expectations, and power dynamics through interaction with students. In this research I examine how race shapes professors' perceptions and experiences in the undergraduate college classroom,

how they manage the emotional demands arising from these experiences, and how the management process affects the nature of their jobs overall.

Research has shown how black scholars' experiences differ from those of their white counterparts, particularly in regard to role conflict, isolation, and a lack of respect and legitimacy as scholars (Aguirre 2000; Baker 1991; Banks 1984; Fields 1996; Menges and Exum 1983; Phelps 1995; Sinegar 1987; Smith and Witt 1993). Surprisingly little of the research, however, addresses the degree to which a professor's race influences his or her experience in the classroom. When it is discussed, it is typically mentioned briefly and/or treated as a minor factor in the professor's routine. Smith and Witt (1993), for example, found that African Americans reported statistically significant higher levels of stress than white professors in regard to service and research, but not teaching. The scale used to measure teaching stress, however, measured the *tasks* of teaching, not the qualitative

Roxanna Harlow, "'Race Doesn't Matter, But . . .': The Effect of Race on College Professors' Experiences and Emotion Management in the Undergraduate College Classroom" from *Social Psychology Quarterly* 66, no. 4 (December 2003): 348–363. Copyright © 2003. Reprinted with the permission of the author and the American Sociological Association.

experience connected to professors' perceptions of the classroom climate, their relationship with students, their feelings about teaching, or the management of these views and feelings in order to teach effectively. Hendrix (1995), Rains (1995), and Moore (1996) found that black and white professors' experiences in the classroom indeed are qualitatively different. Yet because of scope limitations and small sample sizes (with Ns of 6 to 17), it is unclear whether these experiences are due to race or to gender, and the emotional component of teaching has been mostly unexplored.

As Goffman (1963) notes, race is an attribute that people consider when forming opinions about groups or individuals; therefore black professors may find themselves managing a racial stigma in the classroom. Such a stigma, as Feagin and Sikes (1994) explain, eventually can take an emotional toll. In this research I examine how the crediting[1] and the discrediting aspects of race differentially shape black[2] and white professors' experiences with undergraduate teaching and classroom emotion management. Because this area of research is largely unexplored, the answers to these questions provide greater insight into racial differences in faculty members' experiences in the classroom. They help us as well to understand how differences in emotional labor and management may create more and different work for professors, depending on their social status characteristics.

EMOTIONAL LABOR AND MANAGEMENT

Hochschild (1983) discusses emotion as a workplace commodity, and estimates that one-third of the American workforce engages in emotional labor. While most jobs require us to deal with our emotions in some way (e.g., holding back anger at the boss), she distinguishes between this type of emotion work and emotional labor. Emotion work is the process of handling our daily, personal emotions; emotional labor involves evoking, performing, and managing emotions that are a required aspect of a job or occupation. Emotion management is the process of handling emotions in both personal (emotion work) and professional (emotional labor) spheres.

Emotional labor and management can be understood as a form of impression management (Goffman 1959; Wood 2000). According to Goffman (1959), impression management is the process through which people project a self-image that is consistent with how they want to be seen by others. Goffman believed that the ability to mask one's true emotions while providing the appropriate emotional display is the true test of a high-quality social performance. College teaching requires extensive emotional labor; professors try to perform and evoke emotions such as enthusiasm and excitement while also managing or suppressing their own immediate feelings and moods (Bellas 1999; Harlow 2002). These performances are affected, however, by the degree to which students and teachers begin their relationship with a mutual acceptance of the professor's status and identity.

IDENTITY AND AFFECT CONTROL THEORY

Identity theory states that a person's behavior is directly connected to her or his conception

---

[1] Goffman (1963) defines a stigma as a discrediting attribute. It is difficult to fully understand the process of devaluing certain characteristics, however, without discussing how we come to value other characteristics. Crediting attributes, then, add or have the potential to add value or credibility to a person or a group of people. This concept is useful for understanding the relational nature of stigma, and how the valued and the devalued are integrally tied together. Jason Jimerson originally named and conceptualized this idea in personal discussions.

[2] In this study, the terms black and African American are used interchangeably to refer to black people acculturated in the United States.

of self, and that these conceptions are shaped in part by responses from others through interaction (Stryker 1992). According to this theory, we all have multiple identities that are arranged hierarchically: that is, some identities are more relevant than others from situation to situation. For professors in the classroom, their identity as teacher tends to be one of the most central and most salient at that moment, and they perform in certain ways so as to reinforce that identity.[3] If it is not confirmed through interactions with students, a negative emotional effect may result. According to affect control theory, when our conception of self is not confirmed, our emotions provide the cue that things are going wrong. We then adjust our definition of a situation or change our behavior so as to correct the emotional dissonance (Heise 1989).

Similar to affect control theory, Burke (1991) discusses "the control-system view of the identity process" (p. 838). He explains that when a person's understanding of her or his own identity (the identity standard) in a social situation is inconsistent with feedback from others in that situation (inputs), that person becomes distressed. To resolve this feeling, the person changes her or his behavior (outputs) in an effort to alter the external feedback in a way that is consistent with the internally defined identity. Burke notes that matching one's identity standard with others' inputs can involve a complex cycle of interactions. Ultimately, however, these two must match; otherwise, high levels of stress

result. In this paper I seek, in part, to explain what self-definitions professors are trying to establish with their classroom performances, and how these vary by race. If the definitions are not confirmed through interactions with students, what are the emotional consequences for professors, and how are they managed?

Race is what Cohen (1982) defines as a diffuse status characteristic: that is, even though a particular status may be irrelevant to a task, persons of high status are considered more competent. Therefore black professors' identity performances may involve providing "proof" in any number of ways to justify their presence in a high-status position. As Rakow (1991) observes, the statuses of white, male, and professor are all high, and thus are compatible and even anticipated. For African Americans, however, their racial status is inconsistent with their faculty status; therefore they may find themselves doing "tiring 'identity work'" (Rakow 1991, 10) in order to reconcile students' perceptions with their own. The findings presented here show that race affects the amount of work professors do in the classroom; negotiating a racial stigma creates emotion work and labor for African American professors beyond that required of their white peers.

Data and Methods

From February through November 1999, I conducted 58 in-depth interviews with 29 white and 29 African American faculty members at a large Midwestern state university with a 91 percent white student population. Twenty-six respondents were female; 32 were male. They included 22 assistant professors, 27 associate professors, and nine full professors, ranging in age from 30 to 65 with a mean age of 44. Eighteen of the men and six of the women taught in traditionally applied fields

---

[3]An important aspect of identity theory is the concept of identity salience: the likelihood that an identity will be invoked at a particular point in time (Stryker 1992). I use the terms *central* and *salient* here because I am also referring to the concept of psychological centrality (Stryker and Serpe 1994). Psychological centrality pertains to the likelihood that an identity will be most important or most central for a person at a particular point in time. Centrality implies an awareness of the importance of the identity; salience does not (Stryker and Serpe 1994).

such as business and health science; 14 men and 20 women were housed in the humanities or social sciences. I included only full-time tenure-track faculty members who taught at least one undergraduate course. I excluded professors in the School of Music because students were evaluated differently there. I targeted faculty members acculturated in the United States so that respondents' understandings of race and racial dynamics would be comparable.

The sample selection was based on the population of black professors meeting the above criteria; then I matched them with white participants of similar gender, rank, and department or area of study. Of the 30 black faculty members who qualified for the study, 29 agreed to participate. Of the corresponding white faculty members whom I contacted, only two did not participate. This response rate was extremely high (97% black and 94% white) in view of the time commitment asked of the participants.

The semistructured interview consisted of 37 open-ended questions and lasted, on average, 75 minutes. I (an African American) asked the professors about their anxiety on the first day of class, their teaching style, the level of students' energy in their classes, students' opinions of the respondents, how they would like to be viewed by students, and other subjects. Questions directly related to their social status were not raised until midway through the interview, when I asked about students' positive and negative views of the respondents, and whether they felt that their own race or gender affected any of those views. Because I kept the initial questions race-neutral (in regard to the professor), the race-related responses to those questions were generated on their own, and were a product of what was most important to the respondents at that time. The remainder of the interview dealt with topics such as challenges to authority, how the respondents

handled those challenges, concerns about teaching, and job stress. I ended the interview with a general question about racism and sexism.

Findings

RACIAL DIFFERENCES IN FACULTY MEMBERS' PERCEPTIONS

"Race doesn't matter, but . . ." The black faculty members in my sample were aware of the negative stereotypes associated with their racial group, and often commented on the continued existence of racial problems in society today. Although they had a sophisticated understanding of macro social processes and how they affected racial inequality, almost half of the black professors were reluctant to claim that their race mattered to students, or that race influenced their classroom experience in any negative way. Problems related to racial issues were often internalized ("It's my own fault for thinking about it too much") or downplayed altogether (see Table 1). For example, one professor stated, "Race is always an issue," but then went on to emphasize regional differences that he felt were more important. He explained, "Just in general, getting over the, if you will, racial divide, I really haven't had any problems like that here. I just try to understand my students" (Respondent 25: black male).

Race was "always an issue" on a macro level, but this professor wanted to make clear that he personally had no problem with a "racial divide." Similarly, after pondering the effect of race on his teaching, another professor stated, "Uh, the race thing? In the sense that I'm aware that I'm black, but—I'm not sure . . . but I don't really think that it's going to make a difference in the classroom" (Respondent 23: black male).

Although these two professors expressed doubts about the significance of their race in

Table 1 Self-Reported Classroom Experiences, by Race and Gender

	% of African American Professors			% of White Professors		
	Men (n = 16)	Women (n = 13)	Total (N = 29)	Men (n = 16)	Women (n = 13)	Total (N = 29)
Initially Downplayed or Internalized Their Racialized Classroom Experiences[a]	50	31	41	n/a	n/a	n/a
Believe Students Immediately Notice Their Racial Status	75	92	83	6	0	3
Believe Students Question Their Intellectual Authority (Competency/Qualifications)	94	54	76	6	8	7
Feel They Must Prove Their Competence/Intelligence	56	54	55	6	15	10
Received Inappropriate Student Challenges to Intellectual Authority	44	23	34	0	15	7
Racial Double Standard (White Advantage)	50	77	62	25	8	17

[a]This experience is not applicable to white professors because, for the most part, they did not interpret their classroom work in a racialized way.

the classroom, they also expressed an awareness of their subordinate racial status as well as their rarity in the academy.[4] They believed that as soon as they stepped into the classroom, students were surprised by their race and/or noticed it immediately (see Table 1).

The data, then, produced seemingly contradictory statements about the effect of race on these professors' classroom experiences. After downplaying it initially, they then proceeded to explain how, in fact, race mattered significantly. Most of these professors felt that students stereotyped them: 76 percent of the black professors reported that students

questioned their competency, qualifications, and credibility (see Table 1).

In essence, most black professors felt that their classes always contained at least some students who questioned their right to hold the status of professor. For example, immediately after Respondent 23 stated that he did *not* think his race made a difference in the classroom, he went on to explain that he *had* been concerned about his race because most of the students were white and had never seen a black professor before, especially in his discipline. As a result, he made an extra effort to appear qualified and knowledgeable:

I wanted them to know that I know what I'm talking about, and that I'm really well qualified to teach what I teach. And I want them to know that I'm here because of my skills and my ability and that I can do a really good job. And so it's very important to me that when I teach, that comes across, because people will try to challenge you. (Respondent 23: black male)

Similarly, after being asked, "Do you think your race or gender affects students' positive or negative views of you?" Respondent 25, who had said he had no problems with the "racial divide," added:

Undoubtedly. Now exactly how, I'm not totally sure . . . but I did have a very, very interesting experience, though, my first semester with a black student. . . . And he said to me after about the third lecture of the class . . . "Dr. [his name], I'm so glad that you're here. I've never had a black professor before. And you're competent too." Well, I was glad that he was glad to see me . . . but his statement "and you're competent too" was very interesting coming from him. Now if that was coming from him, just think of what maybe some white kid from some rural farm town in [the state] is thinking when I stand up in front of him, [who] doesn't know me from Adam. (Respondent 25: black male)

Like Respondent 23, this faculty member may not have had problems with the racial divide, but he believed that his race influenced how students viewed him and his ability to teach. Although these responses from black professors initially sounded contradictory, the contradiction is resolved when understood in the context of a management strategy (to be discussed later), which enabled them to function effectively day to day.

In contrast to the black professors, some white male professors downplayed their intellectual presence in order to seem more approachable to students.

I think that initially the main thing one's doing is not trying to make oneself seem knowledgeable because they're going to think that [I'll be that way] as a professor. I think it's a matter of trying to make oneself seem approachable and accessible, so for me there's a certain element of calculated self-deprecation. (Respondent 47: white male)

This difference in classroom reality for black and for white professors was illustrated in part by faculty members' reports of students' challenges to their classroom authority.

"I really do know what I'm talking about." Although few men of either race reported concerns about their physical authority in the classroom (the right to be in charge, organize the course, assign materials, and discipline students), black men reported that students resisted their intellectual authority—that is, their knowledge and competency (see Table 1). This was particularly the case for black assistant professors.

Black women also felt that their competency was questioned, but overall they were more likely to report challenges to their physical rather than their intellectual authority.[5] Young black women at the assistant and associate levels were the most likely to report challenges to both their competence and their control over the classroom. Explaining this dynamic, Respondent 34 (black female) noted that students do not usually see black people in positions of power, especially black women. As a result, they may doubt black women's academic and leadership capabilities. Commenting on the social structural factors shaping students' often unconscious attitudes about blackness, femininity, and intelligence, this professor went on to explain how looking young simply exacerbated the problem for such women.

This question of competency was an issue even for professors who taught predominantly nonwhite classes and/or classes on race-related topics. For example, when asked, "When students see you're their professor,

[5]Describing the "cult of true womanhood," Hill-Collins noted that "'true' women possessed four cardinal virtues: piety, purity, submissiveness, and domesticity" (1991, 71). Thus, although black women (like black men) felt that students doubted their competence, they also struggled, in ways that the men did not, with issues of authority in regard to classroom presence (physical authority) as they tried to balance students' expectations of "submissiveness" and "domesticity" with power and control.

what do you think they're thinking?" Respondent 32 (black female) replied, "So when I walk into the class, they know it's a class dealing with black people. I walk in as a black professor. I think to some degree it probably legitimates the content. . . ." The remainder of her response was surprising, however:

> And I think when I walk in there, other things go through their minds. Probably whether or not I'm good, whether or not I'm tough, whether or not this is going to be a blow-off class for them, whether I'm an affirmative action professor, whether I'm going to be one of these attitudes kind of professor, whether I'm going to be a racist professor, whether I'm going to be the kind of professor who makes white people feel bad about what has happened to black people in America.[6]

Despite the course topic, this professor believed that her race triggered for students negative stereotypes about black people (in regard to competence and browbeating about racism), and black women in particular (in regard to anger and attitude). Another professor similarly explained that his blackness gave him credibility in teaching race-related topics. He then added:

> But then on the other hand there's always an undercurrent of "He's black, he couldn't possibly know what he's talking about." And a lot of that will come more from black students than white. 'Cause a lot of our people have internalized those kinds of ideas, you know. That's what they've been taught. (Respondent 30: black male)

He went on to explain how he states his credentials on the first day of class in an effort to counteract the negative stereotypes that students of all races have internalized.

---

[6]Several black professors used the term *affirmative action professor* or *affirmative action hire* to indicate that students thought they were unqualified. This is not to say that they themselves equated affirmative action with a lack of qualification. They seemed aware, however, that many students viewed affirmative action as the hiring of unqualified people of color.

The black professors' responses on these issues differed sharply from those of white faculty members. In reply to the question "When students see you're their professor, what do you think they're thinking?" one professor stated:

> I don't know if I've ever thought about what they were thinking. . . . I suspect that there is some response to the fact that I am still pretty young and female. I suspect perhaps now there is some feeling of "Is this a graduate student or professor?" I don't know if I ever thought about that. (Respondent 21: white female)

Similarly, another professor responded:

> I'm not sure I know exactly. I think I probably look a little young . . . but otherwise, I don't think that there's much about me that really makes me stand out specifically . . . . I don't think I make a very striking first impression or anything. (Respondent 28: white male)

Responses such as "I don't know" or "I never thought about that before" were common among white faculty members answering this question; these were followed by comments on how their age (and, in the case of women, their gender) might play a role in what students thought. White professors usually did not have to anticipate students' reactions to phenotypic cues, though such anticipation was commonplace for black professors. In contrast to the black faculty members, most white faculty members, especially white males, took students' confidence in them for granted: 76 percent of black professors felt that students called their qualifications into question, in contrast to only 7 percent of white professors (see Table 1).

The white professors had hardly considered how their racial status might shape students' personal and professional evaluations of them. When asked, "Do you feel that your race or gender affects students' positive or negative views of you?" white women were most likely to focus on their gender alone. White men often overlooked the crediting aspects of both their gender and their race. When Respondent

20, for example, was asked if his race and gender shaped students' attitudes, he replied:

> I don't think so. In my department, there's more women than men. . . . I mean there's a complex mix of faculty, and I don't think it makes any difference to any [students] really. . . . For example, we have black faculty, we have faculty from other countries, we have a lot of women [faculty], I told you. I think that for some of [the students] it's a fairly new experience, something they may not have thought about in their high school, especially, or their home towns. But . . . I don't think it matters a lot to them. (Respondent 20: white male)

In response to this question, another professor replied:

> Ohhh, I don't think so. I don't think so. I mean, it probably helps to be a white male but it's really hard to know. You know, the only reason why it may help is that they see me in them. . . . They look at me and say, well, this guy is kinda like me, so—I have no proof of that and I really have no way of knowing if that's really even to any great advantage. (Respondent 31: white male)

Although these professors were skeptical that there was any benefit to being a white male, many of the black faculty members in my sample felt that in fact it was a great advantage.

"THAT'S WRONG": CHALLENGES AND IMPRESSION MANAGEMENT

To resist negative stereotyping, the black professors in my sample often performed competence and authority by projecting a strict, authoritative demeanor, making students aware of their professional achievements, and (for black women) reminding students to call them Doctor or Professor rather than by their first name, Ms., or Mrs. Although women were more likely than men to describe their classroom style as authoritative, this distinction broke down along racial lines: 69 percent of white female respondents reported that they were authoritative in the classroom, while all of the black women did so. Among the men, 44 percent of the black faculty members considered their style to be authoritative, in contrast to only 19 percent of the white respondents (see Table 2). In addition,

Table 2 Self-Reported Presentation and Evaluation, by Race and Gender

	% of African American Professors			% of White Professors		
	Men (n = 16)	Women (n = 13)	Total (N = 29)	Men (n = 16)	Women (n = 13)	Total (N = 29)
Authoritative	44	100	69	19	69	41
Reminds Students to Call Them by Their Appropriate Title	13	69	38	0	31	14
Evaluated by Students as Cold/Mean/Intimidating	0	62	28	0	15	7
Evaluated by Students as Too Hard/Demanding	44	62	52	19	38	28
Felt Physically Threatened by a Student	0	31	14	0	8	3
Validation Regarding Classroom Performance Is Internal	56	46	52	19	0	10
Classroom Problems Decline with Age	25	54	38	6	54	28

69 percent of black women felt that they had to remind students to call them Doctor or Professor, but only 31 percent of white women reported doing so.

In spite of their efforts to demonstrate competency, black professors reported more challenges to their intellectual authority than did their white counterparts (see Table 1). In most of these challenges, as described by the professors, students questioned their knowledge directly or indirectly in a way that was inappropriate or disrespectful. The challenges included arguments on basic points of the discipline (e.g., a student might argue that the sociological imagination is not defined as the professor defined it), questioning the validity of lecture material, and more indirect forms of resistance. Describing a challenge by a white student, one professor stated:

> First of all, he simply thought he knew everything, and that he certainly couldn't learn anything from me. And [he] went so far as to say, when I was trying to explain something, . . . "That's wrong, that's just wrong, that's not true.". . . This is very, very difficult because at the same time, you can't go off on him because you've got to be respectful and you've got to be this professional person and stuff, but it's very, very hurtful, you know, particularly from someone who was not an excellent student. (Respondent 45: black male)

While this professor was trying to manage his anger, he was also managing the frustration and "hurt" caused by the doubts to his competency from a student he believed was not even particularly bright.

In addition to direct challenges such as this, black professors discussed how students challenged them in indirect ways. In the following account, as in the situation described above, a student doubted the veracity of the class lecture material. The professor recounted what the student did to confirm her information:

> [The student] tells me that he was having trouble believing what I said, and that he went over to the [discipline] department to see if he could get that documented and validated. And I said, "And?" And he said, "Well, I asked some [discipline] professors and they said that such a document existed and that you were telling the truth." And I said, "Uh-huh." . . . Some students don't believe what I have to say and they will have to go and ask somebody white before they believe it. (Respondent 32: black female)

According to this respondent's account, although the student did not challenge her knowledge directly in class, the fact that he went to another professor in her discipline, specifically a white male professor, to confirm her information was an indirect challenge to her knowledge and intellectual authority over the class and the material. She added that she believed such double-checking of her material was quite frequent.

CONSEQUENCES OF RACIALIZED CLASSROOM EXPERIENCES

"I have to be perfect." For most of the black professors, one consequence of the challenges to their intellectual authority was a need to prove their competence to students (see Table 1). They were particularly conscious about doing well because they did not want to reinforce negative attitudes about black people's intelligence. This pressure to be a racial model often manifested itself in overpreparation and in a hyperawareness of speech patterns or mistakes of any kind. One professor stated:

> Given that I'm the only one [black female], you start to think, well God, you know, are people lookin' at what I do? And they've never seen a black female teaching in [the department]. [The discipline is] for white males. . . . So you always have that doubt. And it makes you a little nervous. Makes you want to do that much better so that you don't have to worry about it. . . . (Respondent 19: black female)

Another professor explained:

> When I first started teaching, I felt as though I had to be almost perfect. . . . And even the

first couple of years here, if I would misspeak in terms of making a mistake, I always felt as though students would stereotype me, so I always felt as though I couldn't make a mistake. I always felt as though I had to be perfect in terms of the content of the lecture, the delivery of the lecture. . . . And I just think that if we have more black faculty members who are here, Latino and otherwise, I could feel increasingly the freedom to not be perfect. (Respondent 33: black male)

These professors felt pressure not only to prove individual competence, but also, as reflected in the above quotes, to be perfect for the whole race because people might interpret any negative personal performance as a reflection on African Americans overall.

In addition to the pressure to be perfect, black professors were coping with the frustration of receiving what they viewed as differential treatment by students: 62 percent of black professors raised the issue of a racial double standard (see Table 1). Overall they had the sense that white professors automatically commanded students' respect while black professors had to earn it. Respondents also felt that white professors were thought to be smarter, less biased, and more legitimate as faculty members. One professor explained:

I give my credentials the first day of class. And I do feel to some extent I have to, and I know nobody else [in this department] does. . . . So tomorrow I'll stand in front of class and tell them all that I've done and blah, blah, blah. . . . I've found if I don't do that, I don't get the respect that I would deserve. I'd get more people challenging what I say about [the discipline]. (Respondent 42: black male)

As the only nonwhite professor in his department, this respondent felt that the double standard lay in the need to prove his competence, unlike his white colleagues. The white professors in my sample tended to report that their intellectual authority over classroom material was assumed and taken for granted.

Another professor commented as follows on the double standard:

There are many black professors here at [the school] that think there's like a tax, OK—a black tax—on their course evaluations. So like say, if they got a 2.5 on their evaluation. That's equivalent to like a 2.8 for a white professor of comparable quality. That may be true and it may not be true; I don't really know.[7] (Respondent 25: black male)

Although he expressed his doubts about the actual existence of a "black tax," this respondent implied, at the very least, that the presence of a quantitative double standard was not implausible.

In addition to the frustration arising from a racial double standard, some black professors felt that their white colleagues did not understand how greatly their classroom experiences differed qualitatively:

[S]tudents expect the traditional hierarchy of society to prevail in the class. That is, white male on the top, and a black woman on the bottom. And they can't get ready for the fact that a black woman is teaching this class! And that the [white male teaching assistants] are not in charge . . . You know, I think that if I were white, that I wouldn't have to go through those sorts of things in my classroom . . . but at every turn I have to remind students that I am the professor. I'm not just the instructor . . . I have a PhD . . . I have to tell students, "Look. I graduated *summa cum laude,* I got my master's and my PhD . . . I published these books and these articles . . ." to let them know that, you know, I may be black, but what you think about in terms of what it means to be black is not necessarily what I am, if it's a negative perception . . . being uneducated and being illiterate and not able to think and basically being an affirmative action kind of a person. So those are the kinds of things that I think make my job more difficult. Much more difficult. And

---

[7]At this university, the items on the course evaluations are scored on a scale from 0 (lowest) to 4 (highest).

it's unfortunate that the so-called standardized evaluation process that we have been using in colleges and universities [does] not take these things into consideration. In fact, if you raise [the subject], the college will look at you like you're crazy because they don't deal with that. And they're actually being honest because they don't understand the sheer level of complexity on the part of the professor and the student in dealing with these kinds of issues. So I'm not blaming my colleagues. I'm just saying they're really very ignorant {pause} about what goes on in my classes, and the extent to which I have to use measures above and beyond what they have to use to even survive in the classroom. (Respondent 15: black female)

As stated above, some black professors sensed that people did not *get it*. They felt that people did not understand how being black made teaching a different job for them than if they had been white.

"THE ANGRY BLACK WOMAN": INTERSECTIONS OF GENDER AND RACE

While research has shown that white female faculty members struggle for respect and authority in the college classroom (Baker and Copp 1997; Harlow 2002; Martin 1984; Statham, Richardson, and Cook 1991),[8] black women confronted the burden of negotiating both femaleness and blackness. One respondent replied as follows to the question "Do you feel that your race or gender affects [students'] positive or negative views of you?":

I definitely believe that there's something to this business about me being angry and not opening up. I'm just so aware of this whole black woman as, you know, angry person kind of myth. Somehow that we're like 70 percent attitude. . . . But at the same time, I'm like look,

I'm not gonna be skinnin' and grinnin' Sambo every day. . . . I think they don't allow me the room to be serious, and I really do think that's about the "angry black woman with much attitude" myth, you know? . . . I do feel like some students expect that I'm gonna be more maternal, and if I don't live up to that, then the only place that's familiar to them that they can go in terms of judgments is "Oh, then she must have an attitude." So I'm not like "Oh come here, honey, let me hug you, feel my bosom" kind of thing, right . . . but I really do feel like I don't have options. That there are these sorts of two caricatures of black womanhood that they're familiar with, and that somehow I have to work within those. (Respondent 9: black female)

In other words, in the case of black women who do not fulfill the "motherly" expectation and who spend time doing serious work in class, students may interpret their seriousness or businesslike approach within the framework of stereotypical images of black femininity: that is, that black women are angry and have an attitude. Although both white and black women reported efforts to avoid being seen as mean or cold, black female faculty members were more likely to report actual evaluations by students as mean, cold, or intimidating. Black women also were more likely to report physical or verbal threats by students (see Table 2).

EMOTION MANAGEMENT STRATEGIES

For many professors, especially women, age and experience reduced some of the problems they faced in the college classroom (see Table 2). Negative constructions of blackness endure, however, so black professors had to rely on long-term strategies to manage the racial component of teaching.

"I don't have this problem, but . . ." As stated earlier, many black professors initially downplayed the effects of their race in the classroom; doing so helped them manage the overall

---

[8] I also found that women's emotional labor in the classroom is more extensive than men's. Emotional labor due to gender, however, functions differently than emotional labor due to race. This paper focuses only on the racial differences.

frustration of a double standard due to racism. By reconceptualizing a group problem such as racism as a problem unique to an individual's pedagogical strategies, black professors gained a greater sense of control over their classrooms and felt less like prisoners of students' negative social conditioning. One professor explained that some of his black peers faced racial difficulties in the classroom, but he did not experience this problem:

> And I say this from the perspective of some of my peers, particularly black professors that I'm familiar with from all around the nation. Quite frankly they have a difficult time, some of 'em, dealing with large white classrooms. . . . Some of that, in my opinion, is not just the problem of dealing with a lot of white students. The problem is themselves! If they would just be themselves and stop trying to live up to some ideal that they think other people are looking for, they'd be fine in a lot of occasions. . . . I know [that] a lot of the white majority students, [when] they see a young black professor, they're gonna try 'em, OK. It's just that simple. . . . The question is, you know, is there a center there? Are you centered enough to just know that you have a job to do, and just go ahead and do it, and be yourself, and that should be enough, and if it's not, well, you're probably in the wrong profession. (Respondent 25: black male)

On the one hand, this professor acknowledged the structural constraints that are placed on black professors because of the stigmatization of blackness ("white majority students, they see a young black professor, they're gonna try 'em"). At the same time, however, he emphasized that such classroom dynamics did not pertain to him ("I say this from the perspective of some of my peers"). Thus it was a problem that ultimately depended on how an individual "centered" himself or herself, even though he heard such comments from black professors everywhere. Through this interpretation of the issue, he managed individually what would otherwise have been an insurmountable structural problem.

Similarly, when I asked Respondent 16, a black female, if she felt that her race or gender affected students' positive or negative views of her, she replied, "Oh I'm sure it does, but I don't know how. I'm sure it does. I'm certain it does." I then asked how she could be so certain if she was not even sure how students' views were affected. She replied:

> Well, because in our society, race matters. It matters. And because it matters, then I think there are some students who probably do look at my race. However, I'm not a very race-conscious person. . . . I think I present myself such that people will see me as a friendly person, as an outgoing person, as a competent person, and for those reasons they would not then assume negative traits about me based on my ethnicity. And I think if I'm doing my work well in the classroom, that even though students might see me initially as being an African American teacher, that at the end they ought to see me as the professor, as a human agent in the classroom trying to bring about creative intellectual change. And I do think that I don't recall any of my students focusing unduly on my race. (Respondent 16: black female)

Once again, this professor acknowledged the social structural constraints of race ("in our society, race matters"), but then went on to exempt herself from these potential effects by saying that if she focused on doing her job well, students would not care about such things. Both by distancing herself from the structural impact of race and by not caring about what students thought (just "doing my work well in the classroom"), she alleviated some of the potential frustration of having to deal with stereotypes, the fear of being perfect, double standards, and the rest. "I don't care what other people think." The idea of "just doing my job," "centering," and "looking internally" was common among most of the black faculty members (see Table 2). Many explained that as long as they did their job well, what they looked like would ultimately be irrelevant to students. By adopting this attitude, they decreased the emotion management involved in worrying about stereotyping, credibility, and so forth. In explaining how he felt at the beginning of a new semester, one professor stated:

> [W]hen I walk into the classroom, I'm excited to get things started, and I feel very, very confident about my skills . . . and I don't worry about other people's politics anymore. Kind of like I have an internal focus, rather than an external focus about what other people think about me. It's more important how I feel about me. *I finally came to rest with that* (emphasis added). (Respondent 8: black male)

This professor later expressed pride in his new degree of emotional control in the classroom. Not only did he have to learn to reject consistently negative images of himself, he also had to learn how to suppress his anger in order to teach effectively.

Another professor explained that she *wanted* to stop caring about students' perceptions, but was continuing to struggle with this difficult form of emotion management. In reply to a question about how much she enjoyed teaching, she stated:

> I really try to do it the best way that I can do it. But sometimes it's pretty difficult because I just get tired of dealing with these issues. And I feel that I've been put upon. And I feel that [because] I have to deal with issues that other people don't have to deal with. . . . So I should just forget about it and go into the classroom and do the best job that I can. And that's what I try to do. But some days it is really a challenge. . . . Some of my colleagues just go into class and talk, and, you know, that's it. (Respondent 15: black female)

Frustrated by the fact that she could not, like her white colleagues, simply go into class and lecture without concerns about racism and stereotyping, this respondent realized that she had to stop caring so much about students' views. At the same time, she observed that just doing the best job she could while ignoring her emotions was extremely difficult.

Analysis and Discussion

Consistent with findings by Feagin and Sikes (1994), many black faculty members were reluctant to say that their race mattered in the classroom, and looked for other reasons to explain their racialized experiences.[9] Ultimately, however, they expressed frustration about what they considered to be students' challenges to their intellectual authority. Yet despite this frustration, black professors also discussed how their race was beneficial to them in the classroom: many noted that black students were often happy to see that they had a black professor. In addition, they felt that their race increased their legitimacy when they were teaching on racial topics.

According to their reports, however, this legitimacy had rigid boundaries. Students may have felt that African American professors brought their personal experiences to topics of race, thus providing an "authentic" understanding of the issue. Yet at the same time, these professors discussed how their race detracted from their credibility in regard to students' perceptions of their *intellectual* knowledge of the material: that is, the scholarly, "objective" assessment of racial issues. Thus, although students might accept as legitimate certain experiential knowledge transmitted by the professor, black professors simultaneously might face doubts of their competency regarding their intellectual interpretations of the course work. Adding to the professors' frustration was the

---

[9]Half of the black men at some point downplayed the effect of their race in the classroom, but only one-third of the black women did so. This difference may exist because black women faced both gender and race discrimination, and so were less likely to downplay racial factors when the gender issues they faced were so widely acknowledged. Therefore their discussion of gender difference also integrated race: they discussed the experience of being *black* women in the classroom.

fact that both white and nonwhite students doubted their academic abilities.

Research by Chambers, Lewis, and Kerezsi (1995) adds credence to the view that students question black professors' competency. They found that white students generally continue to perceive African Americans negatively, particularly when "situations involve close social contact . . . or when African Americans are not cast in stereotypical roles" (p. 55). They argued that white students may view black professors as ineffective and may question their competency. In addition, after Hendrix (1998) interviewed students to explore the influence of race on professors' credibility, she found that overall, black professors were considered less credible than white professors, particularly when the course subject was not directly connected to their race.

Because of doubts about credibility, I found a heightened concern, particularly among black assistant professors, about making a mistake in class. Although some of this fear may have been due to lack of tenure, the junior professors stated explicitly that their concerns about tenure stemmed from their research, not their teaching. Their responses were consistent with findings by Aguirre (2000), who argued that because of nonwhite faculty members' small numbers and minority status, white students view them solely as affirmative action hires (which they interpret incorrectly as unqualified hires). These perceptions by students contribute to an environment in which faculty members of color may feel that they must "be overachievers in a context where [w]hite faculty are not themselves overachievers" (Aguirre 2000, 72).

As a result of this pressure to overachieve, "minority faculty may perceive themselves as occupying a contradictory role in the academic workplace—outsiders but expected to be model citizens in academe," as they try to prove that they are equal to white faculty members (Aguirre 2000, 51). The large amount of physical and emotional impression management involved in trying to convince students of their competence and their right to be in charge would be eliminated if students identified immediately with the professor and associated that identity with intellect and professionalism. In this study, most white professors did not mention challenges to their competency, an indication that they did not need to constantly prove and project intellectual authority.

In contrast to their white colleagues, a mistake in class by black professors could be interpreted as incompetence; such an interpretation reinforces negative stereotypes and reflects negatively on black people as a whole. Not only did black professors carry the weight of knowing that their performance might symbolize the potential of an entire racial group, but many had white colleagues who might not have noticed or acknowledged the differences in their jobs due to race. Most of the white professors in the sample did not observe the possibility of racial differences in the classroom.

Being a credit to the race, while also experiencing the frustration of a racial double standard as well as denials from white colleagues that such a double standard exists, requires black professors to manage both personal and professional emotions far more extensively than their white peers. This is particularly the case for younger black professors: because they have less experience, they may struggle harder than their seasoned colleagues to win a sense of control over their ability to be effective. This challenge is intensified by the feeling that their knowledge as professors is already devalued because they are black. This dynamic is complicated further by gender: the black female respondents reported the effects of both gender and racial stereotypes as they worked to maintain their physical and intellectual presence in the classroom. Hill-Collins (1991) discusses four cultural conceptualizations of black womanhood that historically have perpetuated black women's subordinate status. Two of these are relevant here. Probably the most common and most widespread is the mammy—the nurturing, obedient, asexual black woman. Another is the matriarch—the "overly aggressive, unfeminine women" (Hill-Collins 1991, 74) who prevent the men in their lives from asserting their masculinity. According to Hill-Collins (1991), "the matriarch is essentially a failed mammy, a negative stigma applied to those African-American women who dared to violate the image of the submissive, hard-working servant" (p. 74). Thus the evaluations as mean, cold, angry, and attitudinal that so many of the black female respondents reported receiving (see Table 2) are consistent with this matriarch image: that is, their gender is also racialized. Black female professors seem to be allowed even less "room to be serious" (Respondent 9: black female) than their white female counterparts, who also struggle against stereotypical gender expectations. For those black women who did not succeed in walking the fine line between masculinity and femininity, students were even more likely to interpret their serious and/or professional behavior as over-aggressive and insufficiently subservient.

To be effective in the classroom, black professors had to learn how to manage the frustration of a racial double standard and the pressure of representing an entire racial group. Trying not to care about students' stereotypical views emerged as a key management strategy. If they could ignore this type of negative feedback, the professors could gain a greater sense of control over the emotional and physical labor of the classroom.

If (as stated by identity theory) our conception of self is shaped in part by responses from others through interaction, and if our behavior is often shaped by our desire to have our conception of self reinforced (Stryker 1992), then professors' classroom performances are in part an effort to reinforce, through students, an identity as a good, knowledgeable professor. Many black faculty members, however, reported that such an identity was not

reinforced for them through students, in part because of broader cultural understandings of blackness as inferior. Therefore, to function effectively in the classroom, they had to diminish or even eliminate the importance of interaction with students for defining and confirming their identity as teacher.

Thus the data showed that more than half of the black faculty members engaged in *selective identity construction*. This process can be defined as selectively incorporating responses from interactions that confirm conceptions of self, while rejecting responses that conflict with such conceptions, regardless of the significance of that interaction in defining a highly central or salient identity. For example, in spite of the centrality of the teacher identity in the classroom, many of the black professors learned to ignore identity cues from interactions with students that challenged their professorial identity. Instead they developed and reinforced their teacher identity through other means: positive interactions with students, interactions with friends, family, and peers, and internal strength. They emphasized selecting out interactions that contradicted their self-perceptions; meanwhile they maintained an internal focus so that their professor status was validated from within, not by students.

This process of maintaining an internal focus, however, involves extensive emotion management. According to affect control theory, as stated earlier, when our conception of self is not confirmed, we adjust our definition of a situation or change our behavior so as to relieve the resulting emotional tension (Heise 1989). The black professors who were the most satisfied with teaching, however, worked to ignore those emotional cues altogether instead of paying attention to the cues and trying constantly to change their behavior in order to correct students' perceptions of them. These professors learned to suppress and (in some cases) ultimately eliminate feelings of frustration, anger, or inadequacy in order to diminish the importance of those nonconfirming inter-actions; thus students' responses would no longer be integral to shaping their conceptions of self or their professorial identity.

Instead of adjusting their actions or the def-inition of the situation to change how they felt, as affect control theory would predict, these professors learned how to change how they felt in an effort to change, at some point, the definition of the situation. That is, by ignor-ing emotional cues from negative interactions with students, and by focusing solely on con-firming their identity internally, they hoped, through their display of confidence and com-petence, to ultimately change how students viewed them and regarded black professors in general. Respondent 45 (black male) explained that this process required a movement from "conventional thinking" and "conventional reality" to "the new way of thinking."

For this professor, "conventional thinking" occurs when black professors accept as important the stereotypical ways in which students may view and/or interact with them. By changing their behavior in response to these interactions—by overpreparing, citing credentials, dressing up, or growing frustrated—professors give power and validation to that "conventional reality" and "conventional truth": that is, students will doubt the competence of black professors, and blackness will be stigmatized. The "new way" of thinking, however, requires such a firm ground-ing in one's sense of self and identity that inter-action with students no longer serves to shape that identity. In other words, ideas about black inferiority ("conventional truth") are marginal-ized in that individual's reality and ultimately lose power.

Once this emotion management has been accomplished, the emotional labor in the class-room becomes much easier because one can focus on projecting excitement, enthusiasm, and friendliness without the need also to man-age fear, frustration, and anger. When a profes-sor can focus solely on the traditional aspects of the job, her or his feelings of enjoyment, relaxation, and confidence can increase, with the effect of potentially undermining students' negative stereotypes about blackness. Contrary to Burke's (1991) notion of the identity process, selective identity construction saves profes-sors from experiencing high levels of stress, even when students' perceptions do not match professors' self-concepts.

Although these black professors acknowl-edged racism as a systemic problem, by con-structing their professorial identity selectively they were able to lessen the individual-level effect of race bias in order to function effectively in the classroom. When one professor was asked how racism and sexism influenced the way he thought about life in general, he replied:

> I think it influences it a lot. You know, despite my point that it seems silly to spend a lot of time and energy worrying about these things, these things do matter, especially in America. . . . So I think it matters a great deal, but it doesn't much matter to me. (Respondent 35: black male)

As this professor stated succinctly, people's pre-conceptions have the power, on a societal level, to affect the life chances of entire groups of peo-ple, and therefore are critically important. Yet although people are not insulated from the social and cultural effects of such judgments, they must live their lives as individuals. In that respect, in order to avoid paralysis by racism, other peo-ple's opinions must "not much matter."

Conclusion

When black and white faculty members teach, they function in disparate realities. White pro-fessors operate in a social space where white-ness is crediting and privileged, but is invisible and thus is taken for granted; African American professors function in a space where black-ness is discrediting and devalued. The find-ings reported here suggest that these cultural and structural understandings of blackness and whiteness consequently shape the way in which black and white professors experience the college classroom and understand, interpret, and manage those experiences. Because these results are based on faculty experiences at a large, predominantly white university, further research is needed in settings that differ in size, region, and racial composition. In addition, an exploration of the classroom experiences of other nonwhite and international faculty members would be instructive.

The reality for many African American professors is that there will always be students who question their competency, credentials, and ability to teach and assess students' work. This reality, combined with the weight of representing the entire race, can be emotionally draining, particularly for young faculty members who may spend hours poring over lectures so as not to be anything less than perfect or totally prepared. To manage the frustrations resulting from a racial double standard, and to be effective in the classroom, my black respondents learned to stay cognizant of existing macro-level racial barriers while diminishing the importance of those barriers on the microlevel in order to prevent racism from debilitating them in their everyday lives.

References

Aguirre, Adalberto. 2000. *Women and Minority Faculty in the Academic Workplace.* San Francisco: Jossey-Bass.

Baker, Fostenia. 1991. "A Study of Black Faculty Perceptions of Hiring, Retention and Tenure Processes in Major White Universities." PhD dissertation, Department of Educational Leadership, George Washington University, Washington, DC.

Baker, Phyllis, and Martha Copp. 1997. "Gender Matters Most: The Interaction of Gendered Expectation, Feminist Course Content, and the Pregnancy in Student Course Evaluations." *Teaching Sociology* 25: 29–43.

Banks, William. 1984. "Afro-American Scholars in the University." *American Behavioral Scientist* 27: 325–38.

Bellas, Marcia L. 1999. "Emotional Labor in Academia: The Case of Professors." *Annals of the American Academy of Political and Social Science* 561: 96–110.

Burke, Peter. 1991. "Identity Processes and Social Stress." *American Sociological Review* 56: 836–49.

Chambers, Tony, Jacqueline Lewis, and Paula Kerezsi. 1995. "African American Faculty and White American Students: Cross-Cultural Pedagogy in Counselor Preparation Programs." *The Counseling Psychologist* 23: 43–62.

Cohen, Elizabeth G. 1982. "Expectation States and Interracial Interaction in School Settings." *Annual Review of Sociology* 8: 209–35.

Feagin, Joe, and Melvin Sikes. 1994. *Living With Racism.* Boston: Beacon.

Fields, Cheryl. 1996. "A Morale Dilemma." *Black Issues in Higher Education* 13: 22–23, 25–26, 28–29.

Gallop, Jane. 1997. *Feminist Accused of Sexual Harassment.* Durham: Duke University Press.

Goffman, Erving. 1959. *The Presentation of Self in Everyday Life.* Garden City, NY: Anchor Books.

———. 1963. *Stigma.* New York: Simon and Schuster.

Harlow, Roxanna. 2002. "Teaching As Emotional Labor: The Effects of Professors' Race and Gender on the Emotional Demands of the Undergraduate College Classroom." PhD dissertation, Department of Sociology, Indiana University, Bloomington.

Heise, David. 1989. "Effects of Emotion Displays on Social Identification." *Social Psychology Quarterly* 52: 10–21.

Hendrix, Katherine. 1995. "Professor Perceptions of the Influence of Race on Classroom Dynamics and Credibility." Presented at the annual meetings of the Western States Communication Association, February 10–14, Portland, OR.

———. 1998. "Student Perceptions of the Influence of Race on Professor Credibility." *Journal of Black Studies* 28: 738–63.

Hill-Collins, Patricia. 1991. *Black Feminist Thought.* New York: Routledge.

Hochschild, Arlie R. 1983. *The Managed Heart.* Berkeley: University of California Press.

Jacobs, Walter. 1999. "Learning and Living Media Culture in the College Classroom: An Autoethnography of a Possible Postmodern Space." PhD dissertation, Department of Sociology, Indiana University, Bloomington.

Martin, Elaine. 1984. "Power and Authority in the Classroom: Sexist Stereotypes in Teaching Evaluations." *Signs* 9: 482–92.

Menges, Robert, and William Exum. 1983. "Barriers to the Progress of Women and Minority Faculty." *Journal of Higher Education* 54: 123–44.

Moore, Valerie Ann. 1996. "Inappropriate Challenges to Professional Authority." *Teaching Sociology* 24: 202–206.

National Center for Education Statistics. 1997. *1997 Integrated Postsecondary Education Data System, Fall Staff Survey.* Washington, DC: U.S. Department of Education.

Phelps, Rosemary. 1995. "What's in a Number? Implications for African American Faculty at Predominantly White Colleges and Universities." *Innovative Higher Education* 19: 255–68.

Rains, Frances. 1995. "Views From Within: Women Faculty of Color in a Research University." PhD dissertation, Department of Educational Leadership and Policy Studies, Indiana University, Bloomington.

Rakow, Lana. 1991. "Gender and Race in the Classroom: Teaching Way out of Line." *Feminist Teacher* 6: 10–13.

Sinegar, Lee Alton. 1987. "Coping With Racial Stressors: A Case Study of Black Professors in White Academe." PhD dissertation, Department of Counseling, George Washington University, Washington, DC.

Smith, Earl, and Stephanie Witt. 1993. "A Comparative Study of Occupational Stress Among African American and White University Faculty: A Research Note." *Research in Higher Education* 34: 229–41.

Statham, Anne, Laurel Richardson, and Judith Cook. 1991. *Gender and University Teaching.* Albany: SUNY Press.

Stryker, Sheldon. 1992. "Identity Theory." Pp. 871–76 in Edgar Borgatta and Marie Borgatta (eds.), *Encyclopedia of Sociology.* New York: Macmillan.

Stryker, Sheldon, and Richard Serpe. 1994. "Identity Salience and Psychological Centrality: Equivalent, Overlapping, or Complementary Concepts?" *Social Psychology Quarterly* 57: 16–35.

Wood, Elizabeth Anne. 2000. "Working in the Fantasy Factory: The Attention Hypothesis and the Enacting of Masculine Power in Strip Clubs." *Journal of Contemporary Ethnography* 29: 5–31.

Questions

1. What sort of emotion labor is involved in being a college professor? Why does Professor Harlow conclude that professors of color must do more emotion labor than white professors?

2. Reflect upon your experiences in school. What sort of emotion labor is required to play the student role? Do you think that the amount of emotion labor required from students tends to differ by race and gender?

3. Recall Mills' distinction (reading 1) between personal troubles and public issues. Do the professors studied by the author of this article tend to regard the extra effort they think they must make to prove themselves as professors, to be personal troubles or public issues?

    In your judgment, what are the differences in the experiences of white professors and professors of color—personal troubles or public issues?

4. Other research has shown that nonwhite professors generally have to work harder to get the same scores on their teaching evaluations. In view of the evidence presented by Professor Harlow, why do you think that is so?

36
CONFESSIONS OF A NICE NEGRO, OR WHY I SHAVED MY HEAD

Robin D. G. Kelley

No matter how much they distort reality, stereotypes exist and have an impact on people's lives. In this 1995 article, Robin Kelley recounts his experiences with what, to him, was a new stereotype.

It happened just the other day—two days into the new year, to be exact. I had dashed into the deserted lobby of an Ann Arbor movie theater, pulling the door behind me to escape the freezing winter winds Michigan residents have come to know so well. Behind the counter knelt a young white teenager filling the popcorn bin with bags of that awful pre-popped stuff. Hardly the enthusiastic employee; from a distance it looked like she was lost in deep thought. The generous display of body piercing suggested an X-generation flower child—perhaps an anthropology major into acid jazz and environmentalism, I thought. Sporting a black New York Yankees baseball cap and a black-and-beige scarf over my nose and mouth, I must have looked like I had stepped out of a John Singleton film. And because I was already late, I rushed madly toward the ticket counter.

The flower child was startled: "I don't have anything in the cash register," she blurted as she pulled the bag of popcorn in front of her for protection.

"Huh? I just want one ticket for *Little Women*, please—the two-fifteen show. My wife

and daughter should already be in there." I slowly gestured to the theater door and gave her one of those innocent childlike glances I used to give my mom when I wanted to sit on her lap.

"Oh, god . . . I'm so sorry. A reflex. Just one ticket? You only missed the first twenty minutes. Enjoy the show."

Enjoy the show? Barely 1995 and here we go again. Another bout with racism in a so-called liberal college town; another racial drama in which I play the prime suspect. And yet I have to confess the situation was pretty funny. Just two hours earlier I couldn't persuade Elleza, my four-year-old daughter, to put her toys away; time-out did nothing, yelling had no effect, and the evil stare made no impact whatsoever. Thoroughly frustrated, I had only one option left: "Okay, I'm gonna tell Mommy!" Of course it worked.

So those five seconds as a media-made black man felt kind of good. I know it's a product of racism. I know that the myth of black male violence has resulted in the deaths of many innocent boys and men of darker hue. I know that the power to scare is not real power. I know all that—after all, I study this stuff for a living! For the moment, though, it felt good. (Besides, the ability to scare with your body can come in handy, especially when you're trying to get a good seat in a theater or avoid long lines.)

I shouldn't admit this, but I take particular pleasure in putting fear into people on the look-out for black male criminality mainly because those moments are so rare for me. Indeed, my *inability* to employ blackmaleness as a weapon is the story of my life. Why I don't possess it, or rather possess so little of it, escapes me. I grew up poor in Harlem and Afrodena (the Negro West Side of Pasadena/Altadena, California). My mom was single during my formative preadolescent years, and for a brief moment she even received a welfare check. A hard life makes a hard nigga, so I've been told.

Never an egghead or a dork, as a teenager I was pretty cool. I did the house-party circuit on Friday and Saturday nights and used to stroll down the block toting the serious Radio Raheem boombox. Why, I even invaded movie theaters in the company of ten or fifteen hooded and high-topped black bodies, colonizing the balconies and occupying two seats per person. Armed with popcorn and Raisinettes as our missiles of choice, we dared any usher to ask us to leave. Those of us who had cars (we called them hoopties or rides back in that day) spent our lunch hours and precious class time hanging out in the school parking lot, running down our Die Hards to pump up Cameo, Funkadelic, Grandmaster Flash from our car stereos. I sported dickies and Levis, picked up that gangsta stroll, and when the shag came in style I was with it—always armed with a silk scarf to ensure that my hair was laid. Granted, I vomited after drinking malt liquor for the first time and my only hit of a joint ended abruptly in an asthma attack. But I was cool.

Sure, I was cool, but nobody feared me. That I'm relatively short with dimples and curly hair, speak softly in a rather medium to high-pitched voice, and have a "girl's name" doesn't help matters. And everyone knows that light skin is less threatening to white people than blue-black or midnight brown. Besides, growing up with a soft-spoken, uncharacteristically passive West Indian mother deep into East Indian

religions, a mother who sometimes walked barefoot in the streets of Harlem, a mother who insisted on proper diction and never, ever, ever used a swear word, screwed me up royally. I could never curse right. My mouth had trouble forming the words—"fuck" always came out as "fock" and "goddamn" always sounded like it's spelled, not "gotdayum," the way my Pasadena homies pronounced it in their Calabama twang. I don't even recall saying the word "bitch" unless I was quoting somebody or some authorless vernacular rhyme. For some unknown reason, that word scared me.

Moms dressed me up in the coolest mod outfits—short pant suits with matching hats, Nehru jackets, those sixties British-looking turtlenecks. Sure, she got some of that stuff from John's Bargain Store or Goodwill, but I always looked "cute." More stylish than roguish. Kinda like W. E. B. Du Bois[1] as a toddler, or those turn-of-the-century photos of middle-class West Indian boys who grow up to become prime ministers or poets. Ghetto ethnographers back in the late sixties and early seventies would not have found me or my family very "authentic," especially if they had discovered that one of my middle names is Gibran, after the Lebanese poet Kahlil Gibran.

Everybody seemed to like me. Teachers liked me, kids liked me; I even fell in with some notorious teenage criminals at Pasadena High School because *they* liked me. I remember one memorable night in the ninth grade when I went down to the Pasadena Boys' Club to take photos of some of my partners on the basketball team. On my way home some big

---

[1]W. E. B. Du Bois (1868–1963) was the first African American to earn a PhD from Harvard University (1895). He taught sociology at several universities, was a strong advocate for racial integration, and in 1909 founded the National Association for the Advancement of Colored People. Ultimately, Du Bois lost faith in the possibility of integration and began to promote segregation. He was dismissed from the NAACP and moved to Ghana, where he lived until his death.—Ed.

kids, eleventh-graders to be exact, tried to take my camera. The ringleader pulled out a knife and gently poked it against my chest. I told them it was my stepfather's camera and if I came home without it he'd kick my ass for a week. Miraculously, this launched a whole conversation about stepfathers and how messed up they are, which must have made them feel sorry for me. Within minutes we were cool; they let me go unmolested and I had made another friend.

In affairs of the heart, however, "being liked" had the opposite effect. I can only recall having had four fights in my entire life, all of which were with girls who supposedly liked me but thoroughly beat my behind. Sadly, my record in the boxing ring of puppy love is still 0–4. By the time I graduated to serious dating, being a nice guy seemed like the root of all my romantic problems. I resisted jealousy, tried to be understanding, brought flowers and balloons, opened doors, wrote poems and songs, and seemed to always be on my knees for one reason or another. If you've ever watched "Love Connection" or read *Cosmopolitan*, you know the rest of the story: I practically never had sex and most of the women I dated left me in the cold for roughnecks. My last girlfriend in high school, the woman I took to my prom, the woman I once thought I'd die for, tried to show me the light: "Why do you always ask me what I want? Why don't you just *tell* me what you want me to do? Why don't you take charge and *be a man*? If you want to be a real man you can't be nice all the time!"

I always thought she was wrong; being nice has nothing to do with being a man. While I still think she's wrong, it's an established fact that our culture links manhood to terror and power, and that black men are frequently imaged as the ultimate in hypermasculinity. But the black man as the prototype of violent hypermasculinity is as much a fiction as the happy Sambo. No matter

what critics and stand-up comics might say, I know from experience that not all black men—and here I'm only speaking of well-lighted or daytime situations—generate fear. Who scares and who doesn't has a lot to do with the body in question; it is dependent on factors such as age, skin color, size, clothes, hairstyle, and even the sound of one's voice. The cops who beat Rodney King and the jury who acquitted King's assailants openly admitted that the size, shape, and color of his body automatically made him a threat to the officers' safety.

On the other hand, the threatening black male body can take the most incongruous forms. Some of the hardest brothas on my block in West Pasadena kept their perms in pink rollers and hairnets. It was not unusual to see young black men in public with curlers, tank-top undershirts, sweatpants, black mid-calf dress socks, and Stacey Adams shoes, hanging out on the corner or on the basketball court. And we all knew that these brothas were not to be messed with. (The rest of the world probably knows it by now, too, since black males in curlers are occasionally featured on "Cops" and "America's Most Wanted" as notorious drug dealers or heartless pimps.)

Whatever the source of this ineffable terror, my body simply lacked it. Indeed, the older I got and the more ensconced I became in the world of academia, the less threatening I seemed. Marrying and having a child also reduced the threat factor. By the time I hit my late twenties, my wife, Diedra, and I found ourselves in the awkward position of being everyone's favorite Negroes. I don't know how many times we've attended dinner parties where we were the only African Americans in the room. Occasionally there were others, but we seemed to have a monopoly on the dinner party invitations. This not only happened in Ann Arbor, where there is a small but substantial black population to choose from, but in the Negro mecca of Atlanta, Georgia. Our hosts always felt comfortable asking us "sensitive" questions about race that they would not dare ask other black colleagues and friends: What do African Americans think about Farrakhan? Ben Chavis? Nelson Mandela? Most of my black students are very conservative and career-oriented—why is that? How can we mend the relations between blacks and Jews? Do you celebrate Kwanzaa? Do you put anything in your hair to make it that way? What are the starting salaries for young black faculty nowadays?

Of course, these sorts of exchanges appear regularly in most black autobiographies. As soon as they're comfortable, it is not uncommon for white people to take the opportunity to find out everything they've always wanted to know about "us" (which also applies to other people of color, I'm sure) but were afraid to ask. That they feel perfectly at ease asking dumb or unanswerable questions is not simply a case of (mis)perceived racelessness. Being a "nice Negro" has a lot to do with gender, and my peculiar form of "left-feminist-funny-guy" masculinity—a little Kevin Hooks, some Bobby McFerrin, a dash of Woody Allen—is regarded as less threatening than that of most other black men.

Not that I mind the soft-sensitive masculine persona—after all, it is the genuine me, a product of my mother's heroic and revolutionary child-rearing style. But there are moments when I wish I could invoke the intimidation factor of blackmaleness on demand. If I only had that look—that Malcolm X/Mike Tyson/Ice Cube/Larry Fishburne/Bigger Thomas/Fruit of Islam look—I could keep the stupid questions at bay, make college administrators tremble, and scare editors into submission. Subconsciously, I decided that I had to do something about my image. Then, as if by magic, my wish was fulfilled.

Actually, it began as an accident involving a pair of electric clippers and sleep deprivation—a bad auto-cut gone awry. With my lowtop fade on the verge of a Sly Stone afro,

I was in desperate need of a trim. Diedra didn't have the time to do it, and as it was February (Black History Month), I was on the chitlin' lecture circuit and couldn't spare forty-five minutes at a barber shop, so I elected to do it myself. Standing in a well-lighted bathroom, armed with two mirrors, I started trimming. Despite a steady hand and what I've always believed was a good eye, my hair turned out lopsided. I kept trimming and trimming to correct my error, but as my flat-top sank lower, a yellow patch of scalp began to rise above the surrounding hair, like one of those big granite mounds dotting the grassy knolls of Central Park. A nice yarmulke could have covered it, but that would have been more difficult to explain than a bald spot. So, bearing in mind role models like Michael Jordan, Charles Barkley, Stanley Crouch, and Onyx (then the hip-hop group of the hour), I decided to take it all off.

I didn't think much of it at first, but the new style accomplished what years of evil stares and carefully crafted sartorial statements could not: I began to scare people. The effect was immediate and dramatic. Passing strangers avoided me and smiled less frequently. Those who did smile or make eye contact seemed to be deliberately trying to disarm me—a common strategy taught in campus rape-prevention centers. Scaring people was fun for a while, but I especially enjoyed standing in the line at the supermarket with my bald head, baggy pants, high-top Reeboks, and long black hooded down coat, humming old standards like "Darn That Dream," "A Foggy Day," and "I Could Write a Book." Now *that* brought some stares. I must have been convincing, since I adore those songs and have been humming them ever since I can remember. No simple case of cultural hybridity here, just your average menace to society with a deep appreciation for Gershwin, Rodgers and Hart, Van Heusen, Cole Porter, and Jerome Kern.

Among my colleagues, my bald head became the lead subject of every conversation. "You look older, more mature." "With that new cut you come across as much more serious than usual." "You really look quite rugged and masculine with a bald head." My close friends dispensed with the euphemisms and went straight to the point: "Damn. You look scary!" The most painful comment was that I looked like a "B-Boy wannabe" and was "too old for that shit." I had to remind my friend that I'm an OBB (Original B-Boy), that I was in the eleventh grade in 1979 when the Sugar Hill Gang dropped "Rapper's Delight," and that *his* tired behind was in graduate school at the time. Besides, B-Boy was not the intent.

In the end, however, I got more questions than comments. Was I in crisis? Did I want to talk? What was I trying to say by shaving my head? What was the political point of my actions? Once the novelty passed, I began getting those "speak for the race" questions that irritated the hell out of me when I had hair. Why have *black men* begun to shave their heads in greater numbers? Why have so many black athletes decided to shave their heads? Does this new trend have some kind of phallic meaning? Against my better judgment, I found myself coming up with answers to these questions—call it an academician's reflex. I don't remember exactly what I said, but it usually began with black prizefighter Jack Johnson, America's real life "baaad nigger" of the early twentieth century, whose head was always shaved and greased, and ended with the hip-hop community's embrace of an outlaw status. Whatever it was, it made sense at the time.

The publicity photo for my recent book, *Race Rebels*, clearly generated the most controversy among my colleagues. It diverged dramatically from the photo on my first book, where I look particularly innocent, almost angelic. In that first photo I smiled just enough to make my dimples visible; my eyes gazed

away from the camera in sort of a dreamy, contemplative pose; my haircut was nondescript and the natural sunlight had a kind of halo effect. The Izod shirt was the icing on the cake. By contrast, the photograph for *Race Rebels* (which Diedra set up and shot, by the way) has me looking directly into the camera, arms folded, bald head glistening from baby oil and rear window light, with a grimace that could give Snoop Doggy Dogg a run for his money. The lens made my arms appear much larger than they really are, creating a kind of Popeye effect. Soon after the book came out, I received several e-mail messages about the photo. A particularly memorable one came from a friend and fellow historian in Australia. In the course of explaining to me how he had corrected one of his students who had read an essay of mine and presumed I was a woman, he wrote: "Mind you, the photo in your book should make things clear—the angle and foreshortening of the arms, and the hairstyle make it one of the most masculine author photos I've seen recently????!!!!!!"

My publisher really milked this photo, which actually fit well with the book's title. For the American Studies Association meeting in Nashville, Tennessee, which took place the week the book came out, my publisher bought a full-page ad on the back cover of an ASA handout, with my mug staring dead at you. Everywhere I turned—in hotel elevators, hallways, lobbies, meeting rooms—I saw myself, and it was not exactly a pretty sight. The quality of the reproduction (essentially a high-contrast xerox) made me appear harder, meaner, and crazier than the original photograph.

The situation became even stranger since I had decided to abandon the skinhead look and grow my hair back. In fact, by the time of the ASA meeting I was on the road (since abandoned) toward a big Black Power Afro—a retro style that at the time seemed to be making a comeback. Worse still, I had come to participate in a round-table discussion on black hair! My paper, titled "Nap Time: Historicizing the Afro," explored the political implications of competing narratives of the Afro's origins and meaning. Overall, it was a terrific session; the room was packed and the discussion was stimulating. But inevitably the question came up: "Although this isn't directly related to his paper, I'd like to find out from Professor Kelley why he shaved his head. Professor Kelley, given the panel's topic and in light of the current ads floating about with your picture on them, can you shed some light on what is attractive to black men about baldness?" The question was posed by a very distinguished and widely read African American literary scholar. Hardly the naif, he knew the answers as well as I did, but wanted to generate a public discussion. And he succeeded. For ten minutes the audience ran the gamut of issues revolving around race, gender, sexuality, and the politics of style. Even the issue of bald heads as phallic symbols came up. "It's probably true," I said, "but when I was cutting my hair at three-o'clock in the morning I wasn't thinking 'penis'." Eventually the discussion drifted from black masculinity to the tremendous workloads of minority scholars, which, in all honesty, was the source of my baldness in the first place. Unlike the golden old days, when doing hair was highly ritualized and completely integrated into daily life, we're so busy mentoring and publishing and speaking and fighting that we have very little time to attend to our heads.

Beyond the session itself, that ad continued to haunt me during the entire conference. Every ten minutes, or so it seemed, someone came up to me and offered unsolicited commentary on the photo. One person slyly suggested that in order to make the picture complete I should have posed with an Uzi. When I approached a very good friend of mine, a historian who is partly my Jewish mother and partly my confidante and *always* looking out for my best interests, the first words out of her mouth were, "Robin, I hate that picture! It's the worst picture of you I've ever seen. It doesn't do you justice. Why did you let them use it?"

"It's not that bad," I replied. "Diedra likes it—she took the picture. You just don't like my bald head."

"No, that's not it. I like the bald look on some men, and you have a very nice head. The problem is the photo and the fact that I know what kind of person you are. None of your gentleness and lovability comes out in that picture. Now, don't get a swelled head when I say this, but you have a delightful face and expression that makes people feel good, even when you're talking about serious stuff. The way you smile, there's something unbelievably safe about you."

It was a painful compliment. And yet I knew deep down that she was telling the truth. I've always been unbelievably safe, not just because of my look but because of my actions. Not that I consciously try to put people at ease, to erase conflict and difference, to remain silent on sensitive issues. I can't quite put a finger on it. Perhaps it's my mother's politeness drills? Perhaps it's a manifestation of my continuing bout with shyness? Maybe it has something to do with the sense of joy I get from stimulating conversations? Or maybe it's linked to the fact that my mom refused to raise me in a manner boys are accustomed to? Most likely it is a product of cultural capital[2]—the fact that I *can* speak the language, (re)cite the texts, exhibit the manners and mannerisms that are inherent to bourgeois academic culture. My colleagues identify with me because I can talk intelligently about their scholarship on their terms,

---

[2]The concept of cultural capital has gained currency through the work of Marxist sociologist Pierre Bourdieu, who uses the term to refer to specific skills and competencies (for example, the ability to use language and other social skills) that middle- and upper-class parents are able to pass on to their children. Ownership of cultural as well as economic capital provides advantages to members of the middle and upper classes and increases the probability of their success.—Ed.

which invariably has the effect of creating an illusion of brilliance. As Frantz Fanon said in *Black Skin, White Masks,* the mere fact that he was an articulate *black* man who read a lot rendered him a stunning specimen of erudition in the eyes of his fellow intellectuals in Paris.

Whatever the source of my ineffable lovability, I've learned that it's not entirely a bad thing. In fact, if the rest of the world could look a little deeper, beyond the hardcore exterior—the wide bodies, the carefully constructed grimaces, the performance of terror—they would find many, many brothas much nicer and smarter than myself. The problem lies in a racist culture, a highly gendered racist culture, that is so deeply enmeshed in the fabric of daily life that it's practically invisible. The very existence of the "nice Negro," like the model-minority myth pinned on Asian Americans, renders the war on those "other," hardcore niggas justifiable and even palatable. In a little-known essay on the public image of world champion boxer Joe Louis, the radical Trinidadian writer C. L. R. James put it best: "This attempt to hold up Louis as a model Negro has strong overtones of condescension and race prejudice. It implies: 'See! When a Negro knows how to conduct himself, he gets on very well and we all love him.' From there the next step is: 'If only all Negros behaved like Joe, the race problem would be solved'" (1946).

Of course we all know this is a bunch of fiction. Behaving "like Joe" was merely a code for deference and patience, which is all the more remarkable given his vocation. Unlike his predecessor Jack Johnson—the bald-headed prizefighter who transgressed racial boundaries by sleeping with and even marrying white women, who refused to apologize for his "outrageous" behavior, who boasted of his prowess in every facet of life (he even wrapped gauze around his penis to make it appear bigger under his boxing shorts)—Joe Louis was America's hero. As James put it, he was a credit to his race, "I mean the human race."

(Re)presented as a humble Alabama boy, God-fearing and devoid of hatred, Louis was constructed in the press as a raceless man whose masculinity was put to good, patriotic use. To many of his white fans, he was a man in the ring and a boy—a good boy—outside of it. To many black folks, he was a hero because he had the license to kick white men's butts and yet maintain the admiration and respect of a nation. Thus, despite similarities in race, class, and vocation, and their common iconization, Louis and Johnson exhibited public behavior that reflected radically different masculinities.

Here, then, is a lesson we cannot ignore. There is some truth in the implication that race (or gender) conflict is partly linked to behavior and how certain behavior is perceived. If our society, for example, could dispense with rigid, archaic notions of appropriate masculine and feminine behavior, perhaps we might create a world that nurtures, encourages, and even rewards nice guys. If violence were not so central to American culture—to the way manhood is defined, to the way in which the state keeps African American men in check, to the way men interact with women, to the way oppressed peoples interact with one another—perhaps we might see the withering away of white fears of black men. Perhaps young black men wouldn't feel the need to adopt hardened, threatening postures merely to survive in a Doggy-Dogg world. Not that black men ought to become colored equivalents of Alan Alda. Rather, black men ought to be whomever or whatever they want to be, without unwarranted criticism or societal pressures to conform to a particular definition of manhood. They could finally dress down without suspicion, talk loudly without surveillance, and love each other without sanction. Fortunately, such a transformation would also mean the long-awaited death of the "nice Negro."

Not in my lifetime. Any fool can look around and see that the situation for race and gender relations in general, and for black males in particular, has taken a turn for the worse—and relief is nowhere in sight. In the meantime, I will make the most of my "nice Negro" status. When it's all said and done, there is nothing romantic or interesting about playing Bigger Thomas. Maybe I can't persuade a well-dressed white couple to give up their box seats, but at least they'll listen to me. For now. . . .

Reference

James, C. L. R. 1946. "Joe Louis and Jack Johnson." *Labor Action,* July 1.

Questions

1. Have you ever been a victim of stereotyping—for example, based on your gender, race, ethnicity, sexual orientation, or social class? If you have, how did it make you feel?

2. Early in the article Kelley refers to the "media-made black man." What did he mean by this?

3. Does a shaved head have a different meaning for a black man than for a white man? In other words, would people find a white man with a shaved head to be scary? Why or why not?

4. Kelley says that "any fool can look around and see that the situation for race and gender relations in general, and for black males in particular, has taken a turn for the worse—and relief is nowhere in sight." To what extent do you agree with this assessment?

37

THE MODEL MINORITY MYTH

Asian Americans Confront Growing Backlash

Yin Ling Leung

In this 1987 article, Yin Ling Leung reveals something of a social paradox: Members of some groups in our society are singled out for discriminatory treatment because they are judged by the dominant group to be "inferior," whereas others are singled out for discrimination because they are judged "superior." Note that here, the terms *Asians* and *Asian Americans* refer to a wide range of peoples, including Cambodians, Chinese, Filipinos, Hmong, Japanese, Koreans, Laotians, Thais, and Vietnamese.

The once predominant media caricatures of Asians such as the effeminate Charlie Chan, the evil Fu Manchu, the exotic dragon-lady Suzy Wong or the docile, submissive Mrs. Livingston are giving way to a more subtle but equally damaging image. The emerging picture of Asians as hardworking, highly educated, family-oriented, and financially successful—in short, a "model minority"—appears benign at first, even beneficial. However, Asians are experiencing a growing backlash against their "model minority" status. The pervasive perception that Asian Americans are "making it," even surpassing whites despite their minority status, is resulting in discriminatory college admittance practices and a rise in anti-Asian sentiment.

What is now being coined the "model minority myth" began to take root in the late 1960s, after increasing numbers of Asian immigrants came to the U.S. under the Immigration Act of 1965.[1] A 1966 *U.S. News and World Report* article, entitled "Success Story of One Minority Group in the U.S.," portrayed Asian Americans as hardworking and uncomplaining, and implied that discrimination is not an obstacle for Asian Americans. A rash of similar articles followed, each attempting to reveal the "formula" responsible for Asian American success and prosperity.

The increased numbers of Southeast Asian refugees (the Hmong, Vietnamese, Laotian, and Kampuchean/Cambodians) and the increased immigration from Taiwan, Korea and Hong Kong have made Asians the second-fastest-growing minority population in the U.S. With this increase in numbers, the media has increased its focus on the "success stories" of Asian Americans as a whole. Articles in popular magazines such as *Newsweek*, *U.S. News and World Report* and others, with titles

Yin Ling Leung, "The Model Minority Myth: Asians Confront Growing Backlash" from *Minority Trendsetter* (Winter 1987): 5–7. Reprinted with the permission of *Minority Trendsetter*, Center for Third World Organizing.

[1]Center for Third World Reporting. 1987. *Minority Trendsletter*, Winter, pp. 5–7.

like "Asian-Americans: A 'Model Minority,'" "The Drive to Excel," "A Formula for Success," "The Promise of America," and "The Triumph of Asian Americans," perpetuate a distorted image of universal Asian-American success. One article in *Fortune* magazine portrayed Asians as a super competitive force, or "super minority," outperforming even the majority white population.

Myth Versus Reality

A closer examination of the facts, however, reveals holes in both the "model minority" and "super minority" myths. For example, 1980 census figures place the mean family income for Asian American families in the U.S. at $26,456—nearly $3,000 higher than white families. These figures dramatically change, however, if adjusted for the number of workers per family. Because Asians tend to have more workers per family, the total income of a family reflects less per individual. In addition, over 64 percent of Asian Americans live in urban areas of San Francisco, Los Angeles, New York and Honolulu, where the incomes and cost of living are correspondingly higher.

The model minority myth also masks the complexity of Asians in America and the different realities they face. In fact, Asian Americans come from sharply distinct backgrounds which determine their life in the U.S. Many of the "successful" Asian immigrants touted by the media as exemplifying the model minority phenomenon come from families that have been in the states for many generations or from aristocratic, elite, educated, economically advantaged backgrounds in their home countries. For example, the early Vietnamese refugee boat people were from wealthier and more educated communities than the more recent refugees from Vietnam. In addition, immigrants from China, Japan, and Korea tend to come from relatively more privileged backgrounds.

The more recent immigrants from Southeast Asia, like the Hmong, Laotian, Kampuchean/Cambodian, and the Vietnamese refugees arriving after 1976, do not mirror the image of instant success that the media perpetuates. These hundreds of thousands of Southeast Asian refugees suffer not only from language difficulties, but also from deep-seated emotional and psychological disorders, resulting from the trauma they experienced in the war-torn countries of Southeast Asia. Asian refugees also face limited work opportunities, substandard wages and lack of health benefits and unhealthy working conditions.

Another facet to [the] model minority myth is the belief that all Asians excel academically. There is no disputing that Asian Americans are "overrepresented" in the nation's colleges and universities. Asians make up approximately 3.7 million or 1.6 percent of the total U.S. population, but comprise 8 to 18 percent of enrollment in the nation's top colleges and universities. At the University of California at Berkeley, Asian students make up a quarter of the student population.

The media links Asian "success" in education with their strong familial bonds. This is, to some extent, an accurate portrayal. Many Asian cultures believe that social mobility is directly tied to education and therefore spend a disproportionate amount of family income on education, as compared to white families. Because it is a considerable sacrifice for most immigrant families to send their children to college, Asian students are often urged by their parents to pursue "safer" professions, such as medicine, engineering and other fields where the economic payback is proportionate to the number of years (and dollars) invested in education.

Even in these "safe" professions, however, Asians are discovering that quiet achievement and good job performance may not amount to promotions. A *Newsweek* article recently pointed to a phenomenon of Asian middle-management professionals, especially in corporate business fields, who "top-out," reaching a plateau beyond which their employers will not promote them.

Backlash: Asians Face Discrimination

Repercussions of the model minority myth on Asian Americans could be described as "the many being punished by the success of a few." Asians of all classes and generations are experiencing a rise in anti-Asian sentiment. This anti-Asian sentiment is expressed both through subtle, systematic discrimination, particularly in higher education, and through racially motivated violence.

Because of the disproportionate numbers of Asian Americans in the nation's universities, some colleges are denying Asians affirmative action consideration. At Princeton University, for example, where Asians make up approximately 8.5 percent of the entering class, admissions officials no longer consider Asian Americans as a minority group, despite federal regulations which define them as a protected subgroup.

Other prestigious colleges and universities are systematically excluding qualified Asians through the application of heavily subjective criteria. At the University of California at Berkeley, for example, despite a 14 percent rise in applications between 1983 and 1985, the number of Asian Americans admitted to UCB dropped 20 percent in 1984.

The Asian American Task Force on UC Admissions, which conducted a seven-month study, found that the university had temporarily used a minimum SAT verbal score to disqualify applicants. While Asian Americans excel on the math sections of the SAT, their national average on the verbal portion of the test was under 400. The Task Force also found that UCB now relies more heavily on subjective criteria for freshman admissions. For the fall of 1987, grades and test scores will determine only 40 percent of admittees, while 30 percent will be chosen by subjective factors which tend to operate against Asians.

According to Henry Der, executive director of Chinese for Affirmative Action: "Qualified Asian students are being excluded from the Berkeley campus in substantial numbers. It is apparent that UC policy changes are conscious attempts to limit the growth of Asian students, to the benefit of qualified white students."

Discriminatory practices at UC Berkeley point to a nationwide trend. At Harvard University, where Asians make up 10.9 percent of the first-year class, admitted Asian students had scores substantially higher than white students who were admitted. At Brown University, a study conducted by Asian American students found that Asian American admittance rates in the early 1980s had been consistently lower than the all-college admittance rate.

There is increasing evidence that these and other select schools are designing "hidden quotas" to exclude otherwise qualified Asian applicants. For example, a recent survey of Asian American applicants at Stanford demonstrated that popular images of Asians as narrowly-focused math and science students influenced how admissions officers judged Asians for entrance to college campuses. Just as "regional diversity" was used as a mechanism to keep Jews, who tended to be concentrated in metropolitan areas like New York and Los Angeles, out of elite institutions prior to World War II, "extra-curricular and leadership" criteria are functioning in a similar manner for certain Asians. The Stanford study found that although Asian Americans participated in nearly the same proportion as whites in high school sports, in equal numbers in music and in greater numbers in social, ethnic and community organizations, "intentional or unintentional" biases have made many applicants the victims of racial stereotypes.

Black conservative Thomas Sowell and other neoconservatives applaud the divorce of Asians from their minority status. Sowell believes that this will cause schools to be just as rigorous in selecting Asian students as they are at selecting majority white students. In this way, he continues, students will not be mismatched with their schools, a problem he attributes to quota requirements.

Anti-Asian Sentiment Rising

The model minority myth, coupled with the rising economic prowess of Pacific Rim Asian countries and the corresponding economic downturn in the U.S., has given rise to an increase in anti-Asian violence. In 1981, the Japanese American Citizens League recorded seven cases in which anti-Asian sentiment was expressed verbally, legislatively or physically; in 1982 they recorded four; in 1983, 20; in 1984, 30; in 1985, 48.

One explanation for this rise in anti-Asian violence is that Asians are being used as scapegoats[2] for the nation's economic problems. Both business and labor have waged explicitly anti-Asian media campaigns portraying Japanese competition as an explanation for the ills of American industry.

The case of Vincent Chin dramatically demonstrates the potential impact of such campaigns. Chin, a 27-year-old Chinese American resident of Detroit, was bludgeoned to death by two white unemployed auto workers. The two men, who were merely fined and put on probation, mistook him for Japanese. They saw Chin as a representative of the Japanese automobile imports business, which they blamed for the loss of their jobs. Violence against Asian refugees and immigrants who compete for scarce resources in low-income communities has also dramatically increased.

The Asian Community Responds

Asian Americans are contradicting the very stereotype of the hardworking, uncomplaining minority by protesting the discriminatory practices in the nation's colleges and in the job market. For example, the Chinese American Legal Defense Fund, a Michigan-based organization, has filed suit against UC Berkeley and several other elite institutions, including Stanford, Princeton, Yale, and MIT. They charge that campuses have imposed "secret quotas" on Asians because of their growing enrollments. In another case, Yat-Pang Au, valedictorian of San Jose's Gunderson High School, with "top test scores and an impressive array of extracurricular activities," is threatening a civil rights suit against UC Berkeley for denying his entrance to the competitive College of Engineering.

At least one school has responded to this pressure by re-examining its admittance policies. A recent study of Asian student admission at Stanford, Brown, Harvard, and Princeton by John H. Bunzel and Jeffrey K. D. Au, both from Stanford, found that Stanford was the only university to buck the trend of declining Asian admissions. The 1986 entering class of Asian Americans increased from 119 last year to 245 this year. Asians at Stanford make up 15.6 percent of the class, still lower than UC Berkeley, where 26.5 percent of this year's entering class are Asian Americans.

Mobilizations against anti-Asian violence have also begun on the national and the community level. The Japanese American Citizens League, the Violence Against Asians Taskforce,

---

[2]The concept of scapegoat comes to us from the Old Testament. As told in Leviticus (16:10), on the day of Atonement, the sins of the Jewish people were heaped upon the head of a goat who was then "let go . . . into the wilderness." The term *scapegoat* thus literally means "escaping goat." Today, the concept is used to refer to people who, though they may be completely innocent of any offense, are singled out, blamed, and punished for the misfortunes of others.—Ed.

Chinese for Affirmative Action, and other Asian groups have monitored incidents of anti-Asian violence and pressured the U.S. Commission on Civil Rights and other government bodies to confront and investigate the problem. Projects such as the Coalition to Break the Silence and the Community Violence Prevention Project, both in Oakland, CA, are fighting to raise community consciousness on the issue through community forums and legislative testimony. The Coalition to Break the Silence has also developed ties with other organizations doing similar work in Los Angeles, New York, and Boston.

Questions

1. What does Leung mean by "backlash"? Can you think of any other examples of this phenomenon?

2. Some people who oppose affirmative action and quotas for blacks and Hispanics are nonetheless in favor of setting limits on how many Asian Americans should be admitted to colleges and universities. What could explain this apparent contradiction?

3. For individual Asian Americans, what difficulties might be caused by being stereotyped as a "model minority"?

38

TALES OUT OF MEDICAL SCHOOL

Adriane Fugh-Berman, M.D.

Research has shown that although boys and girls may sit in the same classrooms with the same teachers, they receive much different educations: "From grade school through graduate school Female students are more likely to be invisible members of classrooms" (Sadker and Sadker, *Failing at Fairness: How America's Schools Cheat Girls*, 1994). In this 1992 walk down memory lane, Adriane Fugh-Berman illustrates the nature of the invisibility and what happens when the "girls" try to change things.

With the growth of the women's health movement and the influx of women into medical schools, there has been abundant talk of a new enlightenment among physicians. Last summer, many Americans were shocked when Frances Conley, a neurosurgeon on the faculty of Stanford University's medical school, resigned her position, citing "pervasive sexism." Conley's is a particularly elite and male-dominated subspecialty, but her story is not an isolated one. I graduated from the Georgetown University School of Medicine in 1988, and while medical training is a sexist process anywhere, Georgetown built disrespect for women into its curriculum.

A Jesuit school, most recently in the news as the alma mater of William Kennedy Smith, Georgetown has an overwhelmingly white, male and conservative faculty. At a time when women made up one-third of all medical students in the United States, and as many as one-half at some schools, my class was 73 percent male and more than 90 percent white.

The prevailing attitude toward women was demonstrated on the first day of classes by my anatomy instructor, who remarked that our elderly cadaver "must have been a Playboy bunny" before instructing us to cut off her large breasts and toss them into the thirty-gallon trash can marked "cadaver waste." Barely hours into our training, we were already being taught that there was nothing to be learned from examining breasts. Given the fact that one out of nine American women will develop breast cancer in her lifetime, to treat breasts as extraneous tissue seemed an appalling waste of an educational opportunity, as well as a not-so-subtle message about the relative importance of body parts. How many of my classmates now in practice, I wonder, regularly examine the breasts of their female patients?

My classmates learned their lesson of disrespect well. Later in the year one carved a tick-tack-toe on a female cadaver and challenged others to play. Another gave a languorous sigh after dissecting female genitalia, as if he had just had sex. "Guess I should have a cigarette now," he said.

Ghoulish humor is often regarded as a means by which med students overcome fear and anxiety. But it serves a darker purpose as well: Depersonalizing our cadaver was good preparation for depersonalizing our patients later. Further on in my training an ophthalmologist would yell at me when I hesitated to place a small instrument meant to measure eye

Adriane Fugh-Berman, M.D., "Tales Out of Medical School" from *The Nation* (January 20, 1992). Reprinted with permission from the January 20, 1992 issue of *The Nation*. For subscription information, call 1-800-333-8536. Portions of each week's Nation magazine can be accessed at http://www.thenation.com.

pressure on a fellow student's cornea because I was afraid it would hurt. "You have to learn to treat patients as lab animals," he snarled at me.

On the first day of an emergency medicine rotation in our senior year, students were asked who had had experience in placing a central line (an intravenous line placed into a major vein under the clavicle or in the neck). Most of the male students raised their hands. None of the women did. For me, it was graphic proof of inequity in teaching; the men had had the procedure taught to them, but the women had not. Teaching rounds were often, for women, a spectator sport. One friend told me how she craned her neck to watch a physician teach a minor surgical procedure to a male student; when they were done the physician handed her his dirty gloves to discard. I have seen a male attending physician demonstrate an exam on a patient and then wade through several female medical students to drag forth a male in order to teach it to him. This sort of discrimination was common and quite unconscious: The women just didn't register as medical students to some of the doctors. Female students, for their part, tended (like male ones) to gloss over issues that might divert attention, energy or focus from the all-important goal of getting through their training. "Oh, they're just of the old school," a female classmate remarked to me, as if being ignored by our teachers was really rather charming, like having one's hand kissed.

A woman resident was giving a radiology presentation and I felt mesmerized. Why did I feel so connected and involved? It suddenly occurred to me that the female physician was regularly meeting my eyes; most of the male residents and attendings made eye contact with only the men.

"Why are women's brains smaller than men's?" asked a surgeon of a group of male medical students in the doctors' lounge (I was in the room as well, but was apparently invisible). "Because they're missing logic!" Guffaws all around.

Such instances of casual sexism are hardly unique to Georgetown, or indeed to medical schools. But at Georgetown female students also had to contend with outright discrimination of a sort most Americans probably think no longer exists in education. There was one course women were not allowed to take. The elective in sexually transmitted diseases required an interview with the head of the urology department, who was teaching the course. Those applicants with the appropriate genitalia competed for invitations to join the course (a computer was supposed to assign us electives, which we had ranked in order of preference, but that process had been circumvented for this course). Three women who requested an interview were told that the predominantly gay male clinic where the elective was held did not allow women to work there. This was news to the clinic's executive director, who stated that women were employed in all capacities.

The women who wanted to take the course repeatedly tried to meet with the urologist, but he did not return our phone calls. (I had not applied for the course, but became involved as an advocate for the women who wanted to take it.) We figured out his schedule, waylaid him in the hall and insisted that a meeting be set up.

At this meeting, clinic representatives disclosed that a survey had been circulated years before to the clientele in order to ascertain whether women workers would be accepted; 95 percent of the clients voted to welcome women. They were also asked whether it was acceptable to have medical students working at the clinic; more than 90 percent approved. We were then told that these results could not be construed to indicate that clients did not mind women medical students; the clients would naturally have assumed that "medical student" meant "male medical student." Even if that were true, we asked, if 90 percent of clients did not mind medical students and 95 percent did not mind women, couldn't a reasonable person assume that female medical students would be acceptable? No, we were informed. Another study would have to be done.

We raised formal objections to the school. Meanwhile, however, the entire elective process had been postponed by the dispute, and the blame for the delay and confusion was placed on us. The hardest part of the struggle, indeed, was dealing with the indifference of most of our classmates—out of 206, maybe a dozen actively supported us—and with the intense anger of the ten men who had been promised places in the course.

"Just because you can't take this course," one of the men said to me, "why do you want to ruin it for the rest of us?" It seemed incredible to me that I had to argue that women should be allowed to take the same courses as men. The second or third time someone asked me the same question, I suggested that if women were not allowed to participate in the same curriculum as men, then in the interest of fairness we should get a 50 percent break on our $22,500 annual tuition. My colleague thought that highly unreasonable.

Eventually someone in administration realized that not only were we going to sue the school for discrimination but that we had an open-and-shut case. The elective in sexually transmitted diseases was canceled, and from its ashes arose a new course, taught by the same man, titled "Introduction to Urology." Two women were admitted. When the urologist invited students to take turns working with him in his office, he scheduled the two female students for the same day—one on which only women patients were to be seen (a nifty feat in a urology practice).

The same professor who so valiantly tried to prevent women from learning anything unseemly about sexually transmitted diseases was also in charge of the required course in human sexuality (or, as I liked to call it, heman sexuality). Only two of the eleven lectures focused on women; of the two lectures on homosexuality, neither mentioned lesbians. The psychiatrist who co-taught the class treated us to one lecture that amounted to an apology for rape: Aggression, even hostility, is normal in sexual relations between a man and a woman, he said, and inhibition of aggression in men can lead to impotence.

We were taught that women do not need orgasms for a satisfactory sex life, although men, of course, do; and that inability to reach orgasm is only a problem for women with "unrealistic expectations." I had heard that particular lecture before in the backseat of a car during high school. The urologist told us of couples who came to him for sex counseling because the woman was not having orgasms; he would reassure them that this is normal and the couple would be relieved. (I would gamble that the female half of the couple was anything but relieved.) We learned that oral sex is primarily a homosexual practice, and that sexual dysfunction in women is often caused by "working." In the women-as-idiots department, we learned that when impotent men are implanted with permanently rigid penile prostheses, four out of five wives can't tell that their husbands have had the surgery.

When dealing with sexually transmitted diseases in which both partners must be treated, we were advised to vary our notification strategy according to marital status. If the patient is a single man, the doctor should write the diagnosis down on a prescription for his partner to bring to her doctor. If the patient is a married man, however, the doctor should contact the wife's gynecologist and arrange to have her treated without knowledge of what she is being treated for. How to notify the male partner of a female patient, married or single, was never revealed.

To be fair, women were not the only subjects of outmoded concepts of sexuality. We also received anachronistic information about men. Premature ejaculation, defined as fewer than ten thrusts(!), was to be treated by having the man think about something unpleasant, or by having the woman painfully squeeze, prick or pinch the penis. Aversive therapies such as these have long been discredited.

Misinformation about sexuality and women's health peppered almost every course (I can't recall any egregious wrongs in biochemistry). Although vasectomy and abortion are among the safest of all surgical procedures, in our lectures vasectomy was presented as fraught with long-term complications and abortion was never mentioned without the words "peritonitis" and "death" in the same sentence. These distortions represented Georgetown's Catholic bent at its worst. (We were not allowed to perform, or even watch, abortion procedures in our affiliated hospitals.) On a lighter note, one obstetrician assisting us in the anatomy lab told us that women shouldn't lift heavy weights because their pelvic organs will fall out between their legs.

In our second year, several women in our class started a women's group, which held potlucks and offered presentations and performances: A former midwife talked about her profession, a student demonstrated belly dancing, another discussed dance therapy and one sang selections from *A Chorus Line.* This heavy radical feminist activity created great hostility among our male classmates. Announcements of our meetings were defaced and women in the group began receiving threatening calls at home from someone who claimed to be watching the listener and who would then accurately describe what she was wearing. One woman received obscene notes in her school mailbox, including one that contained a rape threat. I received insulting cards in typed envelopes at my home address; my mother received similar cards at hers.

We took the matter to the dean of student affairs, who told us it was "probably a dental student" and suggested we buy loud whistles to blow into the phone when we received unwanted calls. We demanded that the school attempt to find the perpetrator and expel him. We were told that the school would not expel the student but that counseling would be advised.

The women's group spread the word that we were collecting our own information on possible suspects and that any information on bizarre, aggressive, antisocial or misogynous behavior among the male medical students should be reported to our designated representative. She was inundated with a list of classmates who fit the bill. Finally, angered at the school's indifference, we solicited the help of a prominent woman faculty member. Although she shamed the dean into installing a hidden camera across from the school mailboxes to monitor unusual behavior, no one was ever apprehended.

Georgetown University School of Medicine churns out about 200 physicians a year. Some become good doctors despite their training, but many will pass on the misinformation and demeaning attitudes handed down to them. It is a shame that Georgetown chooses to perpetuate stereotypes and reinforce prejudices rather than help students acquire the up-to-date information and sensitivity that are vital in dealing with AIDS, breast cancer, teen pregnancy and other contemporary epidemics. Female medical students go through an ordeal, but at least it ends with graduation. It is the patients who ultimately suffer the effects of sexist medical education.

Questions

1. According to Fugh-Berman's account, the gender ratio was usually skewed at Georgetown's medical school. In your judgment, would there be less sexism if the ratio of men and women was more equal? Why or why not?

2. To what extent might it be said that the women medical students were victims of hate crimes? What would be the motive behind these attacks?

39

AFTERWORD

The Sociological Eye and Its Blinders

Randall Collins

As we neared the end of the twentieth century, many people paused to take stock of where we had come from and where we might be heading. Randall Collins was among those moved to such millennial musings. He was asked by the editors of *Contemporary Sociology* to answer some hard questions: Is there a core to sociology? Should there be? What do sociologists have in common that makes them members of the same discipline?

Does sociology have a core? Yes, but it is not an eternal essence; not a set of texts or ideas, but an activity.

This is not the same as saying the discipline of sociology will always exist. Sociology became a self-conscious community only in the mid-1800s, about five generations ago, and has been an academic discipline for four generations or less. Disciplines go in and out of existence. The very concept of disciplinary specialization as we know it was created in the Napoleonic period at the time of reorganization of the French Academies, as Johan Heilbron has shown in *The Rise of Social Theory* (1995). There is no guarantee that any particular discipline will remain fixed. Biology, a discipline first recognized by Auguste Comte, has repeatedly shifted its boundaries, combining with physics and chemistry, or spinning off genetics and ecology, making up a shifting array of new fields. Discoveries do not respect administrative boundary lines. Major advances in research or theory tend to pull followers after

Randall Collins, "The Sociological Eye and Its Blinders" from *Contemporary Sociology* 27, no. 1 (January 1998): 2–7. Reprinted with the permission of the American Sociological Association and the author.

them, who institutionalize themselves in turn for a while in some organizational form, if only until the next big round of discovery.

In much the same way, sociologists keep forming hybrid communities on their borders, for example, with economics, literary theory, or computer science. In recent decades, hybrid disciplines have split off from, overlapped with, or encroached upon sociology as criminal justice, ethnic studies, gender studies, management, science and technology studies (i.e., what was once "sociology of science"), and no doubt more to come. There is nothing to lament in this. A glance at the history of long-term intellectual networks, and of academic organizations, shows that branching and recombining are central to what drives intellectual innovation. (The pattern of such long-term networks is documented in my *The Sociology of Philosophies* [1998].)

Sociology, like everything else, is a product of particular historical conditions. But I also believe we have hit upon a distinctive intellectual activity. Its appeal is strong enough to keep it alive, whatever its name will be in the future and whatever happens to the surrounding institutional forms. The lure of this activity is what drew many of us into sociology.

One becomes hooked on being a sociologist. The activity is this: It is looking at the world around us, the immediate world you and I live in, through the sociological eye.

There is a sociology of everything. You can turn on your sociological eye no matter where you are or what you are doing. Stuck in a boring committee meeting (for that matter, a sociology department meeting), you can check the pattern of who is sitting next to whom, who gets the floor, who makes eye contact, and what is the rhythm of laughter (forced or spontaneous) or of pompous speechmaking. Walking down the street, or out for a run, you can scan the class and ethnic pattern of the neighborhood, look for lines of age segregation, or for little pockets of solidarity. Waiting for a medical appointment, you can read the professions and the bureaucracy instead of old copies of *National Geographic*. Caught in a traffic jam, you can study the correlation of car models with bumper stickers or with the types of music blaring from radios. There is literally nothing you can't see in a fresh way if you turn your sociological eye to it. Being a sociologist means never having to be bored.

But doesn't every discipline have its special angle on all of reality? Couldn't a physicist see the laws of motion everywhere, or an economist think of supply curves of whatever happens in everyday life? I still think sociology is uniquely appealing in this respect. What physicists or chemists can see in everyday life is no doubt rather banal for them, and most of their discoveries in recent centuries have been made by esoteric laboratory equipment. Fields like economics, it is true, could probably impose an application of some of their theories upon a great many things. But for virtually all disciplines, the immediate world is a sideshow. For sociologists, it is our arena of discovery, and the source at which we renew our energies and our enthusiasm.

In saying this, I don't mean to say that the only true sociologists are the practitioners of ethnographic or participant observation, or that the core of sociology is limited to

Goffman-style microsociology. I do think that all of us who are turned on by sociology, who love doing what we do, have the sociological eye. It is this that gives us new theoretical ideas and makes alive the theories that we carry from the past. The world a sociologist can see is not bounded by the immediate microsituation. Reading the newspaper, whether the business section or the personal ads, is for us like an astronomer training his or her telescope on the sky. Where the ordinary reader is pulled into the journalistic mode, reading the news through one or another political bias or schema of popular melodrama, the sociological eye sees suggestions of social movements mobilizing or winding down, indications of class domination or conflict, or perhaps the organizational process whereby just this kind of story ended up in print, defined as news. For us, novels depict the boundaries of status groups and the saga of social mobility, just as detective stories show us about backstages. Whatever we read with the sociological eye becomes a clue to the larger patterns of society, here or in the past. The same goes for the future: Today's sociologists are not just caught up in the fad of the Internet; they are already beginning to look at it as another frontier for sociological discovery.

I want to claim, in short, that all kinds of sociologists, microethnographers and statisticians, historical comparativists and theorists alike, have the sociological eye. I think that virtually all of the most productive sociologists among us do. We all went through a gestalt switch in our way of looking at the world, sometime early in our careers, that was the key moment in our initiation into sociology. Having become initiated, I suppose, one can also become burned out. The vision fades; everyday life becomes just everyday; the newspapers become just a little jolt of political clichés to go along with the morning orange juice; sociology becomes just life at the office, number crunching or writing reviews on yet another meta-critique on the lives of dead Germans. Sure, we can lose the vision and the enthusiasm. But the initiation lingers; the gestalt switch is still there to be switched on. We can always reenergize ourselves by getting back to the source: Turn on the sociological eye and go look at something. Don't take someone else's word for what there is to see, or some common cliché (even a current trendy one), above all not a media-hype version of what is there; go and see it yourself. Make it observationally strange, as if you'd never seen it before. The energy comes back. In that way, I suspect, sociologists are probably more energized by their subject matter than practitioners of virtually any other discipline.

Now I want to thicken the plot. Turning on the sociological eye is the main way that many of us became sociologists, but it isn't the only way. There is another recruitment path, which also acts as a continuing source of energy and commitment. This is the path of social activism. Many, perhaps most of us, became interested in sociology because we belonged to social movements or had social commitments. We wanted to do something to change society, help people, fight injustice, and elevate the oppressed. This image of sociology has long been foremost in the public eye. In an earlier generation, people used to confuse "sociology" with "socialism," or more recently with "social work." The 1960s gave another radical jolt to this trajectory, along with a repetition of the pattern of putting down one's elders for not being up with today's crusade. We of the '60s generation have been experiencing the turn that comes, in time, of being on the receiving end of the same process.

There are complications in the career of activist commitment too; there can be burnout, and also institutionalization, so that researching one's favorite oppressed group also becomes just another day at the office. But here, too, it remains possible to reawaken the old energy surge by making contact with the source: that is, get in touch with a movement that is still mobilized, feed one's energies into it, and receive back the stepped-up current that comes from solidarity and commitment. Old lefties

(and, more precisely, old New Lefties) can get a surge in their commitment by intellectual action that carries forward the old targeting of opponents. World-system theory, for instance, is not just another academic specialty, for those who work in it; there is a political resonance that makes even such arcane topics as trade routes in the Ottoman Empire into opportunities to grapple with the history of the capitalist beast. Sociology is full of people who have passion, who care deeply about their subject, because so many of us came in through the activist side.

This is a second reason why sociology is so distinctive. Although politically committed persons and former or current activists work throughout the academic world, in few disciplines does activism mesh so directly with one's immediate work as in sociology. Sociology is nearly the most politicized and activist of all fields. (In recent years literature, which resembles sociology in several of the respects I have been discussing, has probably come to rival sociology in ideological intensity.) Probably the only disciplines that are even more thoroughly politicized than sociology are relatives of sociology, such as ethnic studies, black studies, and women's studies, which were created as hybrids between academic departments and activist movements.

Now to the crux of the drama. Sociology has two core commitments: what I have called the "sociological eye" and social activism. They can be combined; some people have both of them, simultaneously or in differing strengths at different times in their careers. And one can become burned out from both, so the entire population of those of us who are nominally called "sociologists" array ourselves all across this two-dimensional grid. Much of the conflict within sociology goes on between those who are at the peak intensities of the two different commitments.

In the late 1950s, C. Wright Mills' *The Sociological Imagination* castigated mere "abstracted empiricists" and "grand theorists" for losing what Mills regarded as the true sociological commitment to an activist critique and reconstruction of society. Today, James Rule in *Theory and Progress in Social Science* (1997) makes a parallel critique, charging that sociology is full of specialized intellectual movements caught up in self-generated problems, spinning technicalities of their own devising. For Rule, movements as diverse as rational choice, network analysis, and feminist theory all share the pathology of turning inward on themselves, surrounding themselves with a wall of esoteric vocabulary, and losing sight of the first-order questions of perennial concern: the conditions of stratification, social disruption, and violence. It is possible to be sympathetic to the spirit of Mills' and Rule's critiques and still to see the larger dimensions of the intellectual conflict. Mills' targets (Lazarsfeld, Parsons, Merton) and many of Rule's targets also had the sociological eye; these were (and are) sociologists who have turned on their vision, seeing something around us that the ordinary eye doesn't see, whether it be latent functions (in one of the older examples) or network structures (in one of the newer ones).

From the point of view of the committed activist, those sociologists who don't work on burning social problems seem like incomprehensible duffers or backsliding traitors to the cause; the activist commitment makes it hard to see that there is a driving commitment on the other side too, just an entirely different one. Erving Goffman, hiding out backstage in the mental hospital, was not merely seeing patients and psychiatrists through official or even counterofficial eyes, but was making his own distinctively sociological discoveries of how the construction of normalcy and of the self takes place. From the activist viewpoint, the judgment on other sociologists' work tends to be "if you're not part of the solution you're part of the problem." From the point of view of the voyager with the sociological eye, the activist is just someone who has already made up his or her mind and is no longer open to seeing anything new.

Perhaps the purest recent formulation of the viewpoint of the sociological eye is the preface to the second edition of Donald Black's *The Social Structure of Right and Wrong* (1998). Black regards the activist mentality as the biggest blinder to seeing the social pattern: For right and wrong, the categories by which the activist works are themselves socially variable attitudes arising from particular configurations of conflict, social control, and conflict management. For Black, categories such as crime, or ethnic or gender identity, are mere folk concepts that need to be dissolved into the analytical space of "pure sociology." Black is positively glowing from his sociological eye, almost like a Hindu tantric seer looking down and through us mere mortals below.

The two versions of sociological commitment, at their most intense, are like opposing gestalts; one impedes even bare awareness of what can be seen through the other. A recent example of the contretemps that can result is the public reception of Arlie Hochschild's *The Time Bind* (1997). Throughout her career, Hochschild's work has been a blend of the sociological eye and activist commitment, although (Hochschild is a student of Erving Goffman) the sociological eye tends to predominate. Hochschild treads on dangerous ground, because she chooses to study topics that are at the heart of current public controversy; yet she does not let the commitment dictate what she *sees*, and she goes willingly down the pathways opened by unexpected discoveries.

Research on *The Time Bind* began with a puzzle: Hochschild noticed that relatively few people were taking advantage of family-friendly employment policies allowing shorter hours, part-time work, parental leave, or flexible time. A politically conventional diagnosis today would be to blame economic pressure or subtle organizational coercion. Hochschild instead began to see the situation through a new gestalt: For many middle-class people, work and home were changing places. The successes of the middle-class women's movement were now producing unforeseen consequences. Home was becoming more of a hassle (already documented in Hochschild's previous book, *The Second Shift* [1989]), particularly as employed women work longer paid hours and still receive relatively little help from their husbands at home. One response, Hochschild perceived, was to gradually abandon the home battle, shifting the emotional center of one's life to one's work. Along with this has gone a large institutional shift: Family life has gotten deskilled, dependent upon commercial services for everything from food preparation to child care and entertainment. The Taylorized factory of the early twentieth century, with its efficiency-oriented speed-up, has invaded the home just at the time that modern participative management techniques have made middle-class workplaces more emotionally friendly. Hochschild perceives that the spate of services for children, of how-to books and courses on dealing effectively with family situations, even the very concept of "quality time" with one's children, are a kind of speed-up in the home, putting scientific home management to work to manipulate emotions as well as diets and minutes. For Hochschild, the entire gestalt of work and family is shifting; the divorce rate of broken marriages needs to be seen in the light of "marriages" to a place of employment, with job terminations as a second, sometimes counterbalancing "divorce rate."

My point is that Hochschild's sociological imagination was lit up at some point in her research. The starting point involved fairly standard feminist issues in the public arena, but what she came to see was filled with ironic resonances of a prior history of sociological discovery: the industrial management movement of the earlier part of the century, the "emotion work" that Hochschild herself had earlier uncovered in her study of airline flight attendants (*The Managed Heart* [1983]), the interplay between the official frontstage ideals (in this case, of how a contemporary parent is supposed to deal with one's children) and the backstage reality of how people make out amid the pressure of institutions. It is exploring these resonances, I am sure, that drew Hochschild

deeper and deeper into her research; the sociological eye has a way of pulling you down its wilderness paths. These same resonances give the book much of its appeal for sociologists.

At the same time, *The Time Bind* has been greeted with public controversy. Most people do not have the sociological eye; public political discourse is carried out in the language of parties and movements, and everything published is assessed as a move for or against a partisan position. Hochschild has been attacked for undermining the family leave act, for blaming working mothers for emotionally abandoning their children, for misperceiving the fight of working women against the pressures of corporate organization. Hochschild's response in the public press has been to stick to her vision: Her critics are closing their eyes on an unexpected reality they are afraid to see. Some of Hochschild's critics are sociologists, and some of the attack is not mere lay mentality against the professional sociologist: It is the perennial inner conflict of our discipline, the movement activist stance against the sociological eye. Some of the controversy over Hochschild's work mixes both dimensions; there are technical issues at stake involving research methods, the scope of interpretations based on Hochschild's particular slice of data, and underlying images of what kinds of families existed in an earlier historical period. Some of the activist critique of Hochschild's unwelcome findings is carried out on the terrain of technical argument. And indeed she may well be faulted in some of these aspects, such as the complexity of causes of why employees don't take off more time from work.

Yet the importance of Hochschild's vision remains; however specialized her research sample, she points to a cutting edge of social change. The puzzle over leave time was just the point of entry into a larger insight. Hochschild's sociological eye illuminates because it gives us a new gestalt, a way of making sense of what has happened to the entire complex of work-and-home as we pass a historical watershed. When examined analytically instead of moralistically, it is not a question of denouncing or defending contemporary outsourcing of child care, home care, entertainment, and emotional support; nor of nostalgia for another era in which indeed middle-class women were confined to craft work or domestic labor. I think Hochschild's critics are mistaken in assuming that she has merely warped the activist scale of evaluations, and in not understanding the seriousness of a commitment to seeing as much as one can with one's sociological eye, however unsettling the news may be.

The two sources of sociologists' commitment often struggle against each other. If we have to choose between them, I say we must choose the sociological eye; if that is lost, all is lost. Without it, even sociological activists lose their creativity and their credibility with the public, appearing only as purveyors of facts chosen by persons whose minds are already made up. But unless there is all-out war between the factions, we can live with the struggle, and even prosper from it. Sociology is fortunate that it has so much built-in energy, so much intellectual commitment—even if those commitments sometimes are at cross-purposes.

Yet it is not always so. Sometimes the intensities are at more moderate levels, where blending is easier. And sometimes both commitments are high, but the sociological eye is wonderfully appropriate for what the social activist wants to reveal. Good examples are the urban ethnographies of street life by Elijah Anderson, *Streetwise* (1990) and *The Code of the Streets* (forthcoming). Anderson has a Goffmanian eye for the nuances of signals and signs given off in public, at the same time that he presents the dilemmas of social interaction in a racially mixed, physically dangerous neighborhood. A good-hearted activist with no other resources than the best intentions, or an angry activist full of righteousness, could not have written these books; it takes a sociological eye. And what the sociological eye saw is now revealed to the rest of us who read Anderson's books. Probably the sociological eye will always be the possession of a little group of devotees within the larger society. But the border between sociologists and lay people isn't fixed, and some of what we see can cross over. Sometimes it expands other people's vision.

References

Anderson, Elijah. 1990. *Streetwise: Race, Class and Change in an Urban Community.* Chicago: University of Chicago Press.

———. forthcoming. *The Code of the Streets.*

Black, Donald. 1998. *The Social Structure of Right and Wrong.* 2d ed. Orlando: Academic Press.

Collins, Randall. 1998. *The Sociology of Philosophies: A Global Theory of Intellectual Change.* Cambridge, MA: Harvard University Press.

Heilbron, Johan. 1995. *The Rise of Social Theory.* Minneapolis: University of Minnesota Press.

Hochschild, Arlie. 1983. *The Managed Heart.* Berkeley: University of California Press.

———. 1989. *The Second Shift: Working Parents and the Revolution at Home.* New York: Viking.

———. 1997. *The Time Bind: When Work Becomes Home and Home Becomes Work.* New York: Metropolitan Books.

Rule, James B. 1997. *Theory and Progress in Social Science.* Cambridge: Cambridge University Press.

Questions

1. Collins says that the core of sociology is the "sociological eye." What is that?

2. Why does Collins say that activism can be a blinder to sociological eyes?

3. Based on all that you've learned in your sociology class, why is it so difficult for "lay people" to see the world through sociological eyes?